Communications
in Computer and Information Science 198

David C. Wyld Michal Wozniak
Nabendu Chaki Natarajan Meghanathan
Dhinaharan Nagamalai (Eds.)

Advances in Computing and Information Technology

First International Conference, ACITY 2011
Chennai, India, July 15-17, 2011
Proceedings

Springer

Volume Editors

David C. Wyld
Southeastern Louisiana University, Hammond, LA 70402, USA
E-mail: david.wyld@selu.edu

Michal Wozniak
Wroclaw University of Technology, 50-370 Wroclaw, Poland
E-mail: michal.wozniak@pwr.wroc.pl

Nabendu Chaki
University of Calcutta, Calcutta, India
E-mail: nchaki@gmail.com

Natarajan Meghanathan
Jackson State University Jackson, MS 39217-0280, USA
E-mail: nmeghanathan@jsums.edu

Dhinaharan Nagamalai
Wireilla Net Solutions PTY Ltd, Melbourne, VIC, Australia
E-mail: dhinthia@yahoo.com

ISSN 1865-0929 e-ISSN 1865-0937
ISBN 978-3-642-22554-3 e-ISBN 978-3-642-22555-0
DOI 10.1007/978-3-642-22555-0
Springer Heidelberg Dordrecht London New York

Library of Congress Control Number: 2011931559

CR Subject Classification (1998): I.2, H.4, C.2, H.3, D.2, F.1

Typesetting: Camera-ready by author, data conversion by Scientific Publishing Services, Chennai, India

Printed on acid-free paper

Springer is part of Springer Science+Business Media (www.springer.com)

Preface

The 4th International Conference on Network Security & Applications (CNSA 2011) was held in Chennai, India, during July 15–17, 2011.The conference focuses on all technical and practical aspects of security and its applications for wired and wireless networks. The goal of this conference is to bring together researchers and practitioners from both academia and industry to focus on understanding the present-day security threats and to propose and discuss counter-measures to defend against such attacks. In the past few years, the enthusiastic participation of a large number of delegates in different AIRCC–organized conferences, like the International Conference on Network Security and Applications (CNSA), International Conference on Networks and Communications (NECOM), International Conference on Web and Semantic Technology (WEST), International Conference on Wireless and Mobile Networks (WIMON), the First International Conference on Advances in Computing and Information Technology (ACITY), reflect the fact that the parent body of the Academy and Industry Research Collaboration Center (AIRCC) is successful in providing a platform toward promoting academic collaboration. We believe that this spirit of co-working was further strengthened during CNSA 2011.

The CNSA 2011, NECOM 2011, WEST 2011, WIMoN 2011 and AICTY 2011 committees invited original submissions from researchers, scientists, engineers, and students that illustrate research results, projects, survey works, and industrial experiences describing significant advances in the areas related to the relevant themes and tracks of the conferences.

Thanks to the authors whose effort as reflected in the form of a large number of submissions for CNSA 2011 on different aspects of network security including Web security, cryptography, performance evaluations of protocols and security application, etc. All the submissions underwent a scrupulous peer-review process by a panel of expert reviewers. Besides the members of the Technical Committee, external reviewers were invited on the basis of their specialization and expertise. The papers were reviewed based on their technical content, originality, and clarity. The entire process, which includes the submission, review, and acceptance processes, was done electronically. This hard work resulted in the selection of high-quality papers that expand the knowledge in the latest developments in networks security and applications.

There were a total of 1,285 submissions to the conference, and the Technical Program Committee selected 195 papers for presentation at the conference and subsequent publication in the proceedings. The book is organized as a collection of papers from the 4th International Conference on Network Security and Applications (CNSA 2011), the Third International Conference on Networks and Communications (NeCoM 2011), the Third International Conference on Web and Semantic Technology (WeST 2011), the Third International Conference on

Wireless and Mobile Networks (WiMoN 2011), and the First International Conference on Advances in Computing and Information Technology (ACITY 2011). This small introduction incomplete would be without expressing our gratitude, and thanks to the General and Program Chairs, members of the Technical Program Committees, and external reviewers for their excellent and diligent work. Thanks to Springer for the strong support. Finally, we thank all the authors who contributed to the success of the conference. We also sincerely wish that all attendees benefited academically from the conference and wish them every success in their research.

David C. Wyld

Michal Wozniak
Nabendu Chaki
Natarajan Meghanathan
Dhinaharan Nagamalai

Organization

General Chairs

David C. Wyld	Southeastern Louisiana University, USA
S. K. Ghosh	Indian Institute of Technology, Kharagpur, India
Michal Wozniak	Wroclaw University of Technology, Poland

Steering Committee

Krzysztof Walkowiak	Wroclaw University of Technology, Poland
Dhinaharan Nagamalai	Wireilla Net Solutions PTY LTD, Australia
Natarajan Meghanathan	Jackson State University, USA
Nabendu Chaki	University of Calcutta, India
Chih-Lin Hu	National Central University, Taiwan
Selma Boumerdassi	CNAM/CEDRIC, France
John Karamitsos	University of the Aegean, Samos, Greece
Abdul Kadhir Ozcan	The American University, Cyprus
Brajesh Kumar Kaushik	Indian Institute of Technology - Roorkee, India

Program Committee Members

A.P. Sathish Kumar	PSG Institute of Advanced Studies, India
Abdul Aziz	University of Central Punjab, Pakistan
Abdul Kadir Ozcan	The American University, Cyprus
Ahmed M. Khedr	Sharjah University, UAE
Alejandro Garces	Jaume I University,Spain
Andy Seddon	Asia Pacific Institute of Information Technology, Malaysia
Ashutosh Dubey	NRI Institute of Science and Technology, Bhopal, India
Ashutosh Gupta	MJP Rohilkhand University, Bareilly, India
Atilla Elci	Toros University, Turkey
Atilla Elci	Eastern Mediterranean University, Cyprus
B. Srinivasan	Monash University, Australia
Babak Khosravifar	Concordia University, Canada
Balaji Sriramulu	drsbalaji@gmail.com
Balakannan S.P.	Chonbuk National University, Jeonju, Korea
Balasubramanian Karuppiah	MGR University, India
Bhupendra Suman	IIT Roorkee, India
Bong-Han Kim	Cheongju University, South Korea

Boo-Hyung Lee	KongJu National University, South Korea
Carlos E. Otero	The University of Virginia's College at Wise, USA
Chandra Mohan	Bapatla Engineering College, India
Charalampos Z. Patrikakis	National Technical University of Athens, Greece
Chih-Lin Hu	National Central University, Taiwan
Chin-Chih Chang	Chung Hua University,Taiwan
Cho Han Jin	Far East University, South Korea
Cynthia Dhinakaran	Hannam University, South Korea
Danda B. Rawat	Old Dominion University, USA
David W. Deeds	Shingu College, South Korea
Debasis Giri	Haldia Institute of Technology, India
Dimitris Kotzinos	Technical Educational Institution of Serres, Greece
Dong Seong Kim	Duke University, USA
Durga Toshniwal	Indian Institute of Techniology, India
Emmanuel Bouix	iKlax Media, France
Farhat Anwar	International Islamic University, Malaysia
Firkhan Ali Bin Hamid Ali	Universiti Tun Hussein Onn Malaysia, Malaysia
Ford Lumban	Gaol University of Indonesia
Genge Bela	Joint Research Centre, European Commission, Italy
Girija Chetty	University of Canberra, Australia
Govardhan A.	JNTUH College of Engineering, India
H.V. Ramakrishnan	MGR University, India
Haller Piroska	Petru Maior University, Tirgu Mures, Romania
Henrique Joao Lopes Domingos	University of Lisbon, Portugal
Ho Dac Tu	Waseda University, Japan
Hoang Huu Hanh	Hue University, Vietnam
Hwangjun Song	Pohang University of Science and Technology, South Korea
Jacques Demerjian	Communication & Systems, Homeland Security, France
Jae Kwang Lee	Hannam University, South Korea
Jan Zizka	SoNet/DI, FBE, Mendel University in Brno, Czech Republic
Jayeeta Chanda	jayeeta.chanda@gmail.com
Jeong-Hyun	Park Electronics Telecommunication Research Institute, South Korea
Jeong-Hyun	Park Electronics Telecommunication Research Institute, South Korea
Jeyanthy N.	VIT University, India
Jivesh Govil	Cisco Systems Inc., USA
Johann Groschdl	University of Bristol, UK

John Karamitsos	University of the Aegean, Greece
Johnson Kuruvila	Dalhousie University, Canada
Jose Enrique Armendariz-Inigo	Universidad Publica de Navarra, Spain
Jungwook Song	Konkuk University, South Korea
K.P. Thooyamani	Bharath University, India
Kamaljit I. Lakhtaria	Saurashtra University, India
Kamalrulnizam Abu Bakar	Universiti Teknologi Malaysia, Malaysia
Khamish Malhotra	University of Glamorgan, UK
Kota Sunitha	G.Narayanamma Institute of Technology and Science, Hyderabad, India
Krzysztof Walkowiak	Wroclaw University of Technology, Poland
Lu Yan	University of Hertfordshire, UK
Lus Veiga	Technical University of Lisbon, Portugal
M. Rajarajan	City University, UK
Madhan K.S.	Infosys Technologies Limited, India
Mahalinga V. Mandi	Dr. Ambedkar Institute of Technology, Bangalore, Karnataka, India
Marco Roccetti	Universty of Bologna, Italy
Michal Wozniak	Wroclaw University of Technology, Poland
Mohammad Mehdi Farhangia	Universiti Teknologi Malaysia (UTM) Malaysia
Mohammad Momani	University of Technology Sydney, Australia
Mohsen Sharifi	Iran University of Science and Technology, Iran
Murty Ch.A.S.	JNTU, Hyderabad, India
Murugan D.	Manonmaniam Sundaranar University, India
N. Krishnan	Manonmaniam Sundaranar University, India
Nabendu Chaki	University of Calcutta, India
Nagamanjula Prasad	Padmasri Institute of Technology, India
Nagaraj Aitha	IT Kamala Institute of Technology and Science, India
Natarajan Meghanathan	Jackson State University, USA
Nicolas Sklavos	Technological Educational Institute of Patras, Greece
Nidaa Abdual Muhsin Abbas	University of Babylon, Iraq
Omar Almomani	College of Arts and Sciences Universiti Utara Malaysia
Parth Lakhiya	parth.lakhiya@einfochips.com
Paul D. Manuel	Kuwait University, Kuwait
Phan Cong Vinh	London South Bank University, UK
Polgar Zsolt Alfred	Technical University of Cluj Napoca, Romania
Ponpit Wongthongtham	Curtin University of Technology, Australia
Prabu Dorairaj	Wipro Technologies, India
R. Thandeeswaran	VIT University, India
R.M. Suresh	Mysore University
Rabindranath berA	Sikkim Manipal Institute of Technology, India
Raja Kumar M.	National Advanced IPv6 Center (NAv6), Universiti Sains Malaysia, Malaysia

Rajendra Akerkar	Technomathematics Research Foundation, India
Rajesh Kumar Krishnan	Bannari Amman Institute of Technology, India
Rajesh Kumar P.	The Best International, Australia
Rajeswari Balasubramaniam	Dr. MGR University, India
Rajkumar Kannan	Bishop Heber College, India
Rakhesh Singh Kshetrimayum	Indian Institute of Technology, Guwahati, India
Ramayah Thurasamy	Universiti Sains Malaysia, Malaysia
Ramin Karimi	Universiti Teknologi Malaysia
Razvan Deaconescu	University Politehnica of Bucharest, Romania
Reena Dadhich	Govt. Engineering College Ajmer, India
Rituparna Chaki	rituchaki@gmail.com
Roberts Masillamani	Hindustan University, India
S. Bhaskaran	SASTRA University, India
Sagarmay Deb	Central Queensland University, Australia
Sajid Hussain	Acadia University, Canada
Salah M. Saleh Al-Majeed	Esses University, UK
Saleena Ameen	B.S. Abdur Rahman University, India
Salman Abdul Moiz	Centre for Development of Advanced Computing, India
Sami Ouali	ENSI, Campus of Manouba, Manouba, Tunisia
Samodar Reddy	India School of Mines, India
Sanguthevar Rajasekaran	University of Connecticut, USA
Sanjay Singh	Manipal Institute of Technology, India
Sara Najafzadeh	Universiti Teknologi Malaysia
Sarada Prasad Dakua	IIT-Bombay, India
Sarmistha Neogy	Jadavpur University, India
Sattar B. Sadkhan	University of Babylon, Iraq
Seetha Maddala	CBIT, Hyderabad, India
Serban	Ovidius University of Constantza, Romania
Sergio Ilarri	University of Zaragoza, Spain
Serguei A. Mokhov	Concordia University, Canada
Seungmin Rho	Carnegie Mellon University, USA
Sevki Erdogan	University of Hawaii, USA
Shivan Haran	Arizona state University, USA
Shriram Vasudevan	VIT University, India
Shubhalaxmi Kher	Arkansas State University, USA
Solange Rito Lima	University of Minho, Portugal
Sriman Narayana Iyengar	VIT University, India
Subir Sarkar	Jadavpur University, India
Sudip Misra	Indian Institute of Technology, Kharagpur, India
Suhaidi B. Hassan	Office of the Assistant Vice Chancellor, Economics Building
Sundarapandian Vaidyanathan	Vel Tech Dr. RR & Dr. SR Technical University, India

SunYoung Han	Konkuk University, South Korea
Susana Sargento	University of Aveiro, Portugal
Swarup Mitra	Jadavpur University, Kolkata, India
Tsung Teng Chen	National Taipei University, Taiwan
Virgil Dobrota	Technical University of Cluj-Napoca, Romania
Vishal Sharma	Metanoia Inc., USA
Wei Jie	University of Manchester, UK
William R. Simpson	Institute for Defense Analyses, USA
Wojciech Mazurczyk	Warsaw University of Technology, Poland
Yannick Le Moullec	Aalborg University, Denmark
Yedehalli Kumara Swamy	Dayanand Sagar College of Engineering, India
Yeong Deok Kim Woosong	University, South Korea
Yuh-Shyan Chen	National Taipei University, Taiwan
Yung-Fa Huang	Chaoyang University of Technology, Taiwan

External Reviewers

Abhishek Samanta	Jadavpur University, Kolkata, India
Amit Choudhary	Maharaja Surajmal Institute, India
Anjan K.	MSRIT, India
Ankit	BITS, PILANI, India
Aravind P.A.	Amrita School of Engineering, India
Cauvery Giri	RVCE, India
Debdatta Kandar	Sikkim Manipal University, India
Doreswamyh Hosahalli	Mangalore University, India
Gopalakrishnan Kaliaperumal	Anna University, Chennai, India
Hameem Shanavas	Vivekananda Institute of Technology, India
Hari Chavan	National Institute of Technology, Jamshedpur, India
Kaushik Chakraborty	Jadavpur University, India
Lavanya	Blekinge Institute of Technology, Sweden
Mydhili Nair	M. S. Ramaiah Institute of Technology, India
Naga Prasad Bandaru	PVP Siddartha Institute of Technology, India
Nana Patil	NIT Surat, Gujrat
Osman B. Ghazali	Universiti Utara Malaysia, Malaysia
P. Sheik Abdul Khader	B.S.Abdur Rahman University, India
Padmalochan Bera	Indian Institute of Technology, Kharagpur, India
Pappa Rajan	Anna University, India
Pradeepini Gera	Jawaharlal Nehru Technological University, India
Rajashree Biradar	Ballari Institute of Technology and Management, India
Ramin Karimi	University Technology, Malaysia
Reshmi Maulik	University of Calcutta, India
Rituparna Chaki	West Bengal University of Technology, India

S.C. Sharma	IIT - Roorkee, India
Salini P.	Pondichery Engineering College, India
Selvakumar Ramachandran	Blekinge Institute of Technology, Sweden
Soumyabrata Saha	Guru Tegh Bahadur Institute of Technology, India
Srinivasulu Pamidi	V.R. Siddhartha Engineering College Vijayawada, India
Subhabrata Mukherjee	Jadavpur University, India
Sunil Singh	Bharati Vidyapeeth's College of Engineering, India
Suparna DasGupta	suparnadasguptait@gmail.com
Valli Kumari Vatsavayi	AU College of Engineering, India

Technically Sponsored by

Software Engineering & Security Community (SESC)
Networks & Communications Community (NCC)
Internet Computing Community (ICC)
Computer Science & Information Technology Community (CSITC)

Organized By

ACADEMY & INDUSTRY RESEARCH COLLABORATION CENTER (AIRCC)
www.airccse.org

Table of Contents

Advances in Computing and Information Technology

Output Regulation of the Unified Chaotic System

Sundarapandian Vaidyanathan

R & D Centre, Vel Tech Dr. RR & Dr. SR Technical University
Avadi-Alamathi Road, Avadi, Chennai-600 062, India
sundarvtu@gmail.com
http://www.vel-tech.org/

Abstract. This paper investigates the problem of output regulation of the unified chaotic system (Lu, Chen, Cheng and Celikovsky, 2002). Explicitly, state feedback control laws to regulate the output of the unified chaotic system have been derived so as to track the constant reference signals. The control laws are derived using the regulator equations of C.I. Byrnes and A. Isidori (1990), who solved the problem of output regulation of nonlinear systems involving neutrally stable exosystem dynamics. Numerical simulations are shown to illustrate the results.

Keywords: Unified chaotic system, output regulation, nonlinear control systems, feedback stabilization.

1 Introduction

Output regulation of control systems is one of the very important problems in control systems theory. Basically, the output regulation problem is to control a fixed linear or nonlinear plant in order to have its output tracking reference signals produced by some external generator (the exosystem). For linear control systems, the output regulation problem has been solved by Francis and Wonham (1975, [1]). For nonlinear control systems, the output regulation problem has been solved by Byrnes and Isidori (1990, [2]) generalizing the internal model principle obtained by Francis and Wonham [1]. Byrnes and Isidori [2] have made an important assumption in their work which demands that the exosystem dynamics generating reference and/or disturbance signals is a neutrally stable system (Lyapunov stable in both forward and backward time). The class of exosystem signals includes the important particular cases of constant reference signals as well as sinusoidal reference signals. Using Centre Manifold Theory [3], Byrnes and Isidori have derived regulator equations, which completely characterize the solution of the output regulation problem of nonlinear control systems.

The output regulation problem for linear and nonlinear control systems has been the focus of many studies in recent years ([4]-[14]). In [4], Mahmoud and Khalil obtained results on the asymptotic regulation of minimum phase nonlinear systems using output feedback. In [5], Fridman solved the output regulation problem for nonlinear control systems with delay, using Centre Manifold Theory [3]. In [6]-[7], Chen and Huang obtained results on the robust output regulation for output feedback systems with nonlinear exosystems. In [8], Liu and Huang obtained results on the global robust output regulation problem for lower triangular nonlinear systems with unknown control direction. In [9], Immonen obtained results on the practical output regulation for bounded

D.C. Wyld et al. (Eds.): ACITY 2011, CCIS 198, pp. 1–9, 2011.

linear infinite-dimensional state space systems. In [10], Pavlov, Van de Wouw and Nijmeijer obtained results on the global nonlinear output regulation using convergence-based controller design. In [11], Xi and Ding obtained results on the global adaptive output regulation of a class of nonlinear systems with nonlinear exosystems. In [12]-[14], Serrani, Marconi and Isidori obtained results on the semi-global and global output regulation problem for minimum-phase nonlinear systems.

In this paper, the output regulation problem for the chaotic system [15] has been solved using the regulator equations [2] to derive the state feedback control laws for regulating the output of the Coullet chaotic system for the important case constant reference signals (set-point signals). The unified chaotic system is an important chaotic system proposed by J. Lu, G. Chen, D.Z. Cheng and S. Celikovsky ([15], 2002) and this chaotic system bridges the gap between Lorenz system ([16], 1963) and Chen system ([17]. The unified chaotic system includes Lorenz system, Chen system and Lü system ([18], 2002) as special cases.

This paper is organized as follows. In Section 2, a review of the solution of the output regulation for nonlinear control systems and regulator equations has been presented. In Section 3, the main results of this paper, namely, the feedback control laws solving the output regulation problem for the unified chaotic system for the important case of constant reference signals has been detailed. In Section 4, the numerical results illustrating the main results of the paper have been described. Section 5 summarizes the main results obtained in this paper.

2 Review of the Output Regulation for Nonlinear Control Systems

In this section, we consider a multi-variable nonlinear control system modelled by equations of the form

$$\dot{x} = f(x) + g(x)u + p(x)\omega \tag{1}$$

$$\dot{\omega} = s(\omega) \tag{2}$$

$$e = h(x) - q(\omega) \tag{3}$$

Here, the differential equation (1) describes the *plant dynamics* with state x defined in a neighbourhood X of the origin of $\mathbb{R}^n$ and the input u takes values in $\mathbb{R}^m$ subject to the effect of a disturbance represented by the vector field $p(x)\omega$. The differential equation (2) describes an autonomous system, known as the *exosystem*, defined in a neighbourhood W of the origin of $\mathbb{R}^k$, which models the class of disturbance and reference signals taken into consideration. The equation (3) defines the error between the actual plant output $h(x) \in \mathbb{R}^p$ and a reference signal $q(\omega)$, which models the class of disturbance and reference signals taken into consideration.

We also assume that all the constituent mappings of the system (1)-(2) and the error equation (3), namely, f, g, p, s, h and q are C^1 mappings vanishing at the origin, *i.e.*

$$f(0) = 0,\ g(0) = 0,\ p(0) = 0,\ h(0) = 0 \text{ and } q(0) = 0.$$

Thus, for $u = 0$, the composite system (1)-(2) has an equilibrium $(x, \omega) = (0, 0)$ with zero error (3).

A *state feedback controller* for the composite system (1)-(2) has the form

$$u = \alpha(x, \omega) \tag{4}$$

where α is a $\mathcal{C}^1$ mapping defined on $X \times W$ such that $\alpha(0,0) = 0$. Upon substitution of the feedback law (4) in the composite system (1)-(2), we get the closed-loop system given by

$$\begin{aligned} \dot{x} &= f(x) + g(x)\alpha(x, \omega) + p(x)\omega \\ \dot{\omega} &= s(\omega) \end{aligned} \tag{5}$$

State Feedback Regulator Problem [2]:

Find, if possible, a state feedback control law $u = \alpha(x, \omega)$ such that

(1) [*Internal Stability*] The equilibrium $x = 0$ of the dynamics

$$\dot{x} = f(x) + g(x)\alpha(x, 0)$$

is locally exponentially stable.

(2) [*Output Regulation*] There exists a neighbourhood $U \subset X \times W$ of $(x, \omega) = (0, 0)$ such that for each initial condition $(x(0), \omega(0)) \in U$, the solution $(x(t), \omega(t))$ of the closed-loop system (5) satisfies

$$\lim_{t \to \infty} \left[h(x(t)) - q(\omega(t)) \right] = 0. \qquad \blacksquare$$

Byrnes and Isidori [2] have solved this problem under the following assumptions.

(H1). The exosystem dynamics $\dot{\omega} = s(\omega)$ is *neutrally stable* at $\omega = 0$, *i.e.* the system is Lyapunov stable in both forward and backward time at $\omega = 0$.

(H2). The pair $(f(x), g(x))$ has a *stabilizable* linear approximation at $x = 0$, *i.e.* if

$$A = \left[\frac{\partial f}{\partial x} \right]_{x=0} \quad \text{and} \quad B = \left[\frac{\partial g}{\partial x} \right]_{x=0},$$

then (A, B) is stabilizable, which means that we can find a gain matrix K so that $A + BK$ is Hurwitz. ■

Next, we recall the solution of the output regulation problem derived by Byrnes and Isidori [2].

Theorem 1. *[2] Under the hypotheses (H1) and (H2), the state feedback regulator problem is solvable if, and only if, there exist* $\mathcal{C}^1$ *mappings* $x = \pi(\omega)$ *with* $\pi(0) = 0$ *and* $u = \phi(\omega)$ *with* $\phi(0) = 0$*, both defined in a neighbourhod of* $W^0 \subset W$ *of* $\omega = 0$ *such that the following equations (called the* **regulator equations***) are satisfied:*

(1) $\frac{\partial \pi}{\partial \omega} s(\omega) = f(\pi(\omega)) + g(\pi(\omega))\phi(\omega) + p(\pi(\omega))\omega$

(2) $h(\pi(\omega)) - q(\omega) = 0$

When the regulator equations (1) and (2) are satisfied, a control law solving the state feedback regulator problem is given by

$$u = \phi(\omega) + K[x - \pi(\omega)] \tag{6}$$

where K *is any gain matrix such that* $A + BK$ *is Hurwitz.* ■

3 Output Regulation of the Unified Chaotic System

The unified chaotic system ([15], 2002) is one of the paradigms of the three-dimensional chaotic models described by the dynamics

$$\begin{aligned} \dot{x}_1 &= (25\alpha + 10)(x_2 - x_1) \\ \dot{x}_2 &= (28 - 35\alpha)x_1 + (29\alpha - 1)x_2 - x_1 x_3 + u \\ \dot{x}_3 &= x_1 x_2 - \tfrac{1}{3}(8 + \alpha)\, x_3 \end{aligned} \tag{7}$$

where x_1, x_2, x_3 are the state variables, u is the control and $\alpha \in [0, 1]$.

In ([15], 2002), Lu, Chen, Cheng and Celikovsky showed that the system (7) bridges the gap between the Lorenz system ([16], 1963) and the Chen system ([17], 1999). Obviously, the system (7) becomes the original Lorenz system for $\alpha = 0$, while the system (7) becomes the original Chen system for $\alpha = 1$. When $\alpha = 0.8$, the system (7) becomes the *critical* system or the Lü system ([18], 2002). Moreover, the system (7) is always chaotic in the whole interval $\alpha \in [0, 1]$.

In this paper, we solve the problem of output regulation for the unified chaotic system (7) for tracking of the constant reference signals (*set-point signals*).

The constant reference signals are generated by the scalar exosystem dynamics

$$\dot{\omega} = 0 \tag{8}$$

It is important to note that the exosystem given by (8) is neutrally stable, because the exosystem (8) admits only constant solutions. Thus, the assumption (H1) of Theorem 1 holds trivially.

Linearizing the dynamics of the unified chaotic system (7) at $x = 0$, we get

$$A = \begin{bmatrix} -(25\alpha + 10) & 25\alpha + 10 & 0 \\ 28 - 35\alpha & 29\alpha - 1 & 0 \\ 0 & 0 & -\tfrac{1}{3}(\alpha + 8) \end{bmatrix} \quad \text{and} \quad B = \begin{bmatrix} 0 \\ 1 \\ 0 \end{bmatrix}.$$

The system pair (A, B) can be expressed as

$$A = \begin{bmatrix} A_1 & 0 \\ 0 & \lambda^\star \end{bmatrix} \quad \text{and} \quad B = \begin{bmatrix} B_1 \\ 0 \end{bmatrix}$$

where the pair

$$A_1 = \begin{bmatrix} -(25\alpha + 10) & 25\alpha + 10 \\ 28 - 35\alpha & 29\alpha - 1 \end{bmatrix} \quad \text{and} \quad B_1 = \begin{bmatrix} 0 \\ 1 \end{bmatrix}$$

is completely controllable and the uncontrollable mode of A is

$$\lambda^\star = -\frac{1}{3}(\alpha + 8) < 0$$

for all $\alpha \in [0, 1]$.

Thus, the system pair (A, B) is stabilizable and we can find a gain matrix

$$K = [\, K_1 \quad 0 \,] = [\, k_1 \quad k_2 \quad 0 \,]$$

so that the eigenvalues of $A_1 + B_1 K_1$ can be arbitrarily assigned in the stable region of the complex plane. (The uncontrollable mode $\lambda^\star$ will always stay as a stable eigenvalue of $A + BK$.) Thus, the assumption (H2) of Theorem 1 also holds.

Hence, we can apply Theorem 1 to completely solve the output regulation problem for the unified chaotic system (7) for the tracking of constant reference signals generated by the exosystem dynamics (8).

Case (A): Constant Tracking Problem for x_1

Here, we consider the tracking problem for the unified chaotic system (7) with the exosystem dynamics (8) and the tracking error equation

$$e = x_1 - \omega \tag{9}$$

Solving the regulator equations for this tracking problem, we obtain the unique solution

$$\begin{aligned} \pi_1(\omega) = \omega, \ \ \pi_2(\omega) = \omega, \ \ \pi_3(\omega) &= \tfrac{3\omega^2}{8+\alpha} \\ \phi(\omega) &= \tfrac{3\omega}{8+\alpha}\left[\omega^2 + (2\alpha - 9)(8+\alpha)\right] \end{aligned} \tag{10}$$

Using Theorem 1 and the solution (10) of the regulator equations, we obtain the following result.

Theorem 2. *A state feedback control law solving the constant tracking problem for x_1 for the unified chaotic system (7) is given by*

$$u = \phi(\omega) + K[x - \pi(\omega)],$$

where ϕ and $\pi = [\, \pi_1 \quad \pi_2 \quad \pi_3 \,]$ are as given in Eq. (10) and the gain matrix K is given by $K = [\, K_1 \quad 0 \,]$ with K_1 chosen so that $A_1 + B_1 K_1$ is Hurwitz. ■

Case (B): Constant Tracking Problem for x_2

Here, we consider the tracking problem for the unified chaotic system (7) with the exosystem dynamics (8) and the tracking error equation

$$e = x_2 - \omega \tag{11}$$

Solving the regulator equations for this tracking problem, we obtain the unique solution

$$\begin{aligned} \pi_1(\omega) = \omega, \ \ \pi_2(\omega) = \omega, \ \ \pi_3(\omega) &= \tfrac{3\omega^2}{8+\alpha} \\ \phi(\omega) &= \tfrac{3\omega}{8+\alpha}\left[\omega^2 + (2\alpha - 9)(8+\alpha)\right] \end{aligned} \tag{12}$$

Using Theorem 1 and the solution (12) of the regulator equations, we obtain the following result.

Theorem 3. *A state feedback control law solving the constant tracking problem for x_2 for the unified chaotic system (7) is given by*

$$u = \phi(\omega) + K[x - \pi(\omega)],$$

where ϕ and $\pi = [\, \pi_1 \quad \pi_2 \quad \pi_3 \,]$ are as given in Eq. (12) and the gain matrix K is given by $K = [\, K_1 \quad 0 \,]$ with K_1 chosen so that $A_1 + B_1 K_1$ is Hurwitz. ■

Case (C): Constant Tracking Problem for x_3

Here, we consider the tracking problem for the unified chaotic system (7) with the exosystem dynamics (8) and the tracking error equation

$$e = x_3 - \omega \tag{13}$$

Solving the regulator equations for this tracking problem, we obtain the unique solution

$$\begin{aligned} &\pi_1(\omega) = \sqrt{\tfrac{\omega(8+\alpha)}{3}}, \ \ \pi_2(\omega) = \sqrt{\tfrac{\omega(8+\alpha)}{3}}, \ \ \pi_3(\omega) = \omega \\ &\phi(\omega) = (6\alpha - 27 + \omega)\sqrt{\tfrac{\omega(8+\alpha)}{3}} \end{aligned} \tag{14}$$

Using Theorem 1 and the solution (14) of the regulator equations, we obtain the following result.

Theorem 4. *A state feedback control law solving the constant tracking problem for x_3 for the unified chaotic system (7) is given by*

$$u = \phi(\omega) + K[x - \pi(\omega)],$$

where ϕ and $\pi = [\,\pi_1 \quad \pi_2 \quad \pi_3\,]$ are as given in Eq. (14) and the gain matrix K is given by $K = [\,K_1 \quad 0\,]$ with K_1 chosen so that $A_1 + B_1K_1$ is Hurwitz. ■

4 Numerical Simulations

We consider the constant reference signal as $\omega \equiv 2$.

For numerical simulations, we choose the gain matrix $K = [\,K_1 \quad 0\,]$ where

$$K_1 = [\,k_1 \quad k_2 \quad 0\,]$$

is determined using Ackermann's formula [19] so that $A_1 + B_1K_1$ has stable eigenvalues $\{-2, -2\}$.

Case (A): Constant Tracking Problem for x_1

Here, we take $\alpha = 0$ so that the unified system (7) becomes the Lorenz system [16]. A simple calculation gives $K = [\,K_1 \quad 0\,] = [\,-34.4 \quad 7.0 \quad 0\,]$. Let $x(0) = (8, 9, 4)$.

The simulation graph is depicted in Figure 1 from which we see that the state $x_1(t)$ tracks the signal $\omega \equiv 2$ in 6 sec.

Case (B): Constant Tracking Problem for x_2

Here, we take $\alpha = 0.8$ so that the unified system (7) becomes the Lü system [18]. A simple calculation gives $K = [\,K_1 \quad 0\,] = [\,-26.1333 \quad 3.8 \quad 0\,]$. Let $x(0) = (6, 5, 8)$.

The simulation graph is depicted in Figure 2 from which we see that the state $x_2(t)$ tracks the signal $\omega \equiv 2$ in about 14 sec.

Case (C): Constant Tracking Problem for x_3

Here, we take $\alpha = 1$ so that the unified system (7) becomes the Chen system [17]. A simple calculation gives $K = [\,K_1 \quad 0\,] = [\,-24.1143 \quad 3.0 \quad 0\,]$. Let $x(0) = (7, 1, 4)$.

The simulation graph is depicted in Figure 3 from which we see that the state $x_3(t)$ tracks the signal $\omega \equiv 2$ in about 35 sec.

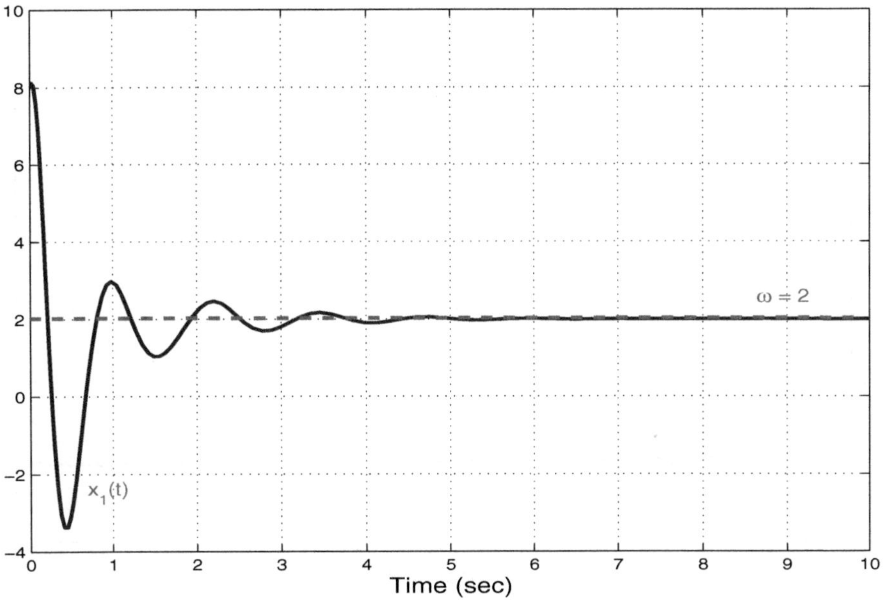

Fig. 1. Constant Tracking Problem for x_1

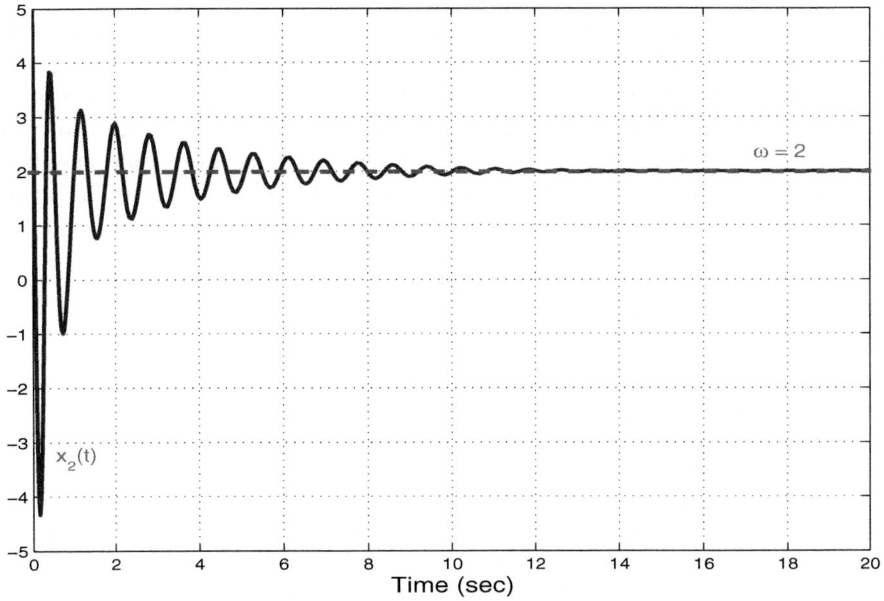

Fig. 2. Constant Tracking Problem for x_2

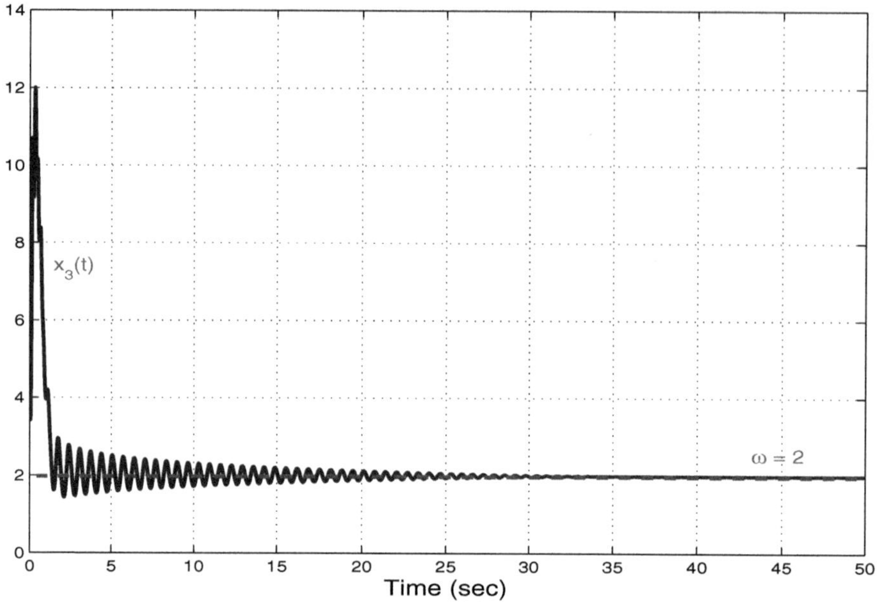

Fig. 3. Constant Tracking Problem for x_3

5 Conclusions

In this paper, the output regulation problem for the unified chaotic system (2002) has been studied in detail and a complete solution for the output regulation problem for the unified chaotic system has been presented as well. Explicitly, using the regulator equations (Byrnes and Isidori, 1990), state feedback control laws for regulating the output of the unified chaotic system have been derived. Simulation results have been also discussed in detail for various special cases of unified chaotic system, *viz.* Lorenz system, Lü system and Chen system.

References

1. Francis, B.A., Wonham, W.M.: The internal model principle for linear multivariable regulators. J. Applied Math. Optim. 2, 170–194 (1975)
2. Byrnes, C.I., Isidori, A.: Output regulation of nonlinear systems. IEEE Trans. Automat. Control. 35, 131–140 (1990)
3. Carr, J.: Applications of Centre Manifold Theory. Springer, New York (1981)
4. Mahmoud, N.A., Khalil, H.K.: Asymptotic regulation of minimum phase nonlinear systems using output feedback. IEEE Trans. Automat. Control. 41, 1402–1412 (1996)
5. Fridman, E.: Output regulation of nonlinear control systems with delay. Systems & Control Lett. 50, 81–93 (2003)
6. Chen, Z., Huang, J.: Robust output regulation with nonlinear exosystems. Automatica 41, 1447–1454 (2005)

7. Chen, Z., Huang, J.: Global robust output regulation for output feedback systems. IEEE Trans. Automat. Control. 50, 117–121 (2005)
8. Liu, L., Huang, J.: Global robust output regulation of lower triangular systems with unknown control direction. Automatica 44, 1278–1284 (2008)
9. Immonen, E.: Practical output regulation for bounded linear infinite-dimensional state space systems. Automatica 43, 786–794 (2007)
10. Pavlov, A., Van de Wouw, N., Nijmeijer, H.: Global nonlinear output regulation: convergence based controller design. Automatica 43, 456–463 (2007)
11. Xi, Z., Ding, Z.: Global adaptive output regulation of a class of nonlinear systems with nonlinear exosystems. Automatica 43, 143–149 (2007)
12. Serrani, A., Isidori, A.: Global robust output regulation for a class of nonlinear systems. Systems & Control Lett. 39, 133–139 (2000)
13. Serrani, A., Isidori, A., Marconi, L.: Semiglobal output regulation for minimum phase systems. Int. J. Robust Nonlinear Contr. 10, 379–396 (2000)
14. Marconi, L., Isidori, A., Serrani, A.: Non-resonance conditions for uniform observability in the problem of nonlinear output regulation. Systems & Control Lett. 53, 281–298 (2004)
15. Lü, J., Chen, G., Cheng, D.Z., Celikovsky, S.: Bridge the gap between the Lorenz system and the Chen system. Internat. J. Bifur. Chaos. 12, 2917–2926 (2002)
16. Lorenz, E.N.: Deterministic nonperiodic flow. J. Atmos. Scien. 20, 131–141 (1963)
17. Chen, G., Ueta, T.: Yet another chaotic attractor. Internat. J. Bifur. Chaos. 9, 1465–1466 (1999)
18. Lü, J., Chen, G.: A new chaotic attractor coined. Internat. J. Bifur. Chaos. 12, 659–661 (2002)
19. Ogata, K.: Modern Control Engineering. Prentice Hall, New Jersey (1997)

Global Chaos Synchronization of Hyperchaotic Bao and Xu Systems by Active Nonlinear Control

Sundarapandian Vaidyanathan and Suresh Rasappan

R & D Centre, Vel Tech Dr. RR & Dr. SR Technical University
Avadi-Alamathi Road, Avadi, Chennai-600 062, India
sundarvtu@gmail.com
http://www.vel-tech.org/

Abstract. This paper investigates the global chaos synchronization of hyperchaotic systems, viz. synchronization of identical hyperchaotic Bao systems (Bao and Liu, 2008), and synchronization of non-identical hyperchaotic Bao and Xu systems. Active nonlinear feedback control is the method used to achieve the synchronization of the chaotic systems addressed in this paper. Our theorems on global chaos synchronization for hyperchaotic Bao and Xu systems are established using Lyapunov stability theory. Since the Lyapunov exponents are not required for these calculations, the active control method is effective and convenient to synchronize identical and different hyperchaotic Bao and Xu systems. Numerical simulations are also given to illustrate and validate the various synchronization results derived in this paper.

Keywords: Chaos synchronization, nonlinear control, hyperchaotic Bao system, hyperchaotic Xu system, hyperchaos, active control.

1 Introduction

Chaotic systems are dynamical systems that are highly sensitive to initial conditions. This sensitivity is popularly referred to as the butterfly effect [1]. Chaos synchronization problem was first described by Fujisaka and Yemada [2] in 1983. This problem did not receive great attention until Pecora and Carroll ([3]-[4]) published their results on chaos synchronization in early 1990s. From then on, chaos synchronization has been extensively and intensively studied in the last three decades ([3]-[25]). Chaos theory has been explored in a variety of fields including physical [5], chemical [6], ecological [7] systems, secure communications ([8]-[10]) etc.

Synchronization of chaotic systems is a phenomenon that may occur when two or more chaotic oscillators are coupled or when a chaotic oscillator drives another chaotic oscillator. Because of the butterfly effect which causes the exponential divergence of the trajectories of two identical chaotic systems started with nearly the same initial conditions, synchronizing two chaotic systems is seemingly a very challenging problem.

In most of the chaos synchronization approaches, the master-slave or drive-response formalism is used. If a particular chaotic system is called the *master* or *drive* system and another chaotic system is called the *slave* or *response* system, then the idea of the synchronization is to use the output of the master system to control the slave system so that the output of the slave system tracks the output of the master system asymptotically.

D.C. Wyld et al. (Eds.): ACITY 2011, CCIS 198, pp. 10–17, 2011.

Since the seminal work by Pecora and Carroll ([3]-[4]), a variety of impressive approaches have been proposed for the synchronization for the chaotic systems such as PC method ([3]-[4]), t he sampled-data feedback synchronization method ([10]-[11]), OGY method [12], time-delay feedback approach [13], backstepping design method [14], adaptive design method ([15]-[18]), sliding mode control method [19], active control method ([20], [21]), etc.

Hyperchaotic system is usually defined as a chaotic system with at least two positive Lyapunov exponents, implying that its dynamics are expanded in several different directions simultaneously. Thus, the hyperchaotic systems have more complex dynamical behaviour which can be used to improve the security of a chaotic communication system. Hence, the theoretical design and circuit realization of various hyperchaotic signals have become important research topics ([22]-[24]).

This paper has been organized as follows. In Section 2, we give the problem statement and our methodology. In Section 3, we derive results for the chaos synchronization of two identical hyperchaotic Bao systems ([25], 2008). In Section 4, we discuss the synchronization of hyperchaotic Xu ([26], 2009) and hyperchaotic Bao systems. Section 5 contains the conclusions of this paper.

2 Problem Statement and Our Methodology

Consider the chaotic system described by the dynamics

$$\dot{x} = Ax + f(x) \tag{1}$$

where $x \in \mathbb{R}^n$ is the state of the system, A is the $n \times n$ matrix of the system parameters and f is the nonlinear part of the system. We consider the system (1) as the *master* or *drive* system.

As the *slave* or *response* system, we consider the following chaotic system described by the dynamics

$$\dot{y} = By + g(y) + u \tag{2}$$

where $y \in \mathbb{R}^n$ is the state of the slave system, B is the $n \times n$ matrix of the system parameters, g is the nonlinear part of the system u is the controller of the slave system.

If $A = B$ and $f = g$, then x and y are the states of two *identical* chaotic systems. If $A \neq B$ and $f \neq g$, then x and y are the states of two *different* chaotic systems. In the active nonlinear control approach, we design a feedback controller which synchronizes the states of the master system (1) and the slave system (2) for all initial conditions $x(0), z(0) \in \mathbb{R}^n$.

If we define the synchronization error as

$$e = y - x, \tag{3}$$

then the synchronization error dynamics is obtained as

$$\dot{e} = By - Ax + g(y) - f(x) + u \tag{4}$$

Thus, the global synchronization problem is essentially to find a feedback controller so as to stabilize the error dynamics (4) for all initial conditions, *i.e.*

$$\lim_{t \to \infty} \|e(t)\| = 0 \tag{5}$$

for all initial conditions $e(0) \in \mathbb{R}^n$.

We use the Lyapunov stability theory as our methodology. We take as a candidate Lyapunov function

$$V(e) = e^T P e,$$

where P is a positive definite matrix. Note that V is a positive definite function by construction. We assume that the parameters of the master and slave systems are known and that the states of both systems (1) and (2) are measurable.

If we find a feedback controller u so that

$$\dot{V}(e) = -e^T Q e$$

where Q is a positive definite matrix, then V is a negative definite function on $\mathbb{R}^n$. Thus, by Lyapunov stability theory [27], the error dynamics (4) is globally exponentially stable and hence the states of the master system (1) and slave system (2) are globally exponentially synchronized.

3 Synchronization of Identical Hyperchaotic Bao Systems

In this section, we apply the active nonlinear control method for the synchronization of two identical hyperchaotic Bao systems ([25], 2008). Thus, the master system is described by the hyperchaotic Bao dynamics

$$\begin{aligned} \dot{x}_1 &= a(x_2 - x_1) + x_4 \\ \dot{x}_2 &= cx_2 - x_1 x_3 \\ \dot{x}_3 &= x_1 x_2 - b x_3 \\ \dot{x}_4 &= k x_1 + d x_2 x_3 \end{aligned} \tag{6}$$

where x_1, x_2, x_3, x_4 are the state variables and a, b, c, d, k are positive real constants.

The slave system is also described by the hyperchaotic Bao dynamics

$$\begin{aligned} \dot{y}_1 &= a(y_2 - y_1) + y_4 + u_1 \\ \dot{y}_2 &= cy_2 - y_1 y_3 + u_2 \\ \dot{y}_3 &= y_1 y_2 - b y_3 + u_3 \\ \dot{y}_4 &= k y_1 + d y_2 y_3 + u_4 \end{aligned} \tag{7}$$

where y_1, y_2, y_3, y_4 are the state variables and u_1, u_2, u_3, u_4 are the nonlinear controllers to be designed.

The four-dimensional Bao system (6) is hyperchaotic when

$$a = 36, \;\; b = 3, \;\; c = 20, \;\; d = 0.1 \;\text{ and }\; k = 21. \tag{8}$$

The synchronization error is defined by

$$e_i = y_i - x_i, \quad (i = 1, 2, 3, 4) \tag{9}$$

A simple calculation yields the error dynamics as

$$\begin{aligned}
\dot{e}_1 &= a(e_2 - e_1) + e_4 + u_1 \\
\dot{e}_2 &= ce_2 - y_1 y_3 + x_1 x_3 + u_2 \\
\dot{e}_3 &= -be_3 + y_1 y_2 - x_1 x_2 + u_3 \\
\dot{e}_4 &= ke_1 + d(y_2 y_3 - x_2 x_3) + u_4
\end{aligned} \tag{10}$$

We choose the nonlinear controller as

$$\begin{aligned}
u_1 &= -ae_2 - (k+1)e_4 \\
u_2 &= -(c+1)e_2 + y_1 y_3 - x_1 x_3 \\
u_3 &= -y_1 y_2 + x_1 x_2 \\
u_4 &= -e_4 - d(y_2 y_3 - x_2 x_3)
\end{aligned} \tag{11}$$

Substituting the controller u defined by (11) into (10), we get

$$\dot{e}_1 = -ae_1 - ke_4, \quad \dot{e}_2 = -e_2, \quad \dot{e}_3 = -be_3, \quad \dot{e}_4 = -e_4 + ke_1 \tag{12}$$

We consider the candidate Lyapunov function

$$V(e) = \frac{1}{2} e^T e = \frac{1}{2} \left(e_1^2 + e_2^2 + e_3^2 + e_4^2 \right) \tag{13}$$

which is a positive definite function on $\mathbb{R}^4$.

Differentiating V along the trajectories of (12), we find that

$$\dot{V}(e) = -ae_1^2 - e_2^2 - be_3^2 - e_4^2 \tag{14}$$

which is a negative definite function on $\mathbb{R}^4$ since a and b are positive constants.

Thus, by Lyapunov stability theory [27], the error dynamics (12) is globally exponentially stable. Hence, we have proved the following result.

Theorem 1. *The identical hyperchaotic Bao systems (6) and (7) are exponentially and globally synchronized for any initial conditions with the nonlinear controller u defined by (11).* ■

Numerical Results

For the numerical simulations, the fourth order Runge-Kutta method with time-step 10^{-6} is used to solve the two systems of differential equations (6) and (7) with the parameter values as given in (8) and the active nonlinear controller u defined by (11).

The initial values of the master system (6) are taken as

$$x_1(0) = 10, \quad x_2(0) = 5, \quad x_3(0) = 20, \quad x_4(0) = 15$$

and the initial values of the slave system (7) are taken as

$$y_1(0) = 2, \quad y_2(0) = 25, \quad y_3(0) = 5, \quad y_4(0) = 30$$

Figure 1 shows that synchronization between the states of the master system (6) and the slave system (7) occur in about 4 seconds.

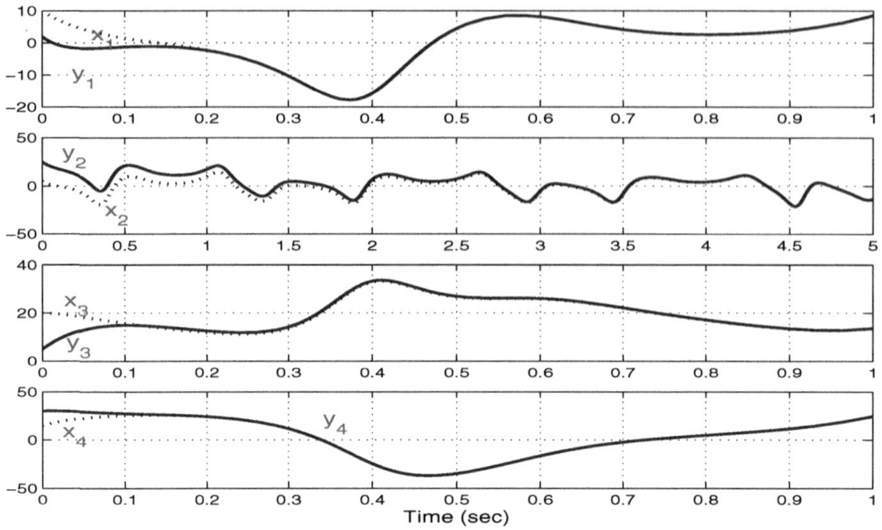

Fig. 1. Synchronization of the Identical Hyperchaotic Bao Systems

4 Synchronization of Hyperchaotic Bao and Xu Systems

In this section, the nonlinear control method is applied for the synchronization of two different hyperchaotic systems described by the hyperchaotic Xu system ([26], 2009) as the master system and the hyperchaotic Bao system ([25], 2008) as the slave system.

The dynamics of the hyperchaotic Xu system, taken as the master system, is described by

$$\begin{aligned}\dot{x}_1 &= \alpha(x_2 - x_1) + x_4 \\ \dot{x}_2 &= \beta x_1 + r x_1 x_3 \\ \dot{x}_3 &= -\gamma x_3 - l x_1 x_2 \\ \dot{x}_4 &= x_1 x_3 - m x_2\end{aligned} \tag{15}$$

where x_1, x_2, x_3, x_4 are the state variables and $\alpha, \beta, \gamma, r, l, m$ are positive real constants.

The dynamics of the hyperchaotic Bao system, taken as the slave system, is described by

$$\begin{aligned}\dot{y}_1 &= a(y_2 - y_1) + y_4 + u_1 \\ \dot{y}_2 &= c y_2 - y_1 y_3 + u_2 \\ \dot{y}_3 &= y_1 y_2 - b y_3 + u_3 \\ \dot{y}_4 &= k y_1 + d y_2 y_3 + u_4\end{aligned} \tag{16}$$

where y_1, y_2, y_3, y_4 are the state variables and u_1, u_2, u_3, u_4 are the nonlinear controllers to be designed.

The four-dimensional Xu system (15) is hyperchaotic when

$$\alpha = 10, \;\; \beta = 40, \;\; \gamma = 2.5, \;\; r = 16, \;\; l = 1 \text{ and } m = 2. \tag{17}$$

The synchronization error is defined by

$$e_i = y_i - x_i, \quad (i = 1, 2, 3, 4) \tag{18}$$

A simple calculation yields the error dynamics as

$$\begin{aligned}
\dot{e}_1 &= a(e_2 - e_1) + e_4 + (a - \alpha)(x_2 - x_1) + u_1 \\
\dot{e}_2 &= ce_2 + cx_2 - \beta x_1 - y_1 y_3 - r x_1 x_3 + u_2 \\
\dot{e}_3 &= -be_3 + (\gamma - b)x_3 + y_1 y_2 + l x_1 x_2 + u_3 \\
\dot{e}_4 &= ke_1 + kx_1 + mx_2 + dy_2 y_3 - x_1 x_3 + u_4
\end{aligned} \tag{19}$$

We choose the nonlinear controller as

$$\begin{aligned}
u_1 &= -ae_2 - (k+1)e_4 + (\alpha - a)(x_2 - x_1) \\
u_2 &= -(c+1)e_2 - cx_2 + \beta x_1 + y_1 y_3 + r x_1 x_3 \\
u_3 &= (b - \gamma)x_3 - y_1 y_2 - l x_1 x_2 \\
u_4 &= -e_4 - kx_1 - mx_2 - dy_2 y_3 + x_1 x_3
\end{aligned} \tag{20}$$

Substituting the controller u defined by (20) into (19), we get

$$\dot{e}_1 = -ae_1 - ke_4, \quad \dot{e}_2 = -e_2, \quad \dot{e}_3 = -be_3, \quad \dot{e}_4 = -e_4 + ke_1 \tag{21}$$

We consider the candidate Lyapunov function

$$V(e) = \frac{1}{2} e^T e = \frac{1}{2} \left(e_1^2 + e_2^2 + e_3^2 + e_4^2 \right) \tag{22}$$

which is a positive definite function on $\mathbb{R}^4$.

Differentiating V along the trajectories of (21), we find that

$$\dot{V}(e) = -ae_1^2 - e_2^2 - be_3^2 - e_4^2 \tag{23}$$

which is a negative definition on $\mathbb{R}^4$ since a and b are positive constants.

Thus, by Lyapunov stability theory [27], the error dynamics (21) is globally exponentially stable. Hence, we have proved the following result.

Theorem 2. *The non-identical hyperchaotic Xu system (15) and hyperchaotic Bao system (16) are exponentially and globally synchronized for any initial conditions with the nonlinear controller u defined by (20).* ∎

Numerical Results

For the numerical simulations, the fourth order Runge-Kutta method with time-step 10^{-6} is used to solve the two systems of differential equations (15) and (16) with the parameter values as given in (17) and the active nonlinear controller u defined by (20).

The initial values of the master system (15) are taken as

$$x_1(0) = 20, \quad x_2(0) = 10, \quad x_3(0) = 8, \quad x_4(0) = 12$$

and the initial values of the slave system (16) are taken as

$$y_1(0) = 12, \quad y_2(0) = 26, \quad y_3(0) = 15, \quad y_4(0) = 20$$

Figure 2 shows that synchronization between the states of the master system (15) and the slave system (16) occur in about 3 seconds.

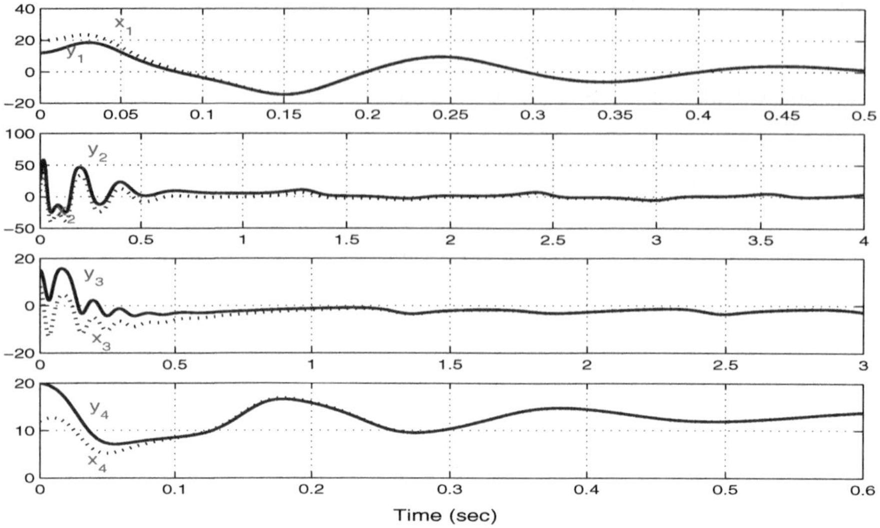

Fig. 2. Synchronization of the Hyperchaotic Xu and Bao Systems

5 Conclusions

In this paper, we have used nonlinear control method based on Lyapunov stability theory to achieve global chaos synchronization for the identical hyperchaotic Bao systems (2008), and non-identical hyperchaotic Bao system (2008) and hyperchaotic Xu system (2009). Numerical simulations are also given to validate all the synchronization results derived in this paper. Since the Lyapunov exponents are not required for these calculations, the nonlinear control method is very effective and convenient to achieve global chaos synchronization for the global chaos synchronization of hyperchaotic Bao and Xu systems.

References

1. Alligood, K.T., Sauer, T., Yorke, J.A.: Chaos: An Introduction to Dynamical Systems. Springer, New York (1997)
2. Fujikasa, H., Yamada, T.: Stability theory of synchronized motion in coupled-oscillator systems. Progr. Theoret. Phys. 69, 32–47 (1983)
3. Pecora, L.M., Carroll, T.L.: Synchronization in chaotic systems. Phys. Rev. Lett. 64, 821–824 (1990)
4. Pecora, L.M., Carroll, T.L.: Synchronizing chaotic circuits. IEEE Trans. Circ. Sys. 38, 453–456 (1991)
5. Lakshmanan, M., Murali, K.: Chaos in Nonlinear Oscillators: Controlling and Synchronization. World Scientific, Singapore (1996)
6. Han, S.K., Kerrer, C., Kuramoto, Y.: Dephasing and bursting in coupled neural oscillators. Phys. Rev. Lett. 75, 3190–3193 (1995)

7. Blasius, B., Huppert, A., Stone, L.: Complex dynamics and phase synchronization in spatially extended ecological system. Nature 399, 354–359 (1999)
8. Kwok, H.S., Wallace, K., Tang, S., Man, K.F.: Online secure communication system using chaotic map. Internat. J. Bifurcat. Chaos. 14, 285–292 (2004)
9. Kocarev, L., Parlitz, U.: General approach for chaos synchronization with applications to communications. Phys. Rev. Lett. 74, 5028–5030 (1995)
10. Murali, K., Lakshmanan, M.: Secure communication using a compound signal using sampled-data feedback. Applied Math. Mech. 11, 1309–1315 (2003)
11. Yang, T., Chua, L.O.: Control of chaos using sampled-data feedback control. Internat. J. Bifurcat. Chaos. 9, 215–219 (1999)
12. Ott, E., Grebogi, C., Yorke, J.A.: Controlling chaos. Phys. Rev. Lett. 64, 1196–1199 (1990)
13. Park, J.H., Kwon, O.M.: A novel criterion for delayed feedback control of time-delay chaotic systems. Chaos, Solit. Fract. 17, 709–716 (2003)
14. Wu, X., Lü, J.: Parameter identification and backstepping control of uncertain Lü system. Chaos, Solit. Fract. 18, 721–729 (2003)
15. Samuel, B.: Adaptive synchronization between two different chaotic dynamical systems. Adaptive Commun. Nonlinear Sci. Num. Simul. 12, 976–985 (2007)
16. Yu, Y.G., Zhang, S.C.: Adaptive backstepping synchronization of uncertain chaotic systems. Chaos, Solit. Fract. 27, 1369–1375 (2006)
17. Park, J.H., Lee, S.M., Kwon, O.M.: Adaptive synchronization of Genesio-Tesi system via a novel feedback control. Physics Lett. A. 371, 263–270 (2007)
18. Park, J.H.: Adaptive control for modified projective synchronization of a four-dimensional chaotic sytem with uncertain parameters. J. Comput. Applied Math. 213, 288–293 (2008)
19. Yau, H.T.: Design of adaptive sliding mode controller for chaos synchronization with uncertainties. Chaos, Solit. Fract. 22, 341–347 (2004)
20. Chen, H.K.: Global chaos synchronization of new chaotic systems via nonlinear control. Chaos, Solit. Fract. 23, 1245–1251 (2005)
21. Sundarapandian, V., Suresh, R.: Global chaos synchronization for Rössler and Arneodo chaotic systems. Far East J. Math. Sci. 44, 137–148 (2010)
22. Vicente, R., Dauden, J., Colet, P., Toral, R.: Analysis and characterization of the hyperchaos generated by a semiconductor laser object. IEEE J. Quantum Electr. 41, 541–548 (2005)
23. Arena, P., Baglio, S., Fortuna, L., Manganaro, G.: Hyperchaos from cellular neural networks. Electronics Lett. 31, 250–251 (1995)
24. Thamilmaran, K., Lakshmanan, M., Venkatesan, A.: A hyperchaos in a modified canonical Chua's circuit. Internat. J. Bifurcat. Chaos. 14, 221–243 (2004)
25. Bao, B.C., Liu, Z.: A hyperchaotic attractor coined from chaotic Lü system. Chin. Phys. Lett. 25, 2396–2399 (2008)
26. Xu, J., Cai, G., Zheng, S.: A novel hyperchaotic system and its control. J. Uncertain Sys. 3, 137–144 (2009)
27. Hahn, W.: The Stability of Motion. Springer, New York (1967)

Stabilization of Large Scale Discrete-Time Linear Control Systems by Observer-Based Reduced Order Controllers

Sundarapandian Vaidyanathan and Kavitha Madhavan

R & D Centre, Vel Tech Dr. RR & Dr. SR Technical University
Avadi-Alamathi Road, Avadi, Chennai-600 062, India
sundarvtu@gmail.com
http://www.vel-tech.org/

Abstract. This paper investigates the stabilization of large scale discrete-time linear control systems by observer-based reduced order controllers. Sufficient conditions are derived for the design of observer-based reduced order controllers for the large scale discrete-time linear control systems by obtaining a reduced order model of the original linear plant using the dominant state of the system. A separation principle has been established in this paper which shows that the observer poles and controller poles can be separated and hence the pole placement problem and observer design problem are independent of each other.

Keywords: Model reduction; reduced-order controllers; stabilization; dominant state; observers; discrete-time linear systems.

1 Introduction

Reduced-order model and reduced-order controller design for linear control systems has been widely studied in the control systems literature ([1]-[9]). Especially in recent decades, the control problem of large scale linear systems has been an active area of research. This is due to practical and technical issues like information transfer networks, data acquisition, sensing, computing facilities and the associated cost involved which stem from using full order controller design. Thus, there is a great demand for the control of large scale linear control systems with the use of reduced-order controllers rather than the full-order controllers ([1]-[3]).

A recent approach for obtaining reduced-order controllers is via obtaining the reduced-order model of a linear plant preserving the dynamic as well as static properties of the system and then working out controllers for the reduced-order model thus obtained ([4]-[8]). This approach has practical and technical benefits for the reduced-order controller design for large scale linear systems with high dimension and complexity.

The motivation for the observer-based reduced order controllers stems from the fact that the dominant state of the linear plant may not be available for measurement and hence for implementing the pole placement law, only the reduced order exponential observer can be used in lieu of the dominant state of the given discrete-time linear system.

D.C. Wyld et al. (Eds.): ACITY 2011, CCIS 198, pp. 18–27, 2011.

In this paper, we derive a reduced-order model for any linear discrete-time control system and our approach is based on the approach of using the dominant state of the given linear discrete-time control system, *i.e.* we derive the reduced-order model for a given discrete-time linear control system keeping only the dominant state of the given discrete-time linear control system. Using the reduced-order model obtained, we characterize the existence of a reduced-order exponential observer that tracks the state of the reduced-order model, i.e. the dominant state of the original linear plant. We note that the model reduction and the reduced-order observer design detailed in this paper are discrete-time analogues of the results of Aldeen and Trinh [8] for the observer design of the dominant state of continuous-time linear control systems.

Using the reduced-order model of the original linear plant, we also characterize the existence of a stabilizing feedback control law that uses only the dominant state of the original plant. Also, when the plant is stabilizable by a state feedback control law, the full information of the dominant state is not always available. For this reason, we establish a separation principle so that the state of the exponential observer may be used in lieu of the dominant state of the original linear plant, which facilitates the implementation of the stabilizing feedback control law derived. The design of observer-based reduced order controllers for large scale discrete-time linear systems derived in this paper has important applications in practice.

This paper is organized as follows. In Section 2, we derive the reduced-order plant of a given linear discrete-time control systems. In Section 3, we derive necessary and sufficient conditions for the exponential observer design for the reduced order linear control plant. In Section 4, we derive necessary and sufficient conditions for the reduced-order plant to be stabilizable by a linear feedback control law and we also present a separation principle for the observed-based reduced order controller design. In Section 5, we present a numerical example. Conclusions are contained in the final section.

2 Reduced Order Model for the Linear System

Consider a discrete-time linear control system $\mathcal{S}_1$ given by

$$\begin{aligned} x(k+1) &= Ax(k) + Bu(k) \\ y(k) &= Cx(k) \end{aligned} \tag{1}$$

where $x \in \mathbb{R}^n$ is the *state*, $u \in \mathbb{R}^m$ is the *control input* and $y \in \mathbb{R}^p$ is the *output* of the linear system. We assume that A, B and C are constant matrices with real entries of dimensions $n \times n$, $n \times m$ and $p \times n$ respectively.

First, we suppose that we have performed an identification of the *dominant* (*slow*) and *non-dominant* (*fast*) states of the given linear system (1) using the modal approach as described in [9].

Without loss of generality, we may assume that

$$x = \begin{bmatrix} x_s \\ x_f \end{bmatrix},$$

where $x_s \in \mathbb{R}^r$ represents the dominant state and $x_f \in \mathbb{R}^{n-r}$ represents the non-dominant state of the system.

Then the system (1) takes the form

$$\begin{bmatrix} x_s(k+1) \\ x_f(k+1) \end{bmatrix} = \begin{bmatrix} A_{ss} & A_{sf} \\ A_{fs} & A_{ff} \end{bmatrix} \begin{bmatrix} x_s(k) \\ x_f(k) \end{bmatrix} + \begin{bmatrix} B_s \\ B_f \end{bmatrix} u(k)$$
$$y(k) = \begin{bmatrix} C_s & C_f \end{bmatrix} \begin{bmatrix} x_s(k) \\ x_f(k) \end{bmatrix} \tag{2}$$

From (2), we have

$$\begin{aligned} x_s(k+1) &= A_{ss}\, x_s(k) + A_{sf}\, x_f(k) + B_s\, u(k) \\ x_f(k+1) &= A_{fs}\, x_s(k) + A_{ff}\, x_f(k) + B_f\, u(k) \\ y(k) &= C_s x_s(k) + C_f x_f(k) \end{aligned} \tag{3}$$

For the sake of simplicity, we will assume that the matrix A has distinct eigenvalues. We note that this condition is usually satisfied in most practical situations. Then it follows that A is diagonalizable.

Thus, we can find a nonsingular matrix (*modal matrix*) P consisting of the n linearly independent eigenvectors of A such that

$$P^{-1}AP = \Lambda,$$

where Λ is a diagonal matrix consisting of the n eigenvalues of A.

We introduce a new set of coordinates on the state space given by

$$\xi = P^{-1}x \tag{4}$$

Then the plant (1) becomes

$$\begin{aligned} \xi(k+1) &= \Lambda\,\xi(k) + P^{-1}B\,u(k) \\ y(k) &= CP\xi(k) \end{aligned}$$

Thus, we have

$$\begin{bmatrix} \xi_s(k+1) \\ \xi_f(k+1) \end{bmatrix} = \begin{bmatrix} \Lambda_s & 0 \\ 0 & \Lambda_f \end{bmatrix} \begin{bmatrix} \xi_s(k) \\ \xi_f(k) \end{bmatrix} + P^{-1}B\,u(k)$$
$$y(k) = CP \begin{bmatrix} \xi_s(k) \\ \xi_f(k) \end{bmatrix} \tag{5}$$

where Λ_s and Λ_f are $r \times r$ and $(n-r) \times (n-r)$ diagonal matrices respectively.

Define matrices $\Gamma_s, \Gamma_f, \Psi_s$ and Ψ_f by

$$P^{-1}B = \begin{bmatrix} \Gamma_s \\ \Gamma_f \end{bmatrix} \text{ and } CP = \begin{bmatrix} \Psi_s & \Psi_f \end{bmatrix} \tag{6}$$

where $\Gamma_s, \Gamma_f, \Psi_s$ and Ψ_f are $r \times m$, $(n-r) \times m$, $p \times r$ and $p \times (n-r)$ matrices respectively.

From (5) and (6), we see that the plant (3) has the following simple form in the new coordinates (4).

$$\begin{aligned} \xi_s(k+1) &= \Lambda_s \, \xi_s(k) + \Gamma_s \, u(k) \\ \xi_f(k+1) &= \Lambda_f \, \xi_f(k) + \Gamma_f \, u(k) \\ y(k) &= \Psi_s \xi_s(k) + \Psi_f \xi_f(k) \end{aligned} \tag{7}$$

Next, we make the following assumptions:

(H1). *As* $k \to \infty$, $\xi_f(k+1) \approx \xi_f(k)$, i.e. ξ_f *takes a constant value in the steady-state.*
(H2). *The matrix* $I - \Lambda_f$ *is invertible.*

Using (H1) and (H2), we find from Eq. (7) that for large values of k, we have

$$\xi_f(k) \approx \Lambda_f \, \xi_f(k) + \Gamma_f \, u(k)$$

i.e.

$$\xi_f(k) \approx (I - \Lambda_f)^{-1} \, \Gamma_f \, u(k) \tag{8}$$

Substituting (8) into (7), we obtain the reduced-order model of the given linear plant (1) in the ξ coordinates as

$$\begin{aligned} \xi_s(k+1) &= \Lambda_s \, \xi_s(k) + \Gamma_s \, u(k) \\ y(k) &= \Psi_s \, \xi_s(k) + \Psi_f \, (I - \Lambda_f)^{-1} \, \Gamma_f \, u(k) \end{aligned} \tag{9}$$

To obtain the reduced-order model of the given linear plant (1) in the x coordinates, we proceed as follows.

Set

$$P^{-1} = Q = \begin{bmatrix} Q_{ss} & Q_{sf} \\ Q_{fs} & Q_{ff} \end{bmatrix},$$

where Q_{ss}, Q_{sf}, Q_{fs} and Q_{ff} are $r \times r$, $r \times (n-r)$, $(n-r) \times r$ and $(n-r) \times (n-r)$ matrices respectively.

By the linear change of coordinates (4), it follows that

$$\xi = P^{-1} x = Qx.$$

Thus, we have

$$\begin{bmatrix} \xi_s(k) \\ \xi_f(k) \end{bmatrix} = Q \begin{bmatrix} x_s(k) \\ x_f(k) \end{bmatrix} = \begin{bmatrix} Q_{ss} \; Q_{sf} \\ Q_{fs} \; Q_{ff} \end{bmatrix} \begin{bmatrix} \xi_s(k) \\ \xi_f(k) \end{bmatrix} \tag{10}$$

Using (9) and (10), it follows that

$$\xi_f(k) = Q_{fs} x_s(k) + Q_{ff} x_f(k) = (I - \Lambda_f)^{-1} \Gamma_f u(k)$$

or

$$Q_{ff} x_f(k) = -Q_{fs} \, x_s(k) + (I - \Lambda_f)^{-1} \, \Gamma_f \, u(k) \tag{11}$$

Next, we make the following assumption.

(H3). *The matrix* Q_{ff} *is invertible.*

Using (H3), the equation (11) becomes

$$x_f(k) = -Q_{ff}^{-1} Q_{fs}\, x_s(k) + Q_{ff}^{-1}(I - \Lambda_f)^{-1} \Gamma_f\, u(k) \tag{12}$$

To simplify the notation, we define the matrices

$$R = -Q_{ff}^{-1} Q_{fs} \quad \text{and} \quad S = Q_{ff}^{-1} (I - \Lambda_f)^{-1} \Gamma_f \tag{13}$$

Using (13), the equation (12) can be simplified as

$$x_f(k) = R x_s(k) + S u(k) \tag{14}$$

Substituting (14) into (3), we obtain the reduced-order model $\mathcal{S}_2$ of the given linear system $\mathcal{S}_1$ as

$$\begin{aligned} x_s(k+1) &= A_s^\star\, x_s(k) + B_s^\star\, u(k) \\ y(k) &= C_s^\star\, x_s(k) + D_s^\star\, u(k) \end{aligned} \tag{15}$$

where the matrices $A_s^\star, B_s^\star, C_s^\star$ and $D_s^\star$ are defined by

$$A_s^\star = A_{ss} + A_{sf}\, R,\ B_s^\star = B_s + A_{sf}\, S,\ C_s^\star = C_s + C_f R \text{ and } D_s^\star = C_f S \tag{16}$$

3 Reduced Order Observer Design

In this section, we state a new result that prescribes a simple procedure for estimating the dominant state of the given linear control system $\mathcal{S}_1$ that satisfies the assumptions (H1)-(H3).

Theorem 1. *Let $\mathcal{S}_1$ be the linear system described by*

$$\begin{aligned} x(k+1) &= Ax(k) + Bu(k) \\ y(k) &= Cx(k) \end{aligned} \tag{17}$$

Under the assumptions (H1)-(H3), the reduced-order model $\mathcal{S}_2$ of the linear system $\mathcal{S}_1$ can be obtained (see Section 2) as

$$\begin{aligned} x_s(k+1) &= A_s^\star\, x(k) + B_s^\star\, u(k) \\ y(k) &= C_s^\star\, x(k) + D_s^\star\, u(k) \end{aligned} \tag{18}$$

where $A_s^\star, B_s^\star, C_s^\star$ and $D_s^\star$ are defined as in (16).

To estimate the dominant state x_s of the system $\mathcal{S}_1$, consider the candidate observer $\mathcal{S}_3$ defined by

$$z_s(k+1) = A_s^\star z_s(k) + B_s^\star u(k) + K_s^\star \left[y(k) - C_s^\star z_s(k) - D_s^\star u(k) \right] \tag{19}$$

Define the estimation error as $e = z_s - x_s$.

Then $e(k) \to 0$ exponentially as $k \to \infty$ if and only if the matrix $K_s^\star$ is such that $E = A_s^\star - K_s^\star C_s^\star$ is convergent. If $(C_s^\star, A_s^\star)$ is observable, then we can always construct an exponential observer of the form (19) having any desired speed of convergence.

Proof. From Eq. (2), we have

$$x_s(k+1) = A_{ss}\, x_s(k) + A_{sf}\, x_f(k) + B_s\, u(k) \tag{20}$$

Adding and subtracting the term $(A_{sf} - K_s^\star C_f)Rx_s(k)$ in the right hand side of Eq. (20), we get

$$\begin{aligned} x_s(k+1) = (A_{ss} + A_{sf}R - K_s^\star C_f R)x_s(k) + A_{sf}x_f(k) \\ -(A_{sf} - K_s^\star C_f)Rx_s(k) + B_s u(k) \end{aligned} \tag{21}$$

Subtracting (21) from (19) and simplifying using the definitions (16), we get

$$e(k+1) = (A_s^\star - K_s^\star C_s^\star)e(k) - (A_{sf} - K_s^\star C_f)[x_f(k) - Rx_s(k) - Su(k)] \tag{22}$$

As proved in Section 2, the assumptions (H1)-(H3) yield

$$x_f(k) \approx Rx_s(k) + Su(k) \tag{23}$$

Substituting (23) into (22), we get

$$e(k+1) = (A_s^\star - K_s^\star C_s^\star)e(k) = Ee(k) \tag{24}$$

which yields

$$e(k) = (A_s^\star - K_s^\star C_s^\star)^k\, e(0) = E^k\, e(0) \tag{25}$$

From Eq. (25), it follows that $e(k) \to 0$ as $k \to \infty$ if and only if E is convergent.

If $(C_s^\star, A_s^\star)$ is observable, then it is well-known [10] that we can find an observer gain matrix $K_s^\star$ that will arbitrarily assign the eigenvalues of the error matrix $E = A_s^\star - K_s^\star C_s^\star$. In particular, it follows from Eq. (25) that we can find an exponential observer of the form (19) having any desired speed of convergence. □

4 Observer-Based Reduced Order Controller Design

In this section, we first state an important result that prescribes a simple procedure for stabilizing the dominant state of the reduced-order control plant derived in Section 2.

Theorem 2. *Suppose that the assumptions (H1)-(H3) hold. Let $\mathcal{S}_1$ and $\mathcal{S}_2$ be defined as in Theorem 1. For the reduced-order model $\mathcal{S}_2$, the feedback control law*

$$u(k) = F_s^\star\, x_s(k) \tag{26}$$

stabilizes the dominant state x_s if and only if the matrix $F_s^\star$ is such that $A_s^\star + B_s^\star F_s^\star$ is convergent. If the system pair $(A_s^\star, B_s^\star)$ is controllable, then we can always construct a feedback control law (26) that stabilizes the dominant state x_s of the reduced-order model $\mathcal{S}_2$ having any desired speed of convergence. □

In practical applications, the dominant state x_s of the reduced-order model $\mathcal{S}_2$ may not be directly available for measurement and hence we cannot implement the state feedback control law (26). To overcome this practical difficulty, we derive an important theorem, usually called as the *Separation Principle*, which first establishes that the observer-based reduced-order controller indeed stabilizes the dominant state of the given linear control system $\mathcal{S}_1$ and also demonstrates that the observer poles and the closed-loop controller poles are separated.

Theorem 3 (**Separation Principle**). *Suppose that the assumptions (H1)-(H3) hold. Suppose that there exist matrices $F_s^\star$ and $K_s^\star$ such that $A_s^\star + B_s^\star K_s^\star$ and $A_s^\star - K_s^\star C_s^\star$ are both convergent matrices. By Theorem 1, we know that the system $\mathcal{S}_3$ defined by (19) is an exponential observer for the dominant state x_s of the control system $\mathcal{S}_1$. Then the observer poles and the closed-loop controller poles are separated and the control law*

$$u(k) = F_s^\star z_s(k) \tag{27}$$

also stabilizes the dominant state x_s of the control system $\mathcal{S}_1$.

Proof. Under the feedback control law (27), the observer dynamics (19)) of the system $\mathcal{S}_3$ becomes

$$\begin{aligned} z_s(k+1) &= (A_s^\star + B_s^\star F_s^\star - K_s^\star C_s^\star - K_s^\star D_s^\star F_s^\star)\, z_s(k) \\ &\quad + K_s^\star [C_s x_s(k) + C_f x_f(k)] \end{aligned} \tag{28}$$

By (14), we know that

$$x_f(k) \approx R x_s(k) + S u(k) = R x_s(k) + S F_s^\star z_s(k) \tag{29}$$

Substituting (29) into (28) and simplifying using the definitions (16), we get

$$z_s(k+1) = (A_s^\star + B_s^\star F_s^\star - K_s^\star C_s^\star)\, z_s(k) + K_s^\star C_s^\star x_s(k) \tag{30}$$

Substituting the control law (27) into (3), we also obtain

$$x_s(k+1) = A_s^\star x_s(k) + B_s^\star F_s^\star\, z_s(k) \tag{31}$$

In matrix representation, we can write equations (30) and (31) as

$$\begin{bmatrix} x_s(k+1) \\ z_s(k+1) \end{bmatrix} = \begin{bmatrix} A_s^\star & B_s^\star F_s^\star \\ K_s^\star C_s^\star & A_s^\star + B_s^\star F_s^\star - K_s^\star C_s^\star \end{bmatrix} \begin{bmatrix} x_s(k) \\ z_s(k) \end{bmatrix} \tag{32}$$

Since the estimation error e is defined by $e = z_s - x_s$, it is easy from equation (32) that the error e satisfies the equation

$$e(k+1) = (A_s^\star - K_s^\star C_s^\star) e(k) \tag{33}$$

Using the (x, e) coordinates, the composite system (32) can be simplified as

$$\begin{bmatrix} x_s(k+1) \\ e_s(k+1) \end{bmatrix} = \begin{bmatrix} A_s^\star + B_s^\star F_s^\star & B_s^\star F_s^\star \\ 0 & A_s^\star - K_s^\star C_s^\star \end{bmatrix} \begin{bmatrix} x_s(k) \\ e_s(k) \end{bmatrix} = M \begin{bmatrix} x_s(k) \\ e_s(k) \end{bmatrix} \tag{34}$$

where

$$M = \begin{bmatrix} A_s^\star + B_s^\star F_s^\star & B_s^\star F_s^\star \\ 0 & A_s^\star - K_s^\star C_s^\star \end{bmatrix} \tag{35}$$

Since the matrix M is block-triangular, it is immediate that

$$\text{eig}(M) = \text{eig}\left(A_s^\star + B_s^\star F_s^\star\right) \cup \text{eig}\left(A_s^\star - K_s^\star C_s^\star\right) \tag{36}$$

which establishes the first part of the Separation Principle namely that the observer poles are separated from the closed-loop controller poles.

To show that the observer-based control law (27) indeed works, we note that the closed-loop regulator matrix $A_s^\star + B_s^\star F_s^\star$ and the observer error matrix $A_s^\star - K_s^\star C_s^\star$ are both convergent matrices. From Eq. (36), it is immediate that M is also a convergent matrix. From Eq. (35), it is thus immediate that $x_s(k) \to 0$ and $e_s(k) \to 0$ as $k \to \infty$ for all $x_s(0)$ and $e(0)$. □

5 Numerical Example

In this section, we consider a fourth order linear discrete-time control system described by

$$\begin{aligned} x(k+1) &= Ax(k) + Bu(k) \\ y(k) &= Cx(k) \end{aligned} \tag{37}$$

where

$$A = \begin{bmatrix} 2.0 & 0.6 & 0.2 & 0.3 \\ 0.4 & 0.4 & 0.9 & 0.5 \\ 0.1 & 0.3 & 0.5 & 0.1 \\ 0.7 & 0.9 & 0.8 & 0.8 \end{bmatrix}, \quad B = \begin{bmatrix} 1 \\ 1 \\ 1 \\ 1 \end{bmatrix} \tag{38}$$

and

$$C = \begin{bmatrix} 1 & 2 & 1 & 1 \end{bmatrix} \tag{39}$$

The eigenvalues of the matrix A are

$$\lambda_1 = 2.4964, \ \lambda_2 = 1.0994, \ \lambda_3 = 0.3203 \ \text{and} \ \lambda_4 = -0.2161$$

Thus, we note that λ_1, λ_2 are unstable (slow) eigenvalues and λ_3, λ_4 are stable (fast) eigenvalues of the system matrix A.

For this linear system, the dominant and non-dominant states are calculated as in [9]. A simple calculation shows that the first two states $\{x_1, x_2\}$ are the dominant (slow) states, while the last two states $\{x_3, x_4\}$ are the non-dominant (fast) states for the given system (37).

Using the procedure described in Section 2, the reduced-order linear model for the given linear system (37) is obtained as

$$\begin{aligned} x_s(k+1) &= A_s^\star x_s(k) + B_s^\star u(k) \\ y(k) &= C_s^\star x_s(k) + D_s^\star u(k) \end{aligned} \tag{40}$$

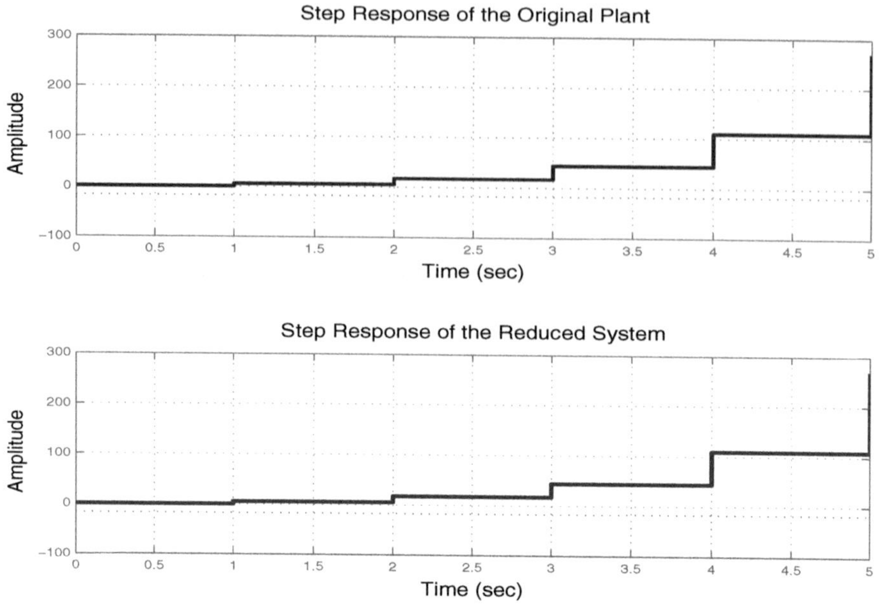

Fig. 1. Step Responses for the Original and Reduced Order Linear Systems

where

$$A_s^\star = \begin{bmatrix} 2.0077 & 1.1534 \\ 0.3848 & 1.5881 \end{bmatrix}, \quad B_s^\star = \begin{bmatrix} 0.8352 \\ 1.1653 \end{bmatrix} \tag{41}$$

and

$$C_s^\star = \begin{bmatrix} 1.0092 & 4.0011 \end{bmatrix} \text{ and } D_s^\star = -0.2904 \tag{42}$$

The step responses of the original plant and the reduced order plant are plotted in Figure 1, which validates the reduced-order model obtained for the given plant.

We note also that the reduced order linear system (40) is completely controllable and completely observable. Hence, we can construct reduced-order observers and observer-based reduced-order controllers for this plant as detailed in Sections 3 and 4.

6 Conclusions

In this paper, sufficient conditions are derived for the design of observer-based reduced order controllers by deriving a reduced order model of the original plant using the dominant state of the original linear system. The observer-based reduced order controllers are constructed by combining reduced order controllers for the original linear system which require the dominant state of the original system and reduced order observers for the original linear system which give an exponential estimate of the dominant state of the original linear system. We established a separation principle in this paper which shows that the pole placement problem and observer design problem are independent of each other.

References

1. Cumming, S.D.: Design of observers of reduced dynamics. Electronics Lett. 5, 213–214 (1969)
2. Forman, T.E., Williamson, D.: Design of low-order observers for linear feedback control laws. IEEE Trans. Aut. Contr. 17, 301–308 (1971)
3. Litz, L., Roth, H.: State decomposition for singular perturbation order reduction - a modal approach. Internat. J. Contr. 34, 937–954 (1981)
4. Lastman, G., Sinha, N., Rosza, P.: On the selection of states to be retained in reduced-order model. IEE Proc. Part D. 131, 15–22 (1984)
5. Anderson, B.D.O., Liu, Y.: Controller reduction: concepts and approaches. IEEE Trans. Auto. Contr. 34, 802–812 (1989)
6. Mustafa, D., Glover, K.: Controller reduction by H-infinity balanced truncation. IEEE Trans. Auto. Contrl. 36, 668–682 (1991)
7. Aldeen, M.: Interaction modelling approach to distributed control with application to interconnected dynamical systems. Internat. J. Contr. 53, 1035–1054 (1991)
8. Aldeen, M., Trinh, H.: Observing a subset of the states of linear systems. IEE Proc. Control Theory Appl. 141, 137–144 (1994)
9. Sundarapandian, V.: Distributed control schemes for large-scale interconnected discrete-tiem linear systems. Math. Computer Model. 41, 313–319 (2005)
10. Ogata, K.: Discrete-Time Control Systems. Prentice Hall, New Jersey (1995)

Review of Parameters of Fingerprint Classification Methods Based on Algorithmic Flow

Dimple Parekh and Rekha Vig

NMIMS University,
Mumbai, Maharashtra 400056, India
{dimple.parekh,rekha.vig}@nmims.edu

Abstract. Classification refers to associating a given fingerprint to one of the existing classes already recognized in the literature. A search over all the records in the database takes a long time, so the aim is to reduce the size of the search space by choosing an appropriate subset of database for search. Classifying a fingerprint images is a very difficult pattern recognition problem, due to the small interclass variability, the large intraclass variability. This paper presents a sequence flow diagram which will help in developing the clarity on designing algorithm for classification based on various parameters extracted from the fingerprint image. It discusses in brief the ways in which the parameters are extracted from the image. Existing fingerprint classification approaches are based on these parameters as input for classifying the image. Parameters like orientation map, singular points, spurious singular points, ridge flow and hybrid feature are discussed in the paper.

Keywords: Singular points, Ridge flow, Orientation map, Spurious singular points, Multiple classifier.

1 Introduction

The authentication of a person requires a comparison of her fingerprint with all the fingerprints in a database. This database may be very large (e.g., several million fingerprints) in many forensic and civilian applications. In such cases, the identification typically has an incongruously long response time. The authentication process can be fastened by reducing the number of comparisons that are required to be performed. A common strategy to achieve this is to partition the fingerprint database into a number of classes. A fingerprint to be identified is then required to be compared only to the fingerprints in a single class of the database based on its features. The well-known Henry's Classification scheme divides a fingerprint structure into three major classes or patterns namely Arch, Loop and Whorl. These classes are further divided by researchers into arch, tented arch, left loop, right loop, double loop and whorl. Figure. 1 displays an algorithmic flow for selection of features and classification of fingerprint. Beginning with generation of orientation map or ridge flow, it follows the flow to be used for different methods for classification.

D.C. Wyld et al. (Eds.): ACITY 2011, CCIS 198, pp. 28–39, 2011.

Orientation map helps to locate singular points. It is possible to get false/spurious singular points while search for genuine singular points. Hybrid class is formed by the combination of the orientation map, ridge flow or real singular points. Features are extracted by using the above techniques followed by classification of fingerprint. These features can be given as input to neural network, clustering algorithm, hidden markov model, rule based approach, genetic algorithm, etc to improve the performance of classification method.

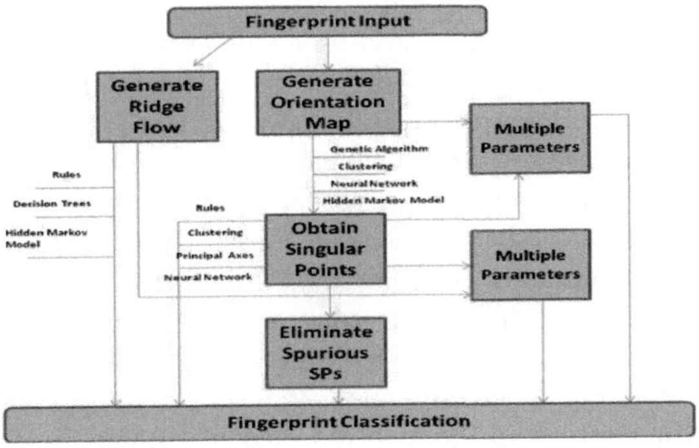

Fig. 1. Algorithmic approach for classifying fingerprint image

2 Related Work

This section glances through various fingerprint classification methods based on the parameters extracted. The following parameters are used for differentiating between various methods: Orientation map, Singular points, spurious singular points, Ridgeline flow and Multiple parameters based methods[31].

2.1 Orientation Map

Orientation map describes the orientation of the ridge-valley structures. The Direction Field can be derived from the gradients by performing averaging operation on the gradients, involving pixels in some neighborhood [23]. Wei and Chen [14] have suggested an improvement in the computation of direction field which gives more accurate information about the ridges and the valleys as shown in figure 2.

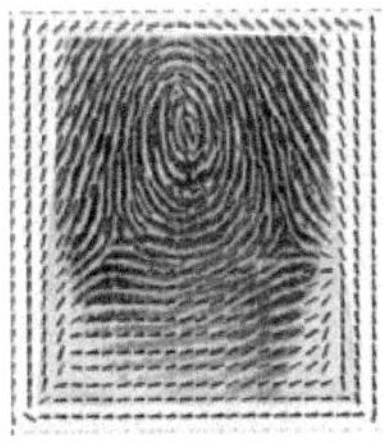

Fig. 2. Smoothed Orientation Field

Cappelli et al. [8] have presented a new approach for fingerprint classification which uses masks for partitioning orientation image. Dynamic masks help to bring stability during partition process. Sylvain et al. [9] uses direction map to capture features which is given to Self Organizing Map for further classification. Guo et al. [10] have presented a statistical approach for fingerprint classification using Hidden Markov Model (HMM). HMM is like a finite state machine in which not only transitions are probabilistic but also output. Feature vector is obtained by getting the local orientation for each block. This observation vector is fed as input to HMM. Krasnjak and Krivec [11] have used quad tree principle to divide the direction map according to homogeneity,which is used as feature vector for neural network using MultiLayer perceptron. Xuejun and Lin [12] have proposed an algorithm based on genetic programming for fingerprint classification. In this paper genetic programming tries to explore a huge search space which cannot be done by human experts.Features are generated from orientation field using genetic programming.

Jiang et al. [13] have given a combined classification approach by performing exclusive and then continuous classification [26]. In exclusive classification, first clustering is performed to form similar groups of data in the database then the query image's orientation field is compared with the cluster representative which reduces search time. In continuous classification the query images orientation map is compared to the fingerprints in the received cluster. Luping Ji, Zhang Yi [15] have presented classification approach using Support Vector Machine (SVM). SVM is a learning theory useful in pattern classification. Four directions (0, $\pi/4$, $\pi/2$, $3\pi/4$) are used for orientation field representation. Fingerprints are then classified using the output of the trained classifier. Sivanandam and Anburajan [16] have used neural network for classification. Jiaojiao Hu, Mei Xie [18] have introduced a classification technique using combination of genetic algorithm and neural network. Orientation field is given as input to genetic programming process. Features are given as input to backpropagation network and Support Vector Machine (SVM) for classification of fingerprints.

2.2 Core and Delta Points

Within the pattern areas of loops and whorls are enclosed the focal points which are used to classify fingerprints. These points are called as core and delta. The delta is that point on a ridge at or in front of and nearest the center of the divergence of the type lines. The core is present when there is atleast one ridge that enters from one side and then curves back, leaving the fingerprint on the same side as shown in figure 3.

Fig. 3. Right Loop with core (red) and delta (green)

Approaches for singularity detection operate on the fingerprint orientation image. Poincare index proposed by Kawagoe and Tojo (1984) is an elegant and practical method to detect singular points. It is computed by algebraically summing the orientation differences between adjacent elements [22]. Poincare index is evaluated for every pixel in the directional image. M.Usman, Assia Khanam [19] have suggested an optimal way of locating core point by extracting the region of interest.

Wang and Zhang [1] have enhanced the fingerprint image to reduce the effect of noise and detected singular points using Poincare Index. Feature Vector is obtained by finding the region of interest [24] using core point. Finally clustering algorithm is used for classification.Liu and Zhang [2],Klimanee and Nguyen [3] and Msizia and Ntsika [5] have preprocessed image and have presented a novel way of locating core and delta points.

Classification is done by defining rules based on the number of singular points.Classification is performed using principal axes in [3]. Srinivasan and Rakesh [4] have proposed a technique based on neural network. They have used PCA (Principal Component Analysis) to reduce the size of the feature space. Singular points detected are then given to SOM (self-organized map) which is an unsupervised learning neural network.

2.3 Ridgeline Flow

The flow of the ridges is an important discriminating characteristic. It is not always easy to effectively extract ridges from noisy fingerprints. It is a parameter more robust than singular points. The ridge line flow is usually represented as a set of curves running parallel to the ridge lines as in figure 4; these curves do not necessarily coincide with the fingerprint ridges and valleys, but they exhibit the same local orientation.

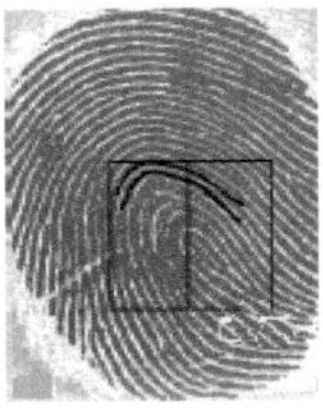

Fig. 4. Tracing of Ridges

Andrew [6] has described a classification technique based on the characteristics of the ridges. Two new classifiers have been presented in the paper. The first classification described is by using Hidden Markov Model (HMM). In fingerprint image the direction changes slowly hence HMM is suitable here for classification. The ridgelines are typically extracted directly from the directional image, then the image is binarized and thinning operation is performed, features are extracted that denotes the ridge behavior. The second classification described is using Decision Trees. Features are extracted and classified using a decision tree approach. Features are extracted at significant points on the ridges and a decision tree is constructed based on the questions about the features and the relationship between those features. Neeta and Dinesh [7] have presented an approach for classification based on ridge flow. To reduce computation high ridge curvature region is extracted using Sobel operator and direction map. HRC is calculated based on the values of the slope within the block. After locating HRC, Ridge tracing is performed. Hye-Wuk and Lee [17] have published classification approach using HMM. Features are extracted from orientation field by locating the direction of the extracted ridge which is then taken as input for HMM for designing fingerprint models.

2.4 Removal of Spurious Singular Points

Accuracy in finding singular points is reduced if the image is of poor quality as shown in figure 5.

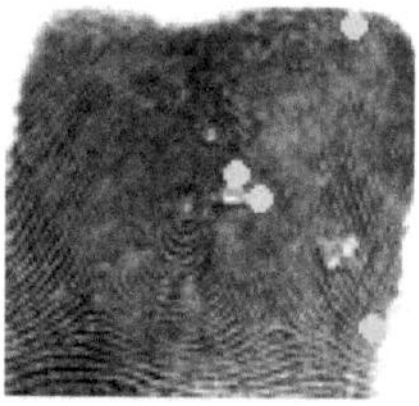

Fig. 5. Spurious Singular Points (yellow)

Zhou et al. [20] work is based on DORIC (Differences of Orientation values along a Circle) feature an extended form of Poincare Index. These are given to Support Vector Machine to design classifier. F.Magalhães et al.[29] uses constraints to remove extra singular points by treating them as centeroid if they are too close and deleting a pair of core and delta if distance between them is less than threshold. N.Johal et al.[30] presents an algorithm to fine tune orientation map by finding the direction of gravity. Blocks are found whose slope is in the range of 0 to pi/2 to obtain singular points.

2.5 Multiple Classifier

Different parameters potentially offer extra information about the patterns to be classified, which may be exploited to improve performance of algorithm.

Jain, Prabhakar, Hong [21] have come up with a novel scheme to represent ridges and valleys of a fingerprint. It uses orientation field to detect core and delta points. 2 stage classification is done, firstly K nearest neighbor to find most likely classes and secondly neural network for further classification.Zhang,Yan [25] have used core and delta points and ridge flow as feature vector. Using singular point, ridge is traced in opposite directions to find the turn number. It then uses rules for classification. Wang,Chen [14] is based on singular points and orientation map. Their feature vector includes number of singular points, angle from delta to core, average of the directions in region of interest. Further, Fuzzy Wavelet Neural Network is used for classification.Wei and Hao [27] have used singular points and ridge flow mthods for feature extraction. In the first level ridgelines are classified and classification is done based on it. In the second level the ridge count between singular points is used for further classification.

3 Conclusion and Future Work

Fingerprint classification is a challenging pattern recognition task that has captured the interest of several researches during the last 30 years. A number of approaches and various feature extraction strategies have been proposed to solve this problem.A Parameter based flow diagram has been generated which will provide a base for the user to understand the approach used for building the algorithm for fingerprint classification. Various approaches of fingerprint classification like rule based, neural network based, genetic algorithm based, ridge flow based reveals that neural network based classification provides better results compared to other techniques. Neural Network using back-propagation algorithm gives good results as it learns complex relationship but it consumes a lot of time for training. In Future we would like explore various pre-processing techniques so as to get accurate orientation map followed by final classification result.

References

1. Wang, S., Zhang, W.W., Wang, Y.S.: Fingerprint Classification by Directional Fields. In: Fourth IEEE International Conference on Multimodal Interfaces (ICMI), pp. 395–399 (2002)
2. Liu, Y., Yuan, S., Zhu, X., Zhang, Y.: A Fingerprint Classification Algorithm Research and Implement. In: Seventh International Conference on Control, Automation, Robotics and Vision (ICARCV 2002), vol. 2, pp. 933–937 (2002)
3. Klimanee, C., Nguyen, D.T.: Classification of Fingerprints using Singular points and their Principal axes. In: IEEE International Conference on Image Processing (ICIP 2004), vol. 2, pp. 849–852 (2004)
4. Srinivasan, T., Shivashankar, S., Archana, V., Rakesh, B.: An Adaptively Automated Five-Class Fingerprint Classification Scheme Using Kohonens Feature map and Fuzzy ant clustering by centroid positioning. In: 1st International Conference on IEEE Digital Information Management, pp. 125–130 (2006)
5. Msizia, I.S., Leke-Betechuoh, B., Nelwamondo, F.V., Msimang, N.: A Fingerprint Pattern Classification Approach Based on the Coordinate Geometry of Singularities. In: IEEE International Conference on Systems, Man, and Cybernetics, USA, pp. 510–517 (2009)
6. Senior, A.: A Combination Fingerprint Classifier. IEEE Transactions on Pattern Analysis and Machine Intelligence 23(10), 1165–1174 (2001)
7. Nain, N., Bhadviya, B., Gautam, B., Kumar, D.: A Fast Fingerprint Classification Algorithm by Tracing Ridge-flow Patterns. IEEE International Conference on Signal Image Technology and Internet Based Systems, 235–238 (2008)
8. Cappelli, R., Lumini, A., Maio, D., Maltoni, D.: Fingerprint Classification by Directional Image Partitioning. IEEE Transactions on Pattern Analysis and Machine Intelligence 21(5), 402–421 (1999)
9. Bernard, S., Boujemma, N., Vitale, D., Bricot, C.: Fingerprint Classification using Kohonen Topology map. In: IEEE International Conference on Image Processing, vol. 3, pp. 230–233 (2001)
10. Guo, H., Ou, Z.-Y., He, Y.: Automatic Fingerprint Classificaiton Based on Embedded Hidden Markov Models. In: IEEE, International Conference on Machine Learning and Cybernetics, vol. 5, pp. 3033–3038 (2003)

11. Krasnjak, D., Krivec, V.: Fingerprint Classification using Homogeneity Structure of Fingerprint's orientation field and Neural Net. In: International Symposium on Image and Signal Processing and Analysis, pp. 7–11 (2005)
12. Tan, X., Bhanu, B., Lin, Y.: Fingerprint Classification based on learned feature. IEEE Transactions on Systems, Man and Cybernetics 35(3), 287–300 (2005)
13. Jiang, X.D., Liu, M., Kot, A.: Fingerprint Identification with Exclusive and Continuous Classification. IEEE Conference on IEA, pp. 1–6 (2006)
14. Wang, W., Li, J., Chen, W.: Fingerprint Classification using Improved Directional Field and Fuzzy Wavelet Neural Network. IEEE Intelligent Control and Automation, 9961–9964 (2006)
15. Ji, L., Yi, Z.: SVM-based Fingerprint Classification using Orientation Field. In: International Conference on Natural Computation, pp. 724–727 (2007)
16. Umamaheshwari, K., Sumathi, S., Sivanandam, S.N., Anburajan, K.K.N.: Efficient Fingerprint Image Classification and Recognition using Neural Network Data Mining. In: IEEE International Conference on Signal Processing, Communications and Networking, ICSCN, pp. 426–432 (2007)
17. Jung, H.-W., Lee, J.-H.: Fingerprint Classification using Stochastic Approach of Ridge Direction Information. In: IEEE International Conference on Fuzzy Systems, pp. 169–174 (2009)
18. Hu, J., Xie, M.: Fingerprint Classification Based on Genetic Programming. In: IEEE International Conference on Computer Engineering and Technology, pp. V6-193–V6-196 (2010)
19. Akram, M.U., Tariq, A., Nasir, S., Khanam, A.: Core Point Detection using Improved Segmentation and Orientation. In: IEEE International Conference on Computer Systems and Applications, pp. 637–644 (2008)
20. Zhou, J., Chen, F., Gu, J.: A Novel Algorithm for detecting Singular Points from Fingerprint Images. IEEE Transactions on Pattern analysis and Machine Intelligence 31(7) (2009)
21. Jain, A.K., Prabhakar, S., Hong, L.: A Multichannel Approach to Fingerprint Classification. IEEE Transactions on Pattern Analysis and Machine Intelligence 21(4), 349–359 (1999)
22. Cho, B.-H., Kim, J.-S., Bae, J.-H., Bae, I.-G., Yoo, K.-Y.: Fingerprint Image Classification by Core Analysis. In: International Conference on Signal Processing Proceedings, ICSP, vol. 3, pp. 1534–1537 (2000)
23. Mohamed, S.M., Nyongesa, H.O.: Automatic Fingerprint Classification System using Fuzzy Neural Techniques. IEEE International Conference on Fuzzy Systems, 358–362 (2002)
24. Malinen, J., Onnia, V., Tico, M.: Fingerprint Classification based on Multiple Discriminant Analysis. In: 9th International Conference on Neural Information Processing (ICONIP 2002), vol. 5, pp. 2469–2473 (2002)
25. Zhang, Q., Huang, K., Yan, H.: Fingerprint Classification based on extraction and analysis of Singularities and Pseudoridges. Visual Information Processing, 2233–2243 (2002)
26. Sha, L., Tang, X.: Combining Exclusive and Continuous Fingerprint Classification. In: International Conference on Image Processing, vol. 2, pp. 1245–1248 (2004)
27. Liu, W., Ye, Z., Chen, H., Li, H.: Ridgeline based 2-Layer Classifier in Fingerprint Classification. In: IEEE International Workshop on Intelligent Systems and Applications, pp. 1–4 (2009)

28. Wang, X., Wang, F., Fan, J., Wang, J.: Fingerprint Classification based on Continuous Orientation Field and Singular Points. In: IEEE International Conference on Intelligent Computing and Intelligent Systems, pp. 189–193 (2009)
29. Magalhães, F., Oliveira, H.P., Campilho, A.C.: A New Method for the Detection of Singular Points in Fingerprint Images. In: Applications of Computer Vision (WACV). IEEE, Los Alamitos (2009)
30. Johal, N.K., Kamra, A.: A Novel Method for Fingerprint Core Point Detection. International Journal of Scientific & Engineering Research 2(4) (2011)
31. Vig, R., Parekh, D.A.: Review of Fingerprint Classification Methods based on Algorithmic Flow. Journal of Biometrics, Bioinfo (2011)

Summary

Table 1. Summary of method for Ridgeline Flow parameter

Sr.No	Approach	Characteristic	Advantages	Disadvantages
1.	A.Senior, 2001	• Hidden Markov Model • Features are extracted by intersecting fiducial lines with ridges. • Classification is done by calculating the probability of data with each class. • Decision Trees - Features are extracted at significant points on the ridges. - Classification is made by constructing a decision tree based on the features extracted. • PCASYS is used to classify fingerprint to improve accuracy.	• Avoids extraction of global features. • Improved accuracy due to combination of classifiers.	• Computation increases • Can lead to over fitting
2.	N. Nain, B. Bhadviya, B. Gutam, D.Kumar and Deepak, 2008	• First stage : High Ridge Curvature region is extracted using Sobel operator. Blocks having slope in the range 0 to 90 are located. • Second stage: Ridge is traced from center in both directions and features are extracted. • Classification is done based on defined conditions for every class.	• Avoids extraction of global features. • Discontinuous ridges are joined by using Gabor filter.	• Classifying a ridge outside HRC leads to wrong results.
3.	H. Jung, J. Lee, 2009	• Ridge Direction is taken as feature. • Markov Model is trained and used for classification.	• Improved Accuracy	• Deciding window size is crucial.

Table 2. Summary of methods for Orientation_Map parameter

Sr. No	Approach	Characteristic	Advantages	Disadvantages
1.	R. Cappelli and A. Lumini, 1999	• It is a guided segmentation process. • It partitions the directional image based on dynamic masks . • Two methods are suggested for classification	• It does not require singularities. • It is rotation and translation invariant.	• Segmentation approach might not always give same result for same image.
2.	S.Bernard, N.Boujemma, D.Vitale, and C.Bricot, 2001	• Image is processed using gabor filter and orientation map is calculated. • Poincare index is used for separation of SPs and is stored as features. • Classification is done using Self Organizing Maps.	• It resolves large intra-class variability.	• Fails on poor quality images. • Training consumes time.
3.	S.Mohamed and H.Nyongesa, 2002	• Directional image in 4 directions is computed from a binarized image. • SPs are calculated using range based on observation. • Features are encoded in a vector and given to fuzzy neural classifier for classification.	• Accurate detection of singular points.	• Generalization can lead to wrong results. • Learning process is time consuming.
4.	H.Guo, Z.Ou and Y.He, 2003	• Orientation field is calculated using gradient method. • Features are extracted block-wise. Vector is formed using orientation field. • Classification is performed using Hidden Markov Model.	• Enhancement of fingerprint image is not required. • Singular points are not required.	• Fails if image quality is low.
5.	L. Sha and X.tang, 2004	• It combines exclusive and continuous classification. • Singularity approach - Exclusive method uses orientation map to classify images. - Continuous method used parameters based on ridges and SPs to classify. • FingerCode approach - Reference point is located using orientation map and FingerCode is generated. - Novel exclusive classification approach is proposed.	• The proposed approach leads to smaller search space thereby saving time.	• Missing SPs will lead to wrong results in singular based method. • SPs are manually located to improve accuracy. • FingerCode method can tolerate missing delta.
6.	X.Tan, B. Bhanu, and Y. Lin, 2005	• Orientation map is based on gradient method. • Computation and feature generation operators are used to generate feature vectors. • Classification is done using Bayesian classifier.	• Search space explored by genetic algorithm is beyond human experts.	• Low quality images can lead to wrong results. • Overfitting can occur.

Table 2. (*continued*)

7.	D.Krašnjak and V.Krivec, 2005	• Orientation map is calculated and divided into 4 tiles. Homogeneity coefficient is computed for every tile till maximum level has reached. • Homogeneity vector constructed is given as input to MultiLayer perceptron for classification.	• Can learn complex relationships more quickly • SPs are not required.	• Training consumes a lot of time. • Requires target values.
8.	X.Jiang, M. Liu and A. Kot, 2006	• Clustering is performed to divide the database into respective classes. • K-means algorithm is used to resolve intra class variability. • Continuous classification is performed after clustering to improve the performance of classification.	• This approach speeds the process of querying the database.	• SPs are required for exclusive classification.
9.	W.Wang, J.Li and W.Chen,2006	• Orientation map is generated using least mean square method. It is further improved by an estimation approach presented in the paper. • Singular points are extracted using Poincare index. • Features are extracted from SPs and given as input to fuzzy wavelet neural network.	• Provides improved accuracy	• Requires accuracy in locating singular points.
10.	K.Umamaheswaril, S. Sumathil,S. Sivanandaml and K. Anburajan, 2007	• Orientation map is generated to fetch the minutiaes using least mean square method. • Feature vector is given as input to Back Propagation network and Learning Vector Quantization for classification	• Improved efficiency and accuracy in classifying images. • Reduced computational complexity due to wavelet compression of feature vector.	• Selecting initial parameter values is sensitive.
11.	Luping Ji and Zhang Yi, 2007	• Least Mean square method is used to generate orientation map. Consistency is calculated to improve quality of orientation field. • Feature vector is computed from the percentage of direction map blocks. • It is given as input to Support Vector Machine for classification.	• Improved accuracy in classifying images. • SPs are not required.	• Training period consumes more time than classification.
12.	J.Hu and M.Xie, 2010	• Orientation map is calculated using gradient method. Features are generated from orientation field using Genetic Programming. • Features are given as input to backpropagation network, if there is ambiguity in classification then SVM is used.	• Combining Backpropagation network with SVM gives better results for classification.	• Overfitting can occur. • Approach is dependent on SPs

Table 3. Summary of methods for Core n Delta parameter

Sr.No	Approach	Characteristic		
			Advantages	Disadvantages
1.	B. Cho, J.Kim, J. Bae, I. Bae, and K.Yoo, 2000	• Poincare Index is used to detect core. • Number and curvature of cores are used for classification.	• Delta is not required for classification.	• False core point is not eliminated completely
2.	Y. Liu, S. Yuan, X. Zhu, Y. Zhang, 2002	• It uses thresholding for preprocessing. • Poincare index is modified to improve accuracy.	• Efficient Classification results.	• More computations due to modified Poincare definition.
3.	S.Wang, W. Zhang and Y. Wang, 2002	• A new feature for fingerprint classification is used to effectively represent the structure of a fingerprint. • K means classifier and 3 nearest neighbor is used for clssification	• Can operate on low quality fingerprint images (missing core and delta).	• More computations due to Euclidean distance.
4.	J.Malinen, V.Onnia, M.Tico, 2002	• Gabor filters are used for feature extraction. • Multiple Discriminant analysis is used for classification.	• It reduces inter-class variance and keeps intra-class variance same.	• Reference point might be lost if cropping is not properly done. • Deciding Singular value and Gabor filter parameters is crucial.
5.	C. Klimanee and D. Nguyen	• Every block is given ridge flow code. Singular points are present in the region where all six codes exists or converge. • Singular point is found in the region where variance is maximum. • Concept of principal axes is used for classification for classes that have same number and type of singular points.	• Accurate location of singular points. • Clearly differentiates arch and tented arch.	• It fails when singular points are not detected.
6.	T.Srinivasan S.Shivashankar Archana.V B.Rakesh,2006	• Features are extracted using PCA (Principal Component Analysis). • Fuzzy ant clustering algorithm is used to find optimal cluster centers. • Classification is done using LVQ2(learning vector quantization) technique and SOM(Self-organizing maps).	• Improves accuracy of classification.	• Computationally complex.

Table 3. *(continued)*

7.	M. Akram, A.Tariq, S. Nasir, A. Khanam,2008	• A novel idea is proposed for gradient based segmentation. Mean of gradients and their standard deviation is calculated. • Orientation filed is estimated accurately. • Core point is located using Poincare Index.	• Works on low quality images. • Optimal Core point is detected.	---
8.	I.Msiza, B. Leke-Betechuoh, F. Nelwamondo and N. Msimang,2009	• Defines new rule-based classifier for classification.	• Can classify fingerprints in case of missing data for loops.	• Will fail if singular points are detected.

Table 4. Summary of methods for removal of spurious singular points

Sr.No	Approach	Characteristic	Advantages	Disadvantages
1.	J.Zhou, F.Chen and J.Gu, 2009.	• It is based on DORIC (Differences of Orientation values along a Circle) feature an extended form of Poincare Index. • A two-stage classifier is designed, first stage, valid SPs are found using their DORIC feature, second stage, classifier is designed using SVM(Support Sector Machine)	• Detects and Eliminates Spurious SPs.	• Images with missing SPs will be rejected.
2.	F.Magalhães, H.Oliveira, A.Campilho, 2009	• Spurious SPs are removed using post-processing constraints after applying Poincare Index. Later DORIC feature is used. • Constraints : - If two Cores or Deltas are too close then they are represented by a centroid. - If the distance between a Core and Delta is less than threshold then both points are deleted.	• More accurate and robust.	• Efficiency degrades rapidly for very poor images, since SPs are not clearly visible.
3.	N.Johal, A. Kamra, 2011	• An algorithm is proposed to fine tune orientation map. • Direction of gravity is obtained to fine tune orientation field block-wise. • Slope ranging between 0 to pi/2, such blocks are located to obtain singular points.	• Gives accurate results.	• Approach fails for images which are too oily or wrinkled.

Adv-EARS: A Formal Requirements Syntax for Derivation of Use Case Models

Dipankar Majumdar[1], Sabnam Sengupta[2], Ananya Kanjilal[3], and Swapan Bhattacharya[4]

[1] RCC Institute of Information Technology, Kolkata – 700015, India
dipankar.majumdar@gmail.com
[2] B.P. Poddar Institute of Management and Technology, Kolkata – 700052, India
sabnam_sg@yahoo.com
[3] B.P. Poddar Institute of Management and Technology, Kolkata – 700052, India
ag_k@rediffmail.com
[4] Jadavpur University, Kolkata – 700032, India
bswapan2000@yahoo.co.in

Abstract. The development of complex systems frequently involves extensive work to elicit, document and review functional requirements that are usually written in unconstrained natural language, which is inherently imprecise. Use of Formal techniques in Requirement Engineering would be of immense importance as it would provide automated support in deriving use case models from the functional requirements. In this paper we propose a formal syntax for requirements called Adv-EARS. We define a grammar for this syntax such that a requirements document in this format can be grammatically parsed and the prospective actors and use cases are automatically derived from the parse tree. The use case diagram is then automatically generated based on the actors and use cases and their relationships. We have used requirements of an Insurance system as a case study to illustrate our approach.

Keywords: Requirements-Engineering, Adv-EARS, Automated Use case derivation, Formal requirements syntax.

1 Introduction

Object Oriented Programming is presently the most widely accepted programming paradigm and UML has become the de-facto standard for modeling an information system based on a given set of functional requirements of an Object Oriented system. However, in most of the cases the functional requirements expressed in natural language needs to be interpreted manually and converted to UML Use case diagrams. Such manual conversion often leads to missing information or incorrect understanding of the user needs. In this paper we define a formal syntax for requirements in a manner similar to natural language such that it is easy to use and understand. Mapping of the grammatical constructs of English has been done in our model named Adv-EARS. This is built upon an earlier work by Marvin et al in [1] who have defined the Easy Approach to Requirements Syntax (EARS). Our model extends a lot on the

D.C. Wyld et al. (Eds.): ACITY 2011, CCIS 198, pp. 40–48, 2011.

basic four constructs and gives the flexibility is expressing any type of requirements. A grammar is then proposed which would parse the Requirements documents written in Adv-EARS and identify the elements of use case diagram from which the latter would be generated automatically.

This would, on one hand, greatly reduce ambiguities and errors in manual conversions. On the other hand, this will ensure a consistent evolution of use case models from requirements which forms the starting point for analysis and design models. Automated support would minimize early errors and provide a foundation for good quality software.

2 Related Work

The objective of our work is to provide automated support for unambiguous interpretation of functional requirements and derivation of Use case models from those requirements. This is only possible through the use of formal techniques. Although there are several proposals to transform a more formal representation into use cases diagrams. For instance, (Stolfa and Radecký, 2004) and (Dijkamn and Joosten, 2002) transforms UML activity diagrams into use case diagrams, and (van Lamsweerde, 2009) transforms goal diagrams into use case diagrams. Formalizations of Textual Requirements to UML Diagrams is however scarce. Hence we here review the research works in the domain of formal specification of requirements.

Mavin et al in [1] put forward the there are three common forms of ambiguity in requirement specification: lexical, referential and syntactical [2]. To overcome such problems that arise because of the association with Natural Language (NL), usage of other notations has been advocated for the specification of user requirements. Z [3], Petri Nets [4] and graphical notations such as Unified Modeling Language (UML) [5, 6] and Systems Modeling Language (SysML) [7] are worth mentioning in this domain of work.

3 Scope of the Work

In this paper we propose a framework for expressing requirements in a formal syntax named Adv-EARS which is parsed by a grammar to identify potential use cases and actors. Our approach then enables automatic derivation of Use case diagrams based on the actors, use cases and their relationships identified from the parser. Use Case identification is a customary procedure in the Requirements Engineering phase, where the potential use-cases are identified along with their intrinsic behavioral pattern(s). These Use-cases are the manifestations of the user requirements at the later part of the Requirements-Engineering process. This automated approach of aspect identification during early part of requirement-engineering phase will be of significant importance. In this paper, we represent the requirements in natural language following a formal syntax as defined in EARS [1]. However, the EARS syntax is not sufficient to enable automatic derivation of use cases. Therefore, we have further extended EARS [1] to include some more constructs to handle the different kinds of requirements and name this as Adv-EARS. We present a Context Free Grammar for the Adv-EARS.

A parser, designed based on the CFG yields a parse tree. The leaf nodes of the parse tree highlight the probable use cases along with the Use-Case Relationships. Consequently, with optional or minor discretionary intervention of the designer, the Use Case diagram can be generated automatically.

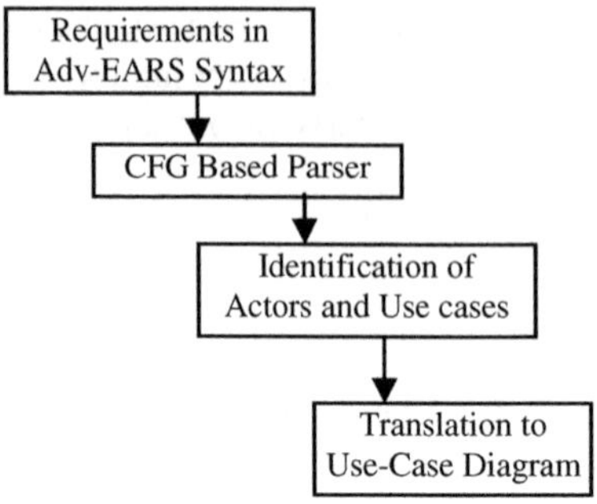

Fig. 1. Diagrammatic representation of our approach

Fig 1 shows the diagrammatic representation of our approach. Textual requirements are represented in a formal language based on Adv-EARS. This structured requirement is parsed using the grammar defined and the parse tree identifies the probable actors, use cases and use case relationships. This information is used to automatically derive the Use case diagram for the system.

4 Derivation of Use-Case Diagram from Requirement

The automatic derivation of use case diagram from requirements expressed in formal syntax comprises of three steps as shown in Fig 1. In the 1st section, we first formally define the software requirement using Adv-EARS model. In the 2nd section, a CFG grammar is defined for parsing the requirements expressed in Adv-EARS. The actors and use cases are identified from the generated parse tree. Finally in the 3rd section we derive the use case diagram from the identified actors and use cases and their relationships.

4.1 The Adv-Ears Model

For the sake of automating the process of Requirements Engineering, we adopt the EARS [1] based Requirements Syntax. The EARS syntax has placed the Requirements under various classification heads: Ubiquitous, Unwanted Behavior, Event Driven and State Driven. The principal objective of this paper is to decompose the phrases identified in EARS [1] further with an aim to identify the involved Entities and Use Cases. Furthermore, the current paper extends the list and thereby adds a new head namely the Hybrid Requirement that is a combination of Event-Driven and Conditional. This is triggered by an event but at the same time having a condition for its execution. This is to take care of requirements that may be of this nature. Moreover the definition of EARS[1] for the existing categories have been also extended and generalized by adding few more different types of syntaxes so that Adv-EARS becomes better suited for use for formal requirement definition.

We use the following codes for the different types of requirements syntax, which are defined in the Table-1 as given below –

Table 1. Requirement Types of Adv-EARS and difference in definition from EARS

UB: Ubiquitous, EV: Event-driven, UW: Unwanted Behavior, ST: State driven, OP: Optional features, HY: Hybrid (Event-Driven and Conditional)

<table>
<tr><th>Req Type</th><th>Definition in EARS</th><th>Definition in Adv-EARS (extensions in bold)</th></tr>
<tr><td>UB</td><td>The <system name> shall <system response></td><td>The <entity> shall <functionality> |
The <entity> shall <functionality> the <entity> for <functionality></td></tr>
<tr><td>EV</td><td>WHEN <optional preconditions> <trigger> the <system name> shall <system response></td><td>When <optional preconditions> the <entity> shall <functionality> |
When <optional preconditions> the <entity> shall perform <functionality> |
When <entity> <functionality> the <entity> shall <functionality></td></tr>
<tr><td>UW</td><td>IF <optional preconditions> <trigger>, THEN the <system name> shall <system response></td><td>IF < preconditions> THEN the <entity> shall <functionality> |
IF < preconditions> THEN the <functionality> of <functionality> shall <functionality> |
IF < preconditions> THEN the <functionality> of <functionality> shall <functionality> to <functionality> |
IF < preconditions> THEN the <functionality> of <functionality> shall <functionality> to <functionality> and <functionality></td></tr>
<tr><td>ST</td><td>WHILE <in a specific state> the <system name> shall <system response></td><td>WHILE <in a specific state> the <entity> shall <functionality> |
WHILE <in a specific state> the <functionality> shall <functionality></td></tr>
<tr><td>OP</td><td>WHERE <feature is included> the <system name> shall <system response></td><td>WHERE <feature is included> the <entity>shall <functionality> |
WHERE < preconditions> the <functionality> shall <functionality> |
WHERE < preconditions> the <functionality> of <functionality> shall <functionality> to <functionality></td></tr>
<tr><td>HY</td><td>Not defined</td><td><While-in-a-specific-state> if necessary the <functionality> shall <functionality> |
<While-in-a-specific-state> if necessary the <entity> shall perform <functionality> |
<While-in-a-specific-state> if < preconditions> the <functionality> shall <functionality></td></tr>
</table>

Summarizing, the contribution of Adv-EARS–

1. Introduction of a new type of Requirement Hybrid (HY) which is an event driven and conditional requirement.
2. Extension of all existing Requirement syntaxes to make it more generic and able to handle more different types of requirements.
3. Instead of <system name> we use <entity> which corresponds to the entities (external & internal) interacting with the software system. These are the nouns and some of them maps to possible actors of the system.
4. Instead of <system response> we use <functionality> which corresponds to the use cases of the software system. These are the verbs and some of them maps to the use cases of the system.

4.2 Generation of Use CASE DIAGRAM from Parse Tree

The parse tree yielded by the CFG as mentioned in the previous section generates the Use Cases at specific points of its leaf nodes as terminal symbols. The probable entities and usecases, which appear as leaf nodes of the parse tree distinctly are identified. A single instance a parse tree having more than one usecases as its leaf nodes indicates the relationship among those usecases. This relationships among one or more Use-Cases determine the Use-case diagram. As a result of which the generation of Use-case diagram becomes entirely mechanized and can highly be automated with minor intervention of the designer.

The key points are:

1. The <functionality> parts of Adv-EARS form the probable use cases of use case diagram.

2. The <entity> parts of Adv-EARS form the actors and/or classes of the system. Minor manual intervention is required to choose the actors of the use case diagram

3. The <functionality> shall <functionality> parts of Adv-EARS form the "includes" relationship of the 1st use case to the 2nd use case.

4. The <functionality> of <functionality> also corresponds to use case relationship. The relationship "includes" or "extends" is decided by the designer.

For example, for a requirement like "If <age is less than 18>, then *perform validation process* shall *invoke error-handler* to reject voter identity application". As per the requirement definition of UW (Unwanted behavior) (3rd case) from Table-1, we can derive the probable actors and use cases corresponding to <entity> and <functionality>

- Use cases: "perform validation process", "invoke error-handler", "reject voter identity application "

- Use case: "perform validation process" holds the <<includes>> relationship with the "invoke error-handler" use case.

Similarly, for the requirement "The *user* shall *login*",
As per the definition of Ubiquitous requirements (UB) in Table-1, we can derive –

- Actor: Applicant, Insurance-Officer
- Use Case: login

The "extends" relationship among the use cases is not within the scope of the use case diagram generated from the parse trees derived from requirements expressed in Adv-EARS format by using a context free grammar. Designer intervention is required to change "includes" to "extends" if required. The generated use case diagram would be a starting point which designers can use as a template to create better designs.

5 Case-Study

We have taken a case study of insurance system to illustrate our approach. This is a common Insurance System followed in most of the Insurance Companies for general and life insurance plans. The following list presents the Requirements Document in Textual form of Natural Language. These are to be formulated according to the EARS Requirements Syntax as shown in earlier section.

Requirements for Insurance System:

1. Applicant logs in to the system
2. Applicant wants to apply for an Insurance Policy
3. Applicant selects an insurance product
4. The policy application form accepts all details from Applicant
5. Underwriting1 performed to validate Applicant details based on product rules
6. Some sample validations –

a. If age > age_limit years, application is rejected
b. If beneficiary is not related to policyholder, application is rejected
c. If profession is risky, application rejected
d. If smoker, set premium value high
e. If user holds previous policies, then policylimit is verified (where a Applicant cannot have policies whose total policy amount exceeds a limit)

7. After underwriting1, if required further details are accepted from Applicant
8. Underwriting2 is performed after new details are obtained
9. Premium is calculated based on product choice and Applicant details
10. Premium payment is accepted
11. If payment is done, policy is created
12. Policy Certificate is generated and issued

5.1 Requirements in Adv-EARS Format

The Requirements Syntax for the Insurance System as presented in Sec 4.1 is reformulated according to the EARS Syntax is presented in the Table-2.

Table 2. Advanced EARS Syntax for Insurance System

Sl. No.	Requirements	Type
1	The *applicant* shall *login*	UB
2	If applicant fails to login then the *login functionality* shall *invoke error-handler*	UW
3	The *applicant* shall *select product details*	UB
4	When product selected the *applicant* shall *provide application details*	EV
5	When application details have been accepted the *Insurance Officer* shall perform *underwriting1*	EV
6	While underwriting1 is performed the *invoke error-handler* shall *handle exceptions*	ST
7	If age is greater than age-limit then the *Checking* of *Underwriting1* shall *invoke Error-Handler* to *reject the application*	UW
8	If profession is risky, then the *Checking* of *Underwriting1* shall *invoke Error-Handler* to *reject the application*	UW
9	If beneficiary is not related to policyholder, then the *Checking* of *Underwriting1* shall *invoke Error-Handler* to *reject the application*	UW
10	Where the beneficiary is a smoker the *Checking* of *Underwriting1* shall *invoke Error Handler* to *set a high value premium.*	OP
11	After underwriting1 is complete, if necessary the *Insurance Officer* shall perform *underwriting2*	HY
12	When underwriting2 is required the *applicant* shall *provide more information*	EV
13	While underwriting2 is performed the *invoke error-handler* shall *handle- exceptions*	ST
14	When underwriting1 and underwriting2 is completed error free the *Insurance Officer* shall *calculate premium*	EV
15	When premium has been calculated the *applicant* shall *make premium payment*	EV
16	If payment fails, the payment-functionality shall *invoke error-handler* to *abort transaction* and *notify user*	UW
17	When payment is done the *Insurance Officer* shall *create policy*	EV
18	When policy issued the *Insurance Officer* shall *generate policy certificate*	EV

5.2 Parse Tree to Use Case Diagram

The above document when fed to the Context Free Grammar presented in section 4.1 for the Advanced EARS Syntax generates a parse tree. The Use Case Diagram, derived from the parse trees yielded by the CFG presented in section 4.2 is shown in Fig 2.

Fig. 2. Use-Case Diagram for Insurance System

6 Discussion and Conclusion

Use of Formal techniques in Requirement Engineering would be of immense importance as it would provide automated support in deriving use case models from the functional requirements. In this paper we propose a formal syntax for requirements called Adv-EARS.

We define a grammar for this syntax such that a requirements document in this format is grammatically parsed and the prospective actors and use cases are automatically derived from the parse tree based on a Context Free Grammar for Adv-EARS. The use case diagram is then automatically generated based on the actors and use cases and their relationships. The Adv-EARS is still extendible and our future work will be to consolidate and present all possible requirements expressed in natural language in Adv-EARS format. Once the Adv-EARS is able to map to most of the constructs of English grammar in a controlled manner, it would take us steps forward in Automated Requirement Engineering, lowering manual intervention and hence lowering the probability of human errors and ambiguity.

References

[1] Mavin, A., Wilkinson, P., Harwood, A., Novak, M.: Easy Approach to Requirements Syntax (EARS). In: 2009 17th IEEE International Requirements Engineering Conference, Atlanta, Georgia, USA, August 31-September 04 (2009)

[2] Warburton, N.: Thinking from A to Z, 2nd edn. Routledge, New York (2000)

[3] Woodcock, J., Davies, J.: Using Z-Specification, Refinement and Proof. Prentice Hall, Englewood Cliffs (1996)
[4] Peterson, J.: Petri Nets. ACM Computing Surveys 9, 223–252 (1977)
[5] Object Management Group, UML Resource Page, http://www.uml.org/
[6] Holt, J.: UML for Systems Engineering: Watching the Wheels, 2nd edn. IEE, Los Alamitos (2004)
[7] Object Management Group, Official OMG SysML Site, http://www.omgsysml.org/
[8] Alexander, I.F., Maiden, N.A.M. (eds.): Scenarios, Stories, Use Cases: Through the Systems Development Life-Cycle. Wiley, Chichester (2004)
[9] Alexander, I.F., Beus-Dukic, L.: Discovering Requirements. John Wiley, Chichester (2009)
[10] Vickers, A., Tongue, P.J., Smith, J.E.: Complexity and its Management in Requirements Engineering. In: INCOSE UK Annual Symposium – Getting to Grips with Complexity, Coventry, UK (1996)
[11] Vickers, A., Smith, J.E., Tongue, P.J., Lam, W.: The ConCERT Ap-proach to Requirements Specification (version 2.0), YUTC/TR/96/01, University of York (November 1996) (enquiries about this report should be addressed to: High-Integrity Systems Engineering Research Group, Department Computer Science, University of York, Heslington, YORK, YO10 5DD, UK)
[12] Hooks, I.: Writing Good Requirements. In: Proceedings of Third International Symposium of INCOSE, vol. 2, INCOSE (1993) [12]
[13] Wiegers, K.: Writing Good Requirements. Software Development Magazine (May 1999)
[14] VOLERE Requirements Specification Template, Atlantic Systems Guild, http://www.volere.co.uk/template.htm
[15] Lauesen, S.: Guide to Requirements SL-07. Template with Examples. Lauesen Publishing (2007)
[16] ASD Simplified Technical English: Specification ASD-STE100. International specification for the preparation of maintenance documentation in a controlled language, Simplified Technical English Maintenance Group (STEMG) (2005)
[17] Fuchs, N. E., Kaljurand, K., Schneider, G.: Attempto Controlled English Meets the Challenges of knowledge Representation, Reasoning, Interoperability and User Interfaces. In: FLAIRS (2006)
[18] Dittrich, K.R., Gatziu, S., Geppert, A.: The Active Database Management System Manifesto: A Rulebase of ADBMS Features. In: Sellis, T.K. (ed.) RIDS 1995. LNCS, vol. 985, pp. 3–20. Springer, Heidelberg (1995)

Tender Based Resource Scheduling in Grid with Ricardo's Model of Rents

Ponsy R.K. Sathiabhama, Ganeshram Mahalingam, Harish Kumar, and Dipika Ramachandran

Madras Institute of Technology, University Departments of Anna University, Chennai, Tamil Nadu, India
ponsy@annauniv.edu, {ganesram.m,harishzz06}@gmail.com, dipika_ramachandran@yahoo.com

Abstract. The policy of resource scheduling determines the way in which the consumer jobs are allocated to resources and how each resource queues those jobs such that the job is finished within the deadline. Tender based scheduling policy requires the resources to bid for job while the consumer processes the bid and awards the job to the lowest bidder. Using an incentive based approach this tender based policy can be used to provide fairness in profit for the resources and successful job execution for the consumers. This involves adjusting the price, Competition Degree (CD) and the job position in the resource queue. In this paper, this model is further extended by incorporating resource categorization and modifying the resource bidding using 'Group Targeting'. The resources are classified using the 'Ricardo's theory of rents' taking into account the speed and type of each resource. This allows the consumer to make his decision using the category of resource along with its price which induces a quality element in the bid processing mechanism. This is modeled using the parameter Quality Degree (QD) introduced in the consumer side. This categorization and modified bid processing result in a scheduling policy closer to market-like behavior.

Keywords: theory of rent, group targeting, quality degree, Maximum pay, resource classification.

1 Introduction

"Grid Computing" refers to the technology that enables access to remote resources and offers high processing power. The basic components of a grid include consumers, resource providers and the Grid Information Server [GIS]. The consumer submits a job to the resources which then schedules the job using a scheduling policy. The Grid information Server helps to locate a resource which can schedule the given job by adding it in its queue. It maintains a list of registered resources and consumers who are the key players in the grid. The scheduling policy will then help to determine how the jobs must be allocated to the resources. There are two aspects to this policy. First it decides which resource the job is allocated to, that is the global scheduling policy. Next it ascertains where in the chosen resource the job can be queued. There are various scheduling policies amongst which the economic policy considered in this paper.

D.C. Wyld et al. (Eds.): ACITY 2011, CCIS 198, pp. 49–57, 2011.

2 Related Work

There are a variety of resources scheduling mechanisms in grid. A scheduling policy must be chosen such that it fits into the characteristics of the given grid environment [4]. Scheduling policy differs with the nature of the jobs that are scheduled. Real time jobs in grid will require resource, processor, storage and bandwidth allocation for streams of data [8] while light weight jobs can be scheduled using AFJS [10].

Scheduling can be done using additional components such as Agents [9] improving scalability and adaptability. Further the scheduling policy can be combined with data transfer technologies such as torrents for data distribution [6]. Economy based scheduling policies operate with price as their primary parameter.

The sequence of scheduling varies among different polices. The sequence which uses double action is discussed in [7]. The scheduling policy must also provide incentives [1] to both the consumer and the resource for participating in the grid. Fairness is one such resource incentive. [5] discusses on-demand fairness wherein fairness can be provided as and when demanded. [3] illustrates the process and benefits of using Java in grid computing.

3 Scheduling Policy

Resource scheduling policy forms the basis in which the jobs of consumers are mapped to the resources in the grid. Resources may vary in number and productivity and hence an efficient scheduling policy must strike a balance between the time required to complete the job and the cost incurred for the same.

3.1 Overview of Economy Based Scheduling

The major advantage of economy based scheduling is the real world scalability, as it works based on price, which is a real world parameter. Further it works in a decentralized environment which eliminates single point failure. The Economy based scheduling entails the fact that the job allocation is done based on the budget and the criteria for meeting the deadline. It provides stability to both resource providers and consumers.

3.2 Tender Based Model

Tender based model is one of the models in the grid scheduling environment where the resource providers compete and bid for the job based on the service they provide (taking the availability of the resources into account) and the cost of undertaking the job. The consumers may also negotiate with the resource providers for getting the job done. The resource consumer submits the job to the resource providers. The various resource providers, then process the requirements of the consumer and bid for the job. The consumer after getting the bids from different resource providers, choose an optimal bid and hand over the job to the selected provider.

This tender model is an incentive based approach [1]. The incentive for the provider is the profit which varies directly with the provider's capability. The incentive for the resource consumer is the successful execution rate. The various steps in the tender model are,

1. The consumer uses the Grid Information Server [GIS] to find the resources which are capable of servicing the consumer needs.
2. The consumer submits the job to all the relevant resources.(Job notification)
3. The resource providers bid for the job.
4. The consumer processes the bid and confirms the submission of the job to a particular resource provider. (Job confirmation)

3.3 Resource Scheduling in Tender Based Model

The global resource scheduling policy determines the resource to which the consumer job must be assigned. The local scheduling policy determines where the job must be placed in the queue and also the variation in the resource characteristics such as price and aggressiveness based on whether the job meets the deadline or not. The local scheduling policy is primarily adopted from [1]. The key parameters used are the Competition Degree (CD), to determine the aggressiveness and the price of the resource. The CD is the probability that a resource does not insert the job into the queue until job confirmation. The job if not inserted, will not influence the acceptance of other jobs by the same resource. Hence higher the CD, the more aggressive the resource is. Further [1] describes four algorithms for scheduling within a resource namely: Job Competing algorithm, which determines whether a job can be accepted to finish within the deadline by the resource and increases the bidding price if the jobs in the queue are reordered to accomplish the same. Local scheduling algorithm, determines where the job should be placed in the resource queue on confirmation such that no penalty in the form of deadline misses is incurred. Even if a penalty is incurred local scheduling algorithm minimizes it and keeps track of it. The third algorithm is the price adjusting algorithm where the price of the resource is varied based on the penalty it has incurred and finally the CD adjusting algorithm adjusts the aggressiveness of the resource based on its consistent performance of meeting the deadline. Here a tender based approach is used as the global scheduling scheme with local scheduling being done as stated above.

The major issues to be addressed in this policy are

1. The initial configuration of the resource price and resource CD
2. The time that the consumer must wait before processing the bid

The consumer offers the job only based on price which does not reflect the real world consumer behavior.

4 Resource Characteristics

Along with the resource characteristics stated in [1], we have expanded it to include resource classification and group targeting. The resource classification is done using the Ricardo's theory of Rents. These additional characteristics are discussed below.

4.1 Ricardo's Model of Rents

Ricardo's theory can be explained with the example of farming [2]. A certain territory has very few settlers but abundant fertile land for growing crops. Assuming farmer A, aspires to start crop cultivation on a piece of land. Since there is a lot of abundant fertile land (meadow land) available, he requests the landlord to lease him the land at a low price. The landlord sees profit in this venture and leases the land. As this trend continues all the meadow land starts getting occupied. Now when another farmer wants to cultivate but finds all the meadow land occupied, he would try to pay more than the existing tenants to take over the land. This gives the landlords a position of power which would allow them to dictate the land prices. But if the prices escalate to such levels that the farmers make no money out of renting a high priced land then they may prefer to shift to the scrub land. Such transitions will continue as the demand for these land increases and will result in another shift to the less productive grasslands. A point to make note of here would be that as the rent price of the grasslands increases it would result in a proportional increase in the scrub land prices and the meadow land prices. That is the low productive land prices will also have a say in the prices of the high productive ones. The above theory can be applied to the resources in the grid and the algorithms of the same are discussed in the implementation.

4.2 Group Targeting

Service providers with brand names have two different sets of customers based on location. They are those who stay in the same location as that of the service provider and those who stay far away. Customers who stay locally access the service provider more frequently than the other customers. Hence the service provider typically offers an incentive primarily by means of a discount to the local customers in order to ensure their frequent access and to stay ahead of competition. At the same time the rare access by other customers can be charged at the normal rate for higher profitability. This kind of offering discount based on a specific parameter is termed as group targeting. The parameters may include location, type of customers etc.,

Location based group targeting is a technique in which specific subset of all the consumers in the grid is targeted by means of a discount in price which results in a higher probability for a given resource to be selected for the jobs of the those consumers. The discount is offered if the consumer is in the same location as that of the resource. This group targeting is helpful in maintaining the stability of the grid by trying to schedule the jobs of consumers into local resources thereby reducing the frequent network transmissions for long distances.

There are instances where the resource provider for a particular job can act as a consumer for another kind of job. Instead of treating the resource and service ends independently group targeting can be applied by keeping track of the set of resources each consumer has taken service from. Some incentive can be offered for a consumer entity wanting a service by the resources which have already utilized the service of the current consumer. The advantage of this kind of group targeting is that it binds two entities and hence offers a high probability of jobs meeting the deadline.

5 Consumer Characteristics

The resource classification and their initial aggressiveness are used by the consumers with the help of two more parameters. They are the Quality degree (QD) associated with the consumer and the Max_Pay (MP) associated with every job a given consumer submits to the grid. The QD is the importance given by the consumer to the quality over price. This is modeled as the probability that a resource will select a higher category resource, categorized using Ricardo's theory, given the resource has choices between different categories. This is restricted by the MP value that constrains the number of choices that a resource can have. MP is the value chosen by the consumer for a particular job stating the maximum amount the consumer is willing to pay to get the job done.

The bid processing must be modified such that the job is not allocated to the lowest bidder. It is done by first eliminating all the bids which have amount above the MP for the given job. After this first round of elimination the number of categories of resources in the existing bids is determined. If only one category is available then the lowest bidder in that category is assigned the job. If there are resources pertaining to more than one category then the QD of the consumer is used to decide which category of resource must be selected. The job is offered to the resource with the minimum amount of bid in the selected category. QD, as stated above, gives the probability that the consumer will choose an expensive high speed resource with category higher than the category of resource it had chosen for its previous job. The consumers initially start with a low value of QD and if they find their job not meeting the deadlines they then increase their QD which in turn increases their probability of choosing a resource with low CD. Thus the selection ensures that the next job of the consumer has more probability of meeting the deadline than the previous job in the low category resource. Further this includes a quality factor for each consumer and hence the job is prevented from being offered based on price alone.

The time that the consumer must wait (T_w) before processing the bids can also be derived from these two parameters. A consumer who demands high quality must wait for more time and hence T_w is directly proportional to the QD of the consumer. If a consumer is willing to pay more it is easier to find a desired resource in a short span of time. Hence T_w is inversely proportional to MP. Hence the time that a consumer must wait can be given as

$$T_w \alpha \ (QD/MP) \tag{1}$$

6 Implementation

6.1 Resource Classification

The features of Ricardo's model can be applied to the resources in the grid environment. The resources are categorized based on the speed into Meadow, Scrubland and Grassland as in the rent theory. The range of speed in each category is determined by the difference in speed of the highest speed resource and the lowest speed resource. This range determines the way in which the resources are classified. Initially the categorization can be done when the resources register with the GIS and it is updated dynamically from time to time. The Meadow and the Grassland resources have the lowest and the highest CD respectively.

```
1. Get the types of Resources
2. For each type 'i' /* type refers to the job a
resource can do */
3. do
4. Max ← Highest Speed of any Resource
5. Min ← Lowest Speed of any Resource
6. Range ← Max - Min
7. For each resource in type 'i'
8. do
9. if ( Max- Range) <= Res_Speed <= Max
10. Grade it as 'M' /* Meadow */
11. else
12. If (Max - 3*Range) <= Res_Speed <= (Max - Range)
13. Grade it as 'S' /* Scrub land */
14. else
15. Grade it as 'G' /* Grassland */
16. end loop
17. end
```

6.2 Resource Pricing

Once the initial price of the lowest speed resource is fixed the price of the other resources can be derived from it. The initial price can be determined by taking into account the scarcity of the resources. If the number of resources is high then the price of the resource is low and vice versa. Hence if the resource is more scarce within the grid then it has high price than the corresponding other resources.

```
1. Order Resource Categories in the increasing fashion
of number of resources available
2. Price the lowest speed resources with P of all types
such that
3. if ( N(Ri) >= N(Rj) )
4. /*N(Rk):Number of resources of type k*/
5. then PL (Ri) <= PL (Rj)
6. /*PL(Rk) Price of lowest speed resource of the type
k*/
7. end if
8. In each type (having M,S,G categories)
9. P[Lowest Speed (S)] ← λ1 * P[Lowest Speed (G)] /* λ1 :
A factor greater than 1 */
10. P[Lowest Speed (S)] ← λ2 * P[Lowest Speed (G)]/* λ2 :
A factor greater than λ1 */
11. Price other resources linearly with respect to
Speed.
```

6.3 Bid Processing

The CD of the resource must vary based on the category of the resource. Since the meadow category resources are more reliable than the other two categories they have the minimum CD. The grassland resources have the maximum CD initially. The CD gets altered by means of the CD adjusting algorithm as suggested by [1]. The initial assignment of aggressiveness helps the consumer in getting better reliable resources as they increase their QD.

```
Wait for time Tw
If (Bid_Amt > Max_Pay)
Remove All the Bids
End if
C ← Number of Categories of Resource remaining
If (C > 1)
use QD to select category 'i' of resource
else
set i ← the category of any resource
R ← the lowest bidder in category 'i'
End if
Allocate job to R
```

7 Performance

7.1 Selection of Bid Processing

The QD of the consumer determines the selection of resource to carry out the job. For a fixed number of five hundred highly overlapping jobs with three consumers and ten resources the selection based on quality given the initial QD is shown graphically in Fig. 1.

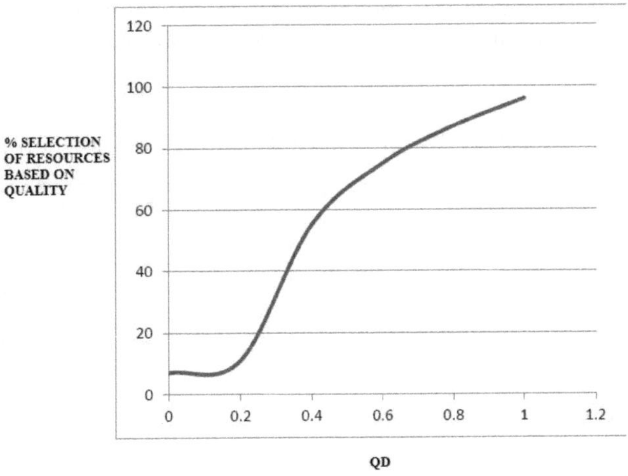

Fig. 1. Percentage of resources selected based on quality and not price with respect to the initial QD setting of the consumers

7.2 Group Targeting in Resource and Consumer Entities

There are entities which can act as both resource and consumer. The percentage of such entities is varied and the percentage of jobs which meet the deadline after group targeting is graphically shown below in Fig. 2.

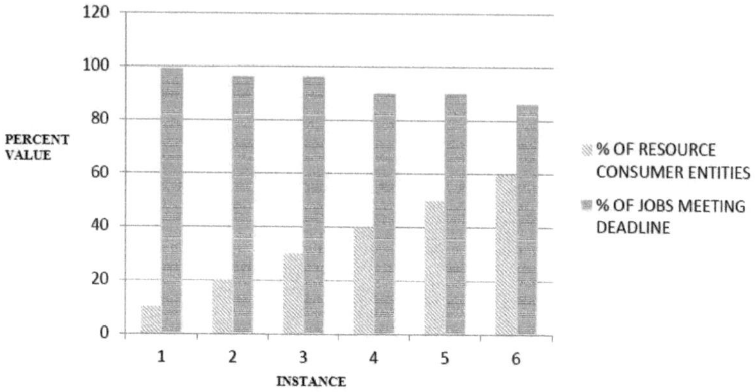

Fig. 2. Percentage of jobs offered based on group targeting between resource consumer entities and the percentage of such jobs meeting deadline

7.3 Deadline with Respect to Affordability

Affordability is given by the average MP with respect to all the jobs. The percentage of jobs meeting the deadline with respect to the affordability is tabulated on Table 1. The conditions for the same are taken to be the presence of only one resource, a total of 500 jobs with the minimum amount equaling 100 and the maximum amount equaling 500 for all the jobs.

Table 1. Deadline with respect to Affordability

Affordability	**% of jobs meeting Deadline**
100	50
200	65
300	75
400	85

8 Conclusion

There are various other economy based scheduling policies, which vary based on bidding and job offering methods. In few cases it might be possible to combine two such policies in order to improve the profitability of the resource and the successful job execution rates. The above mentioned model can be refined using an auction based approach for scarce resources. The resource is set into auction with a base price and the consumers increasingly bid for the resource. The auction can be in a cyclic way where each consumer takes his chance to bid. If the consumer does not bid on his given turn the consumer is eliminated from the auction. This would increase the profitability of scarce resources and the major issue would be the classification of a scarce resource. The other issues include the basis of setting base price for the resource, and the factor by which a consumer must increase the amount in each of its turn to bid.

References

1. Zhu, Y., Xiao, L., Ni, L.M., Xu, Z.: Incentive Based Scheduling for Market-Like Computational Grids. IEEE Transactions on Parallel and Distributed Systems 19(7) (July 2008)
2. Harford, T.: The Undercover Economist, pp. 8–38. Oxford University Press, Oxford (2006)
3. Getov, V., Von Laszewski, G., Philippsen, M., Foster, I.: Multiparadigm Communications in Java for Grid Computing. Communications of the ACM 44(10) (October 2001)
4. Jiang, C., Wang, C., Liu, X., Zhao, Y.: A Survey of Job Scheduling in Grids. In: Dong, G., Lin, X., Wang, W., Yang, Y., Yu, J.X. (eds.) APWeb/WAIM 2007. LNCS, vol. 4505, pp. 419–427. Springer, Heidelberg (2007)
5. Isard, M., Prabhakaran, V., Currey, J., Wieder, U., Talwar, K., Goldberg, A.: Quincy: Fair Scheduling for Distributed Computing Clusters. In: ACM, SOSP 2009 (October 11-14, 2009)
6. Briquet, C., Dalem, X., Jodogne, S., de Marneffe, P.-A.: Scheduling Data-Intensive Bags of Tasks in P2P Grids with BitTorrent-enabled Data Distribution. In: ACM, UPGRADE-CN 2007 (June 26, 2007)
7. Izakian, H., Ladani, B.T., Zamanifar, K., Abraham, A., Snášel, V.: A Continuous Double Auction Method for Resource Allocation in Computational Grids. IEEE, Los Alamitos (2009)
8. Chen, L., Agrawal, G.: A Static Resource Allocation Framework for Grid-based Streaming Applications. Concurrency and Computation: Practice and Experience 18, 653–666 (2006)
9. Cao, J., Jarvis, S.A., Saini, S., Kerbyson, D.J., Nudd, G.R.: ARMS: An agent-based resource management system for grid computing. Scientific Programming 10, 135–148 (2002)
10. Liao, Y., Liu, Q.: Research on Fine-grained Job scheduling in Grid Computing. I.J. Information Engineering and Electronic Business 1, 9–16 (2009)
11. Buyya, R., Abramson, D., Venugopal, S.: The Grid Economy. Proc. IEEE 93(3), 698–714 (2005)
12. Zhu, Y., Xiao, L., Ni, L.M., Xu, Z.: Incentive-Based P2P Scheduling in Grid Computing. In: Proc. Third Int'l Conf. Grid and Cooperative Computing (GCC 2004), p. 209 (2004)
13. Chun, B., Culler, D.: Market-based proportional resource sharing for clusters. Technical Report, University of California, Berkeley (September 1999)

An Adaptive Pricing Scheme in Sponsored Search Auction: A Hierarchical Fuzzy Classification Approach

Madhu Kumari and Kamal K. Bharadwaj

School of Computer and Systems Sciences,
Jawaharlal Nehru University, New Delhi, India
{madhu.jaglan,kbharadwaj}@gmail.co.in

Abstract. Sponsored Search Auctions (SSA) are gaining widespread attention in web commerce community because of their highly targeted customers and billion dollars revenue generating online market. Unlike other form of auctions this class possesses fairly complex interaction among its key players, Users, Advertisers and Search Engines. Therefore research issues pertaining to SSA are being explored with large momentum in eclectic domains e.g. game theory, algorithmic theory and machine learning etc. Though problems related to different pricing schemes in SSA need more focus from researchers especially in analyzing adaptive pricing measures .This work is an effort towards making diligent use of information available in terms of different auctions' situations by ingraining best of major popular pricing schemes in which switching among pricing is made by hierarchical fuzzy classification .Effectiveness of the proposed scheme is illustrated through experimental results.

Keywords: Sponsored Search Auctions, Search Engine, Auctions Contexts, Hierarchical Fuzzy Classification.

1 Introduction

The Internet has made a fundamental change in the way users generate and obtain information thereby facilitating a paradigm shift in consumer search and purchase patterns. In this regard, search engines are able to leverage their value as information location tools by selling advertising linked to user generated queries and referring them to the advertisers. Indeed, the phenomenon of sponsored search advertising where advertisers pay a fee to Internet search engines to be displayed alongside organic (non-sponsored) web search results is gaining ground as the largest source of revenues for search engines. The global paid search advertising market is predicted to have a 37% compound annual growth rate, to more than $33 billion in 2010 and has become a critical component of firm's marketing campaigns. The key Auction Service Provides with most commercial interest, Google, Yahoo! and MSN Live make available to advertisers up to three links above the organic results (these are the mainline slots), up to eight links besides the organic results (sidebar slots) and, more recently, MSN Live even sells links below the organic results (bottom slots). According to a report by Interactive Advertising Bureau and PricewaterhouseCoopers

D.C. Wyld et al. (Eds.): ACITY 2011, CCIS 198, pp. 58–67, 2011.

(2008), the keyword advertising revenue reached $8.5 billion in 2007. By allotting a specific value to each keyword, advertisers only pay the assigned price for the users who actually click on their listing to visit its website in the most prevalent payment mechanism known as cost-per-click (CPC). In comparison to the traditional auctions these auctions have three players, advertiser, search engine and user therefore it becomes quite arduous to understand the nature of interaction and responses of each player towards others. Auctions for sponsored search can be viewed as combinatorial auctions in that bidders have combinatorial (in the search terms and the location of the ad on the search results page) preferences for having ads placed [4]. Furthermore since the search space is much larger than the set of advertisers; it is useful to consider semantic relationship of search terms within pricing algorithms.

Although ongoing exploration of various pricing schemes in SSA is definitely in progress, but literature pertaining to the adaptive pricing scheme based on the contextual information present for the auction is sparse. This paper addresses natural questions like: How to reduce risk factor for auction provider (revenue by ads) and how to use situational information for flexible pricing. The rest of the paper is structured as follows. We have presented related work in the second section. In the third section we explained the terminologies and the forth section wraps the proposed scheme. Experimental results are presented in the fifth section, and the last section concludes the paper with some future extensions to the proposed scheme.

2 Related Work

Sponsored search auctions offers multi-disciplinary research test bed for various tools and techniques. The recent literature focuses on the design and analysis of auction mechanisms are present in [10, 11] whereas major users' preference models are given in [6, 8, 7, 10], effective bidding is explored in [1,12] .[2] Discusses finer lines of research intricacies of SSA and unveils important aspects of these auctions and enforces a need of generalization of the game theoretic techniques to capture the dynamics of SSA. Whereas [6] presents empirical view of complexity of domain and analyzes these auctions to get some patterns over clicked ads. Need and applications of machine learning applications to various aspects of SSA is explained elaborately in [4].

Predicting the probability that users click on ads is crucial to sponsored search because this prediction influences ranking, filtering, placement, and pricing of ads. Ad ranking, filtering and placement have a direct impact on the user experience, as users expect useful ads to be placed in a prominent position on the page. Pricing impacts the advertisers' return on their investment and revenue for the search engine [7]. Whereas [16] analyzes more query oriented feature which are responsible for users attention. Pricing schemes given in [17] are named under hybrid auctions, where an advertiser can make a per-impression as well as a per-click bid, and the auctioneer then chooses one of the two as the pricing mechanism and making use of query specific features to switch among the schemes.

Any stand alone pricing schemes does not perform well under all circumstance. Hence there is a need of adaptive pricing mechanism whose control triggers on situational changes in auction. In the view of above mentioned issues on SSA, this paper proposes an adaptive pricing scheme inspired by [17] and incorporates other schemes too as given in [14].

3 Terminology

Fuzzy Classifiers are the classifiers which use fuzzy sets or fuzzy logic in the course of its training or operation to produce soft labeled classes when used for prediction on new data, for further details [20] can be referred.

Auction context encodes possible configuration of an auction because of entities involved in it (users, search engine and Advertisers). An auction context is defined by three tuple as<*Q, U,A*> where can be defined as:

> ***Q:*** It is to define attributes to the advertising capability of the query under consideration. It can be represented as: *Q*=[*Frequency, QType, AvgSlots*], where *Frequency* is search frequency of query, *QType* is one of four categories [16] and *AvgSlots* are the average number of slots shown in impressions for the query. *QType* is a classification of queries based on the nature of the keywords used in it as defined in [16]. It consists of four classes as Com_Navig (commercial and navigational), Com_Infom (commercial and informational), NCom_Navig (noncommercial and navigational) and NCom_Inform (noncommercial and informational).
>
> ***U:*** U is to reflects users' attention in terms of clicks, popularity (how many different users search the query) and time of query. U can be represented as [*Time, Popularity, AvgClicks*]. *Time* attribute is to classify time periods of search based on the average search volume. It divides continuous time period into three broad categories as Peak Hour (PH), Average Hour (AH) and Odd Hour (OH).

Popularity attribute is to define the popularity quotient of a query among different users. It can be computed by ratio of number different users' issuing this query to the total search volume of the query under consideration.

$$Popularity = \frac{no\ of\ different\ users}{Total\ Frequency} \tag{1}$$

AvgCicks is the percentage of the search volume of a query which eventually registered a click.

> ***A:*** A is to capture advertisers' availability and their monitory contribution for a query. It consists of two attributes as: *A*=[*AvgNoBids, AvgCost*]. *AvgNoBidds* is the average number of qualified Advertisers .This attribute is to capture the average level of competition for a keyword. *AvgCost* is the average of bids submitted by bidders for this query. For a new query it is the current bid offered by any of bidders or zero if no one has bid for it.

Pricing Schemes and Methods: various pricing schemes used in SSA are *Pay Per Impression (PPI)* , *Pay Per Click (PPC*)and *Pay Per Action (PPA).* Most popular pricing methods used by search engines are *Generalized First Price (GFP)* and *Generalized Second Price (GSP),* details of these methods and schemes can be found in [11, 14, 17, 18].

Users Clicking Models are to capture users clicking behavior .These models have explicit knowledge about users' preferences for displayed ads and other contextual information [5].

4 Proposed Scheme

This scheme is to explore the possibility of various pricing scheme over large contextual space of sponsored search arena by exploiting the fact that each auction context is different from others in terms of nature of query, users' attention and number of bidders it attracts. The key idea in the proposed scheme is to classify the auction context (<Q, U, A>) into three fuzzy classes representing different pricing schemes and their memberships reflect auctions' inclination towards a particular class of pricing scheme. Use of fuzzy classification in the proposed scheme is mainly to provide robustness and adaptation to the proposed scheme under dynamic situations. As this work includes hierarchical fuzzy classification therefore we named the proposed scheme as Hierarchical Fuzzy Classification based Pricing (HFCP). Assumptions used in HFCP are as: 1. Advertisers have infinite budget, 2. Users follow Markovian click model as given [5], 3. Advertises' sheer intentions is to display (it includes ad impression, click on ad and any commercial transaction based on ad website) their ads and they submit a bid amount for keywords of interest. 4. Advertisers are already sorted in to keyword pools.

4.1 Classification of Auction's Based on Contexts

Dynamics of interaction among different parties involved in Sponsored search auctions makes its analysis is much more difficult in different dynamic situations [15]. Although it is natural for advertisers to bid upon keywords but they pay to search engine only when their ads are shown or clicked hence it is not clear to advertisers, whether they are buying keywords or clicks. Even form auctioneers' point of view it is not clear what is the right commodity to sell off. Users are most important because their attention decides revenue of search engines and give advertisers' fulfillment of their intent. Due to lack of exact product definition in SSA, it essential to consider any sponsored search auction from all three perspectives e.g. users, advertisers and search engine.

As per the requirement of any fuzzy classification system, the first step is to have a knowledge base, it can be either expert's knowledge or can be learned from some data which describes problem domain. We used Inductive Learning algorithm (See5) [9,13] to extract rules form the data.

As See5 is based on Information gain heuristic, which ignores less informative attribute from the dataset. We could find the most informative attribute are as: frequency of search(*Frequency*), clicked fraction of search(*AvgClicks*), type of the query (*Query Type*), number of bidders in query pool (*AvgNoBids*), average cost of keyword in query(*AvgCost*), average number of shown for query(AvgSlots),time of search(*Time*) and popularity of query among users(*Popularity*).

4.2 Fuzzy Partitioning

This step involves decomposition of variables used in knowledge base into fuzzy sets. We followed mostly semantic decomposition in which each set represents linguistic term [19]. We considered eight attributes for fuzzy space partitioning which are outputs of inductive rules extracted from data. These attributes are decomposed in to three types of fuzzy sets as shown in Fig. 1 and Fig. 2. Membership functions of elements related to each attribute are discussed below.

Fuzzy sets for attributes *AvgSlots* and *AvgCost* follows membership function given by formulas (2) and (3), where interval [a_A ,b_A] is attribute specific interval which depends upon the domain of the attribute.

$$\mu_A^{Low}(x) = \begin{cases} 1 & if\ x \le a_A \\ \left(\frac{b_A - a_A}{b_A}\right) x & if\ a_A < x < b_A \\ 0 & if\ x \ge b_A \end{cases} \tag{2}$$

$$\mu_A^{High}(x) = \begin{cases} 1 & if\ x \ge b_A \\ \left(\frac{x - a_A}{b_A}\right) & if\ a_A < x < b_A \\ 0 & if\ x \le a_A \end{cases} \tag{3}$$

Where $A \in \{AvgSlots, AvgCost\}$ and $x \in Domain(A)$.

Fuzzy sets for attributes *Frequency, Time, Popularity, AvgClicks* and *AvgNoBids* follow membership functions described in Fig. 2. based on formulas (3) ,(4) and (5),

$B \in \{Frequency, Time, Popularity, AvgClicks, AvgNoBids\}$, $v \in \{Low, Medium, High\}$

for *Frequency, Popularity, AvgClicks* and *AvgNoBids*, $v \in \{OH, AH, PH\}$ for *Time*, and $x \in Domain(A)$ and membership function $\mu_B^v(x)$ is defined below

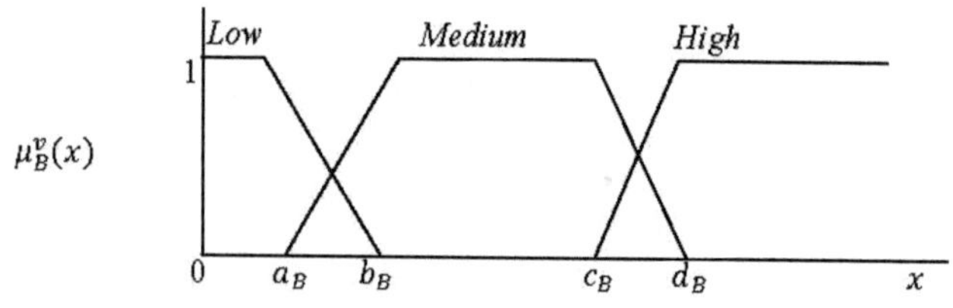

Fig. 1. Membership function of type B attributes ($Frequency, Time, Popularity, AvgClicks, AvgNoBids$), here a_B , b_B, c_B and d_B are dependent specific attributes' domain

$$\mu_B^{Low}(x) = \begin{cases} 1 & if\ x \le a_B \\ \left(\frac{b_B - a_B}{b_B}\right) x & if\ a_B < x < b_B \\ 0 & if\ x \ge b_B \end{cases} \tag{4}$$

$$\mu_B^{Medium}(x) = \begin{cases} \left(\frac{x-a_B}{b_B}\right) & if\ a_B \le x < b_B \\ 1 & if\ b_B \le x < c_B \\ \left(\frac{d_B-c_B}{d_B}\right)x & if\ c_B \le x < d_B \end{cases} \tag{5}$$

$$\mu_B^{High}(x) = \begin{cases} 1 & if\ x \ge d_B \\ \left(\frac{x-c_B}{d_B}\right) & if\ c_B < x < d_B \\ 0 & if\ x \le c_B \end{cases} \tag{6}$$

Fuzzy sets for attribute *QType* composed of two features of query[16] i.e. commercial intent of user and navigational content of query .we divided *QType* domain on two dimensions as commercial(queries which are not commercial are noncommercial) and navigational(queries which are not navigational are informational). It follows membership function described in fig-3 using equations (7) to (9). $\mu_{Navig}(x)$ and $\mu_{Com}(x)$ are memberships of navigational and commercial query respectively. These can be defined as:

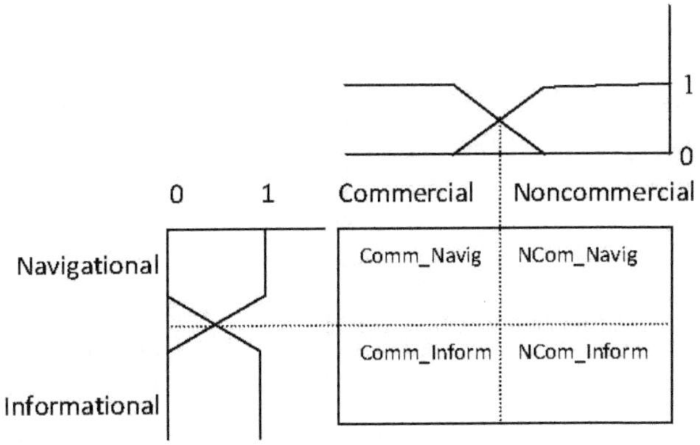

Fig. 2. Membership function for attribute *Qtype*

$$\mu_{Navig}(x) = \begin{cases} 1 & if\ x \le a \\ \left(\frac{b-a}{b}\right)x & if\ a < x < b \\ 0 & if\ x \ge b \end{cases} \tag{7}$$

Where x is a score based on content of keywords in query similarly $\mu_{Com}(x)$ can be computed b y using equation 6 and interval [a, b] chosen accordingly. $\mu_{NCom}(x)$ and $\mu_{Inform}(x)$ can be computed as:

$$\mu_{NCom}(x) = 1 - \mu_{Com}(x) \tag{8}$$

$$\mu_{Inform}(x) = 1 - \mu_{Navig}(x) \tag{9}$$

Based on above equation membership of *Com_Navig, NCom_Navig Com_Inform and NCom_Inform* fuzzy sets can be computed as:

$$\mu_{NCom\_Navig}(x) = \mu_{NCom}(x) \times \mu_{Navig}(x) \tag{10}$$

$$\mu_{Com\_Navig}(x) = \mu_{Com}(x) \times \mu_{Navig}(x) \tag{11}$$

$$\mu_{NCom\_Inform}(x) = \mu_{NCom}(x) \times \mu_{Inform}(x) \tag{12}$$

$$\mu_{Com\_Inform}(x) = \mu_{Com}(x) \times \mu_{Inform}(x) \tag{13}$$

4.3 Hierarchical Fuzzy Classification of Auction Contexts

By following the hierarchical structure of pricing scheme shown in Fig. 4. We propose two level fuzzy classifications. At level1 users' specific features do not play any role hence variables related to query and advertisers are the major attributes for classification.

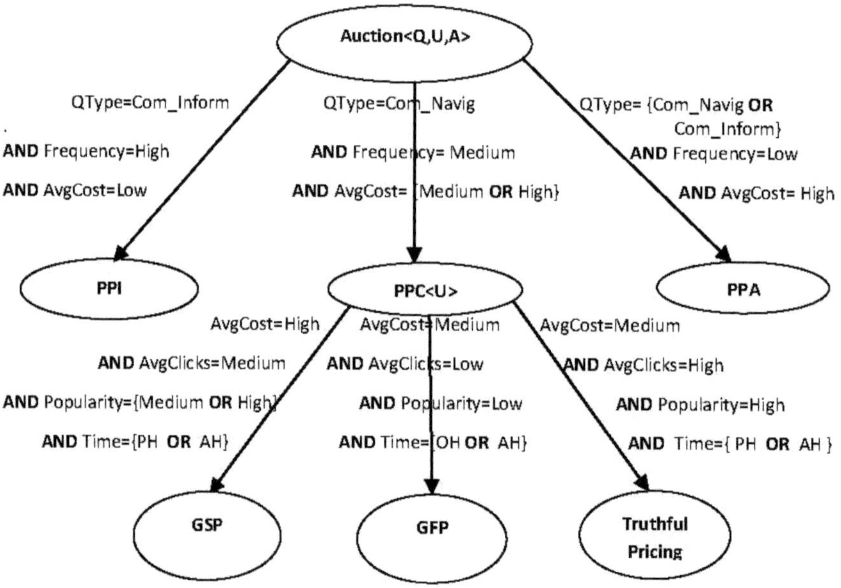

Fig. 3. Generalized extracted patterns from dataset

In the proposed scheme we defined *Pricing Scheme* as a output variable defined by a fuzzy set whose membership value can be computed using center-of-gravity method(COG)[20]. Variables which are not present in the level 1 are shown for ease of representation (actual knowledge base has rules with all variables with their values in such a way that their presence does not affect the membership value of output and it has 31104 rules). A sample rule from this level is shown below.

If *QType*=Com_Inform **AND** *Frequency*=High **AND** AvgCost=Low **Then** *Pricing Scheme* is PPI.

At level 2 of fuzzy classification variables related to users' context are deciding to distribute PPC class in to three major categories GSP,GFP and Truthful Pricing[18]. We introduce another output variable *Pricing Method* whose membership values can be computed by COG method as explained above.A sample rule corresponding to this level is as:

If *QType*=Com_Navig **AND** *Frequency*=Medium **AND** AvgCost=High **AND** AvgClicks=Medium **AND** *Popularity*={Medium **OR** High} **AND** *Time*={PH **OR** AH} **Then** *Pricing Scheme* is PPC **AND** *Pricing Method* is GSP.

Any simple inference mechanisms can be use to extract rules to classify a new context which arrives online. In this work we used min-max inference mechanism experiments and results for the proposed scheme are elaborated in the next section.

5 Experiments and Results

In this paper we used two types of data sets as query based data and advertisers' data. For experimentation and analysis we considered data form query logs and chosen around 45000 commonly searched queries for raw data. This data is further processed to generate data sets for which has both query and users' related features for further analysis. Advertisers' data is generated randomly based on the keywords used in query and commercial viability of a query.

Experimental setup for this paper includes two main steps as applying C.5 on query data sets to obtain background knowledge for HFCP and applying HFCP. In experiments we used Markovian users clicking models as given in[5] We analyzed data from two perspective firstly how a commonly searched query generates under different auction contexts for different pricing schemes(Fig. 5.) and how a pricing scheme performs in terms of revenue for general queries distribution in different auction contexts(Fig. 6.) .

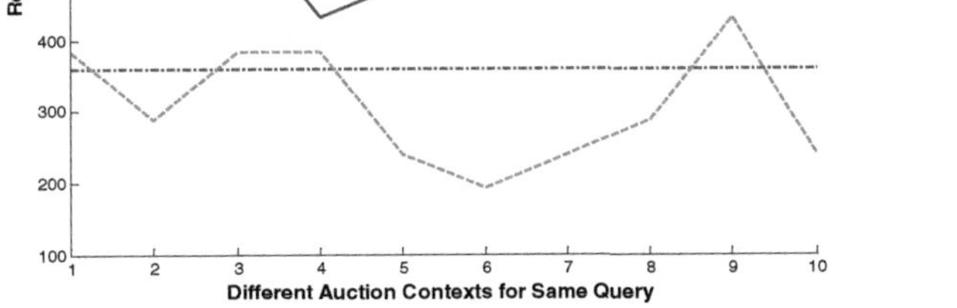

Fig. 4. Analysis of revenue generated by same query (in the batches of 10 to 15 auctions) under different pricing schemes in different auction contexts

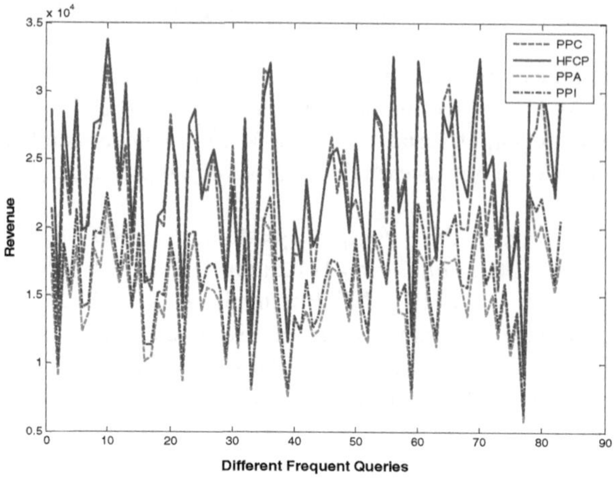

Fig. 5. Analysis of revenue generated by different queries (in the batches of 10 to 15 auctions) under different pricing schemes in different auction contexts

Based on the experiments over ten different queries-advertisers datasets on an average, HFCP performs better: 38% over PPI, 7% over PPC and 47% over PPA in terms of revenue in different on line situations (auction contexts).

6 Conclusion and Future Work

Major thrust of proposed scheme Hierarchical Fuzzy Classification Pricing (HFCP) is to intelligently embed best of the major established pricing schemes (e.g. Pay Per Impression, Pay Per Action and Pay Per Click: GSP, GFP and Truthful Pricing)with a good blend of adaptation to situational changes in Sponsored Search Auctions (SSA) towards profitability and risk minimization among its key players. HFCP scheme is based on hierarchical fuzzy classification to predict soft labels of pricing scheme class using query specific, user specific and Advertiser specific features. As a future work it is to be seen how HFCP scheme performs with different users' preferences and bidding strategies.

References

1. Ghose, A., Yang, S.: An Empirical Analysis of Search Engine Advertising: Sponsored Search in Electronic Markets (working paper). In: SSRN (2009)
2. Feldman, J., Muthukrishnan, S.: Algorithmic Methods for Sponsored Search Advertising, Tutorial. In: SIGMETRICS (2008)
3. Spink, A., Jansen Bernard, J.: Commerce Related Web Search: Current Trends. In: Proceedings 18th Australasian Conference on Information Systems (ACIS 2007), pp. 1–6 (2007)
4. Balcan, M., Blum, A., Hartline, J.D., Mansour, Y.: Sponsored Search Auction Design via Machine Learning. In: Workshop on Sponsored Search Auctions, EC 2005 (2005)

5. Aggarwal, G., Feldman, J., Muthukrishnan, S., Pal, M.: Sponsored search auctions with markovian users. In: Papadimitriou, C., Zhang, S. (eds.) WINE 2008. LNCS, vol. 5385, pp. 621–628. Springer, Heidelberg (2008)
6. Robu, V., La Poutré, H., Bohte, S.: The Complex Dynamics of Sponsored Search Markets? In: Cao, L., Gorodetsky, V., Liu, J., Weiss, G., Yu, P.S. (eds.) ADMI 2009. LNCS, vol. 5680, pp. 183–198. Springer, Heidelberg (2009)
7. Cheng, H., Erick, C.P., Personalized click prediction in sponsored search auctions. In: The Third ACM International Conference on Web Search and Data Mining, New York, USA, pp. 351–360 (2010)
8. Hillard, D., Schroedl, S., Manavoglu, E., Hema, R., Leggetter, C.: Improving Ad Relevance in Sponsored Search. In: The Third ACM International Conference on Web Search and Data Mining, New York, USA, pp. 361–370 (2010)
9. C5.0, Release 2.02 (September 2005), `http://www.rulequest.com/see5-info.html`
10. Varian, H.: Position auctions. International Journal of Industrial Organization 25(6), 1163–1178 (2007)
11. Ostrovsky, M., Edelman, B., Schwarz, M.: Internet advertising and the generalized second price auction: Selling billions of dollars worth of keywords. American Economic Reviews 97(1), 242–249 (2006)
12. Madhu, K., Kamal, B.K.: Fuzzy Logic Based Effective Range Computation and Bidder's Behavior Estimation in Keyword Auctions. In: IEEE 2nd International Advance Computing Conference Patiala, India, February 19-20 (2010)
13. Quinlan, J.R.: C4.5: Programs for Machine Learning. Morgan Kaufmann Publishers, San Francisco (1993)
14. Nazerzadeh, H., Saberi, A., Vohra, R.: Dynamic cost-per-action mechanisms and applications to online advertising. In: WWW 2008, pp. 179–188 (2008)
15. Madhu, K., Kamal, B.K.: Revenue Estimation and Quantification in Sponsored Search Auctions: An Inductive Learning Approach. To appear in ICDEM. LNCS, vol. 6411. Springer, Heidelberg (2010)
16. Ashkan, A., Clarke, C., Agichtein, E., Guo, Q.: Characterizing query intent from sponsored search clickthrough data. In: SIGIR Workshop on Informational Retrieval for Advertising, pp. 15–22 (2008)
17. Ashish, G., Kamesh, M.: Hybrid keyword search auctions. In: WWW 2009, pp. 221–230 (2009)
18. Aggarwal, G., Goel, A., Motwani, R.: Truthful auctions for pricing search keywords. In: EC 2006: The 7th ACM Conference on Electronic Commerce, New York, NY, USA, pp. 1–7 (2006)
19. Klawonn, F., Kruse, R.: Derivation of fuzzy classification rules from multidimensional data. In: Advances in Intelligent Data Analysis, Windsor, Ontario, pp. 90–94 (1995)
20. Cox, E.: The Fuzzy Systems Handbook, 2nd edn. Academic Press Professional, London (1999)

Optimization of Disk Scheduling to Reduce Completion Time and Missed Tasks Using Multi-objective Genetic Algorithm

R. Muthu Selvi and R. Rajaram

Department of Information Technology,
Thiagarajar College of Engineering,Madurai
Tamilnadu,India
{rmsit,rrit}@tce.edu

Abstract. The crucial challenge that decides the success of real-time disk scheduling algorithm lies in simultaneously achieving the two contradicting objectives namely – completion time and missed tasks. This work is motivated toward developing such an algorithm. The goal of this paper is to demonstrate that the simultaneous optimization of completion time and missed tasks produces an efficient schedule for real-time disk scheduling. The objective function is designed to minimize the two parameters. An extensive experimental evaluation to compare the performance of the proposed system vs. other disk scheduling algorithms conducted on 1000 disk request sets. The observations reported that the proposed scheme is a state-of-the-art model offering minimum completion time and missed tasks.

Keywords: disk scheduling, missed tasks, multi-objective optimization.

1 Introduction

The use of spinning magnetic disks for data storage has introduced some interesting problems that have greatly challenged computer systems researchers. In a modern computer, the performance of overall system is directly affected by processor speed, memory and disc capacity and disc speed. Although processor speed and memory capacity are increasing by over 40% per year, evolution of disc speed increases more gradually, growing by only 7% per year [1].

Many modern computer applications require huge amounts of data. In some applications data must be retrieved in real-time. Therefore, disk scheduling has great importance in such systems. Examples of such applications may be found in the multi-media field such as video-on-demand and audio playback systems.

Disk scheduling is the method by which the computer operating systems decides the order in which block I/O operations will be submitted to storage volumes. The operating system uses a disk scheduling technique to determine which request to satisfy. The I/O scheduler is an operating system component whose purpose is to maximize disk performance and to provide quality of service (QoS) between competing disk users.

D.C. Wyld et al. (Eds.): ACITY 2011, CCIS 198, pp. 68–75, 2011.

Traditionally, disk scheduling problem is tackled in two ways. In one approach, more hardwares are added. One example is RAID. It combines multiple physical disks and thereby performance is improved. In another approach, performance and quality of service is improved by improving the software (i.e.) to improve the disk scheduling which efficiently uses the available disk resources. Reordering of disk requests, merging of adjacent requests into single larger requests and delaying a request to the disk drive are the mechanisms used by a disk scheduler.

In this paper, the disk scheduling is formulateed as multi-objective optimization problem. Mmulti-objective genetic Algorithm (MOGA) is used to optimize scheduling of the disk requests. The throughput is maximized by minimizing the computational time for the requests and minimize the number of disk requests missed.

This paper is organized as follows: In Section 2 the work related to the problem is discussed. Section 3 describes the problem. Section 4 briefs the methodology of the proposed MOGA. Section 5 presents the experimental results. Section 6 concludes.

2 Related Work

Walter A. Burkhard et al [2] considered a novel representation scheme for rotational position optimization reducing the required flash memory by a factor of more than thirty thereby reducing the manufacturing cost per drive. The results indicated the existence of workload domains where the step function rpo tables provide very acceptable performance.

Eitan Bachmat [3] considered the problem of estimating the average tour length of the asymmetric TSP arising from the disk scheduling problem with a linear seek function and a probability distribution on the location of I/O requests. Anna Povzner et al [4] have shown that by reserving disk resources in terms of utilization it is possible to create a disk scheduler that supports reservation of nearly 100% of the disk resources, provides arbitrarily hard or soft guarantees depending upon application needs, and yields efficiency as good as or better than best-effort disk schedulers tuned for performance. Timothy Bisson et al [5] have proposed to use the flash memory to reduce write latency by selectively caching write requests to the NVCache. Hai Huang et al [6] proposed a novel technique that dynamically places copies of data in file system's free blocks according to the disk access patterns observed at runtime.

Teorey et al [7] has performed the analysis on various disk scheduling policies. Thomasian et al [8] has proposed some new disk scheduling policies and analyzed them.Zoran Dimitrijev et al [9] presented Semi-preemptible IO, which divides disk IO requests into small temporal units of disk commands to improve the preemptibility of disk access. The evaluation of this prototype system showed that Semi-preemptible IO substantially improved the preemptibility of disk access with little loss in disk throughput and that preemptive disk scheduling could improve the response time for high-priority interactive requests.

A new approach based on Genetic Algorithm (GA) was proposed to schedule disk requests by Mohammad Reza Bonyadi et al [10]. In the proposed method, a simple and robust coding technique has been used while simple genetic operators have been considered. The simulation results showed that the proposed method has less number of missed tasks versus other related works.

3 Problem Description

Consider a set of n disk requests r = {r1r2 .. rn}. Finding a feasible schedule r':rw(1) rw(2) rw(y) rw(n) with minimal completion time and minimal number of requests missed is the goal of real- time disk schedulers. The index function w(i), for i=1 to n, is a permutation of {1,2,y,n}.

For any disk request, time is required to seek the track where the request is located. This time is called as seektime.It is calculated as given in (1)

$$seektime = abs\left(cheadpos - tracknum\right) \quad (1)$$

where

cheadpos: Current head position
tracknum: Track number of the request

To transfer the request from disk to buffer, some time is spent which is called as transfer time.

The completion time of a request is the time to complete the reuest.It is found using (2)

$$c\_time = cur\_time + seektime + transtime \quad (2)$$

where

c_time: Completion time of the request
cur_time: Current time
seektime: Seek time
transtime: Transfer time

Deadline time is the latest time at which disk request should be completed.

Throughput of the disk scheduling is calculated using (3)

$$Throughput = b / c\_time \quad (3)$$

where

b: Data size of the request

Since throughput depends on the completion time of the disk requests, our objective is to minimize the completion time. For real-time applications, missed disk requests are to be reduced.

4 Methodology

4.1 MOGA

Multi-objective optimization problems often deal with conflicting objectives. Many different approaches have been applied to MOGA problems. Aggregation-based approaches use a weighted sum of the objective values as the new objective in a single-objective optimization problem. Criterion-based approaches consider only one objective of a MOGA problem at a time. In the simplest case, the objectives are ranked in order of importance, optimizing each one in turn without degrading the values of the previous objectives.

In this work, the completion time and the number of missed requests are the conflicting objectives. Aggregation-based approach using a weighted sum of the objective values as the new objective in single-optimization problem is used.

4.2 MOGA Pseudo Code

1. Initialize the population. (Any random ordering of the current requests)
2. Traverse the ordering from left to right
3. Calculate the fitness value
4. Apply Elitism
5. Perform crossover
6. Perform mutation
7. Perform Rank-based selection
8. Repeat steps 3-5 till a required number of generations are reached.

4.3 Representation of a Disk Schedule

A chromosome represents the schedule in which the various disk requests are to be processed. The chromosome is an array of n integers, where n is the total number of disk requests to be scheduled. The allele value at the ith entry of a chromosome represents one disk request in the sequence. The gene represents the disk request id which is an integer. Let 1, 2, 3, 4, 5, 6, 7, 8, 9 and 10 be the disk requests. For this example, the representation of the disk request is shown in Fig 1.

3	2	5	6	8	10	1	4	7	9

Fig. 1. Representation of a disk schedule

4.4 Initialization of the Population

Initially the disk request id's are encoded into integers in a continuous fashion. The disk requests are generated randomly. The population size that we have chosen for experiment is 200.

4.5 Fitness Calculation

Fitness value is calculated for each of the chromosome in a population as given in (4)

$$Min\ f(c\_time, m\_request) = \sum_{i=1}^{n} \alpha c\_time_i + \beta m\_request \tag{4}$$

where α, β are coefficients for completion time and number of requests(m_request) respectively.

$\alpha = 100$, $\beta = 10\%$ of α (this is a negative coefficient)

Since the completion time affects the throughput and the performance of the disk scheduler, c_time is given more weightage. Hence, α is chosen as 100.

4.6 Elitism

Elitism is the process of selecting the best chromosomes in a particular generation and retaining them unaffected for the next generation. This is done to overcome the loss of best chromosomes due to the process of crossovers and mutations.The elitism rate that we have chosen is 0.05%.

4.7 Genetic Operators

Cross over that is used in the experiment is Single-Point cross-over. The cross-over rate used in the experiment is 90%. Swap mutation with a rate of 1% is used in the work.Based on the fitness value of each chromosome is ranked. As the objective function is to minimize the fitness value, the chromosome with lowest fitness value is assigned the first rank. Chromosome with lowest rank appears in the next generation.

4.8 Stopping Criterion

In most test cases, the convergence is found at 26th or 27th generation. Therefore, the procedure is repeated for 30 generations.

5 Results and Discussion

5.1 Simulation Environment and Parameters

In the simulation environment, set of read/write requests have been considered that their completion time is calculated using seek time and transfer time. The deadlines of requests are calculated as TimeMultiplier*(TimeoutBase) + (Timeout*(Size/36KB)) where TimeMultiplier is a uniform random number in interval [1-5] and the value of TimeoutBase is 550 for each task. Also, the value of Timeout is 10 and the size parameter is the size of requested data by each request. Table 1 gives the comparison of various population size and fitness values reached. At population size 200, the fitness value reaches the lowest level. The population size is fixed at 200 throughout the experiment. The comparison is shown in Fig 2.The Elitism is done to overcome the loss of best chromosome. Table 2 shows that if elitism is applied, the faster

Table 1. Comparison of population size

Population size	Fitness value	Missed tasks
50	2307	1
100	1802	1
150	1802	1
200	100	0

Table 2. Effect of Elitism

Elitism rate	Convergence	Converging Generation
0	No	-------
1	Yes	7th

convergence is achieved. If elitism size is fixed as 10, the fitness value converges quickly. Hence, esize 10 is used in the experiment. The simulation is done in C. Different types of files such as text (.txt), images (.jpg, .bmp), media (.wma, .avi) are given as input. The size of the file is derived and it is used for the calculation of deadline and throughput, it makes suitable for real time environment.

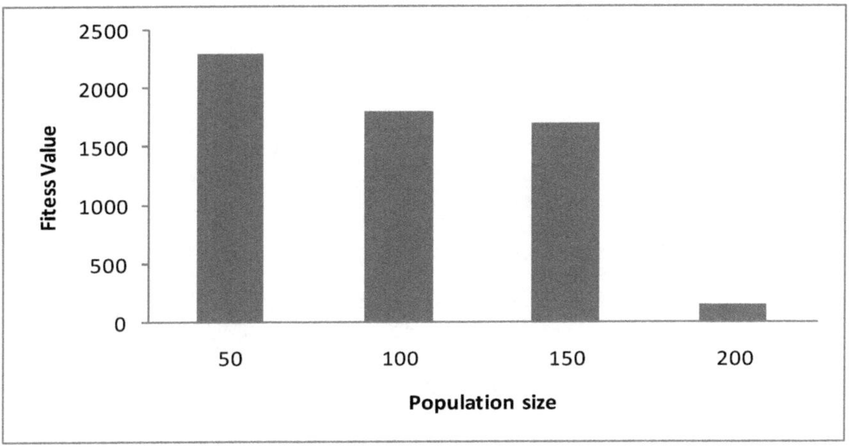

Fig. 2. Population size Vs. Fitness value

5.2 Comparison of Proposed and Existing Algorithms

The experiment is run for 1000 disk requests. The numbers of disk requests are taken as 5, 10 and 15. The throughput and completion time of the proposed work obtained through the experiments are tabulated in Table 3.

Table 3. Throughput and Completion time

Number of requests	Parameters	MOGA	FIFO	SCAN	CSCAN	LOOK	SSTF
5	Throughput (KB/ms)	0.0907	0.04182	0.0644	0.05546	0.06007	0.09078
	Completion Time(ms)	223	484	314	365	337	223
10	Throughput (KB/ms)	27.0795	17.0719	27.0795	19.8811	17.0795	17.0795
	Completion Time(ms)	59	92	59	79	59	59
15	Throughput (KB/ms)	6.3295	4.39274	5.41896	4.98145	4.39274	6.32957
	Completion Time(ms)	316	549	451	479	549	316

5.2.1 Comparison of Completion Time

Fig 3 illustrates that the completion time is reduced by using the proposed work, when compared to the existing algorithms like FIFO, SCAN, CSCAN, LOOK and SSTF. The proposed approach overcomes all the existing algorithms except SSTF. The proposed approach and SSTF show equal performance in reducing the completion time. However, SSTF does not consider deadline and reduce the missed tasks while scheduling the read/write requests.

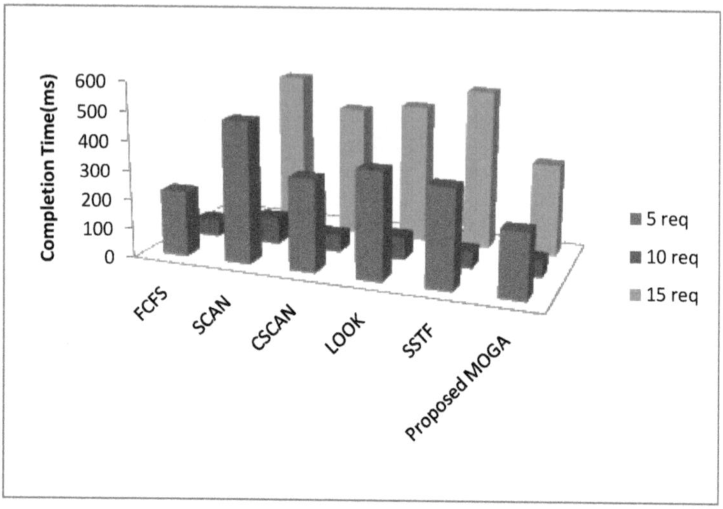

Fig. 3. Comparison of completion time

5.2.2 Comparison of Throughput

Fig 4 compares the throughput of existing algorithms and the proposed work. It illustrates that the throughput is maximized in this approach. The throughput of the

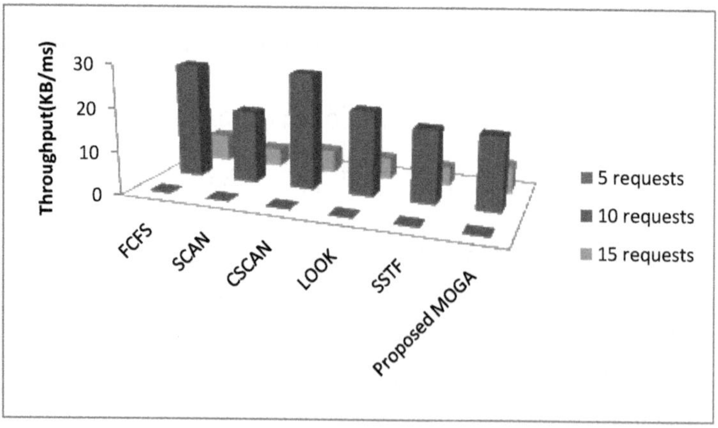

Fig. 4. Comparison of throughput

proposed approach is comparatively equal to SSTF but deadline of read/write requests are not considered in the SSTF algorithm. So, the optimized performance is obtained in this proposal.

6 Conclusion

In this paper, a new approach, MOGA is proposed to optimize the disk requests schedule. In the proposed method, a simple and robust coding technique has been used. To evaluate the proposed method, some scheduling problems have been employed that their parameters were generated randomly. We implemented some famous works and compared with the proposed approach. The simulation results showed that the proposed method produced an optimized schedule versus other related works. It found a trade-off between the conflicting objectives throughput and seek-time.

References

1. Ruemmler, C., Wilkes, J.: An introduction to disc drive modeling. IEEE Computer 27(3), 17–29 (1994)
2. Burkhard, W.A., Palmer, J.D.: Rotational Position Optimization (RPO) Disk Scheduling. In: First Conference on File and Storage Technologies, FAST 2002 (2002)
3. Bachmat, E.: Analysis of disk scheduling, increasing subsequences and space-time. In: v1, Geometry (2006)
4. Povzner, A., Kaldewey, T., Brandt, S.: Efficient Guaranteed Disk Request Scheduling with Fahrrad
5. Bisson, T., Brandt, S.A.: Reducing Hybrid Disk Write Latency with Flash-Backed I/O Requests
6. Huang, H., Hung, W., Shin, K.G.: Dynamic Data Replication in Free Disk Space for Improving Disk Performance and Energy Consumption. In: SOSP 2005 (2005)
7. Teorey, T.J., Pinkerton, T.B.: A Comparative Analysis of Disk Scheduling Policies. Communication of the ACM 15(3), 177–184 (1972)
8. Thomasian, A., Lui, C.: Some new Disk Scheduling Policies and Their performance. In: Proceedings of ACM SIGMETRICS International Conference on Measurement and Modeling of Computer Systems, vol. 30(1), pp. 266–267 (2002)
9. Dimitrijevi, Z., Rangaswami, R., Chang, E.Y.: Systems Support for Preemptive Disk Scheduling. IEEE Transactions on Computers 54(10) (2005)
10. Bonyadi, M.R.: A genetic based disk scheduling method to decrease makespan and missed tasks. Information Systems 35, 791–803 (2010)

Goal Detection from Unsupervised Video Surveillance

Chirag I. Patel[1], Ripal Patel[2], and Palak Patel[3]

[1] Nirma Institute of Technology
Ahmedabad,Gujarat, India
[2,3] BVM Engineering College
Vallabh Vidyanagar, Gujarat, India

Abstract. Unsupervised video surveillance that can automatically learn, predict or detect events can be useful in unsupervised video surveillance that can automatically learn, predict or detect events can be useful in many practical situations. This work describes how many practical situations. This work describes how an unsupervised surveillance can be used in goal detection in basketball videos. We present a system which takes as input a video stream of a basket and an agent trying to hit a goal and produce an analysis of the behavior of the ball in the scene and detect goals. To achieve this functionality, our system relies on two modular blocks. The first-one detects and tracks moving balls in the sequence. The second module takes as input these trajectories and makes decision on a goal versus non goal. We present details of the system, together with results on a number of real video sequences and also provide a quantitative analysis of the results. The approach described here uses object detection and mean-shift tracking to detect and track the basketball in a video. Goal decision is based on the positions of the ball, its current and immediate past positions, in image frame, with respect to a matrix representing the basket.

Keywords: Video surveillance, Event Detection, Viola jones detector.

1 Introduction

Recent development in video acquisition hardware has made possible the acquisition of good quality video streams and increased the scientist's interest in developing video surveillance systems. The development of such systems present several difficulties and one of the most challenging is behavior analysis since it requires the inference of a semantic description of the features (moving regions, trajectories, etc.) extracted from the video stream. The ambitious goal here is to automatically process video streams, acquired in specific situations, in order to characterize the actions taking place and to report any a-priori defined and modeled event in the scene. The difficulties of a direct application of the above algorithm in the domain of video event analysis arise from the uncertainty of the data: from the single view camera video, certain events though very different in their semantic implication are visually apparently same on the image plane.

D.C. Wyld et al. (Eds.): ACITY 2011, CCIS 198, pp. 76–88, 2011.

2 Relevant work

Although the research in the field of unsupervised event detection and learning is at its beginning there are several approaches studied. One of the most widely used techniques is to learn in an unsupervised manner the topology of a Markov model. Another approach is based on variable length Markov models which can express the dependence of a Markov state on more than one previous state. While this method learns good stochastic models of the data it cannot handle temporal relations. A further similar technique is based on hierarchical HMMs whose topology is learned by merging and splitting states ([6]). The advantage of the above techniques for topology learning of Markov models is that they work in a completely unsupervised way. Additionally, they can be used after the learning phase to recognize efficiently the discovered events. On the other hand, these methods deal with simple events and are not capable of creating concept hierarchies. The states of the Markov models do not also correspond always to meaningful events. Another method was proposed in [6] uses inductive logic programming to generalize simple events.

Although being promising, this system was developed only for simple interactions without taking into account any temporal relations. For low-level event detection and learning several standard techniques were also used.

All these approaches perform well in the case of the problem they are specified for but cannot be generalized. Unfortunately, they do not propose a general way of dealing with different types of uncertainty. Study of sports and games videos has not been extensively done. Semantic analysis of sports video generally involves use of cinematic and object-based features. Cinematic features refer to those that result from common video composition and production rules, such as shot types and replays. Objects are described by their spatial, e.g. color, texture, and shape, and spatial-temporal features, such as object motions and interactions [2]. Object-based features enable high-level domain analysis, but their extraction may be computationally costly for real-time implementation. Cinematic features, on the other hand, offer a good trade-off between the computational requirements and the resulting semantics. A good amount of work has been done specially in the field of soccer video analysis. In the literature, object color and One of the most challenging problems in the domain of computer vision and artificial intelligence is video understanding. The research in this area concentrates mainly on the development of methods for analysis of visual data in order to extract and process information about the behavior of physical objects in a scene. Most approaches in the field of video understanding incorporated methods for detection of domain specific events. Examples of such systems use Dynamic Time Warping for gesture recognition [1] or self-organizing networks for trajectory classification [7].The main drawback of these approaches is the usage of techniques specific only to a certain domain which causes difficulties on applying these techniques to other areas Therefore some researchers have adopted a two-steps approach to the problem of video understanding:

- A visual module is used in order to extract visual cues and primitive events.
- This information is used in a second stage for the detection of more complex and abstract behavior patterns.

By dividing the problem into two sub-problems we can use simpler and more domain-independent techniques in each step. The first step makes extensive usage of stochastic methods for data analysis while the second step conducts structural analysis of the symbolic data gathered at the preceding step [6].

The problem of video event recognition has been studied extensively [3]. In most of the approaches explicit models of events are used which are either created manually or learned from labeled data. In this work we focus on the problem of detecting frequent complex activities without a model. In this work an event is a spatial-temporal property of an object in a time interval or a change of such a property. An example of an event at a parking lot is vehicle on the road. For the recognition of events an algorithm was developed in the above work as a component of a system for video event recognition, which in our case is the for video event recognition, which in our case is the texture features are employed to generate highlights and to parse TV soccer programs. Object motion trajectories and interactions are used for football play classification and for soccer event detection [10]. The real time tracking in both systems is achieved by extensive use of a priori knowledge about the system setup, such as camera locations and their coverage. Therefore, their application to our case of basket ball live video/match is limited. Cinematic descriptors are also commonly employed. Li and Sezan summarize football video by play/break and slow-motion replay detection using both cinematic and object descriptors [10]. Scene cuts and camera motion parameters are used for soccer event detection in [11] where usage of very few cinematic features prevents reliable detection of multiple events. Tracking of moving objects in video sequences is a very active research area and there are many approaches which attempt to develop robust techniques for varying video conditions (such as partial or complete occlusions, clutter, noise, etc.).

3 Object Detection

3.1 Viola Jones Object Detection Using Haar Classifier

In our system we have used Viola Jones algorithm to actually detect important objects in our images. Here we have right now applied this to detect the basketball in images. We can also use it to detect the basket in the images. Though the later extension increases automation but we can also use static coordinates to represent a basket as the camera is static. Now we will discuss the theory behind viola jones detector. Thereafter we will present the results of Viola Jones detection on our images.

Theory: The first is the introduction of a new image representation called the "Integral Image" which allows the features used by our detector to be computed very quickly.

The second is a learning algorithm, based on AdaBoost, which selects a small number of critical visual features and yields extremely efficient classifiers. The third contribution is a method for combining classifiers in a "cascade" which allows background regions of the image to be quickly discarded while spending more computation on promising object-like regions [1].Viola Jones algorithm can be mainly understood under the following headings:

3.2 Ada-Boost Based Learning Algorithm

In its original form, the AdaBoost learning algorithm is used to boost the classification performance of a simple learning algorithm (e.g., it might be used to boost the performance of simple perception). It does this by combining a collection of weak classification function to form stronger classifier. In the language of boosting the simple learning algorithm is called weak learner [1]. Ada-boost classifier associates a small weight to classification with greater classification error and similarly greater weights to those with lesser error. Hence, appropriately updating the weights with each classification, it provides us with a strong classifier.

3.3 The Haar Based Classifier

As mention in the approach of viola jones detection, Haar features are computed instead of pixels as they work much faster. Here they use three kinds of feature and these features are easily computed from an intermediate representation of image called integral image. Hence later these images are used to extract features which are given as input to above algorithm to get efficient classifier/strong classifier.

3.4 Cascading of Classifiers

Cascading of classifier reduce the computational time and increase the detection performance [1]. Cascading is a continuous processing of an image through a chain of classifier. If approved by the first classifier it is tested by the second and so on. Disapproval of any images sub window at any classifiers result in rejection of window. And if approved it moves on ahead in the chain of classifiers. Hence this method achieves higher accuracy by decreasing the false positive rates.

4 Results

In our approach we have used a Haar classifier for extraction of features. We run this Haar classifier on an extensive database of positive and negatives of basketball. As, the Haar classifier is, it takes a huge time to learn. But once learning done it provides us with the cascade of classifier which produce real time efficiency. These classifiers are mentioned appropriately in the xml file, which actually is used as a cascade for the Haar classifier, which now detects the basketball in the images. This classifier classifies the image on the basis of features and specific threshold value. Here are some of the numbers before we go on with the results. We have used a dataset of over 890 positives and negatives to train the classifier. These are predominantly images of the ball and not images from our video sequence. Thereafter it took a time in a day to achieve a cascade of classifier. This cascade has around 858 classifiers with their feature and threshold values mentioned accordingly. Some of the results obtained after applying viola jones detector on the input images depicted below.

4.1 Training Images

First we will take a look at the training set. It's divided into the:

Positive training images:

Fig. 1. Training image sample

Negative training images:

Fig. 2. Negative training image sample

Thereafter here are some data, the images from our video sequence.

Fig. 3. Realization of basket matrix

Now here are the results obtained after applying viola jones detector.

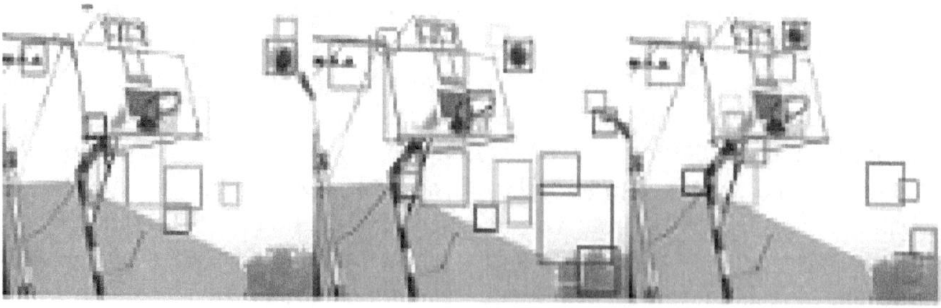

Fig. 4. Result after applying viola jones detector

As observed from the images that some of the images don't yield ideal results which could lead to wrong tracking results. Now the reason behind error is discussed below:

Inappropriate training set: The training set should have been much closer to the images from the video sequence. As training is done before the video shooting error is occurred. Otherwise results are expected much batter.

Quality of the video sequence: As taken in bad light conditions and other videos taken in noisy backgrounds, it causes difficulties to detect ball, especially when it has been trained for different dataset.

Hence the solution which can come up with for decreasing the detection error, after the inappropriate training, is to thin over the possibility of simpler circular filter. But as a rim of basket is circular and other circular objects in the scene might also contribute to detection of more than one circular object. Hence what we have used in our case is change detection. That is discussed in next section.

5 Change Detection

In our system we have used change detection which uses an update model to learn and subtract the background accordingly. We apply this algorithm to have images which have blobs. As we are using change detection hence the blob represents area where change is detected. Thereafter we apply AND operator to the original and background subtracted image and apply viola jones on the resultant image. Here we present some aspect of approach, the concept we have used to come to a decision of using those approach and thereafter the results.

5.1 Some Aspect

In this section we discuss the change based update model for background subtraction. In this method the algorithm detects changes in the scene and marks them as foreground. As the algorithm doesn't learn and updates the model based on the previous image, it can have some errors like blob traces. By blob traces mean, the trace left from the position of a blob in the previous image. Hence even though it is faster than the learning algorithm it is prone to errors of blob traces. This has relevance in our results as explain in following section.

5.2 Concept

The change detected image actually gives us with the blobs which are region of the motion in the image sequence. Hence in an image the main agent of motion is players and basketball. Hence the AND image would only contain aspect and color information of these. Thereafter if we apply viola jones detector over this image it reduce the error tremendously.

5.3 Results

The results with the above approach combined with the viola jones , as can be seen, are much batter. First we will take a look at AND image.

Fig. 5. Original image

Fig. 6. Change detected image

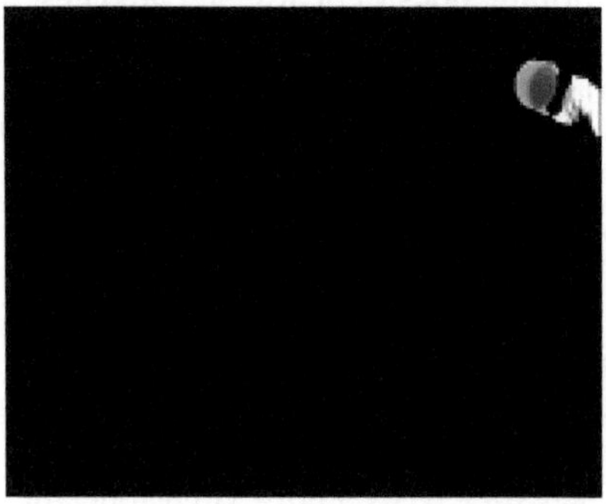

Fig. 7. AND image

Now we will see how viola jone work on this

Fig. 8. Object detection using viola jones

As compared to the previous result it is an improvement as it gives only a single detection. But even with this integrated approach there are flaws which creep in due to use of change detection. These flaws are as follows:

1. Blob traces: blab traces creep in into the AND image and might get tracked as a ball (due to the inaccuracy of our training set). But this still don't affect the result in the end the same blob gets traced.
2. Other agent: These might also creep into give false positive. These affect the results as they are extra detections away from the ball trajectory.

In some of the images there are still errors. As depicted below you can see there are more than one ball detected, Which are in really false positive. The hands of the new agent have been identified as a ball; partially depend on inefficiency of our training set.

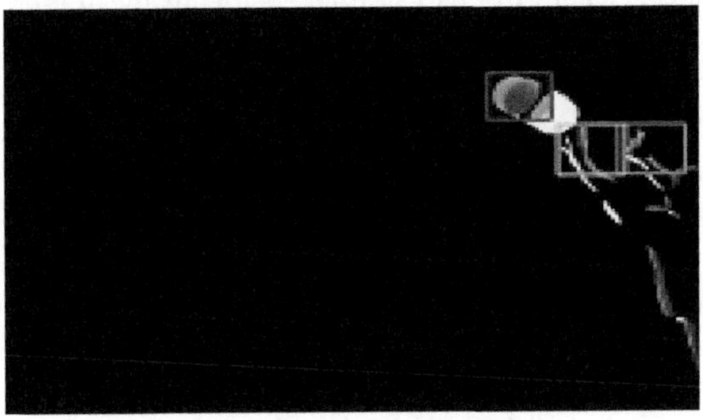

Fig. 9. Error due to true negative

These errors crepe in due to the following reasons:

1. Blob trace: Some of the trace is left by the blob in the update model. Hence sometimes this trace may give the actually appearance of the ball and to be detected. Though being an error it actually doesn't affect the tracking result.

2. Other agent of motion: Other agent of motion may also get in foreground and contribute to ball detection results. As of now we have not removed this error. But we proposed a solution to this. As basketball have a common color, an organgish color, we can compare the color profiles to pinpoint the ball in the AND image.

6 Tracking and Trajectory

In our paper, we used a mean shift algorithm, which is a non-parametric (i.e. kernel) density estimator that optimize smooth similarity function to find the direction of the target movement. The similarity function is obtained by masking the objects color distribution with an epanechnikov kernel, and its smoothness (due to uniformity of kernel profile gradient) allows the use of gradient optimization method. Thus the algorithm focused on a much smaller neighborhood and can outperform the exhaustive search.

In the earlier section we get a blob associate with the ball. Once we have the 'ball' blob we use mean shift based blob tracking on this obtained 'ball' blob. The ball is tracked for more than 98.8% of the frames (in 7872 out of 8000 frames) where the ball is present in the scene. The error present is because once the ball exits a scene or jumps to a new position that is at a distance more than (70-200 pixels) in the image plane the mean shift based tracking often fails to track and associate itself to last position that it was able to tack ball. Since in our case most of the part of image plane is static in the absence of ball, the lost blob stay stationary, and then it takes some frames before the blob can be realized as stationary and then the detection algorithm runs is applied, we lost the ball tracking and trajectory if it reappears in the scene. This happens frequently when the ball rebound from the floor. To analyze the results of event detection of goal versus non-goal, we use the trajectory and the ball position only for the sequence where the ball is tracked for all the frames within those sub-sequences where there is attempt of a hit at the goal basket. In order to get these subsequences we first run the algorithm for tracking described above on the complete sequence of frames, followed by extracting from the obtained frames those sequences that start from a new 'ball ' entering the image plane and end by the blob realized as stationary. Using this we are able to get 89 sequences that represent the event of hit at the goal.

Trajectory information is indirectly used to make decision about the goal. The cases were the ball is very close to camera and hence the blob's velocity vector in pixel per frame is high (120-300 pixels per frame), also in most of our cases the goal attempt is one where the ball has it velocity low (30-90 pixels per frame) since our hits were trajectory where the ball was thrown at low power. This fact is used to distinguish between a hit at the goal and an apparent hit at a goal in the image plane where the ball actually just dips in line with basket at a distance between the lens of camera and a basket.

7 Goal Detection

In above section we have described the tracking now in this section heuristic which we have used in our paper for goal detection is discussed. Our heuristic are not in any way general, but can work effectively with two camera surveillance and goal detection. We will also describe some other ways that were thought in terms of defining the heuristic fro goal detection.

The algorithm used here specific to goal detection in basketball video only. The generality is qualified by the structure of heuristics.

The goal is the event describing the ball passing through (in between) inner circle of the rims of the basket from the top direction (low y axis in the image plane) toward the ground (higher y axis in the image plane).

7.1 Heuristics

To detect the goal, as described above, we use a trajectory (in terms of sequential position in image plane), velocity (direction and magnitude in pixel per frame) and a matrix associated with the basket. The basket matrix is high level representation of basket in the image plane. To make the goal decision earlier, the trajectory is represented in terms of basket matrix where the ball is in proximity to the basket and velocity is downwards and in the range (0-120 pixels per frame).

In a way, the basket matrix is the simplification of pixel area of basket, and the trajectory of the center of the blob of ball is represented in terms of variation of position in the basket matrix instead of in pixels in the image plane.

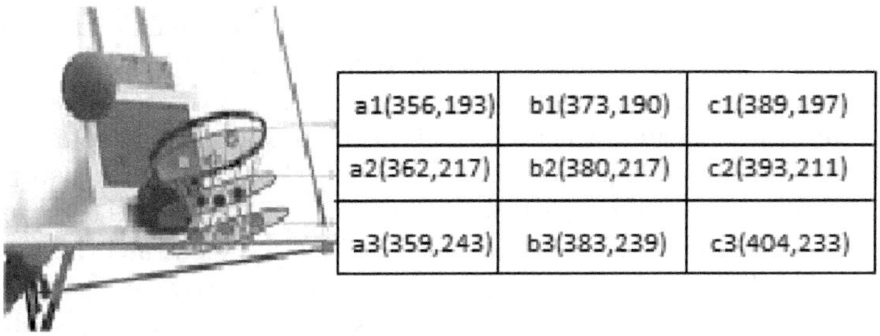

Fig. 10. Realization of basket matrix

This matrix forms a node of graph, and not all paths on this graph is a valid move for a goal to occur. Lets name the first row as a1,b1,c1 and similarly the second row as a2,b2 and c2 and then third as a3,b3 and c3. If ball is in immediately proximity (within 50 pixels to the basket), the trajectory of the ball is also realized in matrix as the value of matrix becomes 1 if it is in the path of ball when goal/no-goal is to be detected. For every frame within of a hit at the goal this matrix is updated if the centre of the ball's blob comes closest to a2 then if the basket matrix has the value 0, then it is updated else not changed. When the ball exits the proximity are of the basket, defined above, the matrix values represent the path of blob and depending on its value, a goal decision is taken.

In the figure 11 we can see the locations of these nodes, and beside is a table that shows their pixel locations. These pixel locations were based on training over just 8 goals and these goals are not the part of data. They are just averages of values and metric to keep these points at same distance.

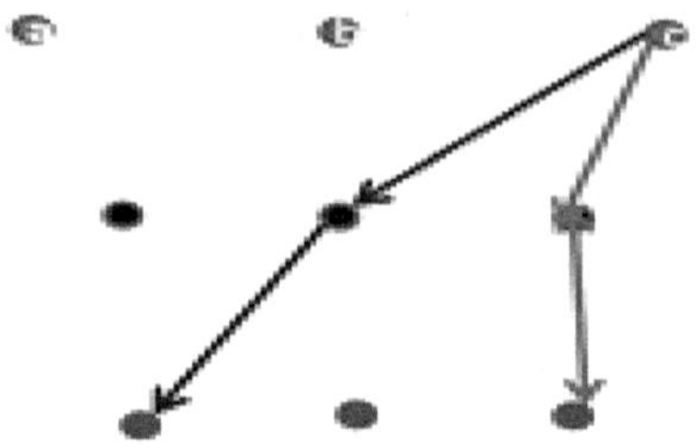

Fig. 11. Goal in basket matrix

Not all sequence of ball position can be considered as goals. The nine points in the basket matrix for a ball that enters in the middle of the basket rim and exits also from the middle would have a basket matrix of

$$\begin{pmatrix} 010 \\ 010 \\ 010 \end{pmatrix}.$$

The top row represents the top face of the rim, similarly, middle and bottom row represent the middle and bottom rows. Some sequences like c1,b2 and c3(figure 11) is common sequence for a successful goal while c1,c2 and c3 is a sequence rarely seen, since a3 represent a situation where the ball hits the inside of rim and then its falling just without rebounding is a very unlikely event. This information along with the velocity direction to conform the ball is actually moving inside the basket, can be used together to decide upon a goal, also the blob's frame speed and size gives clue if the ball is actually entering the basket or just appear to move in such direction in between the camera lens and the basket. Such sequences are also rejected the goals since most of these have a structure of the basket matrix similar to

$$\begin{pmatrix} 010 \\ 001 \\ 000 \end{pmatrix}.$$

Below we can see a goal sequence for the basket matrix obtained as

$$\begin{pmatrix} 010 \\ 001 \\ 010 \end{pmatrix}.$$

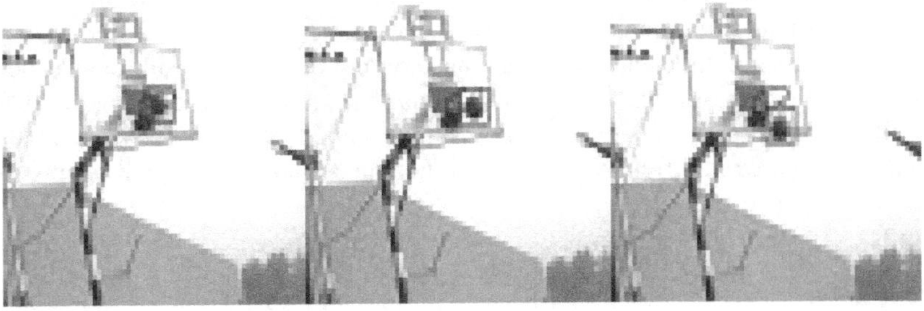

Fig. 12. Goal and its basket matrix

8 Results and Discussion

Above we have discussed our approach to solve the goal detection problem is a basketball video. The algorithm was applied to a video of 8000 frames which has 14 goals and 89 total subsequences when a ball re-enters the scene. Out of this 14 goals all were successfully detected, but the total number of goals detected were 16. 2 misses were counted as goals, which were not easy to detect and only crude algorithm as the above was expected to give some error in detection.

The major cause of the error is the ball that travels downward in a vertical line the camera lens and basket. Even when this happens at a position closer to the lens and further from the basket, it is discarded because of the size and velocity, but the size criterion is not strict since the blobs are associated with the ball having sides sometimes 1-2 times greater than the diameter of the ball, in image plane.
One of the true negative is shown below:

$$\begin{pmatrix} 010 \\ 010 \\ 010 \end{pmatrix}.$$

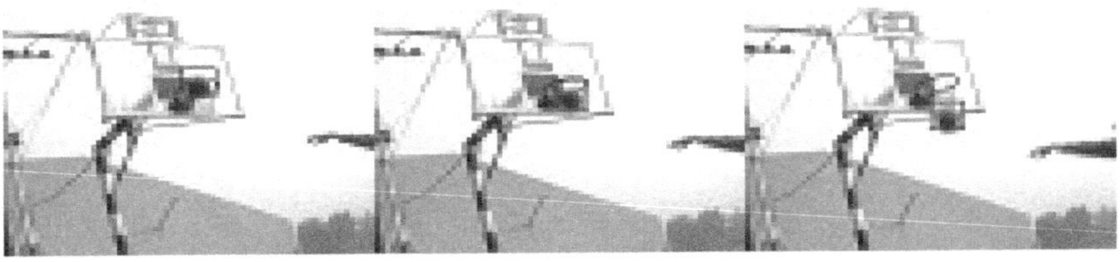

Fig. 13. Goal detected for non-goal

The problem in this case was due to the fact that the ball moved vertically downwards between the camera and the basket falling by path that was just along the central line of the basket (basket matrix in the above figure). Also the ball was very close to the basket and far from the camera which made rejection due to size or velocity hard. This situation is wrongly detected as goal.

The experimental data set was not exhaustive and hence the result cannot be used for any statistical reasoning, but its is obvious that situation like in figure above is very difficult to track and detect using single camera view. The same algorithm running on video from different camera and then the logical and of goal results should give much better results.

References

1. Barmond, M.T., Zuniga, M.: Video understanding framework for automatic behavior recognition. Behavior Research Methods 38, 416–426 (2006)
2. Ekin, A.M., Tekalp, A.: Automatic soccer video analysis and summarization. IEEE Transactions on Image Processing 12, 796–807 (2003)
3. Knodell, R.G., et al.: Formulation and application of a numerical scoring system for accesing histological activity in asymptomatic chronic active hepatitis. Hepatology 1(5), 431–435 (2006)
4. Dee, H.M., Velastin, S.A.: How close are we to solving the problem of automated visual surveillance? Springer, Heidelberg
5. Howell, A., Buxton, H.: Active vision techniques for visually mediated interaction. Image and Vision Computing (12), 861–871 (2002)
6. Medioni, G., Cohen, L., Bremond, F., Hongeng, S., Nevatia, R.: Event detection and analysis from video stream. IEEE Transaction Pattern Analysis Mach. Intell. 23(8), 873–889 (2001)
7. Paul Viola, M.J.: Rapid object detection using boosted cascade o f simple features. In: Conference on Computer Vision and Pattern Recognition (CVPR 2001), vol. 1, p. 511 (2001)
8. Rota, N., Thonnat, M.: Activity recognition from video sequences using declarative models. In: Proceedings of the 14th European Conference on Artificially Intelligence, ECAIOO (2000)
9. Rui, Y., Gupta, A., Acero, A.: Automatically extracting highlights for TV baseball program. ACM Multimedia, 105–115 (2000)
10. Toshev, A., Bremond, F., Thonnat, M.: An apriority based method for frequent composite event discovery in videos. In: ICVS 2006: Proceedings of the Forth IEEE International Conference on Computer Vision Systems, Washingtone DC,USA, p. 10 (2006)
11. Viola, P., Jones, M.: Robust real time object detection, International Journal of Computer Vision (2002)

Data Mining Based Optimization of Test Cases to Enhance the Reliability of the Testing

Lilly Raamesh[1] and G.V. Uma[2]

[1] Research Scholar, Anna University, Chennai 25
lillyraamesh@yahoo.co.in
[2] Asst. Professor/CSE, Anna University, Chennai-25

Abstract. Software testing is any activity aimed at evaluating an attribute or capability of a program or system and determining that it meets its required results. Software testing is important activity in Software Development Life Cycle. Test case selection is a crucial activity in testing since the number of automatically generated test cases is usually enormous and possibly unfeasible. Also, a considerable number of test cases are redundant, that is, they exercise similar features of the application and/or are capable of uncovering a similar set of faults. The strategy is aimed at selecting the less similar test cases while providing the best possible coverage of the functional model from which test cases are generated. Test suite selection techniques reduce the effort required for testing by selecting a subset of test suites. In previous work, the problem has been considered as a single-objective optimization problem. However, real world testing can be a complex process in which multiple testing criteria and constraints are involved. The paper utilizes a hybrid, multi-objective algorithm that combines the efficient approximation of the evolutionary approach with the capability data mining algorithm to produce higher-quality test cases.

Keywords: Test case, test suite, clustering, k-nearest neighbor, multi-objective.

1 Introduction

Software organizations spend considerable portion of their budget in testing related activities. A well tested software system will be validated by the customer before acceptance. The effectiveness of this verification and validation process depends upon the number of errors found and rectified before releasing the system. This in turn depends upon the quality of test cases generated. Through the years a number of different methods have been proposed for generating test cases. A test case is a description of a test, independent of the way a given system is designed. Test cases can be mapped directly to, and derived from use cases. Test cases can also be derived from system requirements. One of the advantages of producing test cases from specifications and design is that they can be created earlier in the development life cycle and be ready for use before the programs are constructed.

D.C. Wyld et al. (Eds.): ACITY 2011, CCIS 198, pp. 89–98, 2011.

2 Software Testing

Software testing is the process of validation and verification of the software product. Effective software testing will contribute to the delivery of reliable and quality oriented software product, more satisfied users, lower maintenance cost, and more accurate and reliable result. However, ineffective testing will lead to the opposite results; low quality products, unhappy users, increased maintenance costs, unreliable and inaccurate results. Hence, software testing is a necessary and important activity of software development process.

2.1 Software Test Suite Optimization

A test case in software engineering is a set of conditions or variables under which a tester will determine whether an application or software system is working correctly or not. The mechanism for determining whether a software program or system has passed or failed such a test is known as a test oracle. In some settings, an oracle could be a requirement or use case, while in others it could be a heuristic. It may take many test cases to determine that a software program or system is functioning correctly. Test cases are often referred to as test scripts, particularly when written. Written test cases are usually collected into test suites. The test suite optimization process involves generation of effective test cases in a test suite that can cover the given System Under Test (SUT) within less time.

In the proposed approach, the test cases are selected by data mining techniques from the Software under Test (SUT). Now, the approach generates a few efficient test cases that can cover the model within less amount of time. Optimization refers to finding one or more feasible solution to one or more objectives. The optimization may be single objective or multi objective. To find globally optimal solutions more reliably multi-objective optimization is used.

2.1.1 Multi-objective Optimization

Multi-objective optimization (or multi-objective programming), also known as multi-criteria or multi-attribute optimization, is the process of simultaneously optimizing two or more conflicting objectives subject to certain constraints. Multi-objective optimization problems can be found in various fields: product and process design, finance, aircraft design, the oil and gas industry, automobile design, or wherever optimal decisions need to be taken in the presence of trade-offs between two or more conflicting objectives. Maximizing profit and minimizing the cost of a product; maximizing performance and minimizing fuel consumption of a vehicle; and minimizing weight while maximizing the strength of a particular component are examples of multi-objective optimization problems.

If a multi-objective problem is well formed, there should not be a single solution that simultaneously minimizes each objective to its fullest. In each case an objective must have reached a point such that, when attempting to optimize the objective further, other objectives suffer as a result. Finding such a solution, and quantifying how much better this solution is compared to many other such solutions, is the goal when setting up and solving a multi-objective optimization problem.

In mathematical terms, the multi-objective problem can be written as:

$$\min_{x} \; [\mu_1(x), \mu_2(x), \ldots, \mu_n(x)]^T$$
$$\text{s.t.}$$
$$g(x) \leq 0$$
$$h(x) = 0$$
$$x_l \leq x \leq x_u$$

where μ_i is the *i*-th objective function, *g* and *h* are the inequality and equality constraints, respectively, and *x* is the vector of optimization or decision variables. The solution to the above problem is a set of Pareto points. Thus, instead of being a unique solution to the problem, the solution to a multi-objective problem is a possibly infinite set of Pareto points.

2.1.2 Solution Methods

There exist many methods to finding a solution to a multi-objective optimization problem, some of which are explained below:

Constructing a single aggregate objective function (AOF)

This is an intuitive approach to solving the multi-objective problem. The basic idea is to combine all of the objective functions into a single functional form, called the AOF, such as the well-known weighted linear sum of the objectives.

The NBI, NC, SPO and DSD methods

The Normal Boundary Intersection (NBI), Normal Contraint (NC), Successive Pareto Optimization (SPO), and Directed Search Domain (DSD) methods solve the multi-objective optimization problem by constructing several AOFs. The solution of each AOF yields a Pareto point, whether locally or globally. The NC and DSD methods suggest two different filtering procedures to remove locally Pareto points. The AOFs are constructed with the target of obtaining evenly distributed Pareto points that give a good impression (approximation) of the real set of Pareto points. The DSD, NC and SPO methods generate solutions that represent some peripheral regions of the set of Pareto points for more than two objectives that are known to be not represented by the solutions generated with the NBI method.

Evolutionary algorithms

Evolutionary algorithms are popular approaches to solving multi-objective optimization. Nowadays, most evolutionary optimizers apply Pareto-based ranking schemes. Genetic algorithms such as the Non-dominated Sorting Genetic Algorithm-II (NSGA-II) and Strength Pareto Evolutionary Approach 2 (SPEA-2) have become standard approaches, although some schemes based on particle swarm optimization and simulated annealing are significant.

Other methods

- Multiobjective Optimization using Evolutionary Algorithms (MOEA).
- PGEN (Pareto surface generation for convex multiobjective instances)
- IOSO (Indirect Optimization on the basis of Self-Organization)

3 Data Mining

Data mining (sometimes called data or knowledge discovery) is the process of analyzing data from different perspectives and summarizing it into useful information - information that can be used to increase revenue, cuts costs, or both. Data mining software is one of a number of analytical tools for analyzing data. It allows users to analyze data from many different dimensions or angles, categorize it, and summarize the relationships identified. Technically, data mining is the process of finding correlations or patterns among dozens of fields in large relational databases.

3.1 Data, Information, and Knowledge

Data
Data are any facts, numbers, or text that can be processed by a computer. Today, organizations are accumulating vast and growing amounts of data in different formats and different databases. This includes:

- operational or transactional data such as, sales, cost, inventory, payroll, and accounting
- nonoperational data, such as industry sales, forecast data, and macro economic data
- meta data - data about the data itself, such as logical database design or data dictionary definitions

Information
The patterns, associations, or relationships among all this *data* can provide *information.* For example, analysis of retail point of sale transaction data can yield information on which products are selling.

Knowledge
Information can be converted into *knowledge* about historical patterns and future trends. For example, summary information on retail supermarket sales can be analyzed in light of promotional efforts to provide knowledge of consumer buying behavior. Thus, a manufacturer or retailer could determine which items are most susceptible to promotional efforts.

4 The Approach

In our method , the Software under Test (SUT) is given as input. The objective of the approach is to generate an efficient test suite that can cover the SUT within less time and cost by applying data mining techniques through the SUT . To maximize the profit of coverage and minimize the total number of test cases needed. The aim of the testing method is to 'cover' the program with test cases that satisfy some fixed coverage criteria such as Statement Coverage or Node Coverage, Branch coverage or Decision Coverage, Decision/Condition Coverage, Multiple Condition Coverage, Path Coverage.

Statement Coverage or Node Coverage : This coverage measures the extent of checks of program behavior. Let Ni be the set of output-defining nodes of SUT subject to test ti, and Vi be the set of covered output defining nodes of SUT subject to test ti.

The optimistic Statement Coverage or Node Coverage of test suite T is $|Vi| / |Ni|$

Branch coverage or Decision Coverage : Branch coverage adequacy criterion verifies whether each control structure (such as an if statement) is evaluated both to true and false conditions.

Branch Coverage % = No. of Branches covered / Total No. of branches

Decision/Condition Coverage : Condition/decision coverage combines the requirements for decision coverage with those for condition coverage. That is, there must be sufficient test cases to toggle the decision outcome between true and false and to toggle each condition value between true and false.

Path Coverage : A test T is considered adequate if it tests all paths. In case the program contains a loop, then it is adequate to traverse the loop body zero time or once.

Code Coverage-In code testing, criteria based on coverage of the building blocks of programs can be used to determine the adequacy of tests. Code coverage is a measure used in software testing. It describes the degree to which the source code of a program has been tested. It is a form of testing that inspects the code directly and is therefore a form of white box testing.

5 Techniques Applied

To optimize the test suite Semantic similarity cluster and k-nearest neighbor algorithm are used. Cluster analysis or clustering is the assignment of a set of observations into subsets (called *clusters*) so that observations in the same cluster are similar in some sense. Clustering is a method of unsupervised learning, and a common technique for statistical data analysis used in many fields, including machine learning, data mining, pattern recognition, image analysis, information retrieval, and bioinformatics. Semantic similarity or semantic relatedness is a concept where a set of documents or terms within term lists are assigned a metric based on the likeness of their meaning / semantic content. This can be achieved for instance by using ontologies to define a distance between test cases (a naive metric), or using statistical means such as a vector space model. There are essentially two types of approaches that calculate topological similarity between ontological concepts:

- Edge-based: which use the edges and their types as the data source;
- Node-based: in which the main data sources are the nodes and their properties.

Other measures calculate the similarity between ontological instances:

- Pairwise: measure functional similarity between two instances by combining the semantic similarities of the concepts they represent
- Groupwise: calculate the similarity directly not combining the semantic similarities of the concepts they represent

The pairwise semantic similarity clustering approach is used to cluster the test cases with functional similarity and the define the distance between the test cases k-nearest neighbor algorithm is used.

The *k*-nearest neighbors algorithm (*k*-NN) is a method for classifying objects based on closest training examples in the feature space. *k*-NN is a type of instance-based learning, or lazy learning where the function is only approximated locally and all computation is deferred until classification. The *k*-nearest neighbor algorithm is amongst the simplest of all machine learning algorithms: an object is classified by a majority vote of its neighbors, with the object being assigned to the class most common amongst its *k* nearest neighbors (*k* is a positive integer, typically small). If $k = 1$, then the object is simply assigned to the class of its nearest neighbor.

The same method can be used for regression, by simply assigning the property value for the object to be the average of the values of its *k* nearest neighbors. It can be useful to weight the contributions of the neighbors, so that the nearer neighbors contribute more to the average than the more distant ones. (A common weighting scheme is to give each neighbor a weight of $1/d$, where d is the distance to the neighbor. This scheme is a generalization of linear interpolation.)

The neighbors are taken from a set of objects for which the correct classification is known. This can be thought of as the training set for the algorithm, though no explicit training step is required. The *k*-nearest neighbor algorithm is sensitive to the local structure of the data.

Nearest neighbor rules in effect compute the decision boundary in an implicit manner. It is also possible to compute the decision boundary itself explicitly, and to do so in an efficient manner so that the computational complexity is a function of the boundary complexity.

```
import java.applet.Applet;
import java.awt.*;
import java.awt.event.ActionListener;
import java.awt.event.ActionEvent;

public class KNN extends Applet implements ActionListener
{   private TextField inputN, inputComplexity, inputK, inputKNN;
  private Button Step1Button, Step2Button, Step3Button;
      private Label errLabel;
  private KNNCanvas theKNNCanvas;
      private Canvas theTruthCanvas;
     private int n, complexity, k, knn;
  private boolean[][] truth;
  private class Sample {
     int x;
     int y;
```

```
      boolean label;    }      Sample[] samples;
   private class Distance {
      double d;
      boolean label;    }      Distance[] distances;
      public void init()
   {              GridBagLayout bag = new GridBagLayout();
                  GridBagConstraints c = new GridBagConstraints();
                     this.setLayout(bag);
                  Label label = new Label("Step 1: Field size(10--80):");
                  bag.setConstraints(label, c);
                  this.add(label);
                   inputN = new TextField("80", 2);
                  bag.setConstraints(inputN, c);
                  this.add(inputN);

                  label = new Label("      complexity(1--100):");
                  bag.setConstraints(label, c);
                  this.add(label);
      inputComplexity = new TextField("5", 2);
                  bag.setConstraints(inputComplexity, c);
      this.add(inputComplexity);
                  Step1Button.addActionListener(this);
                  c.anchor = GridBagConstraints.WEST;
                  c.gridwidth = GridBagConstraints.REMAINDER;
                  bag.setConstraints(Step1Button, c);
                  c.anchor = GridBagConstraints.CENTER;
                  this.add(Step1Button);
                  label = new Label("Step 2: samples(1--2000):");
                  c.gridwidth = 1; // reset to default
                  bag.setConstraints(label, c);
                  this.add(label);
            Step2Button = new Button("Generate Samples");
                  Step2Button.addActionListener(this);
                  c.anchor = GridBagConstraints.WEST;
                  c.gridwidth = GridBagConstraints.REMAINDER;
                    bag.setConstraints(Step2Button, c);
                  c.anchor = GridBagConstraints.CENTER;
                  this.add(Step2Button);
                  label = new Label("Step 3: kNN(1--100):");
                  c.anchor = GridBagConstraints.WEST;
                  c.gridwidth = 1; // reset to default
                  bag.setConstraints(label, c);
                  c.anchor = GridBagConstraints.CENTER;
                  this.add(label);
      inputKNN = new TextField("1", 2);
                  bag.setConstraints(inputKNN, c);
                  this.add(inputKNN);
```

```
Step3Button = new Button("Classify");
            Step3Button.addActionListener(this);
            this.add(Step3Button);
            errLabel = new Label(" ");
            c.anchor = GridBagConstraints.WEST;
            c.fill = GridBagConstraints.BOTH;
            c.gridwidth = GridBagConstraints.REMAINDER;
 bag.setConstraints(errLabel, c);
            this.add(errLabel);
              public void actionPerformed(ActionEvent e)
 {           if (e.getSource() == Step1Button)
            {                    n = new Integer(inputN.getText()).intValue();
            complexity = new Integer(inputComplexity.getText()).intValue();
            k=0; // remove previous samples
            truth = new boolean[n][n];
            int x, y;
            for (x=0; x<n; x++)
                      for (y=0; y<n; y++)
                                truth[x][y] = true;
            for (int i=0; i<complexity; i++)
                      {double w1, w2, b;
                      w1 = Math.random()*2 - 1;
                      w2 = Math.random()*2 - 1;
                      b = Math.random()*n/2;
                      for (x=0; x<n; x++)
                                for (y=0; y<n; y++)
                                          if (w1*(x-n/2)+w2*(y-n/2)+b>0)
                                                    truth[x][y] = !truth[x][y];  }
            theTruthCanvas.repaint();                        }
 else if (e.getSource() == Step2Button)
            {         k = new Integer(inputK.getText()).intValue();
            samples = new Sample[k];
            int i;
            for (i=0; i<k; i++)
            {   samples[i] = new Sample();
               samples[i].x = (int)(Math.random()*n);
               samples[i].y = (int)(Math.random()*n);
               samples[i].label = truth[samples[i].x][samples[i].y];          }
            theTruthCanvas.repaint();                        }
 else if (e.getSource() == Step3Button)
            {int i;
            knn = new Integer(inputKNN.getText()).intValue();
            distances = new Distance[knn];
            for (i=0; i<knn; i++)
            {   distances[i] = new Distance();               }
            theKNNCanvas.repaint();                          }          }
```

```
class KNNCanvas extends Canvas {
        public void paint(Graphics g) {
      int m=5;
      g.setColor(Color.black);
      System.out.println(n);
      g.drawRect(0, 0, n*m+1, n*m+1);
                                      int error = 0;
       for (int x=0; x<n; x++)
          for (int y=0; y<n; y++)
            {
             for (int i=0; i<k; i++){
               double   dist   =   (samples[i].x-x)*(samples[i].x-x)+(samples[i].y-
y)*(samples[i].y-y);
               if (i<knn)
                 {distances[i].d = dist;
                 distances[i].label = samples[i].label;                    }
               else
                 {// go through the knn list and replace the biggest one if possible
                 double biggestd = distances[0].d;
                 int biggestindex = 0;
                 for (int a=1; a<knn; a++)
                   if (distances[a].d > biggestd)
                   {biggestd = distances[a].d;
                    biggestindex = a;                         }
                 if (dist < biggestd)
                   {distances[biggestindex].d = dist;
                   distances[biggestindex].label = samples[i].label;    }}}}}}}}
```

6 Conclusion and Future Work

The optimization of test suite is done in an effective way to enhance the reliability of testing and further this can be enhanced by applying bird flocking technique.

Reference

1. Engström, E., Runeson, P., Skoglund, M.: A systematic review on regression test selection techniques. Information & Software Technology 52(1), 14–30 (2010)
2. Yoo, S., Harman, M., Tonella, P., Susi, A.: Clustering test cases to achieve effective and scalable prioritisation incorporating expert knowledge. In: ACM International Conference on Software Testing and Analysis (ISSTA 2009), Chicago, Illinois, USA, July 19-23, pp. 201–212 (2009)
3. Yoo, S., Harman, M.: Pareto Efficient MultiObjective Test Case Selection. In: ISSTA 2007, London, U.K (July 9-12, 2007)
4. Bleuler, S., Brack, M., Thiele, L., Zitzler, E.: Multiobjective genetic programming: Reducing bloat by using SPEA2. In: Congress on Evolutionary Computation (CEC 2001), Piscataway, NJ, pp. 536–543. IEEE, Los Alamitos (2001)

5. Bleuler, S., Laumanns, M., Thiele, L., Zitzler, E.: PISA - a platform and programming language independent interface for search algorithms. Technical Report 154, Computer Engineering and Networks Laboratory (TIK), Swiss Federal Institute of Technology (ETH) Zurich, Gloriastrasse 35, CH-8092 Zurich, Switzerland (October 2002); Submitted to the Second International Conference on Evolutionary Multi-Criterion Optimization (EMO 2003) (2003)
6. Coello Coello, C.A., Van Veldhuizen, D.A., Lamont, G.B.: Evolutionary Algorithms for Solving Multi-Objective Problems. Kluwer, New York (2002)
7. Corne, D.W., Knowles, J.D., Oates, M.J.: The pareto envelope-based selection algorithm for multiobjective optimisation. In: Schoenauer, M., et al. (eds.) PPSN 2000. LNCS, vol. 1917, pp. 839–848. Springer, Heidelberg (2000)
8. Coello Coello, C.A., Lamont, G.B., Van Veldhuizen, D.A.: Evolutionary Algorithms for Solving Multi-Objective Problems (Genetic and Evolutionary Computation). Springer-Verlag New York, Inc., Secaucus (2006)
9. Deb, K., Kalyanmoy, D.: Multi-Objective Optimization Using Evolutionary Algorithms. John Wiley & Sons, Inc., New York (2001)
10. Deb, K., Agrawal, S., Pratap, A., Meyarivan, T.: A Fast Elitist Non-dominated Sorting Genetic Algorithm for Multi-objective Optimisation: NSGA-II. In: Deb, K., Rudolph, G., Lutton, E., Merelo, J.J., Schoenauer, M., Schwefel, H.-P., Yao, X. (eds.) PPSN 2000. LNCS, vol. 1917, pp. 849–858. Springer, Heidelberg (2000)
11. Do, H., Elbaum, S., Rothermel, G.: Supporting Controlled Experimentation with Testing Techniques: An Infrastructure and its Potential Impact. Empirical Software Engineering 10(4), 405–435 (2005), doi:10.1007/s10664-005-3861-2
12. Elbaum, S., Malishevsky, A.G., Rothermel, G.: Prioritizing test cases for regression testing. In: Proceedings of the 2000 ACM SIGSOFT International Symposium on Software Testing and Analysis, Portland, Oregon, United States, August 21-24, pp. 102–112 (2000), doi:10.1145/347324.348910
13. http://www.en.wikipedia.org/wiki/

An Insight into the Hardware and Software Complexity of ECUs in Vehicles

Rajeshwari Hegde, Geetishree Mishra, and K.S. Gurumurthy

BMS College of Engineering, UVCE, Bangalore, India
rajeshwari.hegde@gmail.com, geetishree@gmail.com,
drksgurumurthy@gmail.com

Abstract. Modern automotives integrate large amount of electronic devices to improve the driving safety and comfort. This growing number of Electronic Control Units (ECUs) with sophisticated software escalates the vehicle system design complexity. In this paper we explain the complexity of ECUs in terms of hardware and software and also we explore the possibility of Common Object Request Broker Architecture (CORBA) architecture for the integration of add-on software in ECUs. This reduces the complexity of the embedded system in vehicles and eases the ECU integration by reducing the total number of ECUs in the vehicles.

Keywords: AUTOSAR, CORBA, ECU, OEM.

1 Introduction

The increasing use of electronic systems in automobiles brings about advantages by decreasing their weight and cost and providing more safety and comfort. The last decade has seen a phenomenal increase in the use of electronic components in automotive systems, resulting in the replacement of purely mechanical or hydraulic-implementations of different functionalities [8]. There are many electronic systems in modern automobiles like antilock braking system (ABS) and Electronic Brakeforce Distribution (EBD), Electronic Stability Program (ESP) and Adaptive Cruise Control (ACC). Such systems assist the driver by providing better control, more comfort and safety. In addition, future x-by-wire applications aim to replace existing braking, steering and driving systems. The developments in automotive electronics reveal the need for dependable, efficient, high-speed and low cost in-vehicle communication [1]. In the earlier days of automotive electronics, each new function was implemented as a stand-alone ECU, which is a subsystem composed of a microcontroller and a set of sensors and actuators. This approach quickly proved to be insufficient with the need for functions to be distributed over several ECUs and the need for information exchanges among functions [7]. Therefore, fundamental architecture of integrated electronic systems in an automobile is important to be designed in order to optimize the total function, cost and productivity [9]. Today, 90% of all innovations are driven by electronics and software. 50-70% of the development costs for an ECU are related to software. Today, premier cars have up to 70 ECUs, connected by 5 system buses

D.C. Wyld et al. (Eds.): ACITY 2011, CCIS 198, pp. 99–106, 2011.

and up to 2500 signals are exchanged by these ECUs [2]. This growing number of ECUs increases the complexity and cost of vehicle development system [3]. Because of the growing system complexity, cost plays a significant role in the development of vehicles. To reduce the vehicle development cost, automotive industrial consortiums are working on standards for automotive electronic systems and software architecture. These standards would increase the commonality and reusability of software in ECU design and reduce the system cost accordingly. The cost, flexibility, extensibility and the need for coping with increased functional complexity in vehicles are changing the fundamental paradigms for the definition of automotive architectures [4]. The complexity of the vehicle systems is also increasing due to the increase in the amount of hardware and software. Instead of isolated functionality on separate ECUs, distributed systems located on several ECUs with a high degree of interaction are introduced [5]. For accurate and efficient development of electronic systems, well defined processes and powerful tools must be used. The transition from the conventional software development approach is being replaced by the model based approach, in order to meet the development time and time to market. The paper is organized as follows. Section 2 deals with the data processing in vehicles. Section 3 deals with the hardware and software in vehicles. Section 4 explains the migration to AUTOSAR. 5 deals with the proposed model to reduce the complexity of electronics and software in vehicles. The paper is concluded in section 6.

2 Data Processing in Vehicles

2.1 Requirements

Highly sophisticated state-of-the-art open-loop and closed-loop control concepts are essential for meeting the demands for function, safety, environmental compatibility and convenience associated with the wide range of automotive subsystems installed in modern-day vehicles.

ECUs developed for use in vehicles all have a similar design. Their structure can be subdivided in the conditioning of input signals, the logic processing of these signals in the microcomputer, and the output of logic and power levels as regulation or control signals [10]. ECUs generally process signals in digital form. Rapid, periodic, real time signals are processed in hardware modules specifically designed for the particular function. This procedure substantially reduces the CPU's interrupt response time requirements.

Originally, data exchange between the ECUs took place via separate wires. However, this type of point-to-point connection is only suitable for a limited number of signals. The introduction of automotive-compatible communication networks for serial transmission of information and data between ECUs has expanded the data transfer capabilities and represents the logical development of autonomous "microcomputers" in vehicles. The generic block diagram of any ECU is shown in the figure3.

The amount of time available for calculations is determined by the control systems. The software contains the actual control algorithms. Depending on the data, an almost unlimited number of logic operations can be established and data records stored and

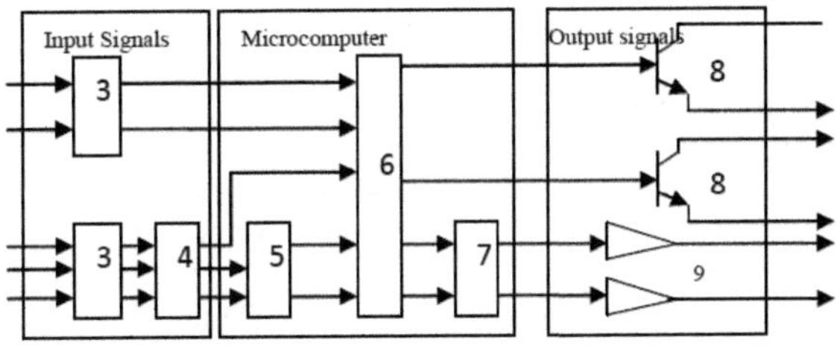

1-Digital input signals 2-analog input signals 3-Protective circuit
4-Amplifier, filter 5-ADC 6-DSP 7-DAC 8-Circuit Breaker 9-Power Amplifier

Fig .1. Signal Processing in the Control Unit

processed in the form of parameters, characteristic curves and multidimensional program maps. For more complex requirements in the field of image processing, the use of digital signal processor is becoming more widespread [10].

3 Hardware and Software in Vehicles

Modern cars of today carry more hardware and computation power than the Apollo spaceship that flew to the moon. They carry up to 80 controllers connected by up to 5 different bus systems connected to numerous sensors and actuators as well as a multimedia human machine interface and external devices such as mobile phones, personal digital assistants [18]. Many automotive ECUs implement most of their functionality in real-time software systems. Thus, ensuring the availability of the software system is essential to guaranteeing the dependable operation of the ECU. Each ECU is a system embedded with software. It's no longer possible to study an ECU as a stand-alone system. The automotive industry is facing the challenge of the rapidly growing significance of software and software-based functionalities. Research has shown that software complexity is a major reason for project delay and cost overrun. AutoSAR is a very recent international effort to address the issue of complexity management of highly integrated ECUs for future requirements[11]. The watchdog is a major design mechanism being used in ECUs to compensate for transient system failures and maintain availability. It is an external circuit/processor that monitors the CPU of an ECU. The application software running on the CPU periodically sends a signal to the watchdog indicating that it is still functioning. If a failure occurs in the ECU software, it would not be able to send this signal, and thus the watchdog would determine that a system failure has occurred. Once the watchdog detects a failure, it triggers a system reset to recover the system and resume normal operation[6]. Table 1 shows ECU software categories [10]. The emission related control ECU includes engine control and transmission control ECUs. They are safety critical and need to collaborate to produce the driving power and distribute it appropriately to the wheels.

Table 1. ECU software categories

Sl. No	ECU software category	Attributes
1	Emission related control ECU	-Safety critical -Emission regulation compliance -Less user interface -Long product life cycle
2	Non Emission related control ECU	-vehicle usability concern -safety regulation(concern) -less user interface -long product life cycle
3	Telematic ECU	-service commitment -conditional user interface complexity -medium product life cycle
4	Infotainment ECU	-less safety related -fancy user interface -neat feature size -adapting consumer electronic features -shorter product life cycle
5	Off-board ECU	-interacts with on-board system -adaptive to multiple vehicle models

It consists of software components that include the RTOS, network control, application control, sensor control, actuator control, on-board diagnostic and the self-test component. Non emission related ECU controls the vehicle electrical and mechanical parts to fulfill non-emission related vehicle system functions. Being with control-oriented software attribute, the architecture of this ECU is similar to the emission related control ECU. Telematic ECU furnishes vehicle driver with additional value-added services, it needs to fulfill the service commitment promoted by the carmaker or the service provider. Off-board ECU interacts with the on-board electronics through vehicle bus to examine their operation status. It hooks to the vehicle bus through the cable that connects to the vehicle test connector[10].

3.1 Autoelectronic Innovations

The automotive electronics market has been growing faster than the overall electronics market and much faster than actual vehicle production. For the next several years, research predicts that automotive electronics will grow at a rate of more than seven percent. Over the course of this decade, the worldwide market for automotive electronics is expected to double [13]. In fact, many industry observers expect electronic components to account for 40% of total car production costs in the near future. Electronic components currently comprise some 20-30% of total costs for all car categories, and this figure is expected to reach 40% or so by 2015 [12]. A generic presentation of any automotive subsystem shall be as depicted in Fig.2.

The main factor behind the rapid increase in the proportion of electronic components used in motor vehicles is the crucial role that electronics plays in developing optimal technological solutions to the four main issues that automakers face today: 1) improving drivability, 2) enhancing safety features, 3) lowering

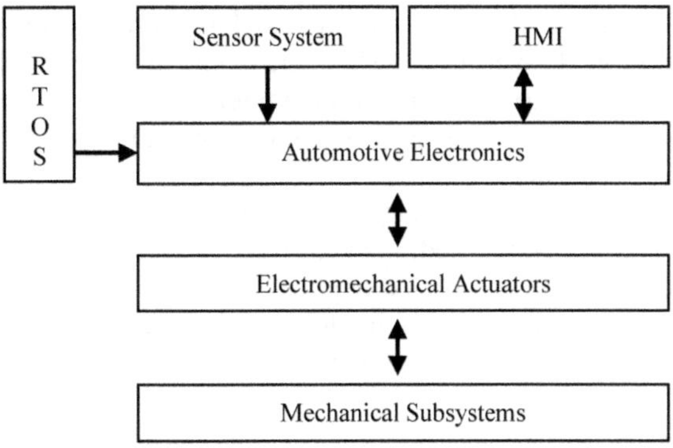

Fig. 2. A generic Automotive Subsystem

environmental burden, and 4) realizing greater operational reliability. Drivers have always demanded safety and reliability, but now that the rate of car ownership is reaching unprecedented heights, they are also insisting on ease of driving. Automakers must now also address environmental issues, which have become a topic of growing concern. The effective application of electronics technology is absolutely vital to the automotive industry as viable solutions to these four key issues.

As a result of technological progress promoted by electronics, electronics technology has become indispensable to ensuring reliability. In particular, as the code size of software for microcomputer control continues to expand, ensuring the reliability of software has become a crucial matter for the automakers. The proportion of man-hours devoted to software development has been rising sharply. This forces the OEMs to redesign their entire development systems to allow efficient development of highly reliable, large-scale software programs. As part of this initiative, OEMs are promoting standardization of software development implementing AUTOSAR standards.

4 Migration to AUTOSAR

The increasing complexity of software implementations parallels increasing supply-chain complexity. Software developers design their components based on requirement definitions from the OEMs or Tier 1 suppliers, who are later responsible for their integration. The AUTOSAR development partnership which includes several OEM manufacturers, Tier 1 suppliers, and tool and software vendors, has been created to develop an open industry standard for automotive software architectures. To achieve the technical goals of modularity, scalability, transferability, and function reusability, AUTOSAR provides a common software infrastructure based on standardized interfaces for the different layers [14].

The migration to AUTOSAR in vehicles does not happen at once. Instead, every OEM is applying various migration scenarios depending on what kind of products are suitable at the developing phase of the specific models. BMW already started migration by applying a network and an ECU migration process. The migration of a vehicle's E/E-network to AUTOSAR will follow a step-by-step approach. Starting with a few ECUs, especially those with a new hardware platform, more and more ECUs will be migrated over time [15]. The great advantage of the AUTOSAR standard is the possibility to integrate a high amount of functionality into one ECU in a controlled way. Such development projects involve multiple suppliers and address many cross-domain interfaces.

The need to concentrate on a common stack of infrastructure software is addressed by AUTOSAR with well-specified, standardized basic software that closes the gap between microcontroller hardware and application software. The technical concept of the AUTOSAR approach is a layered model, which is new in the software design for automotive applications. [16]. Fig. 3 shows the layered software architecture.

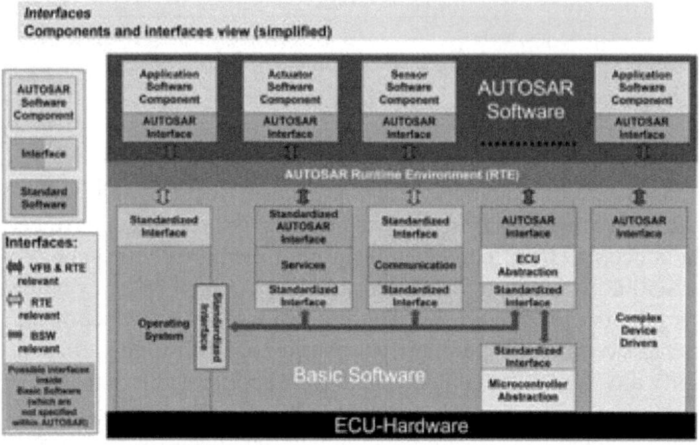

Fig. 3. AUTOSAR layered software architecture [19]

The AUTOSAR layered architecture is offering all the mechanisms needed for software and hardware independence. The upper layer is dedicated to the applications; the lower part, the infrastructure, is containing the basic software layer and the Run Time Environment (RTE) [17].

The basic software layer containing the 53 Basic Software Modules is organized in 3 layers providing the different levels of abstraction from the hardware (Fig.3): the ECU and the microcontroller ; the upper layer, hardware independent, is providing services to the applications software via the RTE.

5 Proposed Model to Reduce Electronics and Software Complexity in Vehicles

To reduce the complexity of electronics in modern vehicle, OEMs are struggling to integrate as many software components as possible into the existing ECU, without degrading the performance of the ECU. In this paper, we propose a new architecture to support ad-on software to the existing ECU, using CORBA middleware which is language, location and platform independent [20]. Fig. 4 shows the proposed model to add the new software to the existing ECU.

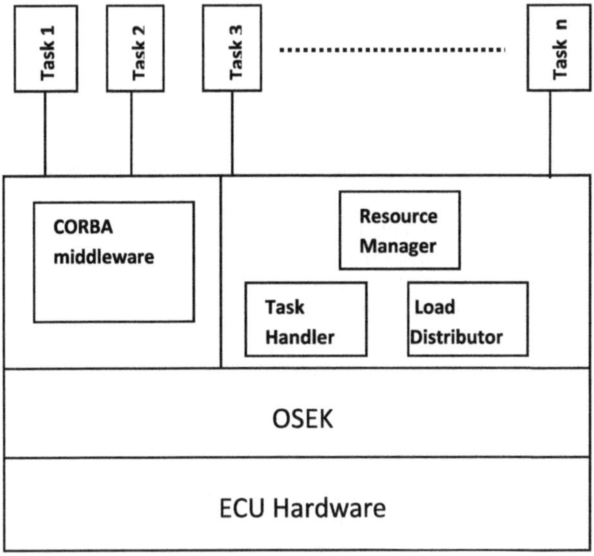

Fig. 4. CORBA middleware Architecture

In the proposed architecture, OSEK Real Time Operating System (RTOS) has been considered with a focus on reusability of application software, and transferable improvement(Hardware, network a non-depending interface). CORBA middleware is a software layer that connects and manages different tasks running on an ECU. It consists of three components, resource manager, load distributer and task handler. When a new task is to be run on the existing ECU, it is detected by the task handler. The task handler of each ECU communicates with other ECUs to know the status of the available resources. The resource handler allocates the resources required for the new task. Depending on the availability of the resources, load distributor assigns the task to the specific ECU. Each ECU is given a unique ID. The ECU with the highest ID is the master and is responsible for the control of the ECUs in the network. If the master ECU fails, a new master will be chosen with the aid of the Bully algorithm which is a method for dynamically selecting a coordinator by the ID. When a new task is detected by all the ECUs, the ECU with less CPU load and the required hardware will execute the new task.

6 Conclusion

In this paper, we addressed the issues on the deployment of electronics and software in vehicles. It is expected that 40% of total cost of the vehicles will be due to the electronics and software. OEMs working towards improvising the legacy software using AUTOSAR. The load sharing and load balancing mechanisms are finding way to reduce the complexity of ECU hardware in vehicles to improve the performance. We also presented CORBA middleware architecture for executing Add-on software, which reduces the need for a new ECU when new features are to be added to the existing system, thereby reducing the complexity of the electronics and software involved in vehicles.

References

1. Chakraborty, S., Ramesh, S.: Programming and Performance Modelling of Automotive ECU Networks. In: 21st International Conference on VLSI Design. IEEE, Los Alamitos (2008)
2. Keskin, U.: In-Vehicle Communication Networks: A Literature Survey (July 28, 2009), http://alexandria.tue.nl/repository/books/652514.pdf
3. NAvet, N., Song, Y., Simonot-Lion, F., Wilwert, C.: Trends in Automotive Communication Systems. Proceedings of the IEEE 93(6) (June 2005)
4. Furukawa, Y., Kawamura, S.: Automotive Electronics: System, Software, and Local Area Network. In: CODES+ISSS 2006, Seoul, Korea, October 22-25 (2006)
5. Frischkorn, H.-G.: Automotive Software: An emerging Domain, A Software Perspective. In: Automotive Software Workshop (2004)
6. See, W.-B.: Vehicle ECU Classification and Software Architectural Implications, http://dspace.lib.fcu.edu.tw/jspui/bitstream/2377/3458/1/ce07ics002006000008.pdf
7. Di Natale, M., Sangiovanni-Vincentelli, A.L.: Moving From Federated to Integrated Architectures in Automotive: The Role of Standards, Methods and Tools. Invited paper, IEEE (2010)
8. Michailidis, A., Spieth, U., Ringler, T., Hedenetz, B., Kowalewski, S.: Test Front Loading in Early Stages of Automotive Software Development Based on AUTOSAR. In: IEEE 2010 (2010)
9. BOSCH Automotive Handbook, 7th edn., pp. 1086–1087. Bentley Publishers
10. Broy, M.: Automotive Software and Systems Engineering. In: IEEE 2005 (2005)
11. Vo, G.N., Lai, R., Garg, M.: Building Automotive Software Component within the AutoSAR Environment - A case study. In: Ninth International Conference on Quality Software (2009)
12. Shelton, C., Martin, C.: Using Models to Improve the Availability of Automotive Software Architectures. In: Fourth International Workshop on Software Engineering for Automotive Systems (SEAS 2007). IEEE, Los Alamitos (2007)
13. Nagabhushana, B.S., Hegde, R., Hegde, V.: Avenues and Technologies for Information in Automotive Industries. In: National Conference on ICSA, Chennai (2006)
14. http://e2af.com/trend/071210.shtml
15. Sangiovanni-Vincentelli, A., Di Natale, M.: Embedded System Design for Automotive Applications. In: IEEE 2007 (2007)
16. Fürst, S.: Challenges in the Design of Automotive Software. In: EDAA 2010 (2010)
17. Fennel, H., Bunzel, S., Heinecke, H., Bielefeld, J., Fürst, S., Schnelle, K.-P., et al.: Achievements and exploitation of the AUTOSAR development partnership. In: CTEA 2006 (2006)
18. http://www.autosar.org
19. Kinkelin, G., Gilberg, A., Delord, B., Heinecke, H., Fürst, S., Moessinger, J., et al.: AUTOSAR on the Road. In: CTEA 2008 (2008)
20. Hegde, R., Gurumurthy, K.S.: CORBA Architecture for the Integration of Add-on Software in Automotive Systems. Journal of Communication and Computer 7(10) (Serial No.71) (October 2010) ISSN 1548-7709

Local Binary Patterns, Haar Wavelet Features and Haralick Texture Features for Mammogram Image Classification Using Artificial Neural Networks

Simily Joseph and Kannan Balakrishnan

Department of Computer Applications,
Cochin University of Science and Technology, Kochi, India
{simily.joseph,mullayilkannan}@gmail.com

Abstract. The objective of this study is the classification of mammogram images into benign and malignant using Artificial Neural Network. This framework is based on combining Local Binary Patterns, Haar Wavelet features and Haralick Texture features. The study shows the importance of Computer Aided Medical Diagnosis in successful decision making by calculating the likelihood of a disease. This multi feature approach for classification obtains an average classification accuracy of 98.6% for training, validation and testing.

Keywords: Machine Learning, Classification, Breast Cancer, CAD.

1 Introduction

Identification and classification of breast abnormalities is an active research area. Breast cancer is affecting the health and lives of millions and millions of women world over. The study by ICMR (Indian Council for Medical Research) says that one in 22 women in India is at the risk of breast cancer. The number of breast cancer patients increases by one in every 2 minutes [1]. Breast cancer statistics shows that in both Urban and rural area the number of affected patients increases. Early detection of breast cancer plays an important role in the diagnostic process. Early detection is important for the complete cure of breast cancer. Masses and microcalcifications are not always cancerous even though they are considered as an early indication of breast cancer. Mammography is the best cost effective method for breast cancer detection [2]. A regular mammographic check up is recommended for women above 50 years.

Tumors are of two types, benign and malignant. Mammogram can easily detect the signs of abnormality. Benign tumors are not cancerous but malignant tumors are cancerous. In mammogram benign tumors appears to be larger in size [3]. Depending on the size of tumor, whether it begins in the ducts or lobules and the degree of spreading breast cancer is classified into 7 types. 1: Ductal Carcinoma In-Situ (DCIS) – is a type of early breast cancer found inside the ductal system. It is not invasive and can be treated successfully. 2: Infiltrating Ductal Carcinoma (IDC) - Represents 78% of all malignancy, appears as well circumscribed areas on mammogram. 3: Medullary Carcinoma - Account for 15% of all breast cancer types, presents the cell that resembles the medulla of brain. 4: Infiltrating Lobular Carcinoma - Appears as a

D.C. Wyld et al. (Eds.): ACITY 2011, CCIS 198, pp. 107–114, 2011.

subtle thickening in the upper-outer quadrant of the breast. This type represents 50% of all type of breast cancer. 5: Tubular Carcinoma- Represents about 2% of all breast cancer processes a distinct tubular structure when viewed under a microscope. 6: Mucinous Carcinoma-Represents approximately 1% to 2% of all breast carcinoma. The differentiating features are mucus production and the presence of poorly defined cells. 7: Inflammatory Breast Cancer (IBC) - It is a rare type, aggressive in nature and causes the lymph vessels to become blocked. The abnormalities in breast tissue can be microcalcifications, Circumscribed lesions, and Speculated lesions [4]. The efficiency of visual examination of mammogram by radiologists can be increased by obtaining a second opinion from computer aided diagnosis systems.

2 Related Works

In recent years different attempt has been made by scientist for the detection and classification of mammogram abnormalities. A cost sensitive method for detection of masses in mammogram using local binary patterns has been proposed by Ning Li [5]. Use of Artificial Neural Networks for mammogram image classification using spatial Graylevel Dependence (SDLD) matrices is proposed in reference [6]. Another method using Haralick texture features also uses ANN for classification [7]. Classification using Multilayer Perceptrons and support Vector Machines based on multi domain features extracted from mammogram images is studied in [8].The use of Gabor wavelets at different frequency scale and orientation for the classification of mammogram image by Support Vector Machine is proposed by Ioan B. [9]. Classification of mammographic lesions using wavelet transform is presented in references [10,11].

3 Proposed System

We proposes a novel approach for classifying mammogram abnormalities by extracting local binary patterns, Haralick texture features and Har wavelet features. The proposed system uses 140 mammogram images of size 1024*1024 from the Mammographic Image analysis Society (MIAS) [12]. The images are in medio-laterl oblique view. The images possess three kinds of background tissues namely Fatty, Fatty-glandular and Dense-glandular. The abnormalities present are calcification, well defined/circumscribed masses, speculated masses, ill-defined masses, architectural distortion and asymmetry. There exist normal, benign and malignant types of mammograms. Image Preprocessing, Feature Extraction and Classification are the main.

3.1 Image Preprocessing

Image preprocessing is performed in order to generate optimal results. The different preprocessing operations applied are noise removal, contrast stretching and edge detection. Digital images are affected by noise during acquisition and transformation. The performance of image processing operations is highly affected by the presence of noises. Mean filters are used for removing the noises. The Sobel operator used for edge detection performs a 2-D spatial gradient measurement on an image to find the approximate absolute gradient magnitude at each point in an input image. Vertical and horizontal derivatives are generated using a convolution kernel. The gradient magnitudes are finally plotted. In contrast stretching the range of intensity values are spanned to a desired intensity levels there by increases the visibility.

3.2 Feature Extraction

The extraction of intelligible features from medical image is very important in proper decision making. Features should carry enough details of the image that are needed for further processing. The features are extracted either globally or locally . In global extraction the whole image is described and in local extraction only part of the image is described. The proposed system extracts texture features for image classification. Texture is the visual patterns of homogeneity [13]. It contains information about the structural arrangements of objects and their relationships. It is concerned with the spatial distribution of gray tones. As visual contents are homogeneous, texture informations are ideal for medical image analysis .This system extracts LBP (Local binary pattern) texture descriptors , Haralick texture features and Haar wavelet features.

3.2.1 Local Binary Pattern Descriptors

LBP (Local Binary Pattern) - a gray scale invariant when used for classification shows good performance [14]. LBP describes local primitives such as curved edges, points, spot, flat areas etc. To generate LBP code for a neighborhood, the weight assigned to each pixels are multiplied with a numerical threshold. The process is repeated for a set of circular samples. As a result the local binary patterns are said to be rotation invariant. Texture over a neighborhood of pixels can be defined as the joint distribution of the gray value of a central pixel of the neighborhood say g_c and gray value of circular pixels located at distance P.

$$T = t(g_c, g_0, g_1, \dots, g_{p-1}). \tag{1}$$

The factorized joint distribution of the difference of central pixels and each pixel in the neighborhood can be represented as:

$$T \approx t(g_c)t(g_0 - g_c, \cdots, g_{p-1} - g_c). \tag{2}$$

To make this invariant against all transformations the signs of the difference are also considered.

$$T \approx t(s(g_0 - g_c), \cdots, s(g_{p-1} - g_c)). \tag{3}$$

$$s(x) = \begin{cases} 1 & x \geq 0 \\ 0 & x < 0 \end{cases}$$

By assigning weight , this difference is converted to a Local Binary Pattern Code which is equivalent to the local texture.

$$LBP_{P,R}(x_c x_c, y_c) = = \sum_{p=0}^{p-1} s(g_p - g_c)\, 2^P. \tag{4}$$

This equation results in the generation of 2^P LBP values.

3.2.2 Haar Discrete Wavelet Transform

DWT (Discrete Wavelet Transform) is widely used in computer Vision applications. Haar wavelet is discontinuous and similar to a bipolar step function. It is the only orthogonal wavelet. Haar wavelet transform calculates a set of wavelet coefficients. Decomposition at different are possible. In this study a 2 level decomposition is performed. A 2 level decomposition divides the grayscale image into 7 sub bands as shown in figure 1. The wavelet features from the image details are calculated and used for classification.

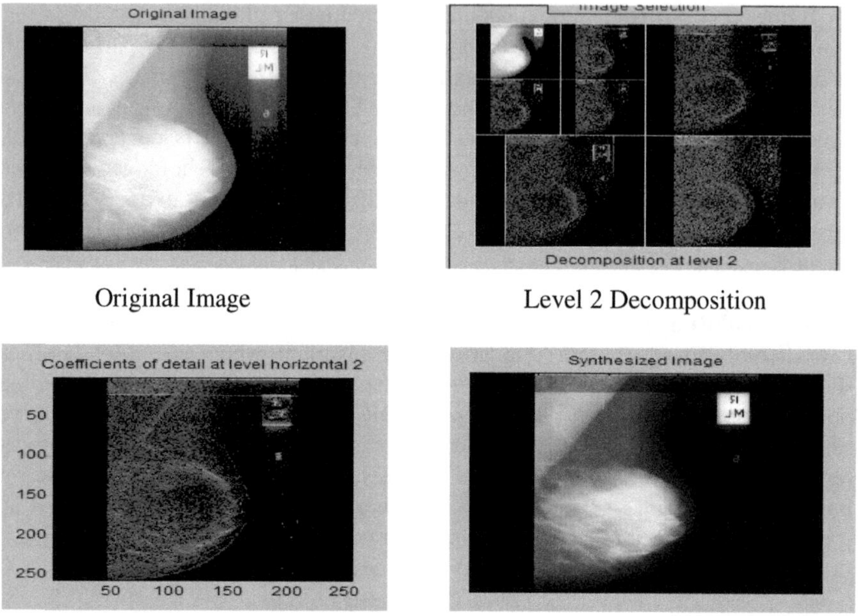

Original Image | Level 2 Decomposition

Coefficient of detail at horizontal level 2 | Synthesized Image

Fig. 1. Sample of Wavelet Decomposition

3.2.3 Haralick Texture Features

Greylevel Co-occurance Matrix **Pd**[i,j] is defined by first specifying a displacement vector **d**=(dx,dy) and counting all pairs of pixels separated by **d** having grey levels i and j. GLCM contains information about the position of pixels having similar grey level values. Haralick Texture features [15] such as Entropy, Contrast, Correlation, Energy, and Homogeniety are extracted from the Greylevel Co-occurrence Matrix.

- Energy $= \sum_i \sum_j P_d^{\,2}(i,j)$.

Entropy $= -\sum i \sum j P_d(i,j) \log P_d(i,j)$.

Contrast $= \sum i \sum j \, (i-j)^2 P_d(i,j)$.

$$\text{Homogeneity} = \sum i \sum j \frac{P_d(i,j)}{1+|i-j|} .$$

$$\text{Correlation} = \frac{\sum i \sum j\,(i-\mu_x)(i-\mu_y)P_d\,(i,j)}{\sigma_x \sigma_y} .$$

4 Classification Using Neural Networks

Classification is the process of predicting class labels of the unknown records. Given a database with a set of items D= { d_1, d_2, d_3, d_4...d_n}. Classification is the process of assigning class labels C={ c_1,c_2,c_3......c_m} to the data items. The entire data set is grouped into training set and test set. Using the training data set, the classifier, builds a model capable of generalizing new test cases. The power of Artificial neural Networks in training and classification has been explored by many scientist over the years [16]. Figure 2 shows the architecture of the multilayer perceptron. Design of the architecture of the neural network is important. The selection of parameters such as number of layers and the number of neurons in each layer affects the accuracy .

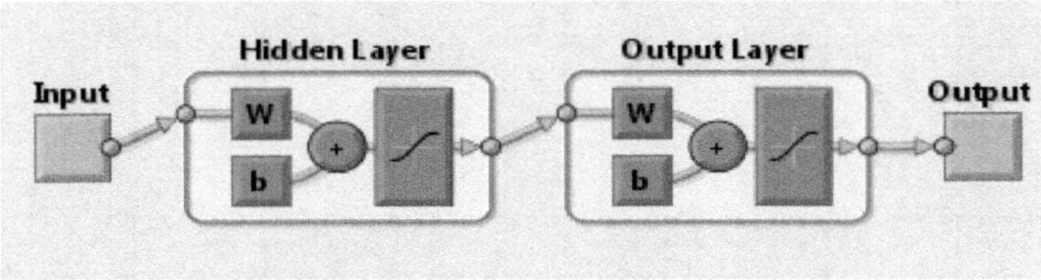

Fig. 2. A sample model of a Multilayer Perceptron

Multilayer Perceptrons are feed forward neural networks. These are trained using backpropagation algorithm. The network is trained to get the desired output. The required output is obtained by forming a linear combination of multiple inputs and by applying some activation function. The proposed architecture consists of two-layer-feed-forward network with hidden layer of Sigmoid and output layer. The weight adjustment in Backpropagation algorithm occurs along the steepest descent way where the function decreases rapidly. But the convergence will be slow. The use of conjugate algorithms makes the convergence fast. Scaled conjugate gradient algorithm is introduced in order to reduce the extra time required in conjugate gradient algorithm for line search of input data [17] . In general the weight adjustment can be represented using the following equation.

$$y=\varphi(\textstyle\sum_{i=1}^{n} w_i\, x_i + b)=\varphi(w^T x + b) .$$

Where w denotes the vector of weights, x is the vector of inputs, b is the bias and is the activation function.

5 Performance Evaluations

The network is trained using the features extracted from the mammogram images. Out of the 140 images, 98 samples are used for training and according to the generated error the network is adjusted..The remaining data is equally split for testing and validation.

In the data set 56 images are benign, 42 are malignant and 42 are normal mammograms.

The result obtained for the network architecture with 20 neurons is shown below. The table summarizes the result with Mean Squared Error which is the average squared difference between required and obtained output and Percent Error which gives the fraction of misclassified samples.

Table 1. Results of Mammogram Image classification

	Samples	MSE	%E
Training:	98	1.93770e-2	5.10204e-0
Validation:	21	2.74281e-2	4.76190e-0
Testing:	21	5.30413e-2	9.52380e-0

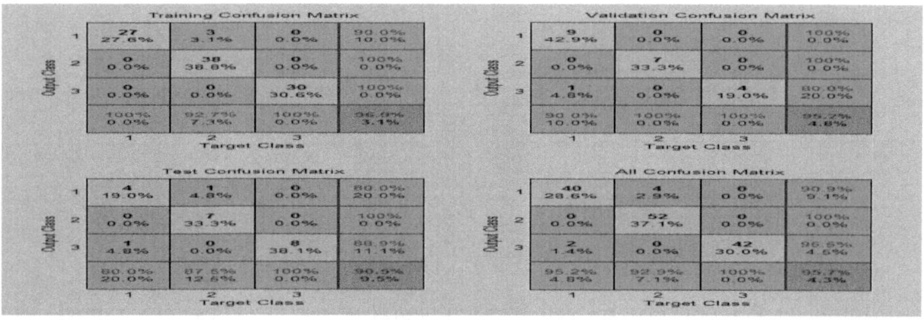

Fig. 3. Confusion Matrix

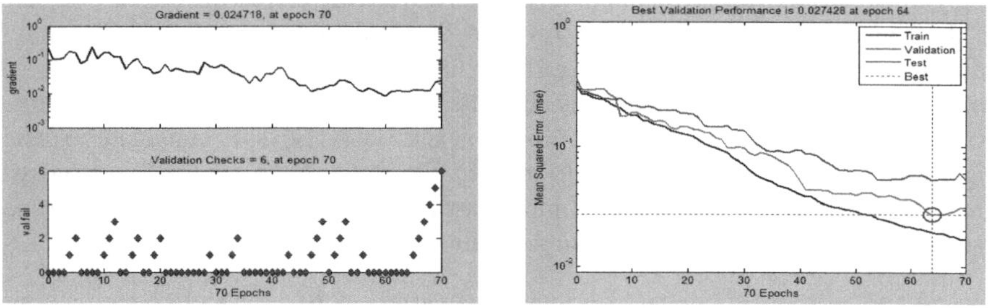

(a) (b)

Fig. 4. (a)Training state (b) Performance of the classifier

After the learning process the overall classification performance was 95.7%. When the network architecture is adjusted by changing the number of neurons to 50 and adjusting some parameters, better results are obtained. The final results are shown in the following figures. For training, the network gives an accuracy of 98% . During training 2 benign images were misclassified into normal, for validation and testing 100 % accuracy is obtained . The average accuracy for the classification is 98.6%. As the classification of malignant into benign is more dangerous than any other classification the proposed method can be treated as an excellent approach because none of the malignant case is misclassified which is important in cancer diagnosis and further treatment.

Table 2. Results of Mammogram Image classification

	Samples	MSE	%E
Training:	98	3.61169e-2	2.04081e-0
Validation:	21	2.30532e-2	0
Testing:	21	2.98685e-2	0

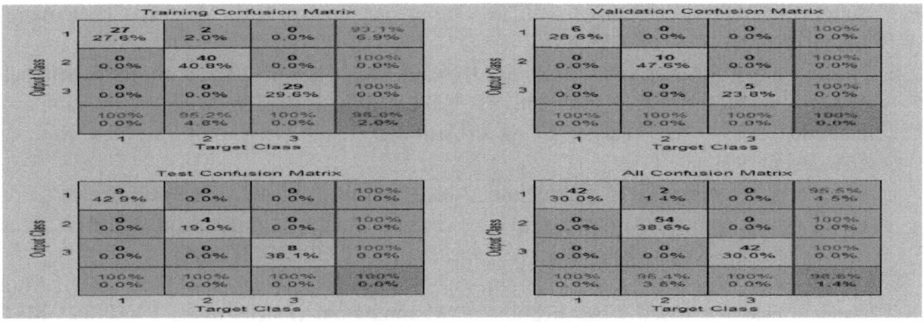

Fig. 5. Confusion Matrix

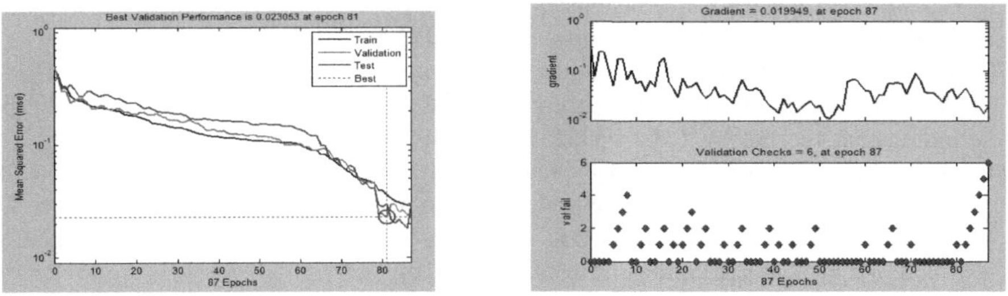

(a) (b)

Fig. 6. (a)Training state (b) Performance of the classifier

6 Conclusion and Future Work

The proposed method of classification focused on the extraction of texture features. The classification result shows the importance and significance of the used features namely Local Binary Patterns Haar Wavelet features and Haralick Texture features, and the power of Backpropagation learning algorithm. The future work will focus on the extraction of features from the region of interest.

References

1. Yao, Y.: Segmentation of breast cancer mass in Mammograms and detection using Magnetic Resonance Imaging. IEEE Image Processing Soc. J. (2004)
2. Nishikawa, R.M.: Current status and future directions computer- aided diagnosis in mammograph. Computerized Medical Imaging and Graphics 31(4), 224–235 (2007)
3. Prabhu Shetty, K., Udupi, V.R., Saptalakar, B.K.: Wavelet Based Microcalcification Detection on Mammographic Images. IJCSNS International Journal of Computer Science and Network Security 9(7) (July 2009)
4. Villegas, O.O.N., De, H., Dominguez, J.O., Sanchez, V.G.C., Gutierrez Casas, E.D., Salgado, G.R.: Rules and feature extraction for microcalcification detection in digital mammograms using neuro-symbolic hybrid system and undecimated filter banks. WSEAS Transactions on Signal Processing 4(8), 484–493 (2008)
5. Li, N., Zhou, H.-J., Guo, Q.-J., Yang, Y.: A Cost-Sensitive Cascaded Method for Automatic Mass Detection. In: IEEE Conference on Systems, Man and Cybernetics, Singapore, pp. 3454–3458 (2008)
6. Heang-Ping, C., Berkman, S., Nicholas, P., Mark, A.H., Kwok, L.L., Dorit, D.A., Mitchell, M.G.: Computerized Classification of Malignant and Benign Microcalcifications on mammograms: texture analysis Using an Artificial Neural Network. Phys. Med. Biol. 42, 549–567 (1997)
7. Ribeiro, P.B., Schoabel, S., Patrocinio, A.C.: Improvement in ANN Performance of the Best Texture Features from Breast Massess in Mammography Images. In: World Congress on Medical Physics and Biomedical Engineering, pp. 2439–2442 (2006)
8. Arfan Jaffar, M., Ahmed, B., Hussain, A., Naveed, N., Jabeen, F., Mirza, A.M.: Multi domain Features based Classification of Mammogram Images using SVM and MLP. Information and Control, 1301–1304 (2009)
9. Ioan, B., Gacsadi, A.: Gabor Wavelet Based Features for Medical Image Analysis and Classification. In: IEEE International Symposium on Applied Science in Biomedical and Communication Technologies, Bratislava, pp. 1–4 (2009)
10. Vijaya, K.G., Ambalika, S.: Contrast Enhancement of Mammographic Images Using Wavelet Transform. In: IEEE International Conference on Computer Science and Information Technology, India, pp. 323–327 (2010)
11. Dellepiane, S.G., Minetti, I., Dellepiane, S.: A Hierarchical Classification Method for Mammographic Lesions Using Wavelet Transform and Spatial Features. In: Bolc, L., Tadeusiewicz, R., Chmielewski, L.J., Wojciechowski, K. (eds.) ICCVG 2010. LNCS, vol. 6374, pp. 324–332. Springer, Heidelberg (2010)
12. Suckling, J., et al.: The Mammographic Image Analysis Society Digital Mammogram Database Exerpta Medica. International Congress Series, vol. 1069, pp. 375–378 (1994)
13. Chen, C.H., Pau, L.F., Wang, P.S.P.: The Handbook of Pattern Recognition and Computer Vision, 2nd edn., pp. 207–248. World Scientific Publishing Co., Singapore (1998)
14. Harwood, D., Ojala, T., Pietikäinen, M., Kelman, S., Davis, S.: Texture classification by center-symmetric auto-correlation, using Kullback discrimination of distributions. Center for Automation Research, University of Maryland, CAR-TR-678 (1993)
15. Haralick, R.M., Shanmugham, K., Dinstein, I.: Textural features for image classification. IEEE Transactions on Systems Man and Cybernetics SMC-3(6), 610–621 (1973)
16. Joseph, S., Balakrishnan, K.: Comparison of MLP, SVM, J48 Classifiers for Mammogram Image Classification, Kerala (2010)
17. Møller, M.F.: A Scaled Conjugate Gradient Algorithm for Fast Supervised Learning MLP. Neural Networks 6, 525–533 (1993)

A Hybrid Genetic-Fuzzy Expert System for Effective Heart Disease Diagnosis

E.P. Ephzibah

School of Information Technology and Engineering,
VIT University, Vellore,
TamilNadu, India
ep.ephzibah@vit.ac.in.

Abstract. This paper presents a genetic algorithm (GA)-based fuzzy logic approach for computer aided disease diagnosis scheme. The aim is to design a fuzzy expert system for heart disease diagnosis. The designed system is based on Cleveland Heart Disease database. Originally there were thirteen attributes involved in predicting the heart disease. In this work genetic algorithm is used to determine the attributes that contribute more towards the diagnosis. Thirteen attributes are reduced to six attributes using genetic search. Fuzzy expert system is used for developing knowledge based systems in medicine. The proposed system uses Mamdani inference method. The system designed in Matlab software can be viewed as an alternative for existing methods to distinguish of heart disease presence.

Keywords: Genetic Algorithms, Fuzzy logic, Medical data, Disease diagnosis.

1 Introduction

Genetic algorithms are known to be one of the best methods for search and optimization problems. Feature selection is the task of identifying and selecting a useful subset of pattern-representing features from a large set of features. The number of features increases as the dimensionality expands. The benefits of feature selection are facilitating data visualization and understanding, reducing the measurement and storage requirements, reducing training time, defying the curse of dimensionality to improve prediction performance. The objective is finally to construct and select subsets of features that are useful to build a good predictor [1]. A subset of useful features may exclude redundant but relevant features. After generating the best feature subset it is used for classification. Fuzzy set theory and fuzzy logic are highly suitable for developing knowledge based systems in medicine for diagnosis of diseases. In this paper it is discussed about how genetic algorithms and fuzzy logic combine together for efficient and cost effective diagnosis of heart disease.

This paper is organized as follows. In section 2 related work is explained. In section 3 the proposed technique is described. In section 4 experimental results are presented in order to prove the significance and efficiency of the proposed technique. Finally section 5 summarizes the conclusion.

D.C. Wyld et al. (Eds.): ACITY 2011, CCIS 198, pp. 115–121, 2011.

2 Related work

Experimental results have shown that genetic algorithms are able to reach a relative good score in a quite small number of generations, for function optimization. They refine the solution space trying to identify the exact optimal solution of the function. There are a good number of methods which reached high classification accuracies using the dataset taken from UCI machine learning repository. Among these, [2] Tool Diag, RA obtained 50.00% classification accuracy by using IB1- 4 algorithm. [2] WEKA, RA obtained a classification accuracy of 58.50% using InductH algorithm while ToolDiag, RA reached to 60.00% with RBF algorithm. [2] Again, WEKA, RA applied FOIL algorithm to the problem and obtained a classification accuracy of 64.00%. [2] MLP+BP algorithm that was used by ToolDiag, RA reached to 65.60%. [2] The classification accuracies obtained with T2, 1R, IB1c and K* which were applied by WEKA, RA are 68.10%, 71.40%, 74.00% and 76.70%, respectively. [2] Robert Detrano used logistic regression algorithm and obtained 77.0% classification accuracy. [15] According to Sellappan Palaniappan, Rafiah Awang, Naïve Bayes gives the highest probability (95%) with 432 supporting cases, followed by Decision tree (94.93%) with 106 supporting cases, and Neural Network (93.54%) with 298 supporting cases. Naïve Bayes appears to be most effective as it has the highest percentage of correct predictions (86.53%) for patients with heart disease, followed by Neural Network (with a difference of less than 1%) and Decision Trees.

3 Proposed Method

The proposed method is based on the Cleveland Clinic Foundation dataset [3]. This dataset is used to diagnose the presence of heart disease based on the various medical tests carried out on a patient. It contains elements of two classes: patients with and without heart disease. There are about 303 instances and 76 attributes. Only 14 attributes out of 76 has been identified to be effective and necessary attributes. According to the proposed method only six attributes are considered. Genetic algorithm is a class of optimization procedure used to solve problem that involves a search to find the optimal solution. GAs operate iteratively on a population of chromosomes, each one of which represents a candidate solution to the problem at hand, properly encoded as a string of symbols(e.g. binary). A randomly generated set of such chromosomes form the initial population from which the GA starts its search. Three basic genetic operators guide this search: selection, crossover, and mutation. The genetic search process is iterative: evaluating, selecting, and recombining chromosome string in the population during each iteration (generation) until reaching some termination condition. Evaluation of each chromosome is based on a fitness function. It determines which of the candidate solutions are better. The GA combines selection, crossover, and mutation operators with the goal of finding the best solution to the problem by searching until the specified criterion is met.

A fuzzy set is a collection of distinct elements with a varying degree of relevance or membership. The membership function takes interval values between 0 and 1. These values express the degrees with which each object is compatible with the properties or features that are distinctive to the collection. A fuzzy set is a generalization of the concept of a set whose characteristic function takes only binary values. A fuzzy inference model can be created using the properties of fuzzy set. The knowledge base of a fuzzy inference system is to link the fuzzified inputs with the associated reasoning mechanism.

There are two major models of fuzzy system, Mamdani [4] and Takagi-Sugeno (T-S) [5] fuzzy systems. The main difference between these two types of fuzzy systems lies in the consequent variable of fuzzy rules. Mamdani type fuzzy systems use linguistic fuzzy sets as consequent variables in fuzzy rules, whereas the T-S type fuzzy systems employ a linear combination of input variables as a rule consequent variable. This work has been implemented using Mamdani type.

Based on the experts' (Doctors') knowledge the fuzzy rules were generated. The generated rules help us to predict the disease using fuzzy tool in Matlab. The input is the set of all the selected features and the output of the system is to get a value 1 or 0 that indicates the presence or absence of the disease.

4 Experimental Results

The table below gives the list of attributes selected by genetic algorithm using MATLAB version:7.3.0.

Table 1. List of selected features from Cleveland Heart disease data set

S No:	*Att No:	+Att No:	Attributes
1	9	3	cp:Chest Pain Type
2	10	4	trestbps: resting blood pressure
3	38	9	exang: exercise induced angina
4	32	8	thalach: Maximum heart rate achieved
5	40	10	oldpeak: ST depression induced by exercise
6	44	12	ca: no.of major vessels

* Attribute Number out of 76
\+ Attribute Number out of 14

Input fields are therefore chest pain type (CPT), resting blood pressure(RBP), exercise (EXER), Maximum heart rate (HR), old peak (ST depression induced by exercise relative to rest), ca –the number of vessels colored(CA). The output field refers to the presence of heart disease in the patient. The following are the membership function diagrams of the input features:

(i) Chest pain type: (CPT) This input feature has four values
1=typical angina
2=atypical angina
3=non-anginal pain
4=asymptomatic

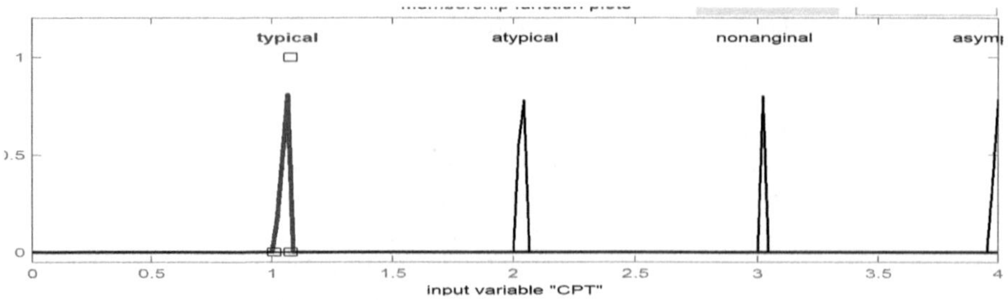

(ii) Resting blood pressure (RBP): Under this input variable there are four fuzzy sets namely, low, medium, high and very high. Membership functions of "Low" and "Very high" sets are trapezoidal and membership functions of "medium" and "high" sets are triangular.

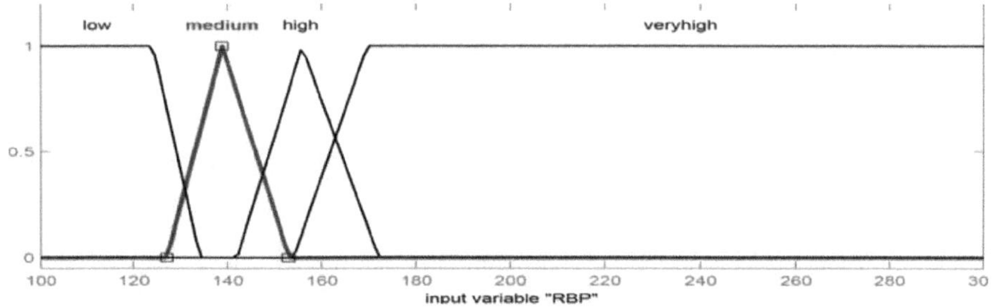

(iii) Exercise (EXER): This input field has just 2 values (0, 1) and one fuzzy set (true).

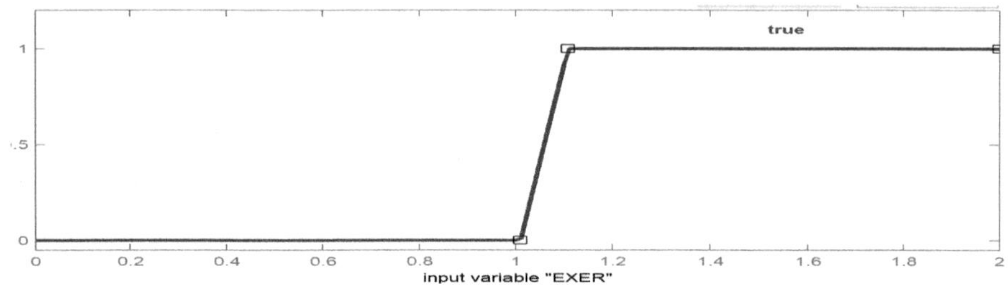

(iv) Old peak: Old peak field has 3 fuzzy sets (Low, Risk and Terrible). Membership functions of "Low" and "Terrible" fuzzy sets are trapezoidal and membership function of "Risk" fuzzy set is triangular.

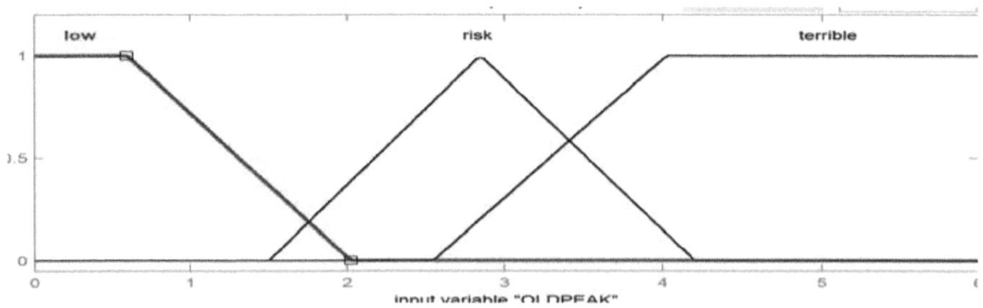

(v) Maximum Heart rate (HR): In this field, we have 3 linguistic variables (fuzzy sets) (Low, Medium and High). Membership functions of "Low" & "High" fuzzy sets are trapezoidal and membership function of "Medium" fuzzy set is triangular.

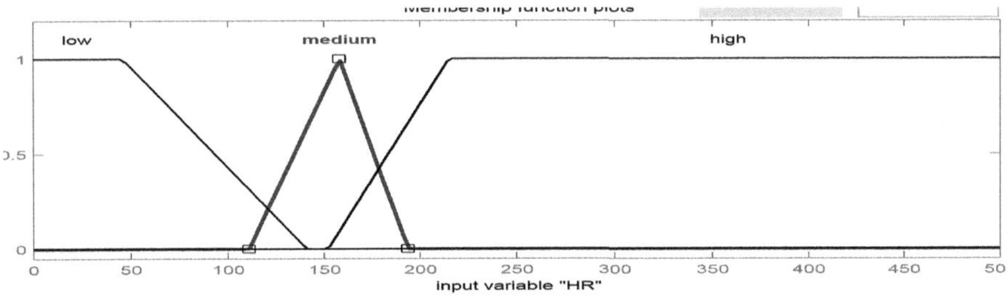

(vi) No. of vessels colored (CA) : In this field there are four fuzzy sets zero, one, two and three.

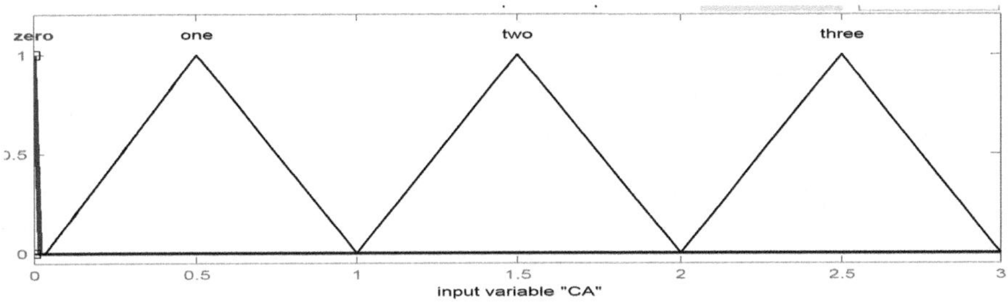

5 System Testing

The output shows the presence or absence of heart disease in a patient given the values for the input features. There are two fuzzy sets, "healthy" & "sick". The membership functions of "healthy" and "sick" are trapezoidal.

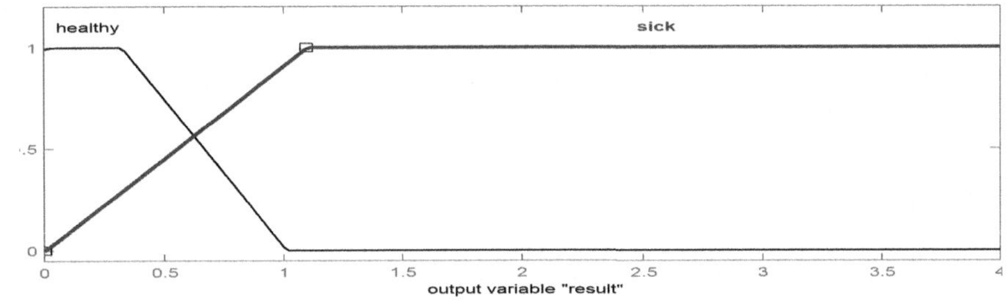

The picture given below is the rule viewer: heart disease. Given an instance for which the result is "sick", the rule viewer correctly points out the presence of the disease.

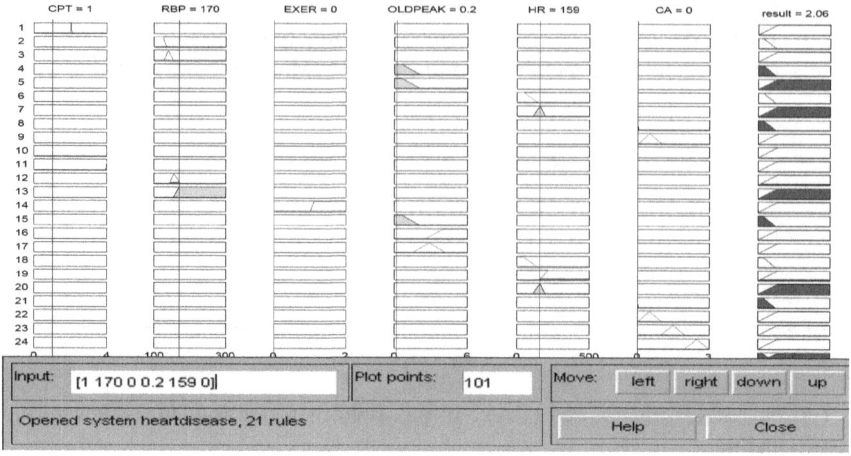

Table 2. System Testing

Chest Pain Type	Resting blood pressure	Exercise induced angina	Oldpeak:	Maximum heart rate achieved	No. of major vessels	Predicted Output
1	170	0	0.2	159	0	"Sick"
3	172	0	0.5	162	0	"Healthy"

6 Conclusion

In this paper a system that combines genetic algorithms and fuzzy expert system is proposed. Genetic algorithm is used to determine the attributes which contribute more towards the diagnosis of heart ailments which indirectly reduces the number of tests which are needed to be taken by a patient. Designing of this system with fuzzy in comparison with other methods improves results. The experts knowledge plays a very important role in framing the fuzzy inference system. The explained model proves to be more efficient in diagnosing heart disease. Furthermore, it has been proven to be competitive with state of the art classifiers like Naïve Bayes, Decision tree, Classification via clustering and SVM classifier.

References

1. Guyon, I., Elisseeff, A.: An introduction to variable and feature selection. Journal of Machine Learning Research 3, 1157–1182 (2003)
2. Polata, K., Guneşa, S., Tosunb, S.: Diagnosis of heart disease using artificial immune recognition system and fuzzy weighted pre-processing. Pattern Recognation (2007)
3. Detrano, R.: V.A. Medical Center, Long Beach and Cleveland Clinic Foundation
4. Zimmermann, H.-J.: Fuzzy Set Theory - And its Applications, 3rd edn. Kluwer Academic Publishers, Dordrecht (1997)

5. Takagi, T., Sugeno, M.: Fuzzy identification of systems and its applications to modeling and control. IEEE Transactions on Systems, Man, and Cybernetics 15, 116–132 (1985)
6. Zadeh, L.A.: Fuzzy Sets. Information and Control 8, 338–353 (1965)
7. Goldberg, D.E.: Genetic Algorithms in Search, Optimization and Machine Learning. Addison-Wesley, Reading (1989)
8. Allahverdi, N., Torun, S., Saritas, I.: Design of a fuzzy expert system for determination of coronary heart disease risk. In: International Conference on Computer Systems and Technologies - CompSysTech 2007 (2007)
9. Kwong, C.K., Chang, K.Y., Tsim, Y.C.: A genetic algorithm based knowledge discovery system for the design of fluid dispensing processes for electronic packaging. Expert Systems with Applications 36(2), 3829–3838 (2008)
10. Shapiro, J.: Genetic algorithms in machine learning. In: Paliouras, G., Karkaletsis, V., Spyropoulos, C.D. (eds.) ACAI 1999. LNCS (LNAI), vol. 2049, pp. 146–168. Springer, Heidelberg (2001)
11. Zhu, F., Guan, S.: Feature selection for modular GA-based classification. Applied Soft Computing, 381–393 (2004)
12. Booker, L.B., Goldberg, D.E., Holland, J.H.: Classifier systems and genetic algorithms. Artificial Intelligence 40(1-3), 235–282 (1989)
13. Soler, V., Roig, J., Prim, M.: Finding Exceptions to Rules in Fuzzy Rule Extraction. In: KES 2002, Knowledge-based Intel. Information Engineering Systems, part 2, pp. 1115–1119 (2002)
14. Parthiban, L., Subramanian, R.: Intelligent heart disease prediction system using CANFIS and Genetic Algorithm. International Journal of Biological Life Sciences (2007)
15. Palaniappan, S., Awang, R.: Intelligent Heart Disease Prediction System Using Data Mining Techniques. In: International Conference on Computer Systems and Applications, AICCSA 2008, pp. 108–115. IEEE/ACS (2008)

Genetic Algorithm Technique Used to Detect Intrusion Detection

Payel Gupta and Subhash K. Shinde

Pillai's Institute of Information Technology,
Bharti Vidyapeeth Institute of Technology
Mumbai,Maharashtra
payel.gupta@gmail.com
skshinde@rediffmail.com

Abstract. The paper content is genetic algorithm based intrusion detection system. It is a simulation type system comes under networking area. The first system in the line is an anomaly-based IDS implemented as a simple linear classifier. This system exhibits high both detection and false-positive rate. For that reason, we have added a simple system based on *if-then* rules that filter the decision of the linear classifier and in that way significantly reduces false-positive rate. In the first step of our solution we deploy feature extraction techniques in order to reduce the amount of data that the system needs to process. Hence, our system is simple enough not to introduce significant computational overhead, but at the same time is accurate, adaptive and fast due to genetic algorithms. The model is verified on KDD99 benchmark dataset.

Keywords: Intrusion detection system, Anomaly based IDS, False positive rate, false negative rate.

1 Introduction

Intrusion detection is becoming an increasingly important technology that monitors network traffic and identifies network intrusions such as anomalous network behaviors, unauthorized network access, and malicious attacks to computer systems. There are two general categories of intrusion detection systems (IDSs): misuse detection and anomaly detection. Misuse detection systems detect intruders with known patterns [3]. Anomaly detection systems identify deviations from normal network behaviors and alert for potential unknown attacks [3].They exhibit higher rate of false alarms, but they have the ability of detecting unknown attacks and perform their task of looking for deviations much faster [2].

Genetic Algorithms (GA) are search algorithms based on the principles of natural selection and genetics. GA evolves a population of initial individuals to a population of high quality individuals, where each individual represents a solution of the problem to be solved. Each individual is called chromosome, and is composed of a predetermined number of gene. The quality of each rule is measured by a fitness function as the quantitative representation of each rule's adaptation to a certain environment. The procedure starts from an initial population of randomly generated individuals. Then the

D.C. Wyld et al. (Eds.): ACITY 2011, CCIS 198, pp. 122–131, 2011.

population is evolved for a number of generations while gradually improving the qualities of the individuals in the sense of increasing the fitness value as the measure of quality. During each generation, three basic genetic operators are sequentially applied to each individual with certain probabilities, i.e. selection, crossover and mutation [6]. In this work we are presenting a genetic algorithm (GA) approach for classifying network connections. GAs is robust, inherently parallel, adaptable and suitable for dealing with the classification of rare classes. Moreover, due to its inherent parallelism, it offers a possibility to implement the system using reconfigurable devices without the need of deploying a microprocessor. In this way, the implementation cost would be much lower than the cost of implementing traditional IDS providing at the same time higher level of adaptability, as these devices can be dynamically reconfigured. Here we further investigate a combination of two GA based intrusion detection systems. The first system in the line is an anomaly- based IDS implemented as a simple linear classifier. This system exhibits high both detection and false-positive rate. For that reason, we have added a simple system based on *if-then* rules that filter the decision of the linear classifier and in that way significantly reduces false-positive rate. We actually create a strong-classifier built upon weak-classifiers, but without the need to follow the process of boosting algorithm as both of the created systems can be trained separately [1].

2 Motivation

Some of the best-performed techniques used in the state-of-the-art apply GA [4], combination of neural networks and C4.5, genetic programming(GP) ensemble, support vector machines, fuzzy logic , clustering techniques , hidden Markov models, junction tree algorithm, Naïve Bayes Classifier, ant colonies, etc. All of the techniques mentioned above have two steps: training and testing. The systems have to be constantly retrained using new data since new attacks are emerging every day. The advantage of all GA or GP-based techniques lies in their easy retraining. It's enough to use the best population evolved in the previous iteration as initial population and repeat the process, but this time including new data. Thus, our system is inherently adaptive which is an imperative quality of IDS [1].

Some of the shortcomings of above techniques are as follows:-

2.1 Clustering Technique (k-means Algorithm)

K-means has been used for clustering data for decades. However, it has two shortcomings in clustering large data sets: number of clusters dependency and degeneracy. Number of clusters dependency is that the value of k is very critical to the clustering result. Degeneracy means that the clustering may end with some empty clusters. This is not what we expect since the classes of the empty clusters are meaningless for the classification [7].

2.2 Support Vector Machine (SVM)

SVM is slow for large size problems. To solve this problem many decomposition methods can be used which decomposes a large QP problem into small sub-problems of size two. The Sequential Minimal Optimization (SMO) algorithm has been used for decomposition of two classes SVMs, in this algorithm. The LIBSVM is adopted to train and test every SVM [8].

2.3 Naïve Bayes Classifier

As a naïve Bayesian network is a restricted network that has only two layers and assumes complete independence between the information nodes. This poses a limitation to this research work. In order to alleviate this problem so as to reduce the false positives, active platform or event based classification may be thought of using Bayesian network [9].

2.4 Hidden Markov Model

Although using sensors improves the quality of the data being processed by our algorithms, we still have to deal with the "false positive" problem. This problem originates from the fact that most, if not all, network sensors adhere to the philosophy that it is preferable to include many erroneously identified intrusions in the input data stream (false positives) rather than to miss one real intrusion (false negative). In addition, our input data originally suffered from the alert repetition problem: a single alert type or a set of alert types being repeated over and over. A drawback of the algorithm is its considerable price, as it has O(Tn2) complexity. Since n is the number of the states, i.e. the number of normal user activity patterns in the database, its value could be significant in the case of a large system. Another disadvantage of the anomaly based IDS in general is the creation of the database containing the user profiles, which could be a task of considerable difficulty [10].

2.5 Junction Tree Algorithm

The drawback of the described method is its considerable computational price, since it has *O(TM2)* complexity. Since *M2* is the cardinality of the clique state space, its value could be significant in the case of a large system. Another disadvantage of the anomaly based IDS in general is the creation of the database containing the user profiles, which could be a task of considerable difficulty and requires some period of time the system is unprotected[11].

2.6 Fuzzy Logic

When using fuzzy logic, it is often difficult for an expert to provide "good" definitions for the membership functions for the fuzzy variables. We have found that genetic algorithms can be successfully used to tune the membership functions of the fuzzy sets used by our intrusion detection system. Each fuzzy membership function can be defined using two parameters. [12].

Thus we are using genetic algorithm for solving the problem of intrusion detection. Benefits of GA are as follow:-

- GAs are intrinsically parallel, since they have multiple offspring, they can explore the solution space in multiple directions at once. If one path turns out to be a dead end, they can easily eliminate it and continue working on more promising avenues, giving them a greater chance by each run of finding the optimal solution.

- Due to the parallelism that allows them to implicitly evaluate many schemas at once, GAs are particularly well-suited to solving problems where the space of potential solutions is truly huge - too vast to search exhaustively in any reasonable amount of time, as network data is.
- Working with populations of candidate solutions rather than a single solution and employing stochastic operators to guide the search process permit GAs to cope well with attribute interactions and to avoid getting stuck in local maxima, which together make them very suitable for dealing with classifying rare class, as intrusions are.
- System based on GAs can easily be re-trained, which provides the possibility of evolving new rules for intrusion detection. This property offers the adaptability of a GA-based system, which is an imperative quality of an intrusion detection system having in mind the high rate of new attacks' emerging [1].
- Generally good at finding acceptable solutions to a problem reasonably quickly.
- Free of mathematical derivatives.
- No gradient information is required.
- Free of restrictions on the structure of the evaluation function.
- Fairly simple to develop.
- Do not require complex mathematics to execute.
- Able to vary not only the values, but also the structure of the solution.
- Get a good set of answers, as opposed to a single optimal answer.[6]

3 Review of Literature

GA evolves a population of initial individuals to a population of high quality individuals, where each individual represents a solution of the problem to be solved. Each individual is called chromosome, and is composed of a predetermined number of genes [14]. The quality of each rule is measured by a fitness function as the quantitative representation of each rule's adaptation to a certain environment. The procedure starts from an initial population of randomly generated individuals. Then the population is evolved for a number of generations while gradually improving the qualities of the individuals in the sense of increasing the fitness value as the measure of quality. During each generation, three basic genetic operators are sequentially applied to each individual with certain probabilities, i.e. selection, crossover and mutation. The algorithm flow is presented in Fig. 1. Determination of the following factors has the crucial impact on the efficiency of the algorithm: selection of fitness function, representation of individuals and the values of GA parameters (crossover and mutation rate, size of population, threshold of fitness value). Determination of these factors usually depends on the application. In our work we have employed two simple fitness functions [5].

[Start] Generate random population of n chromosomes (suitable **solutions** for the problem).[Fitness] Evaluate the fitness f(x) of each chromosome x in the population.[New population] Create a new population by repeating the following steps until the new population is complete.1 [Elitism] Select the best chromosome or chromosomes to be carried over to the next generation. 2 [Selection] Select two parent

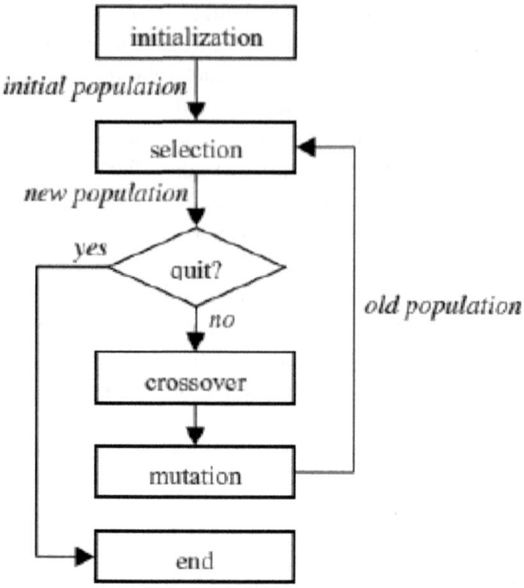

Fig. 1. Genetic Algorithm Flowchart

chromosomes from a population according to their fitness (the better fitness, the bigger chance to be selected). Selection can be done "with replacement", meaning that the same chromosome can be selected more than once to become a parent.3 [Crossover] with a crossover probability pc, cross over the parents, at a randomly chosen point, to form two new offspring If no crossover is performed, an offspring is the exact copy of parents.4 [Mutation] with a mutation probability pm, mutate two new offspring at each locus.5 [Accepting] Place new offspring in the new population.6 [Replace] Replace the old generation with the new generated. 7[Test] If the end condition is satisfied, stop, and return the best solution in current population.8 [Loop] Go to step 2.

3.1 Selection

This operator selects the chromosome in the population for reproduction. The more fit the chromosome, the higher its probability of being selected for reproduction. Thus, selection is based on the survival-of-the-fittest strategy, but the key idea is to select the better individuals of the population, as in tournament selection, where the participants compete with each other to remain in the population. The most commonly used strategy to select pairs of individuals is the method of roulette-wheel selection, in which every string is assigned a slot in a simulated wheel sized in proportion to the string's relative fitness. This ensures that highly fit strings have a greater probability to be selected to form the next generation through crossover and mutation. After selection of the pairs of parent strings, the crossover operator is applied to each of these pairs. It is useful to distinguish between the *evaluation function* and the *fitness function* used by a genetic algorithm. The evaluation function, or objective function, provides a measure of performance with respect to a particular set of parameters. The fitness function transforms that measure of performance into an allocation of reproductive opportunities. The evaluation of a string representing a set of parameters is independent of the evaluation of any other string. The fitness of that string, however, is always defined with respect to other members of the current population. When individuals are modified to produce new individuals, they are said to be *breeding* [13]. Selection determines which individuals are chosen for breeding (recombination) and how many offspring each selected individual produces. The individual (chromosome or string) is first evaluated by a fitness function to determine the quality. During testing an individual receives a grade, known as its *fitness*, which indicates how good a solution it is. The period in which the individual is evaluated and assigned fitness is known as *fitness assessment*. Good chromosomes (those with the highest fitness function) survive and have offspring, while those chromosomes furthest removed or with the lowest fitness function are culled. Constraints on the chromosomes can be modelled by penalties in the fitness function or encoded directly in the chromosomes' data structures [7].

3.2 Crossover and Mutation

3.3.1 One-Point Crossover

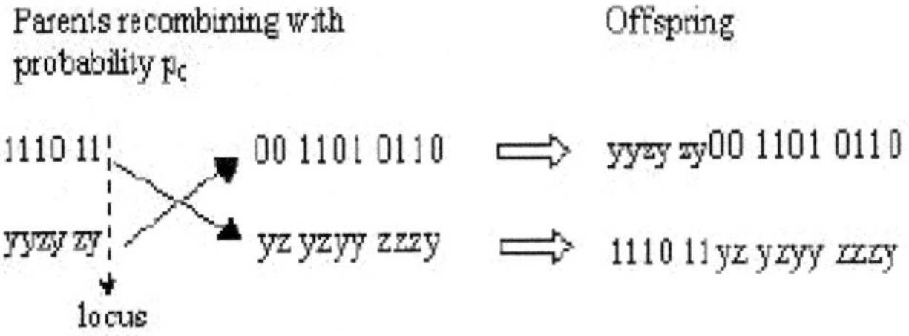

3.3.2 Two-Point Crossover

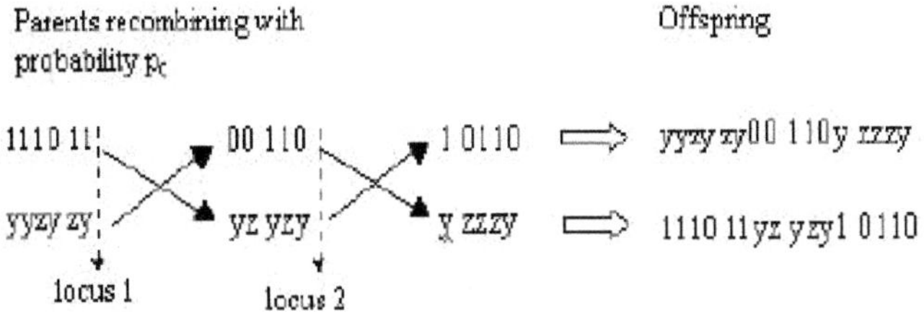

3.3.3 Uniform Crossover

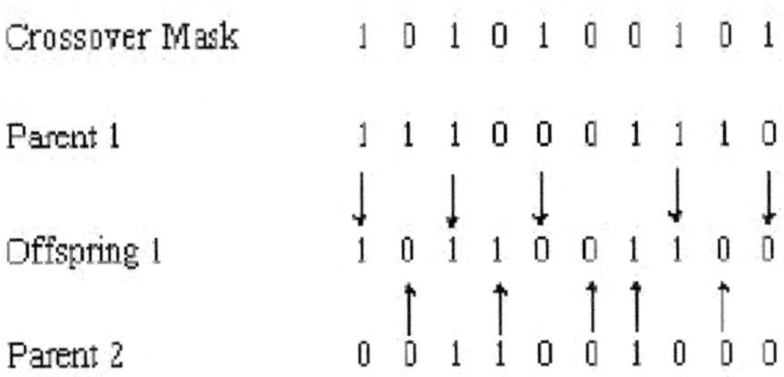

Uniform crossover

4 Strategy

Three common problems of intrusion detection systems are speed, accuracy and adaptability which can be overcome by using Genetic algorithm approach. The main feature of this system is the use of genetic algorithm for intrusion detection. The system shows the simulation of Genetic algorithm as applied to KDD dataset for identifying attacks from set of connections. The speed issue arises from the extensive amount of data that needs to be monitored in order to observe the entire situation. We are deploying a different approach. Instead of defining different attack scenarios, we extract the features of network traffic that are likely to take part in an attack. The implemented IDS is a serial combination of two IDSs. The complete system is presented in Fig. 2. The first part is a linear classifier that classifies connections into normal ones and potential attacks. Due to its very low false-negative rate, the decision that it makes on normal connections is considered correct. But, as it exhibits high false-positive rate, if it opts for an attack, its decision has to be re-checked. This re-checking is performed by a rule-based system whose rules are trained to recognize normal connections. This part of the system exhibits very low false-positive rate, i.e. the probability for an attack to be incorrectly classified as a normal connection is very low. In this way, the achieved false-positive rate of the entire system is significantly reduced while maintaining high detection rate. As our system is trained and tested on KDD99 dataset, the election of the most important features is performed once at the beginning of the process. Implementation for a real-world environment, however, would require performing the feature selection process before each training step [1].

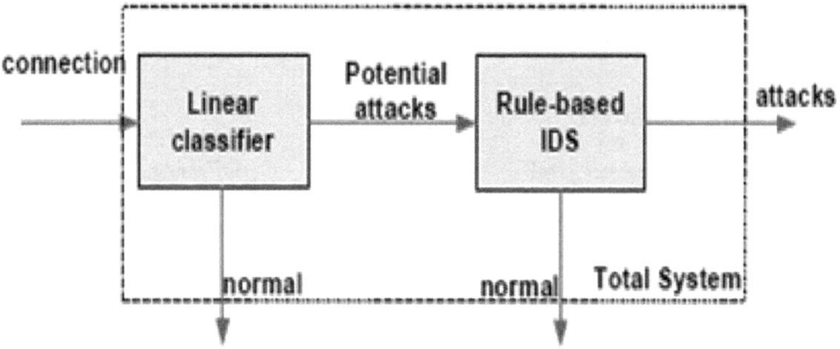

Fig. 2. Block diagram of the system

The linear classifier is based on a linear combination of three features. The features are identified as those that have the highest possibility to take part in an attack by deploying PCA .In our approach, instead of using the principal components (PCs) as new variables; we use the information in the PCs to find important variables in the original dataset. We first calculate the PCs, and then study the screed plot which shows the sorted eigenvalues from bigger towards smaller as a function of the eigenvalue index, so as to determine the number of *k* important variables to keep. Next, we consider the eigenvector corresponding to the smallest eigenvalue (the least important PC), and discards the variable that has the largest (absolute value) coefficient in that vector. Then, we consider the eigenvector corresponding to the second smallest eigenvalue, among the variables not discarded earlier. The process is repeated until only k variables remain. The selected features and their explanations are presented in Table. In the Appendix we give the selected features for different dimensions of the feature set obtained by the same algorithm.

Attack Types

A connection is a sequence of TCP packets starting and ending at some well defined times, between which data flows to and from a source IP address to a target IP address under some well defined protocol. Each connection is labeled as either normal, or as an attack, with exactly one specific attack type. Each connection record consists of about 100 bytes. Attacks fall into four main categories:

- DOS: denial-of-service, e.g. sync flood;
- R2L: unauthorized access from a remote machine, e.g. guessing password;
- U2R: unauthorized access to local super user (root) privileges, e.g., various ``buffer overflow" attacks;
- probing: surveillance and other probing, e.g., port scanning.[15]

The second part of the system (Fig.2) is a rule-based system, where simple *if-then* rules for recognizing normal connections are evolved [1]. Each rule is an *if-then* clause, which contains a "condition" and an "outcome The feature "Attack name" is used in the "outcome" part, which indicates the classification of a network record (at training stage) or connection (at intrusion detection stage) when the "condition" part of a rule is matched.

NAME OF FEATURES	EXPLANATION
Service	Destination service (e.g. telnet, ftp)
hot	Number of hot indicators
Logged in	1 if successfully logged in, 0 if not

Fig. 3. Feature used to describe normal connections

An example of a rule is given in the following:

if *(service="http"* ***and*** *hot="0"* ***and*** *logged_in="0")* ***then*** *normal;*
Other probable conditions are:-

if *(service="smtp"* ***and*** *hot="0"* ***and*** *logged_in="1")* ***then*** *normal;*
if *(service="finger"* ***and*** *hot="0"* ***and*** *logged_in="0")* ***then*** *normal;*
if *(service="domain_u"* ***and*** *hot="0"* ***and*** *logged_in="0")* ***then*** *normal;*
if *(service="telnet"* ***and*** *hot="0"* ***and*** *logged_in="1")* ***then*** *normal;*
if *(service="eco_i"* ***and*** *hot="0"* ***and*** *logged_in="0")* ***then*** *normal;*
if *(service="ntp_u"* ***and*** *hot="0"* ***and*** *logged_in="0")* ***then*** *normal;*

Precicion =(tp)/(tp+fp) Recall=tp/(tp+fn)
F-measure:-

$$F=2 *\{(precision * recall)/(precision + recall)\}$$

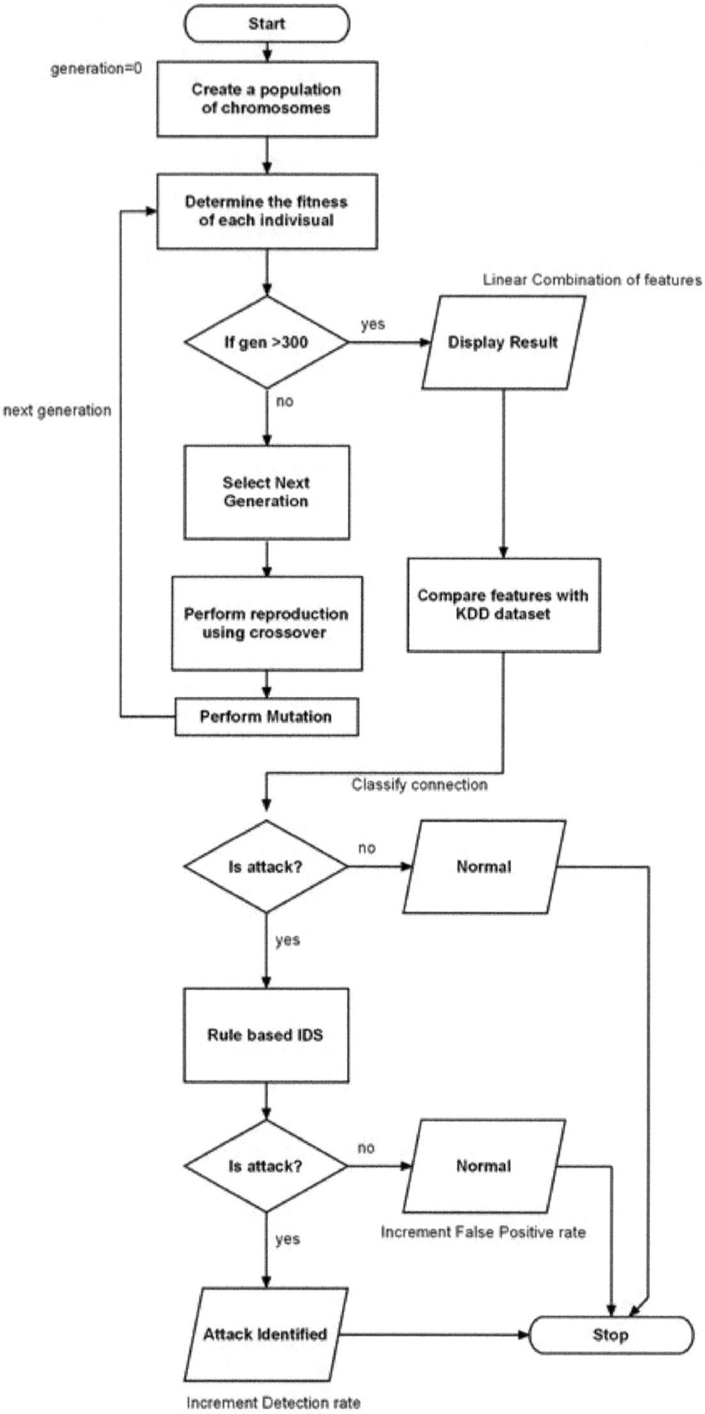

Fig. 4. Flow of the system

6 Conclusion

The networks having many connections cannot be physically shown. But we are trying to develop an application which shows various connections. And using genetic algorithm we will be searching and identifying normal and attack connections. With the help of this we can calculate false positive rate of the system. Large number of connections can be used as we are using genetic algorithm. Instead of using probable connections we can use probable features which are prone to attacks.

References

[1] Bankovic, Z., Moya, J.M., Araujo, Á., Bojanic, S., Nieto-Taladriz, O.: Genetic algorithm based solution for intrusion detection. ETSI Telecomunicaci6n, Universidad,Politécnica de Madrid, pp. 192–199 (2009)

[2] Bankovic, Z., Stepanovic, D., Bojanic, S., Nieto-Taladriz, O.: Improving Network Security using Genetic Algorithm Approach. ETSI Telecomunicaci6n, Universidad, Politécnica de Madrid (July 27, 2007)

[3] Gong, R.H., Zulkernine, M., Abolmaesumi, P.: A Software Implementation of a Genetic Algorithm Based Approach to Network Intrusion Detection. Queen's University Kingston, Ontario (2005)

[4] Chittur, A.: Model Generation for an Intrusion Detection System Using Genetic Algorithms. Ossining High School Ossining, NY (2005)

[5] Weiss, G.M.: Mining with Rarity: A Unifying Framework 6(1)

[6] A.A.R. Townsend. Genetic Algorithms – a Tutorial (July 2003)

[7] Haines, J.W., Rossey, L.M., Lippmann, R.P., Cunningham, R.K.: Extending the DARPA Off-Line Intrusion Detection Evaluations, Lincoln Laboratory, Massachusetts Institute of Techonology (2001)

[8] Mulay, S.A.: Intrusion Detection System Using Support Vector Machine and Decision Tree, Maharashtra, India, vol. 3 (2010)

[9] Panda, M., Patra, M.R.: Network Intrusion Detection Using NaÏVe Bayes, Department of E &TC Engineering, G.I.E.T., Gunupur, India, vol. 7 (December 2007)

[10] Yamini, S.: Intrusion Detection Systems using Hidden Markov Models. RVS College of Arts & Science, Sulur

[11] Nikolova, E., Jecheva, V.: Anomaly Based Intrusion Detection Based on the Junction Tree Algorithm. Burgas Free University, Faculty for Computer Science and Engineering, Bulgeria (2007)

[12] Goyal, A., Kumar, C.: GA-NIDS: A Genetic Algorithm based Network Intrusion Detection System, Evanston, Illinois

[13] Li, W.: Using Genetic Algorithm for Network Intrusion Detection, Mississippi State University, Mississippi State (2002)

[14] Yao, J.T., Zhao, S.L., Saxton, L.V.: A study on fuzzy intrusion detection, University of Regina

[15] Owais, S., Snasel, V., Kromer, P., Abraham, A.: Survey: Using Genetic Algorithm Approach in Intrusion Detection Systems Techniques. In: 7th Computer Information Systems and Industrial Management Applications, CISIM 2008, pp. 300–307 (2008)

Online Delaunay Triangulation Using the Quad-Edge Data Structure

Chintan Mandal and Suneeta Agarwal

Department of Computer Science and Engineering
Motilal Nehru National Institute of Technology, India
chintanmandal@gmail.com
suneeta@mnnit.ac.in

Abstract. Previous works involving the Online Delaunay triangulation problem required that the incoming request lies within the triangulation or a predefined initial triangulation framework, which will contain all the incoming points. No mention is made for Online Delaunay triangulation when the request point lies outside the triangulation, which also happens to be the unbounded side of the Convex Hull of the triangulation. In this work, we give a solution for the Online Delaunay triangulation Problem for incoming request points lying in the unbounded side of the Convex Hull bounding the Delaunay triangulation as well for points lying inside the triangulation. We use the Quad-Edge data structure for implementing the Delaunay triangulation.

Keywords: Online algorithms, Delaunay triangulation, Convex Hull, Quad-Edge data structure.

1 Introduction

For a given set of points $P = \{p_1, p_2, \ldots, p_n\}$ in the Euclidean 2D plane, triangulation is the planar subdivision of the plane into a set of non-overlapped regions. The subdivision contains a finite set of edges meeting at a common endpoint from the given set of points. If the minimum angle of all the angles of the triangles is considered, then the configuration of triangles in which the minimum angle is maximized conforms the triangles to be Delaunay. The boundary of the Delaunay triangulation is the convex hull of the given set of points. The online Delaunay triangulation problem is to update the present configuration of a Delaunay triangulation to a new Delaunay triangulation when a new point joins the present set of points.

Guibas, Knuth and Sharir[6] developed a randomized incremental algorithm for Delaunay triangulation (DT) which they claimed to be "more online". Randomized incremental algorithms[2] developed for DT consider the set of points in a large infinite triangle, where one vertex of the triangle is at the highest point amongst the given sample points and another two vertices at very large distances not in the triangle[12]. Devillers, Meiser and Teillaud[3] discusses insertion and deletion of points using a Delaunay Tree, which maintains a hierarchy of records

D.C. Wyld et al. (Eds.): ACITY 2011, CCIS 198, pp. 132–141, 2011.

of all the triangles which has been deleted or added. Mostafavi et.al[8] also gave a fully dynamic algorithm(a more generalized algorithm having both addition and deletion queries) for the DT based on the QE data structure. They form an "initial frame" of a triangle and then points are inserted individually. Search for the triangle which bounds the point is done by "walking" from some initial triangle edge in a given configuration. However, most of the works do not give a generalized situation when the arriving point could lie outside the convex hull.

In this present work we solve the problem for points going to join the present DT when the request point can lie inside or outside the present convex hull(CH). We have implemented the DT with the Quad-Edge data structure, which inclusive of keeping the triangulation structure as a planar graph, also helps in swapping edges easily.

The rest of the paper is organized as follows: section 2 gives a brief recount of online algorithms, relevant data structures used in our work; section 3 gives a discussion of our proposed algorithms. The paper concludes with a brief conclusion of the work.

2 Background Theory

An algorithm is online if it solves for successive inputs or requests, without having any knowledge about the future inputs or requests. Online algorithms do not have an absolute performance unlike an offline algorithm. In an offline algorithm, the inputs are known in advance, preprocessing is possible and an absolute performance can be obtained. The performance of an "online algorithm" is measured in terms of the ratio between the total cost of the online algorithm for all the requests in the request sequence and the cost of an optimal offline algorithm for the same set of inputs as a batch.This ratio is known as the ***Competitive Ratio(K)***. An online algorithm is considered good if K is small[9].

The convex hull(CH) and the Delaunay triangulation(DT) is an intimate problem for solving many other problems in computational geometry. The CH is the smallest convex polygon bounding a given set of points in 2D. They arise in problems relating to GIS and computer graphics for identifying object boundaries[2,11]. [Fig. 1] shows two triangulation configurations for the same set of points - $P1$, $P2$, $P2$ and $P4$. In [Fig. 1a], the minimum angle of the angles of the triangle pair $\triangle P1P2P3$ and $\triangle P1P3P4$ is *greater* than the minimum angle of the angles in the triangle pair $\triangle P1P2P4$ and $\triangle P2P3P4$[Fig. 1b]. To check that two adjacent triangles are Delaunay, one checks if the circumcircle of one the triangles contains the farthest point of the adjacent triangle. In [Fig. 1], the circumcircle around $\triangle P1P2P3$ encloses the point $P4$ confirming them not be Delaunay. Swapping the edge $P1P3$ with $P2P4$ makes the pair of triangles $\triangle P1P2P4$ and $\triangle P2P3P4$ to be Delaunay. This is referred as the incircle test.

The Quad-Edge(QE)[5,1,10] data structure was proposed by Guibas and Stolfi to help to maintain the triangulation planar subdivisions structures. The QE is an edge based data structure i.e. it keeps information about the edges or sides

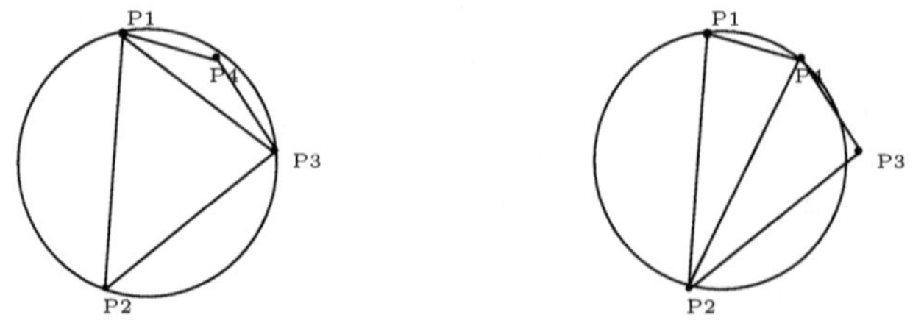

(a) Failure of InCircle() on $\triangle P1P2P3$ as $P4$ is inside $\bigcirc P1P2P3$

(b) InCircle() on $\triangle P1P2P4$ and $P3$ is outside $\bigcirc P1P2P4$

Fig. 1. InCircle() conditions for Delaunay triangulation

which make the triangle. Three QEs represents the three edges of a triangle. Each QE consists of two oppositely directed half edges[1]($\boldsymbol{E}$ **and** $\boldsymbol{E}$**.Sym()**) as shown in [Fig. 2a] facing two adjacent triangles based on that QE. [Fig. 2a] also shows the different algebraic operators as discussed in [5], which has symmetric properties. In [Fig. 2b], QE BC has two half edges, $\overrightarrow{BC}$ facing $\triangle ABC$ and $\overrightarrow{CB}$ facing $\triangle BCD$. As each half edge of the QE faces a triangle, information about the triangle can be added to the half edge which it faces. We refer to it as the *Face Number*, which is also the triangle number, which the half edge is facing.

A triangulation can also be referred to as a Planar Straight Line Graph(PSLG). A PSLG is a planar graph which is embedded in the plane and an edge of the graph is mapped to the corresponding straight line on the plane. The edge weights of the PSLG is the distance of the straight line to which it is mapped. Each QE representing a line/edge of a PSLG keeps information of four extra references to its neighboring edges and vertices with which the edge or planar line is connected to. Updation is done by updating the different pointers of the new QE which is formed from the old QE which is deleted when swapping of edges or even when new edges are added to the structure. The total updation takes constant time, but the intermediate steps, each also having constant time, being many, makes the total process slow[13]. However, we prefer the QE data structure for its easy manipulation of swapping of the edges, its loyalty in keeping with the triangulation manifold and the simple operators having constant time for traversing the edges of the triangulation.

Below is a list of some functions on QE which are mentioned in our present work:

1. E.**FaceNumber()** : This returns the $Face\_Number$ which the half edge E is facing. *If* $Face\_Number$ *of the half edge, E, is 0, then E faces the unbounded side of the CH of the triangulation.* In [Fig. 2b], $\overrightarrow{BC}$.FaceNumber()= 1.
2. E.**Face**($Face\_Number$) : This function returns the half edge of the QE which is facing the triangle $Face\_Number$.In [Fig. 2b], $ABCDEF$ is a PSLG with the respective QE on each edge of the triangle is shown. QE AB is

[1] This half edge is different to the Half-Edge data structure, also referred to as *Doubly Connected Edge List*[10].

represented with two half edges $\overrightarrow{AB}$ and $\overrightarrow{BA}$. As $\overrightarrow{BA}$ faces the unbounded side of CH, $\overrightarrow{BA}$ has $Face\_Number = 0$ and $\overrightarrow{AB}$ has $Face\_Number = 1$, which is the face number of $\triangle ABC$ numbered 1.

3. **FindOppositeVertex**(HalfEdge E) : This returns the opposite vertex of the half edge of the triangle the half edge E is facing e.g. in [Fig. 6b], FindOppositeVertex($\overrightarrow{SD}$) returns point P.
4. **Swap**(HalfEdge E) : This function swaps the QE associated with half edge E joining the opposite vertices of the associated QE. This function comes useful for swapping edges when the DT condition fails for adjacent triangles of QE. The function returns a half edge of the swapped QE.

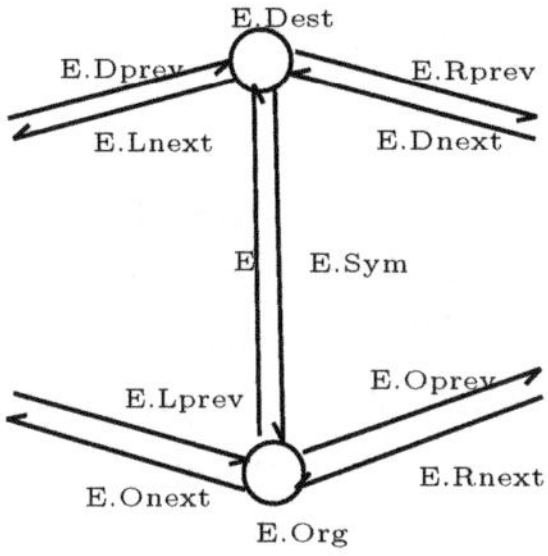

(a) Quad Edge[10]

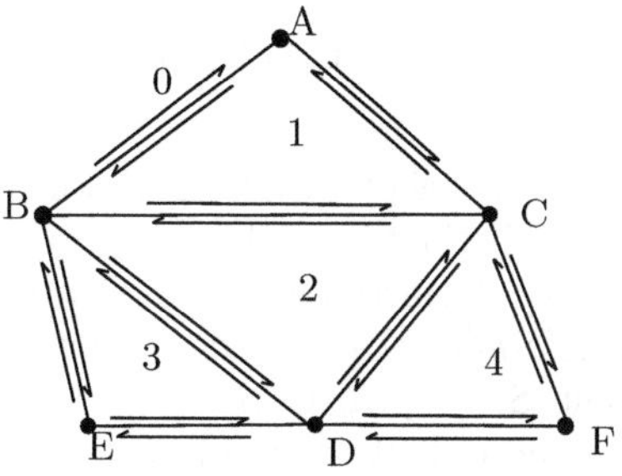

(b) PSLG showing the Quad-Edge for each edge

Fig. 2. Quad-Edge data structure and PSLG with its corresponding representation with its Quad-Edge

3 Discussion of the Proposed Algorithms

$R(r_1, r_2, ..., r_n)$ is a sequence of requests, where each request is a point to be placed in the 2D-Euclidean plane and a DT is to be obtained including the request point. The point can be such that it can be outside the CH or inside the Delaunay triangulated CH. Thus, the problem could be stated as two sub-problems, the former when the point lies outside the CH, and the point has to be added to the previously formed CH and a new DT formed subsequently. The latter problem deals with forming the DT when the point lies inside the present DT-ed CH. We use the QE data structure for storing the triangulation.

The algorithm for online DT(OnlineDelaunayTriangulation()) is divided into two parts as previously discussed, one finding whether the incoming point lies outside or inside the CH and the other, modifying the present DT to accommodate the new incoming point into a new DT configuration. Here, booleans $is\_Outside\_Convex\_Hull$ and PML_G_PMR, List *AddedEdges*, int *Req* are all global variables which are accessed by all the other algorithms. List is a storage data structure or container for accumulating the QEs. $PSLG$ and $PSLG\_DT$ are graph variables which are in fact connected structure of the QEs. $PSLG\_DT$ denotes a PSLG which conforms to DT, while the former only denotes only a PSLG. *Req* is an integer value denoting the incoming request point identifier.

```
Input: P_RequestSequence = {p1, p2, ..., pn}
Output: PSLG_DT(p1, p2, ..., pn)
/* The variables is_Outside_Convex_Hull, AddedEdges, PML_G_PMR, PSLG, PSLG_DT
   are all global variables which could be accessed by all the other algorithms. */
boolean is_Outside_Convex_Hull
List AddedEdges
integer Req
Graph PSLG, PSLG_DT
boolean PML_G_PMR ← false
PSLG_DT ← FormTheFirstTriangle(p1, p2, p3)
while (Req ≠ n) do
   is_Outside_Convex_Hull = isOutsideConvexHull(p_Req)
   if (is_Outside_Convex_Hull ≡ false) then
      LocateTriangle(p_Req)
   end if
   CreateDelaunay(PSLG, p_Req)
   Req ← Req + 1
end while
```

Fig. 3. Algorithm OnlineDelaunayTriangulation()

In OnlineDelaunayTriangulation()[Fig. 3], the simplest case, the first triangle (FormTheFirstTriangle(p_1, p_2, p_3)) is formed from the first three requests. The triangle formed also is a CH for three points and a PSLG which is also DT($PSLG\_DT$) as a circumcircle of the triangle does not contain any other point. Subsequently, from the fourth request, we check first if the point lies outside the CH. If isOutsideConvexHull() return $False$, then the point lies inside the CH. As the inside of the CH is triangulated, the next problem lies in finding the bounding triangle for the point in the PSLG_DT(LocateTriangle()). The final step is to obtain a new DT(CreateDelaunay()) from the PSLG changed from the $PSLG\_DT$ due to the triangles formed by the addition of a new point. isOutsideConvexHull()[Fig. 7] returns $True$ if the point lies in the unbounded side of the CH else $False$. If the point lies in the unbounded region of the CH, $PSLG\_DT$ is updated with point added to the structure to form a PSLG. The algorithm traverses linearly along the CH from any random half edge, *Edge*, having face value 0. The algorithm has two cycles; the first one trying to search for the first supporting line and the second, searching for the second supporting line if the first one exists. Supporting lines are searched based on OrientationOfPoint(Point S,Point D,Point P), which finds the orientation of the point P with respect to the line $\overrightarrow{SD}$[Fig. 6a]. The orientation of the point can be found by calculating the area of the triangle(e.g. $\triangle SDP$), which can be positive, negative or zero, in constant time[11]. If the individual orientations of the request point P_{Req} with respect to the lines joining M(origin of the *present_edge*) to R(origin of the next edge in the counterclockwise direction) and L(origin of the previous edge in the clockwise direction) respectively is same, then the line $\overrightarrow{P_{Req}M}$ is a supporting line[Fig. 5a]. Existence of the first supporting line confirms for the second. After the first supporting line is found, traversing the CH searching for the subsequent supporting line, will rest on the comparison of $\angle PML$ and $\angle PMR$. If $\angle PML < \angle PMR$[Fig. 4b], then traversing is done by choosing *Edge*.Lnext() i.e. we traverse the CH in the clockwise direction along the same face else we traverse in the opposite direction in the anti-clockwise direction through *Edge*.Lprev()[Fig. 4a] for searching the second supporting line. However, while searching for the first supporting line on the CH boundary, if *present_edge* edge meets the initial starting edge, we come to the conclusion that the request point is inside the CH. Finding the angles $\angle PML$ and $\angle PMR$ takes O(1) time.

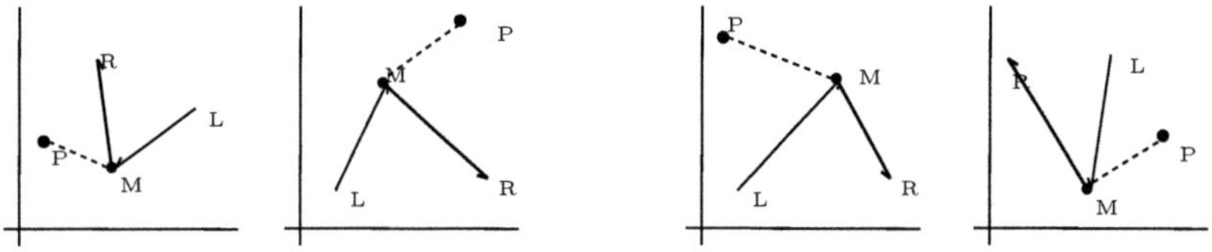

(a) $\angle PML > \angle PMR$ (b) $\angle PML < \angle PMR$

Fig. 4. Relation between the $\angle PML$ and $\angle PMR$ for searching the supporting lines on the Convex Hull

(a) Supporting Lines: $\overrightarrow{P\_ReqP4}$ and $\overrightarrow{P\_ReqP2}$ (b) Convex Hull on updation with point *P_Req*

Fig. 5. The changed Convex Hull after the supporting lines have been found

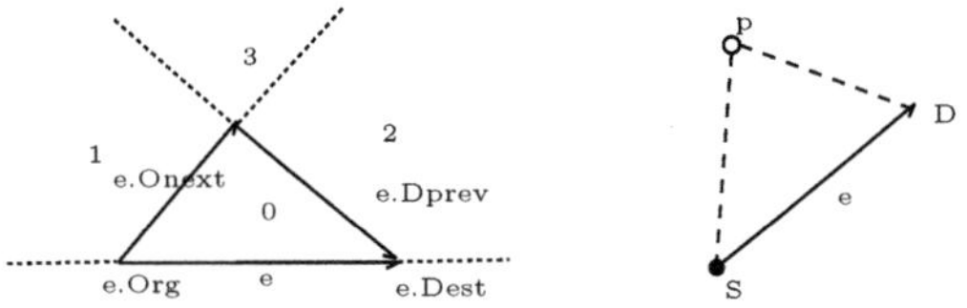

(a) Orientation of a Point with respect to an edge(**e**)[1] (b) Angle of Point P w.r.t. a line segment $\overrightarrow{SD}$

Fig. 6

After i stages/requests, the total number of points in the configuration is i and the number of points on the CH is $k(k < i)$. When a new request at stage $(i{+}1)$, P_{Req} arrives, the search for the first supporting line along the CH is at most along $O(k-1)$ edges in the clockwise direction of the same face, in case no supporting line(s) are found. However, if one of the supporting lines is found, then the search for the second supporting line might require again require a search through a $O(k'-1)$ (k$'$ < k)edges. Thus, the search for the two supporting lines is linear in order of O(k). All the edges traversed while searching for the second supporting line[11] are stored in the List *AddedEdges*. After the second supporting line has been found, the origin of the edges stored in the *AddedEdges* list with P_{Req} are joined, making sure that the half edges facing the outside CH of the supporting edges has a *Face Number* 0[Fig. 5b]. All the other half edges can have face value of the new triangles, which it is facing. The half edges facing the first triangle formed from the first three request point have a face value 1. This updation of the graph *PSLG_DT* transforms it to a *PSLG*.

```
Input: PSLG_DT(p_1, ..., p_{i-1}),Point p_i
Output: is_Outside_Convex_Hull
boolean found_first_supporting_line ← false
HalfEdge present_edge ← QuadEdge.Face(0).Lnext()
PML_G_PMR ← false
while (True) do
   Point M = present_edge.Org()
   Point L = present_edge.LPrev().Org()
   Point R = present_edge.LNext().Org()
   orientation1 ← OrientationOfPoint(R, M, P)
   orientation2 ← OrientationOfPoint(L, M, P)
   if (orientation1 ≡ orientation2) then
      if (found_first_supporting_line ≡ False) then
         found_first_supporting_line ← False
         if (∠PML ≥ ∠PMR) then
            PML_G_PMR ← true
         end if
         AddedEdges.Pushback(present_edge)
         if (PML_G_PMR ≡ False) then
            present_edge ← present_edge.Lprev()
         else
            present_edge ← present_edge.Lnext()
         end if
      else
         AddedEdges.Pushback(present_edge)
         is_Outside_Convex_Hull ← True
      end if
   end if
   if (orientation1 ≠ orientation2) then
      if (found_first_supporting_line ≡ False) then
         present_edge ← present_edge.Lnext()
         if (present_edge ≡ Edge.Face(0)) then
            break
         end if
      end if
      if (found_first_supporting_line ≡ True) then
         AddedEdges.PushBack(present_edge)
         if (PML_G_PMR ≡ False) then
            present_edge ← present_edge.Lprev()
         else
            present_edge ← present_edge.Lnext()
         end if
      end if
   end if
end while
if (is_Outside_Convex_Hull ≡ True) then
   for all (HalfEdge Edge ∈ AddedEdges) do
      Join Edge.Org() with p_i
   end for
end if
return is_Outside_Convex_Hull
```

Fig. 7. Algorithm isOutsideConvexHull()

In LocateTriangle()[Fig 8], if the point lies inside the triangulation, then the triangle is located and edges are joined with the incoming point and the other three vertices of the bounding triangle(lines 35 - 38). In our work, we have implemented the procedure for locating a triangle by "walking" proposed by Brown and Faigle[1] who showed that the algorithm proposed by Guibas[5] does not terminate for certain configurations of triangles. It is observed that if we consider the QEs along the CH, half edges facing the unbounded side are directed in a clockwise direction and they represent a circular linked-list if the first triangle formed is connected with sides $\overrightarrow{p_1, p_2}$, $\overrightarrow{p_2, p_3}$ and $\overrightarrow{p_3, p_1}$. The edges joined with P_{Req} and the vertices of the bounding triangle is added to list *AddedEdges*. This updation of the graph *PSLG_DT* transforms it to a *PSLG*.

```
Input: PSLG_DT(p_1, ..., p_{i-1}),Point p_i
Output: PSLG(p_1, ..., p_i)
 1: /* The input to the algorithm is p_i while PSLG_DT() is globally available in OnlineDelaunay-
    Triangulation(). QuadEdge can be any randomly selected Quad Edge along the boundary of
    the CH in PSLG_DT. */
 2: HalfEdge E = QuadEdge.Face(0).Sym()
 3: boolean is_bounded_triangle ← False
 4: if LeftOf(P,E) then
 5:    E ← E.Sym()
 6: end if
 7: while (is_bounded_triangle ≡ False) do
 8:    choose_line ← 0
 9:    if LeftOf(p_i,E.Onext())≡ False then
10:       choose_line ← choose_line + 1
11:    end if
12:    if (LeftOf(p_i,E.Dprev())≡ False) then
13:       choose_line ← choose_line + 2
14:    end if
15:    if (choose_line ≡ 0) then
16:       return E
17:    end if
18:    if (choose_line ≡ 1) then
19:       E ← E.Onext()
20:    end if
21:    if (choose_line ≡ 2) then
22:       E ← E.Dprev()
23:    end if
24:    if (choose_line ≡ 3) then
25:       /* Calculate the angle between the Point p_i and and edge */
26:       ∠angle1 ←CalAngPtSeg(p_i,E.Onext())
27:       ∠angle2 ←CalAngPtSeg(p_i,E.Dprev())
28:       if (∠angle1 ⩽ ∠angle2) then
29:          E ← E.Onext()
30:       else
31:          E ← E.Dprev()
32:       end if
33:    end if
34: end while
35: for all (Vertices in the Bounding Triangle) do
36:    Join vertex_i(i = 1, 2, 3) of enclosing triangle of p_i
37:    Add edge to List AddedEdges
38: end for
```

Fig. 8. Algorithm LocateTriangle()[1]

CreateDelaunay()[Fig. 9] transforms the *PSLG* obtained from either of the two above algorithms to a *PSLG_DT*. The triangles of the *PSLG* which are checked for Delaunay condition are adjacent to the edges in the *AddedEdges* list for the request point lying outside the CH. If the point lies inside a triangle, the adjacent triangles checked for Delaunay are along the edges which are next in the anti-clockwise direction to the edges in the list *AddedEdges*. The Delaunay condition is checked by the InCircle() test for points in the polygon of which the QE is a diagonal, and if it fails, the edge in question is swapped(SwapEdge(HalfEdge E)) with the edge joining the other two points of the quadrilateral formed by the combination of the adjacent triangles(Lines 16-20). The function SwapEdge(HalfEdge E) returns the halfedge whose origin point is P_{Req}.

```
Input: PSLG(p1, ..., pi)
Output: PSLG_DT(p1, ..., pi)
 1: ListF ← AddedEdges.Front()
 2: ListE ← AddedEdges.End()
 3: Edge E
 4: if (is_bounded_triangle) then
 5:    if (PML_G_PMR) then
 6:       ListF ← ListF + 1
 7:    else
 8:       ListE ← ListE − 1
 9:    end if
10: end if
11: while (ListF < ListE) do
12:    if (is_Outside_Convex_Hull ≡ False) then
13:       E ← ListF.Lnext()
14:    end if
15:    Point P1 ←FindOppositeVertex(E)
16:    Point P2 ←FindOppositeVertex(E.Sym())
17:    if (CircumCircle(E.Org(),P1,E.Dest(),P2)< 0) then
18:       HalfEdge E  ⟵ SwapEdge(E)
19:       HalfEdge E1 ⟵ CreateDelaunayAdjacent(E.Dprev(),PSLG)
20:       HalfEdge E2 ⟵ CreateDelaunayAdjacent(E.Rprev(),PSLG)
21:    end if
22:    ListF ← ListF + 1
23: end while
```

Fig. 9. Algorithm CreateDelaunay()

Four edges of the polygon, which has the swapped edge as a diagonal, become candidates to be checked as Delaunay edges but one has only to check two edges of the polygon, which does not have P_{Req} as its end point[4,7]. This is be done recursively by using Algorithm CreateDelaunayAdjacent()[Fig. 10].

```
Input: PSLG(p1, ..., pi), HalfEdge E
Output: PSLG_DT(p1, ..., pi)
Point P1 ←FindOppositeVertex(E)
Point P2 ←FindOppositeVertex(E.Sym())
if (CircumCircle(E.Org(),P1,E.Dest(),P2)< 0) then
   HalfEdge E  ⟵ SwapEdge(E)
   HalfEdge E1 ⟵ CreateDelaunayAdjacent(E.Dprev(),PSLG)
   HalfEdge E2 ⟵ CreateDelaunayAdjacent(E.Rprev(),PSLG)
end if
```

Fig. 10. Algorithm CreateDelaunayAdjacent()

4 Conclusion

We have given a solution to the online Delaunay triangulation problem for query points lying inside and outside the convex hull formed by the Delaunay triangulation using the Quad-Edge data structure. Previous solutions to this problem considered query points to only lie inside the triangulation of the existing points or a large triangular frame containing all the query points. Also, the problem of the online convex hull, which was treated as a different problem from the online Delaunay triangulation is combined here while solving for the online Delaunay triangulation by our proposed algorithm. As the dual of DT is the Voronoi diagram of the given points and QE keeps information about both information about the triangulation and its dual, the problem can also be reformulated for the online Voronoi diagram for the given points.

References

1. Brown, P.J.C., Faigle, C.T.: A robust efficient algorithm for point location in triangulations. Technical Report UCAM-CL-TR-728, University of Cambridge, Computer Laboratory (February 1997)
2. de Berg, M., van Kreveld, M., Overmars, M., Schwarzkopf, O.: Computational Geometry: Algorithms and Applications, 3rd edn. Springer, Heidelberg (2008)
3. Devillers, O., Meiser, S., Teillaud, M.: Fully dynamic delaunay triangulation in logarithmic expected time per operation. Comput. Geom. Theory Appl. 2, 55–80 (1992)
4. De Floriani, L., Puppo, E.: An on-line algorithm for constrained delaunay triangulation. CVGIP: Graphical Models and Image Processing 54(4), 290–300 (1992)
5. Guibas, L., Stolfi, J.: Primitives for the manipulation of general subdivisions and the computation of voronoi. ACM Trans. Graph. 4, 74–123 (1985)
6. Guibas, L.J., Knuth, D.E., Sharir, M.: Randomized incremental construction of delaunay and voronoi diagrams. In: Paterson, M. (ed.) ICALP 1990. LNCS, vol. 443, pp. 414–431. Springer, Heidelberg (1990)
7. Hjelle, Ø., Dæhlen, M.: Triangulations and Applications (Mathematics and Visualization). Springer-Verlag New York, Inc., Secaucus (2006)
8. Mostafavi, M.A., Gold, C., Dakowicz, M.: Delete and insert operations in voronoi/delaunay methods and applications. Comput. Geosci. 29, 523–530 (2003)
9. Motwani, R., Raghavan, P.: Randomized Algorithms. Cambridge University Press, Cambridge (1997)
10. Nielsen, F.: Visual Computing: Geometry, Graphics, and Vision. Charles River Media / Thomson Delmar Learning (2005)
11. Preparata, F.P., Shamos, M.I.: Computational geometry: an introduction. Springer-Verlag New York, Inc., New York (1985)
12. Schäfer, M.: Computational Engineering - Introduction to Numerical Methods. Springer-Verlag New York, Inc., Secaucus (2006)
13. Shewchuk, J.: Triangle: Engineering a 2d quality mesh generator and delaunay triangulator. In: Lin, M., Manocha, D. (eds.) FCRC-WS 1996 and WACG 1996. LNCS, vol. 1148, pp. 203–222. Springer, Heidelberg (1996), doi:10.1007/BFb0014497

A Novel Event Based Autonomic Design Pattern for Management of Webservices

Vishnuvardhan Mannava[1] and T. Ramesh[2]

[1] Department of Computer Science and Engineering, KL University, Vaddeswaram, 522502, A.P, India
vishnu@klce.ac.in
[2] Department of Computer Science and Engineering, National Institute of Technology, Warangal, 506004, A.P, India
rmesht@nitw.ac.in

Abstract. A system is said to be adaptive if its behavior automatically changes according to its context.Systems based on the service-oriented architecture (SOA) paradigm must be able to bind arbitrary Web services at runtime.Web services composition has been an active research area over the last few years. However, the technology is still not mature yet and several research issues need to be addressed. In this paper, we propose an autonomic design pattern that describes the dynamic composition and adaptation of Web services based on the context. This pattern is primarily an extension of the Case-based Reasoning, Strategy, Observer Design Patterns.We proposed a framework where service context is configurable to accomodate the needs of different users and can adapt to dynamic changing environments.This permits reusability of a service in different contexts and achieves a level of adaptiveness and contextualization without recoding and recompiling of the overall composed services. The execution of adaptive composite service is provided by an observer model. Three core services, coordination service, context service, and event service, are implemented to automatically schedule and execute the component services, that adapt to user configured contexts and environment changes at run time. We demonstrate the benefits of our proposed design pattern by an experimental setup with implementation without generating stubs at the client side.

Keywords: Autonomic computing, Web Service, UDDI, Observer Pattern, Strategy Pattern, Adaptive Patterns, Case-based Reasoning, Dynamic service composition, Stub.

1 Introduction

Advances in software technologies and practices have enabled developers to create larger, more complex applications to meet the ever increasing user demands. In today's computing environments, these applications are required to integrate seamlessly across heterogeneous platforms and to interact with other complex applications. The unpredictability of how the applications will behave and interact in a widespread, integrated environment poses great difficulties for system

D.C. Wyld et al. (Eds.): ACITY 2011, CCIS 198, pp. 142–151, 2011.

testers and managers. Autonomic computing proposes a solution to software management problems by shifting the responsibility for software management from the human administrator to the software system itself. It is expected that autonomic computing will result in significant improvements in terms of system management, and many initiatives have begun to incorporate autonomic capabilities into software components.

On the other hand as applications grow in size, complexity, and heterogeneity in response to growing computational needs, it is increasingly difficult to build a system that satisfies all requirements and design constraints that it will encounter during its lifetime. Furthermore, many of these systems are required to run continuously, disallowing downtimes while code is modified. As a result, it is important for an application to self-adapt in response to changing requirements and environmental conditions. Autonomic computing has been proposed to meet this need, where a system manages itself based on high-level objectives from a systems administrator. Due to their high complexity, adaptive and autonomic systems are difficult to specify, design, verify, and validate. In addition, the current lack of reusable design expertise that can be leveraged from one adaptive system to another further exacerbates the problem.

Web services, and more in general Service-Oriented Architectures (SOAs), are gathering a considerable momentum as the technologies of choice to implement distributed systems and perform application integration. Although tremendous efforts and results have been made and obtained in Web service composition area[2,3], the technology is still not mature yet and requires significant efforts in some open research areas[7,9]. A current trend is to provide adaptive service composition and provisioning solutions that offer better quality of composite Web services[9,4,6] to satisfy the user needs. The pervasiveness of the Internet and the proliferation of interconnected computing devices (e.g., laptops, PDAs, 3G mobile phones) offer the technical possibilities to interact with services anytime and anywhere. For example, business travelers now expect to be able to access their corporate servers, enterprise portals, e-mail, and other collaboration services while on the move. Since the contexts of users, either human beings or enterprises, are varied, it is essential that service composition embraces a configurable and adaptive service provisioning approach (e.g., delivering the right service in the right place at the right time). Configuration allows the same service to be reused in different contexts without low-level recoding and recompilation of the service.On the other hand reconfiguration allows the system to change dynamically according to environments reducing the down time.

This paper is structured as follows Section 2 provides the related work. Section 3 describes Web services.Section 4 illustrates the adaptive patterns. Section 5 elaborates the proposed autonomic pattern and its structure. Section 6 summarizes this paper and concludes with possible future direction.

2 Related Work

There are publications reporting the service composition strategies and architectures of Web services. According to a review[4] of dynamic Web services composition techniques the service composition strategies are classified as Static Composition, Semi-dynamic Composition and Dynamic Composition based on the time of composition plan creation and service binding times. The authors[4] reviewed that there are eight categories of composing related services from atomic services to form a complex service. Dynamic Web service composition is a complex and very challenging task in Web services as the composition plan is generated at runtime based on the requester's complex service request. The authors have summarized how plans are generated at runtime to compose the services from atomic services and the architectures that support the orchestration of services dynamically. The authors[9] have developed the CCAP system (Configurable Composition and Adaptive Provisioning of composite services) that provides a system infrastructure for distributed, adaptive, context-aware provisioning of composite Web services. They have[9] illustrated how simple services are configured at run time to form a complex service. They all isolated the freedom of dynamic publishing, un-publishing, discovery and binding at runtime from the UDDI registry.

There are publications reporting the reconfiguration of the system dynamically to adapt to the changing environments.The author[8] proposed adaptive patterns that help in developing dynamically adaptive systems.All the available literature focused on either the service delivery or the reconfiguration of the system at runtime but not both simultaneously.

In this paper we present a pattern based framework that makes the system to adapt based on changes, events dynamically.On change adaptation deals with the monitoring of service health while on event adaptation focuses on delivering the client requests by discovery and compose a new services without recompiling the existing the services.

3 Web Services Framework

Web service is a new paradigm to deliver application services on Web and enables a programmable Web, not just an interactive Web. Web service is the third generation in the Web evolution after static HTML and interactive Web development such as PERL, ASP, JSP, and others. Web services are typical black box-reusable building block components in the distributed computing.

3.1 Web Service Architecture

There are three important components in Web services architecture. Figure 1 shows the Web service requester (simplified client) on the left, the Web service provider on the right, and the Web service registry on the top. A Web services provider must publish/register its services with a Universal Description, Discovery, and Integration (UDDI) registry so that it can be accessed by any Web services requester globally. It just looks like a phonebook, where all businesses register their phones there for customers to look up services. A customer

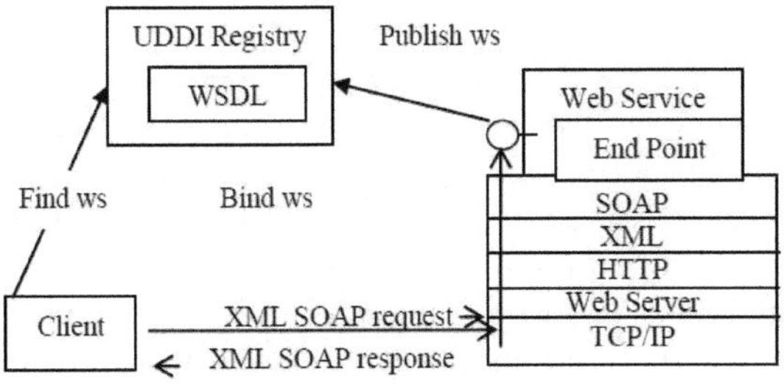

Fig. 1. Web Service Architecture

must look up the phonebook either on-line or by phonebook unless a customer knows the phone number before.

4 Adaptive Design Patterns

A design pattern is a general and reusable solution to a commonly recurring problem in design.An adaptive design pattern provides solution for the construction of adaptive systems.There are twelve adaptation design patterns harvested thus far along with their intentions[8].Table 1 enumerates the patten template.

Table 1. Adaptation Design Patterns Template

Pattern Name	A unique handle that describes the pattern.
Classification	Facilitates the organization of patterns according to their main objective.
Intent	A brief description of the problem(s) that the pattern addresses.
Context	Describes the conditions in which the pattern should be applied.
Motivation	Describes sample goals and objectives of a system that motivate the use of the pattern.
Structure	A representation of the classes and their relationships depicted in terms of UML class diagrams.
Participants	Itemizes the classes depicted in the Structure field and lists and their responsibilities.
Behavior	Provides UML state or sequence diagrams to represent how a pattern achieves its main objective.
Consequences	Describes how objectives are supported by a given pattern and lists the trade-offs and outcomes of applying the pattern.
Constraints	Contains LTL and A-LTL templates and a prose description of the properties that must be satisfied by a given design pattern instantiation.
Related Patterns	Additional design patterns that are commonly used in conjunction.
Known Uses	Lists sources used to harvest design pattern.

5 Proposed Pattern

This pattern provides framework for how Web services are invoked without recompiling the existing services and how an observer pattern[5] can be used to notify the changes. Proposed pattern is amalgamation of Strategy, observer and faade design patterns. To demonstrate this we have considered a Online Book Store application as an example where an user can bind to the services provided by different book vendors at run time without worrying about the client side proxy stubs and the administrator is relieved from monitoring the system health. we have given the java skeleton code not the complete implementation

5.1 Proposed Pattern Structure

The proposed pattern structure is given in figure 2.

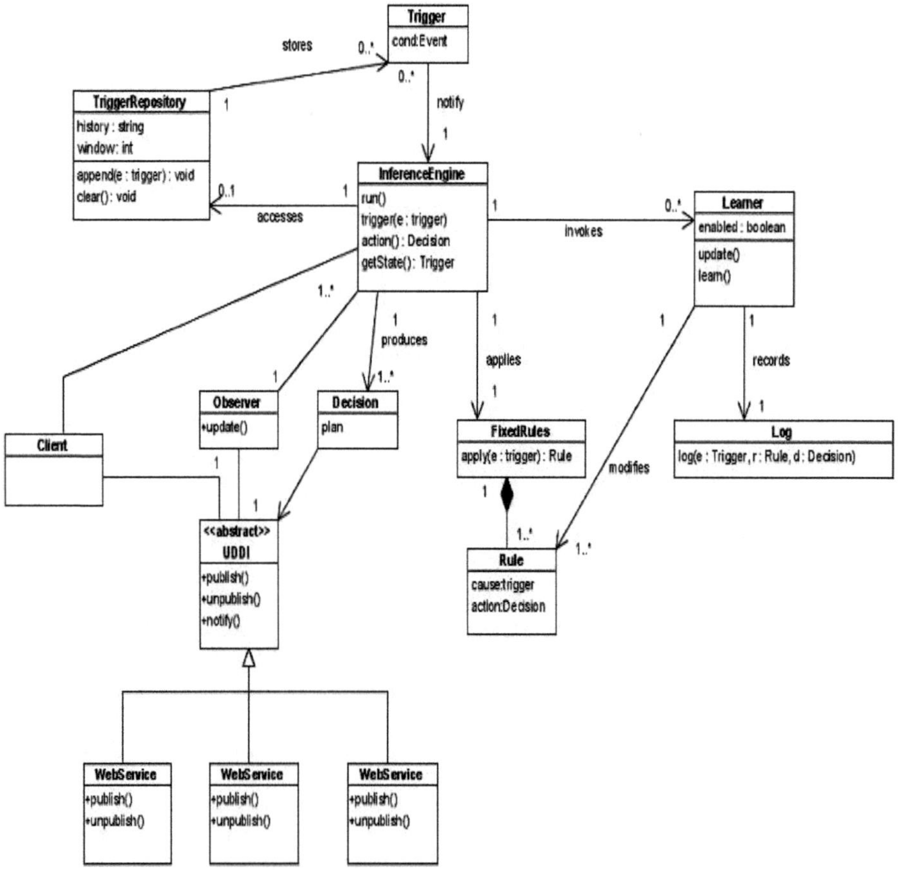

Fig. 2. UML class diagram for the adaptive pattern

5.2 Participants

- **Client:** Is an SOA or an application using the services published in the UDDI.
- **UDDI:** Is a common interface for all the service providers to register their services.
- **Web Service:** Implements the service that the provider exposes to the outside world.
- **Decision:** This class represents a reconfiguration plan that will yield the desired behavior in the system.
- **Fixed Rules:** This class contains a collection of Rules that guide the Inference Engine in producing a Decision. The individual Rules stored within the Fixed Rules can be changed at run time.
- **Inference Engine:** This class is responsible for applying a set of Rules to either a single Trigger or a history of Triggers and producing an action in the form of a Decision.
- **Learner:** Applies on-line and statistical-based algorithms to infer new Rules in the system. This is an optional feature of the Case-based Reasoning design pattern.
- **Log:** This class is responsible for recording which reconfiguration plans have been selected during execution. Each entry is of the form Trigger-Rule-Decision.
- **Rule:** Represents a relationship between a Trigger and a Decision. A Rule evaluates to true if an incoming Trigger matches the Trigger contained in the Rule.
- **Trigger:** This class contains relevant information about what caused the adaptation request. A Trigger should at least provide information about the error source, the timestamp at which the error was observed, the type of error observed and whether it has occurred before or not. Additional information may be included as required.
- **Trigger Repository:** Contains a history of Triggers. This history can be used by the Learner class to identify trends that may warrant further reconfigurations.

5.3 Related Patterns

1. **Event Monitor:** Clients use the Event Monitor pattern when there is no discernable event notification mechanism available on a target Web Service or when the available mechanism does not adequately fit the needs of the client.
2. **Publish/Subscribe:** The Publish/Subscribe pattern is an evolution of the Observer pattern. Whereas the Observer pattern relies on registration directly with a particular Web Service, the Publish/Subscribe pattern decouples the service that delivers notifications from the service that receives notification. This allows multiple services to send the same notification; it also abstracts the responsibility for event delivery and subscriber registration to a common class.

3. **Adaptive Strategy pattern:** Define a self-adaptive strategy, exposing to the client a single strategy referencing the best available concrete strategy, only requiring from the client an access to the environment information that can be used to choose the best strategy
4. **Case-based Reasoning:**Apply rule-based decision-making to determine how to reconfigure the system.

5.4 Consequences

1. Interprocess communication may be necessary to implement within the client computer.
2. The notifications can be sent with HTTP but also as email with SMTP.
3. Dynamic selection from UDDI registry can be done without proxy stubs generation.
4. Relieves the system administrator from high end tasks like monitoring the system status and reconfiguring the system.

6 Proposed Pattern Approach

This pattern works in two folds one is Onchange adaptation and another is Onaction adaptation.

6.1 Onchange Adaptation

Onchange adaptation is triggered by the changes in the environment which include the publication of new service,un-availability of the existing services in the UDDI registry etc. and these are observed by the inference engine making use of the Observer pattern[5] which acts as a trigger on the inference engine and based on the trigger the engine will get the rules from the fixed rules class.If a reconfiguration is warrant then the engine will create a decision and applies it on the UDDI in turn configuring the Webservice that caused the change.After successful action it then logs the event, rule and decision in the log.If it is a new rule then rule is updates in the trigger repository making the system to learn new rules.The sequence diagram for the same is shown figure 3.

6.2 Onevent Adaptation

Onevent adaptation is triggered by the user when a service is required.The user when requests for a service then the inference engine will get the status of the UDDI by exploiting the Observer pattern[5].After getting the operational status of the UDDI it will query for the rules from the fixed rules and decides whether a reconfiguration is necessary.If necessary it will take the decision and applies it on the UDDI.After the completion of the reconfiguration the UDDI will serve the client request and the client invoke the service dynamically without generating the stubs at runtime.This approach eliminates the burden of recompilation the overall services and generation of client stubs.The sequence diagram is shown in figure 4.

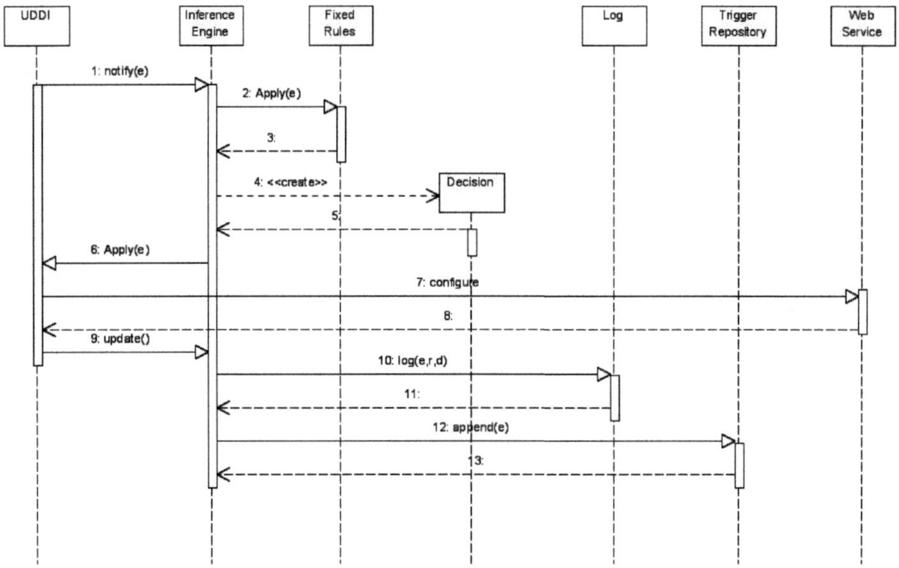

Fig. 3. Sequence diagram for OnChange adaptation scenario

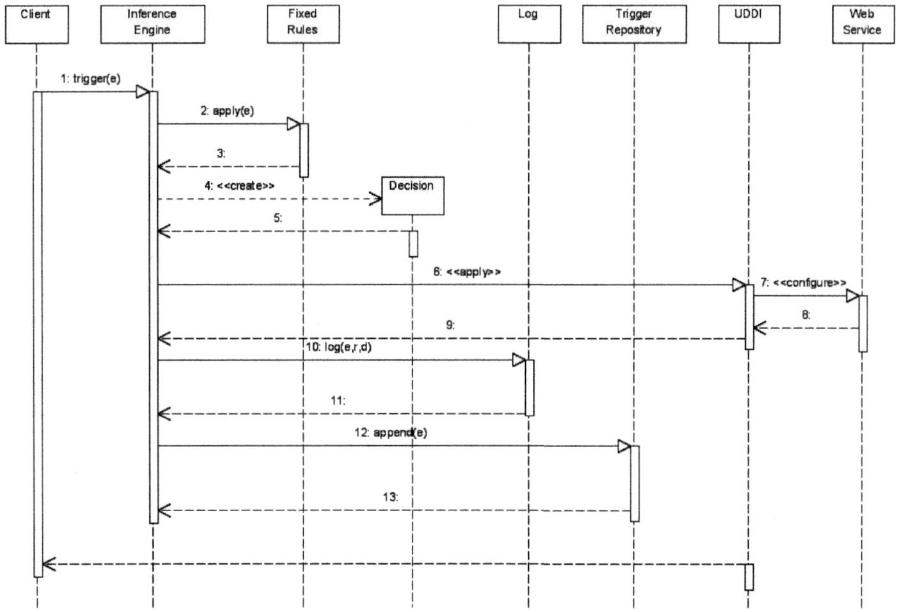

Fig. 4. Sequence Diagram for Onevent adaptation scenario

7 Case Study

To test the efficiency of the proposed pattern we have implemented it by defining the services and registered them with the UDDI registry using JUDDI[1].We have collected the profiling data using the built-in profiler of NetBeans IDE and plotted a graph where X-axis represents the runs and Y-Axis refers to the time.The server latency may effect the profiling time but it is negligible since the registry is hosted on the localhost.The graph is shown in figure 5.

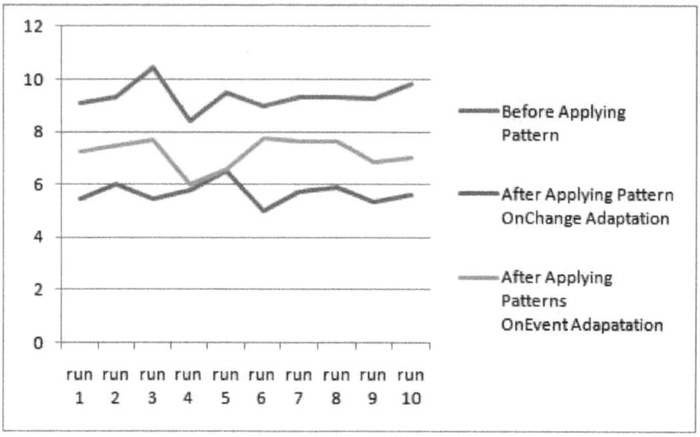

Fig. 5. Profiling Data

8 Conclusion and Future Work

In this paper we have proposed an autonomic pattern easing the invocation and composition of services dynamically at runtime without recompiling the existing services and shown how the behaviour of the composed services changes reflecting the changes made to the WSDL file dynamically without worrying about the proxy stubs generation.This pattern harvests the development of autonomic system that can able to reconfigure itself based on the environmental changes. An interesting direction of future research concerns incorporating WSDM to monitor the composed services, performance of the orchestration engine and to manage or to reconfigure among them at runtime dynamically.

References

1. jUDDI - an open source java implementation of the Universal Description, Discovery, and Integration (UDDI) specification for web services, `http://ws.apache.org/juddi/`
2. Agarwal, V., Dasgupta, K., Karnik, N., Kumar, A., Kundu, A., Mittal, S., Srivastava, B.: A service creation environment based on end to end composition of web services. In: Proceedings of the 14th International Conference on World Wide Web, WWW 2005, pp. 128–137. ACM, New York (2005)

3. Charfi, A., Mezini, M.: Middleware services for web service compositions. In: Special Interest Tracks and Posters of the 14th International Conference on World Wide Web, WWW 2005, pp. 1132–1133. ACM, New York (2005)
4. D'Mello, D.A., Ananthanarayana, V.S., Salian, S.: A review of dynamic web service composition techniques. In: Advanced Computing. CCIS, vol. 133, pp. 85–97. Springer, Heidelberg (2011)
5. Gamma, E., Helm, R., Johnson, R., Vlissides, J.: Design patterns: elements of reusable object-oriented software. Addison-Wesley Professional, Reading (1995)
6. Harrer, A., Pinkwart, N., McLaren, B.M., Scheuer, O.: The scalable adapter design pattern: Enabling interoperability between educational software tools. IEEE Trans. Learn. Technol. 1, 131–143 (2008)
7. Milanovic, N., Malek, M.: Current solutions for web service composition. IEEE Internet Computing 8, 51–59 (2004)
8. Ramirez, A.J.: Design Patterns for Developing Dynamically Adaptive Systems. Master's thesis, Michigan State University, East Lansing, Michigan (August 2008)
9. Sheng, Q.Z., Benatallah, B., Maamar, Z., Ngu, A.H.H.: Configurable composition and adaptive provisioning of web services. IEEE T. Services Computing 2(1), 34–49 (2009)

Towards Formalization of Ontological Descriptions of Services Interfaces in Services Systems Using CL

Amit Bhandari[1] and Manpreet Singh[2]

[1] Department of Computer Sc & Engg, RIMT-MAEC, Mandi Gobindgarh, Punjab, India
amitbhandari@ieee.org
[2] UCOE, Punjabi University, Patiala, Punjab, India
msgujral@yahoo.com

Abstract. With the advent of semantic technologies, the Internet is moving from Web 2.0 to Web 3.0. Social Networks, Semantic Web, Blogs, etc are all components of Web 3.0. In this paper, we intend to formally represent the description of the service systems proposed by expressing the constraints and capabilities of the system in standards-based language; Common Logic. We translate and represent the WSML ontology, web-services, relations, axioms and other entity metadata descriptions of the system in ISO Common Logic. Also, the temporal constraints of the system discussed are represented using service policies. The extended service policies (WS-Policy Language) are discussed for representing the temporal constraints of the system.

1 Introduction

We represent machine-readable metadata ontologies specified in first-order-logic as described in this paper. This specification not only describes the normal constraints of the system but also extends the discussion to temporal constraints for various services in the system along with the capabilities and requirements of the system services which are described using service policies. Further, we formally specify the capabilities and requirements of system services described in WSML ontologies using standard ISO/IEC 24707:2007 Common Logic specification [1, 2]. ISO/IEC 24707:2007 is a standard family of logic-based languages based on First-Order Logic (FOL)/First-Order Semantics. The dialects included in Common Logic[1] (the ISO/IEC 24707:2007 standard) are: the Common Logic Interchange Format (CLIF), the Conceptual Graph Interchange Format (CGIF), and XML-notation for Common Logic (XCL). The components of CL include entities, relations, quantification, negation, iteration, and concept, i.e., we can formally specify an ontology using CL. It has been presented in various researches [4-9] that ontology can be specified formally using some specification language which can be either a standards-based language or non-standard language. We aim to represent the temporal-system described in Section 3 using Common Logic (CL), which further can be modeled using Web Services Modeling Ontologies (WSMO) [10]. We model ontologies and services identified in the system using WSML-Full [11]. Moreover, for representing the temporal state of

[1] Common Logic is referred as CL later in the text.

D.C. Wyld et al. (Eds.): ACITY 2011, CCIS 198, pp. 152–161, 2011.

system, we extend WS-Policy [12, 13] and WS-ServiceAgreement [14] so that time-based characteristics of the systems services can be represented.

In this paper, we translate temporal policy language to WSML-Full ontologies which are then formally specified using CL. The ontologies, services, relations and axioms in the system have been identified. We have described and modeled the system using WSML in our previous work [15, 16]. By mapping the temporal service policies presented in this paper in WSML and then formally representing them using standardized language (CL), we benefit from the tools and the expertise that is expected and bound to adhere with a standards-based approach.

This paper is divided into four sections below; Section 2 presents the domain knowledge which introduces with the WSML, CL and the policy framework used in the paper. Section 3 presents the case study of the system and the processes which are temporal in nature. Section 4 formally specifies the system in CL by translating the modeled system in CL. Section 5 presents the conclusion and future scope of work.

2 Domain Knowledge

2.1 Service Policies

The specification of the policies can be similar to the one as given by using WS-Policy based temporal execution system specified and implemented in [17-20]. The WS-Policy Language has been proposed by the joint effort of Microsoft, IBM, SAP and others [12]. We apply the temporal execution system as specified in [16] for describing the temporal constraints of the system since it uses WS-Policy language and it has many advantages for selecting this kind of services policies:

- It is very easier to convert the constraints specified in WSPL to CL than from any other language to CL.
- Specifying the temporal constraints in XML-format (WSPL) makes it easier to implement.
- Formal verification and Model checking can be easily applied on the overall specifications of the system; rather than applying the modular-approach.

The WSPL used in the description of the system has the syntax as specified in Figure-1. Based on the fact whether the assertion is false or true, the temporal constraints specified in place of service-policy will be evaluated. For specifying the temporal characteristics of the system, we use the temporal policy language extension to WS-Policy. The temporal constraints of the system using Microsoft Office Web Apps in an enterprise are also discussed in [16].

The policy assertions specified in <wsp:All></wsp:All> component can describe the services behavior and is generally evaluates to a boolean value. If the policy assertion evaluates to *true* value, then the service behavior is as predicted and service of the system are offered as usual; however, if the policy assertion evaluates to *false* value in the system, the service requests of the system are denied from being offered. The assertions are mapped to the time when the services of the system are being expected to be offered and when it is being expected to be denied.

```
<wsp:Policy
 xmlns:sp='http://namespace.com/secpol'
 xmlns:wsp='http://namespace.com/wspol' >
  <wsp:ExactlyOne>
   ( <wsp:All>
    ( ... )*
    </wsp:All> )*
  </wsp:ExactlyOne>
<wsp:Policy>
```

Fig. 1. Example of policy assertion in WSPL

2.2 Common Logic

The common logic is an abstract first order semantic logic for specifying ontologies using any of the dialects CLIF, CGIF, XCL. The CLIF syntax is given by ISO 14977:1996 Extended Backus-Naur Form (EBNF) [3]. The Table-1 presents a comparison between the specification coverage of CL, description logic ontology languages such as WSML-DL, OWL-DL, WSML-Full, WSML-Rule.

The CLIF specification for the statement "If *a person has a valid unique identifier then he will be able to have an account in a bank*" is as shown in Figure-2.

```
(forall ((x Person))
   (if (isValid(x.UniqueId)) (and (Bank y) (exists
((Account x y)))))
```

Fig. 2. Specification of statement using CLIF

With the help of CL, we can easily specify WSML or OWL ontologies but the reverse is not possible since CL is of abstract nature and it can be thought of as intermediate form before laying down of any concrete specification for the system. For example, in our scenario, we will first specify the ontologies, web services including capabilities, interfaces etc. to an intermediate one, i.e. CL specification; then later, the temporal constraints of the system and the intermediate form (CL-spec) is concretely-specified. The abstract specification of ontologies, web-services, relations, axioms, etc. helps to remove the bindings that are there in the WSML or OWL description.

2.3 Ontologies

Ontology engineering is used for conceptualizing and representing the knowledge. The knowledge presented in ontology is a first-oder-logic (FOL) with monotonous automata as specified in WSML [11]. We use WSML for describing the ontologies of the system. Web Services Modeling Language (WSML) is available in five variants; Core, Flight, Description Logic, Rule and Full. Each of them can specify ontology, web-service, goals and mediators. However, the difference lies in the specification of the WSML and the constraints on including various entities. While describing a web-service, it may not be mandatory to describe capability while using WSML-DL; however, the capability and interface definition becomes mandatory binding in case of WSML-Full. The other entities of WSML are concept, relations, axioms, capabilities, interfaces, etc.

An example of concept description of ontology for a Person is as shown in Figure-3. The concept Person can be thought of as a class in WSML along with its attributes. The data-type of the attributes is also described along with the definition of the class or concept Person. This gives a binding of the type of attribute with the concept and further with other entities of the WSML. However, in CL, there is no such way of defining any variable before use and the variables are normally used without describing the data-type as shown in Figure-3.

Table 1. Formal component availability in the WSML, OWL and CL

Components	CL	WSML-DL	WSML-Rule	WSML-Full	OWL-Full
Classical Negation (neg)	√	√	×	√	√
Existential Quantification	√	√	×	√	√
Disjunction	√	√	×	√	√
Meta Modeling	√	×	√	√	√
Default Negation (naf)	√	×	√	√	√
LP Implication	√	×	√	√	√
Integrity Constraints	√	×	√	√	√
Function Symbols	√	×	√	√	√
Unsafe Rules	√	×	√	√	×

3 System Description

We have formally described system scenarios previously in [15, 16] using web services modeling toolkit (WSMT) [22]. Also, in [16], the temporal characteristics and constraints of the services are described using extended-WSPL framework. We extend the discussion of system described in [16], where-in the office web apps [21] is deployed in a SaaS platform for an enterprise, named OOSE; along with the temporal constraints for the employees of the OOSE enterprise. The layered system overview with various components interacting with each other is as shown in Figure-4.

The component web services layer in the layered overview of services in OOSE enterprise contains

- *Word Viewing Service* (WVS), responsible for rendering of the word document in the browser
- *Excel Calculation Service* (ECS), responsible for calculation of all the formula fields in the spreadsheet along with the rendering of the spreadsheet in the browser.
- *PowerPoint Service* (PS), responsible for slideshow display in the browser and managing the rich-slide display. For images embedding in the slides like PNG support in slides, PS extends the required services from eXtensible Application Markup Language (XAML).

- *PowerPoint Broadcast Service* (PBS), responsible for broadcasting of the power-point slides to multiple clients and providing streaming services of the same.
- *Visio Service* (VS), responsible for rendering of the visio document which may contain a UML diagram for a project, an organization chart.

```
concept Person
    FirstName ofType _string
    LastName ofType _string
    Age ofType _integer
    DateOfBirth ofType _date
    UniqueIdentifier ofType _string
    PermanentAccountNo ofType _string
    DrivingLicenseNo ofType _string
    EmployeeNo ofType _string
```

Fig. 3. Description of a *concept* using WSML

The service cloud refers to SaaS deployment of the services so that mobility in the service access and the ease-of-use of the target application is achieved as discussed in [16]. We have also raised the point of technology convergence for the selection of SaaS as platform deployment for the services and applications of OOSE. Collectively, the web services, and applications layer is referred as OOSE Services Cloud (OSC).

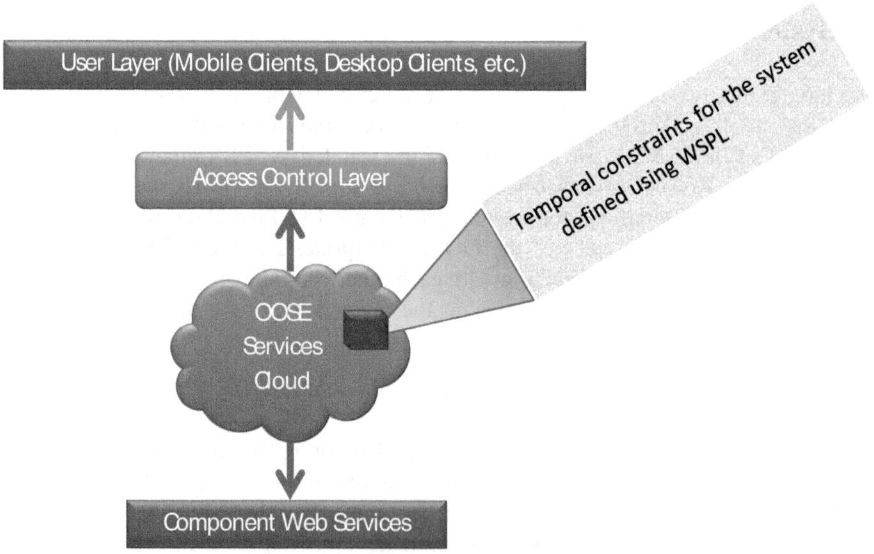

Fig. 4. Layout of services in OOSE enterprise

The temporal constraints for the system act as component of OSC, i.e., it is one of the services offered by OSC which provides temporal characteristics and constraints for the system using extended-WSPL. Since, SaaS implementation is done for the given scenario, an authorization framework is required to grant access rights to the services offered by OSC to multiple users.

The temporal constraints of the system are represented using WSPL as described earlier. The entities to be included for specifying temporal constraints have been identified as; start-date, end-date, and timestamp. The start-date signifies date-time when the web-service is initialized, the end-time signifies the date-time when web-service should deny providing any service. The timestamp specifies the date-time of writing the policy. So, a policy assertion will be true if the web-service can provide service and a policy assertion will be evaluated as false if the web-service end-date has expired, i.e., it has denied of providing any services to the requestor. An example service policy assertion for specifying start-date, end-date for a web-service is as shown in Figure-5.

```
<wsp:Policy
 xmlns:sp='http://oose.org/secpol'
 xmlns:wsp='http://w3.org/ns/wspol' >
  <wsp:ExactlyOne>
   <wsp:All>
    <tsp:StartDate>01/11/2011</tsp:StartDate>
    <tsp:EndDate>01/11/2012</tsp:EndDate>
    <tsp: Timestamp >01/10/2011 07:53:12
AM</tsp:Timestamp>
    </wsp:All>
  </wsp:ExactlyOne>
<wsp:Policy>
```

Fig. 5. Temporal services policies assertions in WSPL

4 Ontology Specification

The ontologies and web-services described for the system discussed in Section 3 are specified in CL. We use the ontology description given in [16], and extend it for specification in CLIF. The meta-tokens defined by CLIF project are used for defining the mappings between the ontology and web-services descriptions and the CLIF specification.

4.1 Ontology Specification

The concept-level mapping of WSML structure with CLIF structure is defined in Table-2.

Table 2. Concept-level mapping of WSML-Construct and CLIF Expression

WSML Construct	CLIF Expression
concept SharepointAppPool appPool ofType SharepointAppPool	(exists(SharepointAppPool OfficeOntology) (and(SharepointAppPool x) (x#appPool definedAs wsml:objectType(SharePointAppPool))));
concept User userName ofType _string firstName ofType _string lastName ofType _string encryptedPassword ofType _string	(exists(User OfficeOntology) (and(User x) (x#userName definedAs wsml:string) (x#firstName definedAs wsml:string) (x#lastName definedAs wsml:string) (x#encryptedPassword definedAs wsml:string)));
concept WordDocument fileAttributes ofType _string fileName ofType _string fileSize ofType _integer author ofType _string renderer ofType _object	(exists(WordDocument OfficeOntology) (and (WordDocument x) (x#fileAttributes definedAs wsml:string) (x#fileName definedAs wsml:string) (x#fileSize definedAs wsml:integer) (x#author definedAs wsml:string) (x#renderer definedAs wsml:object)));

For representing the class properties, for example, in case of defining concept 'User', we use '#' operator and the use of the operator is obvious.

4.2 WS-Level Meta-terms in CLIF

In the web services-level meta-terms in CLIF, we identify web services defined in WSML and translate the description into CLIF expression as shown in Table-3. For identifying various entities of WSML construct in CLIF, we've used wsml:capability to denote capability, wsml:interface to denote interface, wsml:choreography to denote choreography, and so on. The denotion of the WSML-entities in CLIF is obvious.

Table 3. WS-level mapping of WSML-Construct and CLIF Expression

WSML Construct	CLIF Expression
webservice WVS capability WVSCapability nonFunctionalProperties discovery#discoveryStrat egy hasValue discovery#LightweightRul eDiscovery endNonFunctionalProperti es interface WordDocument choreography WVSUserInterface orchestration ExcelCalcService interface HostDocumentService interface EmbeddedDocCompositeServ ice orchestration PowerPointService	(exists(OfficeOntology WVS) (and (WVS x) (OfficeOntology p) (wsml:capabilityOf WVS(discoveryStrategy hasValue lightWeightRuleDiscovery)) (wsml:interface(wordDocum ent existsIn p)) (wsml:choreography(wSUser Interface existsIn p)) (wsml:orchestration(excel CalcService existsIn p)) (wsml:interface(hostDocum entInterface definedBy p)) (wsml:orchestration embeddedDocCompositeServi ce existsIn p)));

5 Conclusion and Future Work

In this section we present the conclusions drawn from the text of this paper and the directions of future scope of work:

- By translating and mapping WSML to CL, we have shown that WSML-Full is an expressive subset of CL.
- The ontology description of the system models the temporal constraints or characteristics as discussed in the case study of the system, hence the CL specification of the system is bound to include those constraints.
- Finally, because of little support of the CL with model checkers, and provers; we will further specify the abstract CL specification to some concrete specification which has support for model checkers, provers, etc. and also implement the need for an access control framework in the system as shown in Figure-3.

References

1. International Standards Office, ISO 24707/2007 Information Technology - Common Logic (CL): a framework for a family of logic-based languages. ISO, Geneva (2007), http://www.iso.org/iso/catalogue_detail.htm?csnumber=39175
2. Menzel, C.: Common Logic - Motivations and Some Gentle Theory. Presentation delivered at Semtech 2008 Workshop (2008), http://www.cl.tamu.edu/
3. International Standards Office, ISO 14977/1996 Information Technology – Syntactic Metalanguage – Extended BNF. ISO, Geneva (2007), http://www.iso.org/iso/catalogue_detail.htm?csnumber=26153
4. Wang, H. H., Saleh, A., Payne, T., Gibbins, N.: Formal Specification of OWL-S with Object-Z. In: Proceedings of the First ESWC Workshop on OWL-S: Experiences and Future Directions, Austria (2007)
5. Wang, H.H., Saleh, A., Payne, T., Gibbins, N.: Formal Specification of OWL-S with Object-Z: the Static Aspect. In: Proceedings of the 2007 IEEE/WIC/ACM International Conference on Web Intelligence, pp. 431–434. IEEE Press, New York (2007)
6. Corcho, Ó., Gómez Pérez, A.: A Roadmap to Ontology Specification Languages. In: Dieng, R., Corby, O. (eds.) EKAW 2000. LNCS (LNAI), vol. 1937, pp. 80–96. Springer, Heidelberg (2000)
7. Roman, D., Kifer, M., Fensel, D.: WSMO Choreography: From Abstract State Machines to Concurrent Transaction Logic. In: Bechhofer, S., Hauswirth, M., Hoffmann, J., Koubarakis, M. (eds.) ESWC 2008. LNCS, vol. 5021, pp. 659–673. Springer, Heidelberg (2008)
8. Wang, H.H., Gibbins, N., Payne, T., Sun, J.: A Formal Model of Semantic Web Service Ontology (WSMO) Execution. In: Proceedings of 13th IEEE International Conference on Engineering of Complex Computer Systems, pp. 111–120. IEEE Press, New York (2008)
9. Wang, H.H., Gibbins, N., Payne, T., Sun, J.: A Formal Semantic Model of the Semantic Web Service Ontology (WSMO). In: Proceedings of 12th IEEE International Conference on Engineering Complex Computer Systems, pp. 74–86. IEEE Press, New York (2007)
10. Roman, D., Lausan, H., Keller, U., Oren, E., Busseler, C., Kifer, M., Fensel, D.: D2v1.0. Web Service Modeling Ontology (WSMO), http://www.wsmo.org/2004/d2/v1.0/
11. Steinmetz, N., Toma, I. (eds.) D16.1v1.0 WSML Language Reference (2008), http://www.wsmo.org/TR/d16/d16.1/v1.0/
12. Vedamuthu, A. S., Orchard, D., Hirsch, F., Hondo, M., Yendluri, P., Boubez, T., Yalcinalp, U.: Web Services Policy 1.5 – Framework. W3C Recommendation (2007), http://www.w3.org/TR/ws-policy/
13. IBM developerWorks, Web Services Policy Framework, http://www.ibm.com/developerworks/library/specification/ws-polfram/
14. Andrieux, A., et al.: Web Services Agreement Specification (WS-Agreement), http://www.ogf.org/documents/GFD.107.pdf
15. Bhandari, A., Singh, M.: Formal Description of Services Interfaces of SMAL Services in Services Computing Environment. In: 2011 International Conference on Network Communication and Computer, pp. 58–62 (2011)
16. Bhandari, A., Singh, M.: Towards Ontology-based Services Interfaces in Services Systems based Environment. International Journal of Computer Applications 15(6), 19–24 (2011)

17. Mathes, M., Heinzl, S., Freisleben, B.: WS-TemporalPolicy: A WS-Policy extension for Describing Service Properties with Time Constraints. In: Annual IEEE International Computer Software and Applications Conference, pp. 1180–1186. IEEE Press, New York (2008)
18. Heinzl, S., Seiler, D., Juhnke, E., Freisleben, B.: Exposing Validity Periods of Prices for Resource Consumption to Web Service Users via Temporal Policies. In: Proceedings of the 11th International Conference on Information Integration and Web-based Applications & Services, pp. 235–242. ACM Press, New York (2009)
19. Tosic, V., Erradi, A., Maheshwari, P.: WS-Policy4MASC – A WS-Policy Extension Used in the MASC Middleware. In: Proceedings of the 2007 IEEE International Conference on Services Computing, pp. 458–465. IEEE Press, New York (2007)
20. Kallel, S., Charfi, A., Dinkelaker, T., Mezini, M., Jmaiel, M.: Specifying and Monitoring Temporal Properties in Web services Compositions. In: Proceedings of the Seventh IEEE European Conference on Web Services, pp. 148–157. IEEE Press, New York (2009)
21. Microsoft Technet, Understanding Office Web Apps (Installed on SharePoint 2010 Products) (2010), `http://technet.microsoft.com/en-gb/library/ff431685.aspx`
22. Kerrigan, M.: D9.1v0.2 Web Service Modeling Toolkit (WSMT), `http://www.wsmo.org/TR/d9/d9.1/v0.2/20050425/`

Advanced Data Warehousing Techniques for Analysis, Interpretation and Decision Support of Scientific Data

Vuda Sreenivasarao[1] and Venkata Subbareddy Pallamreddy[2]

[1] Dept.of Computer Science & Engg, St.Mary's College of Engg & Tech, JNTU Hyderabad
[2] Dept. of Computer Science & Engg, QIS College of Engg & Tech, JNTU Kakinada

Abstract. R & D Organizations handling many Research and Development projects produce a very large amount of Scientific and Technical data. The analysis and interpretation of these data is crucial for the proper understanding of Scientific / Technical phenomena and discovery of new concepts. Data warehousing using multidimensional view and on-line analytical processing (OLAP) have become very popular in both business and science in recent years and are essential elements of decision support, analysis and interpretation of data. Data warehouses for scientific purposes pose several great challenges to existing data warehouse technology. This paper provides an overview of scientific data warehousing and OLAP technologies, with an emphasis on their data warehousing requirements. The methods that we used include the efficient computation of data cubes by integration of MOLAP and ROLAP techniques, the integration of data cube methods with dimension relevance analysis and data dispersion analysis for concept description and data cube based multi-level association, classification, prediction and clustering techniques.

Keywords: Scientific Data Warehouses, On-line analytical processing (OLAP), Data Mining, On-Line Analytical Mining (OLAM), DBM, Data Cubes.

1 Introduction

R & D Organizations handling many Research and Development projects produce a very large amount of Scientific and Technical data. The analysis and interpretation of these data is crucial for the proper understanding of Scientific / Technical phenomena and discovery of new concepts. Data warehousing and on-line analytical processing (OLAP) are essential elements of decision support, which has increasingly become a focus of the database industry. Many commercial products and services are now available, and all of the principal database management system vendors now have offerings in these areas. Decision support places some rather different requirements on database technology compared to traditional on-line transaction processing applications. Data Warehousing (DW) and On-Line.

Analytical Processing (OLAP) systems based on a dimensional view of data are being used increasingly in traditional business applications as well as in applications such as health care and bio-chemistry for the purpose of analyzing very large amounts of data. The use of DW and OLAP systems for scientific purposes raises several new

D.C. Wyld et al. (Eds.): ACITY 2011, CCIS 198, pp. 162–174, 2011.

challenges to the traditional technology. Efficient implementation and fast response is the major challenge in the realization of On-line analytical mining in large databases and scientific data warehouses. Therefore, the study has been focused on the efficient implementation of the On-line analytical mining mechanism. The methods that I used include the efficient computation of data cubes by integration of MOLAP and ROLAP techniques, the integration of data cube methods with dimension relevance analysis and data dispersion analysis for concept description and data cube based multi-level association, classification, prediction and clustering techniques. I describe back end tools for extracting, cleaning and loading data into a scientific data warehouse; multidimensional data models typical of OLAP; front end client tools for querying and data analysis; server extensions for efficient query processing; and tools for metadata management and for managing the warehouse. These methods will be discussed in detail.

2 OLAP+ Data Mining On-Line Analytical Mining

On-line analytical processing (OLAP) is a powerful data analysis method for multi-dimensional analysis of data warehouses. Motivated by the popularity of OLAP technology, I use an On-Line Analytical Mining (OLAM) mechanism for multi-dimensional data mining in large databases and scientific data warehouses. I believe this is a promising direction to pursue for the scientific data warehouses, based on the following observations.

1 Most data mining tools need to work on integrated, consistent, and cleaned data, which requires costly data cleaning, data transformation and data integration as pre-? Processing steps. A data warehouse constructed by such pre-processing serves as a Valuable source of cleaned and integrated data for OLAP as well as for data mining.
2 Effective data mining needs exploratory data analysis. A user often likes to traverse flexibly through a database, select any portions of relevant data, analyze data at different granularities, and present knowledge/results in different forms. On-line analytical mining provides facilities for data mining on different subsets of data and at different levels of abstraction, by drilling, pivoting, filtering, dicing and slicing on a data cube and on some intermediate data mining results. This, together with data/knowledge visualization tools, will greatly enhance the power and flexibility of exploratory data mining.
3 It is often difficult for a user to predict what kinds of knowledge to be mined beforehand, by integration of OLAP with multiple data mining functions. On-line analytical mining provides flexibility for users to select desired data mining functions and swap data mining tasks dynamically.However, data mining functions usually cost more than simple OLAP operations. Efficient implementation and fast response is the major challenge in the realization of On- line analytical mining in large databases and scientific data warehouses. Therefore, our study has been focused on the efficient implementation of the On-line analytical mining mechanism. The methods that I used include the efficient computation of data cubes by integration of MOLAP and ROLAP techniques, the integration of data cube methods with dimension relevance

analysis and data dispersion analysis for concept description and data cube based multi- level association, classification, prediction and clustering techniques. These methods will be discussed in detail in the following subsections.

2.1 Architecture for On-Line Analytical Mining

An OLAM engine performs analytical mining in data cubes in a similar manner as an OLAP engine performs on- line analytical processing. Therefore, it is suggested to have an integrated OLAM and OLAP architecture as shown in below Figure.1., where the OLAM and OLAP engines both accept users on-line queries (instructions) and work with the data cube in the analysis Furthermore, an OLAM engine may perform multiple data mining tasks, such as concept description, association, classification, prediction, clustering, time-series analysis, etc. Therefore, an OLAM engine is more sophisticated than an OLAP engine since it usually consists of multiple mining modules which may interact with each other for effective mining in a scientific data warehouse.

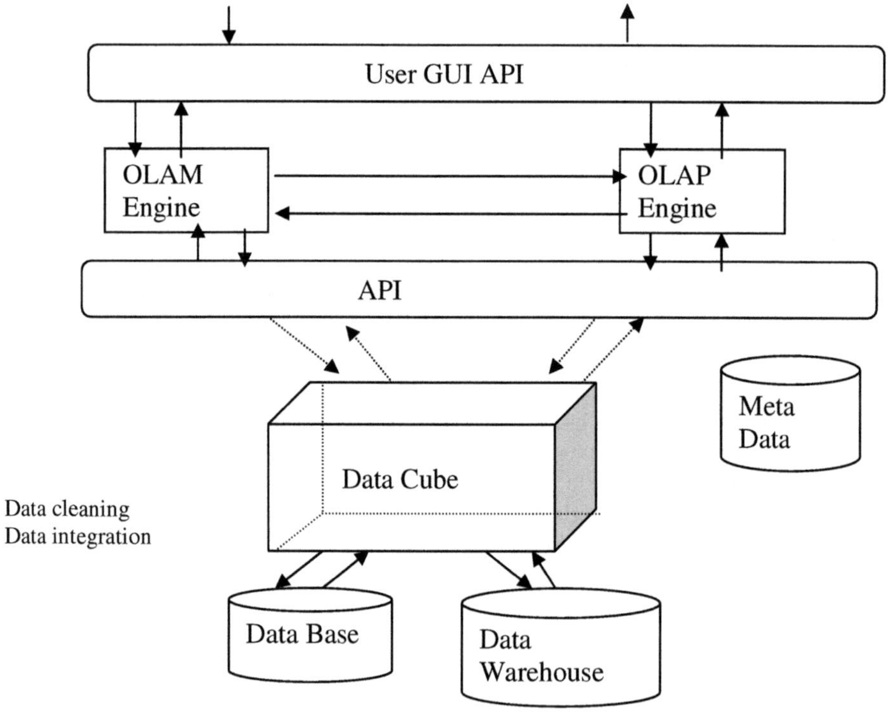

Fig. 1. An integrated OLAM and OLAP architecture

Since some requirements in OLAM, such as the construction of numerical dimensions, may not be readily available in the commercial OLAP products, I have chosen to construct our own data cube and build the mining modules on such data cubes. With many OLAP products available on the market, it is important to develop on-line analytical mining mechanisms directly on top of the constructed data cubes and OLAP engines. Based on our analysis, there is no fundamental difference between the data cube required for OLAP and that for OLAM, although OLAM analysis may often involve the analysis of a larger number of dimensions with finer granularities, and thus require more powerful data cube construction and accessing tools than OLAP analyses. Since OLAM engines are constructed either on customized data cubes which often work with relational database systems, or on top of the data cubes provided by the OLAP products, it is suggested to build online analytical mining systems on top of the existing OLAP and relational database systems rather than from the ground up.

2.2 Data Cube Construction

Data cube technology is essential for efficient on-line analytical mining. There have been many studies on efficient computation and access of multidimensional databases. These lead us to use data cubes for scientific data warehouses.

The attribute-oriented induction method adopts two generalization techniques (1) attribute removal, which removes attributes which represent low-level data in a hierarchy, and (2) attribute generalization which generalizes attribute values to their corresponding high level ones. Such generalization leads to a new, compressed generalized relation with count and/or other aggregate values accumulated. This is similar to the relational OLAP (ROLAP) implementation of the roll-up operation. For fast response in OLAP and data mining, the later implementation has adopted data cube technology as follows, when data cube contains a small number of dimensions, or when it is generalized to a high level, the cube is structured as compressed sparse array but is still stored in a relational database (to reduce the cost of construction and indexing of different data structures). The cube is pre-computed using a chunk-based multi-way array aggregation technique. However, when the cube has a large number of dimensions, it becomes very sparse with a huge number of chunks. In this case, a relational structure is adopted to store and compute the data cube, similar to the ROLAP implementation. We believe such a dual data structure technique represents a balance between multidimensional OLAP (MOLAP) and relational OLAP (ROLAP) implementations. It ensures fast response time when handling medium-sized cubes/cuboids and high scalability when handling large databases with high dimensionality. Notice that even adopting the ROLAP technique, it is still unrealistic to materialize all the possible cuboids for large databases with high dimensionality due to the huge number of cuboids it is wise to materialize more of the generalized, low dimensionality cuboids besides considering other factors, such as accessing patterns and the sharing among different cuboids. A 3-D data cube/cuboids can be selected from a high- dimensional data cube and be browsed conveniently using the DBMiner 3-D cube browser as shown in Figure.2. Where the size of a cell (displayed as a tiny cube) represents the entry count in the corresponding cell, and the brightness of the cell represents another measure of the cell. Pivoting, drilling, and slicing/dicing operations can be performed on the data cube browser with mouse clicking.

2.3 Concept Description

Concept/class description plays an important role in descriptive data mining. It consists of two major functions, data characterization and data discrimination (or comparison).

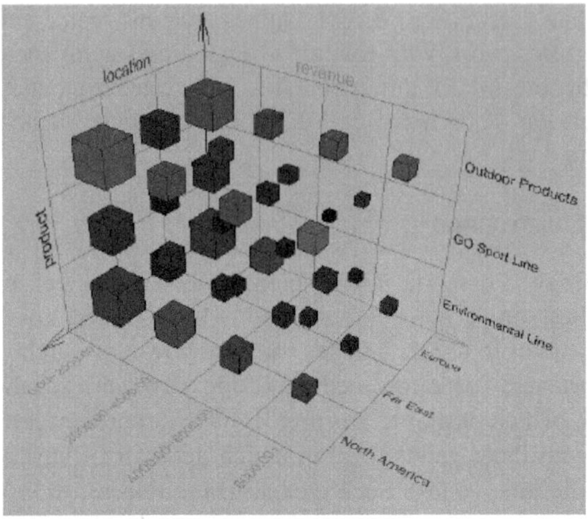

Fig. 2. Browsing of a 3-dimensional data cube in DBMiner

Data characterization summarizes and characterizes a set of task-relevant data by data generalization. Data characterization and its associated OLAP operations, such as drill-down and roll-up (also called drill-up).

2.4 Database System Architecture

The Database System used for the scientific data warehouses can use a centralized architecture, containing ETL, Data Warehousing, OLAP and Data Mining in a single platform. The overall system architecture is seen in below Figure.3.

This type of architecture can reduce the administration costs because of its single platform, and also reduces the implementation costs. This Architecture supports faster deployment and improved scalability and reliability.

The OLAP in this type architecture can empower end user to do own scientific analysis, can give ease of use. This also provides easy Drill Down facility to the users. This architecture can provide virtually no knowledge of tables required for the users. This architecture can also improve exception analysis and variance analysis.

This architecture gives user the multidimensional view of data and can provide easy Drill Down, rotate and ad-hoc analysis of data. It can also support iterative discovery process. It can provide unique descriptions across all levels of data. The DB modifies & summarizes (store aggregates) of the scientific data and adds historical information to the DB.

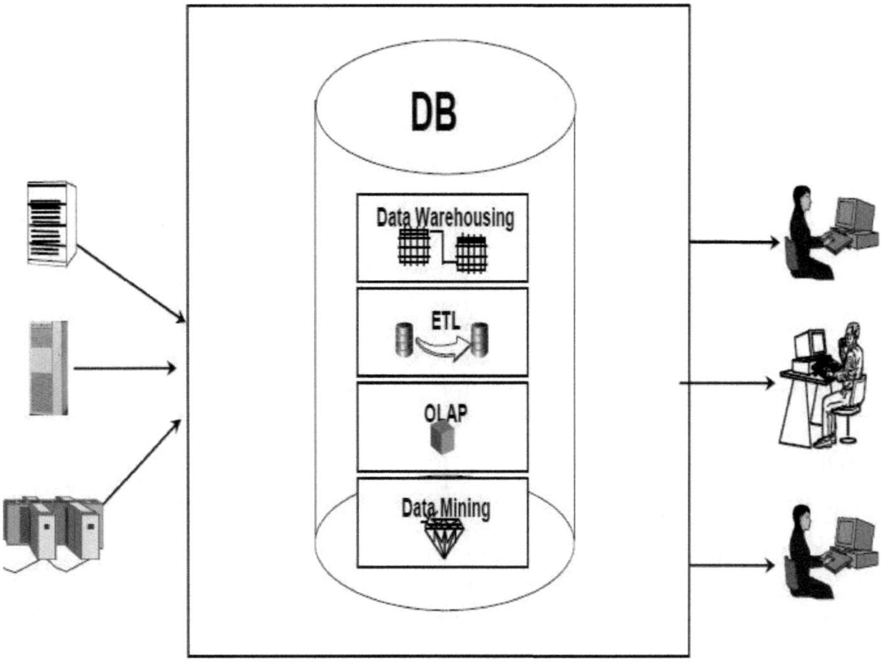

Fig. 3. Database System Architecture

3 OLAP++ System Architecture

The overall architecture of the OLAP++ system is seen in Figure.4. The object part of the system is based on the OPM tools that implements the Object Data Management Group (ODMG) object data model and the Object Query Language (OQL) on top of a relational DBMS, in this case the ORACLE RDBMS. The OLAP part of the system is based on Microsoft's SQL Server OLAP Services using the Multi- Dimensional expressions (MDX) query language.

When a SumQL++ query is received by the Federation Coordinator (FC), it is first parsed to identify the measures, categories, links, classes and attributes referenced in the query. Based on this, the FC then queries the metadata to get information about which databases the object data and the OLAP data reside in and which categories are linked to which classes. Based on the object parts of the query, the FC then sends OQL queries to the object databases to retrieve the data for which the particular conditions holds true. This data is then put into a "pure" SumQL statement (i.e. without object references) as a list of category values.

This SumQL statement is then sent to the OLAP database layer to retrieve the desired measures, grouped by the requested categories. The SumQL statement is translated into MDX by a separate layer, the "SumQL-to-MDX translator", and the data returned from OLAP Services is returned to the FC. The reason for using the

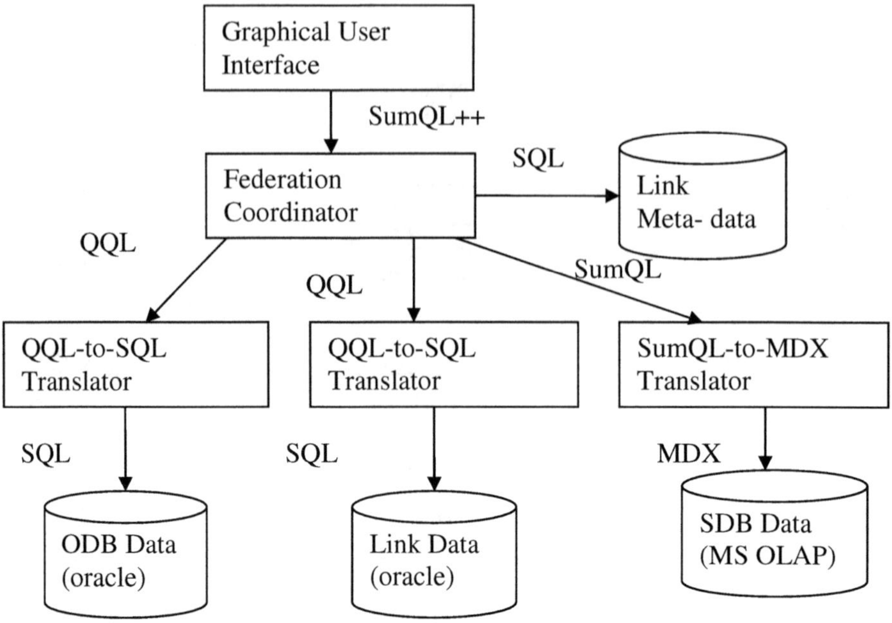

Fig. 4. OLAP++ Architecture

intermediate SumQL statements is to isolate the implementation of the OLAP data from the FC. As another alternative, we have also implemented a translator into SQL statements against a "star schema" relational database design. The system is able to support a good query performance even for large databases while making it possible to integrate existing OLAP data with external data in object databases in a flexible way that can adapt quickly to changing query needs.

3.1 Back End Tools and Utilities

Data warehousing systems use a variety of data extraction and cleaning tools, and load and refresh utilities for populating warehouses Data extraction from "foreign" sources is usually implemented via gateways and standard interfaces (such as Information Builders EDA/SQL, ODBC, Oracle Open Connect, Sybase Enterprise Connect, Informix Enterprise Gateway).

Data Cleaning: Since a data warehouse is used for decision making, it is important that the data in the warehouse be correct. However, since large volumes of data from multiple sources are involved, there is a high probability of errors and anomalies in the data. Therefore, tools that help to detect data anomalies and correct them can have a high payoff. Some examples where data cleaning becomes necessary are: inconsistent field lengths, inconsistent descriptions, inconsistent value assignments, missing entries and violation of integrity constraints. Not surprisingly, optional fields in data entry forms are significant sources of inconsistent data. There are three related, but somewhat different, classes of data cleaning tools. Data migration tools allow simple transformation rules to be specified; e.g., "replace the string gender by sex". Warehouse Manager from Prism is an example of a popular tool of this kind. Data scrubbing tools use domain-specific knowledge (e.g., postal addresses) to do the scrubbing of data. They often exploit parsing and fuzzy matching techniques to accomplish cleaning from multiple sources. Some tools make it possible to specify the "relative cleanliness" of sources. Tools such as Integrity and Trillum fall in this category. Data auditing tools make it possible to discover rules and relationships (or to signal violation of stated rules) by scanning data. Thus, such tools may be considered variants of data mining tools. For example, such a tool may discover a suspicious pattern (based on statistical analysis) that a certain car dealer has never received any complaints.

Load: After extracting, cleaning and transforming, data must be loaded into the warehouse. Additional preprocessing may still be required: checking integrity constraints; sorting; summarization, aggregation and other computation to build the derived tables stored in the warehouse; building indices and other access paths; and partitioning to multiple target storage areas. The load utilities for data warehouses have to deal with much larger data volumes than for operational databases. There is only a small time window (usually at night) when the warehouse can be taken offline to refresh it. Sequential loads can take a very long time, e.g., loading a terabyte of data can take weeks and months! Hence, pipelined and partitioned parallelisms are typically exploited 6. Doing a full load has the advantage that it can be treated as a long batch transaction that builds up a new database. While it is in progress, the current database can still support queries; when the load transaction commits, the current database is replaced with the new one. Using periodic checkpoints ensures that if a failure occurs during the load, the process can restart from the last checkpoint. However, even using parallelism, a full load may still take too long. Most commercial utilities (e.g., RedBrick Table Management Utility) use incremental loading during refresh to reduce the volume of data that has to be incorporated into the warehouse. Only the updated tuples are inserted. However, the load process now is harder to manage. The incremental load conflicts with ongoing queries, so it is treated as a sequence of shorter transactions (which commit periodically, e.g., after every 1000 records or every few seconds), but now this sequence of transactions has to be coordinated to ensure consistency of derived data and indices with the base data.

Refresh: Refreshing a warehouse consists in propagating updates on source data to correspondingly update the base data and derived data stored in the warehouse. There are two sets of issues to consider: *when* to refresh, and *how* to refresh. Usually, the warehouse is refreshed periodically (e.g., daily or weekly). Only if some OLAP queries need current data (e.g., up to the minute stock quotes), is it necessary to propagate every update. The refresh policy is set by the warehouse administrator, depending on user needs and traffic, and may be different for different sources. Refresh techniques may also depend on the characteristics of the source and the capabilities of the database servers. Extracting an entire source file or database is usually too expensive, but may be the only choice for legacy data sources. Most contemporary database systems provide replication servers that support incremental techniques for propagating updates from a primary database to one or more replicas. Such replication servers can be used to incrementally refresh a warehouse when the sources change. There are two basic replication techniques: data shipping and transaction shipping. In data shipping, a table in the warehouse is treated as a remote snapshot of a table in the source database.

After_row: triggers are used to update a snapshot log table whenever the source table changes; and an automatic refresh schedule (or a manual refresh procedure) is then set up to propagate the updated data to the remote snapshot. In transaction shipping (e.g., used in the Sybase Replication Server and Microsoft SQL Server), the regular transaction log is used, instead of triggers and a special snapshot log table. At the source site, the transaction log is sniffed to detect updates on replicated tables, and those log records are transferred to a replication server, which packages up the corresponding transactions to update the replicas. Transaction shipping has the advantage that it does not require triggers, which can increase the workload on the operational source databases. However, it cannot always be used easily across DBMSs from different vendors, because there are no standard APIs for accessing the transaction log. Such replication servers have been used for refreshing data warehouses. However, the refresh cycles have to be properly chosen so that the volume of data does not overwhelm the incremental load utility. In addition to propagating changes to the base data in the warehouse, the derived data also has to be updated correspondingly.

3.2 Conceptual Model and Front End Tools

A popular conceptual model that influences the front-end tools, database design, and the query engines for OLAP is the *multidimensional* view of data in the warehouse. In a multidimensional data model, there is a set of *numeric measures* that are the objects of analysis. Examples of such measures are sales, budget, revenue, inventory, ROI (return on investment). Each of the numeric measures depends on a set of *dimensions,* which provide the context for the measure.

For example, the dimensions associated with a sale amount can be the city, product name, and the date when the sale was made. The dimensions together are assumed to *uniquely* determine the measure. Thus, the multidimensional data views a measure as a value in the multidimensional space of dimensions. Each dimension is described by a set of attributes. For example, the Product dimension may consist of four attributes: the category and the industry of the product, year of its introduction, and the average profit margin. For example, the soda Surge belongs to the category beverage and the food industry, was introduced in 1996, and may have an average profit margin of 80%. The attributes of a dimension may be related via a hierarchy of relationships. In the above example, the product name is related to its category and the industry attribute through such a hierarchical relationship. Another distinctive feature of the conceptual model for OLAP is its stress on *aggregation* of measures by one or more dimensions as one of the key operations; e.g., computing and ranking the *total* sales by each county (or by each year). Other popular operations include *comparing* two measures (e.g., sales and budget) aggregated by the same dimensions. Time is a dimension that is of particular significance to decision support (e.g., trend analysis). Often, it is desirable to have built-in knowledge of calendars and other aspects of the time dimension.

3.3 Front End Tools

The multidimensional data model grew out of the view of business data popularized by PC spreadsheet programs that were extensively used by business analysts. The spreadsheet is still the most compelling front-end application for OLAP. The challenge in supporting a query environment for OLAP can be crudely summarized as that of supporting spreadsheet operations efficiently over large multi-gigabyte databases. Indeed, the Essbase product of Arbor Corporation uses Microsoft Excel as the front-end tool for its multidimensional engine. We shall briefly discuss some of the popular operations that are supported by the multidimensional spreadsheet applications. One such operation is pivoting. Consider the multidimensional schema of Figure.5. represented in a spreadsheet where each row corresponds to a sale. Let there be one column for each dimension and an extra column that represents the amount of sale. The simplest view of pivoting is that it selects two dimensions that are used to aggregate a measure, e.g., sales in the above example. The aggregated values are often displayed in a grid where each value in the (x, y) coordinate corresponds to the aggregated value of the measure when the first dimension has the value x and the second dimension has the value y. Thus, in our example, if the selected dimensions are city and year, then the x-axis may represent all values of city and the y-axis may represent the years. The point (x, y) will represent the aggregated sales for city x in the year y. Thus, what were values in the original spreadsheets have now become row and column headers in the pivoted spreadsheet. Other operators related to pivoting are rollup or drill-down Rollup corresponds to taking the current data object and doing a further group-by on one of the dimensions. Thus, it is possible to roll-up the sales data, perhaps already aggregated on city, additionally by product. The drill-down operation is the converse of rollup. Slice_and_dice corresponds to reducing the dimensionality of the data, i.e., taking a projection of the data on a subset of dimensions for selected values of the other dimensions. For example, we can slice_and_dice sales data for a specific product to create a table that consists of the dimensions city and the day of sale.

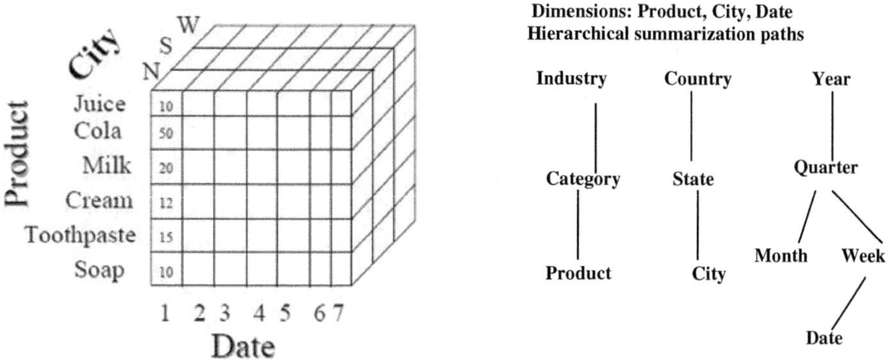

Fig. 5. Multidimensional data

4 Advantages

On-line analytical processing (OLAP) is a powerful data analysis method for multi-dimensional analysis of data warehouses. OLAM engine may perform multiple data mining tasks, such as concept description, association, classification, prediction, clustering, time series analysis, etc. Therefore, an OLAM engine is more sophisticated than an OLAP engine since it usually consists of multiple mining modules which may interact with each other for effective mining. Based on our analysis, there is no fundamental difference between the data cube required for OLAP and that for OLAM, although OLAM analysis may often involve the analysis of a larger number of dimensions with finer granularities, and thus require more powerful data cube construction and accessing tools than OLAP analyses. The attribute-oriented induction method adopts two generalization techniques (1) attribute removal, which removes attributes which represent low-level data in a hierarchy, and (2) attribute generalization which generalizes attribute values to their corresponding high level ones. Such generalization leads to a new, compressed generalized relation with count and/or other aggregate values accumulated. Data warehousing systems use a variety of data extraction and cleaning tools, and load and refresh utilities for populating warehouses Data extraction from "foreign" sources is usually implemented via gateways and standard interfaces. *Data Cleaning, Load, Refresh and After_row* operations can be performed more efficiently. Data cleaning is a problem that is reminiscent of heterogeneous data integration, a problem that has been studied for many years. But here the emphasis is on *data* inconsistencies instead of schema inconsistencies. Data cleaning, as I indicated, is also closely related to data mining, with the objective of suggesting possible inconsistencies. This architecture gives user the multidimensional view of data and can provide easy Drill Down, rotate and ad-hoc analysis of data. It can also support iterative discovery process. It can provide unique descriptions across all levels of data. The OLAP in this type architecture can empower end user to do own scientific analysis, can give ease of use. This also provides easy Drill Down facility to the users. This architecture can provide virtually no knowledge of tables required for the users. This architecture can also improve exception analysis and variance analysis. Provides high query performance and keeps local processing at sources unaffected and can operate when sources unavailable. Can query data not stored in a DBMS through Extra information at warehouse The use of DW and OLAP systems for scientific purposes raises several new challenges to the traditional technology. Efficient implementation and fast response is the major challenge in the realization of On-line analytical mining in large databases and scientific data warehouses. Therefore, the study has been focused on the efficient implementation of the On-line analytical mining mechanism. The methods that I used include the efficient computation of data cubes by integration of MOLAP and ROLAP techniques, the integration of data cube methods with dimension relevance analysis and data dispersion analysis for concept description and data cube based multi-level association, classification, prediction and clustering techniques. I describe back end tools for extracting, cleaning and loading data into a scientific data warehouse; multidimensional data models typical of OLAP; front end client tools for querying and data analysis and tools for metadata management and for managing the warehouse.

5 Conclusions

Data warehousing using multidimensional view and on-line analytical processing (OLAP) have become very popular in both business and science in recent years and are essential elements of decision support, analysis and interpretation of data. Data warehouses for scientific purposes pose several great challenges to existing data warehouse technology. This paper provides an overview of scientific data warehousing and OLAP technologies, with an emphasis on their data warehousing requirements. The methods that I used include the efficient computation of data cubes by integration of MOLAP and ROLAP techniques, the integration of data cube methods with dimension relevance analysis and data dispersion analysis for concept description and data cube based multi-level association, classification, prediction and clustering techniques. I describe back end tools for extracting, cleaning and loading data into a scientific data warehouse; multidimensional data models typical of OLAP; front end client tools for querying and data analysis; server extensions for efficient query processing; and tools for metadata management and for managing the warehouse.

References

1. Microsoft Corporation. OLE DB for OLAP Version 1.0 Specification. Microsoft Technical Document (1998)
2. The OLAP Report. Database Explosion (February 18, 2000), `http://www.olapreport.com/DatabaseExplosion.htm`
3. Pedersen, T.B., Jensen, C.S.: Research Issues in Clinical Data Warehousing. In: Proceedings of the Tenth International Conference on Statistical and Scientific Database Management, pp. 43–52 (1998)
4. Pedersen, T.B., Jensen, C.S., Dyreson, C.E.: Supporting Imprecision in Multidimensional Databases Using Granularities. In: Proceedings of the Eleventh International Conference on Statistical and Scientific Database Management, pp. 90–101 (1999)
5. Pedersen, T.B., Jensen, C.S., Dyreson, C.E.: Extending PractiPre-Aggregation in On-Line Analytical Processing. In: Proceedings of the Twentyfifth International Conference on Very Large Data Bases, pp. 663–674 (1999)
6. Pedersen, T.B., Jensen, C.S.: Multidimensional Data Modeling for Complex Data. In: Proceedings of the Fifteenth International Conference on Data Engineering (1999); Extended version available as TimeCenter Technical Report TR-37
7. `http://www.olapcouncil.org`
8. Codd, E.F., Codd, S.B., Salley, C.T.: Providing OLAP (On-LineAnalytical Processing) to User Analyst: An IT Mandate, Arbor Software's web site, `http://www.arborsoft.com/OLAP.html`
9. Kimball, R.: The Data Warehouse Toolkit. John Wiley, Chichester (1996)
10. Barclay, T., Barnes, R., Gray, J., Sundaresan, P.: Loading Databases using Dataflow Parallelism. SIGMOD Record 23(4) (December 1994)
11. O'Neil, P., Quass, D.: Improved Query Performance with Variant Indices. To appear in Proc. of SIGMOD Conf. (1997)
12. Harinarayan, V., Rajaraman, A., Ullman, J.D.: Implementing Data Cubes Efficiently. In: Proc. of SIGMOD Conf. (1996)

13. Chaudhuri, S., Krishnamurthy, R., Potamianos, S., Shim, K.: Optimizing Queries with Materialized Views. In: Intl. Conference on Data Engineering (1995)
14. Widom, J.: Research Problems in Data Warehousing. In: Proc. 4th Intl. CIKM Conf. (1995)
15. Cattell, R.G.G., et al. (eds.): The Object Database Standard: ODMG 2.0. Morgan Kaufmann, San Francisco (1997)
16. Thomsen, E.: OLAP Solutions. Wiley, Chichester (1997)
17. Winter, R.: Databases: Back in the OLAP game. Intelligent Enterprise Magazine 1(4), 60–64 (1998)
18. Wu, M.-C., Buchmann, A.P.: Research Issues in Data Warehousing (submitted for publication)
19. Levy, A., Mendelzon, A., Sagiv, Y.: Answering Queries Using Views. In: Proc. of PODS (1995)
20. Seshadri, P., Pirahesh, H., Leung, T.: Complex Query Decorrelation. In: Intl. Conference on Data Engineering (1996)
21. Widom, J.: Research Problems in Data Warehousing. In: Proc. 4th Intl. CIKM Conf. (1995); Gupta A., Harinarayan V., Quass D.: Aggregate-Query Processing in Data Warehouse Environments. In: Proc. of VLDB (1995)

Anti-synchronization of Li and T Chaotic Systems by Active Nonlinear Control

Sundarapandian Vaidyanathan[1] and Karthikeyan Rajagopal[2]

[1] R & D Centre, Vel Tech Dr. RR & Dr. SR Technical University
Avadi-Alamathi Road, Avadi, Chennai-600 062, India
sundarvtu@gmail.com
http://www.vel-tech.org/

[2] School of Electronics and Electrical Engineering, Singhania University
Dist. Jhunjhunu, Rajasthan-333 515,India
rkarthiekeyan@gmail.com
http://www.singhaniauniversity.co.in/

Abstract. The purpose of this paper is to study chaos anti-synchronization of identical Li chaotic systems (2009), identical T chaotic systems (2008) and non-identical Li and T chaotic systems. In this paper, sufficient conditions for achieving anti-synchronization of the identical and non-identical Li and T systems are derived using active nonlinear control and our stability results are established using Lyapunov stability theory. Since the Lyapunov exponents are not required for these calculations, the active nonlinear feedback control method is effective and convenient to anti-synchronize the identical and non-identical Li and T chaotic systems. Numerical simulations are also given to illustrate and validate the anti-synchronization results for the chaotic systems addressed in this paper.

Keywords: Active control, anti-synchronization, chaotic systems, Li system, T system, nonlinear control.

1 Introduction

Chaotic systems are dynamical systems that are highly sensitive to initial conditions. This sensitivity is popularly referred to as the *butterfly effect* [1].

Since the pioneering work of Pecora and Carroll [2], chaos synchronization has attracted a great deal of attention from various fields and it has been extensively studied in the last two decades. Chaos theory has been explored in a variety of fields including physical [3], chemical [4], ecological [5] systems, secure communications ([6]-[7]). In the recent years, various schemes such as PC method [2], OGY method [8], active control ([9]-[10]), adaptive control [11], backstepping design method [12], sampled-data feedback synchronization method [13], sliding mode control method [14], etc. have been successfully applied to achieve chaos synchronization. Recently, active control has been applied to anti-synchronize two identical chaotic systems ([15]-[16]) and different hyperchaotic systems [17].

In most of the chaos synchronization approaches, the *master-slave* or *drive-response* formalism is used. If a particular chaotic system is called the *master* or *drive* system

D.C. Wyld et al. (Eds.): ACITY 2011, CCIS 198, pp. 175–184, 2011.

and another chaotic system is called the *slave* or *response* system, then the idea of anti-synchronization is to use the output of the master system to control the slave system so that the states of the slave system have the same amplitude but opposite signs as the states of the master system asymptotically. In other words, the sum of the states of the master and slave systems are expected to converge to zero asymptotically, when anti-synchronization appears.

In this paper, we derive new results for the global chaos anti-synchronization of identical Li systems (2009), identical T systems (2008) and non-identical Li and T systems.

This paper has been organized as follows. In Section 2, we give the problem statement and our methodology. In Section 3, we derive results for the anti-synchronization of identical Li systems ([18], 2009) using active control. In Section 4, we derive results for the anti-synchronization of identical T systems ([19], 2008) using active control. In Section 5, we derive results for the anti-synchronization of Li and T systems using active control. In Section 6, we present the conclusions of this paper.

2 Problem Statement and Our Methodology

Consider the chaotic system described by the dynamics

$$\dot{x} = Ax + f(x), \tag{1}$$

where $x \in \mathbb{R}^n$ is the state of the system, A is the $n \times n$ matrix of the system parameters and f is the nonlinear part of the system. We consider the system (1) as the *master* or *drive* system.

As the *slave* or *response* system, we consider the following chaotic system described by the dynamics

$$\dot{y} = By + g(y) + u \tag{2}$$

where $y \in \mathbb{R}^n$ is the state of the slave system, B is the $n \times n$ matrix of the system parameters, g is the nonlinear part of the system and u is the controller of the slave system.

If $A = B$ and $f = g$, then x and y are the states of two *identical* chaotic systems. If $A \neq B$ and $f \neq g$, then x and y are the states of two *different* chaotic systems.

For the anti-synchronization of the chaotic systems (1) and (2) using active control, we design a feedback controller u, which anti-synchronizes the states of the master system (1) and the slave system (2) for all initial conditions $x(0), y(0) \in \mathbb{R}^n$.

If we define the *anti-synchronization error* as

$$e = y + x, \tag{3}$$

then the error dynamics is obtained as

$$\dot{e} = By + Ax + g(y) + f(x) + u \tag{4}$$

Thus, the global anti-synchronization problem is essentially to find a feedback controller (*active control*) u so as to stabilize the error dynamics (4) for all initial conditions, *i.e.*

$$\lim_{t \to \infty} \|e(t)\| = 0, \quad \forall\, e(0) \in \mathbb{R}^n \tag{5}$$

We use the Lyapunov stability theory as our methodology. We take as a candidate Lyapunov function

$$V(e) = e^T P e,$$

where P is a positive definite matrix. Note that V is a positive definite function by construction. We assume that the parameters of the master and slave systems are known and that the states of both systems (1) and (2) are available for measurement.

If we find a feedback controller u so that

$$\dot{V}(e) = -e^T Q e$$

where Q is a positive definite matrix, then V is a negative definite function on $\mathbb{R}^n$.

Thus, by Lyapunov stability theory [20], the error dynamics (4) is globally exponentially stable and hence the the states of the master system (1) and slave system (2) will be globally exponentially anti-synchronized.

3 Anti-synchronization of Identical Li Systems

In this section, we apply the active nonlinear control method for the anti-synchronization of two identical Li systems ([18], 2009).

Thus, the master system is described by the Li dynamics

$$\begin{aligned} \dot{x}_1 &= a(x_2 - x_1) \\ \dot{x}_2 &= x_1 x_3 - x_2 \\ \dot{x}_3 &= b - x_1 x_2 - c x_3 \end{aligned} \tag{6}$$

where x_1, x_2, x_3 are the state variables and a, b, c are positive real constants.

When $a = 5, b = 16$ and $c = 1$, the Li system (6) is chaotic as shown in Figure 1.

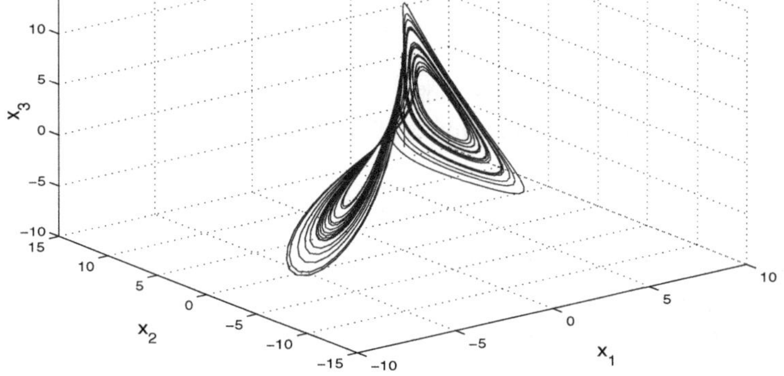

Fig. 1. The Li Chaotic System

The slave system is also described by the Li dynamics

$$\begin{aligned} \dot{y}_1 &= a(y_2 - y_1) + u_1 \\ \dot{y}_2 &= y_1 y_3 - y_2 + u_2 \\ \dot{y}_3 &= b - y_1 y_2 - c y_3 + u_3 \end{aligned} \tag{7}$$

where y_1, y_2, y_3 are the state variables and u_1, u_2, u_3 are the nonlinear controllers to be designed.

The anti-synchronization error is defined by

$$e_i = y_i + x_i, \quad (i = 1, 2, 3) \tag{8}$$

A simple calculation yields the error dynamics as

$$\begin{aligned} \dot{e}_1 &= a(e_2 - e_1) + u_1 \\ \dot{e}_2 &= -e_2 + y_1 y_3 + x_1 x_3 + u_2 \\ \dot{e}_3 &= 2b - c e_3 - (x_1 x_2 + y_1 y_2) + u_3 \end{aligned} \tag{9}$$

We choose the nonlinear controller as

$$\begin{aligned} u_1 &= -a e_2 \\ u_2 &= -y_1 y_3 - x_1 x_3 \\ u_3 &= -2b + x_1 x_2 + y_1 y_2 \end{aligned} \tag{10}$$

Substituting the controller u defined by (10) into (9), we get

$$\begin{aligned} \dot{e}_1 &= -a e_1 \\ \dot{e}_2 &= -e_2 \\ \dot{e}_3 &= -c e_3 \end{aligned} \tag{11}$$

We consider the candidate Lyapunov function

$$V(e) = \frac{1}{2} e^T e = \frac{1}{2} \left(e_1^2 + e_2^2 + e_3^2 \right) \tag{12}$$

which is a positive definite function on $\mathbb{R}^3$.

Differentiating V along the trajectories of (11), we find that

$$\dot{V}(e) = -a e_1^2 - e_2^2 - c e_3^2 \tag{13}$$

which is a negative definite function on $\mathbb{R}^3$ since a and c are positive constants.

Thus, by Lyapunov stability theory [20], the error dynamics (11) is globally exponentially stable. Hence, we have proved the following result.

Theorem 1. *The identical Li chaotic systems (6) and (7) are exponentially and globally anti-synchronized with the active nonlinear controller u defined by (10).* ■

Numerical Results

For the numerical simulations, the fourth order Runge-Kutta method with time-step 10^{-6} is used to solve the two systems of differential equations (6) and (7). We take the parameter values as $a = 5, b = 16$ and $c = 1$ so that the two Li systems (6) and (7) are chaotic. The active controller u is defined by (10).

The initial values of the master system (6) are taken as

$$x_1(0) = 28, \;\; x_2(0) = 12, \;\; x_3(0) = 10$$

and the initial values of the slave system (7) are taken as

$$y_1(0) = 16, \;\; y_2(0) = 25, \;\; y_3(0) = 30$$

Figure 2 shows the anti-synchronization between the states of the master system (6) and the slave system (7).

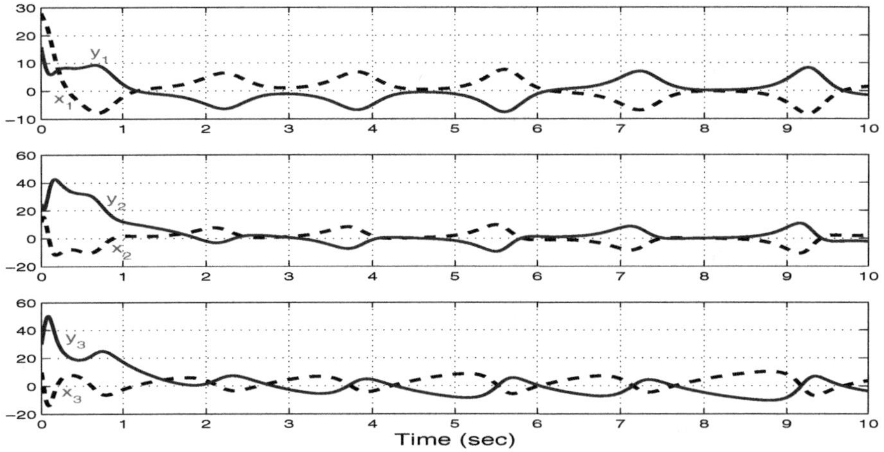

Fig. 2. Anti-synchronization of the Identical Li Chaotic Systems

4 Anti-synchronization of Identical T Systems

In this section, we apply the active nonlinear control method for the anti-synchronization of two identical T systems ([19], 2008).

Thus, the master system is described by the T dynamics

$$\begin{aligned} \dot{x}_1 &= \alpha(x_2 - x_1) \\ \dot{x}_2 &= (\gamma - \alpha)x_1 - \alpha x_1 x_3 \\ \dot{x}_3 &= -\beta x_3 + x_1 x_2 \end{aligned} \tag{14}$$

where x_1, x_2, x_3 are the state variables and α, β, γ are positive real constants.

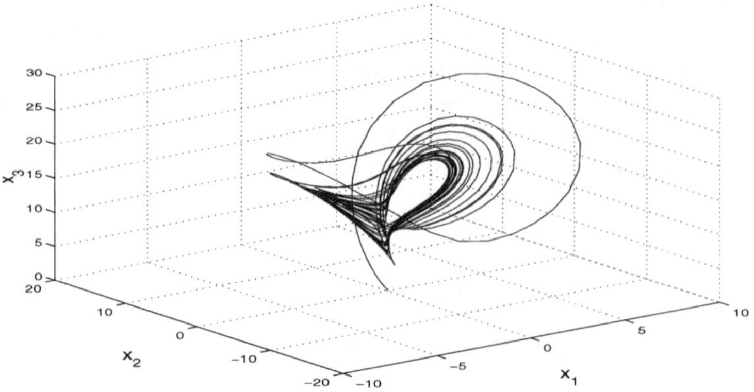

Fig. 3. The T Chaotic System

When $\alpha = 2.1, \beta = 0.6$ and $\gamma = 30$, the T system (14) is chaotic as shown in Figure 3.

The slave system is also described by the T dynamics

$$\begin{aligned}\dot{y}_1 &= \alpha(y_2 - y_1) + u_1\\ \dot{y}_2 &= (\gamma - \alpha)y_1 - \alpha y_1 y_3 + u_2\\ \dot{y}_3 &= -\beta y_3 + y_1 y_2 + u_3\end{aligned} \tag{15}$$

where y_1, y_2, y_3 are the state variables and u_1, u_2, u_3 are the nonlinear controllers to be designed.

The anti-synchronization error is defined by

$$e_i = y_i + x_i, \quad (i = 1, 2, 3) \tag{16}$$

A simple calculation yields the error dynamics as

$$\begin{aligned}\dot{e}_1 &= a(e_2 - e_1) + u_1\\ \dot{e}_2 &= (\gamma - \alpha)e_1 - \alpha(y_1 y_3 + x_1 x_3) + u_2\\ \dot{e}_3 &= -\beta e_3 + y_1 y_2 + x_1 x_2 + u_3\end{aligned} \tag{17}$$

We choose the nonlinear controller as

$$\begin{aligned}u_1 &= -\alpha e_2\\ u_2 &= (\alpha - \gamma)e_1 - e_2 + \alpha(y_1 y_3 + x_1 x_3)\\ u_3 &= -y_1 y_2 - x_1 x_2\end{aligned} \tag{18}$$

Substituting the controller u defined by (18) into (17), we get

$$\begin{aligned}\dot{e}_1 &= -\alpha e_1\\ \dot{e}_2 &= -e_2\\ \dot{e}_3 &= -\beta e_3\end{aligned} \tag{19}$$

We consider the candidate Lyapunov function

$$V(e) = \frac{1}{2}\, e^T e = \frac{1}{2}\, \left(e_1^2 + e_2^2 + e_3^2\right) \tag{20}$$

which is a positive definite function on $\mathbb{R}^3$.

Differentiating V along the trajectories of (19), we find that

$$\dot{V}(e) = -\alpha e_1^2 - e_2^2 - \beta e_3^2 \tag{21}$$

which is a negative definite function on $\mathbb{R}^3$ since α and β are positive constants.

Thus, by Lyapunov stability theory [20], the error dynamics (19) is globally exponentially stable. Hence, we have proved the following result.

Theorem 2. *The identical T chaotic systems (14) and (15) are exponentially and globally anti-synchronized with the active nonlinear controller u defined by (18).* ∎

Numerical Results

For the numerical simulations, the fourth order Runge-Kutta method with time-step 10^{-6} is used to solve the two systems of differential equations (14) and (15). We take the parameter values as $\alpha = 2.1, \beta = 0.6$ and $\gamma = 30$ so that the two T systems (14) and (15) are chaotic. The active controller u is defined by (18).

The initial values of the master system (14) are taken as

$$x_1(0) = 10, \;\; x_2(0) = 22, \;\; x_3(0) = 30$$

and the initial values of the slave system (15) are taken as

$$y_1(0) = 26, \;\; y_2(0) = 40, \;\; y_3(0) = 14$$

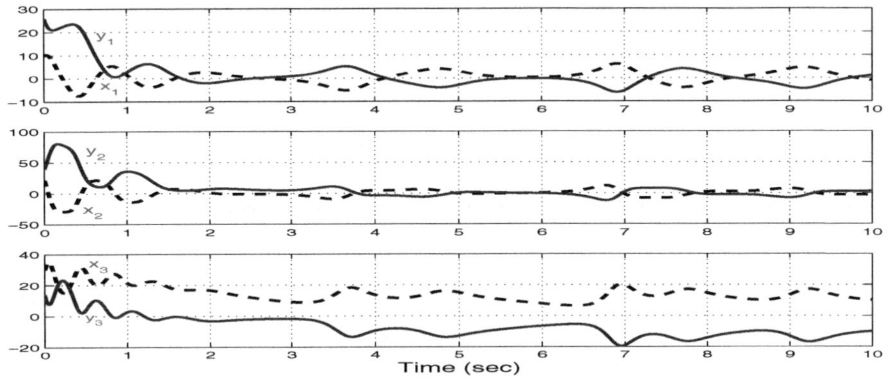

Fig. 4. Anti-synchronization of the Identical T Chaotic Systems

Figure 4 shows the anti-synchronization between the states of the master system (14) and the slave system (15).

5 Anti-synchronization of Li and T Chaotic Systems

In this section, we apply the active nonlinear control method for the anti-synchronization of non-identical Li and T chaotic systems.

As the master system, we consider the Li system ([18], 2009) described by

$$\begin{aligned}\dot{x}_1 &= a(x_2 - x_1)\\ \dot{x}_2 &= x_1x_3 - x_2\\ \dot{x}_3 &= b - x_1x_2 - cx_3\end{aligned} \tag{22}$$

where x_1, x_2, x_3 are the states of the system and a, b, c are positive real constants.

As the slave system, we consider the T system ([19], 2008) described by

$$\begin{aligned}\dot{y}_1 &= \alpha(y_2 - y_1) + u_1\\ \dot{y}_2 &= (\gamma - \alpha)y_1 - \alpha y_1y_3 + u_2\\ \dot{y}_3 &= -\beta y_3 + y_1y_2 + u_3\end{aligned} \tag{23}$$

where y_1, y_2, y_3 are the states of the system, α, β, γ are positive real constants and u_1, u_2, u_3 are the nonlinear controllers to be designed.

The anti-synchronization error is defined by

$$e_i = y_i + x_i, \quad (i = 1, 2, 3) \tag{24}$$

A simple calculation yields the error dynamics as

$$\begin{aligned}\dot{e}_1 &= \alpha(e_2 - e_1) + (a - \alpha)(x_2 - x_1) + u_1\\ \dot{e}_2 &= (\gamma - \alpha)e_1 - e_2 + y_2 - (\gamma - \alpha)x_1 - \alpha y_1y_3 + x_1x_3 + u_2\\ \dot{e}_3 &= b - \beta e_3 + (\beta - c)x_3 + y_1y_2 - x_1x_2 + u_3\end{aligned} \tag{25}$$

We choose the nonlinear controller as

$$\begin{aligned}u_1 &= -\alpha e_2 - (a - \alpha)(x_2 - x_1)\\ u_2 &= -(\gamma - \alpha)y_1 - y_2 + \alpha y_1y_3 - x_1x_3\\ u_3 &= -b - (\beta - c)x_3 - y_1y_2 + x_1x_2\end{aligned} \tag{26}$$

Substituting the controller u defined by (26) into (25), we get

$$\begin{aligned}\dot{e}_1 &= -\alpha e_1\\ \dot{e}_2 &= -e_2\\ \dot{e}_3 &= -\beta e_3\end{aligned} \tag{27}$$

We consider the candidate Lyapunov function

$$V(e) = \frac{1}{2}\, e^T e = \frac{1}{2}\, \left(e_1^2 + e_2^2 + e_3^2\right) \tag{28}$$

which is a positive definite function on $\mathbb{R}^3$.

Differentiating V along the trajectories of (27), we find that

$$\dot{V}(e) = -\alpha e_1^2 - e_2^2 - \beta e_3^2 \tag{29}$$

which is a negative definite function on $\mathbb{R}^3$ since α and β are positive constants.

Thus, by Lyapunov stability theory [20], the error dynamics (27) is globally exponentially stable. Hence, we have proved the following result.

Theorem 3. *The Li system (22) and the T system 23) are exponentially and globally anti-synchronized with the active nonlinear controller u defined by (26).* ■

Numerical Results

For the numerical simulations, the fourth order Runge-Kutta method with time-step 10^{-6} is used to solve the two systems of differential equations (22) and (23) with the active nonlinear controller u defined by (26). The parameter values are chosen so that the Li and T systems exhibit chaotic behaviour, *i.e.*

$$a = 5,\ b = 16,\ c = 1,\ \alpha = 2.1,\ \ \beta = 0.6 \ \text{ and } \ \gamma = 30$$

The initial values of the master system (22) are taken as

$$x_1(0) = 32,\ \ x_2(0) = 24,\ \ x_3(0) = 12$$

and the initial values of the slave system (23) are taken as

$$y_1(0) = 20,\ \ y_2(0) = 11,\ \ y_3(0) = 28$$

Figure 5 shows the anti-synchronization between the states of the master system (22) and the slave system (23).

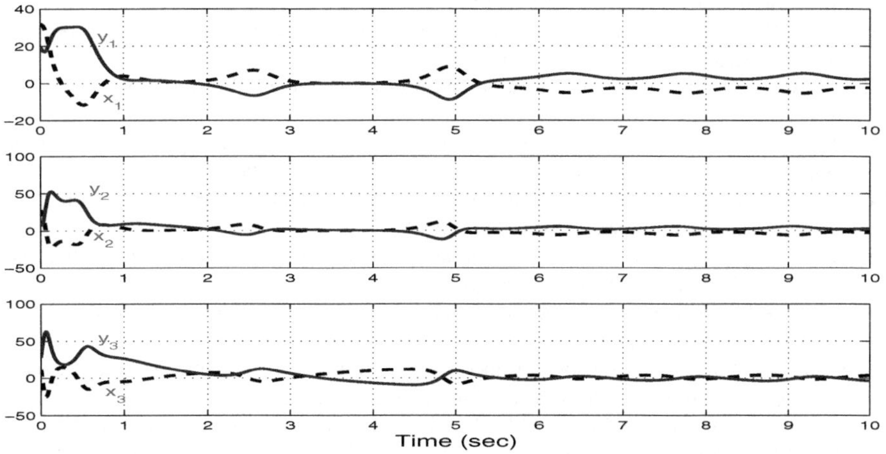

Fig. 5. Synchronization of the Li and T Chaotic Systems

6 Conclusions

In this paper, we have used nonlinear control method based on Lyapunov stability theory to achieve global chaos synchronization for the identical Li systems (2009), identical T systems (2008) and non-identical Li and T systems. Numerical simulations are also given to illustrate the effectiveness of the synchronization schemes derived in this paper. Since the Lyapunov exponents are not required for these calculations, the nonlinear control method is very effective and convenient to achieve global chaos synchronization for the chaotic systems addressed in this paper.

References

1. Alligood, K.T., Sauer, T., Yorke, J.A.: Chaos: An Introduction to Dynamical Systems. Springer, New York (1997)
2. Pecora, L.M., Carroll, T.L.: Synchronization in chaotic systems. Phys. Rev. Lett. 64, 821–824 (1990)
3. Lakshmanan, M., Murali, K.: Chaos in Nonlinear Oscillators: Controlling and Synchronization. World Scientific, Singapore (1996)
4. Han, S.K., Kerrer, C., Kuramoto, Y.: Dephasing and bursting in coupled neural oscillators. Phys. Rev. Lett. 75, 3190–3193 (1995)
5. Blasius, B., Huppert, A., Stone, L.: Complex dynamics and phase synchronization in spatially extended ecological system. Nature 399, 354–359 (1999)
6. Cuomo, K.M., Oppenheim, A.V.: Circuit implementation of synchronized chaos with application to communication. Phys. Rev. Lett. 71, 65–68 (1993)
7. Kocarev, L., Parlitz, U.: General approach for chaotic synchronization with applications to communications. Phys. Rev. Lett. 74, 5028–5031 (1995)
8. Ott, E., Grebogi, C., Yorke, J.A.: Controlling chaos. Phys. Rev. Lett. 64, 1196–1199 (1990)
9. Ho, M.C., Hung, Y.C.: Synchronization of two different chaotic systems by using generalized active control. Phys. Lett. A. 301, 424–428 (2002)
10. Chen, H.K.: Global chaos synchronization of new chaotic systems via nonlinear control. Chaos, Solit. Fract. 23, 1245–1251 (2005)
11. Lu, J., Wu, X., Han, X., Lu, J.: Adaptive feedback synchronization of a unified chaotic system. Phys. Lett. A. 329, 327–333 (2004)
12. Wu, X., Lü, J.: Parameter identification and backstepping control of uncertain Lü system. Chaos, Solit. Fract. 18, 721–729 (2003)
13. Murali, K., Lakshmanan, M.: Secure communication using a compound signal using sampled-data feedback. Applied Math. Mech. 11, 1309–1315 (2003)
14. Yau, H.T.: Design of adaptive sliding mode controller for chaos synchronization with uncertainties. Chaos, Solit. Fract. 22, 341–347 (2004)
15. Li, G.H.: Synchronization and anti-synchronization of Colpitts oscillators using active control. Chaos, Solit. Fract. 26, 87–93 (2005)
16. Hu, J.: Adaptive control for anti-synchronization of Chua's chaotic system. Phys. Lett. A. 339, 455–460 (2005)
17. Zhang, X., Zhu, H.: Anti-synchronization of two different hyperchaotic systems via active and adaptive control. Internat. J. Nonlinear Sci. 6, 216–223 (2008)
18. Li, X.F., Chlouverakis, K.E., Xu, D.L.: Nonlinear dynamics and circuit realization of a new chaotic flow: A variant of Lorenz, Chen and Lü. Nonlinear Anal. 10, 2357–2368 (2009)
19. Tigan, G., Opris, D.: Analysis of a 3-D chaotic system. Chaos, Solit. Fract. 36, 1315–1319 (2008)
20. Hahn, W.: The Stability of Motion. Springer, New York (1967)

Message Encoding in Nucleotides

Rahul Vishwakarma[1], Satyanand Vishwakarma[2], Amitabh Banerjee[3], and Rohit Kumar[4]

[1] Tata Consultancy Services, Chennai, India
derahul@ieee.org
[2] National Institute of Technology - Patna, India
Electronics and Communication Engineering
[3] HCL Technologies Ltd, India
[4] SRM University, India
Computer Science and Engineering

Abstract. This paper suggests a message encoding scheme in nucleotide strand for small text les. The proposed scheme leads to ultra high volume data density and depends on adoption of transformation algorithms like, Burrow-Wheeler transformation and Move to Front for generating better context information. Huffman encoding further compresses the transformed text message. We used a mapping function to encode message in nucleotide from the binary strand and tested the suggested scheme on collection of small text size les. The testing result showed the proposed scheme reduced the number of nucleotides for representing text message over existing methods.

Keywords: encoding, nucleotides, compression, text files.

1 Introduction

DNA consists of double stranded polymers of four different nucleotides: adenine (A), cytosine (C), guanine (G) and thymine (T). The primary role of DNA is long-term storage of genetic information. This feature of DNA is analogous to a digital data sequence where two binary bits 0 and 1 are used to store the digital data. This analogous nature of DNA nucleotide with Binary Bits can be exploited to use artificial nucleotide data memory [1] [2]. For example, small text message can be encoded into synthetic nucleotide sequence and can be inserted into genome of living organisms for long term data storage. Further, to enhance the data density for encoded message, original text message can be compressed prior to encoding.

Currently, there exist many losses-less compression algorithms for large text les. All of them need sufficient context information for compression, but context information in small le (50 kB to 100 kB) is difficult to obtain. In small les, context information is sufficient context information only when we process them by characters. Character based compression is most suitable for small les up to 100 kB. Thus we need a good compression algorithm [3], which requires only small context or we need an algorithm that transforms data into another form. An alternative approach

D.C. Wyld et al. (Eds.): ACITY 2011, CCIS 198, pp. 185–191, 2011.

is to use Burrow Wheeler transform followed by Move to Front transform. The Huffman encoding is used to convert the original file into compressed one.

The paper suggests a compression scheme for small text message with an introduction of mapping table to encode the data into nucleotide sequence to increase the data density. The organization of paper will be as follows: Section 2 presents a method for data preparation using transforms and compression scheme. Section 3 describes the mapping function for encoding the message into nucleotide sequence. Section 4 describes the method for message encoding and retrieval. Section 5 shows the performance result, and Section 6 contains the conclusion of this paper.

2 Prior Works

There has been much advancement in the use of DNA as a data storage device. One of the most critical step in the realization of biological data storage is the conversion of digital data to nucleotide sequence. Below are few mentioned works which tried to encode the information to be stored in biological sequence.

Battail proposed the idea of using hereditary media as a media for information transmission in communication process.[4] Shuhong Jiao devised a code for DNA based cryptography and steganocryptography and implemented in artificial component of DNA.[5] Nozomu Yachie used keyboard scan codes for converting the information to be encoded into hexadecimal value and finally binary values. The last step was to translate the bit data sequence into four multiple oligonucleotide sequence. This was mapped with the nucleotide base pairs.[6] Chinese University of Hong Kong used Quaternary number system to transform the information for mapping it to nucleotides. First they obtained ASCII vale of the information and used the mapping table 0=A, 1=T, 2=C and 3=G for the formation of nucleotide strand. In this method of encoding nucleotides the number of binary bits used for representing the digital information was same as the nucleotide strand. [7].

3 Data Preparation

3.1 Context Information

Currently there are many compression methods that require good context in order to achieve a good compression ratio. One of them is Burrow Wheeler transform [8] [9]. BWT can achieve good compression ratio provided that there is a sufficient context which is formed by frequent occurrence of symbols with same or similar prefixes. Maximizing the context leads to better compression ratio. The Burrow Wheeler algorithm is based on the frequent occurrence of symbol pairs in similar context and it uses this feature for obtaining long strings of the same characters. These strings can be transformed to another form with move to front (MTF) transformation.

3.2 Compression

We used statistical compression method [10] to compress the data obtained after transformation. The chosen statistical compression scheme was Huffman encod-ing [11].

Input consists of alphabet A and set W represented in equation (1) and (2) respectively. Output is a set of binary sequence in equation (3), which must satisfy the goal (4) for all the codes with the given condition [12].

$$A = \{a_1, a_2,\ldots,a_n\} \tag{1}$$

$$W = \{w_1, w_2,\ldots,w_n\} \tag{2}$$

$$w_i = weight(a_i), 1<i< n$$

$$C(A,W) = \{c_1, c_2,\ldots,c_n\} \tag{3}$$

$$L(C) = \sum_{i=1}^{n} w_i \times length(i) \tag{4}$$

$$L(C) \leq L(T)$$

4 Mapping Function

4.1 Mapping Table

Mapping table consists of binary bits and nucleotides. Binary value is repre-sented as 0 and 1. Nucleotides are represented as A, C, G and T. Four binary bits are represented by two nucleotide base pairs resulting in sixteen such combinations as shown in Mapping Table [13]. The reason for choosing four bits for two nucleotides is that the output of Huffman encoding here is Hexadecimal value (radix =16). So we need sixteen such combinations to represent this in binary and then nucleotides.

Mapping Table

Binary - nts.	Binary - nts.	Binary - nts.	Binary - nts.
0000 - AA	0100 - AC	1000 - AG	1100 - AT
0001 - CA	0101 - CC	1001 - CG	1101 - CT
0010 - GA	0110 - GC	1010 - GG	1110 - GT
0011 - TA	0111 - TC	1011 - TG	1111 - TT

4.2 Encryption

The encoded message must be encrypted in order to maintain its security [14]. For this purpose One time pad encryption is used. The requirement for one time pad is that the number of bits of random key must be the same length as of the message to be encoded. The encryption is processed character by character. The secrecy property of the encrypted message depends upon the generated random pad and the decryption of the message is impossible without knowing the true random key and makes it mathematically unbreakable [15].

5 Messgae Encoding and Retrieval

We have implemented the data encoding in nucleotides by integrating the transformation algorithm with statistical compression scheme. Here we have demonstrated our encoding and message retrieval scheme on small text: OPERATION BARBAROSSA.

The first step was to perform Burrow wheeler transform and move to front transform on the original text. This was done to generate better context infor-mation and obtain high compression ratio.

The security of the encoded message was maintained by encryption method. The encryption method used was One Time Pad where a randomly generated binary strand was XORed with the binary strand obtained from Huffman en-coding. We used a random function generator for generating the random binary sequence. Only in the last step, Huffman encoding method was introduced which compressed the original text message to a much smaller size. The next step to-ward message encoding was to use mapping table. The generated binary strand obtained after Huffman encoding was mapped to nucleotides according to the mapping table.

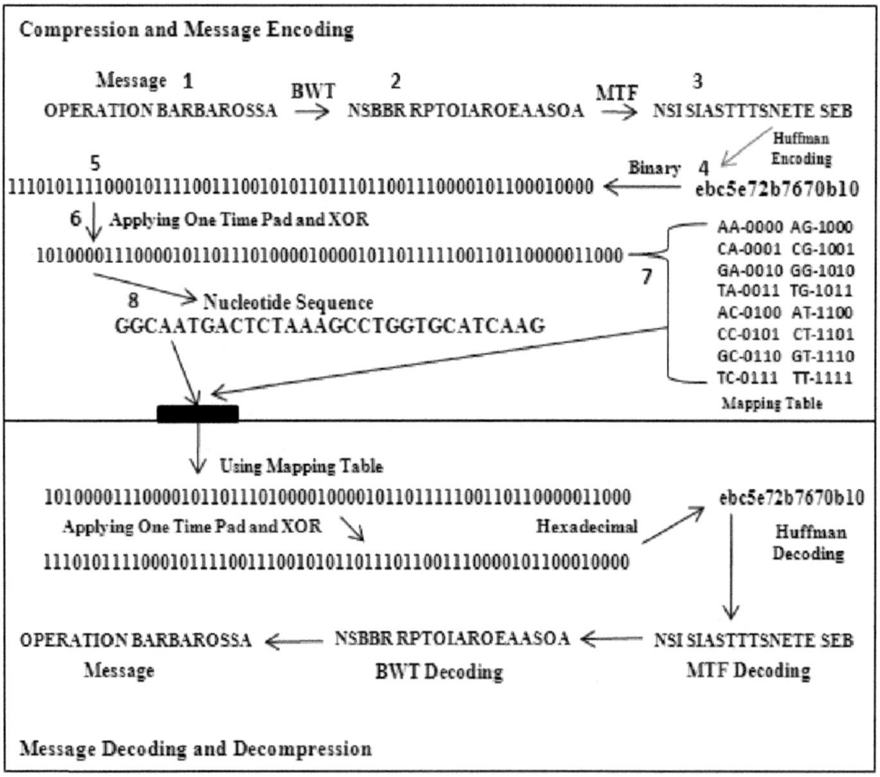

Fig. 1. Message encoding and decoding scheme in nucleotides

Second phase of our work was to convert the encrypted binary strand into nucleotide sequence. Although many other mapping functions can be used, but for our convenience we used two nucleotides to represent four binary bits, as hexadecimal (radix =16) value is being converted to four bit binary representation and thus leading to formulation of original text message in form of nucleotide sequence.

The decoding of message can be performed by reversing the encoding scheme. This is explained in Figure 1. This nucleotide sequence can be arti cially synthesized and inserted into the host to maintain the attributes of hereditary media and durable data storage for intensive period of time [1]. We have not proceeded in implementing the biological protocols to insert the sequence in genome of bacteria.

6 Performance

The suggested method was compared with two different methods on a set of les. The les that we used for testing is available at http://testdata.idlecool.net. This is a collection of single line texts. The original form was used for compression and encoding scheme.

The first method was comparison of nt-1 and nt-3, where nt-1 represents the number of nucleotides used to represent the original text message after converting the text message to binary and mapping it with nucleotides, and nt-3 represents the number of nucleotides obtained after encoding the nucleotide sequence after performing transformation and then applying compression algorithm on the same text message. In this algorithm, Burrow-Wheeler-Transformation and Move to Front transform was applied to the text message.

The comparison in the second method was used for demonstrating the im-portance of context information generation using transformation algorithm. Here we compared nt-2 and nt-3 , where nt-2 represents the number of nucleotides obtained after encoding then nucleotides without applying transformation algorithm and nt-3 with transformation algorithm on the same text le. The compression efficiency was tested with many tests over several les. The size of text les chosen varied from 140 Bits to 700 Bits.

Experimental result showed that the maximal compression efficiency was achieved by applying transformation in the first step. This transformation gen-erates better context information needed to compress text les of very small size (1000 Bytes). Result for encoding nucleotides without performing transform is depicted in the Figure 3. This shows that transformation prior to compression reduces the number of nucleotides to represent the same text message. The mean compression factor for the eight tested le was 2.076. As can be seen form results above, our algorithm for small message is better when incorporated with transformation algorithm. Even though, the difference in compression factor was 0.294. This is a step toward reducing the number of nucleotides for message strand and consecutively reducing the cost factor in artificially synthesizing the nucleotide strand for encoding message.

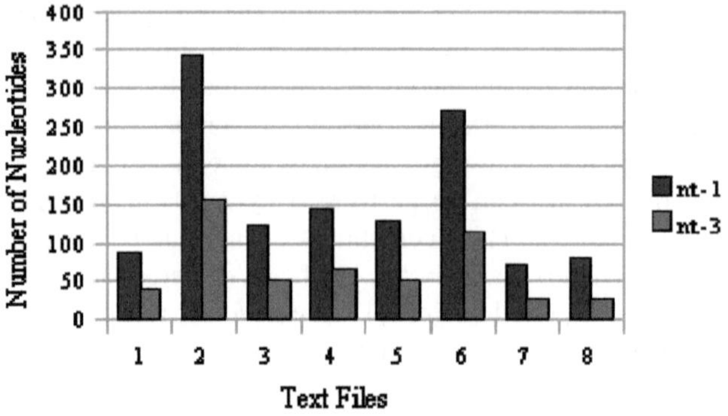

Fig. 2. Comparison between nt-1 and nt-3

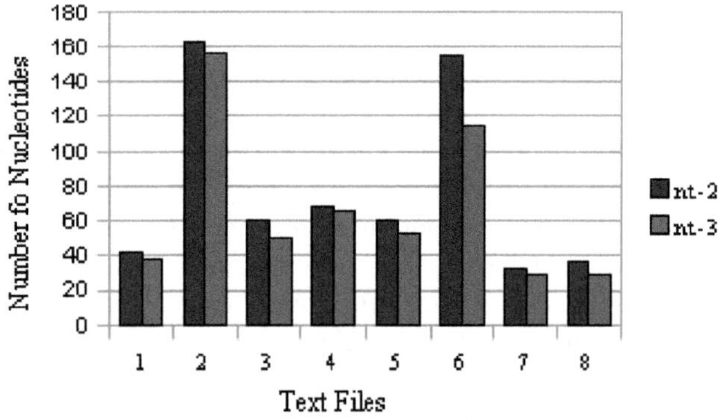

Fig. 3. Comparison between nt-2 and nt-3

7 Conclusion

This paper describes a data encoding method to achieve high volume data den-sity by reducing the number of nucleotides. The primary focus of this study was to encode data for les of very small size.

Data encoding method was performed into two steps. The first step was to compress the original text message. This was achieved using transformation and compression algorithm. Second step was introduction of Mapping table, which finally maps the binary strand to nucleotide sequence.

The contribution of this study are summarized as follows. First, while ma-jority of previous experiments just mapped the binary strand to nucleotide sequence, this study reduced the number of nucleotides to represent the same in-formation, finally reducing the cost factor for artificially synthesizing nucleotide strand in laboratory. Second, this study uses transformation on original text message prior to compression to achieve better context information, resulting in a compression factor of 2.37.

This scheme may be useful for many applications which need to store small message for long period of time, e.g. military implications, signatures of living modified organism (LMOs) and as valuable heritable media. Future work may focus on modification of transformation algorithm and designing other mapping function for encoding nucleotide sequence.

References

1. Cox, J.P.: Long-term data storage in DNA. Trends Biotechnol. 19, 247–250 (2001)
2. Bancroft, C., Bowler, T., Bloom, B., Clelland, C.T.: Long-term storage of information in DNA. Science 293, 1763–1765 (2001)
3. Ziviani, N., Moura, E., Navarro, G., Baeza-Yates, R.: Compression: a key for next-generation text reyrival systems. IEEE Computer 33, 37–44 (2000)
4. Battail, G.: Heredity as an Encoded Communication Process. IEEE Transactions on Information Theory 56(2), 678–687 (2010)
5. Jiao, S., Goutte, R.: Code for encryption hiding data into genomic DNA of living organisms. In: Signal Processing ICSP 2008. pp. 2166–2169 (2008)
6. Yachie, N., Sekiyma, K., Sugahara, J., Ohashi, Y., Tomita, M.: Alignement- Based Approach for Durable Data Storage into Living Organ-isms. Biotechnol. Prog. 23, 501–505 (2007)
7. Chinese University of Hong Kong, `http://www.cuhk.edu.hk/cpr/pressrelease/101124e.htm`
8. Lansky, J., Chernik, K., Vlickova, Z.: Comparison of Text Models for BWT. In: Data Compression Conference, DCC 2007, p. 389 (March 2007)
9. Burrows, M., Wheeler, D.J.: A block-sorting lossless data compression algorithm. Technical Reprot, Digital System Research Center Research Reoprt 124 (1994)
10. Pandya, M.K.: Compression: efficiency of varied compression techniques. Technical Report, University of Brunnel, UK (2000)
11. Huffman, D.A.: A method for the construction of minimum-redundancy codes. Proceedings of IRE 40(9), 1098–1101 (1952)
12. Nelson, M., Gailly, J.L.: The Data Compression Book. M and T Books (1995)
13. Ercegovac, M.D., Lang, T., Moreno, J.: Introduction to Digital Systems. John Wiley and Sons Inc., Chichester (1999)
14. Clelland, C.T., Risca, V., Bancroft, C.: Hiding messages in DNA microdots. Nature 399, 533–534 (1999)
15. Shannon, C.: Communication Theory of Secrecy Systems. Bell System Tech-nical Journal 28(4), 656715 (1949)
16. Arita, M., Ohashi, Y.: Secret signatures inside genomic DNA. Biotechnol. Prog. 20, 1605–1607 (2004)

XIVD: Runtime Detection of XPath Injection Vulnerabilities in XML Databases through Aspect Oriented Programming

Velu Shanmughaneethi, Ra. Yagna Pravin, and S. Swamynathan

Department of Computer Science and Engineering
College of Engineering Guindy Campus
Anna university Chennai, India
shanneethi@nitttrc.ac.in, yagnapravin@gmail.com,
swamyns@annauniv.edu

Abstract. The growing acceptance of XML technologies for documents and protocols, it is logical that security should be integrated with XML solutions. In a web application, an improper user input is root cause for a wide variety of attacks. XML Path or XPath language is used for querying information from the nodes of an XML document. XPath Injection is an attack technique used to exploit applications that construct XPath (XML Path Language) queries from user-supplied input to query or navigate XML documents such as SQL in Databases. Hence, we proposed an approach to detect XPath injection attack in XML databases at runtime through Aspect Oriented Programming (AOP). Our approach intercept XPath expression i.e.) XQuery from the web application through Aspect Oriented Programming (AOP) and parse the XQuery expression to find the inputs to be placed in the expression. The identified inputs are used to design an XML file and it would be validated through a proposed schema. The validation results the correctness of the XQuery.

Keywords: XPath Injection, XQuery, Web Application Security, XSLT, XML Schema, XML Security, Command Injection.

1 Introduction

Web applications have become one of the most important communication channels between various kinds of service providers and clients. This dynamic application offering wide range of services, such as on-line stores, e-commerce, and social network services, etc. To meet seamless communication environment, security has always been vitally important in the information world to ensure the integrity of content and transactions, to maintain privacy and confidentiality, and to make sure information is used appropriately. However, in today's web-based environment, the means for providing that security have changed. Using physical security no longer works as well as it did in the past when all the computing resources were locked in a central computing room with all jobs submitted locally. Efforts to create a single pervasive security infrastructure do not scale effectively to the Internet, due to the heterogeneous nature of hardware and software systems and to conflicting

D.C. Wyld et al. (Eds.): ACITY 2011, CCIS 198, pp. 192–201, 2011.

administrative, application and security requirements. Although application-level firewalls offer immediate assurance of Web application security, but they have drawbacks like requires careful configuration, and they only for a Web application security assessment framework that offers black-boxed testing for identifying Web application vulnerabilities. Among many types of vulnerabilities, command injection vulnerability is quite common and it has become one of the most serious security threats in web applications. A command injection is an exploit of a system weakness to gain access to the system for the purpose of executing malicious code, harvesting user data, and engaging in other activities. In the category of command injection, an XPath Injection attacks may occur when a web site requires user-supplied information to construct an XQuery for XML data. XQuery is a powerful language designed for processing XML data. Today XPath injection is quite common, due to the accelerating use of Web services and use of XML documents instead relational databases or traditional flat files. Hence, XML data is more at risk when it comes to accepting poor input data for XPath parsers.

2 Literature Survey

Researchers have started to contribute in the area of XPath injection and its possible liabilities. Amit Kelvin [2] illustrates the nature of XPath injection attacks and its consequences. The paper presents the possible mechanisms of attacking an XPath query with different samples for each type. Jaime Blasco [3] provides a brief introduction to Xpath Injection Techniques and also compares it with another similar attack namely, SQL injection. The paper also portrays various scenarios where possible attacks can completely retrieve the XML document for a given attack query. It also highlights the un-availability of access rights for these XML databases which can be major reason for attack unlike normal RDBMS. Jinghua and Sven [7] describe the satisfiablility test for a XPath query. This defines the structure of the query and the possible optimization of the query for obtaining a desired result set. Dimitris et al, [4] described a novel way for detecting XPath injections. In this paper the location specific identifiers where used to validate the executable XPath code. These identifiers reflect the call sites within the application. The major disadvantage was any source code change required a training mode for re-assigning the identifiers. Nuno Antunes et al, [5] describe the detection of XPath injection in web services using AOP. They initially, instrumented the web service to intercept all XPath commands executed, and then they generate legitimate workload based on the web service operations through that learn XPath queries and then generated an attack load and finally detect vulnerability by comparison of both set. Gabriel et al [6] presents a framework named AProSec, which is a security aspect for detecting SQL injections and Cross Scripting Site (XSS).The authors define clearly the need for AOP for providing security to web applications.

3 XPath Injection

XPath is a standard language used to refer to parts of an XML document. It can be used directly by an application to query an XML document. Today, many organizations have adopted XML as a data format for everything from configuration files to remote procedure calls. So, like any other application or technology that allows outside user submission data, XML applications can be susceptible to code injection attacks, specifically XPath injection attacks. Moreover, its notation/syntax is always implementation independent, which means the attack may be automated. By sending intentionally malformed information into the web site, an attacker can find out how the XML data is structured, or the way to access data. An attacker may even be able to elevate the privileges on the web site if the XML data is being used for authentication and other transactions.

3.1 XPath Injection Motivation and Consequences

Website defacement which results in an unauthorized change to Web applications is the top motivation for hackers. In XPath injection, when a malicious user can insert arbitrary XPath code into the form fields and URL query parameters in order to inject this code directly into the XPath query parser engine. Doing so would allow a malicious user to bypass authentication (if an XML-based authentication system is used) or to access restricted data from the XML data source. This leads to privilege escalation and information leakage. Consider an application that uses XML database to authenticate its users. The application retrieves the user id and password from a request and forms an XPath expression to query the database. An attacker can successfully bypass authentication and login without valid credentials through XPath injection. Improper validation of user-controlled input and use of a non-parameterized XPath expression enable the attacker to injection an XPath expression that causes authentication bypass. For example, consider the xml document.

```
<?xml version="1.0"?>
<Login xmlns:xsi=http://www.w3.org/2001/XMLSchema-instance
xsi: noNamespaceSchemaLocation = "login.xsd">
<user><uname>shan</username> <passwd>neethi</passwd></user>
<user><uname>neethi</username> <passwd>mughan</passwd></user>
<user><uname>computer</username> <passwd>centre</passwd></user>
<user><uname>tamil</username> <passwd>chenai</passwd></user>
</Login>
```

The above XML document stores information about the registered user for the particular web application. To perform authentication for the user, a web application receives username and password from the user.

```
XPathExpression expr = xpath.compile("//Login/user[username/ text() =
'"+loginID+"'and passwd/text()='"+password+"' ]");
```

The user supplied username and password placed into the appropriate place of the XQuery to perform user validation. The following XQuery is generated in server and it would be sent to xml document for user validation.

```
("//Login/user[username/text()='shan' and passwd/text()='neethi' ]"
```

If the user name and password presented in the XML data then this will return true to the web page otherwise it will return false. This is a simple authentication procedure in web application which uses XML data as back-end service. If the attacker can craft the input, such way that, always the user becomes an authenticated user for a web site by XPath injection. For example the above XQuery can be crafted as the following XQuery

```
let $str := doc("login.xml")/Login/user
        return if ($str/username='shan' and $str/passwd=''or'1'='1' ) then
<b>true</b> else    <b>false</b>
```

Here, the password data is always true in this XQuery. So that, whenever such password is given to the password filed, the user authentication would be treated as a purely authenticated user for the web application. Although this attack grants the attacker access to the application, it does not necessarily grant them access as the most privileged account. In some cases, an attacker can further manipulate the XPath query to force the server to return various parts of the document. Hence, this XPath injection also leads to extracting document structure and modify the document information in addition to escalate privileges.

3.2 Preventive Measures for XPath Injection

XPath injection can be prevented in the same way as SQL injection since XPath injection attacks are much like SQL injection attacks. The common ways to prevent XPath Injections are *Strong input validation, Use of parameterized XPath queries and Use of custom error.* So, the developer has to ensure that the application does accept only legitimate input and another way is use parameterized queries to prevent XPATH injection. Even then, these methods are not consistent to prevent XPath injection in web applications[11]. Hence, we proposed a new approach for effective detection of XPath injection vulnerabilities by schema based validation of the user input that are provided to the web applications.

3.3 Aspect Oriented Programming

An Aspect Oriented Programming (AOP) module is designed to intercept XQuery that arise through the user inputs. Aspect-Oriented Programming (AOP) is a good candidate for designing security issues. AOP has been proposed as a technique for improving separation of concerns in software systems and for adding crosscutting functionalities without changing the business part of the application. AOP provides specific language mechanisms that make possible to address concerns, such as security, in a modular way. This module used for detecting malicious input values given by user for unearthing vulnerabilities present in the web application.

4 Proposed Approach

The proposed system involves a new approach for detecting XPath injection vulnerabilities in web applications shown in figure.1. This approach integrates with Aspect Oriented Programming (AOP) which is used for cross cutting concerns such as security. AOP provides code modularity and involves separation of business logic from common concerns such as logging, security, etc. An AOP plays a major role in the detection of XPath injection vulnerabilities by intercepting XQuery which framed by the input parameters.

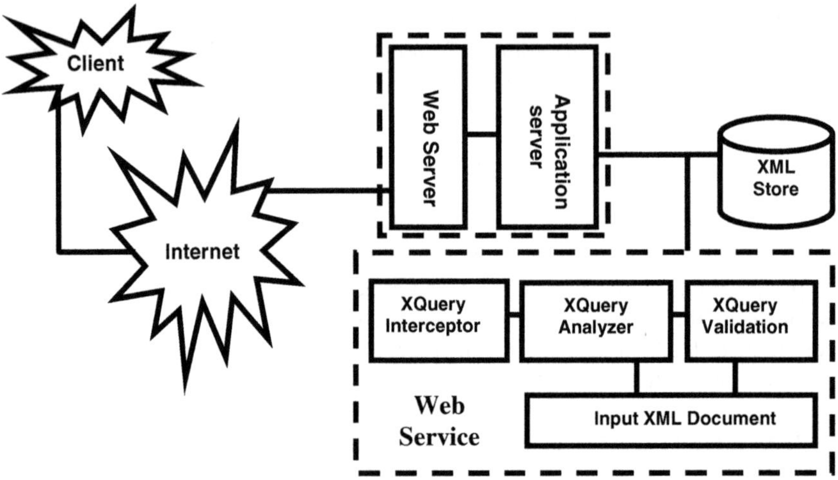

Fig. 1. Proposed XPath Detection Architecture

The above architecture describes the XPath injection detection technique implemented in a tool named XPath Injection Vulnerability Detector (XIVD). When the user provides the required inputs into the web forms, they are then placed into the XQuery in an appropriate place of the application. Finally, the complete XQuery string is generated for processing data transaction on XML databases. The generated (or framed) XQuery string may cause XPath injection in a web application. This attack is possible, only when the user inputs are passed directly to the web application. Sometime, illegitimate inputs may leads to bypass authentication or retrieve privileged XML data. The inputs that lead to XPath injection have to be prevented to run on the XML data. Moreover, the XPath injection is not restricted only by the web form input. It is also possible by HTTP header or by Cookie. But at end, all the inputs would be placed into the XQuery for run on XML data. Hence, our approach analyzes the XQuery for identifying the vulnerabilities and preventing XPath injection.

4.1 XQuery Interception

This module involves intercepting the user input that is would be associated in XQuery in web application. These input parameters are the source of the injection vulnerabilities and can be named as sink points since it provides the attacker with an opportunity to make use of vulnerable code. The input interception module is placed in web service section, which intercepts the input through AOP technique. Once the user provides the input in a client application, these values are given to web application server which in turn sends the input parameters to the web application. These input parameters may consist some of the malicious values. If these malicious values are directly passed to the application then, it may possibly unearth vulnerability. Hence it is necessary to intercept the user input parameters before the actual execution of the web service. The code defined in this module is used for intercepting the query. These methods are used for executing the query in order to obtain the results from the XML databases.

4.2 XQuery Analyzer

In this module the intercepted XQuery is analyzed and the input parameters are obtained in order to detect possible injections. The analyzer basically tokenizes the query and retrieves the input parameter. Different types of queries can also be tokenized in order user inputs. After obtaining the input parameters the detection of possible vulnerability should be done. This process needs to be generic and effective in order to detect any type of possible injection. Though several methods are available, a powerful technique is to use a XML (eXtensible Mark-up Language) file which would be validated by our proposed schema. This file is a well-formed document, platform indepented and provides lesser over head for validation. This module standardizes the detection process by using a simpler and effective way of generating a XML file for user provided inputs. This approach would help in decreasing the false positive rate because the identifying the vulnerabilities becomes more effective. This module is also a part of the AOP layer since this XML file is to be generated for whatever user input that is provided to the web service that connects to a XML database. For example consider the following query

("//Login/user[username/text()='raj' and passwd/text()='any' or '1'='1']")

After intercepting the query, the analyzer obtains the inputs from the query and stores them in a XML document. This document is then further used for validation in order to detect vulnerabilities.

```
<?xml version="1.0" encoding="UTF-8"?>
<XQuery>
<input>raj</input>
<input>any' or '1'='1'</input>
</Query>
```

Fig. 2. Sample XML file for the above query

Figure 2 illustrates a sample XML file that would be generated after the XQuery is intercepted. This XML file consists of only the input parameters that were given as user inputs from the client application. Further this can be used for validation in order to find if any injection is present.

4.3 XQuery Validation

The validation process is to identify the injected parameters with the help of our proposed schema and the generated XML file. Though several validation methods are possible, a XML schema is the most powerful and effective technique. The XML schema can be used to define the structure of the XML document and even provide various constraints for it. The proposed schema is a generalized meta data which define structure and type of user input is shown in figure 4.. Hence in our approach, a well defined XML schema is defined for detecting possible injection characters in the input values provided by the user.

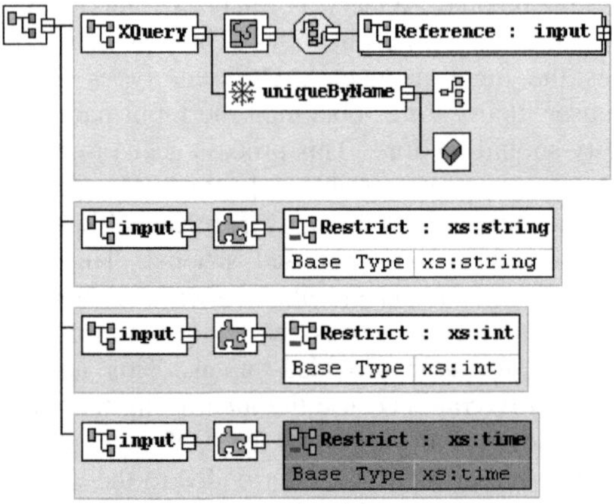

Fig. 3. Partial XML schema definition

The validation process identifies any possible injections in the input values. In case if the validation fails, the execution of the intended operation is stopped and a log file is generated indicating that an injection has occurred. If the validation process is passed, then the operation is allowed to execute and the desired results are obtained. Figure 3 depicts the partial schema for the proposed approach. The schema is vital in detecting injections in the inputs. Inputs can be of any type and hence the schema restricts values for each data type thereby providing an effective validation process.

The XML file generated from the previous module that consists of the user inputs is now validated with a well defined XML schema. If the validation passes then injection is not present in the input parameters, in case of failure the injection is logged in a log file.

Figure 4 illustrates a sample log file generated for a set of attack inputs that were tested. The log file clearly indicates the attack input mismatch with the schema thereby avoiding the injection to take place.

```
Mar 10, 2011 12:26:27 AM
ERROR: cvc-pattern-valid: Value "any or '1'='1'" is not facet-valid with respect to pattern '([a-zA-Z0-9]*[_.'$%^*()]+)' for
type '#AnonType_input'
Mar 9, 2011 1:00:37 AM
Mar 10, 2011 12:26:27 AM
ERROR: cvc-pattern-valid: Value "1=1" is not facet-valid with respect to pattern '([a-zA-Z0-9]*[_.'$%^*()]+)' for type
'#AnonType_input'
Mar 9, 2011 1:16:10 AM
ERROR: cvc-pattern-valid: Value " ' or 'a'='b'" is not facet-valid with respect to pattern '([a-zA-Z0-9]*[_.'$%^*()]+)' for type
'#AnonType_input'.
Mar 10, 2011 12:26:27 AM
ERROR: cvc-pattern-valid: Value "any or '1'='1'" is not facet-valid with respect to pattern '([a-zA-Z0-9]*[_.'$%^*()]+)' for
type '#AnonType_input'
```

Fig. 4. Sample log file generated for different attack inputs

5 Results and Discussions

To evaluate our proposed approach, we have analyzed the performance of the developed tool based on the response time with our XIVD based approach as well as without our approach. The response time in real web environment is collected and tabulated is shown in table1.

Table 1. Response Time Assessment

No. of Test	Response Time Without XIVD module (milli seconds)	Response Time With XIVD module (milli seconds)	Response Time Difference (ms)
1	94.25	125.35	30.85
2	109.25	155.45	46.25
3	156.75	195.35	39.40
4	98.50	115.45	16.95
5	125.45	175.45	50.0
6	156.75	200.50	43.75
7	88.50	140.75	52.25
8	95.45	157.75	62.3
9	112.25	156.50	44.25
10	105.50	135.50	35.0

The response time difference with our proposed approach is very minimal. The time delay between both module could be compromised when to compare the consequences of command injection. The following graph represents pictorial representation of response time assessment.

The following graph in figure 5 shows the comparison of the response time, between the proposed XIVD tool and without it. As shown in the graph, the XIVD does not bring a huge difference in the response time.

X – Axis represents Number of Test
Y – Axis represents Response Time

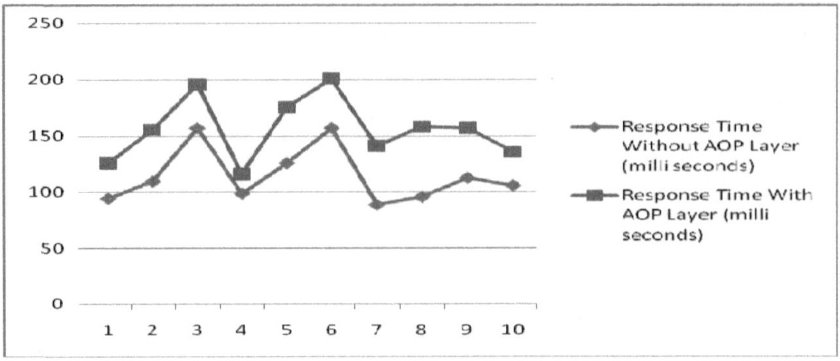

Fig. 5. Sample log file generated for different attack inputs

Since the XIVD is a modular approach, it can be very widely used in the case of security, logging, etc. When compared to other approach the over head was found to better.

6 Conclusion and Future Work

In this paper we have proposed a new approach for detecting XPath injection vulnerabilities using AOP. The AOP based approach is a very effective method for detecting vulnerabilities. Comparing with previous approaches, there can be a significant reduction in overhead and also less number of false positives can be achieved. The main advantage of this approach is that AOP provides modularity as well as avoids the need for changes in the source code of the application. We have analyzed the approach using our tool XIVD, with different web applications and found that the response time is limited. In future, we intend to analyze other forms of web attacks (namely XSS, CSRF) that are more common in the Internet.

References

[1] Su, Z., Wassermann, G.: The Essence of Command Injection Attacks in Web Applications. In: Proceedings of the Thirty Third ACM Symposium on Principles of Programming Languages, South Carolina, pp. 372–382 (2006)

[2] Kelvin, A.: Blind XPath Injection, a whitepaper from Watchfire, Director of Security and Research, Sanctum (2005)

[3] Blasco, J.: Introduction to XPath Injection Techniques. In: Hakin9, Conference on IT Underground, Czech Republic, pp. 23–31 (2007)

[4] Mitropoulos, D., Karakoidas, V., Spinellis, D.: Fortifying Applications against XPath Injection Attacks. In: MCIS 2009: 4th Mediterranean Conference on Information Systems, Athens, pp. 1169–1179 (2009)

[5] Antunes, N., Laranjeiro, N., Vieira, M., Madeira, H.: Effective Detection of SQL/XPath Injection Vulnerabilities in Web Services. In: IEEE International Conference on Services Computing, Portugal, pp. 260–267 (2009)

[6] Hermosillo, G., Gomez, R., Seinturier, L., Duchien, L.: Using Aspect Programming to Secure Web Applications. Journal of Software 6(2), 53–63 (2008)

[7] Groppe, J., Groppe, S.: Filtering unsatisfiable XPath queries. Journal Data & Knowledge Engineering 64(1), 134–169 (2008)

[8] XML Path Language (XPath) version 2.0, `http://www.w3.org/TR/XPath`

[9] OWASP Guide, `http://www.owasp.org/index.php/Blind_XPath_Injection`

[10] Vieira, M., Antunes, N., Madeira, H.: Using Web Security Scanners to Detect Vulnerabilities in Web Services. In: Intl.Conf. on Dependable Systems and Networks, Lisbon (2009)

[11] Laranjeiro, N., Vieira, M., Madeira, H.: Protecting Database Centric Web Services against SQL/XPath Injection Attacks. In: Bhowmick, S.S., Küng, J., Wagner, R. (eds.) DEXA 2009. LNCS, vol. 5690, pp. 271–278. Springer, Heidelberg (2009)

[12] Wu, R., Hisada, H., Ranaweera, R.: Static analysis of web security in generic syntax format. In: The International Conference on Internet Computing (ICOMP 2009), Las Vegas, NV, pp. 58–63 (2009)

[13] Gegick, M., Williams, L.: Toward the use of automated static analysis alerts for early identification of vulnerability- and attack-prone components, Research paper, North Carolina State University, Raleigh, NC (2009)

Multilevel Re-configurable Encryption and Decryption Algorithm

Manoharan Sriram, V. Vinay Kumar, Asaithambi Saranya, and E. Tamarai Selvam

Department of Computer Science and Engineering, Rajalakshmi Engineering College, Anna University, Chennai, Tamil Nadu, India
{sriramm17,vinaykumar1690,saranya.thj}@gmail.com,
selvamets@yahoo.co.in

Abstract. In the existing crypto graphical techniques, to increase the strength of encoding data and to keep the data secured against cryptanalysis, a Multi-Level Encryption algorithm with an Efficient Public Key System is proposed. The Multi-Level encryption steps up the strength of the algorithm by using five keys for encrypting each character, and it makes cryptanalysis impossible without detecting all the five keys. The key generation and distribution method suits the algorithm well, as the purpose of multilevel keys to enhance security step by step is followed while detecting the keys. The proposed algorithm possesses the property of re-configurability in which the logical set of operations performed to encrypt the data can be done in six ways. The keys are not of the static values, and each time a character is encrypted the key value changes, causing intruder getting perplexed. The encrypted data is represented in the patch of color form.

Keywords: Multilevel encryption, Public Key system, Key Counter, Configuration Key ASCII, RGB Color Model.

1 Introduction

The technique which assures secured transmission and reception of data by an encrypted form of information over the network is cryptography. Though cryptography took its effect thousands of years ago, its existence made a greater impact only after the invention of electronic computers [1]. There are many algorithms that have been proposed under the technique of cryptography. Each and every algorithm that has been accepted worldwide is known for its own strength and uniqueness. The newer method of cryptography is subdivided into two types: Secret key cryptography, Public key cryptography [2]. In this paper, a novel cryptographic algorithm is proposed based on public key system, with multi level encryption technique. This multilevel encryption technique has been used in defense messaging system with a different usage of access control at different levels [3]. The applicability of multi level encryption in our algorithm is for increasing the security

D.C. Wyld et al. (Eds.): ACITY 2011, CCIS 198, pp. 202–210, 2011.

level in the proposed algorithm. When, the number of keys used for encryption increases, the strength of algorithm also increases. The algorithm proposed here uses five keys, in which each key lifts the data to the next level of encryption. The five keys generated in the algorithm is based on secret key generated by Diffie hellman key exchange system. Here the encrypted data is sent to the receiving end with the distribution of sender's Public key, common key elements. This avoids the intrusion detection of keys at the transmission channel. The reconfigurable algorithms are well accepted for their dynamic behavior and the idea of reconfigurable encryption using FPGA Designs has been a promotable way for implementing it [4].The paper is structured with the depiction of architecture diagram, the algorithm for encryption and decryption process, encryption technique, decryption technique, and the experimental results of the proposed algorithm.

2 Architecture Diagram and System Design

The basic flow of the algorithm has input section, conversion section followed by encryption [5]. The flow of execution is reverse in decryption process. Fig. 1 represents the architecture diagram of the encryption and decryption process. The input section has the text file which consists of ASCII based characters. The conversion section does the work of converting characters into ASCII format. The three Multilevel Keys -Key1, Key2, and Key3 used to represent R-G-B Color representation respectively is used for Encryption purpose and they result in the stages of partial cipher text 1, 2 and cipher text respectively. It is converted to RGB Color representation and the resultant is an encrypted file which has the patch of colors where each color represents a character [6]. The file is transferred across the network and the decryption process follows the order of converting the cipher text, partial cipher text form of 2 and then 1 using Key3,Key2,Key1 keys respectively. The conversion section involves the conversion of ASCII character to readable text format which is the decrypted and original file. The algorithm for the encryption and decryption process is discussed below in a step by step manner [7]. Key values are applied with module function of 255,after processing each character.

2.1 Encryption Algorithm

Input: Text file, Secret key, Multilevel keys-Key1,Key2,Key3, key counter, configuration key, prime number chart, Configuration key chart,

Output: Encrypted file- RGB color representation of characters.

Method: RGB Encryption ()

Begin

1) Get the text file as input
2) Using Secret key generate Multilevel keys, key counter and Configuration key.
3) Read the configuration key.

4) Get the character of text file and convert it into ASCII format
5) Operate it with Multilevel Key1 using first logical operator of configuration key's order in configuration chart.
6) The resultant is partial cipher text 1 and it is processed with Multilevel Key2 using the second logical operator in configuration chart.
7) The resultant value is partial cipher text 2.Step 6 is repeated with Partial Cipher text 2 and Multilevel Key3 with third logical operator in key chart.
8) The resultant is Cipher text.
9) The partial cipher text 1, partial cipher text 2, cipher text is fed as the input value for R, G, B in RGB model respectively
10) Place the color formed for the character in buffer.
11) Increase the key by the key counter value for the next character encryption.
12) Repeat step 4 to step 11 till the end of file occurs.
13) Place the buffer data in the encrypted file.

End

2.2 Decryption Algorithm

Input: Encrypted file-RGB color representation of characters, Secret key, Multilevel keys-Key1,Key2,Key3,key counter, configuration key, prime number chart, Configuration key chart .

Output: Text file

Method: RGB Decryption ()

Begin

1) Get the encrypted text file
2) Using Secret key generate Multilevel keys, key counter and Configuration key
3) Access the Configuration key and determine the order of logical operations specified in the configuration key chart
4) The RGB color model is determined for each of the character in text file and the six digit hexadecimal RGB code is obtained.
5) The last two digits of the hexadecimal code obtained is the Cipher text, and is logically operated with Multilevel Key3 using third logical operator and this yields Partial Cipher text2.
6) Partial Cipher text2 is operated with Multilevel Key2 using second logical operator and this gives Partial cipher text 1.
7) Step 6 is repeated with partial cipher text 1 and Multilevel Key1 operated by first logical operator.
8) This yields the ASCII character of the text.
9) Convert the ASCII to original text and store it in buffer.
10) Increase the key by the key counter value for each character.
11) Repeat steps 4 to 10 till the end of file occurs
12) Place the buffer data in the decrypted file.

End

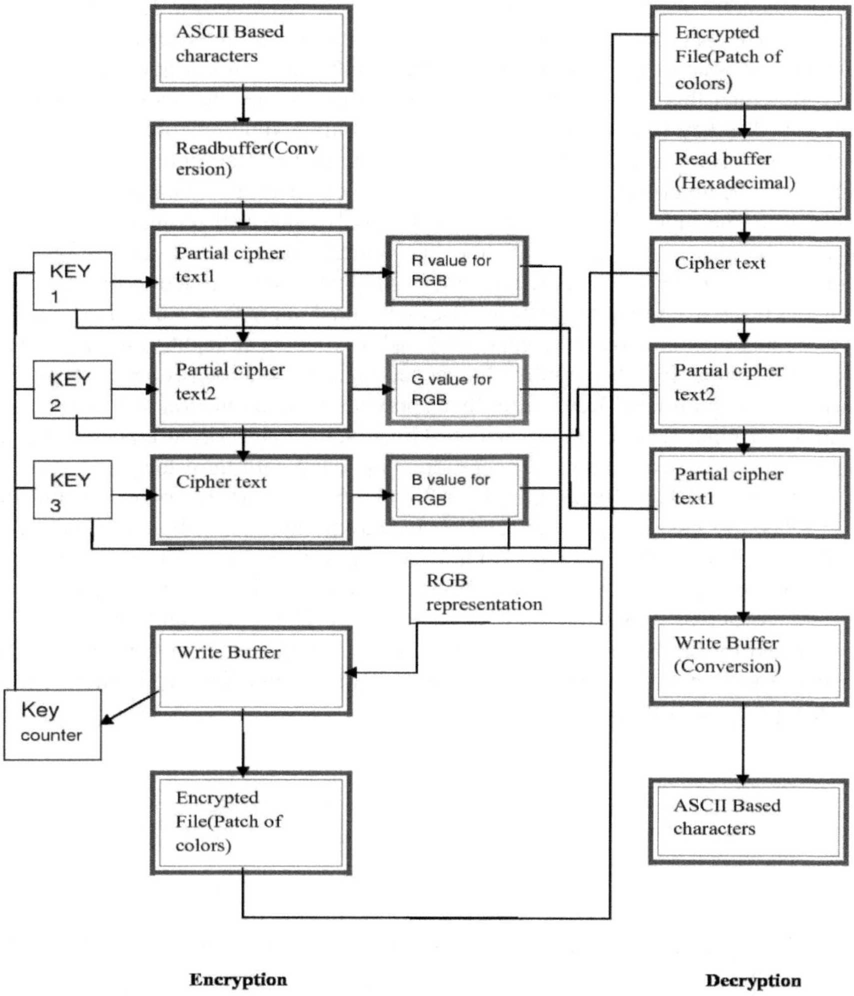

Fig. 1. Architecture diagram of Encryption and Decryption Process

3 Encryption

The multilevel reconfigurable encryption and decryption algorithm enhances the properties of cryptosystem by encrypting the data at multilevel and by designing a reconfigurable encryption method with the dynamic change in key values. Fig 2 represents the flow of encryption process. The algorithm uses the multi level keys along with a key counter and configuration key .The Multilevel keys, Key counter, Configuration key are generated by the secret key, which is generated by diffie hellman Key exchange process. Key generation is discussed in the part of key distribution and generation section. The configuration key, which is generated in key generation process, determines the logical operation structure.

Fig 4 denotes the Configuration key chart for determining the logical operation structure. The key counter, which is based on multilevel keys, contributes to the dynamic key system. The key counter increments the value of key at each character's encryption, and this involves the avoidance of vulnerability that can be posed by a static key. The key values is made to be applied with module function of 255.The set of characters from a text file is fed as an input for the algorithm, which is to be encrypted. The algorithm performs the encryption character by character. A character is read from the input file and its equivalent ASCII value is determined. The ASCII value of the character is applied to the first logical operation (as per configuration chart) with the multilevel Key1, after then applying modulo function of value 255, since 255 is the maximum value of RGB Color model-value for a color. The value we get from this section is partial cipher text1 and it is fed as an input to the RGB color model -Red value, It is then applied for second logical operation (as per configuration chart) with the multilevel Key2, after then applying modulo function of 255.The value is fed as an input to RGB color model –Green value. The partial cipher text 2 we obtained from the second logical operation is operated with third logical operator(as per configuration chart) using multilevel Key3, after then applying modulo function of 255. The resultant is cipher text and is given as an input to RGB color model-Blue value. The RGB value we get from these steps is used to produce the color representation for the corresponding character in the text file, which is the encrypted form of particular character from a source file. The three multilevel keys are incremented by the key counter after encrypting each character in the text file. The process of encryption is repeated till the end of file occurs. The final output will be the encrypted file of RGB color representation.

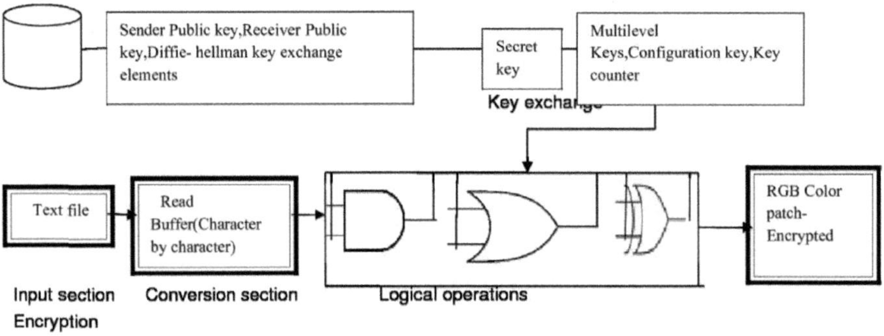

Fig. 2. Encryption Algorithm

4 Decryption

A reverse process of encryption is followed in the decryption process. Fig 3 represents the decryption process. The three multilevel keys, configuration key and key counter are accessed by the receiver through public key system. The RGB color representation of the text file is receipted by the receiver and the configuration key is accessed. The configuration key chart relates the configuration key with the order of logical operations. The reverse order of configuration key chart's order is followed while decrypting the character. The color model's RGB value is the cipher text and also the value of Blue in RGB model. The blue value obtained from the RGB representation is operated using third logical operator(as per configuration key chart) with Multilevel Key3.It cedes partial cipher text 2,which is then operated with Multilevel key 2 using second logical operator. The partial cipher text 1 is obtained which is operated with Multilevel Key1 using first logical operator .This reveal the ASCII value of the original text. Then the ASCII is converted to original text. The key values are incremented by the value of key counter, after decrypting each character, The key counter value is known only at the sender and receiver end. The process of decryption is repeated till the end of file occurs. The final stage is the decrypted form of the original file which is the stream of characters of the source file.

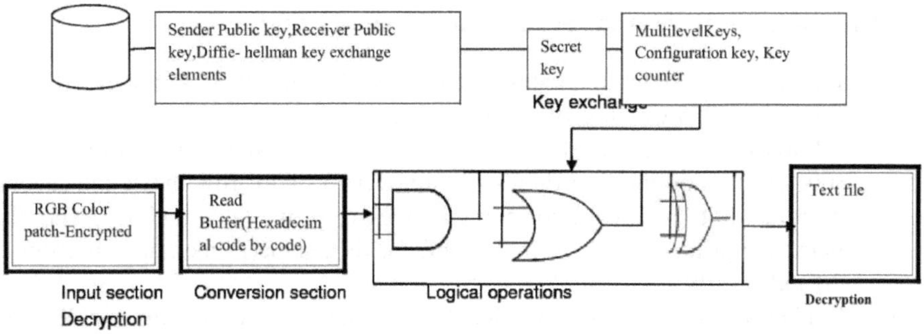

Fig. 3. Decryption Algorithm

5 Key Distribution and Generation

The public key system is followed for the key distribution and key generation process. Diffie–Hellman Key exchange mechanism is used to distribute a secret key. The mathematical flow of the key distribution using Diffie Hellman Key exchange is portrayed here is portrayed here [8].

Let P be a public prime Number and G be a public base, such that G<P and G is a primitive root of P,X be the Sender's Public key, Y be the receiver's public key and A be the Sender's private key, B be the receiver's Private key. S be the secret key to be shared.

At the sender end

$$X=G^A \bmod P \tag{1}$$

At the receiver end

$$Y=G^B \bmod P \tag{2}$$

At the sender end

$$S=Y^A \bmod P \tag{3}$$

At the receiver end

$$S=X^\wedge B \bmod P \tag{4}$$

G=6,P=13,X=6,Y=4.

The secret key S will be 1 for this instance. Secret key 'S' is used to generate all the below keys using key generation process proposed. The keys have the following range

Multilevel Keys-(1,255), Key counter-(1-255), Configuration key-(1-6).

All decimal values obtained in the process are rounded off.

The following steps depict how the keys are generated and how they can be detected at the receiving end.

5.1 Generation of Keys at the Sender and Receiver's End

1) Public key system generates Secret key S, after then applying Modulo function of 255 which gives Multilevel Key1.
2) Multilevel key1 is generated from the above step and it will have range – (001,255).Using the first digit of Multilevel Key1 for row index and second digit of Multilevel Key1 for column index of prime table and accessing the particular prime number from the table yields a value(Prime numbers from 1-20 and 20-40).
3) Taking average of Multilevel Key1 and indexed value of prime table from step 2, gives Multilevel Key 2.
4) Accessing prime table with Multilevel Key 2 values as index, taking average of Multilevel Key 2 and the indexed value of prime table generated from this step gives Multilevel Key3.
5) Taking average of Multilevel -Key1, Key2, Key3 values will give Counter key.
6) Addition of digits of Key counter will yield a value. This is used for finding configuration key. Key1 -0, 6.Key 2-1, 7.Key 3-2, 8, Key 4-3, 9, Key 5-4.Key 6 -5. (if addition of digits is 0 or 6 then Configuration key is 1).

The sender and receiver must generate keys based on the above process The secret key is used to generate the five keys of algorithm. Thus, there is no need of transmitting the keys to receiver and only the encrypted data is sent. The algorithm inherits the advantages of a public key system. Intrusion detection to find the keys is impossible with the proposed mechanism of distributing keys.

6 Configuration Chart

The configuration key chart depicted in Fig. 4. is used for referring the order of the configuration key. The order of logical operation in encryption and decryption is followed according to the configuration key.

Table 1. Configuration Key chart

KEY VALUE	LOGICAL ORDER OF OPERATION
1	XOR AND OR
2	AND OR XOR
3	OR AND XOR
4	AND XOR OR
5	OR XOR AND
6	XOR OR AND

7 Experimental Results

Input: Set of ASCII characters to be encrypted, three multilevel keys, Configuration key, key counter, Configuration key chart

Output: Encrypted form of source file-(Patch of colors from RGB model).

Key constraints:

1) Numerals are preferred for key values.

2) Configuration key of 1-6 is allowed since there are only six logical functionalities in the algorithm

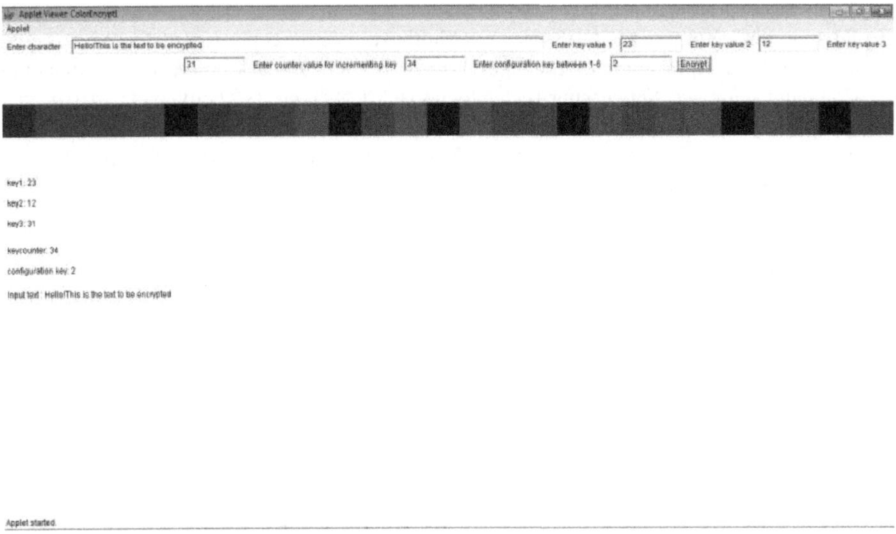

Fig. 4. Experimental result of the proposed algorithm

8 Conclusion and Future Work

Though many cryptographic algorithms exist, the proposed algorithm keeps the data more and more secured by applying multilevel encryption strategy. Since we change the value of keys at each character's encryption, dissimilar colors of same character is attained at different instance. This makes cryptanalysis less possible. The technique of finding the logical operation by intruding is a difficult process as there are six patterns of logical functionalities and the pattern can be observed only if configuration key is found. The technique of public key system for key distribution is employed efficiently for determining three multilevel keys, key counter, configuration key . The main advantage of this algorithm is that the keys are not transmitted with encrypted data. As, the sender generates the secret keys on receiving the public key of receiver and its own private key, and the receiver detects the secret keys using the public key of sender and its own private key, the problem of key detection by the intruder is avoided. Unless, the intruder knows all the five keys, there is zero probability of finding the intended message at the intrusion. The receiver attains the privacy with the assurance of private access of multilevel keys, configuration key and a key counter.

The algorithm is more flexible to accommodate any number of logical operations simply by increasing the number of iterations of logical operations.

The algorithm is proposed on the basis of RGB color model. In future it can be tested with many other color models such as HSB, RGB, CMY, CMYK color models. In the future, the various types of files such as image, video, audio files could be accommodated for encryption by this algorithm.

References

1. History of Cryptography, `http://www.en.wikipedia.org/`
2. Types of Cryptography, `http://www.citrix.com/`
3. Begum, J.N., Kumar, K., Sumathy, V.: Multilevel access control in defense messaging system using Elliptic curve cryptography. In: 2010 International Conference on Computing Communication and Networking Technologies (ICCCNT), pp. 1–9 (July 29-31, 2010)
4. Wang, K.: An Encrypt and Decrypt Algorithm Implementation on FPGAs. In: Fifth International Conference on Semantics, Knowledge and Grid, SKG 2009, pp. 298–301 (October 12-14, 2009)
5. Basicflow of cryptosystem, `http://www.networksorcery.com/`
6. RGB Color chart, `http://www.tayloredmktg.com/`
7. Algorithm structure, `http://www.di-mgt.com/`
8. Diffie-Hellman Key Exchange Protocol, `http://www.iacr.org`

Segmentation of Printed Devnagari Documents

Vikas J. Dongre and Vijay H. Mankar

Department of Electronics & Telecommunication,
Government Polytechnic, Nagpur, India
dongrevj@yahoo.co.in, vhmankar@gmail.com

Abstract. Document segmentation is one of the most important phases in machine recognition of any language. Correct segmentation of individual symbols decides the success of character recognition technique. It is used to decompose an image of a sequence of characters into sub images of individual symbols by segmenting lines and words. Devnagari is the most popular script in India. It is used for writing Hindi, Marathi, Sanskrit and Nepali languages. Moreover, Hindi is the third most popular language in the world. Devnagari documents consist of vowels, consonants and various modifiers. Hence a proper segmentation Devnagari word is challenging. A simple approach based on bounded box to segment Devnagari documents is proposed in this paper. Various challenges in segmentation of Devnagari script are also discussed.

Keywords: Devnagari Character Recognition, paragraph segmentation, Line segmentation, Word segmentation, Machine learning.

1 Introduction

Machine learning and human computer interaction are the most challenging research fields since the advent of digital computers. In Optical Character Recognition (OCR), the text lines, words and symbols in a document must be segmented properly before recognition. Correctness/incorrectness of text line segmentation directly affects accuracies of word/character segmentation and consequently changes the accuracies of word/character recognition [1]. Several techniques for text line segmentation are reported in the literature [2-5]. These techniques may be categorized into three groups as follows: (i) Projection profile based techniques, (ii) Hough transform based techniques, (iii) Thinning based approach. As a conventional technique for text line segmentation, global horizontal projection analysis of black pixels has been utilized in [4, 6]. Piece-wise horizontal projection analysis of black pixels is employed by many researchers to segment text pages of different languages [2, 8]. In piecewise horizontal projection technique, the text-page image is decomposed into horizontal stripes. The positions of potential piece-wise separating lines are obtained for each stripe using horizontal projection on each stripe. The potential separating lines are then connected to achieve complete separating lines for all respective text lines located in the text page image.

D.C. Wyld et al. (Eds.): ACITY 2011, CCIS 198, pp. 211–218, 2011.

Concept of the Hough transform is employed in the field of document analysis in many research areas such as skew detection, slant detection, text line segmentation, etc [7]. Thinning operation is also used by researchers for text line segmentation from documents [9]. In this paper we have proposed a bounded box method for segmentation of documents lines and words and characters. The method is based on the pixel histogram obtained.

The organization of this paper is as follows: In Section 2, we have discussed features of Indian scripts. Section 3 discusses image preprocessing methods. Section 4 details the proposed segmentation approach. Experimental results are discussed in Section 5 and scope for further research is discussed in Section 6.

2 Features of Devnagari Script

India is a multi-lingual and multi-script country comprising of eighteen official languages. Because there is typically a letter for each of the phonemes in Indian languages, the alphabet set tends to be quite large. Hindi, the national language of India, is written in the Devnagari script. Devnagari is also used for writing Marathi, Sanskrit and Nepali. Moreover, Hindi is the third most popular language in the world [1]. It is spoken by more than 500 million people in the world. .Devnagari has 11 vowels and 33 consonants. They are called basic characters. Vowels can be written as independent letters, or by using a variety of diacritical marks which are written above, below, before or after the consonant they belong to. When vowels are written in this way they are known as *modifiers* and the characters so formed are called *conjuncts*. Sometimes two or more consonants can combine and take new shapes. These new shape clusters are known as *compound characters*. These types of basic characters, compound characters and modifiers are present not only in Devnagari but also in other scripts.

All the characters have a horizontal line at the upper part, known as *Shirorekha*. In continuous handwriting, from left to right direction, the shirorekha of one character joins with the shirorekha of the previous or next character of the same word. In this fashion, multiple characters and modified shapes in a word appear as a single connected component joined through the common shirorekha. Also in Devnagari there are vowels, consonants, vowel modifiers and compound characters, numerals. Moreover, there are many similar shaped characters. All these variations make Devnagari Optical Character Recognition, a challenging problem. A sample of Devnagari character set is provided in table 1 to 6.

Table 1. Vowels and Corresponding Modifiers

Vowels:	अ	आ	इ	ई	उ	ऊ	ऋ	ए	ऐ	ओ	औ
Modifiers:		ा	ि	ी	ु	ू	ृ	े	ै	ो	ौ

Table 2. Consonants

क	ख	ग	घ	ङ	च	छ	ज	झ	ञ	ट
ठ	ड	ढ	ण	त	थ	द	ध	न	प	फ
ब	भ	म	य	र	ल	व	श	ष	स	ह

Table 3. Half Form of Consonants with Vertical Bar

क्	ख्	ग्	घ्		च्		ज्	झ्	ञ्	
			ण्	त्	थ्		ध्	न्	प्	फ
ब्	भ्	म्	य्		ल्	व्	श्	ष्	स्	

Table 4. Examples of Combination of Half-Consonant and Consonant

क क क्क	क ल क्ल	घ न घ्न	च ञ च्ञ	ञ च ञ्च	त न त्न	प त प्त	प ल प्ल
ब ब ब्ब	भ न भ्न	म ल म्ल	ल ल ल्ल	श न श्न	श व श्व	श ल श्ल	स न स्न

Table 5. Examples of Special Combination of Half-Consonant and Consonant

क ष क्ष	ज ञ ज्ञ	ट ट ट्ट	ट ठ ट्ठ	त र त्र	द द द्द
द ध द्ध	द व द्व	द व र द्व्र	श र श्र	द भ द्भ	द य द्य

Table 6. Special Symbols

क़	ख़	ग़	ज़	फ़	ड़	ढ़	ं	ँ	:	।	ऽ	ॅ

3 Image Preprocessing

We have collected the printed document pages from different official printed letters in Marathi language. The document pages are scanned using a flat bed scanner at a resolution of 300 dpi. These pixels may have values: OFF (0) or ON (1) for binary images, 0– 255 for gray-scale images, and 3 channels of 0–255 colour values for colour images. Colour image is converted to grayscale by eliminating the hue and saturation information while retaining the luminance. It is further analyzed to get useful information. Such processing steps are explained below.

3.1 Thresholding and Binarization

We have used histogram based properties to binarize the document taken as a data set. The digitized text images are converted into binary images by thresholding using Otsu's method [16]. Original image contains 0 for Object and 1 for background. The image inverted to obtain image such that object pixels are represented by 1 and background pixels by 0.

3.2 Noise Reduction

The noise, introduced by the optical scanning device or the writing instrument, causes disconnected line segments, bumps and gaps in lines, filled loops etc. The distortion including local variations, rounding of corners, dilation and erosion, is also a problem. Prior to the character recognition, it is necessary to eliminate these imperfections [10-11]. It is carried using various morphological processing techniques.

3.3 Skew Detection and Correction

Handwritten document may originally be skewed or skewness may introduce in document scanning process. This effect is unintentional in many real cases, and it should be eliminated because it dramatically reduces the accuracy of the subsequent processes such as segmentation and classification. Skewed lines are made horizontal

Fig. 1. Preprocessed Images (a) Original, (b) segmented (c) Shirorekha removed (d) Thinned (e) image edging

by calculating skew angle and making proper correction in the raw image using Hu moments and various transforms [12-14].

3.4 Thinning

The boundary detection of image is done to enable easier subsequent detection of pertinent features and objects of interest (see fig.1 (a to e)). Various standard functions are now available in MATLAB for above operations [15].

4 Proposed Segmentation Approach

After the image is preprocessed using methods discussed in section 3, we now apply various techniques for segmentation of document lines, words and characters. The process of segmentation mainly follows the following pattern:

1) Identify the page layout. 2) Identify the text lines in the page. 3) Identify the words in individual line. 4) Finally identify individual character in each word.

4.1 Line Segmentation

The global horizontal projection method is used to compute sum of all white pixels on every row and construct corresponding histogram. The steps for line segmentation are as follow:

- Construct the Horizontal Histogram for the image (fig. 2-b).
- Count the white pixel in each row.
- Using the Histogram, find the rows containing no white pixel.
- Replace all such rows by 1 (fig. 2-c).
- Invert the image to make empty rows as 0 and text lines will have original pixels.
- Mark the Bounding Box for text lines using standard Matlab functions (regionprops and rectangle).
- Copy the pixels in the Bounding Box and save in separate file. (separated lines shown in fig. 2-f).

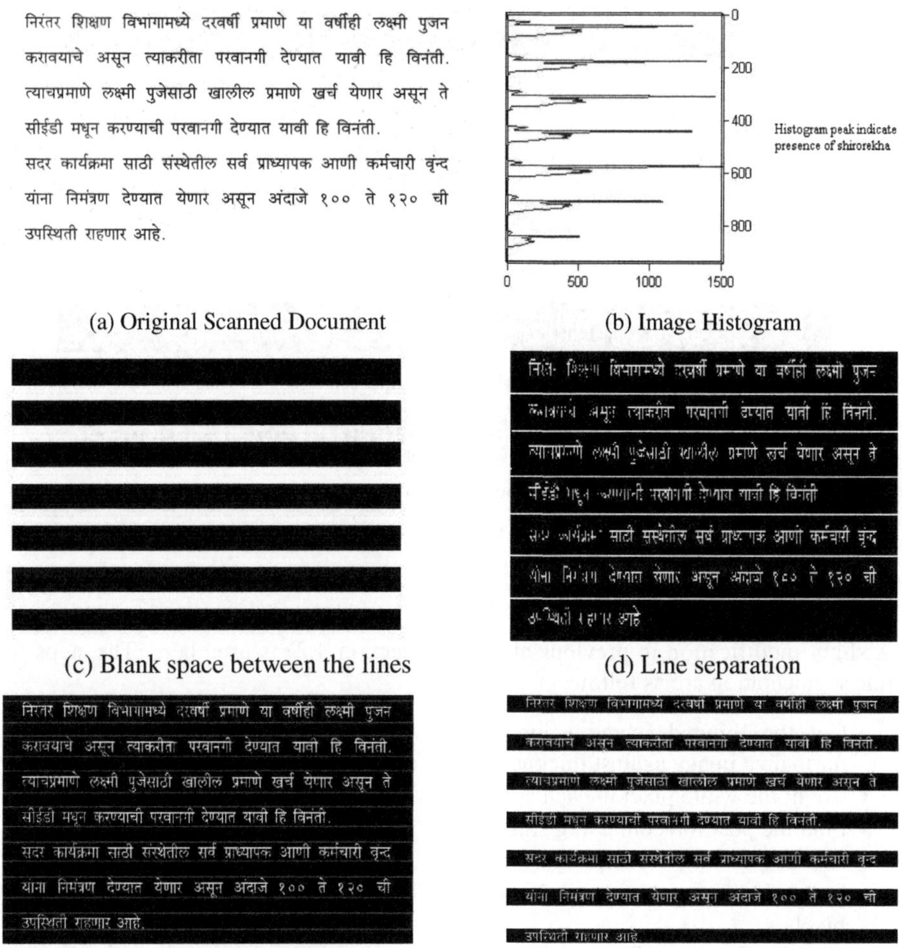

(a) Original Scanned Document (b) Image Histogram

(c) Blank space between the lines (d) Line separation

(e) Regions of interest (f) Segmented lines

Fig. 2. Line Segmentation

4.2 Word Segmentation

The global horizontal projection method is used here to compute sum of all white pixels on every column and construct corresponding histogram. The steps for line segmentation are as follow:

- Construct the Vertical Histogram for the image (fig. 3-b).
- Count the white pixel in each column.
- Using the Histogram, find the columns containing no white pixel.
- Replace all such columns by 1
- Invert the image to make empty rows as 0 and text words will have original pixels.
- Mark the Bounding Box for word. (See fig 3-c)
- Copy the pixels in the Bounding Box and save in separate file. (See fig. 3-d).

(a) Original line

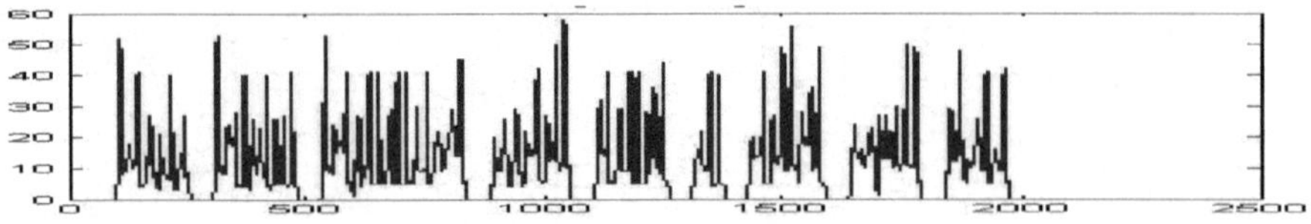

(b) Word Histogram

(c) Regions of interest

(d) Segmented words

Fig. 3. Word Segmentation

4.3 Character Segmentation

A slight modification in previous algorithm (section 4.2) is used here. The steps for line segmentation are as follow:

- Get the thinned image using Matlab bwmorph function. (This is done to normalize image against thickness of the character).
- Count the white pixel in each column.
- Find the position containing single white pixel.
- Replace all such columns by 1.
- Invert the image to make such columns as 0 and text characters will have original pixels.
- Mark the Bounding Box for characters using standard Matlab functions. See fig 4-a.
- Copy the pixels in the Bounding Box and save in separate file. (Separated characters are shown in fig. 4-b).

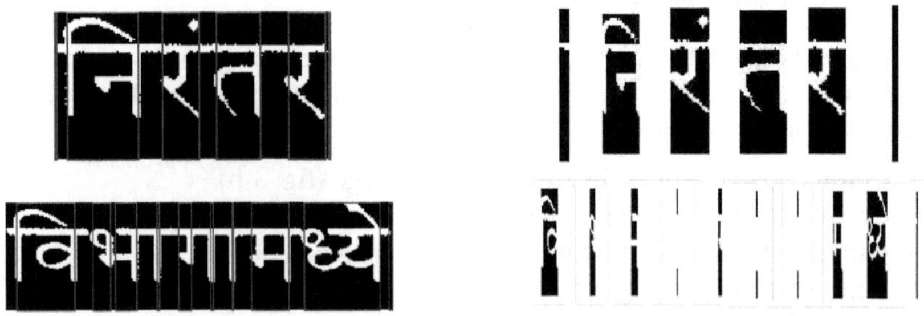

(a) region of Interest (b) segmented characters

Fig. 4. Character segmentation

5 Results and Discussion

Various documents were collected and tested. It is observed that line and word segmentation is done with 100% accuracy, but it is not the same for character segmentation. As shown in figure 4(b), first word having four characters is segmented into six symbols, whereas second word having five characters is segmented into ten symbols. This error is resulted since the words are scanned only from top to bottom. Devnagari is two dimensional script as consonants are modified in many ways to form a meaningful letter. The basic letters can be modified from top, bottom, left or right. For accurate segmentation, all the modifiers must be segmented so that their recognition can be properly done done.

6 Conclusions and Future Work

In this paper, we have presented a primary work for segmentation of lines, words and characters of Devnagari script. 100% successful segmentation achieved in line and word segmentation but character level segmentation needs more effort as it is complicated for Devnagari script. This is challenging work due to following reasons.

- Compound letters are connected at various places. It is difficult to identify exact connecting points for segmentation.
- Upper and lower modifier segmentation needs different approaches.
- Separating anuswara (.) and full stop(.) from noise is critical as both resemble the same. Knowledge of Natural language processing techniques needs to be applied here.
- Handwritten unconnected compound letter segmentation is also critical.
- Handwritten unintentionally connected simple letter segmentation is also critical.

All these issues will be dealt in the future for printed and handwritten documents in Devnagari script by using various approaches.

References

[1] Priyanka, N., Pal, S., Mandal, R.: Line and Word Segmentation Approach for Printed Documents. IJCA Special Issue on Recent Trends in Image Processing and Pattern Recognition 1"RTIPPR", 30–36 (2010)

[2] Wong, K., Casey, R., Wahl, F.: Document Analysis System. IBM J. Res. Dev. 26(6), 647–656 (1982)

[3] Nagy, G., Seth, S., Viswanathan, M.: A prototype document image analysis system for technical journals. Computer 25, 10–22 (1992)

[4] Kumar, V., Senegar, P.K.: Segmentation of Printed Text in Devnagari Script and Gurmukhi Script. IJCA: International Journal of Computer Applications 3, 24–29 (2010)

[5] Pal, U., Datta, S.: Segmentation of Bangla Unconstrained Handwritten Text. In: Proc. 7th Int. Conf. on Document Analysis and Recognition, pp.1128–1132 (2003)

[6] Dongre, V.J., Mankar, V.H.: A Review of Research on Devnagari Character Recognition. International Journal of Computer Applications (0975 – 8887) 12(2), 8–15 (2010)

[7] Pal, U., Mitra, M., Chaudhuri, B.B.: Multi-skew detection of Indian script documents. In: Proc. 6th Int. Conf. Document Analysis Recognition, pp. 292–296 (2001)
[8] Likforman-Sulem, L., Zahour, A., Taconet, B.: Text line Segmentation of Historical Documents: a Survey. International Journal on Document Analysis and Recognition 9(2), 123–138 (2007)
[9] Magy, G.: Twenty years of Document Analysis in PAMI. IEEE Trans. in PAMI 22, 38–61 (2000)
[10] Serra, J.: Morphological Filtering: An Overview. Signal Processing 38(1), 3–11 (1994)
[11] Arica, N., Yarman-Vural, F.T.: An Overview of Character Recognition Focused On Off-line Handwriting. In: C99-06-C-203. IEEE, Los Alamitos (2000)
[12] Cheriet, M., Kharma, N., Liu, C.-L., Suen, C.Y.: Character Recognition Systems: A Guide for students and Practioners. John Wiley & Sons, Inc., Hoboken (2007)
[13] Kapoor, R., Bagai, D., Kamal, T.S.: Skew angle detection of a cursive handwritten Devnagari script character image. Journal of Indian Inst. Science, 161–175 (May-August 2002)
[14] Pal, U., Mitra, M., Chaudhuri, B.B.: Multi-Skew Detection of Indian Script Documents. In: CVPRU IEEE, pp. 292–296 (2001)
[15] Mankar, V.H., et al.: Contour Detection and Recovery through Bio-Medical Watermarking for Telediagnosis. International Journal of Tomography & Statistics 14(S10) (special volume) (Summer 2010)
[16] Jing, G., Rajan, D., Siong, C.E.: Motion Detection with Adaptive Background and Dynamic Thresholds. In: Fifth International Conference on Information, Communications and Signal Processing, Bangkok, W B.4, pp. 41–45 (2005)

About the Authors

Vikas. J Dongre received B.E and M.E. in Electronics in 19991 and 1994 respectively. He served as lecturer in SSVPS engineering college Dhule, (M.S.) India from 1992 to 1994. He Joined Government Polytechnic Nagpur as Lecturer in 1994 where he is presently working as lecturer (selection grade). His areas of interests include Microcontrollers, embedded systems, image recognition, and innovative Laboratory practices. He is pursuing for Ph.D in Offline Handwritten Devnagari Character Recognition. He has published one research paper in international journal and one research paper in international conference.

Vijay H. Mankar received M. Tech. degree in Electronics Engineering from VNIT, Nagpur University, India in 1995 and Ph.D. (Engg) from Jadavpur University, Kolkata, India in 2009 respectively. He has more than 16 years of teaching experience and presently working as a Lecturer (Selection Grade) in Government Polytechnic, Nagpur (MS), India. He has published more than 30 research papers in international conference and journals. His field of interest includes digital image processing, data hiding and watermarking.

An Adaptive Jitter Buffer Playout Algorithm for Enhanced VoIP Performance

Atri Mukhopadhyay[1], Tamal Chakraborty[1], Suman Bhunia[2], Iti Saha Misra[2], and Salil Kumar Sanyal[2]

[1] School of Mobile Computing and Communication, Jadavpur University Salt Lake Campus, Kolkata-700098, India
[2] Dept. of Electronics & Telecommunication Engineering Jadavpur University, Kolkata-700032, India
{atri.mukherji11,tamalchakraborty29,sumanbhunia}@gmail.com, iti@etce.jdvu.ac.in, s_sanyal@ieee.org

Abstract. The QoS standard of a VoIP session degrades if its stringent time requirements are not met. Low end-to-end delay of the voice packets and low packet loss must be maintained. Jitter between voice packets must also be within tolerable limits. Jitter hampers voice quality and makes the VoIP call uncomfortable to the user. Very often, buffers are used to store the received packets for a short time before playing them at equal spaced intervals to minimize jitter. However, this introduces the problem of added end-to-end delay and discarded packets. In this paper, some established adaptive jitter buffer playout algorithms have been studied and a new algorithm has been proposed. The network used for the analysis of the algorithms has been simulated using OPNET modeler 14.5.A. The proposed algorithm kept jitter within a tolerable limit along with drastic reduction of delay and loss compared to other algorithms analyzed in this paper.

Keywords: VoIP, QoS parameters, Adaptive Algorithm, Jitter Buffer playout, Congested network.

1 Introduction

The characteristics of the Internet backbone are time-variant in nature. Its properties are so random and unpredictable that it is not an easy task to statistically determine the way the backbone is going to behave in a future point of time. The reason behind the lack of proper prediction of its characteristics is its dependency on the behavior of the other connections throughout the network [1]. The connectivity may be hampered due to several reasons rendering networking applications ineffectual. The networks suffer from congestion when traffics exceeding the capacity of the network are routed through it. As a result, the data packets suffer high delay and loss while passing through the network. Such delay and loss are unacceptable in case of applications having stringent time requirements. This set of applications is called Real-time applications and they include facilities like Internet Protocol (IP) telephony,

D.C. Wyld et al. (Eds.): ACITY 2011, CCIS 198, pp. 219–230, 2011.

teleconference, etc. Of the various real-time applications, we have concentrated on Voice over IP (VoIP) since it has gained importance over the past few years owing to its low cost and ease of interfacing between data and voice traffic [2].

VoIP applications are not only sensitive to the extent of the delay and loss suffered by the voice packets but also to the inter-arrival jitter, i.e. the variation in delay suffered by consecutive voice packets [2], [3]. Jitter is one of the main factors that degrade the Quality of Service (QoS) in IP networks [4]. This variation in delay is often the result of network congestion. Generally, the VoIP applications send data at a constant rate. So, any alteration in the end-to-end delay suffered by two voice packets means that the time between two events occurring at the source and the time between the events perceived at the receiver are not equal. Such an event is not desired in a VoIP system as it degrades speech quality. Hence, we need some mechanisms to undo this variation in delay that is being incorporated into the voice packets by the network. One of the feasible solutions is the use of some mechanism which aims to reduce the network congestion, e.g. increasing the packet payload size [5]. Congestion can also occur in the intermediate access points. So VoIP performance can also be enhanced by optimizing the access point parameters [6]. But the most effective solution is to store the voice packets for a short time in the receiver buffer before playing it out, thus reducing the jitter [7]. However, using a fixed playout time for every packet is rendered useless if the network characteristics are variable and the voice packets suffer different extent of delay while passing through it [8]. Several algorithms have already been proposed so that the playout time for a voice packet is delayed in accordance with the variation in the network and thus provide better QoS for the VoIP applications. However, if the playout delay is too large, the end-to-end delay suffered by the voice packets is increased beyond acceptable limits and the VoIP performance may become irritating to the user because significant awkwardness occurs between speakers when delay exceeds 200 ms [8]. On the other hand, if the playout delay is too small, voice packets may be discarded due to late arrival [2]. This hampers the voice quality. It is not desirable that the voice packets suffer from either high delay or high loss. So, it is mandatory to obtain an optimum playout time to get the best performance out of a VoIP system.

In this paper, we have analyzed some of the already established adaptive jitter buffer playout algorithms and have tested for their efficiency in several network scenarios. Further, we have also taken a note of their shortcomings and have proposed a new adaptive jitter buffer playout algorithm that provides the optimum QoS to the VoIP application in terms of delay, loss and jitter. The performance of the new algorithm has been tested in varying network scenarios using OPNET simulator. Moreover, its performance has also been compared with the analyzed algorithms.

2 Related Work

A significant research has already been conducted in the quest of finding a suitable adaptive jitter buffer playout algorithm. As already mentioned, finding the proper playout delay is of utmost importance. In order to find out the efficiency of some of the already existing adaptive jitter buffer algorithms, we have studied five algorithms mentioned in [9] and [10].

2.1 Exponential Average Algorithm (EXP-AVG) [9]

In this algorithm, the delay estimate for the ith packet is computed based on RFC 793 algorithm and the variation in the delays is calculated as suggested by Van Jacobson in the calculation of round-trip-time estimates for the TCP retransmit timer [11]. In this algorithm the estimate of the playout delay for packet i is evaluated by the equation (1).

$$P_i = d_i + 4v_i \tag{1}$$

where,
$$d_i = \alpha d_{i-1} + (1-\alpha) n_i \tag{2}$$

$$v_i = \alpha v_{i-1} + (1-\alpha)|d_i - n_i| \tag{3}$$

where, n_i denotes the one-way delay of the ith packet and the value of α is 0.998002 [9].

2.2 Fast Exponential Average Algorithm (F-EXP-AVG) [9]

This algorithm is similar to the previous one. The only difference being that if the current packet's network delay 'n_i' is greater than d_{i-1}, then d_i is given by equation (4).

$$d_i = \beta d_{i-1} + (1-\beta) n_i \tag{4}$$

where, the value of β is 0.75 [9].

2.3 Minimum Delay Algorithm (Min-D) [9]

The primary objective of this algorithm is to minimize the delay. So it uses the minimum value of the network delay suffered by the packets in the current talkspurt to estimate the playout delay of the next talkspurt. Let S_i be the set of all packets received in the talkspurt prior to the one initiated by i. So, the delay estimate for packet i is calculated by (5). Apart from this modification, this algorithm is similar to the EXP-AVG algorithm.

$$d_i = \min_{j \in S_i} \{n_i\} \tag{5}$$

2.4 Spike Detection Algorithm (Spike-Det) [9]

One of the most common phenomena observed in a VoIP system is that some of the packets suddenly suffer from high end-to-end delay. As a result no voice packet reaches the receiver for some time followed by the arrival of a large number of voice packet reaching almost simultaneously. We describe this phenomenon as the 'spike'. The above stated algorithms do not take care of this problem. However, this algorithm seeks to overcome the problem with the incorporation of a spike detection mechanism. When, a spike is detected, the algorithm switches to 'SPIKE' mode and later reverts back to 'NORMAL' mode when the network condition becomes normal.

2.6 Window Algorithm [10]

This algorithm collects the network delays of last few received packets and the delay distribution is updated with every incoming talkspurt. The playout delay of the incoming packet is chosen by obtaining a delay that represents a given percentile among the last few received packets. This algorithm also detects spikes. On detection of a spike, the algorithm stops collecting packet delays. If a talkspurt starts during a spike, then the delay of the first packet of the talkspurt is used as the playout delay for that talkspurt. The efficiency of determination of playout delay for this algorithm depends on the window size, i.e. the number packets considered for recording their delay. If the window is too small, then the estimation of playout delay is likely to be poor. On the other hand, if the window size is too large, large memory is wasted for keeping tracks of long and unnecessary history.

3 The Simulation Setup

We have created the congested network scenario used for the analysis of the above mentioned adaptive jitter buffer playout algorithms and to assess our new algorithm with the help of OPNET 14.5.A. The set up consists of four nodes. Two ethernet4_slip8_gtwy_adv gateways are used to interface an IP cloud to the communicating nodes. The IP cloud simulates the presence of an IP backbone in the communication path of the nodes. The gateways and the IP cloud are connected with PPP_adv link whose data rate can be altered.

It is seen from Fig. 1, that one of the nodes acts as the Voice caller whereas another node acts as the Voice callee. These two nodes exchange voice packets between each other. Both these nodes are configured to use G.726 ADPCM coder with 32 kbps and it produces traffic at a constant rate. The other two nodes, i.e. node 1 and node 2 interchange packets unrelated to the VoIP communication, i.e. the cross traffic. Their communication bit rate varies randomly every second between the lower and upper extremes of 0 kbps and 1000 kbps respectively. The basic purpose of these nodes is to congest the links between the gateways and the IP cloud. It is worth mentioning that in order to simulate various network behavior, we have simulated the network several times with the capacity of the PPP_adv link having the values of 600 kbps, 800 kbps, 1000 kbps, 1200 kbps and 1400 kbps. Thus we have created a varying network, so as to induce variable end-to-end delay to the voice packets exchanged between the pair of voice nodes. The IP cloud serves to simulate the routing functionalities and can also increase the delay and packet loss rate. For simplicity, only the results with network capacities 600 kbps, 1000 kbps and 1400 kbps are shown as they cover the three types of jitter conditions, i.e. a network with high jitter (600 kbps network), a network with moderate jitter (1000 kbps network) and a network with low jitter (1400 kbps network).

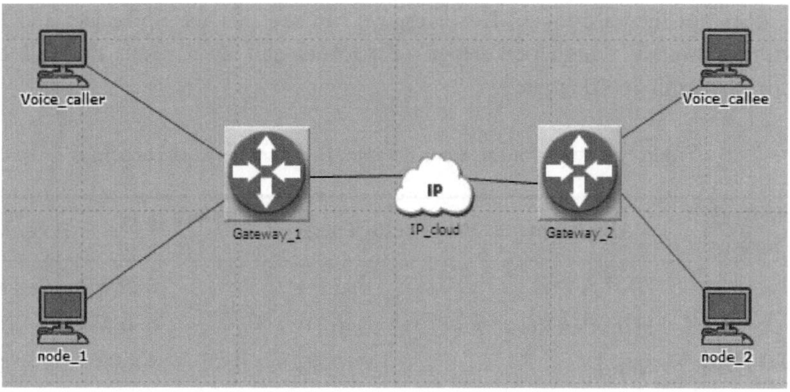

Fig. 1. The OPNET Simulation Setup

4 Analysis of the Existing Adaptive Jitter Buffer Playout Algorithms

The link capacity has been set in accordance with each of the above mentioned values and VoIP call simulations have been carried out between the two voice nodes to study their behavior. The end-to-end delay values for each of the voice packets were noted. Later, these set of readings have been used to implement the various algorithms and then we have compared the results to find out the improvement in VoIP performance, i.e. reduction in jitter.

It is observed from Table 1 that for a network which induces high jitter to the voice packets passing through it (network capacity of 600kbps), the F-EXP-AVG algorithm discards least number of packets, and hence the lowest discard ratio. However, it increases the playout delay to such an extent that the average delay increases beyond a tolerable value and hence the voice quality degrades. The other algorithms induce lower average delay, but discard a large number of voice packets since the packets arrive after the estimated playout time. As a result, the voice call standards go below tolerable limits. The average Mean Opinion Score (MOS) reflects the voice quality offered by each of the algorithms. It is evident that none of the algorithms perform satisfactorily under high jitter conditions.

In a network with moderate congestion (network capacity of 1000 kbps) and consequently moderate jitter, the average delay induced by the algorithms decreases considerably. However, the F-EXP-AVG still imparts higher delay to the voice packets whereas, the Min-D and Spike-Det discards a large number of packets thus suffering from large losses. Further, the performances of the algorithms in a network with low congestion (network capacity 1400 kbps) are also tabulated. Here, we can say that since the inter-arrival jitter for the packets is low, the playout algorithms do not incorporate a significant playout delay to the voice packets. Hence, the end-to-end delay does not increase much. However, we can see that the Spike-Det and Min-D algorithms discard a high percentage of packets and as a result the call quality provided by them gets degraded.

Table 1. Results for the algorithms for different network capacities

Network Capacity	Algorithm	Avg. delay (ms)	Discard ratio (%)	Avg. MOS
600 kbps	EXP-AVG	493.94	6.289	1.0232
	F-EXP-AVG	1446.76	0.482	1.0041
	Min-D	417.80	8.867	1.0191
	Spike-Det	338.17	6.318	1.0461
	Window	341.49	5.524	1.0320
1000 kbps	EXP-AVG	119.83	3.928	1.9114
	F-EXP-AVG	276.46	0.453	2.1900
	Min-D	112.12	6.547	1.6462
	Spike-Det	115.12	6.867	1.6143
	Window	103.63	3.865	1.9386
1400 kbps	EXP-AVG	89.52	0.756	2.8233
	F-EXP-AVG	102.93	0.049	3.4264
	Min-D	88.53	2.681	2.1664
	Spike-Det	87.69	4.728	1.8486
	Window	86.10	0.516	2.9840

5 Proposed Adaptive Jitter Buffer Playout Algorithm

After extensive analysis of some of the existing jitter buffer algorithms, we have come to the conclusion that, when the jitter imparted by the network to the voice packets is very high, the playout delay increases considerably. Moreover, the packet discard ratio also increases beyond tolerable limits. The net result of the above two factors is degradation in the quality of voice in the VoIP session. Our algorithm seeks to reduce the playout delay and packet discard ratio. Our algorithm can be summarized in the following steps which are to be followed as long as the VoIP call continues. We estimate the network characteristics by keeping track of the last '*w*' received packet. We use this accordingly to vary the value of α, where α is a parameter that determines how much a newly received packet depends on the previously received packets. The algorithm is pictorially represented by a flowchart in Fig. 2.

The Proposed Algorithm:

```
1. ni = ith packet network delay, α =0.875;
2. DD = abs(ni - ni-1);  /* DD indicates the absolute
                            value of the difference in
                            network delay of 2 consecutive
                            packets*/
3. IF (i < w)            /* w indicates the number of
                            packets to be considered or the
                            window size */
         find out the inter-quartile range of 'i-1'
   packets;
     ELSE
         find out the inter-quartile range of the last
   'w' packets;
4. IF (inter-quartile range < 5)
          IF (α +0.01< 0.998002)
               α = α +0.01;
          ELSE
               α = 0.998002;
     ELSE
         IF (α - 0.05 > 0.75)
               α = α - 0.05;
         ELSE
               α = 0.75;
5. IF(mode == NORMAL)
         IF (DD > (1 - α) x 100)
               mode = SPIKE;
         ELSE
               goto step 6;
     ELSE IF (ni < α x  ni-1)       /* that is, mode =
   SPIKE */
         mode = NORMAL;
     Else
         goto step 6;
6. IF(mode == SPIKE)
          di = 0.75 x  di-1 + (1-0.75) x  ni;
     ELSE                       /* that is, mode = NORMAL
   */
         IF(new talkspurt)
               di = ni;
         ELSE
               di = α x di-1 + (1 - α) x ni;
7. Y = abs(di - ni) ;
8. vi= 0.998002 x vi-1 + (1-0.998002) x Y;
9. Playout delay = di + 4 vi;
```

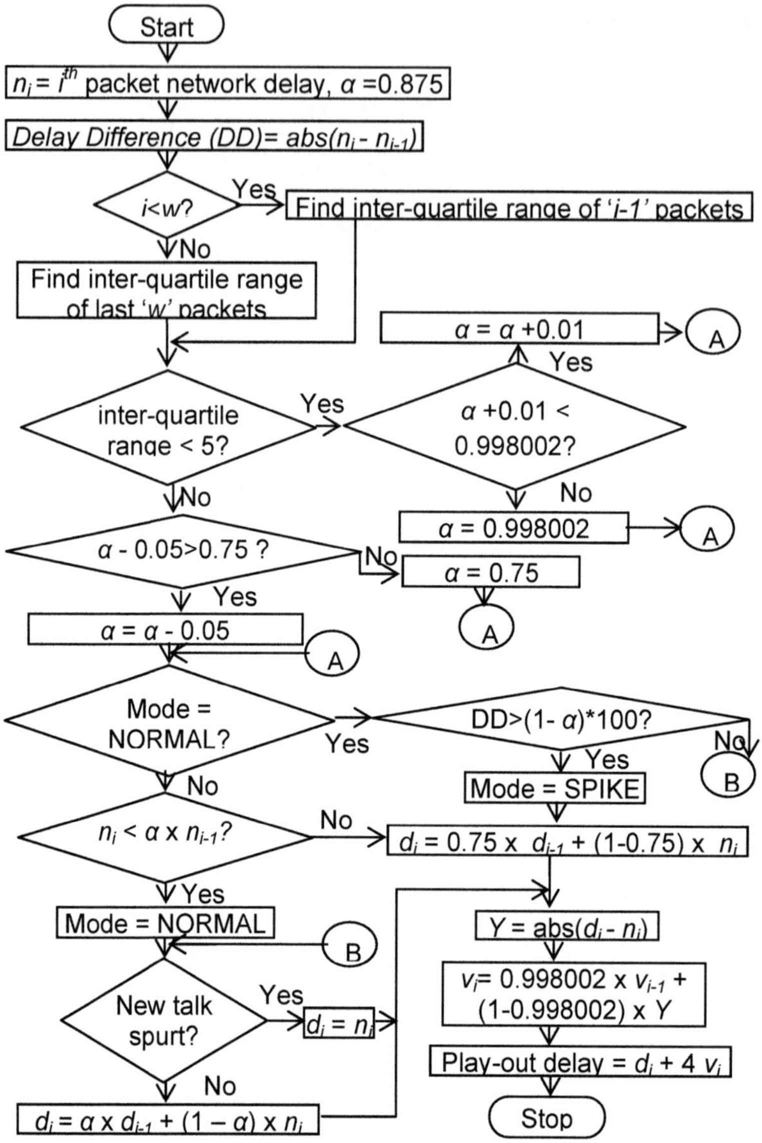

Fig. 2. Flowchart of the Proposed Adaptive Jitter Buffer Playout Algorithm

6 Results

The QoS of a VoIP call can be best described by the MOS value as both the end-to-end delays of the packets and the packet loss are considered for the calculation of the MOS [12]. The proposed algorithm is applied to find out its effectiveness and it gives a better MOS than the other discussed algorithms. The results also show that it reduces jitter considerably.

Table 2. Results for the proposed algorithm for different network capacity

Bandwidth (kbps)	Avg. delay (ms)	Packet Discard Ratio (%)	Average MOS	Improvement in jitter (%)
600	276.93	2.635	1.4508	35.34
800	161.42	2.846	2.0657	38.96
1000	107.80	2.806	2.1059	44.86
1200	92.50	0.664	2.8709	50.19
1400	87.68	0.171	3.2932	54.49

It is seen from Table 2 that the proposed algorithm performs satisfactorily for all of the above network scenarios. In Fig. 3, it is evident that the jitter reduces significantly on applying the proposed adaptive jitter buffer playout algorithm. The average jitter throughout the duration of the call falls from 18.38 ms to 11.88 ms. The results reflect the effectiveness of the algorithm under congested network that impart high jitter to the voice packets passing through it. Fig. 4 and Fig. 5, illustrates the behavior of the algorithm with moderate and low jitter, where the network capacity is 1000kbps and 1400kbps respectively. It is seen that the proposed algorithm reduces jitter considerably and performs well, in all three network scenarios.

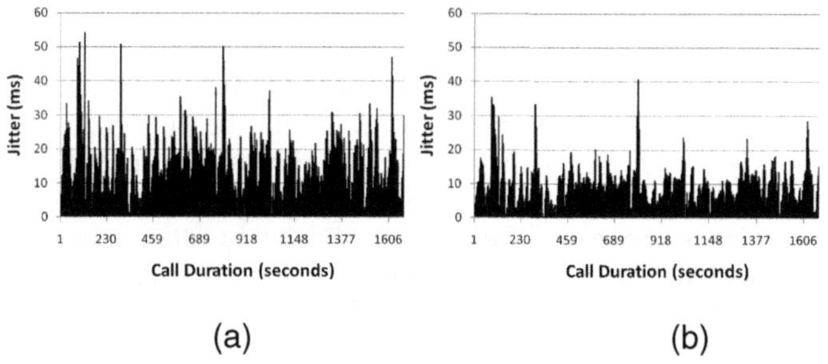

Fig. 3. The Inter-arrival jitter for network capacity of 600 kbps (a) Without playout buffer (b) With proposed algorithm

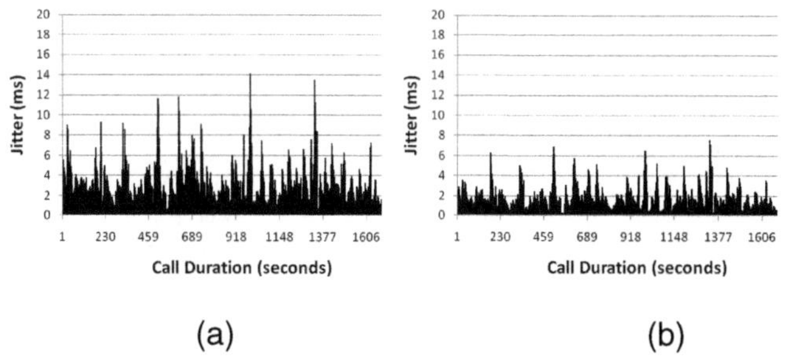

Fig. 4. The Inter-arrival jitter for network capacity of 1000 kbps (a) Without playout buffer (b) With proposed algorithm

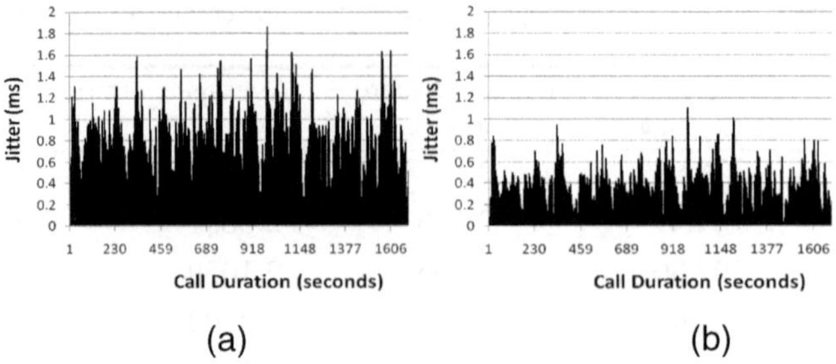

Fig. 5. The Inter-arrival jitter for network capacity of 1400 kbps (a) Without playout buffer (b) With proposed algorithm

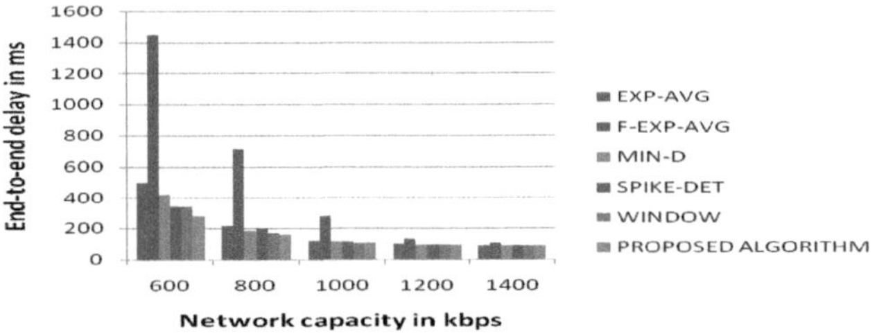

Fig. 6. Comparison of the end-to-end delays of the different algorithms

Further endeavors have been taken in order to find out where the proposed adaptive jitter algorithm stands, when compared with the performances of the other discussed algorithms. Our algorithm has given the lowest end-to-end delay among all the algorithms especially when the network is more congested and the extent of jitter in the voice packets is very high. The end-to-end delay results can be observed in Fig. 6. When examined for packet discard ratio it has been found that our algorithm performs quite well. However, the F-EXP-AVG algorithm has even lower packet discard ratio. The packet discard ratio comparison is illustrated in Fig. 7. Upon further examinations, it is observed that for a congested medium, our algorithm gives the best MOS values. However, for network with very low jitter, F-EXP-AVG gets the edge because of its lower packet discard ratio. The comparative results of MOS values have been included in Fig. 8.

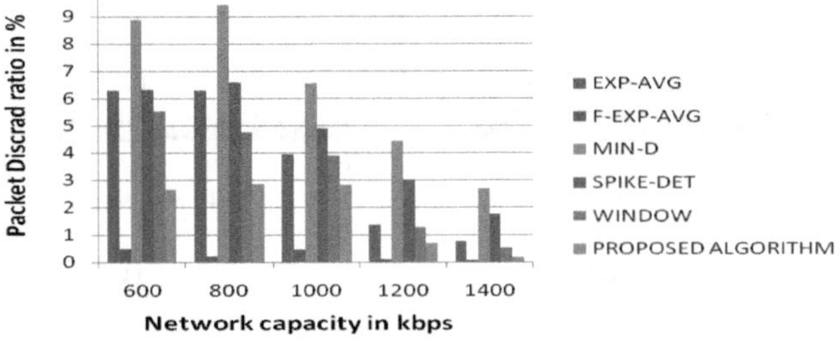

Fig. 7. Comparison of the packet discard ratio of the different algorithms

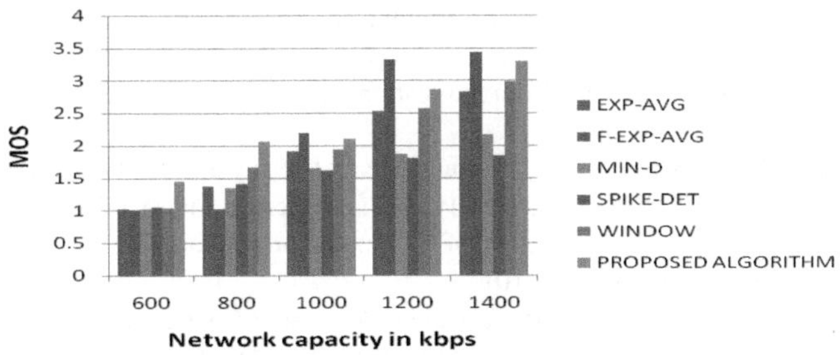

Fig. 8. Comparison of MOS of the different algorithms

7 Conclusion

A congested network transports voice packets with uneven delay. The result of this unevenness is incorporation of jitter in the consecutive voice packets. Jitter is not desirable during a voice call as it leaves the user dissatisfied. Several, algorithms have already been proposed to add a further playout delay to the voice packets in hope of minimizing the jitter. However, selecting the optimum playout delay is a tricky part. These algorithms often under-estimate or over-estimate the network delay of future incoming voice packets, resulting in discarding of the packets or long undesirable end-to-end delay respectively. We have proposed an algorithm that addresses to this problem and properly estimates the network delay of the future incoming voice packets. Our algorithm aims to enhance the QoS of the VoIP session. It seeks to decrease the end-to-end delay and packet discard ratio while allowing a tolerable amount of jitter to be present in the voice packets. The primary aim of our algorithm is to enhance user experience by improving the MOS of the call. We are conducting further studies in order to get even better QoS for the voice calls in a congested network scenario.

Acknowledgements. The authors acknowledge the support from DST, Govt. of India for this work in the form of FIST 2007 Project on "Broadband Wireless Communications" in the Department of ETCE, Jadavpur University.

References

1. Bolot, J.C., Vega-Garcia, A.: Control mechanisms for packet audio in the Internet. In: IEEE Annual Joint Conference of the IEEE Computer Societies. Networking the Next Generation, San Francisco, USA, March 24-28, pp. 232–239 (1996)
2. Davidson, J., Peters, J.: A Systematic Approach to understanding the basics of VoIP, Voice over IP Fundamentals. CISCO press (2000)
3. Khasnabish, B.: Implementing Voice over IP, June 12. John Wiley & Sons, Inc., Chichester (2003)
4. Chi, S., Womack, B.F.: QoS-based adaptive playout scheduling based on the packet arrival statistics: Capturing local channel characteristics. In: 2010 IEEE International Workshop Technical Committee on Communications Quality and Reliability (June 2010), doi: 10.1109/CQR.2010.5619942

5. Mukhopadhyay, A., Chakraborty, T., Bhunia, S., Saha Misra, I., Sanyal, S.K.: Study of enhanced VoIP performance under congested wireless network scenarios. In: Third International Conference on Communication Systems and Networks, 2011, pp. 1–7 (January 4-8, 2011)
6. Chakraborty, T., Mukhopadhyay, A., Saha Misra, I., Sanyal, S.K.: Optimization Technique for Configuring IEEE 802.11b Access Point Parameters to improve VoIP Performance. In: Thirteenth International Conference of Computer and Information Technology, Dhaka, Bangladesh, December 23-25 (2010)
7. Gournay, P., Anderson, K.D.: Performance Analysis of a Decoder-Based Time Scaling Algorithm for Variable Jitter Buffering of Speech Over Packet Networks. In: IEEE International Conference on Acoustics, Speech and Signal Processing (May 2006), doi: 10.1109/ICASSP.2006.1659946
8. McNeill, K.M., Liu, M., Rodriguez, J.J.: An Adaptive Jitter Buffer Play-Out Scheme to Improve VoIP Quality in Wireless Networks. In: IEEE Military Conference (October 2006), doi: 10.1109/MILCOM.2006.302119
9. Ramjee, R., Kurose, J., Towsley, D., Schulzrinne, H.: Adaptive Playout Mechanisms for Packetized Audio Applications in Wide-Area Networks. In: Networking for Global Communications, INFOCOM 1994, June 12-16, vol. 2, pp. 680–688 (1994), doi:10.1109/INFCOM.1994.337672
10. Moon, S.B., Kurose, J., Towsley, D.: Packet audio playout delay adjustment: performance bounds and algorithms. Multimedia Systems 6(1), 17–28 (1998), doi:10.1007/s005300050073
11. Jacobson, V.: Congestion avoidance and control. In: 1988 ACM SIGCOMM Conf., Stanford, pp. 314–329 (August 1988)
12. Cole, R.G., Rosenbluth, J.H.: Voice Over IP Performance Monitoring. ACM SIGCOMM Computer Communication Review 31(2) (April 2001)

Optimizing VoIP Call in Diverse Network Scenarios Using State-Space Search Technique

Tamal Chakraborty[1], Atri Mukhopadhyay[1], Suman Bhunia[2], Iti Saha Misra[2], and Salil Kumar Sanyal[2]

[1] School of Mobile Computing and Communication,
Jadavpur University Salt Lake Campus, Kolkata-700098, India
[2] Dept. of Electronics & Telecommunication Engineering
Jadavpur University, Kolkata-700032, India
{tamalchakraborty29,atri.mukherji11,sumanbhunia}@gmail.com,
iti@etce.jdvu.ac.in, s_sanyal@ieee.org

Abstract. A VoIP based call has stringent QoS requirements with respect to delay, jitter, loss, MOS and R-Factor. Various QoS mechanisms are being implemented to satisfy these requirements. These mechanisms must be adaptive under diverse network scenarios. Moreover such mechanisms must be implemented in proper sequence, otherwise they may conflict with each other. The objective of this paper is to address the problem of adaptive QoS maintenance and sequential execution of available QoS implementation mechanisms with respect to VoIP under varying network conditions. In this paper, we generalize this problem as a state-space problem and thereby solve it. Firstly, we map the problem of QoS optimization into state-space domain and then apply incremental heuristic search. We implement it under various network and user scenarios in a VoIP test-bed to optimize the performance. Finally, we discuss the advantages and uniqueness of our approach.

Keywords: VoIP, QoS, State-space, Heuristic, Incremental Search.

1 Introduction

Voice over Internet Protocol (VoIP) [1] has witnessed rapid growth in recent years owing to ease of network maintenance and savings in operational costs. As it is being widely deployed in office and public networks, maintaining the Quality of Service (QoS) of an ongoing call has assumed utmost importance. Network parameters such as bandwidth, error rate, loss rate, latency, etc. varies with time. With increasing number of users, the issues related to admission control, fairness, scalability, etc also need to be properly addressed. So the QoS optimization techniques must be adaptive.

However, abrupt implementation of these techniques without maintaining proper sequence often results in degraded performance. For example, Random Early Detection (RED) buffer is not advantageous without end-to-end congestion control mechanism [2]. Further, it is observed that often such abrupt implementations of optimization techniques conflict with each other. For example, RED implementation for small buffer size is not better than static queue with tail-drop mechanism [2]. However, buffer size must be kept small to reduce delay in real-time traffic during

D.C. Wyld et al. (Eds.): ACITY 2011, CCIS 198, pp. 231–242, 2011.

congestion. Thus they conflict each other. So the decision to apply appropriate optimization technique is crucial.

This paper aims to generalize the problem of QoS implementation amid diverse scenarios by mapping it as state-space problem. The objective is to maintain adaptive QoS in multiple call scenarios and under diverse network conditions by applying available QoS optimization techniques in proper sequence. Focus is also on prioritizing emergency calls with QoS guarantees.

A state space search is the method of finding Goal state(s) from start state through certain intermediate states [3]. In heuristics based search, each state is given a heuristic and traversing is done following a heuristic function. Incremental search further reuses information from previous searches to speed up current search [4]. Incremental heuristic search combines features of both. So it is selected as this aims to fulfill the aforementioned objective.

2 Proposed Mechanism

The aim is to map the problem of optimizing VoIP over various network links into a state-space domain where the next state from a set of intermediate states is selected based on incremental heuristic search obeying certain constraints. This is defined as a tuple [N, A, S, G]. The state-space scenario for each call is shown in Fig. 1.

- 'S' contains the start state which is defined as the call initiation state with respect to time and having heuristics namely delay, loss and Mean Opinion Score (MOS).
- 'G' contains the call termination state as the Goal state with respect to time along with its related heuristics as stated above.
- 'N' contains all the intermediate states within. An intermediate state is taken as any part of an ongoing call with respect to time along with its related heuristics. Heuristics can be categorized as *Excellent*, *Good*, *Average* and *Poor* based on user satisfaction level. Any intermediate state is derived by variation in the network parameters, significant change in heuristic values and by application of QoS optimization techniques.
- 'A' is a set of arcs from one state to another and is effected by transition functions namely $\delta 1$, $\delta 2$ and $\delta 3$. $\delta 1$ is network triggered and can occur due to changes in network. $\delta 2$ is performed by the user in response to $\delta 1$ and involves applying QoS optimization techniques. $\delta 3$ is again user triggered and maintains QoS in a multiple call scenario.

Every heuristic must obey certain local constraints for each call. Delay and loss must be within 180 ms and 5% respectively. MOS must be at least 2. In multiple call scenario, global constraints are taken as mean of local constraints. Now the proposed algorithm is discussed. It consists of two phases, namely ***analysis*** and ***implementation***. Each call at a particular instant of time is taken as state '*s*' and is associated with two metrics namely $g = \{delay, loss\}_{avg}$ and $h = \{delay_{est}, loss_{est}\}_{avg}$. '*g*' calculates the average of delay and loss for already generated states, as measured by network monitoring tool. '*h*' estimates delay ($delay_{est}$) and loss ($loss_{est}$) for the state to be generated following implementation of QoS mechanism.

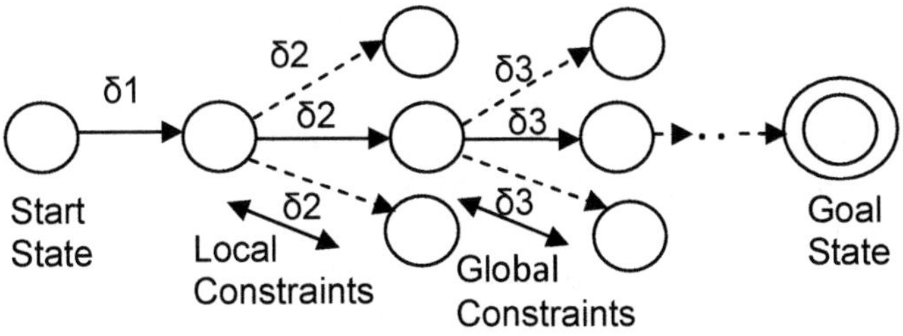

Index

State-Space	Significance In VoIP
Start State	Call Initiation
Goal State	Call Termination
Local Constraints	Constraints for each call
Global Constraints	Constraints in multiple call scenario
δ1	Change in Network Or Heuristics
δ2	Optimization Technique in single call
δ3	Optimization Technique in multiple call scenario
——→	Best ranked action
- - - →	Other actions

Fig. 1. State Space Diagram for the proposed approach

2.1 Analysis Phase

This phase analyzes all possible conditions of network with respect to delay and loss. There can be 4 scenarios that include delay and loss within tolerable limits, worsening of either delay or loss and finally degradation of both. For each scenario, order of implementation of available QoS mechanisms is selected based on its expected performance. Each such mechanism is denoted by action '*a*'. Mathematically, it is denoted by (1) [5].

$$f = \arg\min_{a \in A(s)} h(succ(s, a)) \tag{1}$$

Successor '*succ*' is next state generated due to application of action '*a*' on state '*s*'. *A(s)* denotes set of available actions to optimize state '*s*'. The best ranked action '*a*' is such that by implementing it, '*h*' becomes minimum as denoted by *argmin* function. There are two other functions namely, *one-of (f)* that describes selection of an action from set of suitable actions and *next (f)* that describes selection of next ranked action from set of suitable actions.

2.2 Implementation Phase

As the call starts, initial state is generated with heuristics. With variation in network parameters or significant change in heuristics, new intermediate states are created. The transition function is termed as *δ1*. Each state is monitored to check whether local constraints are satisfied. Each constraint has a '*threshold*'. If the local constraints are violated, *δ2* is applied to bring the heuristics within *threshold*. This implies that the best ranked mechanism is applied as per analyzed results. New states are monitored.

If local constraints are still not satisfied, next ranked action is implemented and so on.

In multiple call scenarios, global constraints must also be satisfied. Calls with low QoS metrics are classified as '*degraded*' calls and the rest as '*accepted*' calls. Existing QoS implementations for *accepted* calls are stopped temporarily and are redirected to the *degraded* calls. As global constraints are satisfied, new states are generated and corresponding transition functions are termed as $\delta 3$. All these states are monitored again and QoS mechanisms are implemented to satisfy local constraints. High priority calls are given weights and global constraints are calculated as weighted mean of local constraints. This approach is represented in Fig. 8. The pseudo-code is given under.

```
1. s:=s_start. //Call initiation state with heuristics.
2. Calculate g_s. //Delay, loss measured for current state
3. IF s ∈ G THEN GOTO step 18.//Goal state is reached.
4. IF g_s>threshold THEN GOTO step 5 ELSE GOTO step 2.
5. s:=s_δ1. Calculate g_s. //New state is generated.
6. a:=one-of(argmin_a∈A(s) h(succ(s,a)).//Select best action.
7. Execute action a.        //Action 'a' is implemented.
8. s:=s_δ2. //New state is generated after action 'a'.
9. Calculate g_s. //Delay, loss measured for current state
10. IF g_s<threshold THEN GOTO step 13 ELSE GOTO step 11.
      /*Local constraints must be satisfied.*/
11. a:=next(argmin_a∈A(s) h(succ(s,a)).//Select next action.
12. Execute action a. GOTO step 8.
13. IF no. of calls>1 THEN GOTO step 14 ELSE GOTO step 3.
14. Classify ongoing calls as accepted calls whose
      g_s<threshold. Rest of the calls is degraded calls.
15. Stop action a ∈ A(s) for accepted calls.
16. Execute action a:=argmin_a∈A(s) h(succ(s,a)) in degraded
      calls.
17. s:=s_δ3. GOTO step 9.//New state is generated after
      action 'a'
18. Calculate g_s for s ∈ G.//Goal heuristics calculated
```

3 Implementation of the Algorithm

3.1 Description of the Test-Bed

Our experimental test-bed, as shown in Fig. 2 consists of fixed and mobile nodes for VoIP communication, wireless access points, a switch and a Session Initiation Protocol (SIP) server. X-Lite [6] is used as the softphone with support for various audio codecs and Group QoS (GQoS). The Brekeke SIP server [7] is SIP Proxy Server and Registrar. ManageEngine VQManager [8] is used to analyze QoS metrics of ongoing call. Further, User Datagram Protocol (UDP) is used with Real-time Transport Protocol (RTP) on top of it.

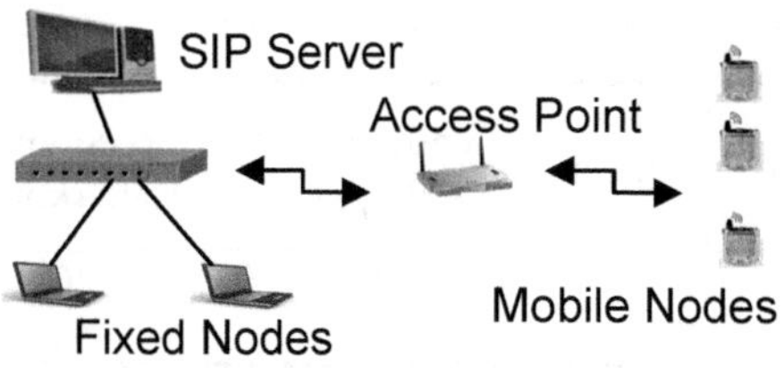

Fig. 2. Experimental Test-Bed

3.2 Test-Bed Analysis Phase

Initially the **effect of buffer size** is studied. Four scenarios are created using Network Emulator for Windows Toolkit (NEWT) [9] as shown in Table 1.

Table 1. Different Network Scenarios

Parameters	Scenario 1	Scenario 2	Scenario 3	Scenario 4
Network Latency in ms	100	100	100	100
Network Loss in %	Nil	Nil	30	30
Buffer Size in packets	Maximum	20	Maximum	20

Table 2. Delay and Loss in each scenario

Scenarios	Max. Delay	Avg. Delay	Max. Loss	Avg. Loss
1	156 ms	112 ms	0 %	0 %
2	39 ms	11 ms	44 %	5 %
3	94 ms	6 ms	61 %	22 %
4	6 ms	1 ms	49 %	21 %

As seen from Table 2, increase in loss rate in network results in degraded performance in terms of packet loss in scenario 4. As buffer size is increased, end-to-end delay increases and retransmissions take place after certain timeout, resulting in further loss as in scenario 3. Even in absence of loss rate, increasing buffer size increases end-to-end delay while decreasing it increases loss as seen in scenarios 1 and 2 respectively. So selection of proper buffer size is important.

It is also observed that if **in/out bit rate in an endpoint** (caller/callee) varies significantly with time, call quality drops and terminates at last. BroadVoice 32 (BV32) [10] is used as the codec and in and out buffer size of an end-point is varied to get the results as shown in Table 3. Fig. 3(b) shows the call termination as the in/out bit rate varies in contrast to Fig. 3(a) where the call continues. Thus it can be inferred that similar buffer sizes and hence comparable bitrates must be maintained for a call to continue successfully.

Table 3. Readings for the variable in/out bit rate in an endpoint

Local-> Remote Buffer size (packets)	Remote-> Local Buffer size (packets)	Sending Rate (kbps)	Receiving Rate (kbps)	Call Duration (sec)
20	20	26	26	1137
90	20	26	54	168

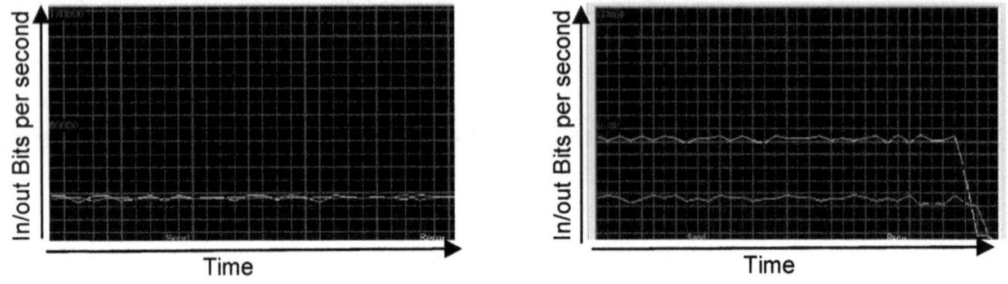

(a) (b)

Fig. 3. Effect of (a) constant in/out bit rate (b) variable in/out bit rate on ongoing call

Further, **effect of active queue management** is studied. Active queues drop packets before queue is full based on certain probabilities and threshold parameters to maintain bursts in flows and fairness among users. Here Random Early Detection (RED) [11] queue is implemented by keeping maximum threshold at 100 and minimum threshold at 50. We create two congested media having 1kbps and 10 kbps Constant Bit Rate (CBR) background traffic. As observed from Table 4, in moderately congested medium, delay and loss are within tolerable limits. Thus it is advantageous than having fixed size buffer. However, increase in congestion increases loss when RED is implemented. So selection of active queue management policy is of utmost importance towards maintaining quality of call.

Table 4. Different Execution Scenarios of RED implementation

Parameters	Background traffic 1 kbps	Background traffic 10 kbps
Average Delay in ms	66	70
Average Loss in %	6	14

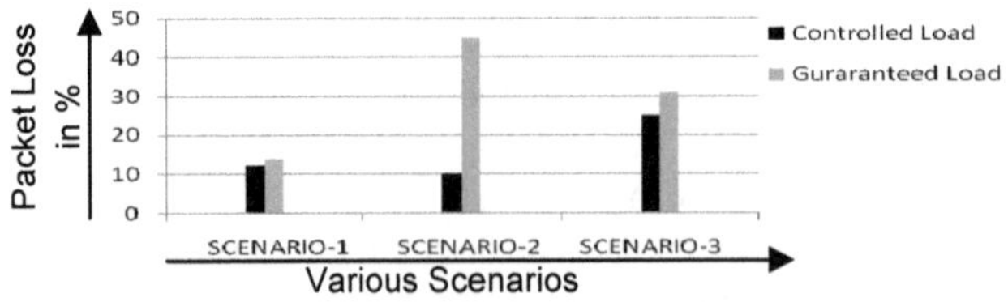

Fig. 4. Effect of Controlled Load and Guaranteed Load on loss in various scenarios

Finally we implement **IntServ model** to optimize VoIP performance. IntServ model proposes 2 service classes [12] namely,

1 Controlled load service [13] for reliable and enhanced best-effort service,
2 Guaranteed load service [14] for applications requiring a fixed delay bound.

Both are implemented in the test-bed for the scenarios as mentioned in Table 1. Experiment results conclude that controlled load service gives better performance in terms of packet loss than guaranteed service in scenarios 1, 2 and 3 as seen in Fig. 4. In scenario 4 which is the most congested scenario, call terminates in 58 seconds and 111 seconds under guaranteed service and controlled load service respectively. So it is concluded that controlled load service is more suited during congestion than guaranteed service.

3.2.1 Selection of Order of Implementation of Optimization Techniques

From analyzed results, the order of implementation is proposed.

- **Case 1:** Both delay and loss are within tolerable range.
  Guaranteed load service is applied to further enhance it.
- **Case 2:** Delay is tolerable but loss is high.
  Buffer size of access points is increased till acceptable value of delay. Further, RED is applied as the next option. If loss persists, third option is to apply FEC technique. Lastly, controlled load service is applied.
- **Case 3:** Loss is less but delay is high.
  The buffer size of access points is decreased till acceptable value of loss. Weighted RED is applied as the next option with random drop type to ensure fairness. Controlled load service is applied as the last option.
- **Case 4:** Both delay and loss are poor.
  Controlled load service is applied. RED is implemented with small difference between maximum and minimum thresholds as next option.

3.3 Test-Bed Implementation Phase

Our proposed approach is initially implemented in a single call scenario in the test-bed as described in Section 3.1. Network conditions are varied using NEWT. Heuristic categories are described in Table 5. Fig. 5 shows the state-space diagram for the call. Heuristics for each state are shown in Table 6 and the transition function for every link is described in Table 7. The average delay is 120 ms and packet loss is 1%. The average MOS is 3.3. Thus the call is of acceptable quality. Readings from VQManager as seen in Fig. 6(a) suggest that loss and delay remain uniform and tolerable in degraded conditions.

Table 5. Category of Heuristics

Heuristic Category	Description
Excellent	Delay<=100 ms, Loss <=1%, MOS>=4
Good	100ms<Delay<=150 ms,1%<Loss<=2%, 3.5<=MOS<4
Average	150ms<Delay<=180 ms,2%<Loss<=5%, 2<=MOS<3.5
Poor	Delay>180 ms, Loss>5%, MOS< 2

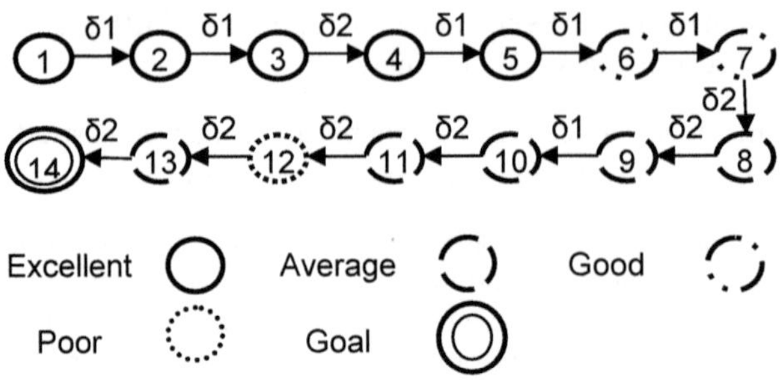

Fig. 5. State transition diagram for the call

Table 6. Heuristics for each state during the call

State	Delay (ms)	Loss(%)	MOS	Duration (s)	Comments
1	6	0	4.4	1	Start State
2	19	0	4.4	420	Excellent
3	85	0	4.4	530	Excellent
4	69	0	4.4	90	Excellent
5	95	0	4.4	350	Excellent
6	131	0	4.4	137	Good
7	147	0	4.4	126	Good
8	169	0	4.4	600	Average
9	164	0	4.4	187	Average
10	160	2	3.3	143	Average
11	169	2	2	136	Average
12	169	2	1.8	136	Poor
13	143	2	2	340	Average
14	163	2	2	250	Goal State

Table 7. Transition function for every link between the states

Link	Transition Functions	Comments
1-2	50 ms latency(δ1)	
2-3	65 ms latency(δ1)	
3-4	Guaranteed service applied(δ2)	Delay decreases to some extent
4-5	80 ms latency(δ1)	
5-6	120 ms latency(δ1)	
6-7	(δ1)	Delay varies significantly
7-8	Buffer size reduced to 50(δ2)	Delay decreases
8-9	Buffer size reduced to 30(δ2)	Delay reaches threshold mark.
9-10	0.01 Loss rate(δ2)	1 out of every 100 packets is lost.
10-11	Buffer size increased to 45(δ2)	To decrease loss & enhance MOS
11-12	Buffer size increased to 60(δ2)	It is done to decrease increasing loss. MOS now becomes uniform.
12-13	RED applied with max threshold of 100 and min threshold of 50(δ2)	As buffer size cannot be increased further due to increase in delay, the next best ranked action is chosen.
13-14	Controlled load is applied(δ2)	MOS gets improved.

The proposed algorithm is implemented in a multiple call scenario. Two calls are made and mapped as state-space diagrams. Fig. 6(b) shows that delay and loss remain tolerable. The heuristic values are shown in Table 8.

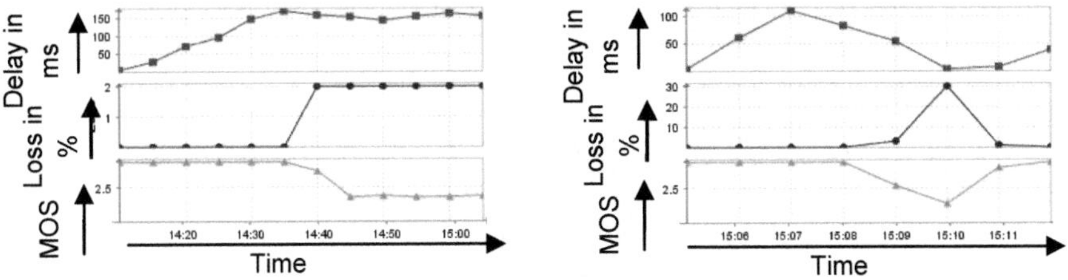

(a) (b)

Fig. 6. Variation of delay, loss and MOS in (a) single and (b) multiple call scenario

Table 8. Heuristic values in multiple call scenario

Parameters	Minimum	Maximum	Average
Delay (ms)	4	110	49
Loss (%)	0	30	5
MOS	1.4	4.4	3.6

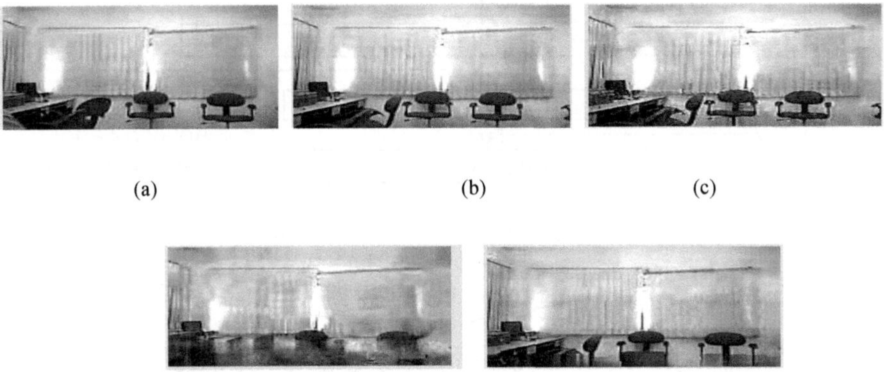

(a) (b) (c)

(d) (e)

Fig. 7. Images during a video call with (a) 0 % (b) 3 % (c) 4 % (d) 6 % (e) 5 % loss

Finally, the algorithm is applied to video call which degrades with increasing network loss as seen in Fig. 7. Applying the algorithm makes it recognizable as in Fig. 7(e). Thus QoS of video call is maintained adaptively.

4 Benefits of the Proposed Algorithm

The benefits of the algorithm are discussed hereby. State-space search has been directed towards finding optimal routes between nodes in various network conditions as in [15]. However, little work as in [16] and [17] has been done with respect to mapping network related problem to state-space problem and solving it. Our proposed

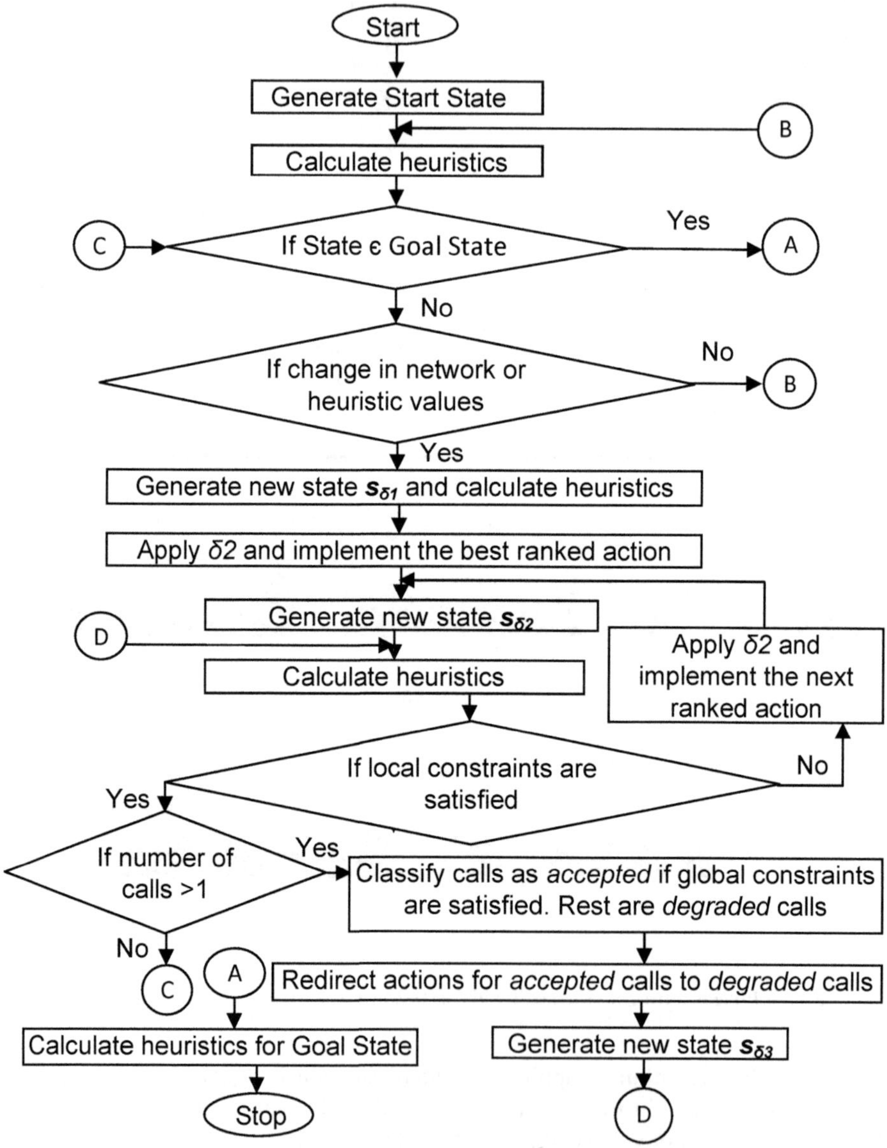

Fig. 8. Flowchart depicting the proposed approach

approach addresses QoS maintenance in real-time systems by mapping it into state-space search problem. This is advantageous as advanced search techniques and new optimizations, for instance as stated in [18] and [19] can be applied. It aims to build automated system which applies transition functions to satisfy constraints, relieving applications from complexities of QoS maintenance and maintaining transparency [20]. From state-space perspective, it satisfies inferential adequacy, inferential efficiency and aquisitional efficiency.

5 Conclusion

In this paper, we have dealt with the problem of adaptive QoS maintenance under dynamic and diverse network conditions and applied optimization techniques accordingly. Test-bed readings verify the fact that application of proposed algorithm in single and multiple voice and video calls keeps delay and loss within threshold limits even as network conditions vary with time. The algorithm further ensures that no conflict arises during application of optimization techniques as proper sequence is maintained among them. While VoIP traffic binds this algorithm to real-time heuristic search, modern optimizations in dynamic search domain can be further applied to state space search approach.

Acknowledgements. The authors deeply acknowledge the support from DST, Govt. of India for this work in the form of FIST 2007 Project on "Broadband Wireless Communications" in the Department of ETCE, Jadavpur University.

References

1. Khasnabish, B.: Implementing Voice over IP. Wiley-Interscience, John Wiley & Sons, Inc., Hoboken (2003)
2. May, M., Bolot, J., Diot, C., Lyles, B.: Reasons not to deploy RED. In: Proc. Seventh International Workshop on Quality of Service, pp. 260–262 (1999)
3. Rich, E., Knight, K.: Artificial Intelligence, 2nd edn. McGraw-Hill Science/Engineering/Math, New York (1990)
4. Koenig, S., Likhachev, M., Liu, Y., Furcy, D.: Incremental Heuristic Search in Artificial Intelligence. AI Magazine 25(2), 99–112 (2004)
5. Koenig, S.: Real-Time Heuristic Search: Research Issues. In: International Conference on Artificial Intelligence Planning Systems, Pennsylvania (June 1998)
6. X-Lite, `http://www.counterpath.com/x-lite.html`
7. Brekeke Wiki, `http://wiki.brekeke.com`
8. ManageEngine VQManager manual, `http://www.manageengine.com`
9. NEWT, `http://research.microsoft.com`
10. Chen, J-H., Lee, W., Thyssen, J.: RTP Payload Format for BroadVoice Speech Codecs, RFC 4298 (December 2005)
11. Branden, B., et al.: Recommendations on Queue Management and Congestion Avoidance in the Internet, RFC 2309 (April 1998)

12. Li, B., Hamdi, M., Lang, D., Cao, X., Hou, Y.T.: QoS-Enabled Voice Support in the Next-Generation Internet: Issues, Existing Approaches and Challenges. IEEE Communications Magazine 38(4), 54–61 (2000)
13. Wroclawski, J.: Specification of the Controlled-Load Network Element Service, RFC 2211 (September 1997)
14. Shenker, S., Partridge, C., Guerin, R.: Specification of Guaranteed Quality of Service, RFC 2212 (September 1997)
15. Zhu, T., Xiang, W.: Towards Optimized Routing Approach for Dynamic Shortest Path Selection in Traffic Networks. In: International Conference on Advanced Computer Theory and Engineering, pp. 543–547 (December 20-22, 2008)
16. Mandal, S., Saha, D., Mahanti, A.: Heuristic search techniques for cell to switch assignment in location area planning for cellular networks. In: IEEE International Conference on Communications, vol. 7, pp. 4307–4311 (June 20-24, 2004)
17. Franqueira, V.: Finding Multi-Step Attacks In Computer Networks Using Heuristic Search And Mobile Ambients. Ph.D Dissertation, University of Twente, Netherlands (2009)
18. Chakraborty, T., Mukhopadhyay, A., Misra, I.S., Sanyal, S.K.: Optimization technique for configuring IEEE 802.11b access point parameters to improve VoIP performance. In: 13th International Conference on Computer and Information Technology (ICCIT), pp. 561–566 (December 23-25, 2010)
19. Mukhopadhyay, A., Chakraborty, T., Bhunia, S., Saha Misra, I., Sanyal, S.K.: Study of enhanced VoIP performance under congested wireless network scenarios. In: Third International Conference on Communication Systems and Networks, 2011, pp. 1–7 (January 4-8, 2011)
20. Aurrecoechea, C., Campbell, A.T., Hauw, L.: A survey of QoS architectures. Multimedia Systems 6(3), 138–151 (1998)

State-Based Dynamic Slicing Technique for UML Model Implementing DSA Algorithm

Behera Mamata Manjari, Dash Rasmita, and Dash Rajashree

Dept of Information Technology, Dept of Computer Science and Engineering
Dept of Computer Science and Engineering,
Siksha 'O' Anusadhan University, Bhubaneswar, India
mamata.siet@gmail.com, {rasmita02,rajashree_dash}@yahoo.co.in

Abstract. Unified Modeling Language has been widely used in software development for modeling the problem domain to solution domain. The major problems lie in comprehension and testing which can be found in whole process. Program slicing is an important approach to analyze, understand, test and maintain the program. It is a technique for analyzing program by focusing on statements which have dependence relation with slicing criterion. Program slicing is of two types (i) Static slicing (ii) Dynamic slicing. Dynamic slicing refers to a collection of program execution and may significantly reduce the size of the program slice because runtime information, collected during execution, is used to compute the program slice. In this paper we introduce an approach for constructing dynamic slice of unified modeling language (UML) using sequence diagram, state chart diagram, class diagram along with the activity diagram. First we construct an intermediate representation known as model dependency graph. MDG combines information extracted from various state diagram. Then dynamic slice is computed by integrating the activity models into the MDG. For a given slicing criterion DSA algorithm traverse the constructed MDG to identify the relevant model element.

Keywords: Program Slicing, Dependency graph, UML Model, DSA algorithm.

1 Introduction

Unified Modeling Language has been widely used in software development for modeling the problem domain to solution domain. It is a result of the evolution of object-oriented modeling languages. It is used for modeling software systems; such modeling includes analysis and design [1]. By an analysis the system is first described by a set of requirements, and then by identification of system parts on a high level. The design phase is tightly connected to the analysis phase. It starts from the identified system parts and continues with detailed specification of these parts and their interaction. For the early phases of software projects UML provide support for identifying and specifying requirements as use cases. Class diagrams or component diagrams can be used for identification of system parts on a high level.

During the design phase class diagrams, interaction diagrams, component diagrams and state chart diagrams can be used for comprehensive descriptions of the different parts in the system.

D.C. Wyld et al. (Eds.): ACITY 2011, CCIS 198, pp. 243–252, 2011.

Analysis of UML models is a challenge since the information about a system is distributed across several model views captured through a large number of diagrams. Analysis of the impact of a change to one model on other elements therefore becomes a non-trivial problem[1][2]. Though UML models are used to reduce the complexity of a problem, but with the increased in product size and complexities, the UML models becomes very large and complex that may involves thousands of interaction among the hundreds of objects. So it becomes very difficult to understand such large model.

Now a day we are dealing with a huge project that may contain hundreds of thousands of lines of code. Here are several situations that all of us might run into, as a tester: Now, you figure out there is somewhere in the program that produce an incorrect output. In order to find where the error comes from, we need to know all previously executed statements that have some effect to the output. Then, now, a bug is found and fixed. But, we cannot guarantee the changed statements will not affect the rest of the program in the future. Studies of software maintainers have shown that approximately **50%** of their time is spent in the process of understanding the code that they are to maintain. So, our goal is to: Reduce the complexity of the program and save the regression testing time. This is possible by breaking the code into small number of pieces.

In this context, we have proposed to use program slicing[8] techniques to decompose large architectures model into small manageable parts. Program slicing is an important approach to analyze, understand, test and maintain the program. It is a technique for analyzing program by focusing on statements which have dependence relation with slicing criterion. Program slicing is of two types (i) Static slicing[2][7] (ii) Dynamic slicing[4][5]. Dynamic slicing refers to a collection of program execution and may significantly reduce the size of the program slice because runtime information, collected during execution, is used to compute the program slice.

In this paper, we concentrate on UML activity diagrams to automatically generate test cases. This paper is organized as follows: A brief discussion on basic concepts is given in the next section. In Section 3 we discuss proposed model. Section 4 describes our Model dependency graph. Section 5 discusses dynamic slicing technique to generate dynamic slice and conclusions are given in Section 7.

2 Basic Concept

In this section, we present an overview of those aspects of UML 2.0 and slicing technique which are relevant to our work.

2.1 Class Diagrams

A class diagram consists of the parts classes, associations and generalizations, and can exist in several different levels. Below is an identification of three different useful levels, starting with the least detailed.

- Conceptual class diagrams (conceptual model), represent concepts of the problem domain

- High level class diagrams (type model), describe static views of a solution to a problem, through a precise model of the information that is relevant for the software system
- Detailed class diagrams (class model), include data types, operations and possibly advanced relations between classes

2.2 Sequence Diagram

UML sequence diagrams are used to model the flow of control between objects. It can be hard to understand the overall flow in a complex system without modeling it. Sequence diagrams model the interactions through messages between objects; it is common to focus the model on scenarios specified by use-cases. It is also often useful input to the detailed class diagram to try to model the specified use cases with sequence diagrams, necessary forgotten operations and relations are usually found. The diagrams consists of interacting objects and actors, with messages in-between them.

2.3 State Chart Diagram

UML State charts are most often used for low level design, like modeling the internal behavior of a complicated class. But they are also useful on a higher level on modeling different states of a whole system; this can be compared to the usage of class diagrams on several levels.

2.4 Activity Diagram

Activity diagrams can be in many places in the design process; sometimes even before use case diagrams for understanding the workflow of a process. But they can also be used for defining how use cases interact or even for detailed design. Basic elements in activity diagrams are activities, branches.

3 Proposed Model

To compute the dynamic slice of the UML model, we structure our work into following steps:

3.1 Development of Various UML Diagram

Given a problem domain, first we have to develop UML model including class diagram along with various sequence diagram and activity diagram.

3.2 Construction of an Intermediate Representation

We propose an intermediate representation for software architecture by integrating various UML diagrams viz., class, and sequence and state-machine diagrams into a single system model. Such a representation would capture all relevant information spread across diverse model views into a single structure and can facilitate effective and efficient slicing.

3.3 Implementation of Dynamic Slicing Algorithm

Based on the constructed intermediate representation, we propose an algorithm for dynamic slicing of UML architectural models using state information. Our slicing algorithm is based on traversing the edges of our intermediate representation for any given scenario execution in the slicing criterion. Through model dependency graph (MDG) traversal, our slicing algorithm would identify the relevant model elements from an architecture based on the dependencies among them to compute dynamic architectural model slice.

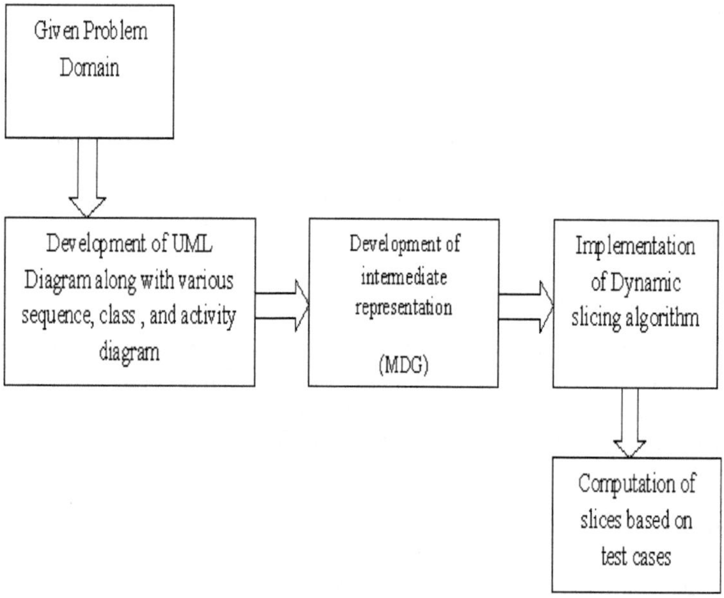

Fig. 1. Proposed Model

4 Model Dependency Graph

In this section, we present an overview of an intermediate representation which we have named Model Dependency Graph(MDG).We first discuss the key elements of MDG and then outline the representation of a generic system using MDG[3]. MDG represents both structural aspects modelled in various class diagrams as well as behavioral aspects modelled in sequence, state-machine and activity diagrams of an architecture. An MDG provides an integrated view of all such UML diagrams.

4.1 MDG Nodes

An MDG consists of different types of nodes that correspond to the elements of either class, or sequence diagrams. The different nodes of the MDG are as follows:

- A class access (CA) node is defined for every class in the UML architectural model.
- A method access (MA) node is defined for every operation of a class.
- An attribute (AT) node is defined for every class attribute.
- A parameter (PR) node is defined for every operation parameter specified in an operation signature.
- A return (RT) node is defined for every return parameter specified in an operation signature.
- A predicate class (PC) node is defined for every combined fragment used in a sequence diagram.
- An interaction (IT) node is defined for every interaction occurrence used in a sequence diagram.

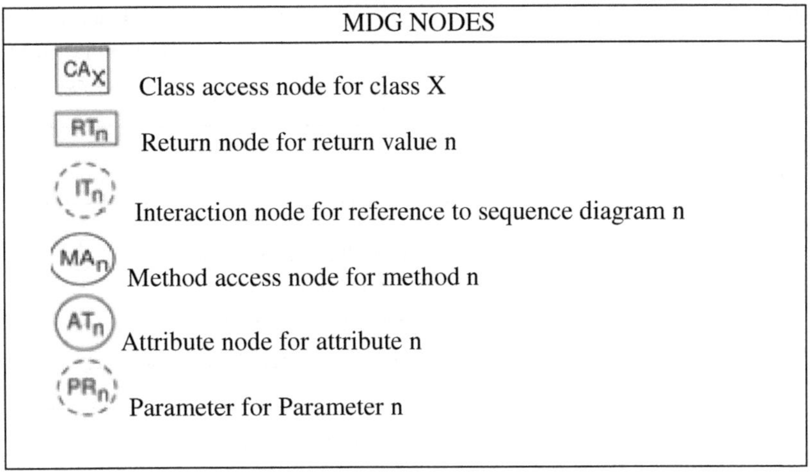

Fig. 2. Different types of MDG nodes

4.2 MDG Edges

The nodes of an MDG can be interconnected by two types of dependence edges namely

- class-induced dependence edges
- interaction-induced dependence

We can classify MDG edges into following based on the type and nature of information available from class, sequence, state machine and activity diagram, respectively.

- Edges of the MDG can be based on the elements in the class diagram. Different types of edges in this category include member dependence, method dependence, data dependence and relationship dependence edges. We call all such dependencies class-induced dependence edges.
- Edges of the MDG can be based on the elements in the sequence diagram. We call all such edges message dependence edges.
- Edges of the MDG can be based on the elements in the state-machine diagram. The data dependence edges in the MDG arising because of specific guard conditions that change an object's state fall under this category. We call all such dependencies state-induced dependence edges.

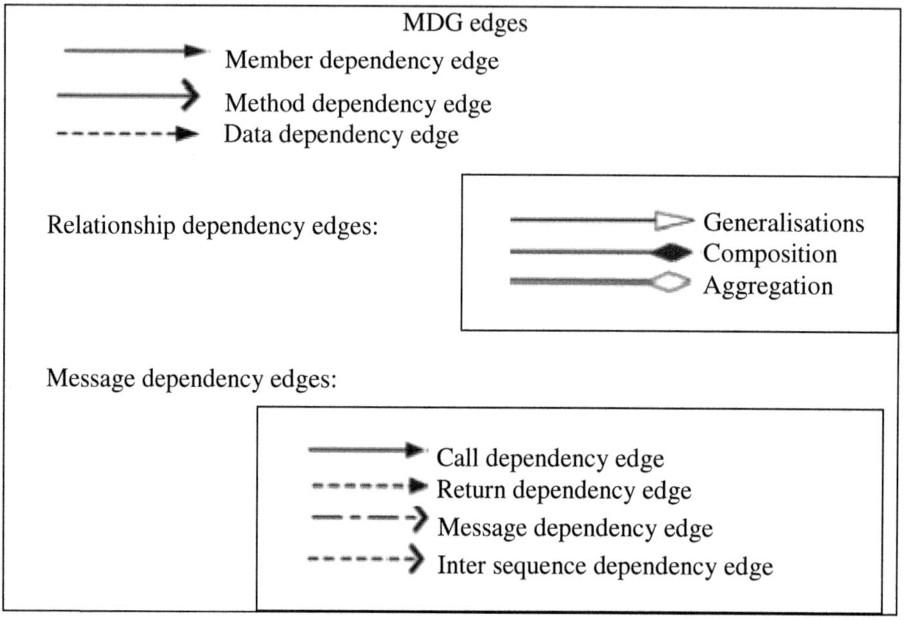

Fig. 3. Different types of edges of MDG

4.3 MDG Construction Technique

We now briefly discuss how class, sequence and activity diagrams can be integrated to construct an MDG. The process of integrating class, sequence and activity diagrams has schematically been shown in Fig. 4. The integration process is carried out over many steps[1][3]. The exact number of steps may vary depending on the number of sequence diagrams present in a given UML model.

In Step-1, an arbitrarily selected sequence diagram SDi along with the information present in different class diagrams is used to construct a partial MDG MDG1. In addition, for all the objects participating in SDi, if the object's corresponding activity diagram AD is available, the object's state information is encompassed on the respective CA nodes in the MDG . Next, the process carried out in Step-1 is repeated

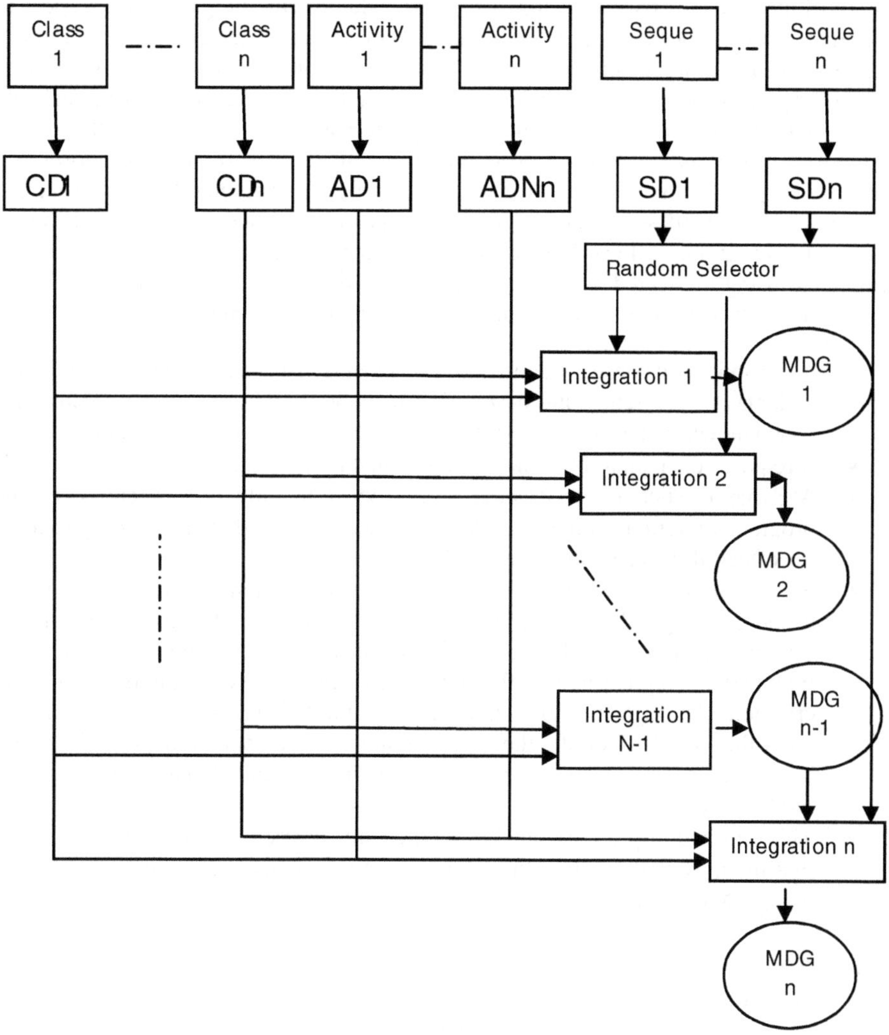

Fig. 4. Integration process for MDG

during Step-2 on another arbitrarily selected sequence diagram SDj. This step also updates MDG1 constructed in previous step, resulting in a partial MDG MDG2.

The same process is repeated till all the sequence diagrams have been considered. For integrating a model with n sequence diagrams, the Step-n will result in MDGn. The MDGn constructed after n steps is the final MDG obtained at the end of integration.

5 Dynamic Slicing Technique

A dynamic program slice is that part of a program that ''affects'' the computation of a variable of interest during program execution on a specific program input[4]. A slice is constituted by the statements that affect the value of the program with respect to the given variable occurrence .The various statements are statements using variables, expressions and assignments and control flow statements. It is an executable portion of the original program whose behavior is, under the same input, indistinguishable from that of the original program on a given variable 'V' at point 'P' in the program[8][9]. Weiser defines a program slice with respect to slicing criterion that consists of program point 's' and a subset of program variables 'v' is now called executable backward static slice. Executable means the slice is required to be an executable program, backward means the direction edges are traversed when a slice is computed using a directed graph and static means they are computed as the solution to a static analysis problem (i.e., without considering the program's input).

- A dynamic slice consists of only those statements that actually affect the value of a variable at a program point for a given execution[9]. It computes those statements which influence the value of a variable occurrence for a specific program.
- It requires the path to be same in the original program and in the slice.
- A dynamic slice is constructed with respect to only one execution of the program (iteration number is taken into account). A dynamic slice preserves the effect of the program for a fixed input.
- Based on the constructed intermediate representation shown in fig 4, we propose an algorithm for dynamic slicing of UML architectural models using state information. Our slicing algorithm is based on traversing the edges of our intermediate representation for any given scenario execution in the slicing criterion. Through model dependency graph (MDG) traversal, our slicing algorithm would identify the relevant model elements from an architecture based on the dependencies among them to compute dynamic architectural model slice.
- This subsection presents our DSA algorithm in pseudocode form. It assumes that the information about the classes and the interactions is available from a given UML model.

```
Algorithm DSA
Requires : SetClass = {CL(1) ... CL(n)}
                    {* Set of classes in a model *}
                     SetInteraction = {I1 ... Im }

Initialization : Graph MDG = NULL
                          List  ScenarioMsgList = NULL

Input : SCd   = [CACL(n) , Smj , DM ]       {* Slicing Criterion *}

Output : DAMS(CACL(n) , Smj , DM )
```

Phase 1 : Incremental extraction of information from structural and behavioral models to construct an MDG

```
                  {* Call a procedure for MDG construction *}
MDG = ConstructMDG(SetClass, SetInteraction);
```

Phase 2 : Traversal of MDG to compute a dynamic slice
for every dependent node traversed from CACL(n) corresponding
to Im (k) ∈ ScenarioMsgList based on DM during execution of
scenario Smj do TraverseMDG(MDG, Im (k), DM);
DAMS(SCd)=Track DynSlice(MDG, Im (k), DM); -
end for
DisplaySlice(DAMS(SCd));
End DSA

- After the slicing criterion is given as an input, DSA computes a dynamic slice on by executing Phase 2 of the algorithm.

6 Test Case Generation

The complexity of testing a system model can be possibly be attributed to the fact that it involves testing a fully integrated system. With increasing complexity of the systems it is expected that a very large set of test cases would be required to achieve full test coverage.Test cases can be generated by identifying all the possible paths in MDG. These can be selectively identified for a particular use case with a specific scenario execution. Once the dynamic slice is computed for a particular slice criterion, it becomes evident that model element is contributed

7 Conclusion

We have proposed a technique for dynamic slicing using state information. Efficiently constructing precise slices of UML architectural models is a difficult problem since the model information is distributed across several diagrams with implicit dependencies among them. We first construct an intermediate representation called MDG.MDG integrates the structural and behavioral aspects of an architectural design. Then test cases are generated based on the path of MDG. The Dynamic slice is calculated based on test criteria. Here DSA algorithm has been imlemented to compute accurate slice.

References

[1] Korel, B., Rilling, J.: Dynamic program slicing methods. Information and Software Technology 40, 647–659 (1998)

[2] Korel, B., Ferguson, R.: Dynamic slicing of distributed programs. Applied Mathematics and Computer Science Journal 2(2), 199–215 (1992)

[3] Korel, B.: Computation of dynamic slices for unstructured programs. IEEE Transactions on Software Engineering 23(1), 17–34 (1997)

[4] Lallchandani, J.T., Mall, R.: Integrated state-based dynamic slicing technique for UML models. The Proceeding of IET Software 4, 55–78 (2010)

[5] Lallchandani, J.T., Mall, R.: Static slicing of UML architectural models. J. Object Technol. 8(1), 159–188 (2009)

[6] Lallchandani, J.T., Mall, R.: Slicing UML Models. PhD thesis, Indian Institute of Technology Kharagpur, West Bengal, India (September 2009)
[7] Lallchandani, J.T., Mall, R.: Dynamic slicing of UML models. Technical Report IIT-CS08-SE-14, Indian Institute of Technology (IIT), Kharagpur, West Bengal, India (April 2008)
[8] N.M. Inc., Magicdraw UML v11.6, http://www.magicdraw.com
[9] Ojala, V.: A slicer for UML state machines. Technical Reports HUT- TCS-B25, Helsinki University of Technology, Laboratory for Theoretical Computer Science (2007)
[10] Object Management Group: Unified modeling language specification, version 2.0 (August 2005), http://www.omg.org
[11] Samuel, P., Mall, R.: A Novel Test Case Design Technique Using Dynamic Slicing of UML Sequence Diagrams. e-Informatica Software Engineering Journal 2(1) (2008)
[12] Tip, F.: A survey of program slicing techniques. J. Programm. Languages 3(3), 121–189 (1995)
[13] Weiser, M.: Program slicing. IEEE Trans. Software Engineering 10(4), 352–357 (1984)

Self Charging Mobile Phones Using RF Power Harvesting

Ajay Sivaramakrishnan[1,*], Karthik Ganesan[1],
and Kailarajan Jeyaprakash Jegadishkumar[2]

B.E Electronics & Communication, II year, SSN College of Engineering,
Old Mahabalipuram Road, SSN Nagar, Tamil Nadu, India
{ajaysivaramakrishnan,karthik1992}@gmail.com
Asst. Professor, Electronics & Communication, SSN College of Engineering,
Old Mahabalipuram Road, SSN Nagar, Tamil Nadu, India
jegadishkj@ssn.edu.in

Abstract. RF power harvesting is one of the diverse fields where still research continues. The energy of RF waves used by devices can be harvested and used to operate in more effective and efficient way. This paper highlights the performance of energy harvesting in an efficient way by using a simple voltage doubler. With slight modifications we attained high output voltage from harvested RF energy. The modified form of existing schottky diode based voltage doubler circuit is presented to achieve high output power for an average input RF power of 20 dBm. The performance of the circuit is studied with simulation results in ADS tools.

Keywords: RF power scavengers, voltage doubler, Impedance matching, resonant circuits.

1 Introduction to RF Energy Harvesting

Nowadays common resource constrained wireless devices operated using battery faces disadvantages as follows:

- Need for main supply to charge drained mobile phone batteries.
- Need to carry charger at all times.
- Use of batteries adds to size.
- Use of Non renewable energy sources.

A viable solution to the above shortcomings is thought of and it is-"Capturing the available energy from the external ambient sources - a technology known as "*Energy Harvesting*" .Other names for this technology are – Power harvesting , energy scavenging and Free energy derived from Renewable Energy.

Elaborating further, Energy harvesters take the necessary fuel from the ambient external sources and obviously available freely for the user, cutting down the cost factor of charging batteries. The external ambient energy sources which are most considered and used for energy harvesting are Wind , Solar , Vibration, Thermoelectric, Temperature Gradient, Radio Frequency (RF) , Acoustic etc. Notable advancements in the low power consuming wireless electronic devices are also a driving factor for thirst in such RF power scavenging technologies.

D.C. Wyld et al. (Eds.): ACITY 2011, CCIS 198, pp. 253–259, 2011.

2 Energy Harvesting through RF

In this paper we focus on energy harvesting technique from electromagnetic energy. Radio waves are present everywhere since it is used for signal transmissions of TV, Radio, Mobile phones etc. Omni directional antennas are the major components used in communication systems to broadcast RF power in KW range. In practice for mobile communication, very few milli-watts of RF power can be scavenged from the atmosphere as the receiver sensitivity of the mobile phone antennas is very high. The major factor for such a tremendous reduction in the transmitted power is absorption by the objects (i.e. obstacles) present in the path of the RF waves and also loss of power in the form of heat in materials where it gets absorbed. Most of the wireless devices like mobile phones consume only microwatts to milliwatts range of power for their operation in sleep & active modes respectively. So we can readily tap the RF power available in the external environment using scavenging circuit and use it to operate our mobile phones. Now, we can see our proposed circuit for achieving such functionality. The figure [1] shown represents the block diagram of various ingredients to design our proposed circuit.

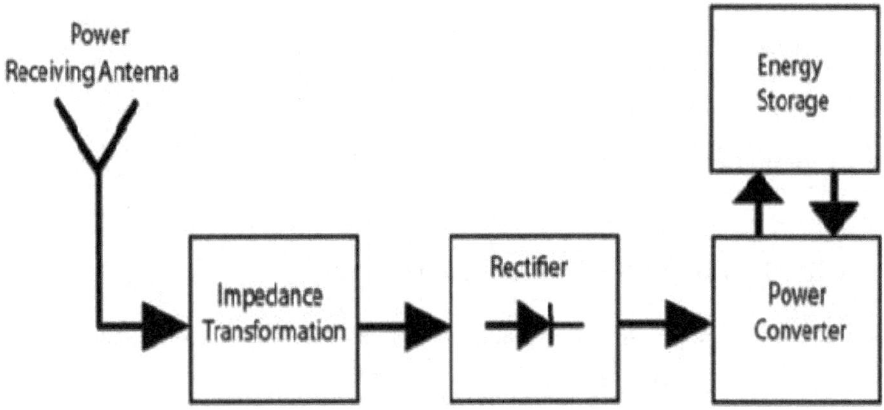

Fig. 1. Block diagram

3 System Overview

The received RF power by an antenna is streamed through a rectifier circuit and then through a power converter circuit which increases the rectified voltage i.e. doubles /triples/quadruples. Finally the converted output DC power can be used for driving the device or it can also be used to recharge batteries. The significance of the Impedance Matching circuit is to match the impedance of antenna with that of rectifier circuit. This achieves higher efficiency in attaining the output power. The input power received by the antenna is transferred to the rectifier circuit only at the resonant frequency. By using impedance transformation circuit, operation of the circuit is restricted to a specific frequency range of 0.9GHz – 1.8GHz which is the operating band for mobile communication.

The figure [2] shown is a basic voltage doubler circuit which receives the input AC voltage.

During the positive half cycle of the input voltage the upper diode will be forward biased whereas the lower diode will be reverse biased because of the polarities with which they are connected with the input side. Thus the upper diode acts as a short circuit whereas the lower diode acts as an open circuit. Thus the upper capacitor charges to +Vm (peak input voltage) through the upper diode with „+" polarity on its upper terminal and a „-„ polarity on its lower terminal.

During the negative half cycle of the input voltage the upper diode will be reverse biased and lower diode will be forward biased because of the polarities with which they are connected with the input side. Thus, the lower diode acts as a short circuit whereas the upper diode acts as an open circuit. Thus the lower capacitor charges to +Vm (peak input voltage) through the lower diode with „+" polarity on its lower terminal and a „-„ polarity on its upper terminal. Because of the half wave rectification by the presence of the diodes in the circuit, the output taken across the two capacitors produces a rectified output voltage of +2Vm i.e. twice the input AC peak voltage.

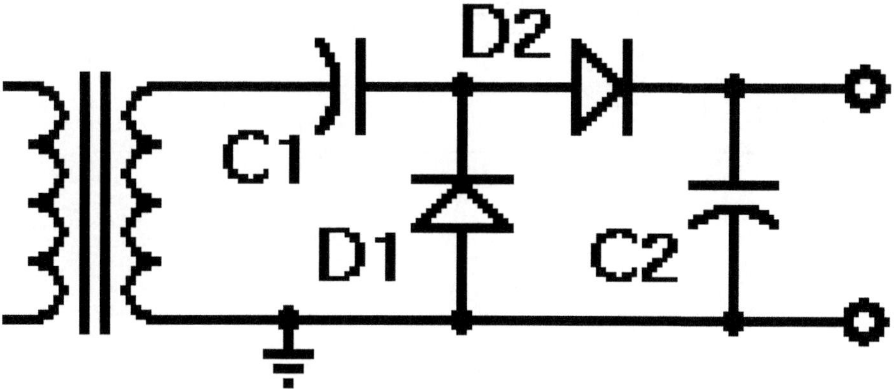

Fig. 2. Basic Voltage doubler circuit

4 Our Proposed Design

Figure [3] shown is our proposed circuit. In our design, in the front end of our circuit, we use ideal power source offering impedance of 50Ω to deliver power ranging from -5dBm to 20dBm. Following the source, we include a resonant circuit to resonate in the frequency range of 0.9GHz to 1.8GHz.

$$f = \frac{1}{2\pi\sqrt{LC}}$$

We attained the resonant circuit by adding inductor to the circuit. In order to achieve a wide band, the quality factor of inductor is reduced by adding resistance to the inductor. This helps us to boost the output power. The same circuit also acts as impedance matching circuit.

Following, we have voltage doubler circuit in our design. During the positive half cycle, diode D1 gets forward biased and charges the capacitor C1. During negative half cycle, diode D2 gets forward biased and charges the capacitor C2. The output is taken across the load resistance RL. This circuit was designed implemented and simulated in ADS tool. The performance of our proposed circuits are described in the following section.

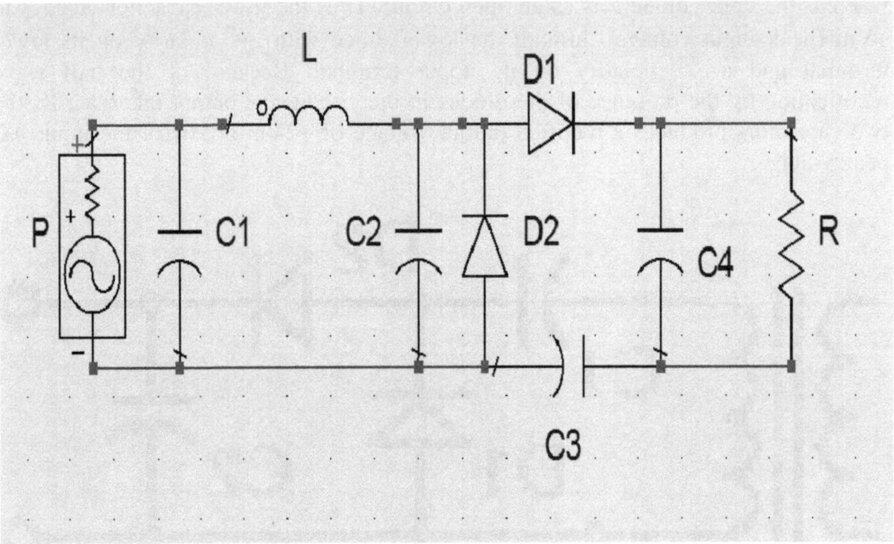

Fig. 3. Circuit for RF energy harvesting

5 Simulation Results

Usually mobile phones receives a power ranging from -5dBm to 40dBm. When the mobile is in active mode or while we are talking over phone, the average signal power received by the receiving antenna of the mobile is an average power of 20 dBm.

Figure [4] and figure [5] are graphs plotted for the input signal of 20dbm which is received by the antenna when the mobile is at active mode.

If the graphs are plotted with 40dbm as input, then the output will be more, which is more than sufficient for the mobile phone to operate.

From Figure [4] and [5] it is obvious that we may get a more efficient and rectified output voltage as well as current for the mobile to work at active state or while talking over phone for the desired operating frequency range of 0.9GHz to 1.9GHz.

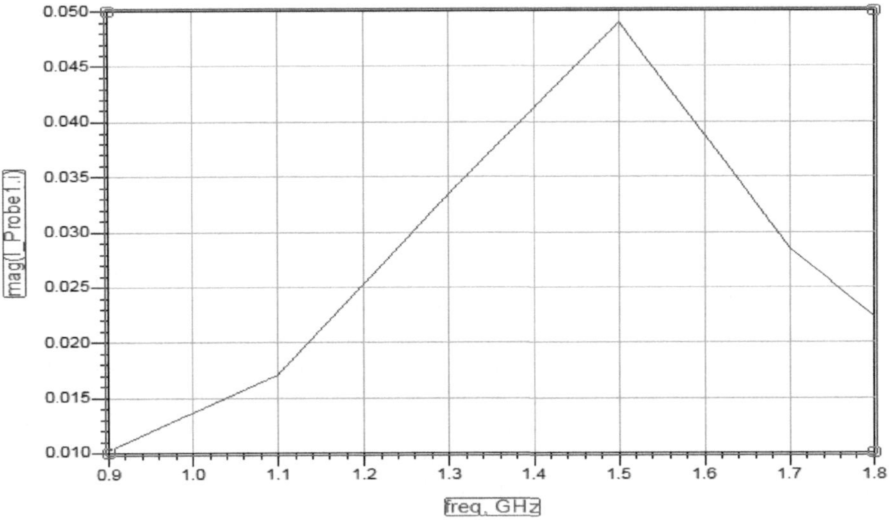

Fig. 4. Graph plotted Current I Vs Frequency

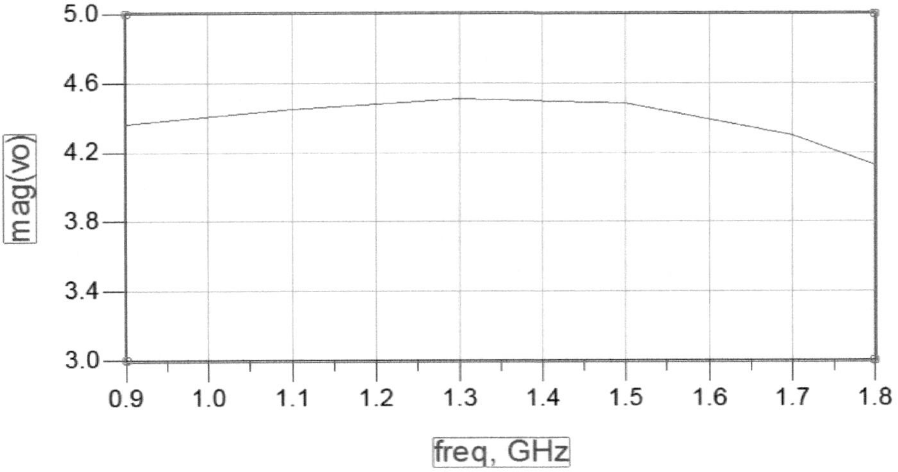

Fig. 5. Graph plotted Output voltage Vo Vs Frequency

6 Major Advantages of the Circuit

The components used here are:

- All schottky diodes of low series resistance which are the best diodes used for operations in RF region. And the switching property of the diode is superior.
- The capacitors used are of values that are easily available.

 The inductor used in the circuit has low inductance value which is smaller in size also easily available.

This proposed circuit can be readily and easily manufactured without the need to order for fabrication thereby proving to be a cost effective one.

7 Conclusion

Our proposed circuit generates a minimum rectified output voltage and current. This output can still be increased by reducing the capacitance values to the range of very low values and increasing the voltage multiplier stages. However this proposed circuit can conveniently capture the RF energy from the environment and convert it to a useful power which can be used to operate the mobile phones. Because of the minimum size of the above circuit, it can easily be implemented in the mobiles without any space constraints. As on whole this circuit can conveniently operate a mobile without the need for charging the battery separately.

References

[1] Brown, W.: The history of power transmission by radio waves. IEEE Transactions on Microwave Theory and Techniques 32(9), 1230–1242 (1984)

[2] Jiang, B., Smith, J.R., Philipose, M., Roy, S., Sundara-Rajan, K., Mamishev, A.V.: Energy scavenging for inductively coupled passive rfid systems. IEEETransactions on Instrumentation and Measurement 56(1), 118–125 (2007)

[3] Mickle, M., Mi, M., Mats, L., CaPelli, C., Swift, H.: Powering autonomouscubic-millimeterdevices. IEEE Antennas and Propagation Magazine 48(1), 11–21 (2006)

[4] Hagerty, J., Helmbrecht, F., McCalpin, W., Zane, R., Popovic, Z.: Recyclingambientmicrowave energy with broad-bandrectenna arrays. IEEETransactions on Microwave Theory and Techniques 52(3), 1014–1024 (2004)

[5] Paing, T., Shin, J., Zane, R.: Z Popovic, Resistor emulation approach to low-power rf energy harvesting. IEEE Transactions on Power Electronics 23(3), 1494–1501 (2008)

[6] Zbitou, J., Latrach, M., Toutain, S.: Hybrid rectenna and monolithic integrated zero-bias microwave rectifier. IEEE Transactions on Microwave Theory and Techniques 54(1), 147–152 (2006)

[7] Shameli, A., Safarian, A., Rofougaran, A., Rofougaran, M., De Flaviis, F.: Power harvester design for passive uhf rfid tag using a voltage boosting technique. IEEE Transactions on Microwave Theory and Techniques 55(6), 1089–1097 (2007)

[8] Seemann, K., Hofer, G., Cilek, F., Weigel, R.: Single - endedultra - low power multistage rectifiers for passive rfid tags at uhf and microwave frequencies. In: IEEE Radioand Wireless Symposium, 2006, pp. 479–482 (January 2006)

[9] Le, T., Mayaram, K., Fiez, T.: Efficient far-field radio frequency energy harvesting for passively powered sensor networks. IEEEJournal of Solid-State Circuits 43(5), 1287–1302 (2008)

[10] Ungan, T., Freunek, M., MUlier, M., Walker, W., Reindl, L.: Wireless energy transmission using electrically small antennas. In: IEEE Radioand Wireless Symposium, RWS 2009, pp. 526–529 (January 2009)

[11] McSpadden, J., Yoo, T., Chang, K.: Theoretical and experimental investigation of a rectenna element for microwave power transmission. IEEE Transactions on Microwave Theory and Techniques 40(12), 2359–2366 (1992)
[12] Pletcher, N., Gambini, S., Rabaey, J.: A 52 J.LW wake-up receiver with -72 dbm sensitivityusing an uncertain-ifarchitecture. IEEEJournal of Solid-State Circuits 44(1), 269–280 (2009)
[13] Harrison, R., Le Polozec, X.: Nonsquarelaw behavior of diode detectors analyzed by the ritz-galerkin method. IEEE Transactions on Microwave Theory and Techniques 42(5), 840–846 (1994)
[14] Geyi, W., Jarmuszewski, P., Qi, Y.: The foster reactancetheorem for antennas and radiation q. IEEE Transactions on Antennas and Propagation 48(3), 401–408 (2000)
[15] Mclean, J.S.: A re-examination of the fundamental limits on the radiation q of electrically small antennas. IEEE Transactions on Antennas and Propagation 44(5), 672 (1996)
[16] Ungan, T., Reindl, L.: Harvesting low ambient rf-sources for autonomous measurement systems. In: Proceedings of IEEE Instrumentation and Measurement Technology Conference, IMTC 2008, pp. 62–65 (May 2008)

A Servey on Bluetooth Scatternet Formation

Pratibha Singh and Sonu Agrawal

RIT, Raipur, Dept. of Computer science & Eng., SSCET, durg, Dept. of Computer sci. & Eng., Raipur, (Chhattisgarh), India
er.pratibha@yahoo.in, agrawalsonu@gmail.com

Abstract. A Bluetooth ad hoc network can be formed by interconnecting piconets into scatternets. The constraints and properties of Bluetooth scatternets present special challenges in forming an ad hoc network efficiently. This paper, the research contributions in this arena are brought together, to give an overview of the state-of-the-art.

Simply stated, Bluetooth is a wireless communication protocol. Since it's a communication protocol, you can use Bluetooth to communicate to other Bluetooth-enabled devices. In this sense, Bluetooth is like any other communication protocol that you use every day, such as HTTP, FTP, SMTP, or IMAP. Bluetooth has a client-server architecture; the one that initiates the connection is the client, and the one who receives the connection is the server. Bluetooth is a great protocol for wireless communication because it's capable of transmitting data at nearly 1MB/s, while consuming 1/100th of the power of Wi-Fi. We discuss criteria for different types of scatternets and establish general models of scatternet topologies. Then we review the state-of-the-art approaches with respect to Bluetooth scatternet formation and contrast them.

Keywords: Bluetooth, Scatternet formation, Piconet, Ad hoc network.

1 Introduction

Bluetooth is a networking technology aimed at low-powered, short range applications. It was initially developed by Ericsson, but is governed as an open specification by the Bluetooth Special Interest Group . Bluetooth is a recently proposed standard for short range, low power wireless communication. Initially, it is being envisioned simply as a wire replacement technology. Its most commonly described application is that of a “cordless computer “consisting of several devices including a personal computer, possibly a laptop, keyboard, mouse, joystick, printer, scanner,etc., each equipped with a Bluetooth card. There are no cable connections between these devices, and Bluetooth is to enable seamless communication between all them, essentially replacing what is today achieved through a combination of serial and parallel cables, and infrared links. However, Bluetooth has the potential for being much more than a wire replacement technology, and the Bluetooth standard was indeed drafted with such a more ambitious goal in mind. Bluetooth holds the promise of becoming the technology of choice for adhoc networks of the future. This is in part because its low power consumption and potential low cost make it an attractive solution for the typical mobile devices used in adhoc networks. This paper includes some previous work done on bluetooth scatternet. This paper is organized as follows.

D.C. Wyld et al. (Eds.): ACITY 2011, CCIS 198, pp. 260–269, 2011.

We briefly describe the salient features of the Bluetooth technology in Section II. We describe key technical challenges that need to be addressed for its successful deployment in large scale adhoc networks in Section III. We discuss certain design objectives in Section IV, and briefly review the existing research in Section V. In section VI ,We describe Survey on researches that had been done previously and we conclude the paper in section VII.

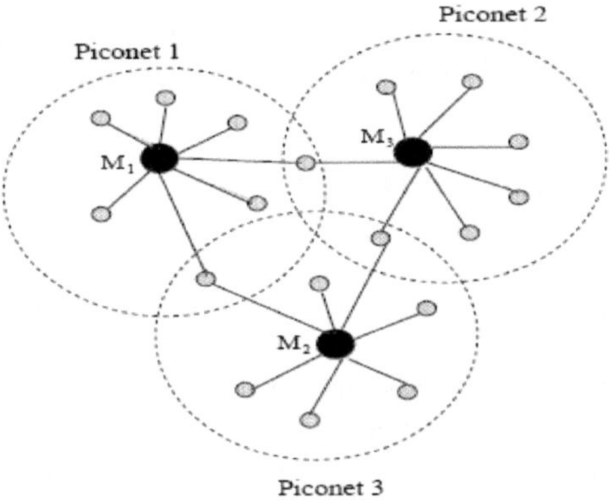

Fig. 1. An example Bluetooth topology is illustrated. The nodes are organized into 3 piconets. The masters of these piconets are M1; M2; M3 respectively. The remaininnodes are the slave nodes or bridge nodes. Slave nodes S1 and S2 can communicate via master M1: Nodes S1 and S3 can communicate via masterM1; bridge B and masterM2.

2 Bluetooth Operation

Bluetooth basics is as follows:

1.Connection establishment
2.Concept of an ad-hoc piconet

In this section, we briefly describe the basic features of a Bluetooth network. Nodes are organized in small groups called *piconets*. Every piconet has a leading node called "master," and other nodes in a piconet are referred to as "slaves." A node may belong to multiple piconets, and we refer to such a node as a "bridge." A piconet can have at most 7 members. Refer to figure 1 for a sample organization. Every communication in a piconet involves the master, so that slaves do not directly communicate with each other but instead rely on the master as a transit node. In other words, Bluetooth provides a half-duplex communication channel. Communication between nodes in different piconets must involve the bridge nodes. A bridge node cannot be simultaneously active in multiple piconets. It is active in one piconet and "parked" in others. Bluetooth allows different activity states for the nodes: active, idle, parked, sniffing. Data exchange takes place between two nodes only when both are active. Activity states of nodes change periodically.

Connecting two devices via Bluetooth requires phases:

1).inquiry: This process consists of a sender broadcasting inquiry packets, which do not contain the identity of the Inquiry sender or any other information.

_ Inquiry Scan: In this state, receiver devices listen for inquiry packets, and upon detection of any such packet, the device broadcasts an inquiry response packet. This contains the identity of the device and its native clock.

2) Page: When paging, a sender device tries to form a connection with a device whose identity and clock are known. Page packets are sent, which contain the sender's device address and clock, for synchronization.

_ Page Scan: In this state a receiver device listens for page packets. Receipt is acknowledged and synchronization between the devices is established

3 Challenges in Bluetooth Design

The Bluetooth specifications have left several design issues open to implementation, when it comes to its use as a networking technology. The objective is to allow designers flexibility so as to cater to the individual network requirements. However for adapting the technology towards large scale deployment in adhoc networks it is imperative that there be a systematic procedure for attaining some of the most common design objectives. We first examine the open issues and then discuss why these need to be carefully "nailed down" in order to satisfy certain universal design objectives. A predominant open issue is how to decide which nodes become masters, slave and bridges. In Bluetooth, nodes are assumed physically equivalent with respect to their Bluetooth capabilities, so that the master and slave states are purely logical. This is a useful feature in the context of adhoc networks where nodes will likely be reasonably homogeneous, but it also introduces several problems. This is because the decision for a node to become slave or master affects the connectivity that will be available to other nodes. In addition, a node needs to decide the number of piconets it should join, and when multiple choices are possible, which subset of piconets to choose. This latter issue arises because a node may have several masters within its communication range. Note that the master of one piconet can participate as a slave in another one. There are multiple facets to the decision of how many piconets a node should join. On one hand, bridge nodes that belong to multiple piconets improve connectivity, which reduces the number of communication hops needed to transfer data between any two nodes and can, therefore, improve overall throughput. On the other hand, the larger the number of piconets a node joins, the larger the associated processing, storage, and most important, communication overhead. This is because a node needs to store certain information about each of the piconets it participates, and furthermore can only be active in one piconet at the time. Specifically, at any one time a node can be active in one piconet and must be parked in the other piconets to which it belongs. Switching from one piconet to another involves a non-negligible processing overhead. In addition, while involved in communications in one piconet, a node is unavailable for communications in all the other piconet. This can also affect throughput, albeit this time negatively, as the participation of one node in multiple piconets proportionally reduces the capacity available for communications between any two of the piconets to which it belongs. Note that the impact of this constraint also depends on whether the node is involved in piconets only as a slave, or whether it is the master of one of the piconets. In the latter case, any period during which the node is acting as a slave in some piconet, corresponds to a communication blackout for all the slaves of the piconet for which it serves as a master. Intuitively, this is an undesirable effect, even if its magnitude depends on the number of nodes involved in the affected piconet. As a matter of fact, the number of slaves that a piconet should have is itself an open issue. The Bluetooth specification imposes an upper bound on this number (7), but performance considerations should also be taken into account. For one, as discussed above, the number of piconets in which a master participates should be different from that of a slave. In general, even in the absence of any other constraints, e.g., assuming all nodes are capable of communicating with all other nodes, the best (throughput wise) configuration in terms of masters, slaves, and bridges is unclear. Having as few masters as possible can increase the number of nodes that are reachable either directly or in a small number of hops. However, it also means that more nodes are sharing the communication channel associated with each master. Similarly, the number of bridge nodes that should exist between different piconets is also unclear. Many bridges can facilitate load distribution and improve connectivity, but this comes at the cost of increasing the complexity of synchronizing communication Schedules an added overhead when switching from piconet to piconet (recall that a node can be active in only one piconet at the time).

For Bluetooth to succeed as a technology on which adhoc networks can be built, it is not only essential to find light-weight solutions to the above problems, but those solutions must be fully distributed. In other words, they should not assume the existence of a central entity with access to the entire system/network state, and nodes decisions should only be based on information about their own state and that of their "neighbors." However, the definition of what a node's neighborhood consists of is itself not clear. Does it consist only of nodes belonging to the same piconet(s), or does it also include other nodes within communication reach? More generally, a neighborhood could be defined as all nodes that are k or less "hops" away (hop count corresponds to the number of masters/piconets that need to be traversed). Clearly there is a trade-off between the accuracy (or optimality) of the decisions that can be made under different scenarios. In general, the more information is available, the better the decisions. However, this comes at the cost of a higher latency, a higher processing cost, and a higher control overhead. It is, therefore, important to identify a design point that is both implementable and capable of providing a reasonably efficient operational solution. One of our goals is to start exploring the space of potential solutions to identify the range of available options.

In this paper, we focus on an initial exploration of some of the above issues that are associated with the problem of "topology formation," when attempting to build an adhoc network based on the Bluetooth technology. These are, however, not the only issues that one would need to address in the context of a Bluetooth adhoc network, and there are many other interesting questions dealing with actual data transmission. For example, how does a master decide the order of data transmission among slaves?. How does a bridge node decide its order of participation in different piconets. The scheduling should be designed so that a master completes its communication with a bridge node while it is active in its piconet. This requires giving priority to bridge nodes as compared to ordinary slaves, and the priority of a bridge node should also depend on the number of piconets it participates in. These issues are closely related to administering different quality of service to different end nodes.

4 Design Objectives

We describe some of our design objectives in deciding how to best form Bluetooth topologies, and subsequently discuss the challenges involved in satisfying these objectives while exploiting the flexibility offered by the Bluetooth specifications. We are primarily concerned with three major objectives:

1. Connectivity,
2. Distributed operation and low overhead,
3. Throughput maximization.

Next, we briefly expand on those three objectives, and what it takes to achieve them.

Maintaining end to end connectivity whenever feasible, i.e., when there exists a selection of node states (slave, bridge, master) that forms a connected topology, is obviously a desirable feature. Let us examine the challenges involved in achieving this objective within the Bluetooth design constraints. Observe first that any Bluetooth topology must satisfy some basic properties. For one, the partitioning of nodes into masters and slaves implies that the graph associated with any Bluetooth topology is a bi-partite graph. This is because both neither masters nor slaves ca communicate directly, and therefore the set of nodes associated with masters only has edges to the set of nodes corresponding to slaves. Similarly, the constraint that a piconet cannot contain more than 7 slaves implies that all nodes associated with masters must have a degree less than or equal to 7. This also implies that if at any time the total number of masters is less than one eighth of the total number of nodes, then certain nodes will not belong to any piconet and thus the topology remains disconnected. These are constraints that any topology formation algorithm must take into account. It is not only the choice of role, i.e., master, slave, or bridge, that is important in determining connectivity, but the order in which nodes are assigned their role is also a key factor. In particular, because connectivity between piconets is ensured through bridge nodes and not all (slave) nodes are capable of playing such a role (the node must be able to "hear" the master of each piconet), connectivity between two piconets may be precluded if the corresponding node attempts to join one of the piconets after the piconet has become full, i.e., already has 7 slaves. This can possibly be fixed by having some slaves relinquish their membership in the piconet, but identifying when this is needed, e.g., connectivity might still exist between the piconets through a multi-hop path, and which node should leave the piconet, is a complex problem. Achieving connectivity is, therefore, a complex and possibly unachievable task, but it provides a benchmark against which heuristics can be evaluated.

Our second design objective, namely a distributed operation and low overhead, is a must for any practical solution. As pointed out earlier, node state changes should be triggered in response to changes in the physical topology. Figure 2 gives an example of how the roles of existing nodes need to be changed to accommodate the arrival of a new node and maintain connectivity. In many instances, detecting and adjusting to topological changes is likely to require a certain amount of communications between nodes. One approach to minimizing overhead is to seek algorithms that rely only on local information, and hence have minimal communication overhead. However, it is unlikely that such simplistic algorithms will be able to efficiently accommodate all possible scenarios. As a result, they will need to incorporate additional design objectives to compensate for their limited decision horizon. For example, a simple strategy would be to seek topologies that have significant redundancy, e.g., connectivity between piconets is achieved through multiple bridges or by having nodes serving as bridges between multiple piconets. Similarly, trying to keep piconet sizes small can improve the odds of success of local strategies.

Our third design objective of maximizing throughput, while obviously desirable, unfortunately adds complexity of its own to an already complex problem. For example, the size of piconets, which plays a role in both determining connectivity and the overhead of any algorithm responsible for maintaining connectivity, also affects the throughput of the network. Consider a piconet with k slaves, and where every slave generates a traffic of intensity r per unit time. Such a configuration, the master needs to support a load of 2kr 2kr per unit time assuming it itself does not generate any traffic (the load on the master increases if the master generates traffic). If the master has a bandwidth of BB, then we must have $2Kr \leq B$ and thus the nodal throughput r r that the piconet supports is inversely proportional to the number of members in the piconet. This would call for keeping K k small, and hence building a topology with many small piconets. On the other hand, a large number of small piconets will lead to long end to end routes, and this in turn may overload the transit piconets and, therefore, also limit the feasible nodal throughput. In general, the selection of the "right" size for piconets depends on how traffic is distributed between nodes and where nodes are located. For example, it is obvious that if nodes AA and B B are within communication range of each other and need to exchange a significant amount of traffic, then they should be assigned to the same piconet. However, other simple configurations do not necessarily yield similarly simple answers. For example, assuming a set of N , N nodes all capable of communicating with each other and a uniform traffic. Pattern, the best topology for such a configuration is not obvious.

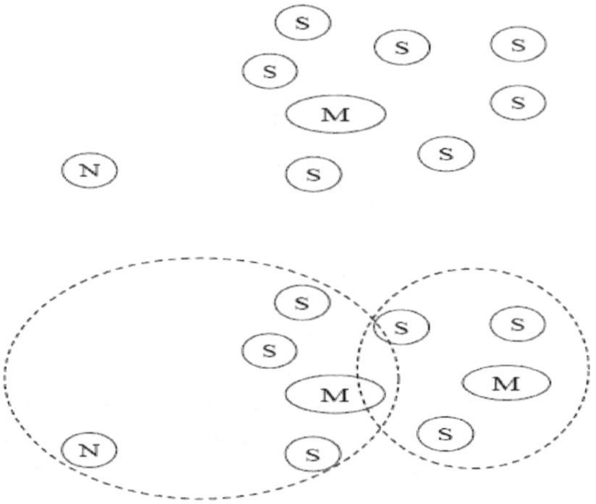

Fig. 2. The effect of arrival of a new node N is illustrated. The nodes labeled S are slaves in a piconet with master labeled M: The new node N is within the transmission range of M only. The piconet has the maximum possible number of members and thus M can not accept node N as its slave. Two different piconets with masters labeled M need to be formed now.

Another factor affecting throughput is the number of piconets a node participates in, and as discussed earlier this number should be different for masters and slaves. There are many possible options to consider, but for the sake of simplicity we propose that a master participate in only one piconet, and that a slave participate in up to K k piconets, where K k is, therefore, the only remaining design parameter. Realistic values for KK are probably 22 or 33: This introduces further constraints on the topology construction algorithm, but they are expected to ensure minimum throughput levels in the network.

5 Related Research

In this section, we mention very briefly a number of previous works that have also been motivated by the need to extend the standard specifications, if the Bluetooth technology is to be used in building adhoc networks.

Salonidis *et. al.* presents a distributed topology construction scheme in Bluetooth networks [6]. The basic assumption behind the scheme is that all nodes are within transmission range of each other. The nodes conduct a leader election algorithm.

The winner knows the identity of all nodes and uses this information to design the desired topology. Thus the algorithm is not scalable if the number of nodes is large. This paper also shows that the average delay involved in synchronizing two nodes (the time spent in the inquiry and the page sequences before the nodes are able to exchange the clock information) is infinite if the nodes have a deterministic sequence of switching between inquiring and inquired (or paging and paged) modes. Bhagwat *et al.* presents a source routing mechanism for Bluetooth networks [1]. Das *et al.* [2] and Johanson *et al.* [4] present distributed scheduling policies for Bluetooth networks.

6 Case Study

This section surveys the current state-of-art for bluetooth scatternet formation platforms.

In [1] A routing protocol which utilizes the characteristics of Bluetooth technology is proposed for Bluetooth-based mobile ad hoc networks. The routing tables are maintained in the master devices and the routing zone radius for each table is adjusted dynamically by using evolving fuzzy neural networks. Observing there exists some useless routing packets which are helpless to build the routing path and increase the network loads in the existing ad hoc routing protocols, they selectively use multiple unicasts or one broadcast when the destination device is out of the routing zone radius coverage of the routing table. The simulation results show that the dynamic adjustments of the routing table size in each master device results in much less reply time of routing request, fewer request packets and useless packets compared with two representative protocols, Zone Routing Protocol (ZRP) and Dynamic Source Routing (DSR).

In [2] work targets small mobile computers with a Bluetooth wireless link. Embedded in cheap robots with data rich sensors, our target does not have enough processing power to do the required analysis on sensor data. We propose the use of parallel processing. In this paper they outline DynaMP, a dynamic message passing architecture. Using an ad-hoc network with on-demand routing based on AODV. DynaMP has a resource discovery mechanism; it distributes code and data using Java class loading, with a caching mechanism to reduce network traffic. They assume the network is unreliable and provide a retry mechanism in distributing the problem.

In [3] this paper studies the optimization of scatternets through the reduction of communication path lengths. After demonstrating analytically that there is a strong relationship between the communication path length on one hand and throughput and power consumption on the other hand, we propose a novel heuristic algorithm suite capable of dynamically adapting the network topology to the existing traffic connections between the scatternet nodes. The periodic adaptation of the scatternet topology to the traffic connections enables the routing algorithms to identify shorter paths between. They evaluate their approach through communicating network nodes, thus allowing for more efficient communications simulations, in the presence of dynamic traffic flows and mobility.

In [4] The vision of ad-hoc networking with Bluetooth includes the concept of devices participating in multiple"piconets" and thereby forming a "scatternet". However, the details of scatternet support for Bluetooth are not specified yet. This paper presents a scheme for Bluetooth scatternet operation that adapts to varying traffic patterns. Basing on sniff mode, it does not require substantial modification of the current Bluetooth specification and may thus be incorporated into currently available Bluetooth products. They present simulation results that confirm the applicability of our approach to realistic scenarios.

In [5] With the growth in the number of devices with an integrated Bluetooth module, the range of applications based on the Bluetooth technology becomes larger, going beyond peer-to-peer use-cases. This paper considers a hybrid network, consisting both of infrastructure and ad hoc parts, referred to as scatternet with infrastructure support. The introduction of the scatternet structure allows to extend the coverage and to enable access of a larger number of users. The formation algorithms are discussed and the importance of synchronization of the formation process for creation of a height- and width-balanced tree topology is illustrated. Simulation results presenting the impact of the link establishment policies on the resulting topology are given.

In [6] this paper addresses the problem of scatternet formation for single-hop Bluetooth based personal area and ad hoc networks, with minimal communication overhead. In a single-hop ad hoc network, all wireless devices are in the radio vicinity of each other, recent scatternet formation schemes by Li, Stojmenovic and Wang are position based and were applied for multi-hop networks. These schemes are localized and can Construct degree limited and connected piconets, without parking any node. They also limit to 7 the number of slave roles in one piconet. The creation and maintenance require small overhead in addition to maintaining location information for one-hop neighbors. In this article they apply this method to single-hop networks; by showing that position Information is then not needed. Each node can simply select a virtual position, and communicate it to all neighbors in the neighbor discovery phase. Nodes then act according to the scheme by Li, Stojmenovic and Wang using such virtual positions instead of real ones. In addition, in this paper they use Delaunay triangulation instead of partial Delaunay triangulation proposed in , since each node has all the information needed. Likewise, they can also apply Minimum Spanning Tree (MST) as the planar topology in our new schemes. Finally, they design experiments to study both the properties of formatted scatternets (such as number and the performances of different localized routing methods on them. The experiments confirm good functionality of created Bluetooth networks in addition to their fast creation and straightforward maintenance.

7 Conclusion

This paper was intended as a brief introduction to the many challenges that the Bluetooth technology faces if it is to succeed as a technology for building adhoc networks and also gives the small description of related work that had been done in this area.. We have described many of the issues that need to be tackled and that have been left unspecified by the current standards. We identified a number of objectives that any solution should aim at meeting, and provided an initial investigation of some of these problems. This is obviously preliminary work, and we are actively investigating many of the problems outlined in this paper. We hope that the paper will also entice others in exploring what we feel is a promising and rich research area.

Acknowledgments

This work was partially supported by Mr. Dipesh Sharma who is Reader of Raipur institute of technology. My special thanks to the Mr. Dipesh sir who have contributed towards development of this work.

References

[1] Huang, C.-J., Lai, W.-K., Hsiao, S.-Y., Liu, H.-Y.: A Bluetooth Routing Protocol Using Evolving Fuzzy Neural Networks
[2] Shepherd, R., Story, J., Mansoor, S.: Parallel Computation in Mobile Systems Using Bluetooth Scatternets and Java
[3] Kall, C.K., Chiasserini, C.-F., Jung, S.: Hop Count Based Optimization of Bluetooth Scatternets
[4] Baatz, S., Frank, M., Küuhl, C., Martini, P., Scholz, C.: Bluetooth Scatternets: An Enhanced Adaptive Scheduling Scheme
[5] Madsen, T.K., Gudmundsson, F., Sverrisson, S., Schwefel, H.P., Prasad, R.: Bluetooth Scatternet with Infrastructure Support: Formation Algorithms
[6] Wang, Y., Stojmenovic, I., Li, X.-Y.: Bluetooth Scatternet Formation for Single-hop Ad Hoc Networks Based on Virtual Positions
[7] Miller, B., Bisdikian, C.: Bluetooth Revealed: The Insider's Guide to an Open Specification for Global Wireless Communications. Prentice-Hall, Englewood Cliffs (2000)
[8] Salonidis, T., Bhagwat, P., Tassiulas, L., Lamaire, R.: Distributed topology construction of Bluetooth personal area networks. In: Proceedings of INFOCOM 2001 (2001)

[9] Salonidis, T., Bhagwat, P., Tassiulas, L.: Proximity awareness and fast connection establishment in bluetooth. In: First Annual Workshop on Mobile and Ad Hoc Networking and Computing, MobiHOC 2000, pp. 141–142 (2000)
[10] Aggarwal, A., Kapoor, M., Ramachandran, L., Sarkar, A.: Clustering algorithms for wireless ad hoc networks. In: Proceedings of the 4th International Workshop on Discrete Algorithms and Methods for Mobile Computing and Communications, Boston, MA, USA, pp. 54–63 (2000)
[11] Kalia, M., Bansal, D., Shorey, R.: Data scheduling ans sar for bluetooth mac. In: Proceedings of IEEE 51st Vehicular Technology Conference, VTC 2000, Tokyo, vol. 2, pp. 716–720 (Spring 2000)
[12] Capone, A., Gerla, M., Kapoor, R.: Efficient polling schemes for bluetooth picocells. In: IEEE ICC 2001, Helsinki, Finland, vol. 7, pp. 1990–1994 (2001)
[13] Golmie, N., Chevrollier, N., ElBakkouri, I.: Interference aware bluetooth packet scheduling. In: Proceedings of IEEE GLOBECOM 2001, pp. 2857–2863 (2001)

Text Mining Based Decision Support System (TMbDSS) for E-governance: A Roadmap for India

Gadda Koteswara Rao and Shubhamoy Dey

Information Systems,
Indian Institute of Management, Indore,
Madhya Pradesh, INDIA
{gkrao,Shubhamoy}@iimidr.ac.in

Abstract. In this digital age most of the government regulations are often available online, similarly with the advent of a number of electronic online forums the opportunity of gathering citizens' petitions and stakeholders' views on government policy has increased greatly, but the volume and the complexity of analyzing unstructured data makes difficult to extract useful information from this data. On the other hand, text mining(TM) has the capability to deal with this type of data. TM techniques can help policy makers by identifying the relatedness between existing regulations and proposed policy drafts. In this article we discuss how text-mining techniques can help in retrieval of information and relationships from unstructured data sources, thereby assisting policy makers in discovering associations between existing policies, proposed policies and citizens' opinions expressed in electronic public forums. In this article, an integrated text mining based architecture for e-governance decision support is presented along with a discussion on the Indian scenario.

Keywords: Text mining techniques, e- governance, public policy, public opinion, decision support systems.

1 Introduction

Data mining was conceptualized in the 1990s as a means of addressing the problem of analyzing the vast repositories of data that are available to mankind, and being added to continuously. Considering the fact that most data (over 80%) is stored as text, text mining has even higher potential [2]. Text mining is a relatively new interdisciplinary field that brings together concepts from statistics, machine learning, information retrieval, data mining, linguistics and natural language processing. It is said to be the discovery by computer of new, previously unknown information by automatically extracting information from different written resources [3]. Text mining is different from mere text search or web search where the objective is to discard irrelevant material to identify what the user is looking for. Essentially, in the context of text search, the user knows what he / she is looking for (in the form of keywords etc.), and the (written) material already exists. In text mining one of the key elements is that the aim is to discover unknown information by linking together existing text data to form new facts or hypotheses. Thus, in many ways text mining is similar to data mining, and indeed regarded by some as an extension of the same. The main point of

D.C. Wyld et al. (Eds.): ACITY 2011, CCIS 198, pp. 270–281, 2011.

departure from the parent discipline of data mining is in the type of data that needs to be analyzed. Whereas data mining deals with mostly numeric structured data, text, the theme of text mining, is regarded as 'unstructured' data. Though, the task of text mining based DSS would seem to be more challenging than that of mining of structured data, the existence of vast amounts of information in electronically available text has led to intense research in text mining techniques, and many of the challenges have been overcome.

The greatest potential of applications of text mining is in the areas where large quantities of textual data is generated or collected in the course of transactions. For example industries like publishing, legal, healthcare and pharmaceutical research, and areas like customer complaints (or feedback) handling and marketing focus group programs would be the best areas of application of text mining.Decision support systems (DSS) help leaders and managers make decisions in situations that are unique, rapidly changing, and not easily specified in advance [01]. Text Mining based DSS (TMbDSS) integrate unstructured textual data with predictive analytics to provide an environment for arriving at well-informed citizen-centric decisions in the context of e-governance.

2 Technical Architecture for TMbDSS

To implement any intelligence system the primary step is the selection of required sources, which in our case is, government policy database, citizens' complaints from relevant web portals, online discussion forums, to allow citizens' to discuss about prestigious government projects and last but not least is social network/media, which have gained immense popularity in modern times, one can also extract the political data from social network /media to understand the stakeholders opinions. As we are talking about the unstructured information from multiple sources and in different formats (pdf, doc, docs, xml, jpg, html etc.) we need use parsing system to transform the documents into the format, which has the capability to handle unstructured/semi-structured data. Next task is the information (keyword/ features) retrieval; it includes tokenization, filtering, stemming, indexing and refinement. However, in some cases traditional keyword extraction techniques may not be able to support, we would then need to implement another technique to extract features which include generic features, domain-specific features and concepts extraction and then refine the regulation database. After the features and information have been stored in the textual/data warehouse, association rule analysis, clustering, categorizing, and summarization can be used to process them into meaningful information.

As per Rao et al [4], Text mining techniques, though relatively new, are considered mature enough to be incorporated into almost all commercial data mining software packages. The features of some popular data mining software that have text mining modules are summarized in their paper. They have observed that text mining has made a transition from the domain of research to that of robust industrial strength technology, and can be used in mission critical applications like e-governance. Figure 1 will help us to understand the Text-Mining based DSS technical architecture. Yue Dai et al, have proposed a similar kind of architecture for a system for competitive intelligence based on analysis in a decision support system model called MinEDec (Mining Environment for Decisions), which is supported by text-mining technologies [5].

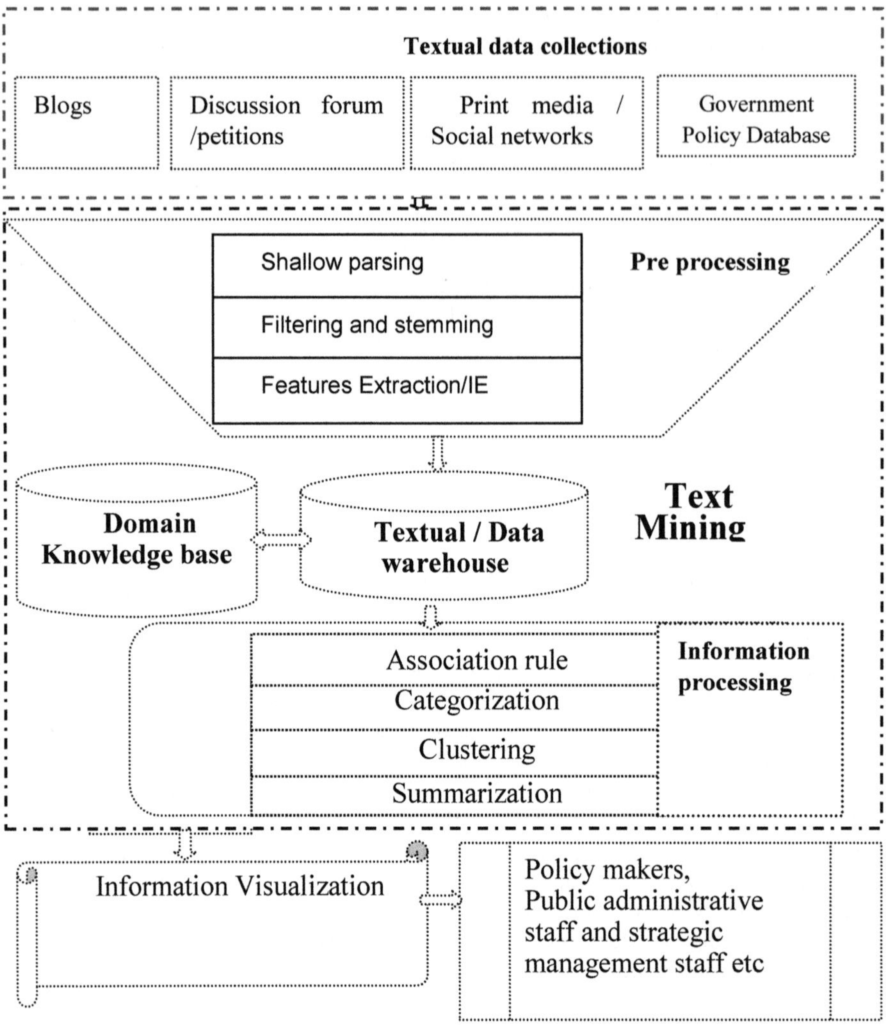

Fig. 1. Text mining Decision support system technical architecture for government

The most widely used text mining techniques are discussed briefly below to enable better understanding of their application in the field of e-governance, citizen participation and e-democracy.

1. Information extraction: Information extraction algorithms identify key phrases and relationships within text. This is done by looking for predefined sequences in text, using a process called 'pattern matching'.
2. Categorization: Categorization involves identifying the main themes of a document by placing the document into a pre-defined set of topics. It does not attempt to process the actual information as information extraction does.

3. Clustering: Clustering is a technique used to group similar documents, but it differs from categorization in that documents are clustered based on similarity to each other instead of through the use of predefined topics. A basic clustering algorithm creates a vector of topics for each document and measures how well the document fits into each cluster.
4. Question answering: Another application area of text mining is answering of question answering, which deals with how to find the best answer to a given question. Question answering can utilize more than one text mining techniques.

3 Text Mining Applications in E-governance

The transformation from conventional government services to E-government services heralds a new era in public services. E-government services can replace the government's traditional services with services of better quantity, quality and reach, and increase citizen satisfaction, using Information and Communication Technology (ICT). E-governance aims to make the interactions between government and citizens (G2C), government and business enterprise (G2B) and inter-government department dealing (G2G) friendly, convenient transparent and less expensive [13]. A growing amount of informative text regarding government decisions, directives, rules and regulations are now distributed on the web using a variety of portals, so that citizens can browse and peruse them. This assumes, however, that the information seekers are capable of untangling the massive volume and complexity of the legally worded documents [7]. Government regulations are voluminous, heavily cross-referenced and often ambiguous. Government information is in unstructured / semi-structured form, the sources are multiple (government regulations comes from national, state and local governments) and the formats are different – creating serious impediment to their searching, understanding and use by common citizens.

In the G2G arena, the government departments are in an even greater need of a system that is able to provide information retrieval, data exchange, metadata homogeneity, and proper information dissemination across the administrative channels of national, regional / state, and local governments [8]. The increasing demand for and complexity of government regulations on various aspects of economic social and political life, calls for advanced knowledge-based framework for information gathering, flow and distribution. For example, if policy makers intend to establish a new act, they need to know the acts related to the same topic that have been established before, and whether the content of the new act conflicts with or has already been included in existing acts [9]. Also, regulations are frequently updated by government departments to reflect environmental changes and changes in policies. Tools that can detect ambiguity, inconsistency and contradiction are needed [9] because the regulations, amended provisions, legal precedence and interpretive guidelines together create a massive volume of semi-structured documents with potentially similar content but possible differences in format, terminology and context. Information infrastructures that can consolidate, compare and contrast different regulatory documents will greatly enhance and aid the understanding of existing regulations and promulgation of new ones.

Government regulations should ideally be retrievable and understandable with ease by legal practitioners, policy makers as well as general public /citizens. Despite many attempts, it is recognized that e-government services are yet to render the desired pro-citizen services and are mostly targeted towards internal efficiency [6]. Kwon et al [15], have proposed a system that helps rule makers understand and respond to the public comments, before finalizing proposed regulations. These public comments are opinion-oriented arguments about the regulations. The facility of identification and classification of main subject of the claims / opinions provided by the tool helps rule-writers preview and summarize the comments. The proposed solution identifies conclusive sentences showing the author's attitude towards the main topic and classifies them to polar classes [15]. The researchers have applied a supervised machine learning method to identify claims using sophisticated lexical and structural features and to classify them by the attitude to the topic: in support of, opposed to, and proposing a new idea [13].

4 Integrating Citizens Voice with E-governance through TMbDSS

It is widely acknowledged that democracy requires well-informed citizens. Information creates trust and is the mechanism for ensuring that politicians serve the electorate. Democracy if effective when there is smooth flow of information between citizens and government [10]. E-governance in its present form has furthered this concept to a certain extent. However, the character of e-governance is mainly one-way flow of information – from the government to the citizens, and authentic citizen participation is absent. With the integration of citizens' participation in the entire process of governance with the help of Information and Communication Technology e-governance evolves into E-democracy and Citizen Participation in policy making can secure democracy, as it generates a continuous flow of information between citizens and the government, helping them in the decision-making process and the citizens can assume a more active role in society, exercising their opinion power with ease and agility [11].

In the usual form of democracy, the general election is the most important citizen participation process. It is significant because it formulates the country's transfer of power from one civilian government to another. Since, elections are intermittent, it is important to have a system in place that has the capability to track public opinion on a more or less continuous basis, and encourage involvement and participation from the electorate on matters of public importance [10]. It is quite possible for citizens' to have different opinions on government proposals. Government can use the online discussion forums and encourage citizens' to discuss on public projects. Once the discussions phase is opened and finished its output are needs to be analyzed so that the underlying trends and preferences of citizens can be incorporated into the decision-making process of the pertinent administrative department [12]. Capturing citizens' opinions through electronic participation / discussion media can be more reliable than traditional methods based on opinions polls and help avoid false opinion declaration. This also drastically changes the methods of surveying citizens' opinion trends as well as the accuracy of the evaluation of their opinions. It reduces the cost, increases reach, and provides almost real time information. Potentially, arguments that led to significant opinion shifts can be detected. However, the volume and the complexity of analyzing unstructured data make this far from straight forward. Text mining can process unstructured data leading to greater understanding of the text in the context of others on the same topic. This is especially important when dealing with expressed public opinion, where the arguments for and against particular positions are important to identify and gauge, but is immensely difficult to extract due their storage in natural language format [13].

Cardeñosa [12] proposes a system, which has the capability to process the messages posted by citizens' on e-message boards, e-mails and open debate threads etc. It collects the messages from online forums, classifies them, identifies the supporting expressions, and extracts the common features and regularities. The system uses association rule mining technique to identify the trend between the citizens' opinions. These rules form the intelligent core of the system. The future refinements and extensions of the system are in the direction of building a more accurate voting pattern prediction system. Fatudimu [14] has applied text-mining techniques on the information collected through newspapers and applied natural language processing (NLP) and association rule mining to extract knowledge and understand the citizens' voice on election issues. Luehrs et al, have discussed about Online Delphi Survey module and also discussed about how citizens' discussions on public issues can be analyzed qualitatively and categorize by using text-mining algorithms based on standard Bayesian inference methods to extract the 'concepts' or main ideas out of a free text and to search for 'similar texts' based on comparison of these concepts [16].Scott et al, says that Social networking sites can be viewed as a new type of online public sphere, and he has discussed about the system which they have implemented to examines the linkage patterns of citizens' who posted links on the Facebook "walls" of Barack Obama, Hillary Clinton,and John McCain over two years prior to the 2008 U.S [17]. Web logging (blogging) and its social impact have recently attracted considerable public and scientific interest. Tae Yano et al have collected blog posts and comments from 40 blog sites focusing on American politics during the period November 2007 to October 2008, contemporaneous with the presidential elections. They have concluded that predicting political discourse behavior is challenging, in part because of considerable variation in user behavior across different blog sites. Their results show that using topic modeling; one can begin to make reasonable predictions as well as qualitative discoveries about language in blogs [18].Muhlberger et. al, have implanted an Interactive Question Answering (QA), and Summarization into a viable learning and discussion facilitation agent called the Discussion Facilitation Agent (DiFA), which will try to keep users(citizens) informed, on the fly, about changes and developments in the deliberation content, and summarize key arguments at the conclusion. [19]. These systems though somewhat futuristic and still in the process of being researched, demonstrate that the concept of participation of citizens' in democratic processes through electronic media is an achievable one. It is also evident from the way these systems work, that text mining capability is the cornerstone of the move towards e-democracy systems.

In Figure-2, the central repository of documents (mostly in unstructured form) has been labeled 'Proposed Govt policies/Govt policies. The citizens are encouraged to record their reactions through the 'public forums / feedback'. Government can also collect data corpus from Social networks. Print/Digital Media contains data in the form of 'Public dialogue and stakeholders opinions. Each of these three corpuses contains huge amount of unstructured/semi structured Data. Knowledge/ insights extracted from these data bases can be used in forming new regulation/policies, understanding citizens' opinions and answering their concerns. The main users of the system are Public Administrative officers (PA Officers), Moderators and Decision makers. It helps in the formulation of new policies, budget analysis, understanding the stakeholders' opinion on national level projects and regulations with the help of text mining tools. Government agencies can better understand social behavior and demands, through analyzing citizens' behavior patterns, information extracted from this can be used to provide citizen centric solution and maintain a closer relationship between government and citizens and enhance the citizens' satisfaction on govt services.

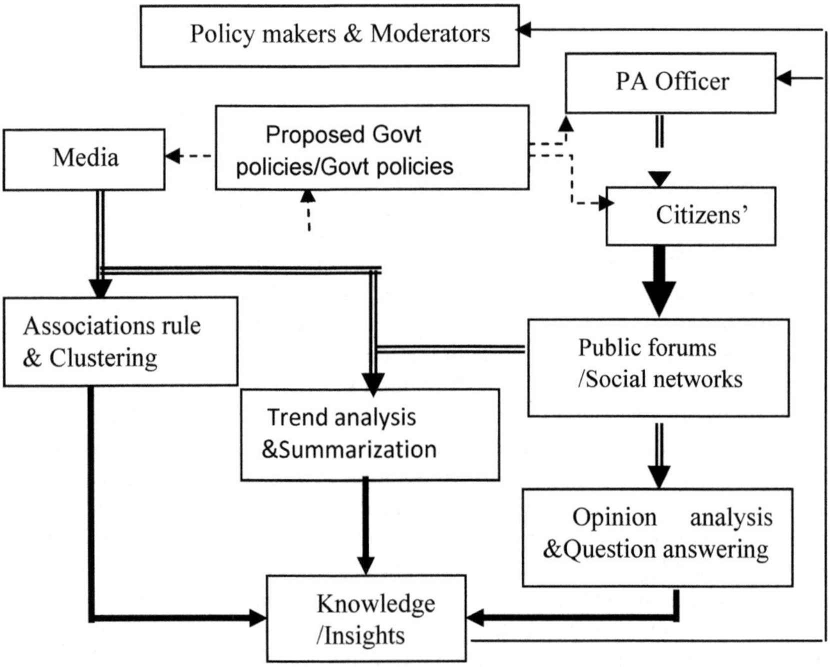

Fig. 2. Citizens' and Stakeholders' participation system

- - - - - - - - - - Access to regulations ——— Access to knowledge
═══ Processing documents ═ ═ ═ Response to citizens' queries
━━━ Knowledge extraction ▬▬▬ citizens' participation

5 E-governance and E-democracy Projects in India

E-governance is about more than streamlining processes and improving services. It's about transforming Governments and renovating the way citizens participate in democracy. Misra, has discussed about the need of Citizen-centric & Criteria-based systems and Involving People in Developing Agenda for Good Governance by receiving citizens' voice. The lack of citizen-centricity in e-government acts as a spanner in the faster growth of Internet penetration in India [20]. Kanungo has discussed about the need of Citizen Centric e-Governance in India and discussed about the need to create a culture of maintaining, processing and retrieving the information through an electronic system and use that information for decision making [21].

5.1 Road Map for Text Mining Based DSS in India

E-Government can advance the agenda on Governance and fiscal reform, transparency, anti- corruption, empowerment and poverty reduction .E-Governance in India has steadily evolved from computerization of Government Departments to initiatives that encapsulate the finer points of Governance, such as citizen centricity, service orientation and transparency. Paramjeet Walia (2009) has discussed about the initiative applications of Information and Communication Technologies (ICTs) in support of e-government initiatives in India [22], National portal of India is initiated as a Mission Mode Project under the National e-governance Plan (NeGP) [23] and other planning initiatives undertaken by the Government of India (GOI) have discussed about the importance of feedback pertaining to utility of the projects, which are part of NeGP and need of a systems to assess the usefulness and impact of e-governance initiatives in India. The plan envisages creation of right environments to implement Government to Government (G2G), Government to Business (G2B), Government to Employee (G2E), and Government to Citizen. Among national portals in the Southern Asia region, India has the highest ranking portal with the highest online services score. It has the most e-services and tools for citizen engagement in the region but not included one among the top 20 countries in e-participation (United Nations E-Government Survey 2010) [24], there is not much literature available on this. Indian government should take the initiative to encourage citizens to send their feedback, complaints, and suggestions through e-portal and discuss various issues on government services in virtual discussion forums.

Gupta, has discussed about the problems with existing systems and implemented an Indian Police Information System and that can be used to extract useful information from the vast crime database maintained by National Crime Record Bureau (NCRB) and find crime hot spots using crime data mining techniques such as clustering etc. [27]. Choudhury, has noted many e-government projects which are running in India (Rural and urban level projects, National level, state level, district level projects and so on) all these projects are taking about G2C and few of them are G2G [28] and we can find very few efforts towards C2G (e-democracy).Monga has discussed about the need of making policy based on computerization to overcome environmental changes and need of series of efforts to achieve this. Need of establishing complete connectivity between various ministries and departments so that transfer of files and papers could be done through Internet thereby choosing efficacious speed as an alternative to manual labor [29]. IIMs are working on Impact assessment of e-government projects, how e-government helps public sector to improve its performance, Critical success factors for individual projects etc.

5.1 1 Multilingual and Cross Lingual Projects in India

India is a multi-lingual (22 official languages) and multi-script Country. As the amount of textual data on the Internet increases, there are also an increasing number of people who want to retrieve information in their native language. Many citizens also have multilingual capabilities that allow them to understand more than one language [25]. It is therefore essential that tools for information processing in local languages are developed in India. Development of technologies in multilingual computing areas involves intensive indigenous R&D efforts due to variety of Indian languages. The focused areas of the Technology Development for Indian Languages Programme in India may be divided into following domains [30]:

-- Translation Systems - Cross Lingual Information Access and Retrieval
-- Linguistic Resources -- Human Machine Interface systems
-- Language processing and Web tools -- Localization and content creation

The CLIA (Cross Lingual Information Access) Project is a mission mode project funded by Government of India; it is an extension of the Cross-Language Information Retrieval paradigm (CLIR) ([25],[26]).By using CLIR users can give queries in their native language and retrieve documents, whether in the same language as the query is, are relevant documents are found in any other language. Gyan Nidhi: Multi-Lingual Aligned Parallel Corpus consists of text in English and 12 Indian languages. It aims to digitize 1 million pages altogether containing at least 50,000 pages in each Indian language and English. Vishleshika is a tool for Statistical Text Analysis for Hindi extendible to other Indian Languages text, it examines input text and generates various statistics, e.g.: Sentence statistics, Word statistics and Character statistics [31]. Karunesh Arora et al (2004), have discussed the process for automatic extraction of phonetically rich sentences from a large text corpus for Indian languages. The importance of such a system and an algorithm to generate a set of phonetically rich sentences from a large text corpus is described along with the results for Hindi language [32]. C-DAC and other R&D centers are working on various projects related to Multilingual Information retrieval, Data Mining, statistics, machine learning and natural language processing projects.

5.2 Steps for TMbDSS

From the available literature, currently running e-government & e-democracy projects in R&D centers' of Indian government and annual report of 2009-2010 from Department of Information Technology India [30], we can conclude that there were not many efforts towards Text mining based citizen-centric solutions using Text Mining. It also needs the centralized initiative but decentralized implementation framework for text mining based DSS. From the definition of Text Mining and currently running ICT projects in India and technologies used in those projects such as CLIR, Text analysis, NLP, Machine Learning, Data Mining, Text mining in tourism and Multi-lingual Information retrieval. One can conclude that India has enough technical experts and domain expertise to start a Text mining project. Fallowing steps may be fallowed for implementation.

- Do the detailed study to find the ways and create a strategic plan
- Resources from Institutes like IITs, ISI, IIMs, C-DAC etc and form an association
    - IITs, ISI and institutes with similar capabilities and competent ,can work on core part of the project
    - C-DAC and IIMs can work as a bridge between R&Ds,Govt and Industry
- Start with an implementation of pilot project at national level to further extend to the states probably in their respective regional languages.

All the national government documents are either in English or Hindi, So India could start a Bi-lingual TMbDSS project by using the fallowing sample architecture.

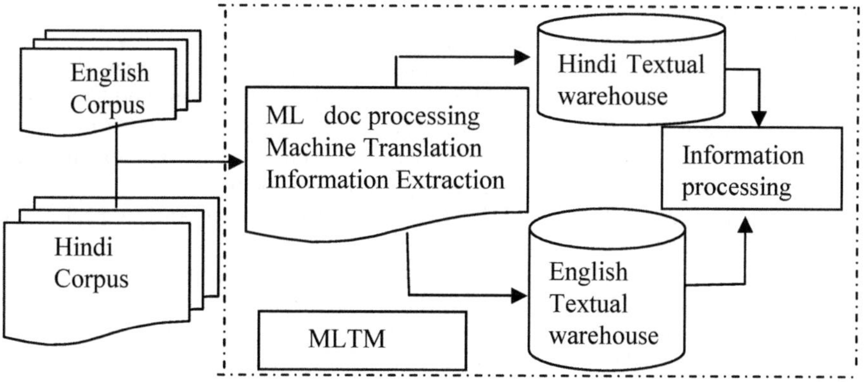

6 Conclusion

In this paper we have discussed need of text mining based DSS for government agencies, various text mining applications developed in e-government &e-democracy, architecture for system development process and then we have proposed a integrated framework which can be used by government organizations' to develop text mining based DSS. We have also studied e-government objectivities and need of Citizen-centric & Criteria-based systems for India and provided a road map for Indian government to start a TMbDSS project.

Reference

[1] Laudon, K.C., Laudon, J.P.: Essentials of Management Information Systems: Managing the Digital Firm. Prentice Hall, London (2004)
[2] McKnight, W.: Building Business Intelligence: text data mining in business intelligence. DM Review, 21–22

[3] Berry, M.W.: Survey of Text Mining: Clustering, Classification and Retrieval. Springer, New York (2004)

[4] Koteswara Rao, G., Dey, S.: Evolution of Text Mining Techniques and Related Applications in E-governance and E-democracy. Proceedings of the IEEE (2010)

[5] Dai, Y., Kakkonen, T., Sutinen, E.: MinEDec: A Decision Support Model that Combines Text Mining with Competitive Intelligence. In: Proceedings of the 9th International Conference on Computer Information Systems and Industrial Management Applications, Cracow, Poland (2010)

[6] Bhatnagar, S.: E-Government: From Vision to Implementation. Sage Publications, India (2004)

[7] Cheng, C.P., Lau, G.T., Law, K.H., Pan, J., Jones, A.: Improving Access to and Understanding of Regulations through Taxonomies. Government Information Quarterly 26(2), 238–245 (2009)

[8] Prokopiadou, G., Papatheodorou, C., Moschopoulos, D.: Integrating knowledge management tools for government information. Government Information Quarterly 21(2), 170–198 (2004)

[9] Shulman, S.W.: eRulemaking: Issues in Current Research and Practice. International Journal of Public Administration 28, 621–641 (2005)

[10] Jefferson, T.: Personal Communication to R. Price (1789)

[11] Maciel, C., Garcia, A.C.: DemIL: an online interaction language between citizen and government. In: Proceedings of the 15th International Conference on World Wide Web, Edinburgh, Scotland, May 23-26, pp. 849–850. ACM Press, New York (2006)

[12] Cardeñosa, J., Gallardo, C., Moreno, J.M.: Text Mining Techniques to Support e-Democracy Systems. In: CSREA EE 2009, pp. 401–405 (2009)

[13] Froelich, J., Ananyan, S., Olson, D.L.: The Use of Text Mining to Analyze Public Input. White paper (2008)

[14] Fatudimu, I.T., Musa, A.G.: Knowledge Discovery in Online Repositories: A Text Mining Approach 22(2), 241–250 (2008) ISSN 1450-216X

[15] Kwon, N., Zhou, L., Hovy, E., Shulman, S.: Identifying and Classifying Subjective Claims. In: Proceedings of the Eighth National Conference on Digital Government Research (dg.o 2007), Philadelphia, PA (2007)

[16] Lührs, R., Malsch, T., Voss, K.: Internet, Discourses and democracy. In: Terano, T., Nishida, T., Namatame, A., Tsumoto, S., Ohsawa, Y., Washio, T. (eds.) JSAI-WS 2001. LNCS (LNAI), vol. 2253, p. 67. Springer, Heidelberg (2001)

[17] Robertson, S.P., Vatrapu, R.K., Medina, R.: The social life of social networks: Facebook linkage patterns in the 2008 U.S. presidential election, Source:dg.o. vol. 390, pp. 6–15 (2008), ISBN:978-1-60558-535-2

[18] Yano, T., Smith, N.A., Cohen, W.W.: Predicting Response to Political Blog Posts with Topic Models. In: NAACL 2009 (2009)

[19] Muhlberger, P., Webb, N., Stromer-Galley, J.: The Deliberative E Rulemaking Project (DeER): Improving Federal Agency Rulemaking Via Natural Language Processing and Citizen Dialogue. In: Proceedings of the 9th Annual International Digital Government Research Conference. ACM International Conference Proceeding Series, vol. 289, p. 403 (2008)

[20] Misra, D.C.: An E-governance Vision for India for 2020: Making India Internet Nation No.1 in the World, Paper contributed to 7th International Conference on e- Governance (ICEG), Indian Institute of Management, Bangalore (April 22-24, 2010)

[21] Kanungo, V.: Citizen Centric e-Governance in India-Strategies for Today, Vision for Future (2007), `http://www.egovindia.org/egovernancepaper.doc`

[22] Walia, P.K.: Access to government information in India in the digital environment. In: World library and Information Congress: 75th IFLA General Conference and Council, Milan, Italy (August 23-27, 2009)

[23] The National e-Governance Plan (NeGP), Meeting of the National e-Governance Advisory Group-NewDelhi (November 12, 2010), http://www.mit.gov.in/sitesupload_files/dit/files/documents/12thNov_NAG_261110.pdf

[24] United Nations E-Government Survey 2010- Leveraging e-government at a time of financial and economic crisis, http://unpan1.un.org/intradoc/groups/public/documents/UNDPADM/UNPAN038853.pdf

[25] Prasenjit Majumder Mandar Mitra Swapan Kumar Parui: Initiative for Indian Language IR Evaluation (2007)

[26] Shukla, V.N.: Natural Language Processing Activities in CDAC, Noida (2010)

[27] Gupta, M., Chandra, B., Gupta, M.P.: Crime Data Mining for Indian Police Information System. In: International Congress on e-government (2008)

[28] Choudhury, S., Kala, C., Sarwan, J.P., Kumar, S.: E-Democracy and Citizen Empowerment through E-Governance and Other e-Initiatives in India, Nepal and Bangladesh-A Case Study (2008)

[29] Monga, A.: E-government in India: Opportunities and challenges (2008)

[30] Information Technology- Annual Report 2009-10 of Government of India- Ministry of Communications & Information Technology, http://www.mit.gov.in/content/annual-plansreports

[31] Shukla, V.N., Arora, K., Gugnani, V.: Digital Library: Language Centered Research, Test Beds and Applications. In: International Conference on Digital Libraries held at New Delhi, India (2004)

[32] Arora, K., Arora, S., Verma, K., Agrawal, S.S.: Automatic Extraction of Phonetically Rich Sentences from Large Text Corpus of Indian Languages. In: Proceedings of International Conference Interspeech 2004-ICSLP, Jeju, Korea, October 4-8 (2004)

IMPACT-Intelligent Memory Pool Assisted Cognition Tool : A Cueing Device for the Memory Impaired

Samuel Cyril Naves

Department of Information Technology,
Sri Sairam Institute of Technology, Anna University, India
cyrilnaves91@gmail.com

Abstract. Memory impairment results from a variety of disease such as Alzheimer, Parkinson, brain trauma and Aging. These people are obsessed with their current state and emotions when dealing with their environment with deteriorating memory in them. There are about 30 million people worldwide afflicted with this instance. They lose their insight into their own condition, forgetting even their loved ones, disability to locate their residence and a myriad of other inabilities. Medicine has evolved fast enough but still there is not a definite method to diagnose or a treatment for their memory loss. The only finding has revealed is due to the depletion of the brain cells and loss in hormone secretion to carry sensory messages. The appropriate reason for this behavior of cells is a mystery unsolved. While not only losing their pensive they develop a cold behavior, socially and emotionally they become unbalanced. The most common form of assistance to them is by caregivers or life logging through writing their reminiscences, taking photos of their surrounding and their close people, mobile phones etc .While all these can be of some form of help to this people it will result only in more stress to their already damaged brain resulting in depression and other mental problems. The proposed tool IMPACT acts like a second brain with a repository of memory comprising of their previous experiences in multimedia format which is sensed and fetched when they come across a similar person or surrounding thus enabling them to recall their senses about that situation engaging cueing interaction.

Keywords: image classification, feature extraction, segmentation, Fuzzy logic, audio recognition, cognition.

1 Introduction

The brain is the most superior organ a human is gifted with enabling him to acquire data, consolidate and retrieve it. The major challenges a person comes across when his brain cells deteriorate causing damage to his cognition capabilities. Many people around the world are diagnosed with memory loss and this disability resulting as a side effect of many diseases is expected to increase many fold.[2] This disease makes a person to lose his current and depress him to sole reliance upon others forgetting their activities, family members and even their purpose in life. IMPACT is the device

D.C. Wyld et al. (Eds.): ACITY 2011, CCIS 198, pp. 282–289, 2011.

designed to trigger the cue of a person enabling him to recall his sense enabling him to know about his past, and direct his present. This device gives the person anew lease of life to lead an independent, active and a stress free life.

2 Background

One out of every hundred people around the world over the age of 50 have been diagnosed with dementia resulting as a side cause of trauma, aging Alzheimer etc.[1] Memory impairment can lead to feelings of uncertainty, irritation, frustration and fear in the person. Living with constant uncertainty about previous experiences can lead to a frightening loss of control in people's lives. [3] Increasingly dependent on a caregiver to help make simple decisions, they are forced to relinquish their life. They can become easily depressed as they struggle with failures with the loss of control that pervades their life. By creating a pool of their memories with sensing their encounter through audio and video format and then offering a quick glimpse into their previous reflection with that situation allow people to reflect on their life and perceive themselves living and experiencing reality continuously through time.

3 Component Specifications

Image Sensor: The image sensor built in is a CMOS sensor which is a type of active pixel sensor. This converts the incoming light into voltage and the transfers to a memory. The technical specification of the sensor suitable will be of

Capturing speed: 50frame per second
Width: 1600
Height: 1200
Aspect ratio: 4:3
Actual pixel count: 1,920,000
Mega pixel: 4
Night vision: Bright white light led.

3.1 Processor

Cortex-A8 processor is used with enabled NEON technology based packed SIMD processing. Registers are considered as vectors of elements of same type. The processor is enabled for accelerating multimedia application. Its frequency ranges from 600MHz to 1GHz with a superscalar micro architecture.

3.2 Memory

A ROM memory is used with a faster access mode for a cache for it. "Smart" memory card architecture is used with significantly increased performance by a fast dynamic random access memory which allows up to 8byte data transfers after every 27 ns after initial access.

3.3 Power

A rechargeable Lithium-ion button cell is used with relatively 1000 mAh is implemented.

3.4 Speaker

A micro speaker is fit in so as to present the user with the recorded sound after comparison of the present sound wave with the previous alias one.

3.5 Microphone

It is built in the power range of 5v so as to capture analog sound and the send it for preprocessing before comparing for an alias sound wave pattern and presenting via speaker giving a glimpse of recording.

Sample Rate: 150 kHz
Bit Rate: 24bit
Polar Patterns: Cardioid, Bidirectional, Omni-directional & Stereo
Frequency Response: 20Hz – 20 kHz
Sensitivity: 4.5mV/Pa (1 kHz)
Max SPL: 80dB k

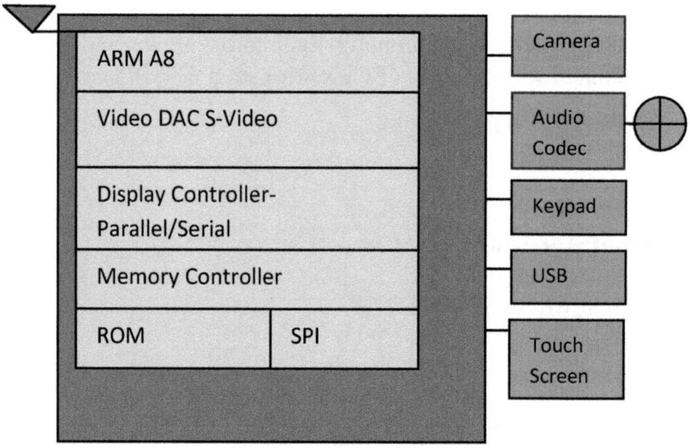

Fig. 1. Block diagram of IMPACT

IMPACT is enabled with an audio and video sensor with live capturing mode so as to record a particular experience of a person directed towards a central memory system in it.[2] It then fetches the already stored comparing with the recently recorded memory by feature matching of either audio or video pattern.

[3] The intelligent memory pool works in a manner to avoid memory clogging causing low access speed. Each and every audio and video is first feature extracted an then stored in the database It stores in only the latest memory associated with that

particular event or person and the existing earlier encounters are automatically deleted thereby avoiding large memory space and fetching delay.

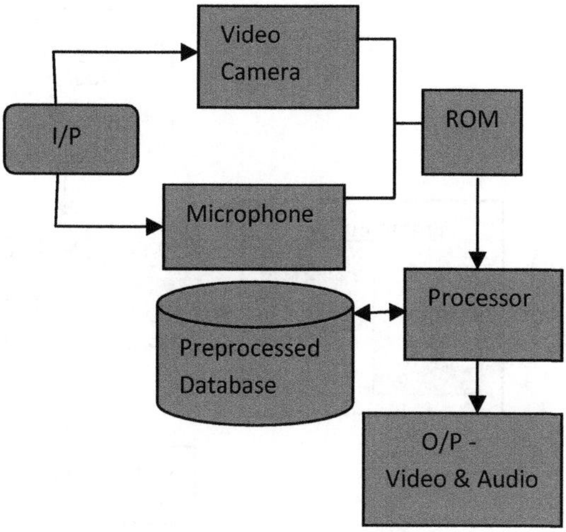

Fig. 2. Working Layout of IMPACT

5 Implementation and Working

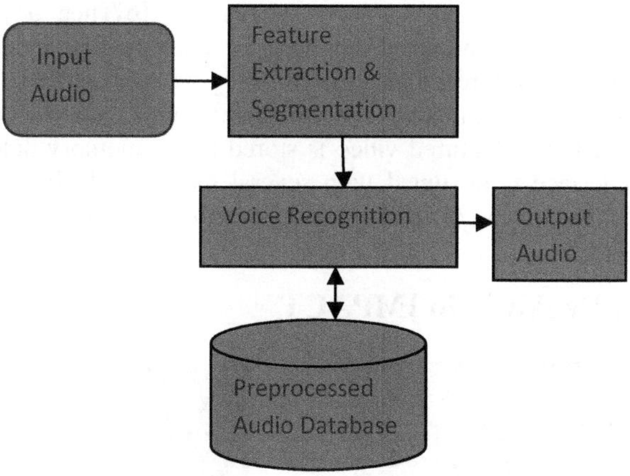

Fig. 3. Functional Block Diagram of Audio Recognition

5.1 Audio Recognition

The audio being recorded with the surrounding of the person i.e. a query audio is processed and segmented and then compared with the already existing featured audio database .After feature matching it is then played to the user allowing him to trigger his cognition. Then the feature extracted query audio is stored in the memory deleting the previous edition of the event.

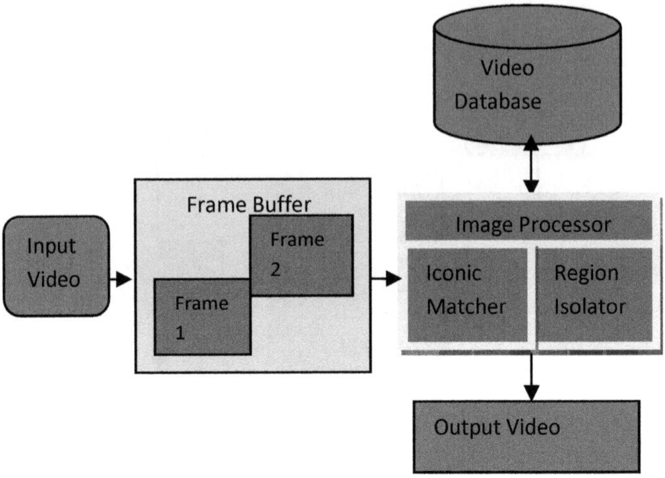

Fig. 4. Functional Block Diagram of Video Recognition

5.2 Video Recognition

The image from the video camera is passed on to a frame buffer following the frame is isolated into regions for each object or regions. [6]Then a feature analyzer computes asset of global and local features for each region and based on those features selects several reference patterns forming an associated attribute memory. This attribute memory is compared and the relative video set is played to the user recollecting his past. The featured video is stored in the memory deleting the earlier one. The user interface is designed with several modes to facilitate the person for options with deletion, storing or fetching memory mode with it.

6 Algorithm Deployed in IMPACT

Fig. 5. Input Video frame

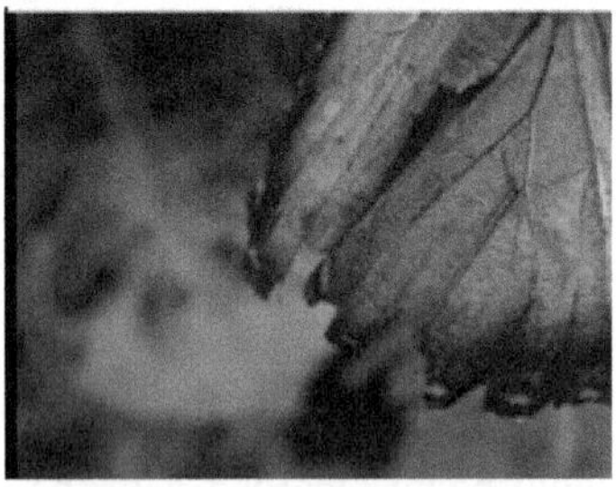

Fig. 6. Region Isolated frame 1

Fig. 7. Region Isolated frame 2

Fig. 8. Region Isolated frame 3

Fig 9. Region Isolated frame 4

6.1 Video Recognition

6.1.1 Preprocessing

In the video recognition a fuzzy logic approach of unified feature matching is done for region based image retrieval.[4] In this each frame is represented by a set of segmented region each of which is characterized by a fuzzy feature reflecting color, texture and shape properties. As a result each frame is associated with a family of fuzzy feature corresponding to regions. Fuzzy features naturally characterize the gradual transition between regions within an image and incorporate the segmentation related uncertainties into the recognition algorithm.

6.1.2 Iconic Matcher

The resemblance of two images is then defined as the overall similarity between two families of fuzzy features and quantified by an iconic matcher, which integrates properties of all the regions in the images. [4]Compared with similarity measures based on individual regions and on all regions with crisp-valued feature representations, the UFM measure greatly reduces the influence of inaccurate segmentation and provides a very intuitive quantification.

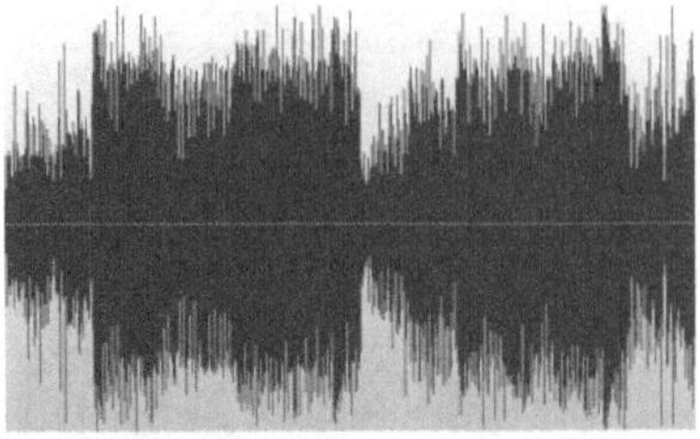

Fig. 10. Cepstral analyzed Query sound wave

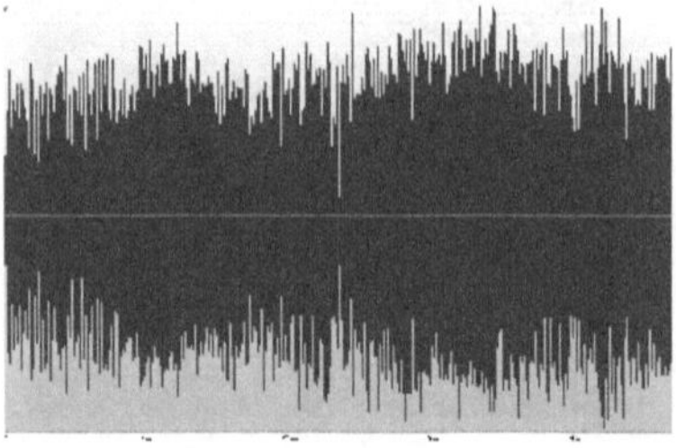

Fig. 11. Cepstral analyzed sound database

6.2 Audio Recognition

6.2.1 Processing

The recorded incoming audio is first processed by neural networks in a way analyzing both text dependent and text independent sound avoiding external disturbances .[5] Each sound wave is extracted of its feature data including cepstral analysis of it.

6.2.2 Feature Matching

Each analyzed sound wave is compared with the already existing feature extracted database, and then if the feature corresponds then the previous audio wave cepstral analysis and the current ones are matched to get the highest occurrence of event.

7 Conclusion

This system IMPACT will allow the person with memory impairment to review a multimedia narrative of an experience as cues to help them not only to recall the experience but to be able to relive the experience. Instead of repetitively asking for assistance, they will be able to use this device as a tablet in recollecting their experience.

8 Future Work

This system has to be deployed with memory impaired individuals and their peers. The effectiveness of the device has to be evaluated and also more concentration has to be dealt in the user interface. Based on caregiver's authored content enhancement of the richness of the review experience has to be done.

References

[1] Alzheimer's Association. Families Care: Alzheimer's Care giving in the United States (2004)

[2] Kawamura, T., Kono, Y., Kidode, M.: Wearable interfaces for a video diary: towards memory retrieval, exchange, and transportation. In: ISWC 2002, pp. 31–38 (2002)

[3] Zhou, X.S., Huang, T.S.: Relevance feedback in image retrieval: A comprehensive review. Multimedia Systems 8, 536–544 (2003)
[4] Zobel, J., Hoad, T.: Detection of video sequences using Compact signatures. ACM Trans. Inf. Syst. 24(1), 1–50 (2006)
[5] Higgins, A.L., Bahler, L., Porter, J.: Speaker verification using randomized phrase prompting. Digital Signal Processing 1, 89–106 (1991)
[6] Melin, P., Acosta, M.L., Felix, C.: Pattern Recognition Using Fuzzy Logic and Neural Networks. In: Proceedings of IC-AI 2003, Las Vegas, USA, pp. 221–227 (2003)

A Secure Authentication System Using Multimodal Biometrics for High Security MANETs

B. Shanthini[1] and S. Swamynathan[2]

[1] Research Scholar
[2] Associate Professor
CSE Department, Anna University, Chennai, India

Abstract. Mobile Adhoc NETworks (MANET) are collections of wireless mobile devices with restricted broadcast range and resources and communication is achieved by relaying data along appropriate routes that are dynamically discovered and maintained through collaboration between the nodes. MANET is a self configuring, dynamic, multi hop radio network without any fixed infrastructure. The main challenge in the design of such networks is how to provide security for the information which is communicated through the network. Biometrics provides possible solutions for this problem in MANET since it has the direct connection with user identity and needs little user interruption.

This proposed Multimodal Biometric-based Authentication Combined Security System provides authentication using face biometrics and security using fingerprint biometrics. The proposed system has three advantages compared to previous works. First, for authentication, eigenface of the sender is generated and is attached to the data to be transferred. Second, to enhance security, the data and the eigenface of the sender is encrypted by using the key which is extracted from the fingerprint biometric of the receiver. Third, to reduce a transmission-based attack, the fingerprint based cryptographic key is randomized by applying a genetic operator. Thus, this security system provides authentication, security and revocability for high security applications in mobile environments.

Keywords: Mobile Ad hoc Networks, User Authentication, Data Security, Face Biometric, Fingerprint Biometric, Genetic Algorithm.

1 Introduction

Mobile ad hoc networks are seen as autonomous that can be quickly formed, on demand, for specific tasks and mission support. Communication generally happens through wireless links, in which nodes within a radio range communicate and coordinate to create a virtual and temporary communication infrastructure for data routing and data transmission. MANET can operate in isolation or in coordination with a wired network through a gateway node participating in both networks. This flexibility along with their self-organizing capabilities, are some of their biggest strengths, as well as their biggest security weaknesses.

D.C. Wyld et al. (Eds.): ACITY 2011, CCIS 198, pp. 290–307, 2011.

The applications of MANET include the foremost situations such as emergency/crisis management, military, healthcare, disaster relief operations and intelligent transportation systems. So message security plays a vital role in data transmission in MANET. However, because of the absence of an established infrastructure or centralized administration, implementation of hard-cryptographic algorithms is a challenging prospect. So, in this paper, we present a novel security system using genetic based biometric cryptography for message security and authentication of the users in mobile ad hoc networks.

1.1 Security Challenges in MANET

Wireless ad hoc networks are vulnerable to various attacks [1]. Adversaries may attempt passive and active attacks to gain unauthorized access to classified information, modify the information, delete the information or disrupt the information flow. The best way to protect data information in a most fine-granular way is by providing security at the application layer. It is highly desirable to handle data confidentiality and integrity in application layer, since this is the easiest way to protect data from altering, fabrication and compromise. With the rapid evolution of wireless technology the reliance of ad hoc networks to carry mission critical information is rapidly growing. This is especially important in a military scenario where strategic and tactical information is sent. Therefore the ability to achieve a highly secure authentication is becoming more critical.

Numerous countermeasures such as strong authentication, encrypting and decrypting the messages using traditional cryptographic algorithms and redundant transmission can be used to tackle these attacks. Even though these traditional approaches play an important role in achieving confidentiality, integrity, authentication and non-repudiation, these are not sufficient for more sensitive applications and they can address only a subset of the threats. Moreover, MANETs [2] cannot support complex computations or high communication overhead due to the limited memory and computation power of mobile nodes.

1.2 Necessity of Biometrics Security

For mission-critical applications such as a military application may have higher requirements regarding data or information security. In such a scenario, we need to design a system which combines user authentication and data security. For that we combine both biometrics and cryptography which overcome the limitations of traditional security solutions. Biometrics refers to the methods for uniquely recognizing humans based upon one or more intrinsic physical or behavioral traits like fingerprints, iris, retina scans, hand, face, ear geometry, hand vein, nail bed, DNA, palm print, signature, voice, keystroke dynamics, and gait analysis etc.

The trade offs among biometric technologies really depend on the application and security level involved. The best biometric technologies [3][4] that can easily be deployable in ad hoc networks are fingerprint and face recognition. Face images have been successfully used in civilian identification for years because of their uniqueness for each individual. As biometrics can't be borrowed, stolen, or forgotten, and forging is practically impossible, it has been presented as a natural identity tool that offers greater security and convenience than traditional methods of personal recognition.

Even though biometric has advantages, it also raises many security and privacy concerns as given below:

i. Biometric is authentic but not secret.
ii. Biometric cannot be revoked or cancelled.
iii. If a biometric is lost once, it is compromised forever.
iv. Cross-matching can be used to track individuals without their consent.

To overcome these disadvantages, instead of using the original biometric, a set of features are taken from it and transformed using genetic algorithm. If a biometric is compromised, it can be simply reenrolled using another feature set and another genetic operation, thus providing revocability and the privacy of the biometric is preserved.

1.3 Genetic Algorithms

Genetic algorithms [5] are a family of computational models inspired by natural evolution. They belong to the field of evolutionary computation and are based on three main operators: Selection selects the fittest individuals, called parents that contribute to the reproduction of the population at the next generation, Crossover combines two parents to form children for the next generation and Mutation applies random changes to individual parents to form children. Two-point crossover operator is used here which has the ability to generate, promote, and juxtapose building blocks to form the optimal strings.

This paper is organized into 4 sections. Section 1 introduces the background and initiatives of the research. It also discusses the challenges of message security, the necessity of biometric security in MANET and Genetic algorithms. Section 2 explains the related research works that has been done to provide security in MANET. Section 3 proposes a new security scheme for MANET which combines genetic algorithm and biometrics. Section 4 analyses the results of various algorithms and section 5 contains conclusion and suggestions for future research.

2 Related Work

A few research works that has been done for data security in MANET, the various approaches of biometric security and Genetic algorithms in security are briefly presented.

Qinghan Xiao [6] introduced a new strategy for authentication of mobile users. Each user has a profile which contains all the information of the ID holders. The group leader also maintains the biometric templates of the group members. Instead of a central authentication server, the group leaders act as distributed authenticators. Each group has a shared cryptographic key which is used for cryptographic communication within the group. The proposed approach is designed for high security small group coalition operations and may not be suitable for enterprise usage.

Jie Liu et al. [7] proposed an optimal biometric-based continuous authentication scheme in MANET which distinguished two classes of authentications: user-to-device and device-to-network. This model focused on the user-to-device class and it can optimally control whether or not to perform authentication as well as which biometrics to use to minimize the usage of system resources.

B Ananda Krishna et al. [8] depicted a model which used multiple algorithms for encryption and decryption. Each time a data packet is sent to the application layer it is encrypted using one of these randomly selected algorithms. When responses are analyzed they give a random pattern and difficult to know neither algorithms nor keys. The proposed scheme worked well for heavily loaded networks with high mobility.

A. Jagadeesan et al. [9] projected an efficient approach based on multimodal biometrics (Iris and Fingerprint) for generating a secure cryptographic key. At first, the minutiae points and texture properties are extracted from the fingerprint and iris images respectively and these features are fused at the feature level to obtain the multi-biometric template. Finally, the multi-biometric template is used for generating a 256-bit cryptographic key.

B. Shanthini et al. [10] explained Cancelable Biometric-Based Security System (CBBSS), where cancelable biometrics is used for data security in mobile ad hoc networks. Fingerprint feature of the receiver is coupled with the tokenized random data by using inner-product algorithm and this product is discretized based on a threshold to produce a set of private binary code which is acting as a cryptographic key in this system.

Kanade S et. al. [11] proposed a simple and effective protocol to securely share crypto-biometric keys which are generated from face and another protocol to generate and share session keys which are valid for only one communication session. This protocol achieves mutual authentication between the client and the server without the need of trusted third party. The stored templates are cancelable. The protocols are evaluated for biometric verification performance on a subset of the NIST-FRGCv2 face database.

B. Shanthini et. al. [12] proposed a security system based on fingerprint biometrics and genetic algorithms. In this proposed approach, a genetic two-point crossover operator is applied on fingerprint feature set and is used for data security in MANETs.

Ae-Young Kim et. al. [13] designed a strong authentication protocol using the fuzzy eigenface vault based on smart card and tested the scheme. The proposed protocol has three advantages. First, to get security, accuracy and convenience they used eigenface in a fuzzy vault scheme which is suitable to combine biometric authentication and cryptography. Second, to enhance security, secret data which is for construction of the fuzzy eigenface vault is saved on a smart card. Third, to reduce a transmission-based attack, a transmission of message is occurred just one time in a login phase. Then, they analyzed security of the proposed protocol and since it has security and convenience, it is suitable for security services that combine biometric-based authentication and cryptography.

B. Shanthini et. al. [14] proposed a security system based on face biometrics and genetic algorithms. In this proposed approach, the face is cropped from the given image and the facial features are extracted which acted as cryptographic key. A genetic two-point crossover operator is applied on facial feature set to randomize the key and is used for encrypting the data transferred within mobile ad hoc networks.

Zarza L et al. [15] explained the context of the study of Genetic Algorithms as an aiding tool for generating and optimizing security protocols. This paper explains how security protocols can be represented as binary strings, how GA tools are used to define genome interpretation in optimization problems.

3 Proposed Work

In this proposed Secure Authentication System the face images are used for authentication and feature set extracted from fingerprint is used for encryption. For randomizing the cryptographic key a genetic two-point crossover operator is applied on fingerprint feature set by which the revocability is achieved. The main objective of the proposed security scheme is to improvise the existing data security approaches for MANET to suit technology enhancements and to study the network performance.

3.1 Overall Processes Invoved in the System

In this approach the facial and fingerprint images of a group of users involved in the communication are stored in the database. From the facial images the actual face is detected, cropped and normalized. Then the eigenface of sender is created and is attached with the actual data. Next, the feature set is extracted from the receiver's fingerprint from which the cryptographic key is generated and is used to encrypt the data and the appended eigenface of the sender. This overall process can be seen in figure 1. At the receiver's end, the reverse process takes place ie the receiver's fingerprint biometric is used for decryption by which the original data and the sender's eigenface are recovered. Now, eigenface recognition method can be used for authentication of the sender.

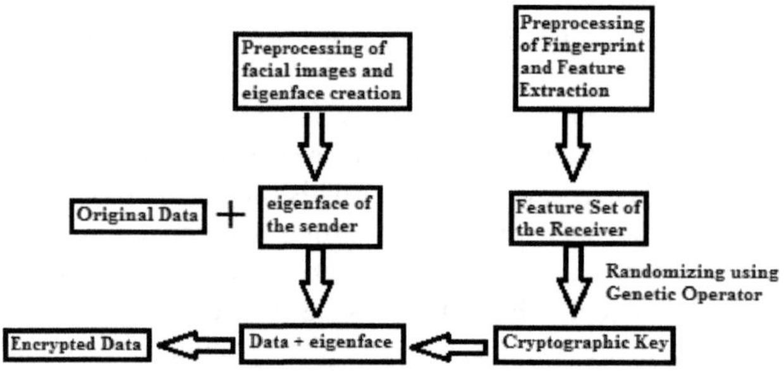

Fig. 1. Overall Processes involved in the sender side

3.2 Preprocessing of Facial Images and Eigenface Creation

3.2.1 Face Detection

In this process, a color based technique is implemented for detecting human faces in images. This method consists of two image processing steps. First, skin regions are separated from non-skin regions. After that, the human face within the skin regions is located and cropped. In order to segment human skin regions from non-skin regions based on color, a reliable *skin color model* of different people is needed [16]. Luminance can be removed from the RGB color representation in the chromatic color space. Chromatic colors are defined by a normalization process shown here: $r = R/(R+G+B)$ & $b = B/(R+G+B)$.

Fig. 2. Sample Face Image Database

Hundred and sixty skin samples were taken from 16 color images, which are shown in figure 2, are used to determine the color distribution of human skin in chromatic color space.

As the skin samples are extracted from color images and they are filtered using a low-pass filter to reduce the effect of noise in the samples. Figure 3 shows the color distribution of these skin samples in the chromatic color space.

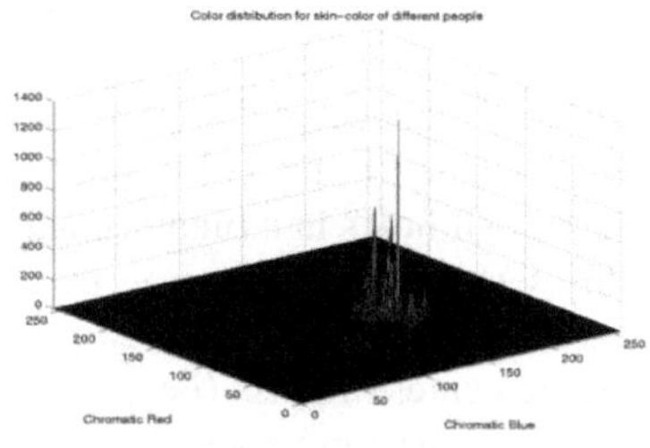

Fig. 3. Color distribution for skin-color of different people

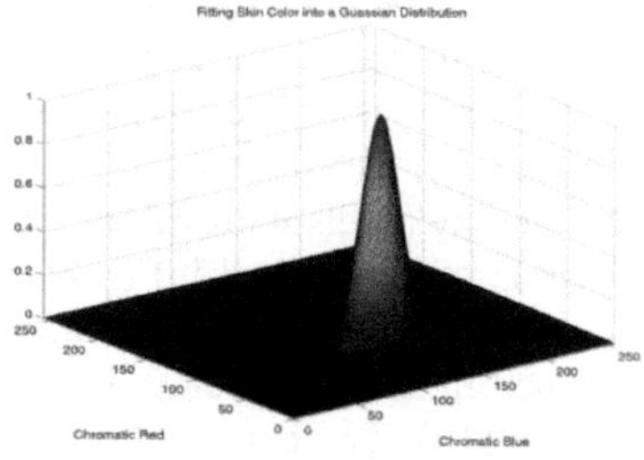

Fig. 4. Gaussian Distribution from skin color

The *color histogram* revealed that the distribution of skin-color of different people are clustered in the chromatic color space and a skin color distribution can be represented by a Gaussian model N(m, C) which is shown in figure 4, where:

$$\text{Mean: } m = E\{x\} \text{ where } x = (r\ b)^T \text{ and Covariance: } C = E\{(x - m)(x - m)^T\}.$$

With this Gaussian fitted skin color model, the likelihood of skin is obtained for any pixel of an image. If a pixel, having transformed from RGB color space to chromatic color space, has a chromatic pair value of (r, b), the *likelihood of skin* for this pixel can then be computed as follows:

$$Likelihood = P(r,b) = \exp[-0.5(x-m)^T C^{-1}(x-m)]$$
$$where : x = (r,b)^T.$$

Hence, this skin color model can transform a color image into a gray scale image such that the gray value at each pixel shows the likelihood of the pixel belonging to the skin. A sample color image and its resulting skin-likelihood image are shown in Figure 5.a and 5.b.

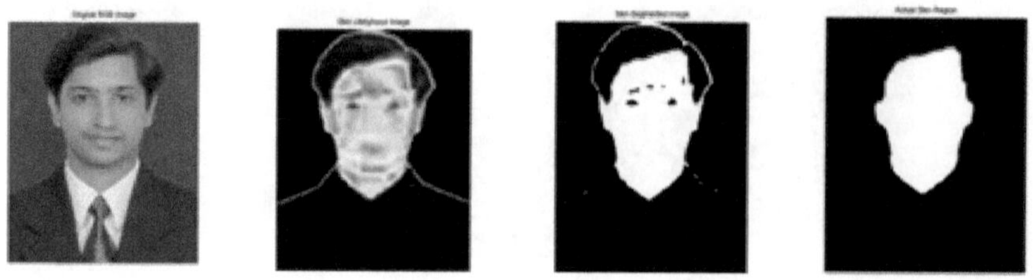

Fig. 5.a. Sample Color Image b. Skin-Likelihood Image c. Skin-Segmented Image d. Actual Skin Region

The skin-likelihood image will be a gray-scale image whose gray values represent the likelihood of the pixel belonging to skin. Since the skin regions are brighter than the other parts of the images, the *skin segmentation* can be done from the rest of the image through a thresholding process. Since people with different skins have different likelihood, an adaptive thresholding process is required to achieve the optimal threshold value for each image. Using this technique the skin-colored regions are effectively segmented from the non-skin colored regions. The skin segmented image resulting from this technique is shown in Figure 5.c.

A *skin region* is defined as a closed region or a set of connected components within the image, which can have 0, 1 or more holes inside it. Its color boundary is represented by pixels with value 1 for binary images. All holes in a binary image have pixel value of zero (black). Figure 5.d. shows the segmented skin region from skin-likelihood image. To study the face region, its area and center of the region is to be determined first. One efficient way is to compute the center of mass (i.e., centroid) of the region [19]. The center of area in binary images is the same as the center of the mass and it is computed as shown below:

$$\bar{x} = \frac{1}{A}\sum_{i=1}^{n}\sum_{j=1}^{m} jB[i,j] \qquad \bar{y} = \frac{1}{A}\sum_{i=1}^{n}\sum_{j=1}^{m} iB[i,j]$$

where B is the matrix of size [n x m] representation of the region and A is the area in pixels of the region. By that way, the center point of the actual face region is found out and is shown in figure 6.a and 6.b. Finally, by using center point the actual face region is cropped, converted into binary image and normalized. Cropped images are shown in figure 6.c and 6.d.

Fig. 6. a. Skin region with center point b. Original image with center point c. Cropped Face region

The sample images are cropped by applying the above said method and are normalized. This is shown in figure 7.

Fig. 7. Cropped and normalized face images

3.2.2 Eigen Face Generation

Eigenfaces are a set of eigenvectors used for human face recognition. A set of eigenfaces can be generated by performing a mathematical process called principal component analysis (PCA) [17] on a large set of human face images. The eigenfaces will appear as light and dark areas that are arranged in a specific pattern. This pattern is how different features of a face are singled out to be evaluated and scored.

This part of the project is to apply the Eigenface approach to recognize someone's face. The problem is to be able to accurately recognize a person's identity and allow the person to access highly secured information. Steps involved in Eigenface creation is explained as follows:

The first step is to obtain a set S with M face images. The images constituting the training set should have been taken under the same lighting conditions, and must be normalized to have the eyes and mouths aligned across all images. They must also be all resampled to the same pixel resolution. Each image is treated as one vector, simply by concatenating the rows of pixels in the original image, resulting in a single row with $r \times c$ elements. The face images shown in figure 7 are converted into gray images, resampled and are used as the input for this method. In our example M = 16 and each image is transformed into a vector of size N and placed into the set.

$$S = \{\Gamma_1, \Gamma_2, \Gamma_3, \ldots\ldots\ldots, \Gamma_M\}$$

The training set and normalized training set are shown in figure 8 and figure 9.

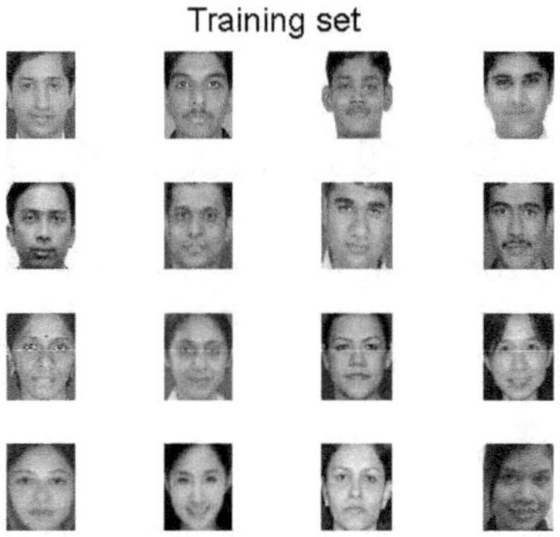

Fig. 8. Training Set Gray images

Fig. 9. Normalized Training Set

After the set is obtained the mean image Ψ is created by using the following formula and is shown in figure 10:

$$\Psi = \frac{1}{M}\sum_{n=1}^{M}\Gamma_n$$

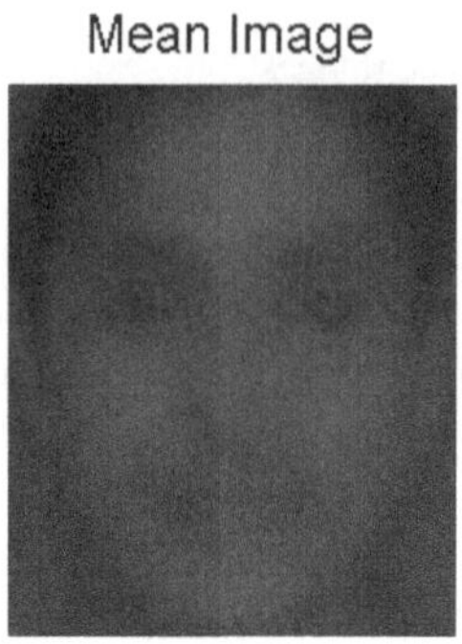

Fig. 10. Mean image

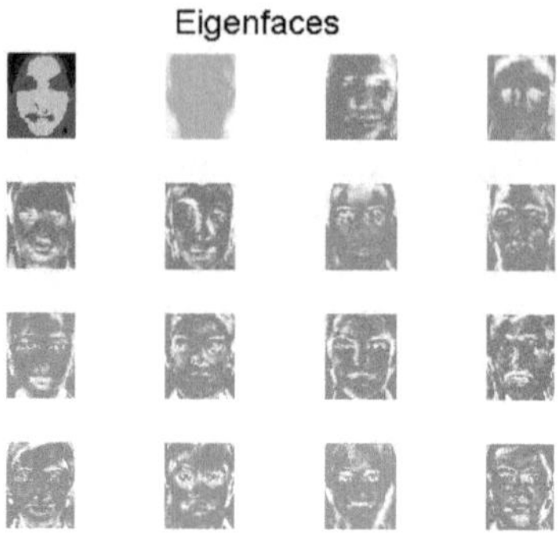

Fig. 11. Eigen Faces

Then the difference Φ between the input image and the mean image is found by using $\Phi_i = \Gamma_i - \Psi$

Next a set of M orthonormal vectors, $\mathbf{u}_n$, is found which best describes the distribution of the data. The kth vector, $\mathbf{u}_k$, is chosen such that

$$\lambda_k = \frac{1}{M}\sum_{n=1}^{M}\left(u_k^T\Phi_n\right)^2$$ is a maximum, subject to $$u_l^T u_k = \delta_{lk} = \begin{cases}1 & \text{if } l = k\\ 0 & \text{otherwise}\end{cases}$$

$\mathbf{u}_k$ and λ_k are the eigenvectors and eigenvalues of the covariance matrix **C.** The covariance matrix **C** in the following manner.

$$C = \frac{1}{M}\sum_{n=1}^{M}\Phi_n\Phi_n^T = AA^T \qquad A = \{\Phi_1, \Phi_2, \Phi_3, \ldots\ldots, \Phi_n\}$$

Since the C matrix is an N2 x N2 matrix, computing its eigenvectors is not computationally feasible. Instead, the eigenvectors vl of the new matrix L = ATA are found which has the same eigenvectors of the matrix C = AAT.

$$L_{mn} = \Phi_m^T\Phi_n$$

Once the eigenvectors, $\mathbf{v}_l$, of the L matrix are found, eigen faces $\mathbf{u}_l$ can also be found by the following formula and the eigen faces of the original images are shown in figure 11.

$$u_l = \sum_{k=1}^{M} v_{lk} \Phi_k \qquad l = 1, \ldots\ldots, M$$

Once the eigen face of the sender is generated that is appended with the original data to be transferred to the receiver and is encrypted by the cryptographic algorithm.

3.3 Preprocessing of Fingerprint and Minutiae Extraction

The fingerprint images are first pre-processed as explained by Akram et. al. [18] to remove noise and irrelevant information present in the images. This is implemented using Matlab. Pre-processing means enhancing the image and it consists of the following steps:

Image Normalization is performed to remove the effect of sensor noise and gray-level background which are the consequence of difference in finger pressure. Normalization is used to standardize the intensity values in an image by adjusting the range of gray-level values so that it lies within a desired range of values.

Image Enhancement enhances the fingerprint image by applying some filters to remove the noises present in the image. The configurations of parallel ridges and valleys with well defined frequency and orientation in a fingerprint image provide useful information which helps in removing undesired noise. The sinusoidal-shaped waves of ridges and valleys vary slowly in a local constant orientation. Therefore, a band-pass filter that is tuned to the corresponding frequency and orientation can efficiently remove the undesired noise and preserve the true ridge and valley structures. Gabor filters have both frequency-selective and orientation-selective properties and have optimal joint resolution in both spatial and frequency domains. Therefore, Gabor filter is used as band-pass filter to remove the noise and preserve true ridge/valley structures.

Fingerprint Image Binarization is to transform the 8-bit gray fingerprint image to a 1-bit image with 0-value for ridges and 1-value for furrows. After the operation, ridges in the fingerprint are highlighted with black color while furrows are white. A locally adaptive binarization method is performed to binarize the fingerprint image. This method transforms a pixel value to 1 if the value is larger than the mean intensity value of the current block (16x16) to which the pixel belongs.

Region of Interest (ROI) [19] is useful to recognize each fingerprint image. The image area without effective ridges and furrows is first discarded since it only holds background information. Then the bound of the remaining effective area is sketched out. To extract the ROI, two steps are followed. The first step is orientation field estimation and the second is intrigued from some morphological methods.

Orientation field estimation representation gives an intrinsic property of the fingerprint images and defines invariant coordinates for ridges and valleys in a local neighborhood. The orientation field of a fingerprint image defines the local orientation of the ridges contained in the fingerprint.

For ROI extraction two morphological operations called ‘open’ and ‘close’ are adopted. The ‘open’ operation can expand images and remove peaks introduced by background noise. The ‘close’ operation can shrink images and eliminate small cavities. Finally the bound area is found by subtracting the closed area from the opened area.

Then the leftmost, rightmost, uppermost and bottommost blocks are thrown away out of the bound so as to get the tightly bounded region containing the bound and inner area.

Ridge Thinning is to eliminate the redundant pixels of ridges till the ridges are just one pixel wide. The full fingerprint image is scanned and in each scan the redundant pixels are marked in each small image window (3x3). Finally all those marked pixels are removed after several scans. For this thinning the built-in morphological thinning function in MATLAB is used.

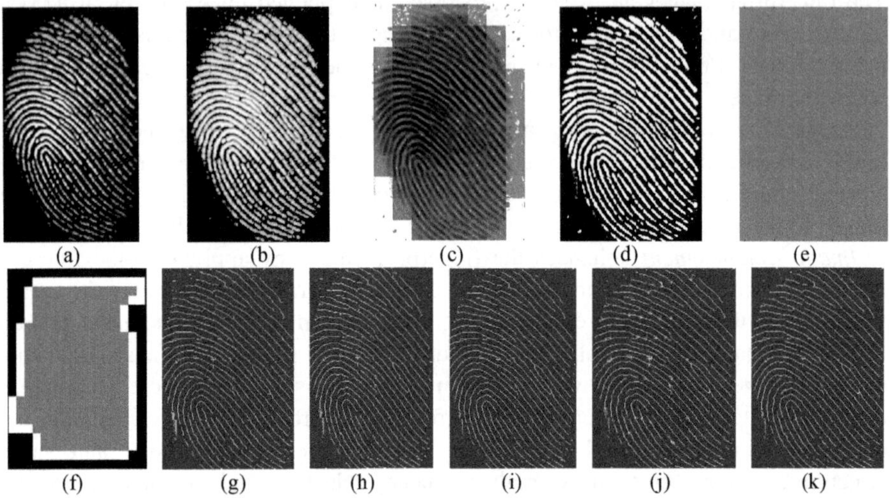

Fig. 12. Fingerprint pre-processing and minutiae extraction (a) Original image (b) Normalized image (c) Enhanced image (d) Binarized image (e) Orientation field map (f) Region of interest (g) Thinned image (h) Removal of H breaks (i) Removal of spikes (j) Extracted minutiae (k) Removal of spurious minutiae.

Removal of H breaks and spikes is done by applying other morphological operations like 'clean', 'hbreak' and 'spur' onto the thinned ridge image.

Marking of fingerprint minutiae is made by following the given procedure. For each 3x3 window, if the central pixel is 1 and has exactly 3 one-value neighbors, then the central pixel is a ridge branch and it is marked. If the central pixel is 1 and has only 1 one-value neighbor, then the central pixel is a ridge ending and it is also marked. Also the average inter-ridge width D is estimated at this stage. The average inter-ridge width refers to the average distance between two neighboring ridges. To approximate the D value, scan a row of the thinned ridge image and sum up all pixels in the row whose value is one. Then divide the row length with the above summation to get an inter-ridge width. Such kind of row scan is performed upon several other rows and column scans are also conducted and finally all the inter-ridge widths are averaged to get the D. Together with the minutia marking, all thinned ridges in the fingerprint image are labeled with a unique ID for further operation. The labeling operation is done by using the morphological operation: BWLABEL.

False Minutia Removal eliminates the spurious minutiae which were occasionally introduced by the earlier stages. For example, false ridge breaks due to insufficient amount of ink and ridge cross-connections due to over inking are not totally eliminated. These false minutiae will significantly affect the accuracy of the system and these are removed.

Finally, the x,y positions of the marked minutiae are stored in a text file and these values are used for generating the cryptographic key. Figure 12 explains the different steps involved in fingerprint image preprocessing.

3.4 Generation of Genetic-Based Biometric Key

In this model all the group members of a small ad hoc network maintain the facial and fingerprint biometric templates of the other group members. Suppose a member wants to send a message to any other member, the feature set taken from the receiver's fingerprint image is undergone into a genetic two-point crossover operation and the result is the cryptographic key in this system. Generation of cryptographic key is shown in figure 13. The same key is generated by the receiver by using his biometric and the same sort of cross over operations and is used for decryption.

If this biometric based key is compromised a new one can be issued by using a different set of fingerprint features and different cross over operation and the compromised one is rendered completely useless. It can also be an application specific that is different sets of fingerprint features can be used with different cross over operations to generate respective cryptographic key for different applications.

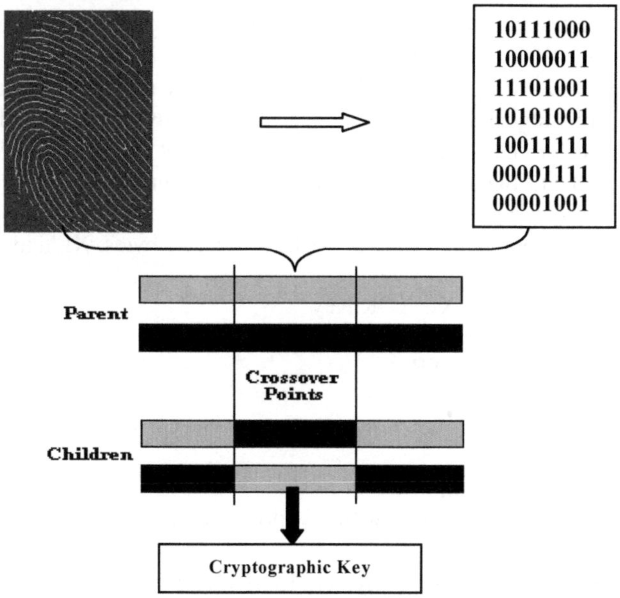

Fig. 13. Generation of cryptographic key from the fingerprint feature set

Example:

Parent	**01011100**	**1010000011111010**	**00110101**
	00110011	**1111000011110000**	**11001100**
		After Crossover	
Children	**01011100**	**1111000011110000**	**00110101**
	00110011	**1010000011111010**	**11001100**

3.5 Securing the Data

Data is secured by applying this cryptographic key to encrypt the actual message appended with the eigen face of the sender using a simple cryptographic algorithm say Fiestel algorithm. The encryption and decryption processes are specified by the formulae:

$$\mathbf{C = E_{KR}(P) \text{ and } P = D_{KR}(C)}$$

where P – Plain Text C - Cipher Text
KR - Key created by Receiver's Biometric
E - Encryption Algorithm D - Decryption Algorithm

In Fiestal algorithm, a block of size N is divided into two halves, of length N/2, the left half called XL and right half called XR. The output of the ith round is determined from the output of the (i-1)th round. Different sub key is used for the iterations. But the number of iterations performed is reduced to show that security can be achieved by using simple algorithm. For example if the plaintext is of 512 bytes, then encryption is performed for every 64 bits with different 64 bit key and the process is repeated until all 512 bytes are encrypted. Fiestel structure is given in figure 14[1].

Algorithm for Encryption**:**

1. Divide the plaintext into two blocks of size, 32 bytes, XL and XR
2. For I = 1 to 32
   Do XL = XL XOR Key
   XR = F (XL) XOR XR
   Swap XL, XR
   Join XL, XR
3. Repeat step 2 until the entire plaintext is encrypted

Algorithm for Decryption**:**

Do the reverse operation of Encryption process.

3.6 Implementation of Security System in MANET

The proposed scheme can be implemented over any unicast routing protocols like DSR or AODV which discover routes as and when necessary and the routes are maintained just as long as necessary. A typical MANET is shown in figure 15. Suppose User A wants to send the message to User C, after the forward and reverse paths are set up by the route discovery method, the data will be sent through that path to the destination C. Before sending the data through that path, the data will be appended with the eigen face of the sender and encrypted by Fiestel algorithm using the genetic based fingerprint biometric key of the receiver. Once the cipher text is received by the receiver, the cipher text is decrypted by reversing the before said processes.

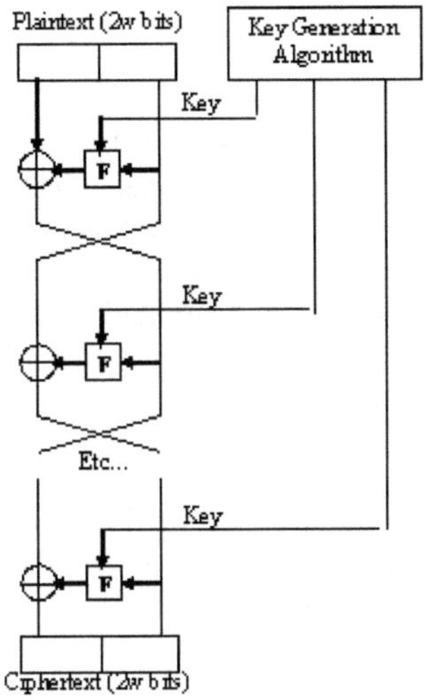

Fig. 14. Fiestel Algorithm without subkeys

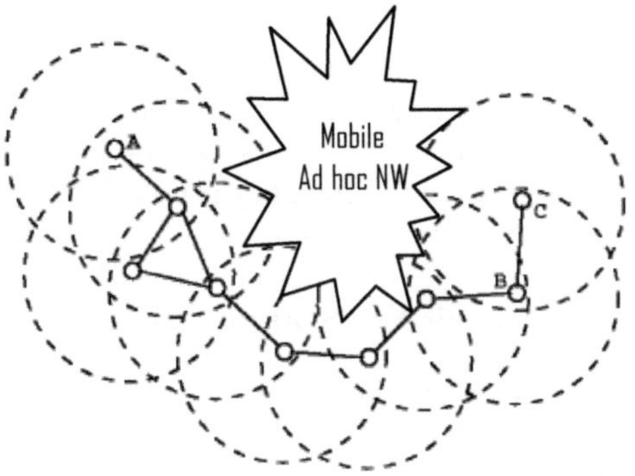

Fig. 15. MANET Structure

4 Security Analysis

4.1 The Security Functions of the Proposed System

- Confidentiality: The privacy of the message is protected by this scheme. Suppose if the attacker wants to derive the original message from the encrypted text, he needs the cryptographic key. The key can be obtained only by using the fingerprint biometric of the receiver. Furthermore the biometric is not used as such instead a cancelable version is used. So, it is computationally infeasible to get the key.
- Authentication: In our proposed scheme, the members of the ad hoc group can authenticate each other through their face biometric. If the receiver wants to verify whether the message is coming from the genuine sender, after decrypting the message he can separate the eigen face and can verify with the sender's face biometric.
- Integrity: In our proposed scheme, the recipient can verify whether the received message is the original one that was sent by the sender. If the attacker changes the cipher text, the original plain text can not be generated after decrypting with the

key created by using receivers biometric. By the property of one-way hash function, it is computationally infeasible for the attacker to modify the cipher text.

4.2 Man-in-the-Middle Attack

An attacker sits between the sender and the receiver and sniffs any information being sent between two ends is called man in the middle attack. Even though the attacker can get the cipher text he cannot view the original message since it is secured using genetic based biometric cryptography.

4.3 Exhaustive Search Attack

If the hacker does not have any information about the solution space or key statistics information, he has to perform an exhaustive search in the entire key space. If the key space is very large, the expected number of guesses by exhaustive search is also very large ie a longer key is more secure under exhaustive search attack. In the proposed approach, since different key is used for different iterations computationally infeasible to get the key by this method.

4.4 Authentic Key Statistics Attack

If the hacker knows the statistics of the authentic keys generated by the key generator system, he may try to guess the keys smartly [20]. Since we use eigen face for authentication it is also not feasible to guess easily and attack the system.

4.5 Device Key Statistics Attack

If the hacker knows the subject space of the system, he may probe the key generation system by inputting the subject information and collecting the statistics of the generated keys. Given such statistics, the hacker may have better ways to guess the cryptographic key. Since such attack focuses on the device the attack is named as device key statistics attack [20]. Our proposed system is intended to provide security for an ad hoc mobile application where each user will be allocated with independent devices and it is not at all possible to hack such system with this attack.

5 Experimental Results

This section reports the analysis of the security parameters like time taken for key generation, encryption and decryption for various algorithms like 3DES192, AES128, AES256 and GBBSS64 [12] in an ad hoc network environment. The graph shown in figure 16 is generated by using the timing measurements given in the following table 1.

From the above chart we can understand that our proposed system achieves relatively high performance than other algorithms and same as GBBSS-64 in terms of less overhead and high security level. Since the key size is very small and algorithm is very simple compared to the other algorithms, the time taken to generate key, encrypt and decrypt is also less but slightly higher than GBBSS-64.

Table 1. Key size and Timing measurements for various algorithms

Encryption Algorithm	Key size Time Complexity Parameters			
	Key Size	Time taken for Key Generation	Time taken for Encryption	Time taken for Decryption
3DES192	192	0.08 ms	0.08 ms	0.07 ms
AES-128	128	0.13 ms	0.1 ms	0.1 ms
AES-256	256	0.13 ms	0.12 ms	0.11 ms
GBBSS-64	64	0,06 ms	0.04 ms	0.03 ms
Proposed System	64	0.08 ms	0.04 ms	0.02 ms

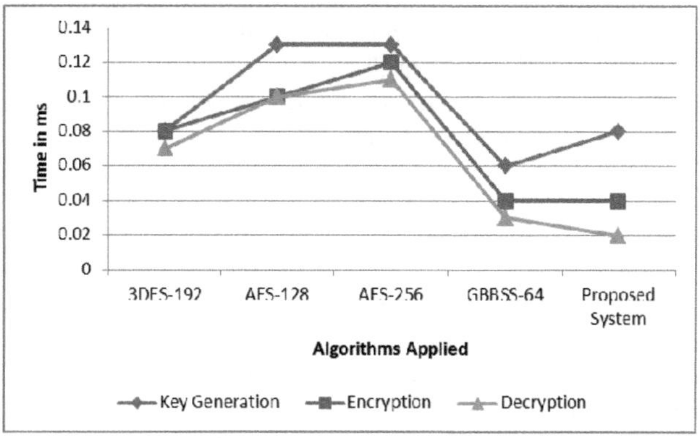

Fig. 16. Timing measurements for various algorithms

Table 2. Security parameters for various algorithms

Encryption Algorithm	Security Parameters			
	Security – Encryption	Authentica-tion	Revocability	Practicality
3DES192	Yes	No	No	No
AES-128	Yes	No	No	No
AES-256	Yes	No	No	No
GBBSS-64	Yes	No	Yes	Yes
Proposed System	Yes	Yes	Yes	Yes

A brief comparison of some of the cryptographic algorithms based on four security related parameters is provided in Table 2. From the above table we can understand that the proposed system provides all compared to other algorithms.

6 Conclusion and Future Work

Although MANET is a very promising technology, challenges are slowing its development and deployment. Traditional security mechanisms are not sufficient for the nodes roaming in a hostile environment with relatively poor physical protection. Therefore to strengthen the encryption algorithm and key, first the advantages of biometrics, cryptography and genetic algorithms are taken into our system. Secondly, security should be achieved by using simple algorithms that involve small inherent delays rather than complex algorithms which occupy considerable memory and delay. Finally, high security ad hoc networks may also need authentication which is also provided in this system.

The method presented in this paper remains as a preliminary approach to realize biometric security in ad hoc networks which needs high security. This approach can be used in very critical, crucial and vital applications where data security and authentication is very important and members who have accessed that data is limited in number like military officers at war-field, scientists in a conference etc. There are many security problems still persist in these types of ad-hoc networks and as a future work, this paper can be extended to solve those problems with different biometrics and also with different multimodal biometrics.

References

1. Stallings, W.: Cryptography and Network Security – Principles and Practices, 3rd edn. Pearson Education, London (2004)
2. Trivedi, A.K., Arora, R., Kapoor, R., Sanyal, S., Abraham, A., Sanyal, S.: Mobile Ad Hoc Network Security Vulnerabilities. IGI Global (2009)
3. Maio, M.D., Jain, A.K., Prabhakar, S.: Handbook of Fingerprint Recognition. Springer, Heidelberg (2003)
4. Li, S.Z., Jain, A.K.: Handbook of Face Recognition. Springer, Heidelberg (2005)
5. Fessi, B.A., Ben Abdallah, S., Boudriga, H.M.: A new genetic algorithm approach for intrusion response system in computer networks. In: IEEE Symposium on Computers and Communications (2009)
6. Xiao, Q.: A Biometric Authentication Approach for High Security Ad hoc Networks. In: Proceedings of IEEE Workshop on Info. Assistance (2004)
7. Liu, J., Richard Yu, F., Lung, C.-H., Tang, H.: Optimal Biometric-Based Continuous Authentication in Mobile Ad hoc Networks. In: Third IEEE International Conference on Wireless and Mobile Computing, Networking and Communications (2007)
8. Ananda Krishna, B., Radha, S., Chenna Kesava Reddy, K.: Data Security in Ad hoc Networks using Randomization of Cryptographic Algorithms. Journal of Applied Sciences 7(24), 4007–4012 (2007)
9. Jagadeesan, A., Thillaikkarasi, T., Duraiswamy, K.: Cryptographic Key Generation from Multiple Biometric Modalities: Fusing Minutiae with Iris Feature. International Journal of Computer Applications 2(6), 975–8887 (2010)
10. Shanthini, B., Swamynathan, S.: A Cancelable Biometric-Based Security System for Mobile Ad Hoc Networks. In: International Conference on Computer Technology (ICONCT 2009), pp. 179–184 (2009)

11. Kanade, S., Petrovska-Delacretaz, Dorizzi, B.: Generating and Sharing Biometrics Based Session Keys for Secure Cryptographic Applications. In: Fourth IEEE International Conference on Biometrics: Theory, Applications and Systems (2010)
12. Shanthini, B., Swamynathan, S.: Data Security in Mobile Ad Hoc Networks using Genetic Based Biometrics. International Journal of Computer Science and Information Security 8(6), 149–153 (2010)
13. Kim, A.-Y., Lee, S.-H.: Authentication Protocol Using Fuzzy Eigenface Vault Based On Moc. In: International Conference on Advanced Communication Technology, pp. 1771–1775 (2007)
14. Shanthini, B., Swamynathan, S.: A Security System using Genetic Based Face Biometrics for MANETs. In: International Conference on Intelligent Systems and /Technology (March 2011) (Selected Paper)
15. Zarza, L., Pegueroles, J., Soriano, M.: Interpretation of Binary Strings as Security Protocols for their Evolution by means of Genetic Algorithms. In: International Conference on Database and Expert Systems Applications (2007)
16. `http://www-cs-students.stanford.edu/~robles/ee368/main.html`
17. Ramesh, R., Kasturi, R., Schunck, B.: Machine Vision, pp. 31–51. McGraw Hill, New York (1995)
18. Usman Akram, M., Tariq, A., Khan, S.A.: Fingerprint Image: pre- and post-processing. International Journal of Biometrics 1(1) (2008)
19. Wu, Z.-l., Li, C.-h. (eds.): Feature Extraction, Foundations and Applications. Springer, Heidelberg (2006)
20. Zhang, W., Zhang, G., Chen, T.: Security analysis for Key generation Systems using Face Images. In: International Conference on Image Processing, pp. 3455–3458 (2004)

Error Detection and Correction for Secure Multicast Key Distribution Protocol

P. Vijayakumar[1], S. Bose[1], A. Kannan[2], V. Thangam[3], M. Manoji[3], and M.S. Vinayagam[3]

[1] Department of Computer Science & Engineering, Anna University, Chennai -25
viji_bond2000@yahoo.com, sbs@cs.annauniv.edu
[2] Department of Information Science & Technology, Anna University, Chennai -25
kannan@annauniv.edu
[3] Department of Computer Science & Engineering, University College of Engineering Tindivanam, India
{vedhathangam,jijimanoji,vinayagamcse}@gmail.com

Abstract. Integrating an efficient Error detection and correction scheme with less encoding and decoding complexity to support the distribution of keying material in a secure multicast communication is an important issue, since the amount of information carried out in the wireless channel is high which produces more errors due to noise available in the communication channel. Moreover, the key must be sent securely to the group members. In this paper, we propose a new efficient Key Distribution Protocol that provides more security and also integrates an encoding method in sender side and decoding method in the receiver side. To achieve higher level of security, we propose Euler's totient function based key distribution protocol. To provide efficient error detection and correction method while distributing the Keying and re-keying information, we introduce tanner graph based encoding stopping set construction algorithm in sender and receiver side of the multicast communication. Two major operations in this scheme are joining and leaving operations for managing multicast group memberships. The encoding and decoding complexity of this approach is computed in this paper and it is proved that this proposed approach takes less decoding time complexity.

Keywords: Multicast Communication, Key Distribution, Euler's Totient Function, Tanner Graph, Pseudo tree, Encoding Stopping set.

1 Introduction

Wireless multimedia services such as pay-per-view, videoconferences, some sporting event, audio and video broadcasting are based upon multicast communication where multimedia messages are sent to a group of members with less computation, communication cost due to the limitation of battery power. In such a scenario only registered members of a group can receive multimedia data. Group can be classified into static and dynamic groups. In static groups, membership of the group is predetermined and does not change during the communication. In dynamic groups,

D.C. Wyld et al. (Eds.): ACITY 2011, CCIS 198, pp. 308–319, 2011.

membership can change during multicast communication. Therefore, in dynamic group communication, members may join or depart from the service at any time. When a new member joins into the service, it is the responsibility of the Group Centre (GC) to disallow new members from having access to previous data. This provides backward secrecy in a secure multimedia communication. Similarly, when an existing group member leaves from any group, he/ not have access she do to future data. This achieves forward secrecy. GC also takes care of the job of distributing the Secret key and Group key to group members.

Most basic key distribution schemes mainly focuses on the domain of key computation which aims at reducing the storage and computation complexity. However, some of the literatures focus on packet loss and packet recovery [10], [14] in turn. In this paper we propose a new key distribution protocol along with error detection and correction techniques. Hence, this approach provides a good approach for the group members to construct the original key even if the keying/Rekeying information's that are sent through the wireless channel are lost. The remainder of this paper is organized as follows: Section 2 provides the features of some of the related works. Section 3 discuses the proposed key distribution protocol and a detailed explanation of the proposed work. Section 4 integrates Error detection and correction with our proposed key distribution method. Section 5 gives the concluding remarks and suggests a few possible future enhancements.

2 Literature Survey

There are many works on key management and key distribution that are present in the literature [1], [2], [8]. In most of the Key Management Schemes, different types of group users obtain a new distributed multicast key for every session update. Among the various works on key distribution, Maximum Distance Separable (MDS) [4] method focuses on error control coding techniques for distributing re-keying information. In MDS, the key is obtained based on the use of Erasure decoding functions [5], [15] to compute session keys by the group members. Here, Group center generates n message symbols by sending the code words into an Erasure decoding function. Out of the n message symbols, the first message symbol is considered as a session key and the group members are not provided this particular key alone by the GC. Group members are given the (n-1) message symbols and they compute a code word for each of them. Each of the group members uses this code word and the remaining (n-1) message symbols to compute the session key. The main limitation of this scheme is that it increases both computation and storage complexity. The computational complexity is obtained by formulating $l_r+(n-1)m$ where l_r is the size of r bit random number used in the scheme and m is the number of message symbols to be sent from the group center to group members. If l_r=m=l, computation complexity is nl. The storage complexity is given by $[log_2L]+t$ bits for each member. L is number of levels of the Key tree. Hence Group Center has to store $n\ ([log_2L]+t\ )$ bits. A new group keying method that uses one-way functions [6] to compute a tree of keys, called the One-way Function Tree (OFT) algorithm has been proposed by David and Alan. In this method, the keys are computed up the tree, from the leaves to the root. This approach reduces re-keying broadcasts to only about *log n* keys. The major limitation of this approach is that it consumes more space. However, time complexity is more important than space complexity. In our work, we focused on reduction of time complexity.

Wade Trappe and Jie Song proposed a Parametric One Way Function (POWF) [3] based binary tree key Management. The storage complexity is given by $\log_a n+2$ keys for a group centre. The amount of storage needed by the individual user is given as $S=a^{L+1}-1/a-1$Keys. Computation time is represented in terms of amount of multiplication required. The amount of multiplication needed to update the KEKs using bottom up approach is $a\log_a n - 1$. Multiplication needed to update the KEKs using top down approach is $C_{tu}= (a-1)\log_a n(\log_a n+1)/2$. The scheme MABS-B [10] provides perfect resilience against packet loss by eliminating the correlation among the packets that are sent. For ensuring such a scheme, Merkle tree which is based on hash functions is constructed and found to be very efficient for providing batch signature and verification. Meanwhile, due to the limitations in MABS-B, an efficient method for multicast communication with forward security, ForwardDiffSig was proposed [14]. This scheme was found to be very efficient in terms of speed, exhibiting low delay even for long keys.

The contribution of this work is that a variation of LDPC (Low Density Parity Check) error correction codes [12], [16-18] has been proposed. LDPC is an error correcting code that constructs a parity check matrix M, which is multiplied with the original data words, d to provide a list of code words, c. If the original data word consists of 8 bits, then LDPC (8, 16) parity check matrix is generated. LDPC codes can also be described by their parity check matrix [19] or tanner graphs. So the degree of the bit node in a tanner graph is equivalent to the column weight of the corresponding column of the parity check matrix. Different Column of a parity matrix will have different column weights. Different row of a matrix will have different row weights.

Initially, Tanner graphs [20] were developed for the process of decoding using LDPC codes, in fact, they can be used for the encoding of LDPC codes [11] In order to provide efficient error correction, and we make use of the idea of Tanner graphs. The Tanner graph may produce pseudo tree [13], based encoding stopping set [12]. In the proposed algorithm, the time complexity of error correction procedure is significantly minimized slightly and the proof is given in section 4.

3 Key Distribution Protocol

3.1 GC Initialization

Initially, the GC selects a large prime number P. This value, P helps in defining a multiplicative group $Z_p{}^*$ and a secure one-way hash function H(.). The defined function, H(.) is a hash function defined from $X \times Y = Z$ where X and Y are non-identity elements of $Z_p{}^*$. Since the function H(.) is a one way hash function, x is computationally difficult to determine from the given function $Z = y^{x} \pmod p$ and y.

3.2 Member Initial Join

Whenever a new user i is authorized to join the multicast group for the first time, the GC sends it (using a secure unicast) a secret key K_i which is known only to the user U_i and GC. K_i is a random element in Z_p*. Using this K_i the Sub Group Keys (SGK) or auxiliary Keys and a Group key K_g are given for that user u_i which will be kept in the user u_i database.

3.3 Rekeying

Whenever some new members join or some old members leave the multicast group, the GC needs to distribute a new Group key to all the current members in a secure way with minimum computation time. When a new member joins into the service it is easy to communicate the new group key with the help of old group key. Since old group key is not known to the new user, the newly joining user can not view the past communication. This provides backward secrecy. Member Leave operation is completely different from member join operation. In member leave operation, when a member leaves from the group, the GC must avoid the use of old Group key/SGK to encrypt new Group key/SGK. Since old members, knows old GK/SGK, it is necessary to use each user's secret key to perform re-keying information when a member departs from the services. In the existing key management approaches, this process increases GC's computation time and communication time. However, the security levels achieved in the existing works are not sufficient with the current computation facilities. Therefore this work focuses on increasing the security level as well as attempts to reduce the communication time.

The GC executes the rekeying process in the following steps:

1. GC defines a one way hash function $h(k_i,y)$ where k_i is the users secret information, y is the users public information and computes its value as shown in equation (1).

$$h(k_i, y) = y^{k_i} (mod\ p) \tag{1}$$

2. GC computes Euler's Totient Function φ(n) [7] for the user u_i using the function $f(k_i, y)$ as shown in equation (2). Next it can compute $f(k_j, y)$ for the user u_j. Similarly it can compute Totient value for 'n' numbers of user if the message has to be sent to 'n' numbers of user.

$$f(k_i, y) = \varphi(h(k_i, y)) \tag{2}$$

3. It also defines a new function $g(k_i,y)$ which is obtained by appending $f(k_i, y)$ with a value 1 in front of it.

$$g(k_i, y) = 1 \parallel f(k_i, y) \tag{3}$$

The purpose of concatenating the value 1 with $f(k_i, y)$ is to provide each user to recover the original keying information. This function is completely different from the function that was used in our previous paper [8]. The main purpose of not using GCD value in this paper is to reduce the computation time. Because computing GCD value for large integers increases computation time.

4. GC computes the new keying information $\gamma_g(t)$ for the new GK K_g to be sent to the group members as shown below.

$$\gamma_g(t) = K_g\ (t) + \prod_{i=1}^{n-1}(g(k_i, y)) \tag{4}$$

5. Perform encoding operation as explained in section 4.1.
6. GC sends the newly computed $\gamma_g(t)$ to the existing group members.

Upon receiving the encoded information from the GC, an authorized user u_i of the current group executes the following steps to obtain the new group key.

1. Perform decoding operation as explained in section 4.2. If there is no error in the received data then process step 2 to 5.
2. Calculate the value $h(k_i, y) = y^{k_i}(mod\ p)$ where K_i is user's secret key and y is the old keying information which is known to all the existing users.
3. Compute $f(k_i, y) = \varphi(h(k_i, y))$
4. Append the value 1 in front of $f(k_i, y)$.
5. A legitimate user u_i may decrypt the rekeying information to get the new group key by calculating the following value.

$$\gamma_g(t) mod\ (1\ \| \ f\ (k_i, y)) \tag{5}$$

3.4 Tree Based Approach

Scalability can be achieved by employing the proposed approach in a key tree based key management scheme to update the GK and SGK. Fig.1. shows a key tree in which, the root is the group key, leaf nodes are individual keys, and the other nodes are auxiliary keys (SGK). In a key tree, the k-nodes and u-nodes are organized as a tree. Key star is a special key tree where tree degree equals group size [9]. In this paper we have discussed about a binary tree based key tree (N=2) wherein the rekeying operation used for member leave case is alone considered. For example, if a member M_8 from the above figure leaves from the group, the keys on the path from his leaf node to the tree's root should be changed. Hence, only the keys, $K_{7,8}$, $K_{5,8}$, $K_{1,8}$will become invalid. Therefore, these keys must be updated. In order to update the keys, two approaches namely top-down and bottom-up are used in the members departure (Leave) operation. In the top-down approach, keys are updated from root node to leaf node. On the contrary, in the bottom-up approach, the keys are updated from leaf node to root node. When member M_9 leaves from the group, GC will start to update the keys, $K_{7,8}$, $K_{5,8}$, $K_{1,8}$ using bottom-up approach. In top-down approach, the keys are updated in the order $K_{1,8}$, $K_{5,8}$, $K_{7,8.}$ The number of multiplications required to perform the rekeying operation is high in top down approach than bottom up approach. So it is a good choice to use bottom up approach in key tree based key management scheme. In binary tree based approach, three updating are required for a group with a size of 8 members. The working principle of the top-down approach process can be described as follows: When a member M_8 leaves from the service, GC computes the Totient value for the remaining members of the group. For simplicity, GC chooses $K_{1,8}$(t-1) (old Group Key) as y. if y value is a primitive root of prime p, then this information is sent as a broadcast message to the remaining (n-1) users.

Next, GC forms the message given in equation (8) and sends the message to all the existing members in order to update the new Group Key using the encoding algorithm explained in section 4.1.

$$\gamma_{1,8}(t) = K_{1,8}\,(t) + \left(g(k_{1,4},\ y) \times g(k_{5,6},\ y) \times g(k_7,\ y)\right) \tag{8}$$

Next update $K_{5,8}$ using,

$$\gamma_{5,8}(t) = K_{5,8}\,(t) + \left(g(k_{5,6},\ y) \times g(k_7,\ y)\right) \tag{9}$$

After the successful updation of Group key, GC will update $K_{7,8}$ using the formula,

$$\gamma_{7,8}(t) = K_{7,8}\,(t) + \left(g(k_7,\ y)\right) \tag{10}$$

In the bottom up approach, the updation of keys follows an organized procedure and the keys are updated using the formula,

$$\gamma_{7,8}(t) = K_{7,8}\,(t) + \left(g(k_7,\ y)\right) \tag{11}$$

The next key to be updated is $K_{1,8}$. This is performed by using the following steps,

$$\gamma_{5,8}(t) = K_{5,8}\,(t) + \left(g(k_{5,6},\ y) \times g(k_{7,8},\ y)\right) \tag{12}$$

$$\gamma_{1,8}(t) = K_{1,8}\,(t) + \left(g(k_{1,4},\ y) \times g(k_{5,8},\ y)\right) \tag{13}$$

After updating all the above keys successfully, it can be sent to the group members by using encoding and decoding techniques by using the methods discussed in Section 4 in order to recover the original key when a key is corrupted.

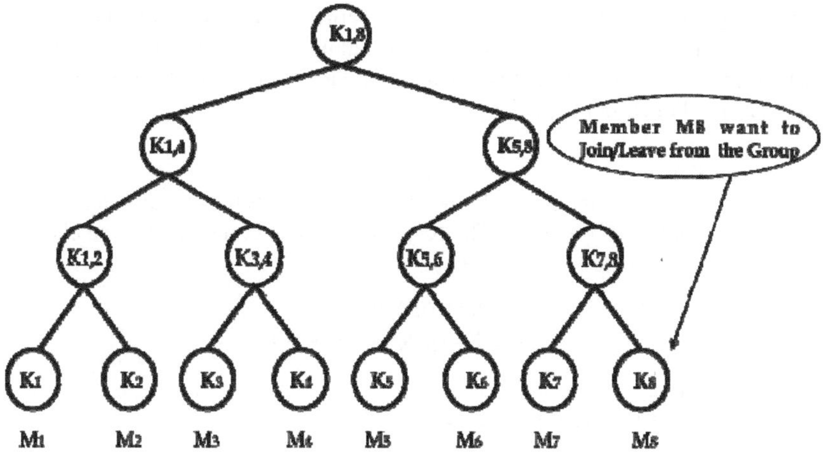

Fig. 1. Binary Tree based Key management Scheme

4 Error Correction Using LDPC Codes

4.1 Encoding at Group Center

Encoding process at group center consists of three phases.

Phase 1: Conversion of original key information bits into binary values (0's and 1's)
Phase 2: Construction of Parity Check Matrix according to size of the key
Phase 3: Construction of Encoding stopping set
Phase 4: Generation and distribution of code words to group members

Algorithm:
Consider an example, where the size of key information is 8 bits. If the original key information bit is 8 bits [1 1 0 1 0 0 1 1] and its corresponding (8, 16) parity check matrix will be generated as mentioned in phase 2 and used as shown below.

$$\begin{pmatrix}
1 & 0 & 0 & 0 & 0 & 0 & 1 & 0 & 0 & 0 & 0 & 0 & 0 & 1 & 0 & 0 \\
0 & 1 & 1 & 1 & 1 & 0 & 0 & 0 & 1 & 0 & 0 & 1 & 1 & 1 & 0 & 0 \\
1 & 0 & 1 & 0 & 0 & 1 & 1 & 0 & 0 & 1 & 1 & 1 & 0 & 0 & 0 & 0 \\
1 & 0 & 0 & 1 & 1 & 0 & 0 & 1 & 0 & 1 & 1 & 0 & 1 & 0 & 1 & 1 \\
0 & 0 & 0 & 0 & 1 & 0 & 1 & 1 & 1 & 0 & 0 & 0 & 0 & 0 & 1 & 0 \\
0 & 0 & 0 & 0 & 0 & 1 & 0 & 1 & 0 & 1 & 0 & 0 & 0 & 1 & 0 & 1 \\
0 & 1 & 0 & 0 & 0 & 0 & 0 & 0 & 1 & 0 & 1 & 0 & 1 & 0 & 0 & 1 \\
0 & 1 & 1 & 1 & 0 & 1 & 0 & 0 & 0 & 0 & 0 & 1 & 0 & 0 & 1 & 0
\end{pmatrix}$$

Parity Check Matrix of (8, 16) LDPC codes

The group members are required to use the same size parity check matrix. From the parity check matrix the GC can construct the Tanner graph. The algorithm coverts the tanner graph into Pseudo tree based Encoding stopping set with maximum bit node degree 3 as explained in [12] .

Reevaluated Bits:
The reevaluated bits r1 and r2 are found in a twofold constraint encoding stopping set with key check nodes C7 and C8. The Key parity check equations for the check nodes C7 and C8 are computed by using Fig. 3.

$$C7 = X11 \oplus X16$$
$$C8 = X4 \oplus X6 \oplus X12 \oplus X15$$

Encoding Process:
The stages of encoding are given below:

1. Fill the values of the information bits in the bottom most level, i.e.,[X5 X6 X7 X10 X11 X12 X14 X15] = [1 1 0 1 0 0 1 1]. Assign X16 = 0 and X4 = 0.
2. Encode the pseudo tree as shown in Fig. 2.and compute the parity bits as follows

$$X8 = X6 \oplus X10 \oplus X14 \oplus X16 = 1$$
$$X1 = X7 \oplus X14 = 1$$

$$X9 = X5 \oplus X8 \oplus X7 \oplus X15 = 1$$
$$X3 = X6 \oplus X1 \oplus X7 \oplus X10 \oplus X11 \oplus X12 = 0$$
$$X13 = X4 \oplus X8 \oplus X1 \oplus X5 \oplus X10 \oplus X11 \oplus X15 \oplus X16 = 0$$
$$X2 = X4 \oplus X9 \oplus X5 \oplus X3 \oplus X13 \oplus X12 \oplus X14 = 1$$

3. Compute the values of key parity check equations C7 and C8 for the diagram shown in Fig.3.

$$C7 = X11 \oplus X9 \oplus X13 \oplus X16 \oplus X2 = 0$$
$$C8 = X4 \oplus X2 \oplus X3 \oplus X6 \oplus X12 \oplus X15 = 1$$

4. Since C7 = 0, C8 = 1, correct values of reevaluated bits X16 = 1, X4 = 0.

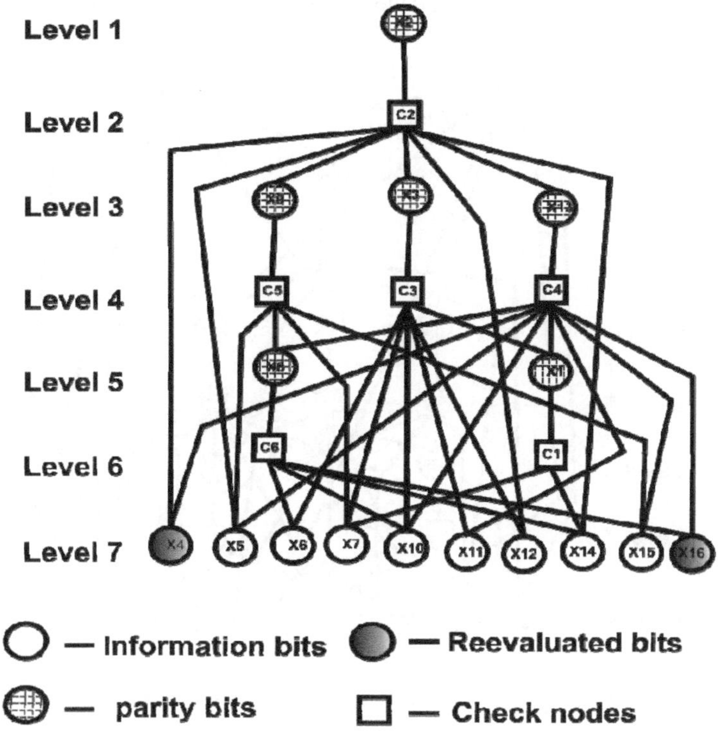

Fig. 2. The Pseudo tree at GC

5. Compute all the parity bits again based on the new values of X16and X4. The encoded code word is [X5 X6 X7 X10 X11 X12 X14 X15 X4 X16 X8 X1 X9 X3 X13 X2] = [1 1 0 1 0 0 1 1 0 1 0 1 0 1 1 0]

4.2 Decoding at Group Members Side

Error correction process at group member's area consists of three phases.

Phase 1: Receives the code words from the group center.

Phase 2: Construction of encoding of stopping set as shown in Fig. 3. according to the parity check matrix used by GC.

Phase 3: Detection of errors by verifying the check node values.
Phase 4: Correction of errors.

Decoding Process:
The code word that is received from the sender is [X5 X6 X7 X10 X11 X12 X14 X15 X4 X16 X8 X1 X9 X3 X13 X2] = [1 1 0 1 0 0 1 1 0 1 0 1 0 1 1 0].After the receipt of the code word, the group members should place the values in the encoding stopping set, and also should verify for the occurrence of errors. On encountering an error, the group members should find out the type of error where in the error can be a single bit error, two bit error,..., n bit error. For any type of errors, there are 3 cases available in the correction of errors and those cases are explained below.

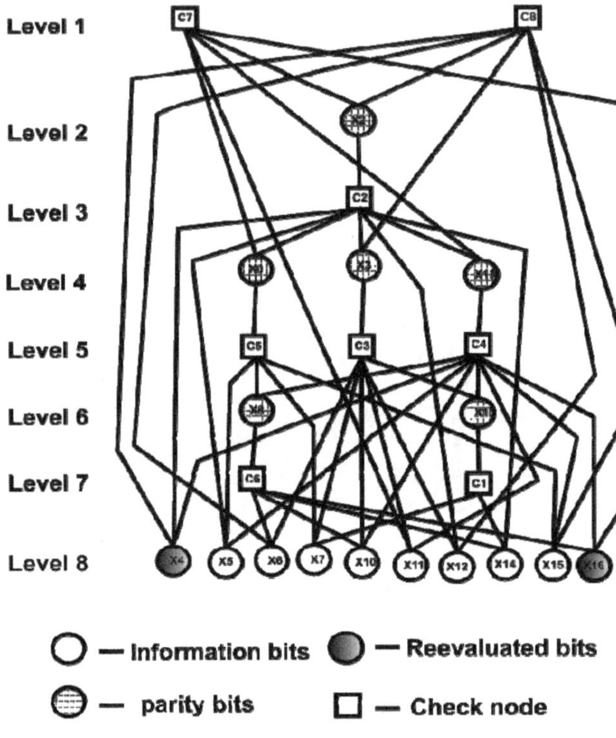

Fig. 3. The Encoding Stopping set at GC

Case 1: Reevaluation Bit

The errors in this case are found to be in the reevaluated bit. For example, [X5 X6 X7 X10 X11 X12 X14 X15 X4 X16 X8 X1 X9 X3 X13 X2] = [1 1 0 1 0 0 1 1 0 0 0 1 0 1 1 0]. The reevaluated bit (X16) value 1 is changed to 0. This is a single bit error type. During the decoding process parity bit values are computed, and during such computation X16 = 0. This does not coincide with the received codeword, where the X16 bit value is 1. Hence, is such a scenario the single bit error has been found. After the conclusion of the occurrence of error, during the correction of errors the reevaluated bits are inverted as [X4 X16] = [0 1]. Even now if the error is not corrected then perform two bit error correction process. Again, the parity bit values are computed from bottom to top (i.e.) calculate all the parity bit values up to reach the last check nodes. If the key check node [C7 C8] values after parity computation are [0 0], then error has been rectified.

Case 2: Key Information Bits

This is the case, where the error has been occurred in the original key information bits or aggregation of information bits and reevaluated bits. Considering the example of received code words as follows, [X5 X6 X7 X10 X11 X12 X14 X15 X4 X16 X8 X1 X9 X3 X13 X2] = [1 1 1 1 0 0 1 1 0 1 0 1 0 1 1 0], X7 information bit value 0 is changed to 1. During the decoding process some parity bit values will be changed and hence the key check node values will not end up as [0 0]. Hence, on finding such error, the correction follows the steps given below:

Step 1: For correcting the error, all combination of reevaluated bits are changed and even after changing if the key check node [C7 C8] values does not become [0 0], migrate to step2.

*Step 2:*This is the final stage of correction wherein, each information bit from left to right in the leaf node are changed until the key check nodes [C7 C8] value becomes [0 0], and the error has been rectified. There are also some cases, where even during such a change the key check node values may not become [0 0] and in such a situation, combination of two, three, ..., n information bits are changed in leaf node from left to right to obtain the key check node value to be [0 0].

Case 3: Parity Bits

In the second case, the error would have occurred in the parity bits: For example, considering the bits received are [X5 X6 X7 X10 X11 X12 X14 X15 X4 X16 X8 X1 X9 X3 X13 X2] = [1 1 0 1 0 0 1 1 0 1 0 1 1 1 1 0]. In this example X9 parity bit value 0 is changed to 1. During the decoding process while calculating the parity bit values, X9 = 0 will be obtained which is not in coincidence with the received codeword, where X9 bit value is 1. This error can be rectified automatically while correcting the information bits. The following proof gives the information regarding the number of changes for the different types of errors.

Lemma:
Any arbitrary LDPC codes has $O(n^2)$ time complexity during decoding process for n bit errors.

Proof:
Let ‘s’ be the number of leaf nodes which includes ‘n’ information bits and ‘r’ re-evaluated bits received from the GC. The received bits are substituted in the encoding stopping set generated at group member’s side. Now we apply the decoding process in encoding stopping set.
An error is said to occur:

1. If the values of the level 1 check nodes (i.e., key check nodes) are not zero.

2. If the computed parity bit values and received parity bit values at each level, in encoding stopping set are unequal.

We need to correct these errors. In case, if the re-evaluated bits are corrupted, then complexity of correcting the re-evaluated bit is 3. Depending upon the number of encoding stopping sets the complexity may increase. If there are two encoding stopping set then the decoding time complexity is 6, in which 3 for first encoding stopping set and another 3 computation for second encoding stopping set and so on. On occurrence of error in the information bits, the following procedure has to be followed.

Since the number of corrupted bits and their position are unknown, we correct them step by step procedure. First we change the 1st bit of the leaf nodes from left to right. Next, we compute the new parity bit values. If the key check node values are equal to zero, then the error is corrected.

Even now, if the key check node values are unequal to zero, then the second bit of the information bit is changed and the procedure is repeated until reaching the last information bits in the leaf level. From this it is very clear that the complexity for correcting one bit error is O(n). If still error persists, the above procedure is repeated for all combination of two information bits. Now the time complexity becomes O(n+(n(n-1)/2)). Even then if the error is uncorrected, then the combination of ‘i’ (i=3,4,…..,n) information bits are changed to calculate the new parity bit value, and the error is corrected. Hence the time complexity for the decoding procedure is $O(n^2)$ as follows. For example if the total number of received information bits is 4 bits and all the four information bits are corrupted, then the decoding time complexity can be computed as shown below.

$$= n + (n (n - \text{op } 1) /2) + ((n - 1) (n - 2) / 2) + 1$$
$$= n + ((n^2 - n)/2) + ((n^2 - 3n + 2)/2) + 1 \quad = n^2 - n + 2 \quad = O(n^2)$$

5 Concluding Remarks

In this paper, a binary tree based key distribution protocol for n bit numbers as the key value has been proposed for creating and distributing keys in order to provide effective security in multicast communications. The major advantages of the work are recovering the original keying information bits if the keying information’s are corrupted. In order to do that we introduced two algorithms in this proposed work. First, Euler’s Totient function is used to achieve higher level of security in the key computation process. Second, Encoding stopping set is constructed in the sender and receiver side in order to verify whether the received key material has no errors. If any error is found in the received key at receiver side, decoding algorithm can correct the error in $O(n^2)$ time. The main advantage of this approach is that the proposed approach can correct n-bit errors in less decoding time. However the main concern of our proposed approach is that it also increases the computation time since the amount of multiplication required is high than the approach discussed in our previous work [8]. The communication time can also be improved by using the N-ary tree based algorithm used in our previous work. Further extensions to this work are to devise techniques to reduce the storage complexity which is the amount of storage required to store the key related information, both in GC and group members’ area.

References

1. Li, M., Poovendran, R., McGrew, D.A.: Minimizing Center Key Storage in Hybrid One-Way Function based Group Key Management with Communication Constraints. Information Processing Letters, 191–198 (2004)
2. Lee, P.P.C., Lui, J.C.S., Yau, D.K.Y.: Distributed Collaborative Key Agreement Protocols for Dynamic Peer Groups. In: Proceedings of the IEEE International Conference on Network Protocols, p. 322 (2002)
3. Trappe, W., Song, J., Poovendran, R., Liu, K.J.R.: Key Management and Distribution for Secure Multimedia Multicast. IEEE Transactions on Multimedia 5(4), 544–557 (2003)
4. Blaum, M., Bruck, J., Vardy, A.: MDS Array Codes with Independent Parity Symbols. IEEE Transactions on Information Theory 42(2), 529–542 (1996)
5. Xu, L., Huang, C.: Computation-Efficient Multicast Key Distribution. IEEE Transactions on Parallel and Distributed Systems 19(5), 1–10 (2008)
6. McGrew, D.A., Sherman, A.T.: Key Establishment in Large Dynamic Groups using One-Way Function Trees. Cryptographic Technologies Group, TIS Labs at Network Associates (1998)
7. Apostol, T.M.: Introduction to Analytic Number Theory, Springer International Students edn., vol. 1, pp. 25–28 (1998)
8. Vijayakumar, P., Bose, S., Kannan, A., Subramanian, S.S.: A Secure Key Distribution Protocol for Multicast Communication. In: Balasubramaniam, P. (ed.) ICLICC 2011. CCIS, vol. 140, pp. 249–257. Springer, Heidelberg (2011)
9. Wong, C., Gouda, M., Lam, S.: Secure Group Communications using Key Graphs. IEEE/ACM Transactions on Networking 8, 16–30 (2000)
10. Zhou, Y., Zhu, X., Fang, Y.: MABS: Multicast Authentication Based on Batch Signature. IEEE Transactions on Mobile Computing 9, 982–993 (2010)
11. Gallager, R.G.: Low-Density Parity Check Codes. MIT Press, Cambridge (1963)
12. Lu, J., Moura, J.M.F.: Linear Time Encoding of LDPC Codes. IEEE Trans. Inf. Theory 57(1), 233–249 (2010)
13. Lu, J., Moura, J.M.F., Zhang, H.: Efficient encoding of cycle codes: A graphical approach. In: Proc. 37th Asilomar Conf. Signals, Systems, and Computers, Pacific Grove, CA, pp. 69–73 (2003)
14. Berbecaru, D., Albertalli, L., Lioy, A.: The ForwardDiffSig Scheme for Multicast Authentication. IEEE/ACM Transactions on Networking 18, 1855–1868 (2010)
15. Mittelholzer, T.: Efficient encoding and minimum distance bounds of Reed-Solomon-type array codes. In: Proc. IEEE Int. Symp. Information theory (ISIT 2002), Lausanne, Switzerland, p. 282 (2002)
16. Lu, J., Moura, J.M.F.: TS-LDPC codes: Turbo-structured codes with large girth. IEEE Trans. Inf. Theory 53(3), 1080–1094 (2007)
17. Johnson, S.J., Weller, S.R.: A family of irregular LDPC codes with low encoding complexity. IEEE Commun. Lett. 7(2), 79–81 (2003)
18. Freundlich, S., Burshtein, D., Litsyn, S.: Approximately lower triangular ensembles of LDPC codes with linear encoding complexity. IEEE Trans. Inf. Theory 53(4), 1484–1494 (2007)
19. Tanner, R.M.: A recursive approach to low complexity codes. IEEE Trans. Inf. Theory IT 27(5), 533–547 (1981)
20. Haley, D., Grant, A., Buetefuer, J.: Iterative encoding of low-density parity-check code. In: Proc. IEEE Globecom, Taipei, Taiwan, ROC, vol. 2, pp. 1289–1293 (2002)

Empirical Validation of Object Oriented Data Warehouse Design Quality Metrics

Jaya Gupta[1], Anjana Gosain[2], and Sushama Nagpal[3]

[1,2] University School of Information Technology,
GGS Indraprastha University, Delhi
jaya_gupta8@yahoo.com, anjana_gosain@hotmail.com
[3] Computer Engineering Dept, Netaji Subhash Institute of Technology, Delhi
sushmapriyadarshi@yahoo.com

Abstract. Data warehouses have been developed that stores information enabling the knowledge worker to make better and faster decisions. As a decision support information system, a data warehouse must provide high level quality of data and quality of service. Various metrics have been defined and theoretical validated to measure the quality of the data warehouse in a consistent and objective manner and if quality measured, it can be managed and improved. Now, in this paper we will use these design quality metrics and empirically validated these metrics by conducting an experiment using regression analysis and deriving the conclusions according to the analysis so that they can be used by researchers and users.

Keywords: Object Oriented Conceptual Modeling, Metrics, Regression Analysis, Empirical Validation.

1 Introduction

Data warehouses have been developed to answer the increasing demands of information required by the top managers and economic analysts of organizations. Quality is the key issue in the building the data warehouse and gives the confidence that particular information meets some context specific quality requirements [8]. A lack of quality in the data warehouse can have disastrous consequences for the organizations. One of the main issues that influence the quality is designing the data warehouse using various data models i.e. conceptual, logical and physical [14]. Conceptual modeling forms the basis of the data warehouse and is concerned with the real world view and understanding of data. Various conceptual model metrics are defined to measure a quality factor in a consistent and objective manner [9] and gives the best ways to help professionals and researchers. Here our goal is to empirically validate the object oriented conceptual model metrics using the correlation and regression analysis technique.

2 Related Work

In this the related work is defined for the two main topics covered in this paper:
(i) Object Oriented Conceptual Multidimensional modeling (ii) Quality metrics proposed in the data warehouse.

D.C. Wyld et al. (Eds.): ACITY 2011, CCIS 198, pp. 320–329, 2011.

2.1 Object Oriented Conceptual Multidimensional Modeling

An approach in [5] has been proposed as an object-oriented (OO) conceptual MD modeling approach. This proposal is a profile of the Unified Modeling Language (UML) which use the standard extension mechanisms (stereotypes, tagged values and constraints) provided by the UML. The extension used the Object Constraint Language OCL for expressing well-formedness rules of new defined elements. Another approach is given in [12] i.e. YAM^2 allows the representation of several semantically related star schemas, as well as summarizability and identification constraints. In [6] the authors propose an approach that provides a theoretical foundation for the use of object-oriented databases and object-relational databases in data warehouse, multidimensional database, and online analytical processing applications.

2.2 Quality Metrics for the Data Warehouses

Metrics are proposed for OO conceptual modeling and theoretical validation and empirical validation is done in [1] but the models taken were few in number. Various OO conceptual model quality metrics are proposed in [4] but are not empirically validated. Si-Said and Prat [3] have proposed some metrics for measuring multidimensional schemas analyzability and simplicity. But these metrics proposed so far has not been empirically validated. Various metrics have been proposed [2] to assure the quality of data warehouse logical models validated both formally and empirically [8]. In [4] authors present a framework to design metrics in which each metric is part of a quality indicator we wish to measure. In [15] there is a review of research in conceptual model quality and identifies the major theoretical and practical issues which need to be addressed.

3 Conceptual Modeling

Multidimensional modeling has been widely accepted as the foundation of data modeling for data warehouses [10]. The first design steps accomplished in data warehouses involve producing a conceptual schema by using a conceptual model that conveniently represents the multidimensional modeling properties. Conceptual modeling describes entity classes, and characteristics i.e. attributes and associations between pairs of those things of significance i.e. relationships. We now need objective metrics for this purpose and we should empirically validate those metrics.

3.1 Object Oriented Conceptual Modeling

In conceptual modeling, we have used the extension of the UML (Unified Modeling Language).This is an object-oriented conceptual approach for data warehouses that easily represents main data warehouse properties at the conceptual level[1].Tables 2 and 3 summarize the defined stereotypes along with a brief description and the corresponding icon in order to facilitate their use and interpretation. These stereotypes are classified into class stereotypes (Table 2) and attribute stereotypes (Table 3).

Table 1. Stereotypes of Class

NAME	DESCRIPTION	ICON
FACT	Classes of this stereotype represent facts in a MD model	#F
DIMENSION	Classes of this stereotype represent dimensions in a MD model	#D
BASE	Classes of this stereotype represent dimension hierarchy levels in a MD model	#B

Table 2. Stereotypes of Attribute [1]

ICON	DESCRIPTION	ICON
OID	It represent OID attributes of fact, dimension or base classes in a MD model	OID
Fact Attributes	It represent attributes of Fact classes in a MD model	FA
Descriptor	It represent descriptor attributes of dimension or base classes in a MD model	D
Dimension Attribute	It represent attributes of dimension or base classes in a MD model	DA

In figure 1, we are interested in analyzing the car sales (Fact Car_Sales) of a big showroom. Here we have taken 20 real world examples of an object oriented data warehouse conceptual model using UML and calculated the values of the metrics.

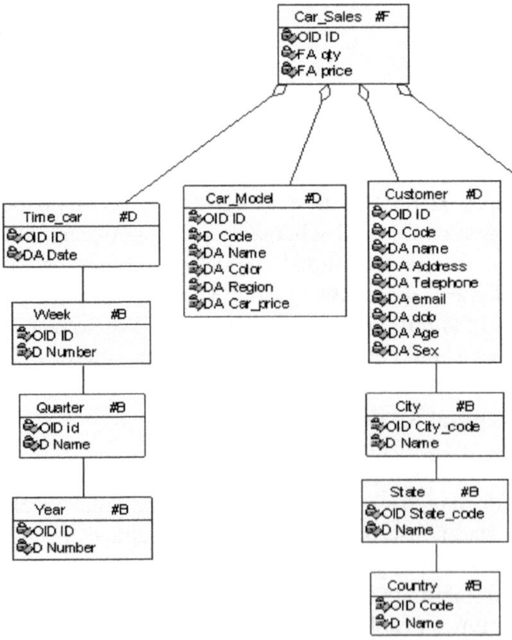

Fig. 1. Example of an object oriented data warehouse conceptual model using UML

3 Metrics Definition

Following are the metrics definition [1] for measuring the understandability of data warehouse conceptual models.

Table 3. Metrics Definition [1]

METRICS	DEFINITION
NDC(S)	Number of dimension classes of the star S (equal to the number of aggregation relationships)
NBC(S)	Number of Base classes of Star S
NC(S)	Total number of classes of the star S NC(S) = NDC(S) + NBC(S) + 1
RBC(S)	Ratio of base classes. Number of base classes per dimension class of the star S
NAFC(S)	Number of FA attributes of the fact class of the star S
NADC(S)	Number of D and DA attributes of the dimension classes of the star S
NABC(S)	Number of D and DA attributes of the base classes of the star S
NA(S)	Total number of FA, D and DA attributes of the star S NA(S) = NAFC(S) + NADC(S) + NABC(S)
NH(S)	Number of hierarchy relationships of the star S
DHP(S)	Maximum depth of the hierarchy relationships of the star S
RSA(S)	Ratio of attributes of the star S. Number of attributes FA divided by the number of D and DA attributes

Table 4. Values of metrics

Metrics/ Schema	NDC	NBC	NC	RBC	NAFC	NADC	NABC	NA	NH	DHP	RSA
S01	4	4	9	1	2	18	4	24	3	3	0.09
S02	3	7	11	2.34	1	13	7	21	3	3	0.05
S03	4	4	9	1	3	17	4	24	2	3	0.14
S04	4	0	5	0	2	23	0	25	0	0	0.08
S05	4	4	9	1	2	20	4	26	2	3	0.08
S06	3	7	11	2.34	2	13	7	22	3	3	0.1
S07	4	5	10	1.25	2	12	5	19	2	3	0.11
S08	3	7	11	2.34	2	15	7	24	2	4	0.09
S09	5	8	14	1.6	2	22	8	32	3	3	0.06
S10	5	4	10	0.8	2	13	4	19	2	2	0.11
S11	5	4	10	0.8	2	21	4	27	2	3	0.08
S12	5	4	10	0.8	2	22	4	28	2	3	0.07
S13	3	4	8	1.37	2	15	4	21	2	3	0.10
S14	3	4	8	1.37	2	16	4	22	2	2	0.1
S15	4	2	7	0.5	2	14	2	18	1	2	0.12
S16	3	0	4	0	4	15	0	19	0	0	0.26
S17	5	7	12	1.4	2	18	7	27	3	4	0.08
S18	4	2	6	0.5	3	12	2	17	1	2	0.21
S19	4	6	10	1.5	2	15	6	23	3	2	0.09
S20	5	3	8	0.6	2	27	3	32	1	3	0.06

4 Experimental Settings

The experimental setting is done to validate the metrics for data warehouse conceptual models for the purpose of evaluating if they are useful with respect of the data warehouse understandability and efficiency.

4.1 Subjects

There are 10 students from the University School of Information Technology, Guru Gobind Singh Indrapastha University, (Delhi) which have participated in the experiment.

We give a set of questions for each schema to all the subjects. For each design, the subjects had to analyze the schema and answer some questions about the design. In this experiment we have taken fix number of questions in each schema Questions for schema car_sales are as follows:-

Schema 1- CAR SALES

1. Which classes do we need to use for knowing the model of the car?
2. Which classes do we need to know that which sales representative has helped in the maximum sales?
3. Which classes do we need to answer the total sales price in a year?
4. If we want to increase our car sales then in which class do we add our promotion advertisement?

The starting time and finish time in which the subjects answers these questions is noted down in seconds and we get the understanding time i.e. time taken to solve the questions.

Table 5. Understanding time

Subject/ Schema	1	2	3	4	5	6	7	8	9	10
S01	60	70	72	58	64	84	74	73	65	50
S02	45	40	56	49	35	41	51	32	29	47
S03	52	45	51	47	40	36	54	41	62	32
S04	35	40	41	36	32	31	28	25	30	26
S05	50	53	51	46	56	65	74	29	35	44
S06	48	39	26	28	37	35	40	27	36	22
S07	32	31	38	26	28	40	34	50	51	41
S08	63	68	75	74	80	59	65	71	78	69
S09	81	86	100	89	79	67	71	86	74	89
S10	56	68	78	45	61	50	53	51	48	89
S11	46	53	52	48	70	68	61	55	42	40
S12	45	53	55	61	60	59	57	45	39	41
S13	40	35	39	25	29	34	31	41	28	27
S14	22	27	36	31	29	34	32	33	24	22
S15	32	37	39	41	45	29	24	26	33	38
S16	38	40	48	36	22	24	29	35	34	27
S17	86	74	96	102	68	67	88	77	84	70
S18	50	45	46	38	29	27	36	37	47	45
S19	56	58	60	84	74	63	41	45	50	61
S20	68	74	77	84	63	59	69	78	81	88

Table 6. Efficiency

Subject/ Schema	1	2	3	4	5	6	7	8	9	10
S01	0.06	0.05	0.05	0.06	0.06	0.04	0.05	0.05	0.04	0.08
S02	0.08	0.1	0.07	0.08	0.11	0.09	0.05	0.12	0.1	0.08
S03	0.07	0.06	0.07	0.04	0.1	0.11	0.07	0.09	0.06	0.12
S04	0.11	0.1	0.09	0.11	0.12	0.09	0.1	0.12	0.13	0.15
S05	0.08	0.07	0.07	0.06	0.07	0.06	0.05	0.06	0.11	0.09
S06	0.08	0.1	0.15	0.14	0.1	0.08	0.07	0.11	0.11	0.09
S07	0.12	0.12	0.1	0.15	0.14	0.1	0.08	0.08	0.07	0.04
S08	0.06	0.05	0.05	0.05	0.05	0.05	0.06	0.05	0.05	0.05
S09	0.04	0.04	0.04	0.04	0.05	0.04	0.05	0.04	0.05	0.04
S10	0.07	0.04	0.05	0.08	0.06	0.08	0.07	0.07	0.08	0.04
S11	0.06	0.05	0.07	0.08	0.05	0.05	0.06	0.07	0.09	0.1
S12	0.06	0.07	0.05	0.06	0.06	0.05	0.05	0.08	0.1	0.09
S13	0.07	0.11	0.1	0.16	0.13	0.11	0.12	0.07	0.14	0.14
S14	0.1	0.11	0.08	0.12	0.13	0.11	0.12	0.12	0.08	0.09
S15	0.09	0.1	0.1	0.09	0.08	0.1	0.16	0.15	0.12	0.1
S16	0.1	0.1	0.08	0.11	0.18	0.16	0.13	0.11	0.11	0.14
S17	0.04	0.05	0.04	0.03	0.05	0.05	0.04	0.05	0.04	0.05
S18	0.08	0.08	0.08	0.1	0.13	0.11	0.11	0.08	0.08	0.08
S19	0.07	0.05	0.06	0.04	0.05	0.06	0.07	0.08	0.08	0.06
S20	0.05	0.05	0.03	0.03	0.06	0.06	0.04	0.03	0.04	0.04

5 Empirical Validation Using Regression Analysis

Regression analysis is also used to understand which among the independent variables are related to the dependent variable, and to explore the forms of these relationships. Regression models involve the following variables:

- The independent variables X.
- The dependent variable *Y*

Correlation is a statistical technique that can show whether and how strongly pairs of variables are related. For example, height and weight are related; taller people tend to be heavier than shorter people.

5.1 Hypothesis

Null Hypothesis H(N): There is no a statistically significant correlation between the metrics and the understandability time of the data warehouse conceptual data models.

Valid hypothesis H(V): There is a statistically significant correlation between the metrics and the understandability time of the data warehouse conceptual data models.

5.2 Variables Used

Here we used two types of variables:-

Independent Variables- The independent variables are the variables for which the effects should be evaluated. In our experiment this variable is metrics being researched. Table 4 presents the values for each metric in each DW conceptual schema provided in the experiment.

Dependent variables: The dependent variable is the time taken to solve the questions.

Efficiency can be calculated as:

$$\text{Efficiency} = \frac{\text{Number of correct answers}}{\text{Time}}$$

5.3 Analysis and Interpretation

We used the data collected in order to test the hypotheses previously formulated. We decided to apply a non-parametric correlational analysis, and parametric correlation analysis avoiding assumptions about the data normality. In this way, we made a correlation statistical analysis using the Kendall Tau's statistic, Spearman Rho and Pearson and we used a level of significance a = 0.05.

The descriptive statistics in which we calculated the mean of the understanding time and the efficiency is calculated by using SPSS Statistical tool.

Based on descriptive statistics i.e. mean we have find the correlation between the dependent and the independent variable using regression analysis.

Table 7. Descriptive Statistics

Mean/ Schema	Mean understanding time	Mean Efficiency
S01	67.00	0.054
S02	42.50	0.088
S03	46.00	0.079
S04	32.40	0.112
S05	50.30	0.072
S06	33.80	0.103
S07	37.10	0.098
S08	30.20	0.052
S09	82.20	0.043
S10	59.90	0.064
S11	53.50	0.068
S12	51.50	0.067
S13	32.90	0.115
S14	29.00	0.106
S15	34.40	0.109
S16	33.30	0.122
S17	81.20	0.044
S18	40.00	0.092
S19	59.20	0.062
S20	74.10	0.042

6 Results

The results of understanding time and the efficiency i.e. correlation and p-value are shown below

Table 8. Results for Understanding time

KENDALL'S TAU											
Metric	**NDC**	**NBC**	**NC**	**RBC**	**NAFC**	**NADC**	**NABC**	**NA**	**NH**	**DHP**	**RSA**
CORRELATION	0.543	0.362	0.449	0.174	-0.148	0.228	0.362	0.411	0.356	0.451	-0.317
P-VALUE	0.003	0.036	0.008	0.296	0.426	0.170	0.036	0.013	0.047	0.013	0.057
SPEARMAN RHO											
Metric	**NDC**	**NBC**	**NC**	**RBC**	**NAFC**	**NADC**	**NABC**	**NA**	**NH**	**DHP**	**RSA**
CORRELATION	0.649	0.461	0.449	0.256	-0.178	0.344	0.461	0.577	0.440	0.562	-0.483
P-VALUE	0.002	0.041	0.008	0.277	0.454	0.138	0.036	0.008	0.052	0.010	0.031
PEARSON											
Metric	**NDC**	**NBC**	**NC**	**RBC**	**NAFC**	**NADC**	**NABC**	**NA**	**NH**	**DHP**	**RSA**
CORRELATION	0.622	0.494	0.603	0.195	-0.215	0.470	0.494	0.691	0.416	0.537	-0.431
P-VALUE	0.003	0.027	0.005	0.409	0.363	0.037	0.027	0.001	0.068	0.015	0.058

Table 9. Results of efficiency

KENDALL'S TAU											
Metric	**NDC**	**NBC**	**NC**	**RBC**	**NAFC**	**NADC**	**NABC**	**NA**	**NH**	**DHP**	**RSA**
CORRELATION	-0.518	-0.398	-0.483	-0.207	0.201	-0.305	-0.398	-0.508	-0.393	-0.464	-0.405
P-VALUE	0.004	0.021	0.004	0.214	0.281	0.067	0.021	0.002	0.028	0.010	0.015
SPEARMAN RHO											
Metric	**NDC**	**NBC**	**NC**	**RBC**	**NAFC**	**NADC**	**NABC**	**NA**	**NH**	**DHP**	**RSA**
CORRELATION	-0.627	-0.483	-0.603	-0.311	0.245	-0.398	-0.483	-0.644	-0.467	-0.563	0.555
P-VALUE	0.003	0.031	0.005	0.182	0.297	0.082	0.031	0.002	0.038	0.010	0.01
PEARSON											
Metric	**NDC**	**NBC**	**NC**	**RBC**	**NAFC**	**NADC**	**NABC**	**NA**	**NH**	**DHP**	**RSA**
CORRELATION	-0.650	-0.536	-0.658	-0.247	0.301	-0.455	-0.536	-0.688	0.416	-0.504	0.511
P-VALUE	0.002	0.015	0.002	0.294	0.197	0.044	0.015	0.001	0.068	0.024	0.021

Analyzing table 8 and 9 we can conclude that there exist a correlation between understandability and metrics, efficiency and metrics as p-value is lower than or equal to a=0.05 and that some metrics are not correlated with time and efficiency.

6.1 Results Summary

The result summary is shown below:

Table 10. Results for understanding time

Metric	**NDC**	**NBC**	**NC**	**RBC**	**NAFC**	**NADC**	**NABC**	**NA**	**NH**	**DHP**	**RSA**
KENDALL TAU	✓	✓	✓	×	×	×	✓	✓	✓	✓	×
SPEARMAN	✓	✓	✓	×	×	×	✓	✓	✓	✓	✓
PEARSON	✓	✓	✓	×	×	✓	✓	✓	×	✓	×

Table 11. Results for efficiency

Metric	NDC	NBC	NC	RBC	NAFC	NADC	NABC	NA	NH	DHP	RSA
KENDALL TAU	✓	✓	✓	×	×	×	✓	✓	✓	✓	✓
SPEARMAN	✓	✓	✓	×	×	×	✓	✓	✓	✓	✓
PEARSON	✓	✓	✓	×	×	✓	✓	✓	×	✓	✓

7 Conclusion

As data warehouse is used for making strategic decisions quality of the information is crucial for any organization. One aspect to assure their quality is to guarantee the quality of the models used in their design (conceptual, logical and physical). In this paper, we have chosen a set of metrics of conceptual modeling in order to assure the quality .We have taken 20 real world schemas examples which helps us measure the understandability and the efficiency of designers and users in working with the schemas. Then, we have performed experiments in order to proof the validity of the metrics. After these experiments we can conclude that several metrics are correlated with the understandability of the models (mainly those measuring the number of elements in the conceptual schema such as the number of classes, associations, attributes, and so on) and with the efficiency of the subjects when dealing with those models (those measuring the number of classes, dimensions, and the number of hierarchy levels defined in dimensions). Now future work is proposal of more quality metrics and validation of those metrics to be used by the researchers.

References

1. Serrano, M., Trujillo, J., Calero, C., Piattini, M.: Metrics for data warehouse conceptual models understandability. Information and Software Technology 49, 851–870 (2007)
2. Serrano, M.A.: Towards Data Warehouse Quality Metrics. In: Proceedings of the International Workshop on Design and Management of Data Warehouses (DMDW 2001), Interlaken, Switzerland (2001)
3. Si-said Cherfi, S., Prat, N.: Multidimensional Schemas Quality: Assessing and Balancing Analyzability and Simplicity. In: Jeusfeld, M.A., Pastor, Ó. (eds.) ER Workshops 2003. LNCS, vol. 2814, pp. 140–151. Springer, Heidelberg (2003)
4. Berenguer, G., Romero, R., Trujillo, J., Bilò, V., Piattini, M.: A Set of Quality Indicators and Their Corresponding Metrics for Conceptual Models of Data Warehouses. In: Tjoa, A.M., Trujillo, J. (eds.) DaWaK 2005. LNCS, vol. 3589, pp. 95–104. Springer, Heidelberg (2005)
5. Luján-Mora, S., Trujillo, J., Song, I.-Y.: Extending UML for multidimensional modeling. In: Jézéquel, J.-M., Hussmann, H., Cook, S. (eds.) UML 2002. LNCS, vol. 2460, pp. 290–304. Springer, Heidelberg (2002)
6. Trujillo, J., Palomar, M., Gómez, J., Song, I.-Y.: Designing Data Warehouses with OO Conceptual Models. IEEE Computer, Special issue on Data Warehouses 34, 66–75 (2001)
7. Serrano, M., Calero, C., Piattini, M.: Validating metrics for data warehouses. IEE Proceedings Software 149(5) (2002)

8. Piattini, M., Caballero, I., Genero, M., Calero, C.: Data Quality and Database Design (1999)
9. Kaiser, M., Klier, M., Heinrich, B.: How to Measure Data Quality – A Metric-Based Approach. In: ICIS Proceedings, Association for Information Systems (2007)
10. Luján-Mora, S.: Multidimensional Modeling using UML and XML, Universidad de Alicante, Spain (2001)
11. Abelló, A., Samos, J., Saltor, F.: YAM^2 (Yet Another Multidimensional Model): An Extension of UML. In: International Database Engineering and Applications Symposium (IDEAS 2002), pp. 172–181. IEEE Computer Society, Edmonton (2002)
12. Vassiliadis, P., Bouzeghoub, M., Quix, C.: Towards Quality-Oriented Data Warehouse Usage and Evolution. In: Jarke, M., Oberweis, A. (eds.) CAiSE 1999. LNCS, vol. 1626, pp. 164–179. Springer, Heidelberg (1999)
13. Romero, R., Mazón, J.-N., Trujillo, J., Serrano, M.A., Piattini, M.: Quality of Data Warehouses. In: Encyclopedia of Database Systems (2009)
14. Peralta, V.: Data Warehouse Logical Design from Multidimensional Conceptual Schemas, Universidad de la República, Uruguay
15. Moody Daniel, L.: Theoretical and practical issues in evaluating the quality of conceptual models: current state and future directions. Data and Knowledge Engineering 44(3), 243–276 (2005)
16. Serrano, M.A., Calero, C., Sahraouni, H.A., Piattini, M.: Emprircal studies to assess the understandability of data warehouse schemas using structural metrics. Software Qual. J (2008)
17. Cruz-Lemus, J.A., Maes, A., Genero, M., Poels, G., Piattini, M.: The impact of structural complexity on the understandability of UML statechart diagrams. Inf. Sci. 180(11), 2209–2220 (2010)

Plagiarism Detection of Paraphrases in Text Documents with Document Retrieval

S. Sandhya and S. Chitrakala

Department of Computer Science and Engineering
Easwari Engineering College, Anna University, Chennai, India
{Sanrsn,ckgops}@gmail.com

Abstract. Retrieval of documents is used for finding relevant documents to user queries and plagiarism is the act of copying the contents of one's work without any acknowledgement. Paraphrasing is a type of plagiarism where the contents from source may be changed. This paper proposes a new document retrieval system and paraphrase plagiarism detection of text documents using multi-layered self organizing map (MLSOM). In the proposed system tree structure is extracted for the document that hierarchically represents the document features as document, pages and paragraphs. To handle the tree-structured documents in an efficient way, MLSOM is used as a clustering algorithm. Using MLSOM the documents can be compared for detecting plagiarism and it finds out the local similarity. Paraphrased plagiarism can be detected by finding the similarity between sentences of two documents which is a kind of local similarity detection.

Keywords: Plagiarism detection, paraphrase, multi-layer self organizing map, sentence similarity.

1 Introduction

Text Retrieval refers to the retrieval of unstructured records, that is, records consisting primarily of free-form natural language text which is also known as Information Retrieval (IR). Of course, other kinds of data can also be unstructured, e.g., photographic images, audio, video, etc. The records that IR addresses are often called "documents". An IR system prepares for retrieval by indexing documents and formulating queries, resulting in document representations and query representations, respectively; the system then matches the representations and displays the documents found and the users selects the relevant items.

Document retrieval (DR) more commonly referred to as Information Retrieval which is the computerized process of producing a list of documents that are relevant to an inquirer's request by comparing the user's request to an automatically produced index of the textual content of documents in the system. Document Retrieval systems are based on different theoretical models, which determine how matching and ranking are conducted. The most prevalent models are Boolean, Vector Space, Probabilistic, and Language Modeling. Within the indexing aspect of each model, the system processes, represents, and weights the substantive content of documents and queries for matching.

D.C. Wyld et al. (Eds.): ACITY 2011, CCIS 198, pp. 330–338, 2011.

The easy access to the Internet has made disseminating knowledge across the world much easier. Documents can easily be searched, copied, saved, and reused for different purposes. Document retrieval (DR) and categorization has also become important in facilitating the handling of large number of documents. As a result, plagiarism detection (PD) has become increasingly important when more information can be electronically exchanged, reused, and copied.

Plagiarism is defined as "the passing off of another person's work as if it were one's own, by claiming credit for something that was actually done by someone else".

The different plagiarism methods are: Copy-paste plagiarism, Paraphrasing, Translated plagiarism, Artistic plagiarism, Idea plagiarism, Code plagiarism and Misinformation of references where the paraphrasing deals with lexical synonymy or substitution of words.

2 Prior and Related Work

The literature survey on document retrieval and plagiarism detection is as follows:

2.1 Document Retrieval

Yates et al [1] presented the basic model for document retrieval namely Boolean model. Boolean model is the earliest and easiest model. It does not use either term frequencies or term weights for the inverted files. Boolean operators- AND, OR, and NOT- are used both for representing the user's need and in the internal matching of the query to the inverted file. The main disadvantage of Boolean model is its inability to relevance rank documents.

Zobel et al [2] presented the probabilistic model for retrieval that assigns the odds of relevance score to each term in a document based on that term's frequency in a set of relevant documents. The issues of probabilistic model are its problematic assumption that probabilities are based on a binary condition of relevance, the assumption of term independence, which is not realistic, and the lack of actual relevance data in the system's initial assignments.

Liu et al [3] describes the language model for retrieving the documents. It is a statistical method for ranking documents in a collection based on the probability that they might have generated the query. The documents in the collection are evaluated and ranked based on the probability of their language model generating that query. Speeding up the retrieval process is an important issue.

Yuqing et al [4] suggested Self Organizing Map (SOM) a versatile neural network used for generating a topologically ordered map and clusters. Based on topologically ordered map of documents, SOM facilities users to find similar documents that are close to each other on the SOM map. SOM is computationally efficient in performing fast DR because it compares a query document with only the neurons instead of all documents in the database. All of the above models for document retrieval rely on term frequency information.

2.2 Plagiarism Detection

The existing works on plagiarism detection is as follows:

Kappe et al [5] gave the three broad categories of detecting textual plagiarism: 1) comparing the query over a database, 2) comparing core sentences/phrases through a search engine, and 3) comparison by stylometric analysis. Kang et al. [6] proposed a method based on linguistically motivated plagiarism patterns that allows partial match when sentences are made different by changing words or structure. Heintze [7] developed a string-matching finger-print based system. It calculates the document fingerprint from character level instead of words. The main disadvantage with this system is it's losing of semantic information.

Monostori et al. [8] used suffix trees to detect plagiarism at a superior speed. It requires less space, but suffix trees do not range well and the algorithm is applicable only to a small data set.

George et al. [9] used document tagging approach for detecting plagiarism. The principle underlying document tagging is to conceal some information (a marker) in source documents so that any re-use of those documents will be evident from the presence of the hidden markers.

Mihai C. Lintean et al [10] uses word semantics and weighted dependencies to compute word similarity.

Issues in existing system:

The issues in the existing system observed from the literature survey are:

- Flat featured documents does not contain any contextual information
- No global and local characteristics of the documents in the legacy DR systems
- Existing models of plagiarism detection detects only direct plagiarism
- Paraphrased plagiarism is difficult to detect as words can be substituted, reordered, splitted etc.

3 Proposed System

From the related work of document retrieval plagiarism detection system it is identified that contextual information of documents and paraphrases are not handled. The proposed system proposes a new document retrieval (DR) and plagiarism detection (PD) system using Multi layer Self-organizing map (MLSOM). In this system a document is represented by a rich-tree structure. Instead of keyword based retrieval, the system compares a full document as a query for efficient document retrieval and plagiarism detection. The tree structure representation of documents is handled in an efficient way using MLSOM algorithm which serves as a clustering algorithm. The tree structure is extracted by partitioning the document into pages and paragraphs where document is at the top layer, paragraphs at the bottom layer. Paraphrased plagiarism of type synonymy can be identified by finding the paragraph similarity between two documents. Paragraphs of the two documents are compared by extracting the sentences and performing the word similarity. The word similarity can be found out by performing semantic similarity computation.

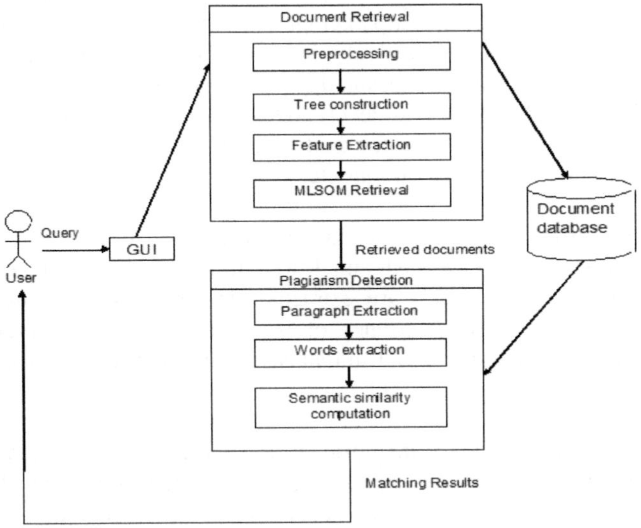

Fig. 1. Architecture of DR and PD of text documents

Fig. 1 gives the architectural model of the proposed system which consists of document retrieval and plagiarism detection system. In document retrieval model, the user gives the query for which the similar documents are retrieved. Preprocessing is done where the words are stemmed to its root, stop words are removed. Then the tree structure is constructed for the document. After tree construction features are extracted for the accurate retrieval of the documents. In plagiarism detection of paraphrase of type synonymy or lexical substitution, paragraph similarity is used. In paragraph similarity check, the sentences of the source and potential (plagiarized) document are extracted for which the word similarity is computed. After the extraction of words semantic similarity is computed. If the similarity of words exceeds the threshold, the document is plagiarized with the synonymy from the source document.

4 System Description

The proposed system contains the following modules:

4.1 Document Retrieval

The document retrieval consists of the following tasks:

Preprocessing: Preprocessing of the documents includes removing non-textual information from the documents and also the articles ("a", "an", "the"), which would disturb the triples while not conveying much information, were removed. After preprocessing of documents has done, tree structure is constructed.

Tree Construction: The documents are partitioned into a tree structure where the document is in the root node, and paragraphs represent the bottom level nodes. Tree structure data can be used effectively for both DR and PD. For DR, similarity between two documents can be measured using the whole tree, where root nodes give global similarity and the second level nodes give the local similarity. The tree structure of the document includes the contextual information as it contains the details of a document like sections, paragraphs etc.

Feature Extraction: For each document word histogram is constructed. The normalized histogram is projected into lower dimensional PCA feature. Based on PCA the features of the nodes are extracted. The word histograms are used for counting the frequency of occurrence of words in a given document. The word histograms are extracted and stored in database which is used in document retrieval and plagiarism detection.

Document Retrieval: In MLSOM retrieval, tree structure is extracted for the query document and the node features are calculated. The nodes are matched from bottom level to top level and the most matched neurons are found. The neurons are sorted in descending order and the associated documents are appended to the retrieval list. The documents in the retrieval list are sorted according the query documents and documents are returned to the user. This sorting helps to retrieve the documents based on relevancy. The MLSOM algorithm for performing the retrieval is given as follows:

MLSOM algorithm:

```
Initialize SOM for all layers
Loop from bottom to top layer
    Create input vector for each node
    Loop for training SOM
find the winner neuron
end of training loop
for each node find final winner neuron until top layer
end of layer loop
```

4.2 Plagiarism Detection

After the retrieval of documents the source and potential document is compared to detect the paraphrasing among the documents. Plagiarism detection consists of the following tasks:

Paragraph Extraction: From the retrieved documents the paragraphs are extracted and it is used to find the sentence similarity for lexical substitution or synonymy in the words from the source and plagiarized documents. Using MLSOM local similarity of the documents is found out.

Word Extraction: From the extracted paragraphs the sentences are delimited in order to perform paraphrase detection among the words in source and plagiarized documents.

Semantic similarity computation: It is used to find the degree of similarity of contents between the source and plagiarized documents when the words in the document are substituted with its synonym. After extracting the words from the paragraphs, word-based similarity is used for detecting the plagiarism where paraphrases can be identified by the comparison of words and if the count exceeds the threshold the document is said to be plagiarized.

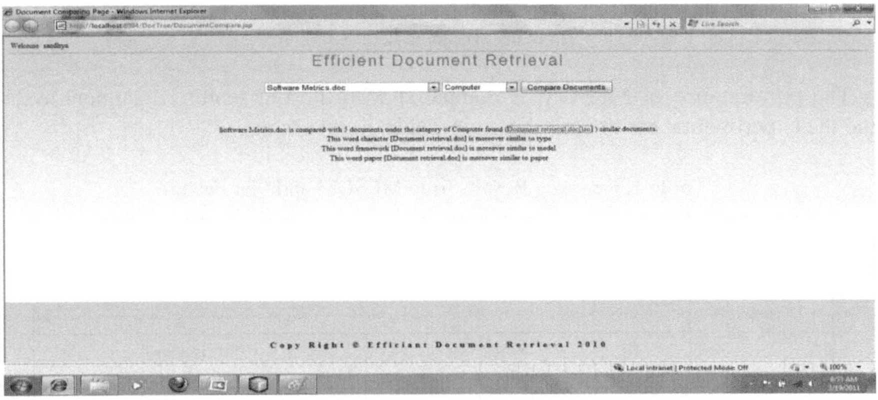

Fig. 2. Paraphrase Detection

Fig. 2 shows the synonymy detected during the comparison of query document with the documents stored in database. A word-to-word comparison is performed to detect the paraphrase (synonymy substitution) of words. For example, the word 'Character' can be paraphrased with its synonym substitute 'type'. Wordnet provides the synset for words and from the word forms, paraphrase is identified.

The SSDP (Semantic Similarity Detection of Paraphrases) algorithm for finding the paraphrases among the documents computes the word similarity by performing the comparison between the query and the retrieved documents.

SSDP Algorithm:

```
begin
initialization of variables
perform document comparison
for each source and plagiarized document
        extract words
        compute word similarity
        save count of word similarity
if count > threshold
        print result as plagiarized
else
        print result as non-plagiarized
end
```

5 Experimental Results

The performance of document retrieval is measured using:

$$\text{precision} = \frac{\text{number of correct documents retrieved}}{\text{number of total documents retrieved}} \tag{1}$$

$$\text{recall} = \frac{\text{number of correct documents retrieved}}{\text{number of total documents in relavant class}} \tag{2}$$

$$\text{F\_score} = \frac{\text{recall} \times \text{precision}}{(\text{recall}+\text{precision})/2} \tag{3}$$

The performance of MLSOM is compared with the flat feature document system and the experimental results are shown in Table 1 and graphs.

Table 1. Retrieval Results from MLSOM and Flat Feature

No of Documents Retrieved	Feature					
	MLSOM			Flat- Feature		
	Precision	Recall	F_score	Precision	Recall	F_score
5	0.72	0.675	0.72	0.5	0.4	0.5
10	0.75	0.75	0.78	0.4	0.375	0.4
15	0.8	0.875	0.8	0.375	0.25	0.375
20	0.875	0.9	0.875	0.2	0.2	0.2

Table 1 shows the comparative results for MLSOM and flat feature with the measures precision, recall and F_score. The performance measures of MLSOM are higher than the flat feature.

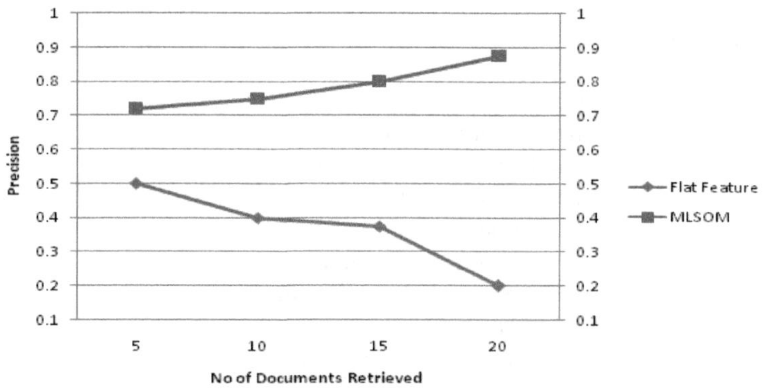

Fig. 3(a). Precision

Fig. 3(a) gives the graph comparing the precision measure comparing MLSOM and flat feature documents. The precision measure of MLSOM is better than the flat feature.

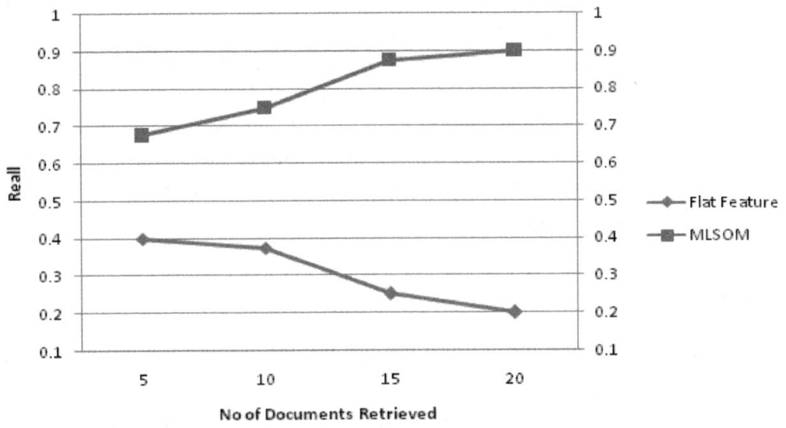

Fig. 3(b). Recall

Fig. 3(b) gives the graph comparing the recall measure of MLSOM and flat feature. The recall measure for MLSOM performs better than flat feature

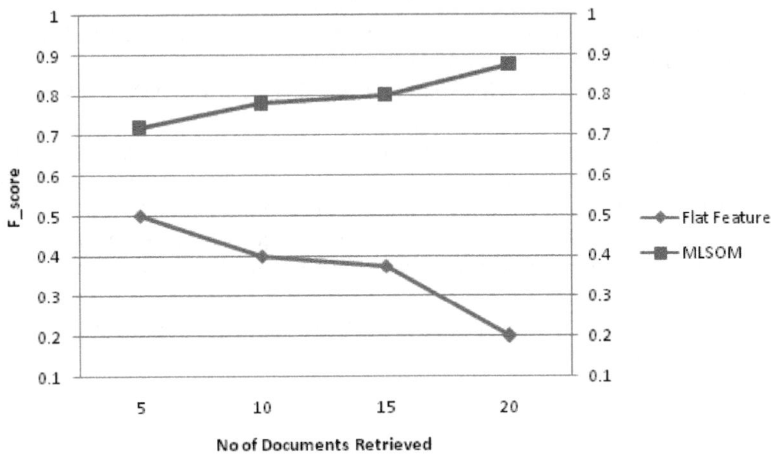

Fig. 3(c). F_score

Fig. 3(c) gives the F_score graph comparing MLSOM and flat feature where the F_score measure for MLSOM is higher than the flat feature.

6 Conclusion

This paper describes the new document retrieval system using MLSOM for retrieving the text documents. SOM has been extended as MLSOM and it is used efficiently for performing both retrieval and plagiarism. The proposed system extracts the tree structure of the documents as it presents the contextual information which was absent in many of the DR models. Tree construction extracts the level-by-level features of the document. As MLSOM incorporates both the global and local characteristics of the documents the performance of retrieving the documents is faster than that of the legacy DR systems. Also MLSOM serves the clustering algorithm and the speed of the retrieval is achieved. The performance results of MLSOM are better while compared with flat featured documents.

References

1. Yates, Neto: Modern Information Retrieval, vol. 15, pp. 750–780. Addison-Wesley/Longman, Reading, MA (1999)
2. Zobel, Moffat: Exploring the similarity space. ACM SIGIR Forum 32(1), 18–34 (1998)
3. Liu, Croft: Statistical Language Modeling for Information Retrieval. In: Cronin, B. (ed.) Annual Review of Information Science & Technology, vol. 38, pp. 556–567 (2004)
4. Lin, Y., Ye, H.: Input Data Representation for Self-Organizing Map in Software Classification. In: Second International Conference on Knowledge Acquisition and Modeling, Callaghan, Australia, pp. 163–195 (2009)
5. Kappe, Zaka: Plagiarism—A survey. Journal of Universal Computing 12(8), 1050–1084 (2006)
6. Kang, N., Gelbukh, A., Han, S.-Y.: PPChecker: Plagiarism pattern checker in document copy detection. In: Sojka, P., Kopeček, I., Pala, K. (eds.) TSD 2006. LNCS (LNAI), vol. 4188, pp. 661–667. Springer, Heidelberg (2006)
7. Heintze: Scalable document fingerprinting. In: Proc. 2nd USENIX Workshop Electron. Commerce, Oakland, CA, pp. 18–21 (November 2007)
8. Monostori, Zaslavsky, Schmidt: MatchDetectReveal: Finding overlapping and similar digital documents. In: Proc. of 21st Century Inf. Resources Manage. Assoc. Int. Conf. Challenges Inf. Technol. Manage., Anchorage, AK, pp. 955–957 (2000)
9. Weir, G.R.S., Gordon, M.A., Macgregor, G.: Technology in plagiarism detection and management. In: 34th ASEE/IEEE Frontiers in Education Conference, Savannah, GA, vol. 13, pp. 351–370 (2004)
10. Lintean, M.C., Rus, V.: Paraphrase Identification Using Weighted Dependencies and Word Semantics. Informatica 34, 19–28 (2010)

An XAML Approach for Building Management System Using WCF

Surendhar Thallapelly, P. Swarna Latha, and M. Rajasekhara Babu

School of Computing Science and Engineering,
VIT University, Vellore, TN, India
{surendharthallapelly2009,pswarnaltha,
mrajasekharababu}@vit.ac.in

Abstract. Building Automation is one of the critical issues in recent scenarios. The process of Building Automation is called as Building automation System (BAS).The BAS includes different kind of information that enables to work towards intelligent building system. There was a Web Services technology for integrating different BAS but it supports only HTTP protocol which is stateless. This paper presents the next generation internet technology Windows Communication Foundation (WCF) to integrate different building automation systems in the development of BAS. WCF includes various contracts which writes and reads Building Automation Control Network (BACnet) data points from BACnet network. These contracts will be called by other enterprise applications for realize BAS integration and get real-time data on BACnet network as a facilities Management.BMS will be applied in a BAS which consists of BACnet network. The applications use sensors, actuators and controllers for controlling Building Management System (BMS). This paper presents a Service Oriented Architecture (SOA) for BMS using WCF and Extensible Application Markup Language (XAML) which will provides client side GUI for BMS reused for different kind of applications. Finally, it discusses about challenges in providing security to BMS.

Keywords: Service Oriented Architecture, Building management system, Building automation system, Windows Communication Foundation, XAML.

1 Introduction

The building management systems used to monitor and control building facilities in BASs. Desktop and Web based BAS have been developed .How ever using traditional Web, Desktop applications same code has to rewritten for each application. Here single XAML is reused between desktop, mobile, browsers and based upon the type of device the application will run. In simple XAML used for seamless user experience of mobile, web and desktop applications. The BAS must be loosely coupled so that the controllers can communicated with any other application. It is difficult to for integration across BASs which may adopt different communication protocols e.g., Lon protocol, bacnet protocol and integrating BAS with existing enterprise applications. Emerging Windows Communication Foundation based on Service Oriented Architecture will solve the problems.

D.C. Wyld et al. (Eds.): ACITY 2011, CCIS 198, pp. 339–345, 2011.

BAS explains functionalities provided by building control system, which is a computerized, intelligent network of electronic devices, designed to monitor and control the mechanical and lighting systems in building. American Society of Heating, Refrigeration and Air-conditioning Engineers (ASHRAE) and Organization for the Advancement of Structured Information Standards (OSAIS) are international organizations to promote the development of service oriented architecture in BAS domain. A Building Automation System (BAS) is an example of a distributed control system. Modern Building Automation System do not only provide improved comfort but offer significant energy cost savings, especially in office buildings and production halls, because of intelligent control systems such as lighting and sunblind functions. The main application of Building Automation System is to increasing user comfort at minimum operational cost and get optimized control schemes for Heating, Ventilation and Control Systems (HVAC), shading and lighting.

In this paper, Windows Communication Foundation and XAML used for developing next generation of BMS.Windows Communication Foundation allow to build distributed and loosely coupled systems E.g. BASs. It will support different types of protocols like tcp, udp. It is stateful protocol. The proposed BMS will applied to an intelligent building whose BAS is within a BACnet network. A set of Windows Communication Foundation endpoints which can read write BACnet data points from the BACnet network based on the BACnet protocol stack. The Windows Communication Foundation service which is installed in the controller can be invoked XAML easily.

The rest of the paper is organized as follows: Section II describes the related work and Section 3 presents the description of architecture of BAS integration based on Windows Communication Foundation. Section 4 describes the proposed development of BAS using Windows Communication Foundation. Section 5 describes challenges in providing security in Building Automation System. Finally, conclusions are presented in section.

2 Related Work

The approaches that have been profoundly established they are standard communication protocol and cross-protocol gateways not met the desired expectations. There is a need for building systems and services integration [9].There exists individual automated building systems for Heating Ventilation and Air condition system and current solutions are not satisfactory level for integrating Building Management Systems [10].The task of building automation and communication Infrastructure that is necessary to required to address integration problems[11].

Sensors will get the HVAC details those details can be accessed by integrated building systems or enterprise applications using service oriented architectures web service[1].Web services can be installed on controllers for providing communication across different protocols[2].Using AJAX and web services installed on controller can provide asynchronously retrieve data from controller using web services[4].Enterprise-wide architecture, for facilities management automation provides BMSs and building automation and control systems will access to additional information that will enable building to be used more effectively [12].

Service oriented architecture and their applicability is building management system and building automation system [6].controlling and managing building automation system through Windows phone mobile [14].Security threats that may arise for building automation system [13].

3 Windows Communication Foundation for BAS Integration

3.1 Principle of Windows Communication Foundation

For integrating different Building Management Systems CORBA (Common Object Request Broker) RMI (Remote Method Invocation), COM (Component Object Model), DCOM (Distributed Component Object Model) is used. They are specific to platform. Although Web Services is platform independent it is stateless and supports only http protocol for communication.

As Building Automation System is example of distributed control system it is based on distributed application's "Service-oriented" architecture. The Windows Communication Foundation is a unified programming model for building service oriented applications. Mainly WCF is used for their purposes-unifications, service orientation, rich integration. Unifications means unifies today's all distributed technologies and used for on-machine, cross machine, and cross internet. Service Orientation means codifies best practices for building distributed applications. Rich integration means integrates with our own distributed stacks and interoperates applications running on other platforms.

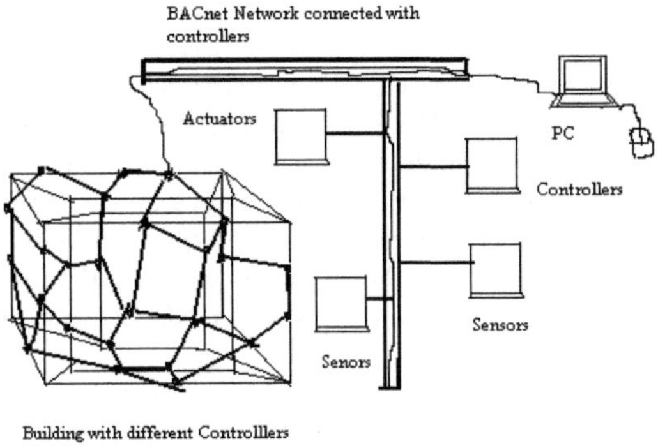

Fig. 1. Sketch map of General BAS with different controllers, sensors, actuators

Compared to Web Services, WCF allows sending messages not only using http, but also using TCP and MSMQ and supports formats other than SOAP, which includes Representational State Transfer Protocol and Plain old XML (POX).It acts as on abstract layer, separating platform and programming language specific details from how application is invoked.

WCF is based on Service Oriented Architecture in which Service Provider who provides service. The Service provider will publish service in Service Broker from which a Requester binds to Service Provider using policy.

3.2 Windows Communication Foundation – Based Architecture for BAS Integration

It includes mainly three different types of integration problems that can be solved. Figure 1 gives a sketch map of BAS integration based on Windows Communication Foundation .The integration of different functional BAS subsystems (security, lighting and so on),integration among different protocols(BACnet, Lon talk) and integration between building automation system and existing enterprise applications. Windows Communication Foundation can be installed in controllers which have strong control functions. Windows Communication Foundation service is not to replace field bus standard communication protocols like bacnet but it adopts existing communication protocols and field bus network.

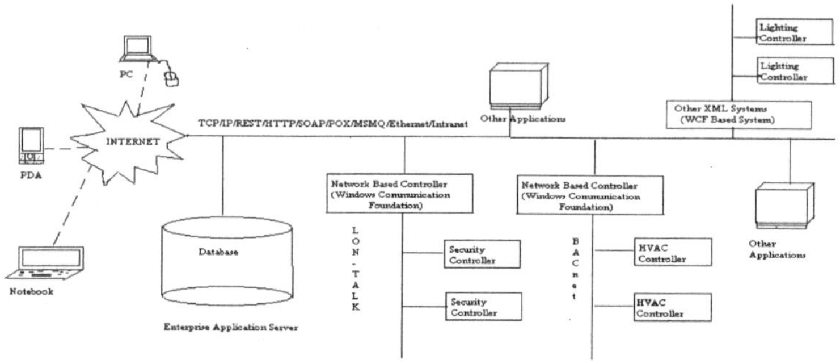

Fig. 2. Sketch map of BAS Integration based on Windows Communication Foundation

Functional components resort to protocol drivers to communicate with field equipments in the field networks Lon talk and BACnet networks. Figure 2 illustrates the software architecture of the BAS integration. These functions are wrapped with public operational contract methods. Here the web server is used for only for browser based applications for storing silver light web pages and will parse specific protocol request (SOAP, REST, and HTTP) and forward request to Windows Communication Foundation Service. For PDA and Multi touch screen will directly access installed Windows Communication Foundation service on BACnet controller.

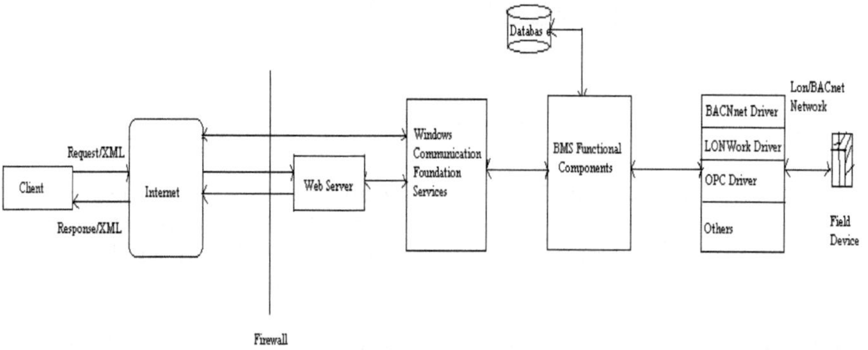

Fig. 3. Windows Communication Foundation based software architecture for Software Integration

The publicly available operational contracts can be invoked by other applications for accessing data on BASs on Internet. These contracts can read and write data to Field Devices.

4 Design of Proposed BMS Using Windows Communication Foundation and XAML

4.1 Brief Description of XAML

XAML is a declarative markup language. It is used for creating rich interactive user interfaces at client side. XAML language is used by Windows Presentation Framework (WPF) and Silverlight.Advantages of XAML are design/code (behavior) separation .At a time both designers and developers can share work and it will take hardware acceleration support to create new levels of visual complexity. For developing desktop applications Windows Presentation Framework used, for browser and pda applications silver light used. XAML language applications will run resolution independently and uses vector based rendering.

4.2 Invoking Windows Communication Foundation Services with XAML

Based on type of device the application will run. If it is browser based application xbap is returned by the server and user modifications will invoke WCF operation contract. Mobile or Touch Screen will invoke proxy of WCF Service from mobile, which will call BACnet device's publically exposed contracts.

The BMS will be applied to a BAS which has BACnet network. The public Windows Communication Framework contracts, which can read and write BACnet data points from the BACnet which can be developed by BACnet protocol stack.

The XAML is reused among Windows Presentation Framework and Silver light applications. So that single application can be used to control pda, touch screen and browser based applications. Here using XAML in phone can access WCF services [6].XAML uses vector based rendering and resolution independent. So XAML will provide rich internet client applications.

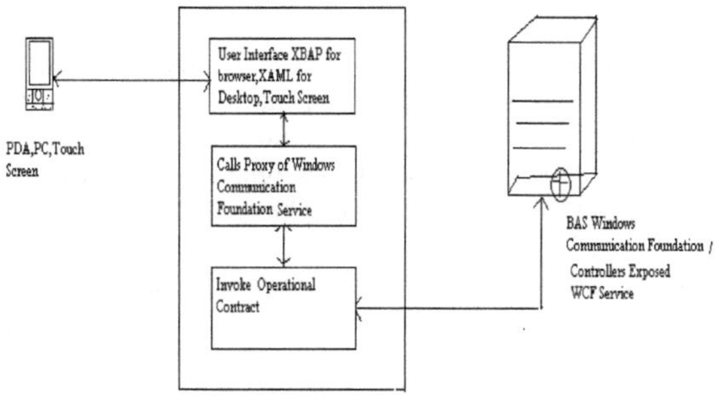

Fig. 4. Architecture for Invoking BAS Windows Communication Foundation with XAML Application

5 Security Issues in Proposed System

The functions that will control building management system i.e., control functions has provided with unauthorized access. The Windows communication Foundation controller can access only after service provider agreement. It prevents malicious access to building management system

6 Conclusions

From the past two decades new protocols are coming in Building Automation System. Integration among these protocols, and integrate existing applications supported by these protocols and supporting new applications always challenge.

Technology is making so many things easier to us. Up to now Web services methods which can read and write BACnet data points from the BACnet network, are developed based on BACnetwork provided, web services are based upon single http protocol and these are stateless. As Windows Communication Foundation which is supporting TCP, REST and so on can be used. In future Windows Communication Foundation which can read and write BACnet data points from the BACnet network which are developed on BACnet network are provided.

XAML is next generation client slide application which can be used by PDA, Multitouch screen Browser and desktop applications. So reusing XAML code among applications will save amount of time and will give high performance as it is Vector based and resolution independent.

Here we propose next generation Building Management System which can real control and monitor Building Automation System using PDA, Touch Screen, Browser and desktop Applications. The BMS can be applied to a typical BAS within a Bacnet.

References

1. Malatras, A., Abolghasem: Web Enabled Wireless Sensor Networks for Facilities Management. IEEE Systems Journal 2(4) (December 2008)
2. Wang, S., Xu, Z., Cao, J., Zhang, J.: A middleware for web service-enabled integration and interoperation of intelligent building systems. Automation in Construction 16, 112–121 (2007)
3. Bai, J., Xiao, H., Yang, X., Zhang, G.: Study on Integration Technologies of Building Automation Systems based on Web Services. In: 2009 ISECS International Technologies of Building Automation System based on Web Services (2009)
4. Bai, J., Xiao, H., Zhu, T., Liu, W., Sun, A.: Design Of a Web-based Building Management System using Ajax and Web Services. In: 2008 International Seminar on Business and Information Management (2008)
5. Neugschwandtner, G., Kastner, W.: Webservices in building automation: Mapping KNX to oBIX. In: IEEE International Conference on Industrial Informatics Vienna, Austria, pp. 87–92 (2007)
6. Malatras, A., Asgari, A.H., Baugé, T., Irons, M.: A service- oriented architecture for building services integration. Journal of Facilities Management 6, 132–151 (2008)
7. `http://wcfguidanceformobile.codeplex.com/`

8. Wang, S., Xie, J.: Integrating Building Management System and facilities management on the Internet. Automation in Construction 11, 707–715 (2002)
9. Wang, S.W., Xie, J.L.: Integrating building management system and facility management on internet. Automation Construction 11(6), 707–715 (2002)
10. Braun, J.E.: Intelligent building systems—Past, present, future. In: Proc. Amer. Control Conf., pp. 4374–4381 (July 2007)
11. Kanstner, W., Neugschwandtner, G., Soucek, S., Michael Newman, H.: Communication Systems for Building Automation and Control. Proceedings of the IEEE 93(6) (June 2005)
12. Wheeler, A.: Commercial applications of wireless sensor Networks using ZigBee. IEEE Common. Mag. 45(4), 70–77 (2007)

Hand Gesture Recognition Using Skeleton of Hand and Distance Based Metric

K. Sivarajesh Reddy[1], P. Swarna Latha[2], and M. Rajasekhara Babu[3]

SCSE, VIT University, Vellore, Tamil Nadu, India - 632014
{ksivarajeshreddy2009,pswarnalatha,mrajasekharababu}@vit.ac.in

Abstract. In this paper we are mainly concerns on the image processing and computer vision concepts for interpretation of gestures .By using gestures we can convey instructions to the machine (computer) or commands to a robots .This is known as Human machine interaction (Human computer interaction (HCI).Hand gestures are an ideal way of exchanging information between human and computer, robots, or any other device. In this paper we are calculating skeleton of the hand by using distance transformation technique and are using for recognition instead of the entire hand, because of its robust nature against translation, rotation and scaling. Skeleton is computed for each and every hand posture in the entire hand motion and superimposed on a single image called as Dynamic Signature of the particular gesture type. Gesture is recognized by using the Image Euclidean distance measure by comparing the current Dynamic Signature of the particular gesture with the gesture Alphabet set.

Keywords: Static Gesture, Local Orientation Histogram (LOH), Euclidean distance, Dynamic Gesture, Skeleton, Dynamic Signature, Image Euclidean Distance (IMED).

1 Introduction

The main idea of this paper is to direct some devices or robots in industries and homes by using hand gestures. For example if we want to switch on and off the devices in a industry from a certain distance by using hand gestures. This hand gesture will control the devices by sending the proper information to the devices; this information will be conveyed by hand gesture. For identifying hand gesture we are making use of the local orientation histograms (LOH),Euclidean distance measure, skeleton concept and image Euclidean distance measure (IMED).

1.1 Hand Gesture

Human Robot Interaction (HRI) or Human Computer Interaction (HCI) having utmost importance in our daily lives. Gesture recognition can be the one of the best approaches in this direction. It is the process in which the gestures made by some user or sender are recognized by the end user like machine or devices. Gesture recognition and classification is one of the interested areas in Machine or computer vision domain.

D.C. Wyld et al. (Eds.): ACITY 2011, CCIS 198, pp. 346–354, 2011.

Gestures are classified as 1.Facial gestures 2.hand Gestures 3.Combination of hand and face gestures. In this paper we mainly concerns on hand gestures.

From the initial intention to the final recognition, gesture follows a motion in space and time [1].Kendon distinguishes the hand gesture into three phases. I.e. a single hand gesture is made of 1. Preparation 2.Stroke 3.Retraction.Among this three phase's stroke carries meaningful information than the other two phases and also it is present between the preparation and retraction. The other two phases consists of moving the arms from the beginning to the rest position and vice versa.

Hand gestures can be categorized as a Static and Dynamic Hand gestures. Static Hand gestures are characterized by the hand posture which is determined by a particular palm-finger configuration. While Dynamic Hand gestures Characterized by start and end stoke of hand and general hand stroke motion [1].

1.2 Hand Gesture Analysis

In this paper analysis of hand gesture is done by vision based technique. Vision based analysis is a natural and difficult one because of limitations of machine vision. Some of the limitations are segmentation of moving hand part against a clutter background, tracking of the hand movement, Skin color of hand for extracting hand part. In this paper properties of an image (intensity values) are used for recognition of hand.

1.3 Gesture Recognition Process

Gesture recognition can be divided into two tasks; 1. Extraction of features 2.Classification. Feature extraction mainly uses the low level information of an image and generates high level information for classification. Features calculated based on distance, velocity, area, centroid, energy information and angle information [2, 3, and 4]. In this paper angle feature was used for identification of static gestures by using Local Orientation Histogram(LOH) and Image Euclidean distance (IMED) measure for dynamic gestures. Image Euclidean Distance (IMED) was used for classification of hand gesture.

2 Proposed Approach

Dynamic signature and Skeleton concept was used for dynamic hand gesture recognition and local orientation histogram for static gesture recognition. In this paper we are considering some assumptions (Constraints) such as.

1. Maintenance of constant distance between the camera and hand
2. Gestures are performed against a black background or uniform background.
3. Gestures are performed in the known region of space.
4. Taking only the Hand images no other body parts for our simplification.
5. Gesture alphabets are priori known to the user.

Generally gesture is a sequence of images Instead of taking all the images considering only some sample of images that will cover the entire motion of gesture, due to this the unwanted information and processing time will be reduced. For identification dynamic gestures in the entire hand movement some start and stop images (posture or static hand gesture) are used. After identification of start posture then only the dynamic hand gesture starts and ends only after identification of stop images. For the identification of start and stop images Local Orientation Histograms (LOH) are used because of the simple and fast calculation. The computation time is less because of dealing directly with pixel values. The Dynamic gesture is the motion present between the start and stop images.

2.1 Preprocessing Stage

This will be done before carrying out the actual processing. The main idea behind this mechanism was removal of the noise and shadows. RGB normalization reduces the intensity variations and removes shadows present in the image. For removal of noises some smoothing techniques and filters was used. Adaptive segmentation of the hand image is carried out because of the skin colors of human beings. Hole filling of hand part also require for filling of the small dots present in the hand area, by using some morphological operations to the hand image. Blob removal is necessary for deletion of the some small dots in the hand image based on the minimum object size. The Object size means the number of white pixels present in the binary image of the corresponding hand image. These all preprocessing steps are required because of Skeleton mainly depends on the Hand segmentation.

2.2 Extracting Features

Here we are mainly using two techniques.

1. Local Orientation Histogram: LOH mainly used for recognition of static gestures (start and stop gestures).It mainly works based on the algorithm proposed by freeman and Roth [6].

2. Dynamic Signature: Dynamic signature means the superimposition of skeleton images on a single image. The Dynamic signature gives the entire motion on a single image itself. The main idea behind using of the skeleton was robust against rotation translation and scaling. In order to perform the gesture classification the gesture notations are already known. A set of samples are required for each gesture.

2.3 Classification Mechanism

The current dynamic signature feature values are compared with database feature values the best match will lead to recognition of the unknown gesture.

3 Preprocessing Steps

The accuracy of the gesture recognition mainly depends on the preprocessing steps. For extracting the hand part background subtraction was used. After histogram based adaptive segmentation applied on image for extracting the hand part. Hole filling algorithm (some morphological operations) used for removal of the black spots in the hand part. Minimum Object size concept was used for removal of white dots present on the hand image. If the object size is less than a particular threshold value then that objects removed from the image.

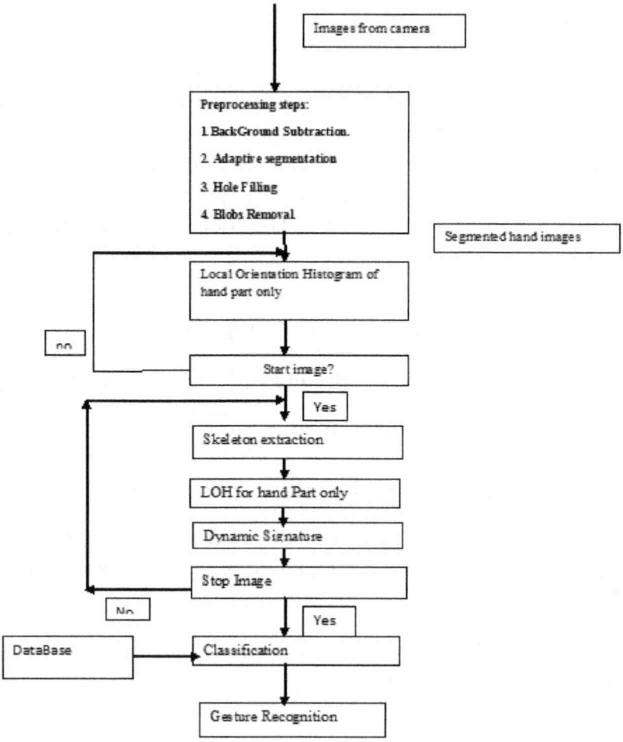

Fig. 1. Gesture Recognition Diagram

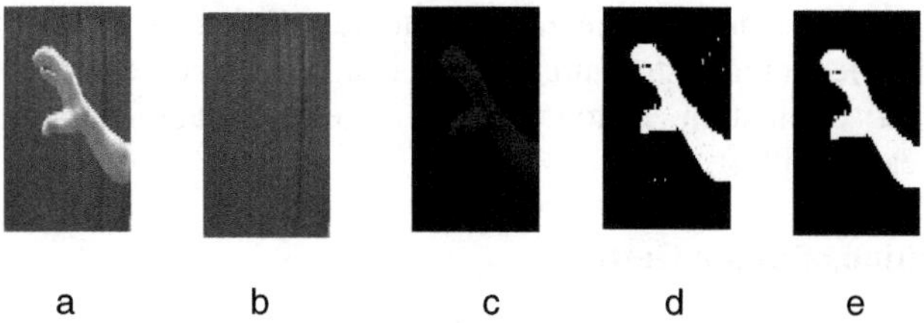

Fig. 2. a. Original Image. b. Background image. c. Background subtraction d. Threshold e. Blob Removal.

4 Static Gesture Recognition

LOH used for static hand gesture recognition. LOH mainly used for recognition of start and stop gesture. The orientation histograms are comparatively easier and simple for computation.

4.1 Local Orientation Histogram

LOH [6] are also easier and faster for computation. LOH are robust against illumination changes. LOH used as features for each gesture and applied on the hand part of the gray image of the original image. The gray level image having hand part against a uniform black background. The local orientations histogram name itself indicates that directions of local gradients. The gradients are obtained by applying the sobel masks along the x and y directions. The sobel edge detection mask values are

$$\text{x-direction}\{0,1,2,-1,0,1,-2,-1,0\} \tag{1}$$

$$\text{y-direction}\{-2,-1,0,-1,0,1,0,1,2\} \tag{2}$$

convolute on the gray hand image. we can get the gradient directions gx and gy.

$$\text{Gradientmagnitude}=\sqrt{gx2+gy2} \tag{3}$$

$$\text{Orientation(or)angle=arctan(gx,gy).} \tag{4}$$

We are eliminating the pixels whose gradient amplitude is less than a mean gradient amplitude multiply by a particular constant(1.5) and for the remaining pixels LOH is calculated.

$$\sum_{m=1}^{M}\sum_{n=1}^{N}\delta(fgradient\,(m,n)-i), \tag{5}$$

where i is the angle in degrees.

i=arctan(gx,gy).

M,and N are image height and widths. $fgradient$ is the matrix of gradient orientations.$\delta(x)$=1 if x=0and zero otherwise. Local Orientation Histogram of static gestures can be seen in [7].

The main idea of using the orientation histogram is that for each gesture there will be a different orientation histogram. If there is a small change in the hand posture it gives different orientation histogram and The calculation of local orientation histogram is easy and fast.

4.2 Recognition of Static Gesture

After finding out the local orientation histogram for a image Euclidean distance measure used for the current and database LOHs.The database having different LOHs for Different static gestures. The minimum Euclidean distance between the current and database is the matched LOH for the current static gesture. The higher number of training samples will leads to high recognition rate.

5 Dynamic Gesture Recognition

Skelton concept used for identification of dynamic gestures. Instead of taking several skeleton images taking single image which will covers entire gesture motion called as Dynamic signature.

5.1 Skeleton Calculation

Dynamic signature is the superimposition of all skeleton images in the gesture. This Dynamic signature covers the entire gesture motion. Skeleton means compact representation of an object and preserves the topology of the object. Skeleton is robust against translation rotation and scaling [8].

Skeleton is extracted by using several methods like by using chamfer distance transform [9, 10], Thinning methods [11] (morphological operations). Skeletons are generated by using opencv's library (open source Package that is developed by Intel.) [12].Distance transformation method used for generating skeleton.

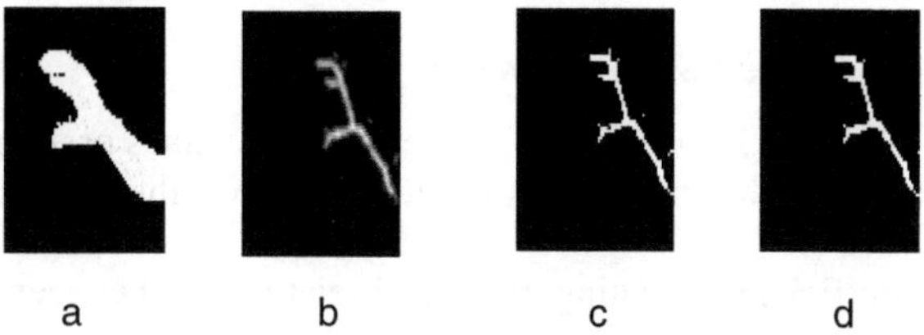

Fig. 3. a. Binary hand image. b. Skelton after applying distance transforms. c.Binary Image of b. d. Noise Removal.

5.2 Dynamic Signature

Dynamic signature means superimposition of all the Skeleton images between the start and stop images. It indicates the entire gesture motion between start and stop images within a single image. Fig 5 indicates the entire gesture motion.

Fig. 4. Dynamic signature

This Dynamic signature mainly having three steps 1.preparation (skeletons are overlaid indicates starting of the gesture.) 2. Stroke (skeletons are apart due to the fast movement of the hand). 3. Resting position (Skeletons are again overlapped).

This Dynamic gesture recognition time mainly depends on the position of the gesture in the image. For improving the robustness we created the extreme left and right positions for gesture. We consider the entire motion between these extreme left and right positions.

5.3 Dynamic Gesture Recognition Process

The recognition performed by comparing the obtained dynamic signature with the database images. The comparison is done by using distance measures. The following distance measures are used for recognition. Euclidean distance measure, Image Euclidean distance measure [15, 16], hausdroff distance [17, 18, 19], Chamfer Distance, baddeleys distance [13, 14].

As in the field of computer vision the most commonly used distance is Euclidean distance. It will discard the image structures and cannot represent the actual relationship between the images. If there is a small variation in the image it will rise to the large Euclidean distance value between two images. Image Euclidean distance measure [15] considers the spatial relationship of the pixels into account .IMED is robust to noise and small deformation.

$$\text{IMED}=\sum_{i=i}^{MN}\sum_{j=1}^{MN} gij(x1i - x2i)(x1j - x2j) \tag{6}$$

Where M and N are image height and width.

X1 is a vector $x1=\{x^1, x2, \text{-----} x^{MN\}}$ x^1, x^2 are intensity values of an image.

Similarly X2 is an another image vector with intensity values of an image $x2=\{x^1, x2, \text{-----} x^{MN\}}$

g^{ij} is thematic coefficient indicating the spatial relationship between pixels .

$$g_{ij}=\frac{1}{2\pi\sigma 2} e^{\left(-\frac{dij*dij}{2\sigma 2}\right)} \tag{7}$$

Where dij is the spatial distance between the pixels on the image lattice and σ is the width parameter.

If pixel1 location is (k,l) and pixel2 location is (k1,l1) then

$$\text{dij is } \sqrt{(k - k1)2 + (l - l1)2} \tag{8}$$

6 Computation Time

The computation time for the dynamic signature is higher because of the skeleton computation, which requires several analyses of the image pixels and also the image Euclidean distance takes lot of computation time because of in this each and every pixel is compared with the each and every pixel of another page.

The computation of the local orientation histogram is easier and takes less processing time because only one time scanning of the image is sufficient for calculation of LOH.

7 Conclusion

Gesture recognition can be done by considering both static gestures and dynamic gestures (Dynamic signature i.e. overlapping of skeleton images).

Static gesture recognition can be done based on freeman –both LOH method [6]for identification of start and stop gestures.LOH calculation is fast and easy one and also robust to illumination changes. The current gesture orientation histogram is compared with the database orientation histograms by using Euclidean distance measure .The best match will have less Euclidean distance value.

The Dynamic signature [7] means the superimposition of all skeleton images. It covers the entire gesture motion in a single image. The current dynamic signature is compared with database dynamic signatures by using image Euclidean distance [15, 16]. The best match having less IMED value. The algorithm is performed on 8 gestures and the recognition rate is 90% in simple conditions (uniform background, limited alphabet, fixed distance between the camera and hand region).

References

1. Pavlovic, V.I., Sharma, R., Huang, T.S.: Visual interpretation of hand gestures for human-computer interaction: a review. IEEE Trans. Pattern Anal. Machine Intell. 19(7), 677–695 (1997)
2. Yoon, H.-S., Soh, J., Bae, Y.J., Yang, H.S.: Hand gesture recognition using combined features of location, angle and velocity. Pattern Recognition 34(7), 1491–1501 (2001)
3. Nayaga, S., Seki, S., Oka, R.: A theoretical consideration of pattern space trajectory for gesture spotting recognition. In: Proc. 2nd IEEE International Conference on Automatic Face and Gesture Recognition (FGR 1996), Killington, Vt, USA, pp. 72–77 (October 1996)
4. Raytchev, B., Hasegawa, O., Otsu, N.: User-independent online gesture recognition by relative motion extraction. Pattern Recognition Letters 21(1), 69–82 (2000)
5. Quek, F.: Unencumbered gestural interaction. IEEE Multimedia 4(3), 36–47 (1996)
6. Freeman, W.T., Roth, M.: Orientation histograms for hand gesture recognition. Tech. Rep. TR-94-03a, Mitsubishi Electric Research Laboratories, Cambridge Research centre, Cambridge, Mass, USA (1995)
7. Lonescu, B., Coquin, D., Lambert, P., Buzuloiu, V.: Dynamic Hand gesture recognition using the skeleton of the hand. EURASIP Journal on Applied Signal Processing (2005)
8. Arcelli, C., Sanniti di Baja, G.: Euclidean skeleton via centre-of-maximal disc extraction. Image and Vision Computing 11(3), 163–173 (1993)
9. Borgefors, G.: Distance transformations in digital images. Computer Vision, Graphics and Image Processing 34(3), 344–371 (1986)
10. Chehadeh, Y., Coquin, D., Bolon, H.: A skeletonization algorithm using chamfer distance transformation adapted to rectangular grids. In: Proc. 13th IEEE International Conference on Pattern Recognition (ICPR 1996), Vienna, Austria, vol. 2, pp. 131–135 (August 1996)
11. Hasthorpe, J., Mount, N.: The generation of river channel skeletons from binary images using raster thinning algorithms. School of Geography, University of Nottingham
12. `http://www.willowgarage.com/pages/software/opencv`
13. Baddeley, A.J.: An error metric for binary images. In: Robust Computer Vision, Wichmann, Karlsruhe, Germany, pp. 59–78 (1992)
14. Coquin, D., Bolon, P.: Applications of Baddeley's distance to dissimilarity measurement between gray scale images. Pattern Recognition Letters 22(14), 1483–1502 (2001)
15. Li, J., Lu, B.-L.: An adaptive image Euclidean distance. China Pattern Recognition 42, 349–357 (2009)
16. Wang, L., Zhang, Y., Feng, J.: On The Image Euclidean Distance. Center for Information Sciences School of Electronics Engineering and Computer Sciences, Peking University Beijing, 100871, China

17. Huttenlocher, D.P., Klanderman, G.A., Rucklidge, W.J.: Comparing images using the Hausdorff distance. IEEE Trans. Pattern Anal. Mach. Intell. 15(9), 850–863 (1993)
18. Vivek, E.P., Sudha, N.: Robust Hausdorff distance measure for face recognition. Pattern Recognition 40(2), 431–442 (2007)
19. Yang, C.H.T., Lai, S.H., Chang, L.W.: Hybrid image matching combining Hausdorff distance with normalized gradient matching. Pattern Recognition 40(4), 1173–1181 (2007)

DWCLEANSER: A Framework for Approximate Duplicate Detection

Garima Thakur[1], Manu Singh[2], Payal Pahwa[4], and Nidhi Tyagi[3]

[1] USIT, Guru Gobind Singh Indraprastha University, India
thakur_garima_27@yahoo.co.in
[2,3] Shobhit University, India
manu.singh1982@gmail.com, mnidhity@rediffmail.com
[4] BPIT, Guru Gobind Singh Indraprastha University, India
pahwapayal@gmail.com

Abstract. Data quality has become a major area of concern in data warehouse. The prime aim of a data warehouse is to store quality data so that it can enhance the decision support systems effectively. Quality of data is improved by employing data cleaning techniques. Data cleaning deals with detecting and removing errors and discrepancies from data. This paper presents a novel framework for detection of exact as well as approximate duplicates in a data warehouse. The proposed approach decreases the complexity involved in the previously designed frameworks by providing efficient data cleaning techniques. In addition, appropriate methods have been framed to manage the outliers and missing values in the datasets. Moreover, comprehensive repositories have been provided that will be useful in incremental data cleaning.

Keywords: Data warehouse, data cleaning, data quality, data mining.

1 Introduction

Data warehouse is subject-oriented, non-volatile, time variant and integrated repository of data to aid the decision support systems of the organization [16]. Data is extracted from multiple heterogeneous operational systems of the organizations and loaded in a data warehouse under a unified schema in order to facilitate reporting and analysis. The prime aim of data warehouses is to maintain data in a manner that enables its usage for other tasks such as Data mining [12]. Data mining is referred to the process of gathering useful and valuable information from a large pool of data [14]. This process of discovering knowledge makes sense only when it discovers the information in a pure form i.e. the information obtained is correct, accurate, unambiguous and consistent. In fact, one of the key aspects of a data warehouse is to store quality enriched data. Data quality can be augmented by data cleaning techniques [2], [8], [10].

Data cleaning is the act of identifying and eradicating inconsistencies and redundancies (often called 'dirty data') from the data [15]. It is an integral component

D.C. Wyld et al. (Eds.): ACITY 2011, CCIS 198, pp. 355–364, 2011.

of a warehousing environment and its need cab be realized in database processing, updating and maintenance. While integrating data from varied information sources numerous discrepancies are generated like- discrepancies in schema formats, naming conventions, syntax errors, missing values, etc. due to numerous reasons [3], [8]. Thus, the prime goal of data cleaning is to improve the quality of data and make it as error-free as possible. A lot of data cleaning techniques have been designed to deal with the dirty data in their own way, but, only a few have been implemented so far.

In this paper we propose a novel data cleaning framework, DWCLEANSER that only handles the exact duplicate fields but also focuses on approximate duplicate data. Moreover, it provides a comprehensive metadata support to the whole cleaning process. In addition, provisions have also been suggested to take care of outliers and missing fields.

The paper is organized as follows. In the next section follows an overview of literatures being reviewed. In section 3, we briefly describe the existing framework. Section 4 highlights the major drawbacks in the existing framework. In section 5 we present our proposed framework DWCLEANSER along with the offered improvements. Our proposed algorithm has been discussed in section 6. In section 7 we draw a comparison between the existing and proposed framework. Lastly, we conclude the paper in section 8.

2 Literature Review

The framework designed in [1] is a sequential, token-based framework that offers fundamental services of data cleaning. The process comprises of six steps like- attribute selection, token formation, cluster creation, computation of similarity, eliminating duplicates and finally merging the cleaned data. The authors have provided a more detailed version of the same framework in [2] where they have discussed about the algorithms and functions to be used in each step.

In [3] the author focuses on the detection and elimination of approximate duplicates by combining three strategies namely, Smith-Waterman algorithm, Priority Queue and Union-Find structures. But, the only limitation was that author did not address the issue of handling singleton records (records that do not match any cluster).

In [5] the authors have suggested improvements in the algorithms discussed in [3]. They have suggested provisions to handle the singleton records and reduced time and space complexity involved in the whole cleaning process.

In [7] the authors have described about the merge-purge techniques where the records are initially sorted and then matched by employing a sliding window approach.

The data quality problems have been classified into single-source and multi-source in [8]. Also they have been discussed at two levels; schema-level and instance-level and emphasized integrating the need to cover schema and instance related data transformations.

The duplicate detection methods have been extended to fuzzy duplicates in [14]. Detection of fuzzy duplicate datasets is very crucial in context of analysis and integration processes.

3 Existing Framework

The framework for data cleaning has been initially designed in [1], and then, further extended in [2]. It is a token-based sequential framework basically designed for detection and elimination of duplicate data in a data warehouse. The framework comprises of six steps described below [1], [2]:

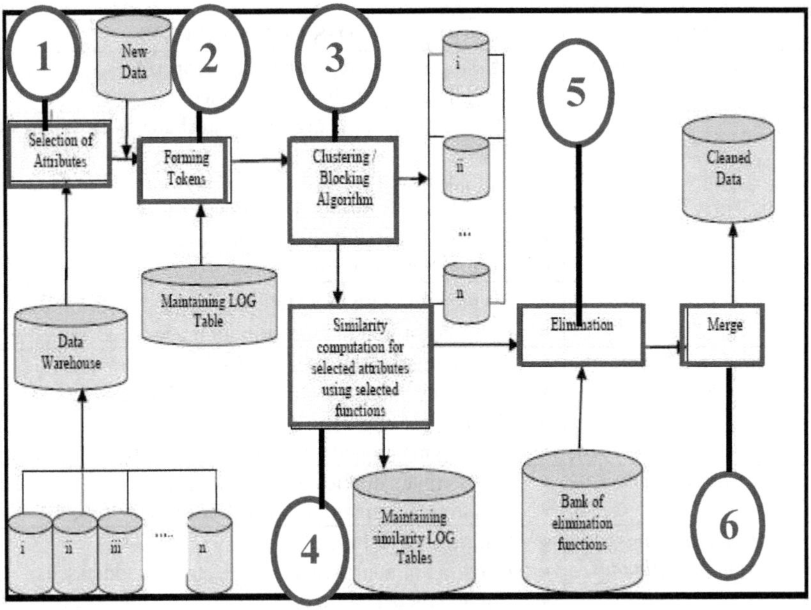

Fig. 1. Existing framework

1) **Selection of attributes:** Attributes are identified and selected for further processing in the following steps.
2) **Formation of tokens:** The selected attributes are utilized to form tokens for similarity computation.
3) **Clustering/Blocking of records:** The blocking/clustering algorithm is used to group the attributes based on the calculated similarity and block-token key.
4) **Similarity computation for selected attributes:** Jaccard similarity method is used for comparing token values of selected attributes in a field.

5) **Detection and elimination of duplicate records:** A rule based detection and elimination approach is employed for detecting and eliminating the duplicates in a cluster or in many clusters.
6) **Merge:** The cleansed data is combined and stored.

4 Pitfalls in Existing Framework

We have presented below the major drawbacks in the framework proposed in [1] and its extended work in [2]. The table summarizes the limitations of each step of the framework design discussed in the previous section.

Table 1. Pitfalls in existing approach

STEPS	DISADVANTAGES
Selection of attributes	• Missing values are not handled properly. • Not all quality attributes discussed. • More emphasis on high rank attributes what about other rankings. • Not addressed the issue that if high ranked attribute fails to detect the duplicates then what will happen. • Integrity constraints not taken into consideration • No highlight on prime attributes or key
Formation of tokens	• Limited focus on LOG tables. • Rules not stored in repository to reduce time and effort
Clustering/Blocking of records	• Approximate duplicates or match not addressed. • Block-key value selection not specified precisely. • Outliers not handled. • Nothing mentioned about the representative of the cluster.
Similarity computation	• Approximate duplicates not handled. • Handling of numeric fields not addressed properly.
Detection and elimination of duplicates	• Outliers not addressed. • Handling of approximate duplicates not addressed. • Limited metadata support.
Merge	• No method of merging specified. • Limited metadata support.

After highlighting the major pitfalls in the existing framework, we have designed a novel framework as described in the following section.

5 Proposed Framework: DWCLEANSER

We have designed an improved framework called DWCLEANSER that will be more effective in handling exact and approximate duplicate detection and their eradication. The devised framework is described below:

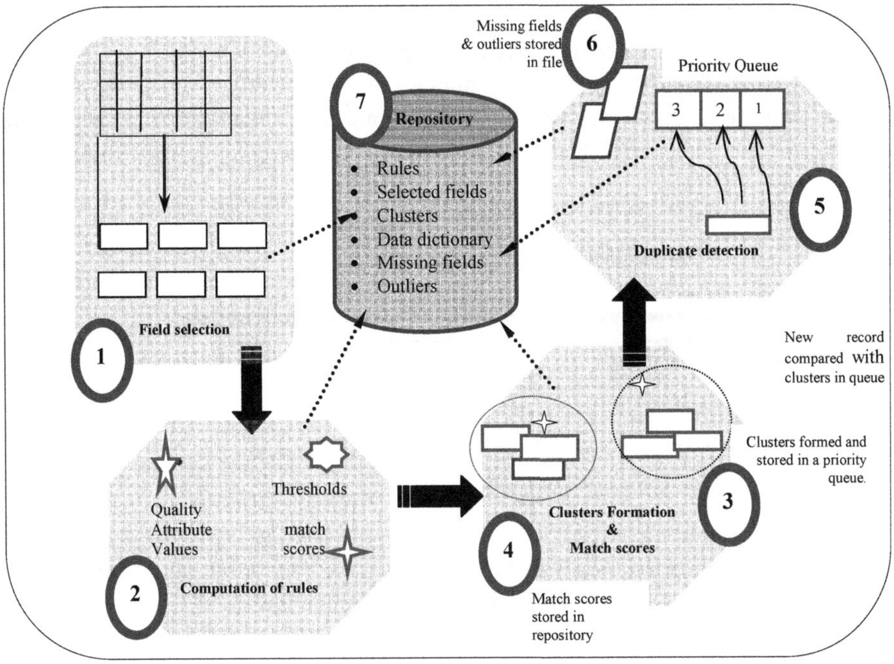

Fig. 2. Proposed Framework

5.1 Field Selection

Data is present in a warehouse in the form of records. Records consist of multiple fields. In this foundation step of the designed framework the records are decomposed into fields. Then these fields are further analyzed for gathering data about their type, relationship with other fields, key fields and integrity constraints like- key fields, checks, assertions, etc so that we have enough metadata about the decomposed fields.

While analyzing fields we might encounter missing data. Missing fields are usually interpreted as one of the following: *(1) value is missing; (2) value not known* [14]. These fields are stored in a separate temporary table and preserved in the repository along with their source record, relation name, data types and integrity constraints if any. Then, they are reviewed by the DBA to verify the reason for their existence. This is necessary because: *(1) if the data is missing it can be recaptured; (2) if the value is not known efforts can be made to gather the data to complete the record or fill the missing field with a valid value.* Moreover, if no valid data can be collected the values is preserved in the repository for further verification and not used in the cleaning procedure. Once the missing field gets filled up it can be treated the same way as other fields in the procedure.

5.2 Computation of Rules

Certain rules are computed that will be utilized during the implementation of the cleaning process. Rules and their computation methodology are as follows:

(1) *Threshold value:*
The threshold value is calculated based on the experiments conducted in [3]. Values lower than the thresholds increase the number of false positives. False positives are records detected as duplicates when in fact they are not. Values above thresholds are not able to detect all duplicates [3], [5]. Values in between can be used to recognize approximate duplicates.

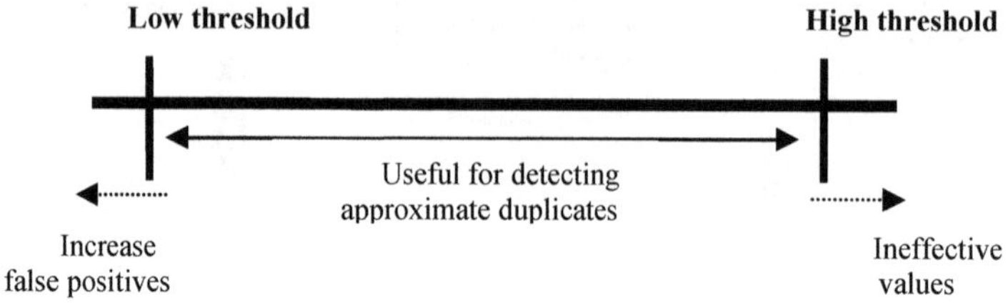

Fig. 3. Threshold values

Fields with high thresholds detect exact duplicate data sets but not always. Hence, we choose a conservative threshold value lower than the threshold so that it may help us in detecting approximate duplicates as well.

(2) *Rules for classification of fields:*
Selected fields are classified on the basis of their data types namely: numeric, characters and strings.

Numeric are the numbers or numeral value fields. Characters are only alphabetic fields. Strings are further decomposed into numeric and character fields [3].

(3) *Rules for data quality attributes:*
The previous framework only focused on 3 quality attributes of data specifically-completeness, accuracy and consistency [5]. In this framework we will formulate rules for calculating values of other quality attribute values as well.

- *Validity:* One criterion for calculating integrity is completeness as mentioned in [6], [8]. The other criterion is validity of tuples or fields in a record [8]. It is calculated as follows [8], [10]:

M= Set of entities in any mini real-world.
R= A relation

$$\textit{Validity} = \frac{\text{No. of tuples in } R \text{ representing entities in } M}{\text{Total no. of tuples in } R} \times 100$$

- *Integrity:* Another criterion for validity is integrity constraints [6], [8].

Check (integrity constraints, if any)
If there are they valid,
Done
If not then,
Review the constraints and validate them
Else
Put assertions.

5.3 Formation of Clusters

For initial cluster formation we use the recursive record matching algorithm [3] with a slight modification that here we can use it for matching of fields rather than whole record. The clusters are stored in priority queue as described in [3]. The highest priority cluster is stored as the head of the queue. Priorities of clusters in the queue are assigned on the basis of their ability to detect duplicates data sets. The cluster that detected the recent match is stored assigned the highest priority, the cluster that detected a duplicate value before it assigned next higher priority and so on [5]. A priority queue data structure provides easy and smooth access and storage mechanism [5].

5.4 Match Score

Match scores are assigned by applying Smith-Waterman algorithm as described in [3]. It is an edit-distance based strategy to assign scores to each good match or a bad miss [5]. The calculations done in this method are stored in a matrix.

5.5 Detection of Exact and Approximate Duplicates

When a new field is to be matched against any data set present in a cluster we use Union-Find structure as discussed in [3]. If it fails in detecting any match then we employ Smith-Waterman which has been described in [3], [5].

5.6 Handling of Outliers and Missing Fields

Records that do not match any of the clusters present are called "outliers". These outliers are referred as 'singleton records' in [3], [5]. These singleton records may be stored in a separate file. This file can be stored in the repository for future analysis and comparisons.

5.7 Updating Metadata/Repository

Metadata and repositories will be an integral part of our proposed framework. We will now discuss the important components of repositories in context of our framework:

1. *Data dictionary:* Will store the information about the relations, their sources, schema, etc.
2. *Rules directory:* All the calculated values of thresholds, quality attributes, matching scores, etc. are stored in this directory for any assistance.

3. *Log files:* They are used to store information about the selected fields and their source record. Another important feature about this file is that it stores the classification of the fields based on their data type explicitly under 3 categories-numeric, strings and characters.
4. *Outlier & Missing field files:* It stores the outliers and missing fields and their related information like-type, source relation, etc.

6 Proposed Algorithm for Duplicate Detection and Elimination

- *Records are decomposed into fields.*
- *Rules are computed for each and every field: optimum threshold values are selected, quality attributes are calculated and classification is made on the basis of data types.*
- *Initial clusters are formed by applying RECURSIVE RECORD MATCHING ALGORITHM in [3], [5] on the fields. And stored in a priority queue data structure. Each cluster has a representative element which is obtained by applying UNION-FIND algorithm.*
- *Whenever a record appears for matching we conduct two passes. In the first pass, it is compared with the representative field of every cluster in the queue.*
- *If a match is found. Then the field is united in that cluster. The cluster is made the head of the queue with the highest priority. Then, we apply UNION-FIND algorithm to find new representative of the cluster [3], [5].*
- *In the next pass we apply SMITH-WATERMAN TECHNIQUE [3], [5] to generate a match score so that we can detect approximate duplicates.*
- *But in case no match is found in both the passes then the field is not discarded. It is compared with the outlier fields stored in a separate file in the same fashion. If it matches with any of the outlier fields it is united with that field to form a cluster and that cluster is moved to the head of the queue.*
- *Else it is stored in the outlier file as another outlier field [5].*

7 Implementation Details

The proposed framework has been implemented in JAVA as front-end for forms & reports and ORACLE 10g as back-end for creation of data warehouse.

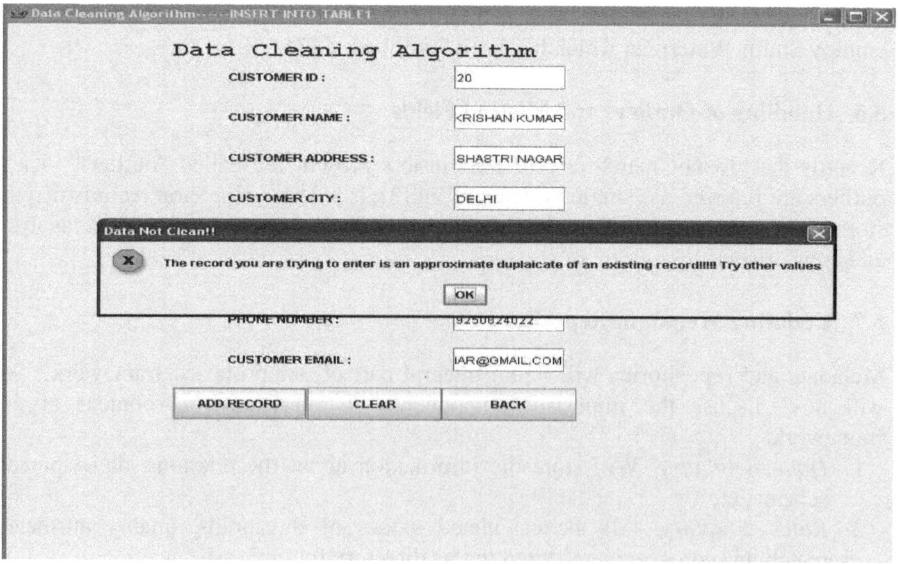

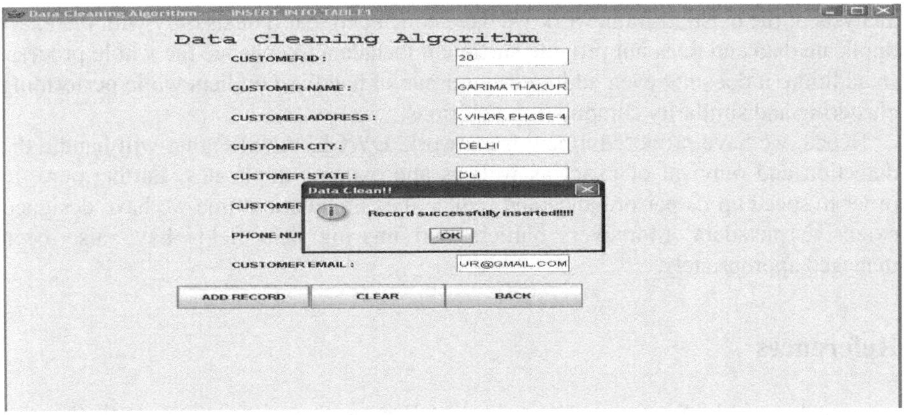

8 Comparison of Existing and Proposed Framework

Table 2. Comparison of the two frameworks

	EXISTING	DWCLEANSER
Focus	Exact duplicates	Duplicate + approximate
Outlier detection	Not addressed	Not addressed
Metadata support	Limited Support in form of LOG tables	Extensive metadata support
Quality attributes	Only 3 attributes computed	More attributes are computed
Clustering techniques	Blocking algorithm + Any clustering technique	Union-find + Priority queue algorithm
Similarity computation	Jaccard function	Edit-distance based Smith-Waterman + Recursive matching
Handling of Missing data	Not addressed	Missing data handled efficiently
Storage structures supported	Not mentioned	Files + Priority queue
Computation time	More: less metadata support, clustering algorithm not specified, similarity function takes time	Less: comprehensive metadata, edit-distance based similarity algorithm, efficient clustering algorithms

9 Conclusion

In this paper we have explored the approach and techniques being followed for detection and removal of duplicate data from a data warehouse. After a thorough analysis of the existing framework we have concluded that it deals only with the exact duplicate data and does not provide sufficient metadata to enhance the whole process. In addition, it does not even addresses the issue of handling outliers while performing clustering and similarity computation functions.

Hence, we have proposed a new framework, DWCLEANSER that will handle the detection and removal of exact as well as approximate duplicates. Furthermore, in order to speed up its performance and reduce the computation time we have designed extensive metadata. Moreover, outliers and missing data fields have also been managed appropriately.

References

1. Tamilselvi, J.J., Saravanan, V.: A Unified Framework and Sequential Data Cleaning Approach for a Data Warehouse. International Journal on Computer Science and Network Security 8 (2008)
2. Tamilselvi, J.J., Saravanan, V.: Detection and Elimination of Duplicate Data Using Token-Based Method for a Data Warehouse: A Clustering based Approach. International Journal of Computational Intelligence Research 5 (2009)
3. Monge, A.: Adaptive Detection of Approximately Duplicate Database Records and the Database Integration Approach to Information Discovery. In: Proceedings of the SIGMOND 1997 Workshop on Data Mining & Knowledge Discovery (1997)
4. Monge, A., Elkan, C.P.: The Field Matching: Problems: Algorithm and Applications. In: SIGMOND workshop on Research Issues on Knowledge Discovery and Data Mining, pp. 276–270 (1996)
5. Pahwa, P., Arora, R., Thakur, G.: An Efficient Algorithm for Data Cleaning. International Journal for Knowledge-Based Organizations (2010) (in press)
6. Marcus, A., Maletic, J.: Data Cleaning: Beyond Integrity Analysis. In: Proceedings of the Conference on Information Quality (2000)
7. Hernandez, A.M., Stolfo, S.J.: Real-World Data is Dirty: Data Cleansing and the Merge/Purge Problem. Data Mining and Knowledge Discovery 2(1), 9–37 (1998)
8. Hang-Hai, D., Erhard, R.: Data Cleaning: Problems & Current Approaches. IEEE Bulletin of the Technical Committee on Data Engineering 24, 4 (2000)
9. Ohanekwu, T., Ezeife, C.: A Token-Based Data Cleaning Technique for Data Warehouse Systems. In: IEEE Workshop on Data Quality in Cooperative Information Systems (2003)
10. Humboldt, F., Müller, H., Christoph, J.: Problems, Methods, and Challenges in Comprehensive Data Cleansing, pp. 5–12. Berlin University (2003)
11. Kononenko, I., Hong, S.J.: Attribute Selection for Modeling. Future Generation Computer Systems 13(2-3), 181–195 (1997) ISSN 0167 – 739X
12. Redman, T.: The Impact of Poor Data Quality on the Typical Enterprise. Communications of the ACM 41(2), 79–82 (1998)
13. Shahri, H.H., Shahri, S.H.: Eliminating Duplicates in Information Integration: An Adaptive Extensible Framework. IEEE Intelligent Systems 21(5), 63–71 (2006)
14. Shahri, H.H., Shahri, S.H., Hellerstein, J., Raman, V.: Potter's Wheel: An interactive Data Cleaning System. In: Proceedings of International Conference on Very Large Databases (2001)
15. Elmasri, R., Navathe, S.B.: Fundamentals of Database Systems. Addison Weasely Pub. Co., Reading (2000) ISBN 0201542633

A Dynamic Slack Management Technique for Real-Time System with Precedence and Resource Constraints

Santhi Baskaran[1] and Perumal Thambidurai[2]

[1] Department of Information Technology
[2]Department of Computer Science & Engg.,
Poncicherry Engineering College, Puducherry – 605014, India
santhibaskaran@pec.edu

Abstract. Energy consumption is a critical design issue in embedded systems, especially in battery-operated systems. Dynamic Voltage Scaling and Dynamic Frequency Scaling allow us to adjust supply voltage and processor frequency to adapt to the workload demand for better energy management. For a set of real-time tasks with precedence and resource constraints executing on a distributed embedded system, we propose a dynamic energy efficient scheduling algorithm with weighted First Come First Served (WFCFS) scheme, which also considers the run-time behaviour of tasks, to further explore the idle periods of processors. Our algorithm is compared with the Service-Rate-Proportionate (SRP) Slack Distribution Technique which uses FCFS and Weighted scheduling schemes. Our proposed algorithm achieves about 6 percent more energy savings and increased reliability over the existing one.

Keywords: Real-time system, Distributed system, Slack, Precedence constraints, Resource Constraints.

1 Introduction

Many embedded command and control systems used in manufacturing, chemical processing, avionics, telemedicine, and sensor networks are mission-critical. These systems usually comprise of applications that must accomplish certain functionalities in real-time [1]. Dynamic voltage scaling (DVS) is an effective technique to reduce CPU energy. DVS takes advantage of the quadratic relationship between supply voltage and energy consumption, which can result in significant energy savings. By reducing processor clock frequency and supply voltage, it is possible to reduce the energy consumption at the cost of performance of processors [2]. Battery powered portable systems have been widely used in many applications. As the quantity and the functional complexity of battery powered portable devices continue to rise, energy-efficient design of such devices has become increasingly important. Also these systems have to concurrently perform a multitude of complex tasks under stringent time constraints. Thus minimizing power consumption and extending battery lifespan while guaranteeing the timing constraints has become a critical aspect in designing such systems. The focus is on task scheduling algorithms to meet timing constraint while minimizing system energy consumption.

D.C. Wyld et al. (Eds.): ACITY 2011, CCIS 198, pp. 365–374, 2011.

In order to make energy efficient, in the scheduling, the execution time of the tasks can be extended up to the worst case delay for each task set. The time gap between the actual execution time and the deadline is called slack time [3]. In real-time system designs, Slack Management is increasingly applied to reduce energy consumption and optimize the system with respect to its performance and time overheads.. In this paper homogeneous distributed embedded systems executing a set of dependent tasks of a real-time application, which are normally represented by a task graph, is considered. The algorithm aims to reduce the energy consumption without missing any deadlines for a hard real-time task and with minimum deadline misses for soft real-time tasks [4]. Resources should be allocated efficiently among tasks and also care should be taken to see that no deadlock occurs [5]. Therefore it is necessary to introduce resource management mechanisms that can adapt to dynamic changes in resource availability and requirement.

This paper is organized in the following way. The related work is addressed in Section 2. The various models used in this work are described in Section 3. Proposed algorithm is described in Section 4. Section 5 discusses the simulation and analysis of results. Finally Section 6 concludes this paper with future work.

2 Related Work

The two most commonly used techniques that can be used for energy minimization in distributed embedded systems are Dynamic Voltage Scaling (DVS) [6] and Dynamic Power Management (DPM) [7]. The application of these system-level energy management techniques can be exploited to the maximum if we can take advantage of almost all of the idle time and slack time in between processor busy times. Hence, the major challenge is to design an efficient scheduling algorithm which can exploit the slack time and idle time of processors in the distributed embedded systems to the maximum. Various energy-efficient slack management schemes have been proposed for these real-time distributed systems. The static scheduling algorithm uses critical path analysis and distributes the slack during the initial schedule [8]. The dynamic scheduling algorithm [9] provides best effort service to soft aperiodic tasks and reduces power consumption by varying voltage and frequencies. Resource adaptation techniques for energy management in distributed real-time systems need to be coordinated to meet global energy and real-time requirements. This issue is addressed based on feedback-based techniques [10],[11] to allocate the overall slack in the entire system.

One of the existing work for distributed embedded real-time system uses Service Rate Proportionate (SRP) slack distribution technique[12] for energy efficiency. Both the Dynamic and the Rate-Based scheduling schemes have been examined with this technique. It introduces SRP a dynamic slack management technique to reduce power consumption. The SRP technique improves performance/overhead by 29 percent compared to contemporary techniques. The existing system do not consider resource constraints among the dependent tasks. Hence to consider resource constraints among dependent real-time tasks, a scheduling algorithm known as Weighted First Come First Served (WFCFS) with an efficient dynamic slack management technique is proposed, such that energy efficiency of the processors increases still maintaining the precedence, resource and timing constraints.

3 Models

In this section, we briefly discuss the system, application, precedence, resource and slack management models that we have used in our work.

3.1 System and Application Model

A distributed embedded system with p homogeneous processors each with its private memory is considered for scheduling the given real-time application. The system requires the complete details of the task processing times (i.e.) the execution time and deadline before program execution. Each processing element (PE) in the system is voltage scalable and, can support continuous voltage and speed changes. We assume that the energy consumption, when the processor is idle, is ignored.

The real-time applications can be modeled by a task graph G = (V,E), where V is the set of vertices each of which represents one computation (task), and E is the set of directed edges that represent the data dependencies between vertices. For each directed edge (v_i, v_j), there is a significant inter-processor communication (IPC) cost when the data from vertex v_i in one PE is transmitted to vertex v_j in another PE. The data communication cost in the same processor can be ignored. Each real-time application has an end-to-end deadline D, by which it has to complete its execution and produce the result.

The frequency selection is influenced by making a task more or less urgent by shifting its deadline back and forth. The range within which the local deadline at node i can be varied is bounded by [S_i−,S_i+]. The values for S can be derived from the local task parameters. If $wcet_i$ represents the worst case execution times of the local task at node i, then

$$S_i^- = wcet_i$$

$$S_i^+ = D - \sum_{j=i+1}^{n} wcet_j$$

3.2 Precedence Model

Tasks of a real-time application considered in this paper have precedence constraints. For example, a task T_i can become eligible for execution only after a task T_j has completed because T_i may require T_j's results. For implementing precedence constraints DAG is used.

Precedence constraints between tasks can also be modelled as resource dependencies. The precedence constraint that T_j precedes T_i is equivalent to the situation where T_i requires a logical resource (before it can start its execution) that is available only after T_j has completed its execution.

Thus, if T_j has completed its execution before T_i arrives, then this logical resource is immediately available for T_i and T_i becomes eligible to execute upon arrival. Furthermore, if T_j has not completed its execution when T_i arrives, then the logical resource is not available and, therefore, T_i is conceptually blocked upon arrival. Later, when T_j completes its execution, the logical resource becomes available and T_i is unblocked.

3.3 Resource Model

To model non-CPU resources and resource requests, we make the following assumptions:

1) Resources are reusable and can be shared, but have mutual exclusion constraints. Thus, only one task can be using a resource at any given time. This applies to physical resources, such as disks and network segments, as well as logical resources, such as critical code sections that are guarded by semaphores.
2) Only a single instance of a resource is present in the system. This requires that a task explicitly specify which resource it wants to access. This is exactly the same resource model as assumed in protocols such as the Priority Inheritance Protocol and Priority Ceiling Protocol [13].
3) A task can only request a single instance of a resource. If multiple resources are needed for a task to make progress, it must acquire all the resources through a set of consecutive resource requests. In general, the requested time intervals of holding resources may be overlapped.
4) We assume that a task can explicitly release resources before the end of its execution. Thus, it is necessary for a task that is requesting a resource to specify the time to hold the requested resource. We refer to this time as HoldTime [14]. The scheduler uses the HoldTime information at run time to make scheduling decisions.

3.4 Slack Management Model

In real-time system designs, slack management is increasingly applied to reduce power consumption and optimize the system with respect to its performance and time overheads. This slack management technique exploits the idle time and slack time of the system through DVS in order to achieve the highest possible energy consumption. In energy efficient scheduling, the set of tasks will have certain deadline before which they should finish their execution and hence there is always a time gap between the actual execution time and the deadline. It is called slack time.

Conventional real-time systems are usually over estimated to schedule and provide resources using the wcet. In average case, real-time tasks rarely execute up to their worst case execution time (wcet). In many applications, actual case execution time (acet) is often a small fraction of their wcet. However, such slack times are only known at runtime through resource reclaimers. This slack is passed to schedulers to determine whether the next job should utilize the slack time or not.

The main challenge is to obtain and distribute the available slack in order to achieve the highest possible energy savings with minimum overhead. But most of these do not address dynamic task inputs. Only a few that attempt to handle dynamic task inputs assume no resource constraints among tasks. But in reality, few tasks need exclusive accesses to a resource. In exclusive mode no two real-time tasks are allowed to share a common resource. If a resource is accessed by a real-time task, it is not left free until the task's execution is completed. Other tasks in need of the same resource must wait until the resource gets freed. Our proposed algorithm handles this issue through the Restriction Vector (RV) [15] algorithm.

Our slack management algorithm decides when and at which voltage should each task be executed in order to reduce the system's energy consumption while meeting the timing and other constraints. Our solution includes two phases: First we use static power management schemes based on wcet to statically assign a time slot to each task. Then we apply dynamic scheduling algorithm to further reduce energy consumption by exploiting the slack arising from the run-time execution time variation. Here a small amount of slack time called unit slack is added to all the tasks and finally we find the subset of tasks that can be allocated this slack time so that total energy consumption is minimized while the deadline constraint is also met.

4 Proposed System

We proposed a new algorithm called Weighted FCFS which increases the efficiency of the system by reducing the total energy consumption. In addition to this, deadline hit ratio is a major factor to be considered in a soft real-time system for better QoS. Our proposed algorithm increases the deadline hit ratio and there by improving the quality of the system.

4.1 System Architecture

Number of tasks and processors are taken as input from the user. Random generator module generates input task parameters required for the scheduling algorithms. The directed acyclic graph is also generated randomly.

In the weighted FCFS method weight is assigned to each task based on the number of tasks on which it depends. First the tasks are inserted into the queue in the non decreasing order of the arrival time. Then the tasks in the queue are sorted according to the increasing order of their weight.

4.2 Restriction Vector (RV) Algorithm

Resource reclaiming [16] refers to the problem of utilizing resources left unused by a task when it executes less than its wcet, because of data-dependent loops and

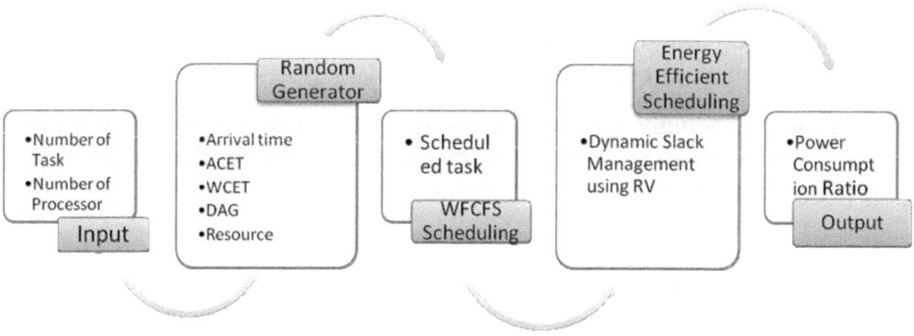

Fig. 1. Overall Architecture of the System

conditional statements in the task code or architectural features of the system, such as cache hits and branch predictions, or both. Resource reclaiming is used to adapt dynamically to these unpredictable situations so as to improve the system's resource utilization and thereby improve its schedulability.

The resource reclaiming algorithm used is a restriction vector (RV) based algorithm proposed in [15] for tasks having resource and precedence constraints. Two data structures namely restriction vector (RV) and completion bit matrix (CBM) are used in the RV algorithm. Each task T_i has an associated p component vector, $RV_i[1 \ldots p]$, where p is the number of processors. $RV_i[j]$ for a task T_i contains the last task in $T_{<i}(j)$ that must be completed before the execution of T_i begins, where $T_{<i}(j)$ denotes the set of tasks assigned to processor P_j that are scheduled in feasible schedule (pre-run schedule) to finish before T_i starts. CBM is an n X p Boolean matrix indicating whether a task has completed execution, where n is the number of tasks in the feasible schedule.

4.3 Dynamic Slack Management Algorithm

The dynamic slack management algorithm for energy efficiency contains three major functions. The first one assigns tasks to the PEs of distributed embedded system. The second function deals with dynamic slack management. The third function calculates the power consumption ratio.

5 Simulation and Analysis of Results

A simulator was developed to simulate voltage scalable processor which dynamically adjusts the processor speed according to the proposed algorithm. A continuous voltage scaling model is used and hence the processor speed can be adjusted continuously from its maximum speed to a minimum speed which is assumed to be 25% of its maximum speed.

For simulation, scheduling task sets and task graphs are generated using the following approach:

- Task sets are randomly generated with parameters such as arrival time, acet, wcet and resource constraints.
- The wcet is taken randomly and acet is also randomly generated such that it is 40 to 100 percent of wcet.
- The overall deadline is generated such that it is always greater than or equal to the sum of acet of all the tasks in DAG.

Task graph is randomly generated using adjacency matrix where 0 represents the tasks that are not dependent on any other tasks and 1 represents the dependency, with varying breadth and depth.

5.1 Performance Parameters

The performance parameters considered for evaluating and comparing our system with the existing system are Deadline Hit ratio and Power Consumption Ratio.

$$\text{Deadline hit ratio} = \frac{\text{Number of times the system meets the deadline}}{\text{Total number of execution}}$$

Deadline hit is defined as the number of input tasks which completes its execution process before its deadline. Deadline hit ratio is defined as the ratio of number of times the system meets the deadline to the total number of execution.

Power consumption ratio is defined as the ratio of power consumed by actual execution time to the power consumed by the sum of actual execution time and slack time.

5.2 Results and Discussion

The comparison of energy consumption between the existing and the proposed algorithms were analyzed. For each set of tasks (varied between 5 to 50) the number of processors is kept constant and the energy consumption for a minimum of ten DAGs are noted. The average values of all those DAGs were calculated. This method was repeated by changing the number of processors and comparison was made between the existing and the proposed algorithms.

Table 1 picturises the power consumed by the existing and proposed algrithms. If the number of processors in the distributed embedded system is two the algorithms were not able to schedule more than 10 tasks, as all task set cases above 10 missed their deadline. From the table it is seen that the average power consumption of the proposed algorithm is 6 percent more than the exixting ones.

Table 1. Comparison of power Consumption between Existing (FCFS,WS) and Proposed (WFCFS) Algorithms

No. of Tasks	P=2			P=4			P=6			P=8			Power Consumption (%)		
	FCFS	WS	WFCFS	FCFS	WS	WFCFS	FCFS	WS	WFCFS	FCFS	WS	WFCFS	FCFS	WS	WFCFS
5	74.8	76.1	71.8	70.7	83.7	74.3	63.3	62.0	60.0	63.3	62	59.0	68.0	70.9	66.0
10	76.6	74.1	76.2	60.3	66.8	62.9	52.3	50.0	57.6	45.4	45.9	42.2	58.7	59.2	59.7
15				51.2	54.4	66.0	55.5	56.7	55.5	47.7	50.3	39.9	51.5	53.8	53.8
20				68.8	72.9	63.6	61.4	58.9	54.5	50.9	59.5	47.3	60.4	63.8	55.1
25				79.0	81.4	68.4	68.6	74.6	59.7	67.1	65.5	60.8	71.5	73.9	63.0
30				80.5	80.0	69.1	72.9	73.1	56.7	67.6	64.2	55.3	73.7	72.4	60.4
35				85.2	85.7	78.7	77.7	77.1	63.0	73.5	70.1	62.7	78.8	77.6	68.1
40				82.5	79.1	76.8	79.0	77.8	71.4	72.2	76.4	60.8	77.9	77.8	69.7
45				85.5	87.6	79.5	78.4	80.8	76.0	79.2	75.4	69.9	81.0	81.3	75.1
50				82.9	87.1	84.9	82.1	82.1	83.1	77.8	81.3	75.0	80.9	83.5	81.0
Average Power Consumption													**70.2**	**71.4**	**65.2**

The deadline hit ratio is also compared among the existing and proposed algorithms by varying the number of tasks from 5 to 50 and the number of processors from 2 to 10. The maximum number of tasks is taken to be 50, because real-time applications with dependent tasks above 50 is very very rare. The number of processors is also limited to 10, as this number itself rare for a distributed embedded system. For sample, the comparison for deadline hit ratio when number of processors p = 4 is shown in Fig. 2. Upto p = 6 the proposed algorithm gives better deadline hit ratio compared to the existing ones. For p>=7, all the algorithms resulted in 100% deadline hit ratio.

Similarly, the comparison for power consumption ratio when number of processors p = 6 is shown in Fig. 3 as a sample. For all cases from p = 2 to 10, proposed algorithm WFCFS with the dynamic slack management technique consumed less power than the existing FCFS and Weighted Scheduling algorithms with the SRP slack management technique, when resource contraint is added to the real-time application in addition to the precedence and time constraints.

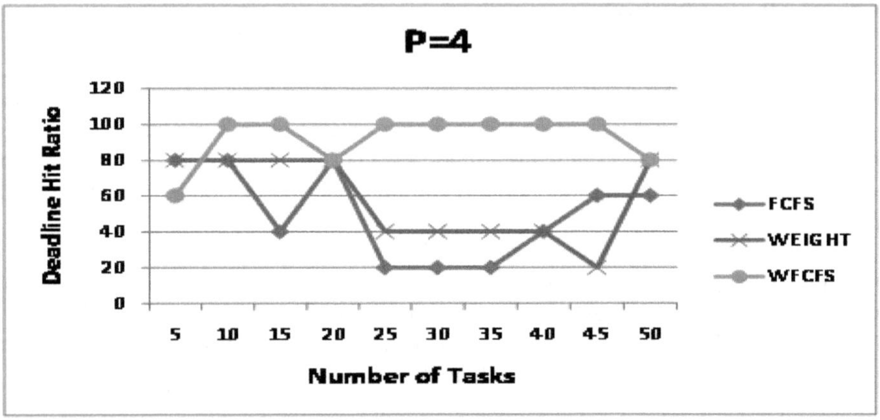

Fig. 2. Comparison Of Deadline Hit Ratio For Existing (FCFS, Weight) and Proposed (Weighted FCFS) Algorithms for No. of Processors (p) is 4

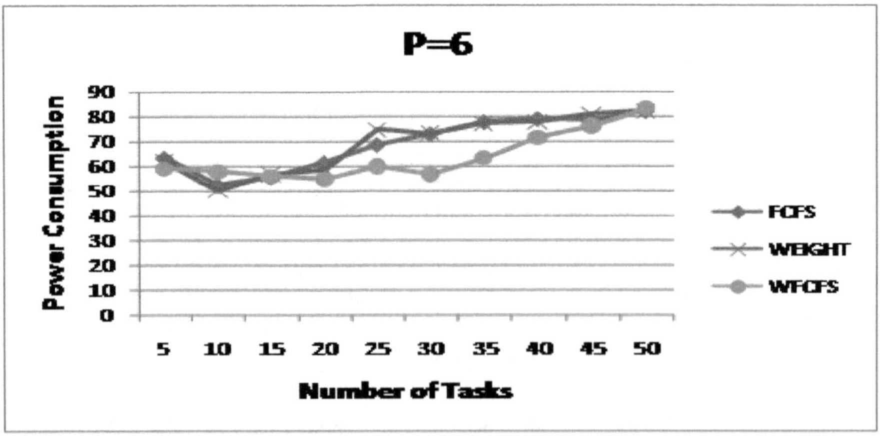

Fig. 3. Comparison of Power Consumption Ratio between Existing (FCFS, Weight) and Proposed (Weighted FCFS) Algorithms for No. of Processors (p) is 6

6 Conclusion

In this work, an energy efficient real-time scheduling algorithm for distributed embedded systems is presented. This scheduling algorithm is capable of handling task graphs with precedence and resource constraints in addition to timing constraints. The major contribution of this work is the development of modified FCFS scheduling algorithm called Weighted FCFS. The proposed dynamic slack distribution technique efficiently utilizes the available slack and in turn increases the efficiency of the system. It also exploits the idle intervals by putting the processor in power down modes to reduce the power consumption. The proposed system increases the deadline hit ratio when compared to the existing system and thus increases the reliability. Simulation results show that almost 6 percent less power is consumed by the proposed algorithm compared with the existing algorithms.

Fault tolerant issues may be considered for such real-time distributed embedded systems as future enhancement. Another important future work may be extending this technique for a heterogeneous distributed real-time system.

References

1. Mahapatra, R.N., Zhao, W.: An Energy-Efficient Slack Distribution Technique for Multimode Distributed Real-Time Embedded Systems. IEEE Transactions on Parallel and Distributed Systems 16(7) (July 2005)
2. Xian, C., Lu, Y.-H., Li, Z.: Dynamic Voltage Scaling for Multitasking Real-Time Systems with Uncertain Execution Times. IEEE Transactions on Computer-Aided Design of Integrated Circuits and Systems 27(8) (August 2008)
3. Acharya, S., Mahapatra, R.N.: A Dynamic Slack Management Technique for Real-Time Distributed Embedded Systems. IEEE Transactions on Computers 57(2) (2008)
4. Yuan, W., Nahrstedt, K.: Energy-efficient soft real-time CPU scheduling for mobile multimedia systems. In: ACM Symposium on Operating Systems Principles, pp. 149–163 (2003)
5. Shen, C., Ramamritham, K., Stankovic, J.A.: Resource reclaiming in multiprocessor real-time systems. IEEE Transactions on Parallel and Distributed Systems 4(4), 382–397 (1993)
6. Ishihara, T., Yasuura, H.: Voltage Scheduling Problem for Dynamically Variable Voltage Processors. In: International Symposium on Low Power Electronics and Design, pp. 197–202 (1998)
7. Benini, L., Bogliolo, A., De Micheli, G.: A Survey of Design Techniques for System-Level Dynamic Power Management. IEEE Transactions on VLSI Systems, 299–316 (2000)
8. Jorgensen, P.B., Madsen, J.: Critical path driven co synthesis for heterogeneous target architectures. In: International Workshop on Hardware/ Software Code, pp. 15–19 (1997)
9. Schmitz, M.T., Al-Hashimi, B.M.: Considering power variations of DVS processing elements for energy minimization in distributed systems. In: International Symposium on System Synthesis, pp. 250–255 (2001)
10. Lu, C., Stankovic, J.A., Tao, G., Son, S.H.: Feedback Control Real- Time Scheduling: Framework, Modeling, and Algorithms. Real-Time Systems Journal, Special Issue on Control-Theoretical Approaches to Real-Time Computing, 85–126 (2002)

11. Baskaran, S., Thambidurai, P.: Power Aware Scheduling for Resource Constrained Distributed Real Time Systems. International Journal on Computer Science and Engineering 02(05), 1746–1753 (2010)
12. Acharya, S., Mahapatra, R.N.: A Dynamic Slack Management Technique for Real-Time Distributed Embedded Systems. IEEE Transactions on Computers 57(2) (2008)
13. Sha, L., Rajkumar, R., Lehoczky, J.P.: Priority Inheritance Protocols: An Approach to Real-Time Synchronization. IEEE Transactions on Computers 39(9), 1175–1185 (1990)
14. Li, P., Wu, H., Ravindran, B., Douglas Jensen, E.: A Utility Accrual Scheduling Algorithm for Real-Time Activities with Mutual Exclusion Resource Constraints. IEEE Transactions on Computers 55(4) (2006)
15. Manimaran, G., Siva ram Murthy, C., Vijay, M., Ramamritham, K.: New algorithms for resource reclaiming from precedence constrained tasks in multiprocessor real-time systems. Journal of Parallel and Distributed Computing 44(2), 123–132 (1997)
16. Shen, C., Ramamritham, K., Stankovic, J.A.: Resource reclaiming in multiprocessor real-time systems. IEEE Transactions on Parallel and Distributed Systems 4(4), 382–397 (1993)

Multi-level Local Binary Pattern Analysis for Texture Characterization

R. Suguna[1] and P. Anandhakumar[2]

[1] Research Scholar, Department of Information Technology
[2] Associate Professor, Department of Information Technology,
Madras Institute of Technology,
Anna University, Chennai-600 044, Tamil Nadu, India
hitec_suguna@hotmail.com, anandh@annauniv.edu

Abstract. Texture is the core element in numerous computer vision applications. The objective of this paper is to present a novel methodology for learning and recognizing textures. A local binary pattern (LBP) operator offers an efficient way of analyzing textures. A multi-level local binary pattern operator which is an extension of LBP is proposed for extracting texture feature from the images. The operator finds the association of LBP operators at multiple levels. This association helps to identify macro features. Depending on the size of the operator, octets are framed and LBP responses of the octets are noted. Their occurrence histograms are combined to frame the texture descriptor. The proposed operator is gray-scale invariant. The operator is computationally simple since it can be realized with few operations in the local neighborhood. A non-parametric statistic named G-Statistic is used in the classification phase. The classifier is trained with images of known texture class to build a model for that class. Experimental results prove that the approach provides good discrimination between the textures.

Keywords: Texture Classification, Multi-level Local Binary pattern, Non-parametric classifier.

1 Introduction

Texture can be used as a measure for interpreting the images. Texture can be regarded as the visual appearance of a surface or material and the visual appearance of the view is captured with digital imaging and stored as image pixels. For a well-defined texture, intensity variations normally exhibit both regularity and randomness, and therefore texture analysis requires careful design of statistical measures. The degrees of randomness and of regularity will be the key measure when characterizing a texture. A surface is taken to be textured if there are large numbers of texture elements (or 'texels') present in it. The components of a texture, the texels, are uniform micro-objects that are placed in an appropriate way to form any particular texture. Image resolution is also very important in texture perception since low-resolution images normally contain very homogenous textures. Textures provide discriminatory information and assists in pattern recognition and segmentation tasks.

D.C. Wyld et al. (Eds.): ACITY 2011, CCIS 198, pp. 375–386, 2011.

Texture plays an important role in natural vision, and it has been widely applied to several surface characterization problems. Haralick et al. [1] applied texture analysis methods to remotely sensed images for doing terrain analysis. They attempted to classify regions of images to predefined classes to form a description of the sensed scene. Oliver [2] used texture analysis and classified regions of SAR images to forest and non-forest classes. Texture has also been utilized for characterizing the surface of more concrete objects. Most of the real-world applications utilize texture analysis. In biomedical engineering and medical image analysis texture has been used for different purposes. Characterization of textured materials is usually very difficult and the goal of characterization depends on the application. The ultimate goal of texture characterization systems is to classify textures into different categories or to recognize different textures.

Typically methods for texture analysis are divided into two main categories with different computational approaches: the stochastic and the structural methods. Structural textures are often man-made and have very regular appearance, for example, of line or square primitive patterns that are systematically located on the surface (e.g. brick walls). In structural texture analysis the properties and the appearance of the textures are described with different rules to specify the kind of primitive elements present in the surface and their location details. Stochastic textures are usually natural and consist of randomly distributed texture elements, which again can be, for example, lines or curves but placed at random (e.g. tree bark). The analysis of these kinds of textures is based on statistical properties of image pixels and regions. There exists other categorization of textures, for example, artificial vs. natural, or micro textures vs. macro textures. Irrespective of the categorization, texture analysis methods try to describe the properties of the textures in a proper way. It depends on the applications what kind of properties should be sought from the textures under inspection and how to do that. This is rarely an easy task.

Applications have different requirements for recognition: usually accuracy is the most important property, but sometimes also speed, usability and configurability should be prioritized. There is no universal recognition method for different texture characterization tasks. In most general image analysis tasks, texture recognition methods must detect different textures in the images, but also consider images on a higher level.

To exploit texture in applications, the measures should be accurate in detecting different texture structures, but still be invariant or robust with varying conditions that affect the texture appearance. Computational complexity should not be too high to preserve realistic use of the methods. Different applications set various requirements on the texture analysis methods, and usually selection of measures is done with respect to the specific application. One of the major problems when developing texture measures is to include invariant properties in the features. In a real-world environment, it is very common that illumination changes over time, and causes variations in the texture appearance. Texture primitives may also rotate and locate in many different ways, which also causes problems. On the other hand, if the features are too invariant, they might not be discriminative enough.

2 Related Work

The gray-level co-occurrence matrix approach is based on studies of the statistics of pixel intensity distributions. The early paper by Haralick et al.[3] presented 14 texture measures and these were used successfully for classification of many types of materials for example, wood, corn, grass and water. However, Conners and Harlow [4] found that only five of these measures were normally used, viz. "energy", "entropy", "correlation", "local homogeneity", and "inertia". However, the size of the co-occurrence matrix is high and suitable choice of d (distance) and θ (angle) has to be made for successful texture classification.

A novel texture energy approach is presented by Laws [5]. This involved the application of simple filters to digital images. The basic filters used were common Gaussian, edge detector, and Laplacian-type filters and they tried to highlight points of high "texture energy" in the image. Ade tried for a revised approach and developed a method using eigen filters[6]. Each eigenvalue that exhibited the variance of the original image were extracted by the corresponding filter. The filters that give rise to low variances were considered as unimportant for texture recognition.

Recent developments include the work with automated visual inspection in work. Manthalkar et al., [7] aimed at rotation invariant texture classification and Pun and Lee [8] aimed at scale invariance. Local frequency analysis had been used for texture analysis.

Ojala T & Pietikäinen M [9] proposed a multichannel approach to texture description by approximating joint occurrences of multiple features with marginal distributions, as 1-D histograms, and combining similarity scores for 1-D histograms into an aggregate similarity score. Ojala T introduced a generalized approach to the gray scale and rotation invariant texture classification method based on local binary patterns [10]. The current status of a new initiative aimed at developing a versatile framework and image database for empirical evaluation of texture analysis algorithms is presented by him.

Another frequently used approach in texture description is using distributions of quantized filter responses to characterize the texture (Leung and Malik), (Varma and Zisserman) [11][12]. Ahonen T, proved that the local binary pattern operator can be seen as a filter operator based on local derivative filters at different orientations and a special vector quantization function [13]. A rotation invariant extension to the blur insensitive local phase quantization texture descriptor is presented by Ojansivu V [14].

3 An Overview of Local Binary Pattern

The local binary pattern (LBP) operator is a very powerful and gray-scale invariant method of analyzing textures. The LBP operator usually combines characteristics of statistical and structural texture analysis. It describes the texture with micro-primitives, often called textons, and their statistical placement rules. Ojala *et al.* (1996) introduced the LBP texture feature to complement and improve the performance of the local image contrast measure. For each pixel in an image, a binary code is produced by thresholding its neighborhood (8 pixels) with the value of the center pixel. A histogram is then constructed to collect up the occurrences of different binary patterns representing different types of curved edges, spots, flat areas etc. tons, and their statistical placement rules.

The original 8-bit version of the LBP operator considers only the eight nearest neighbors of each pixel and it is rotation variant, but invariant to monotonic changes in gray-scale. The dimensionality of the LBP feature distribution can be calculated according to the number of neighbors used. The basic 8-bit LBP can represent 2^8 different local patterns, so the dimensionality of the feature vector is 256. Later, the definiton of the LBP was extended to arbitrary circular neighborhoods of the pixel to achieve multi-scale analysis and rotation invariance (Ojala et al. 2002)[15]. The neighborhood of the center pixel is considered to be circular, and P neighbor samples are selected from the circular perimeter of radius R. Neighbor samples were interpolated on the circle with equal space. In the multi resolution model of the LBP, separate operators at different scales are constructed and the final feature vector is obtained by concatenating individual feature vectors one after another.

Maenpaa et al. [15] introduced the concept of 'uniform' patterns, where the maximum number of bit-wise changes from one to zero or vice versa in the circular neighborhood is limited. Usually the maximum number of bit changes was allowed to be two. With this approach, the number of different binary codes is reduced dramatically, but the discrimination performance remained good.

The derivation of the LBP follows that was represented by Ojala et al. [15]. Texture T is defined as the joint distribution of the gray levels of P+1 (P>0) image pixels:

$$T = t(g_c, g_0, g_1, \ldots, g_{P-1}), \tag{1}$$

where g_c corresponds to the gray value of the center pixel of a local neighborhood. $g_p(p=0,1,2,\ldots,P-1)$ correspond to the gray values of P equally spaced pixels on a circle of radius R (R>0) that form a circularly symmetric set of neighbors.

3.1 Achieving Gray-Scale Invariance

Without losing information, g_c is subtracted from g_p :

$$T = t(g_c, g_0-g_c, g_1-g_c, \ldots, g_{P-1}-g_c) \tag{2}$$

Assuming that the differences are independent of g_c , the distribution is factorized:

$$T = t(g_c)t(g_0-g_c, g_1-g_c, \ldots, g_{P-1}-g_c) \tag{3}$$

Since $t(g_c)$ described the overall luminance of an image, which is unrelated to local image texture, it was ignored and T is represented as

$$T = t(g_0-g_c, g_1-g_c, \ldots, g_{P-1}-g_c) \tag{4}$$

To achieve invariance with respect to any monotonic transformation of the gray scale, only the signs of the differences are considered:

$$T = t(s(g_0-g_c), s(g_1-g_c), \ldots, s(g_{P-1}-g_c)) \tag{5}$$

where

$$s(x) = \begin{cases} 1, x \geq 0 \\ 0, x < 0 \end{cases} \tag{6}$$

Now, a binomial weight 2^p is assigned to each sign $s(g_P-g_c)$ transforming the differences in a neighborhood into a unique LBP code:

$$LBP_{P,R} = \sum_{p=0}^{P-1} s(g_p - g_c)2^p \tag{7}$$

3.2 Achieving Rotation Invariance

For rotation invariance, a transformation was defined as follows:

$$LBP_{P,R}^{ri} = min\{ROR(LBP_{P,R}, i) | i = 0,1, \ldots, P-1\} \tag{8}$$

where the superscript ri stands for "rotation invariant". The function $ROR(x, i)$, circularly shifts the P-bit binary number x, i times to the right.

The concept of "uniform" patterns was introduced in Mäenpää et al [15]. It was observed that certain patterns seem to be fundamental properties of texture, providing the vast majority of patterns, sometimes over 90%. These patterns are called as "uniform" because they have at most two one-to-zero or zero-to-one transitions in the circular binary code.

A uniformity measure U was used to define the "uniformity" of a neighborhood G:

$$U(G_p) = |s(g_{p-1} - g_c) - s(g_0 - g_c)| + \sum_{p=1}^{P-1} |s(g_p - g_c) - s(g_{p-1} - g_c)| \tag{9}$$

Patterns with a U value of less than or equal to two were designated as "uniform". For a bit P bit binary number, the U value was calculated as follows:

$$U(x) = \sum_{p=0}^{P-1} F(x \, xor \, ROR(x, i), p) \tag{10}$$

where x is a binary number. The function (x, i) , extracts the ith bit from a binary number x :

$$F(x, i) = ROR(x, i) \, and \, 1 \tag{11}$$

The rotation invariant uniform $(riu2)$ pattern code for any "uniform" pattern is calculated by simply counting ones in the binary number. All other patterns are labeled "miscellaneous" and given a separate value:

$$LBP_{P,R}^{riu2} = \begin{cases} \sum_{p=0}^{P-1} s(g_p - g_c), U(G_p) \leq 2 \\ P + 1. otherwise \end{cases} \tag{12}$$

4 Proposed Multi Level Local Binary Pattern

An operator is devised by enlarging the spatial support area and combining the association of LBP responses. Existing LBP quantifies the occurrence statistics of individual rotation invariant patterns corresponding to certain micro-features such as spots, flat areas and edges. In our work, we have extended this to capture macro-features. For a given block of image, the squared neighborhood is considered to obtain the LBP value. The LBP operators of size 5x5 and 7x7 are considered for the study. For each operator of specific size, the neighbors of centre pixel are grouped in octets and for each octet the LBP value is computed. Their occurrence histograms are concatenated to form the feature vector. The grouping of neighbors for different operator sizes is shown in Fig. 1.

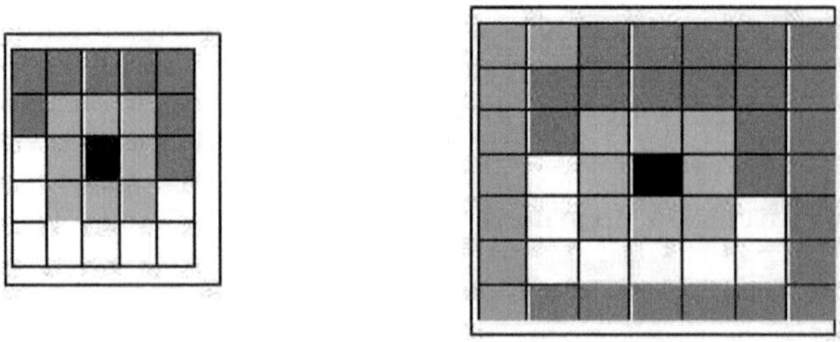

Fig. 1. Octet Representation of 5x5 and 7x7 Operator (Black box represents the centre pixel and other gray shades represent octets)

Our proposed approach has two phases :

- Building a model for Textures
- Recognition of Textures

4.1 Building a Model for Texture Class

Learning of Textures involves capturing the descriptors of each category and building a model for that. The algorithm for building a model for the texture class is given below.

1. For each training image of class Ci
   Perform block processing depending on Operator size
   For each block of the training image
   Extract LBP code for octets
2. Compute the occurrence frequency of LBP Codes for each octet
3. Combine the responses to form a feature vector
4. Build the model probability of that class.

4.2 Recognition of Texture

A non parametric classifier is used to classify the unknown sample. Each sample undergoes block processing and LBP codes are extracted from the octets. The occurrence frequency responses are combined to generate the feature vector of the sample. This is compared with the model histograms of the texture class using G-Statistic measure.

4.3 Non parametric Classification Principle

In classification, the dissimilarity between a sample and a model LBP distribution is measured with a non-parametric statistical test. This measure is called as G statistic and is given as

$$G(S,M) = 2\sum_{b=1}^{B} S_b log\frac{S_b}{M_b} = 2\sum_{b=1}^{B}[S_b logS_b - S_b logM_b] \quad (13)$$

where S and M denote (discrete) sample and model distributions respectively. S_b and $M_b$correspond to the probability of bin b in the sample and model distributions. B is the number of bins in the distributions.

In the classification setting, each class is represented with a single model distribution M^i. Similarly, an unidentified sample texture can be described by the distribution S. L is a pseudo-metric that measures the likelihood that the sample S is from class i . The most likely class C of an unknown sample can thus be described by a simple nearest-neighbor rule:

$$C = {}^{\arg min}{}_{i}L(S, M^{i}) \tag{14}$$

5 Experiments and Results

We demonstrate the performance of our approach with two different problems of texture analysis. Experiment #1 is conducted on datasets to study the performance of the proposed operator for texture classification. Image data includes 16 source textures captured from the Outex database. Experiment #2 involves a new set of images derived from Brodatz album to study the behavior of proposed approach on regular and random textures. Image data included 12 textures from Brodatz album which are classified as regular and random textures. Three different spatial resolutions are realized for $LBP_{P,R}^{riu2}$ with (P,R) values of (8,1), (16,2), (24,3) in the experiments for the corresponding squared neighborhoods as illustrated in Fig.1.

5.1 Experiment #1

The image data included 16 texture classes from Outex database as shown in Fig. 2.

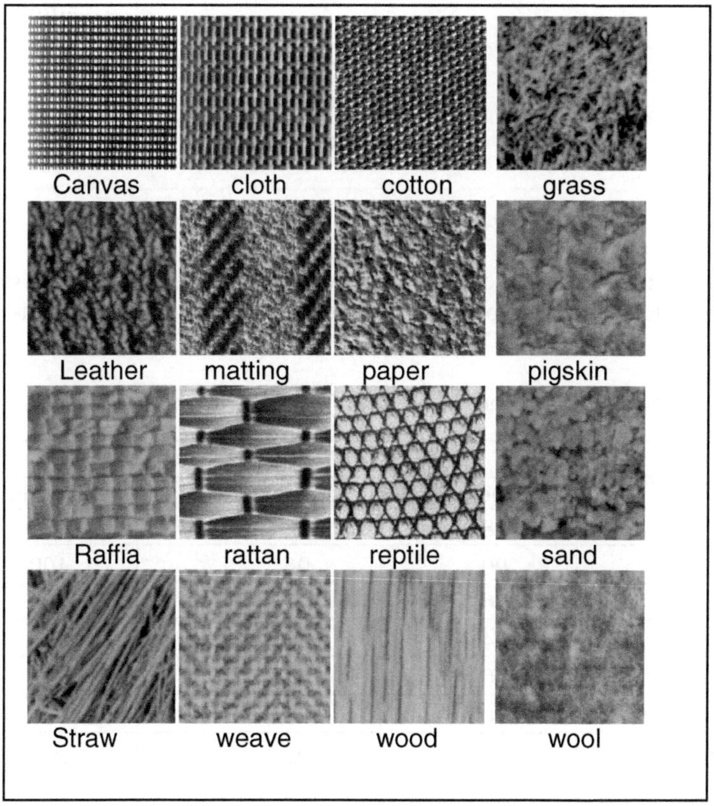

Fig. 2. Sample Images used in Experiment #1

For each texture class, there were sixteen 128x128 source images. In the original experimental setup, the texture classifier was trained with several 32x32 sub images that are extracted from the training image. These sub images are extracted by dividing the source image of size 128x128 into disjoint 32x32 images. From each image 16 samples are extracted and totally 256 samples are generated for each texture class. In other words, 4096 samples are used in the experiment out of which 50% is used for training and remaining for testing. For each texture class, a model histogram is built. The model for the texture classes are shown in Fig, 3.

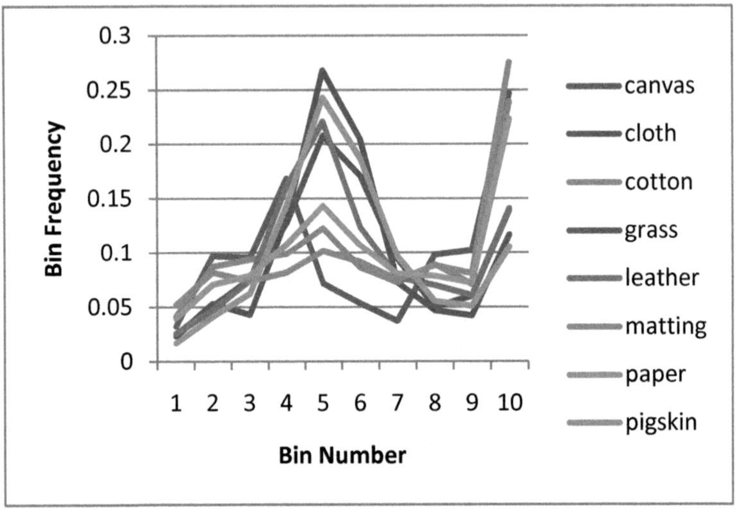

Fig. 3. Model Representation of Textures

Results in Table 1 correspond to the percentage of correctly classified samples. It clearly indicates that the performance is increased with the proposed multi-level LBP operator.

Table 1. Classification Accuracy of Textures on various Operators

Textures	**Classification Accuracy (in %)**		
	3x3 operator	**5x5 operator**	**7x7 operator**
canvas	98	100	100
cloth	90	96	100
cotton	76	100	100
grass	64	70	78
leather	90	84	92
matting	70	80	80
paper	84	92	94
pigskin	46	72	80
raffia	72	68	84

Table 1. *(continued)*

rattan	94	92	96
reptile	84	92	96
sand	48	54	68
straw	78	82	84
weave	70	82	86
wood	90	84	96
wool	68	76	80
Average	76.38	82.75	88.375

5.2 Experiment #2

The behavior of the proposed operator on different texture characteristic is studied. The image data included 12 texture images from Brodatz album which are grouped as regular and random. Sample images are shown in Fig 4. The texture discrimination capability of proposed approach is studied on these sets. Each texture image is of size 64x64. The training dataset consisted of 480 samples (40 samples per texture class) and the test data consisted of 720 samples (60 samples per texture class).

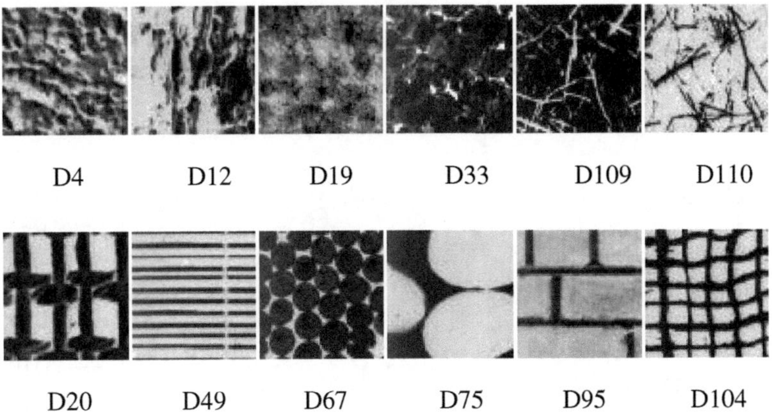

Fig. 4. Sample Images: Top Row contains Random Texture images and Bottom Row has Regular Texture Images

The model Representation of the regular Textures and Random Textures are shown in Fig. 5 and Fig. 6.

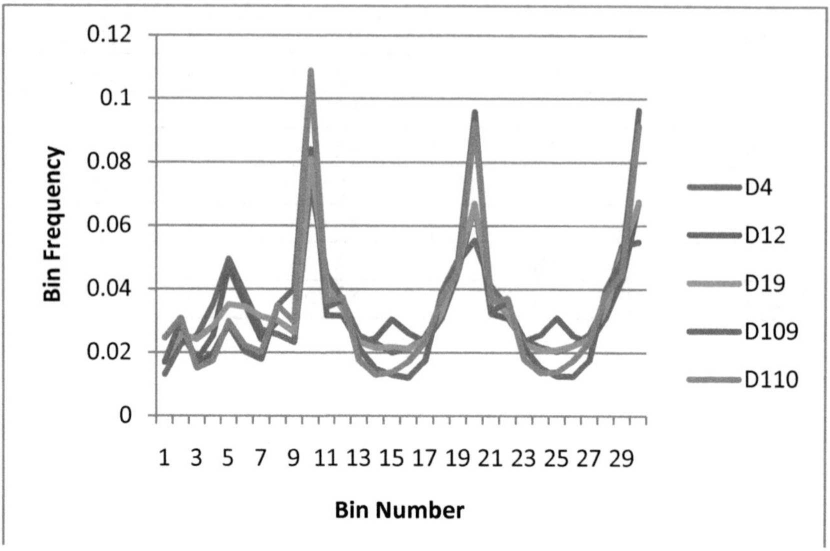

Fig. 5. Model Representation of Regular Textures

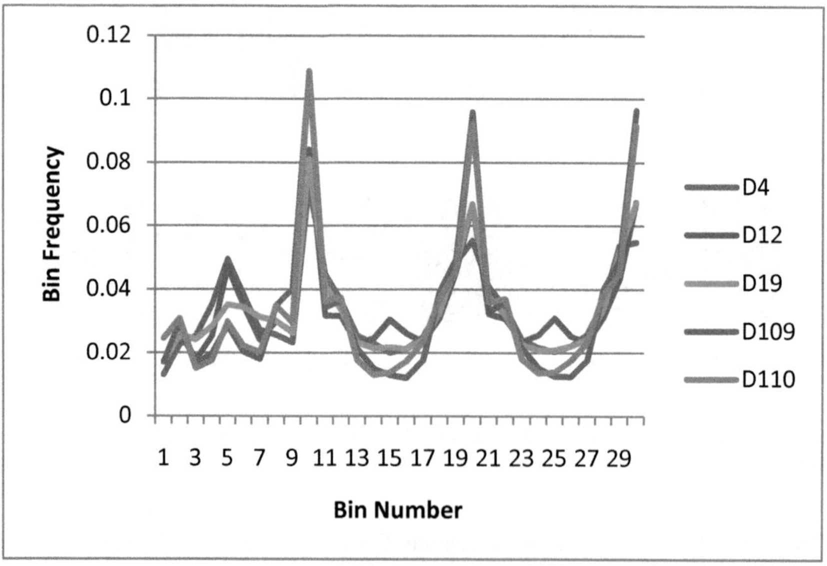

Fig 6. Model Representation of Random Textures

Table 2 presents the classification accuracy of the proposed operator on regular and random textures.

Table 2. Classification Accuracy of Regular and Random Textures

Textures	Classification Accuracy (in %)		
	3x3 operator	5x5 operator	7x7 operator
Regular	97.8	98.3	99.1
Random	95.2	96.8	97.2

We compared the performance of our operator with the LBP operators of circular neighborhood. The proposed operator performance is better than the existing LBP operator.

We have also compared the performance of our feature extraction method with other approaches. Table 6 shows the comparative study with other Texture models.

Table 3. Comparison with other texture models

Texture model	Recognition rate in %
GLCM	78.6
Autocorrelation method	76.1
Laws Texture measure	82.2
LBP (circular neighborhood)	95.8
Our Approach	**97.4**

6 Conclusion

A novel multi level Local Binary Pattern Operator is proposed and their behavior on different texture characteristics are studied. The proposed operator uses squared neighbors and hence no interpolation calculation is required. Also octets are framed based on the size of the operators and hence only one mapping table is sufficient to compute the LBP code. The performance of the proposed operator increases with the operator sizes. It is observed that the efficiency of the proposed operator on regular textures are appreciable.

References

1. Haralick, R.M., Shanmugam, K., Dinstein, I.: Textural feature for image classification. IEEE Transactions on Systems, Man, and Cybernetics SMC-3, 610–621 (1973)
2. Oliver, C.: Rain forest classification based on SAR texture. IEEE Transactions on Geoscience and Remote Sensing 38(2), 1095–1104 (2000)
3. Haralick, R.M.: Statistical and structural approaches to Texture. Proc. IEEE 67(5), 786–804 (1979)
4. Conners, R., Harlow, C.: A theoretical comparison of texture algorithms. IEEE Transactions on Pattern Analysis and Machine Intelligence 2(3), 204–222 (1980)
5. Laws, K.: Textured image segmentation. Ph.D. thesis, University of Southern California, Los Angeles, USA (1980)

6. Ade, F.: Characterization of texture by eigenfilters. Signal Processing 5(5), 451–457 (1983)
7. Manthalkar, R., Biswas, P.K., Chatterji, B.N.: Rotation invariant texture classification using even symmetric Gabor filters. Pattern Recognition Letters 24(12), 2061–2068 (2003)
8. Pun, C.M., Lee, M.C.: Log polar wavelet energy signatures for rotation and scale invariant texture classification. IEEE Trans. Pattern Analysis and Machine Intelligence 25(5), 590–603 (2003)
9. Ojala, T., Pietikäinen, M.: Nonparametric multichannel texture description with simple spatial operators. In: Proc. 14th International Conference on Pattern Recognition, Brisbane, Australia, pp. 1052–1056 (1998)
10. Ojala, T., Pietikäinen, M., Mäenpää, T.: A generalized Local Binary Pattern operator for multiresolution gray scale and rotation invariant texture classification. In: Singh, S., Murshed, N., Kropatsch, W.G. (eds.) ICAPR 2001. LNCS, vol. 2013, pp. 397–406. Springer, Heidelberg (2001)
11. Leung, T., Malik, J.: Representing and recognizing the visual appearance of materials using three dimensional textons. International Journal Computer Vision 43(1), 29–44 (2001)
12. Varma, M., Zisserman, A.: A statistical approach to texture classification from single images. International Journal of Computer Vision 62(1-2), 61–81 (2005)
13. Ahonen, T., Pietikäinen, M.: A framework for analyzing texture descriptors. In: Proc. Third International Conference on Computer Vision Theory and Applications (VISAPP 2008), Madeira, Portugal, vol. 1, pp. 507–512 (2008)
14. Ojansivu, V., Heikkilä, J.: A method for blur and affine invariant object recognition using phase-only bispectrum. In: Campilho, A., Kamel, M.S. (eds.) ICIAR 2008. LNCS, vol. 5112, pp. 527–536. Springer, Heidelberg (2008)
15. Ojala, T., Pietikäinen, M., Mäenpää, T.: Multiresolution Gray-Scale and Rotation Invariant Texture Classification with Local Binary Patterns. IEEE Trans. Pattern Analysis and Machine Intelligence 24(7), 971–998 (2002)

Brain Tissue Classification of MR Images Using Fast Fourier Transform Based Expectation- Maximization Gaussian Mixture Model

Rajeswari Ramasamy[1] and P. Anandhakumar[2]

[1] Research Scholar, Department of Information Technology, MIT campus, Anna University, Chennai-44, India
rajimaniphd@gmail.com
[2] Associate Professor, Department of Information Technology, MIT campus, Anna University, Chennai-44, India
anandh@annauniv.edu

Abstract. This paper proposes MR image segmentation based on Fast Fourier Transform based Expectation and Maximization Gaussian Mixture Model algorithm (GMM). No spatial correlation exists when classifying tissue type by using GMM and it also assumes that each class of the tissues is described by one Gaussian distribution but these assumptions lead to poor performance. It fails to utilize strong spatial correlation between neighboring pixels when used for the classification of tissues. The FFT based EM-GMM algorithm improves the classification accuracy as it takes into account of spatial correlation of neighboring pixels and as the segmentation done in Fourier domain instead of spatial domain. The solution via FFT is significantly faster compared to the classical solution in spatial domain — it is just O(N log $_2$N) instead of O(N^2) and therefore enables the use EM-GMM for high-throughput and real-time applications.

Keywords: Fast Fourier Transform (FFT), Frequency domain, Expectation - Maximization, Gaussian Mixture Model (EM-GMM), Computational complexity, Tissue classification.

1 Introduction

Fully automatic segmentation of brain tissues in Magnetic Resonance Imaging (MRI) is of great interest for clinical studies and research.MRI depends on the response of the magnetic fields to produce digital images that provides structural information about the brain tissue. This noninvasive procedure becomes standard neuro-imaging modality in examining the structures of the brain.

MRI has been known as the best paraclinical examination for lesions which can reveal abnormalities in 95% of the patients [1].The process of interpretation of MR images by a specialist for detection of abnormalities is a difficult and time-consuming task, and result directly depends on the experience of the specialist. A reason for such a difficulty is related to the complexity of images and anatomical borders are having visually vague edges. Therefore an automatic segmentation method to provide an acceptable performance is needed [2].

D.C. Wyld et al. (Eds.): ACITY 2011, CCIS 198, pp. 387–398, 2011.

MRI of the normal brain can be divided into three regions other than background as white matter, gray matter, cerebrospinal fluid (CSF) fluid or vascular structure. Because most brain structures anatomically defined by boundaries of these classes, a method to segment these tissues into these categories is an important step in quantitative morphology of brain.[3].

Classification of human brain in magnetic resonance (MR) images is possible via supervised techniques such as artificial neural networks and support vector machine (SVM) [4] and unsupervised classification techniques unsupervised such as self organization map (SOM) [4] and fuzzy c-means combined with feature extraction techniques.[5].

Other supervised classification techniques, such as k-nearest neighbors (k-NN) also group pixels based on their similarities in each feature image [6, 7, 8, 9] can be used to classify the normal/pathological T2-wieghted MRI images. The use of unsupervised machine learning algorithms (ANN and k-NN) to obtain the classification of images under two categories, either normal or abnormal.[10].

Intensity based methods center around the classification of individual voxels and include methods such as neural network classifiers [11][12], k-nearest neighbor classifier[13],and Gaussian mixture modeling (GMM)[14].

The model suffers from an assumption of spatial independence of voxel intensities. Spatial correlation was encoded by extending GMM to Hidden Markov Random Field (HMRF) model[15].

Statistical approaches to image segmentation based on pixel intensity is the Expectation Maximization algorithm (EM) algorithm. The main disadvantage of EM algorithm is it fails to utilize strong spatial correlation between neighboring pixels. This EM algorithm used along with Gaussian multi resolution algorithm (GMEM) which has high reliability and performance under different noise levels.[16].

2 Materials and Methods

Lustig et al. (2004) discusses a fast and accurate discrete spiral Fourier transform and its inverse. The inverse solves the problem of reconstruction of an image from the acquired MRI data along a spiral k-space Trajectory.[17]. Rowe and Logan (2004)[18], Rowe (2005)[19] and Rowe *et al.* (2007)[20] proposes the use of Fourier transform to reconstruct signal and noise of fMRI data that utilizes the information of phase functions of Fourier transform of images.

The classification performance of Fourier transform was compared with that of wavelet packet transform. Kunttu *et al.* (2003) has applied Fourier transform to perform classification of images.[21]

The techniques of applying Fourier transform in communication and data process are very similar to those to Fourier image analysis, therefore many ideas can be borrowed from is discussed(Zwicker and Fastl, 1999, Kailath, et al.,2000 and Gray and Davisson, 2003).[22],[23],[24]. Similar to Fourier data or signal analysis, the Fourier Transform is an important image processing tool which is used to decompose an image into its sine and cosine components. Comparing with the signal process, which is often using 1-dimensional Fourier transform, in imaging analysis, 2 or higher dimensional Fourier transform are being used. Fourier transform has been widely applied to the fields of image analysis.

Paquet *et al.* (1993)[25] introduced a new approach for the segmentation of planes and quadrics of a 3-D range image using Fourier transform of the phase image. Li and Wilson (1995) established a Multiresolution Fourier Transform to approach the segmentation of images based on the analysis of local information in the spatial frequency domain.[26].

Wu *et al.* (1996) presented an iterative cell image segmentation algorithm using short-time Fourier transform magnitude vectors as class features[27]. Escofet *et al.* (2001) applied Fourier transform for segmentation of images and pattern recognition.[28]. Zou and Wang (2001) proposed a method to exploit the auto-registration property of the magnitude spectra for texture identification and image segmentation. These methods can potentially be applied to many of those previous segmentation problems.[29].

Harte and Hanka, 1997, designed an algorithm for large classification problem using Fast Fourier Transform (FFT). [30].This paper was trying to deal with curse of dimensionality problem, which is the purpose of this paper too. The classification performance of Fourier transform was compared with that of wavelet packet transform. Kunttu *et al.* (2003) applied Fourier transform to perform image classification.[31].

Rowe and Logan (2004), Rowe (2005) and Rowe et al. (2007) used Fourier transform to reconstruct signal and noise of fMRI data utilizing the information of phase functions of Fourier transform of images.[31].

Mezrich (1995) proposes imaging modalities that one can choose the dimension of K-space and therefore choose the proper number of frequencies of the observed signal. Wu et al. (1996) obtained the K-space using so called “short-time Fourier transforms magnitude vectors”. Lustig et al. (2004) also proposed a fast spiral Fourier transform to effectively choose the K-space. Li and Wilson (1995) proposed Laplacian pyramid method to filter out the high frequencies by using a unimodal Gaussian-like kernel to convolve with images. The problem with those selection methods and procedures did not work on the possibility that even some low frequencies are not necessarily important.

A new algorithm is proposed making use of Fast Fourier Transform which works in frequency domain in which a new image is made by summing the product of the kernel weights with the pixel intensity values under the kernel. The previous procedure of moving the kernel around and making new voxel values is the definition of convolution which takes into account of spatial correlation among the neighboring pixels and it combines the advantage of conventional EM algorithm for segmentation.

3 Proposed Work

3.1 System Overview

Figure1 shows the overall system flow diagram.

The proposed system starts with MRI image and noise added to the image and after that FFT is applied. The output of both real and imaginary parts is given as input of EM-GMM algorithm. The image is smoothed in frequency domain and convolution is faster as compared to spatial domain. The output is classified into three classes as white matter, gray matter and cerebrospinal fluid (CSF). The solution via FFT is significantly faster compared to the solution in spatial domain.

3.2 Algorithm for the Proposed Approach

Step 1: Read and display the Input I_0 Image of size M×N.
Step 2: Add Gaussian noise of 0.1 and 0.01 to the input image and apply FFT to each Gaussian noise added images.
Step 3: Apply EM algorithm to the output of Fourier transformed images.
Step 4: Apply Gaussian Mixture Model algorithm to the output of Expectation and Maximization to classify the images into three classes.
Step 5: Assign color to the classified images.
Step 6: Compute segmentation accuracy.
Step7: Display the classified gray matter, white matter and CSF in MRI brain image as segmented image S.

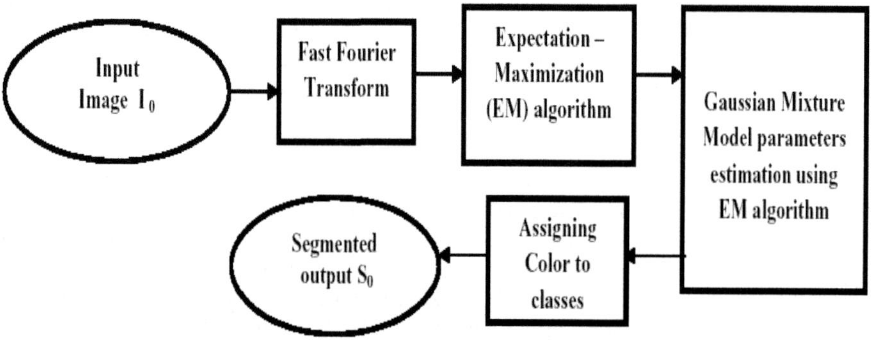

Fig. 1. The Flow chart of FFT based EM-GMM model. The input image I_0 is the image to be segmented and output is the segmented image S_0.

3.3 Data Modeling

Statistical models are used to represent the image data by considering the image as a random processes particularly, a mixture of random processes. The process is assumed to be independently identically distributed functions (iid), a Gaussian distribution functions.

Representing the model by using the equation,

$$f(x_i / \phi) = \sum_{k=1}^{K} p_k G(x_i \mid \theta_k) \tag{1}$$

where K is the number of processes or classes that need to be extracted from the image, $\theta_k \forall k = 1, 2, ...K$ is a parameter vector of class K and its of the form $\left[\mu_{k,} \sigma_k\right]$ such that μ_k, σ_k are the mean and standard deviation of the distribution k respectively, p_k is the mixing proportion of class k($0 < p_k < 1$, $\forall k = 1, 2, ...K$ and $\Sigma k p_k = 1$. x_i is the intensity of pixel i and $\phi = \{p_1, ...p_k, \mu_1, ...\mu_k, \sigma_1, ...\sigma_k\}$ is called as the parameters of the mixture.

3.4 Fast Fourier Transform

A discrete Fourier transform (DFT) converts a signal in the time domain into its counterpart in frequency domain. If (x_i) be a sequence of length N, then its DFT is given by the sequence (F_n)

$$\sum_{kp_k} = 1 \tag{2}$$

An efficient way to compute the DFT is by applying Fast Fourier transform (FFT). By using FFT the computational complexity can be reduced from $O(n^2)$ to $O(n \log n)$. Input signal of the FFT in origin can be a complex and of arbitrary size. The result of the FFT contains the frequency data and the complex transformations.

3.5 Fast Fourier Transform for Image Processing

The need of Fourier Transform arises because of the fact that in MRI/fMRI measurements are not voxel values. Mainly measurements are spatial frequencies. These spatial frequencies got by applying Gx & Gy magnetic field gradients to encode then complex-valued DFT of the object is measured.

3.6 Expectation and Maximization Algorithm

Expectation Maximization is widely used in image processing. Instead of classifying pixels into classes, it is possible to assign the probability belong to classes.

Suppose we are having a random sample $X = \{X_1, X_2, \ldots .. X_n\} \sim f(x/\theta)$.

$$\theta = \arg\max_{\theta} \pi_{i=1}^{n} f(x_i \mid \theta) \tag{3}$$

$$= \arg\max_{\theta} \pi_{i=1}^{n} \ln f(x_i \mid \theta) \tag{4}$$

This optimization problem is nontrivial when f complex is and it gives a motivation for the development of the EM algorithm. The data is augmented with latent (unobserved) data X^c such that the complete data

$$X^c = (X, X^m) \sim f(x^c) = f(x, x^m) \tag{5}$$

The conditional density for the missing data X^m is

$$f(x^m \mid x, \theta) = \frac{f(x, x^m \mid \theta)}{f(x \mid \theta)} \tag{6}$$

Rearranging terms,

$$f(x, \theta) = \frac{f(x, x^m \mid \theta)}{f(x^m \mid x, \theta)} \tag{7}$$

This optimization problem is nontrivial when f is complex and it gives a motivation for the development of the EM algorithm. We augment the data with latent (unobserved) data X^c such that the complete data

$$X^c = (X, X^m) \sim f(x^c) = f(x, x^m) \tag{8}$$

The expected log-likelihood for the complete data by

$$Q(\theta \mid \theta_0, X) = E[\ln f(X^c \mid \theta \mid X, \theta_0)] \tag{9}$$

Maximizing the likelihood as

1. E-step: compute $Q(\theta \mid \hat{\theta}_{j-1}, X)$
2. M-step: maximize $Q(\theta \mid \hat{\theta}_{j-1}, X)$ and take $\theta = \arg\max_{\theta} Q(\theta \mid \theta_{j-1}, X)$

If the above procedure is iterated, we get the sequence of estimators, $\hat{\theta} = \hat{\theta}_0, \hat{\theta}_1, \hat{\theta}_2 \ldots\ldots\ldots$ it converges to the maximum likelihood estimator $\hat{\theta}_0$.

4 Experimental Results

In order to test the performance of proposed algorithm, a good comparison between FFT based EM-GMM algorithm and without applying FFT based EM-GMM introduced. Data set is the manually segmented image of MRI human brain. The performance of FFT based GMM against different noise levels and complex structure of brain MRI images is computed and comparisons are made.

4.1 Segmentation Accuracy

The accuracy of algorithm is computed by using the confusion matrix, where the overall accuracy of segmentation is computed by total number of correctly classified pixels divided by total number of pixels. i.e.

$$\text{AC} = \sum_x (x, x) / \sum_x \sum_y (x, y) \tag{10}$$

The accuracy of any of the class for example class x is computed by dividing the correctly classified pixels of this class over the total number of pixels that have been assigned to this class. i.e

$$\text{AC}_x = (x, x) / \sum_y (x, y) \tag{11}$$

Figure 2 and Figure 3 display the original images and noise variance of 0.001 added to original image. Figure 4 and figure 5 shows the magnitude and phase of Fourier transformed image respectively. obtained by the EM algorithm. The overall accuracies are computed and reported in TABLE I.

The accuracy of segmentation is dropped from 97% to 90% when noise variance increased from 0.01 to 0.1. This algorithm is sensitive to noise it is not suitable for images with heavy noise.

Many of the pixels are misclassified although surrounded pixels are correctly classified and it is due to the fact that EM fails to utilize the strong spatial correlation between neighboring pixels. The reason is that Gaussian mixture assumes that all pixels are independently and identically distributed. This is result got by without applying FFT convolution.

- By moving the kernel around and making new voxel values is the definition of convolution which takes into account of spatial correlation among the neighboring pixels and it combines the advantage of conventional EM algorithm for segmentation. This procedure reduces the number of misclassified pixels because it takes into account of spatial correlation among the neighboring pixels.

Figure 10 shows the speed of execution of FFT based EM-GMM algorithm compared to convolution in spatial domain. It is just O(N log $_2$N) instead of O(N^2) and therefore enables the use EM-GMM for high-throughput and real-time applications.

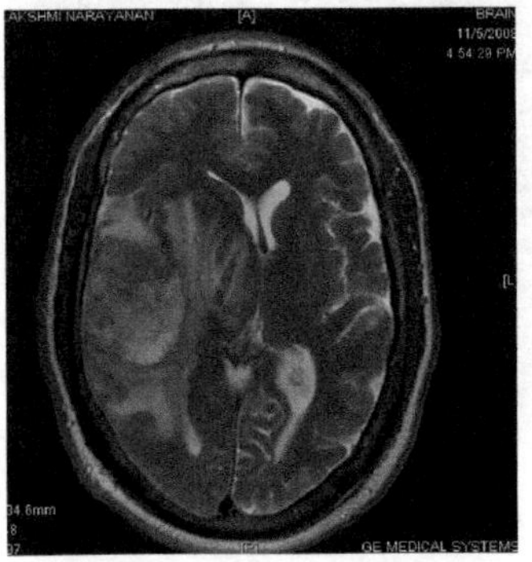

Fig. 2. Original Image

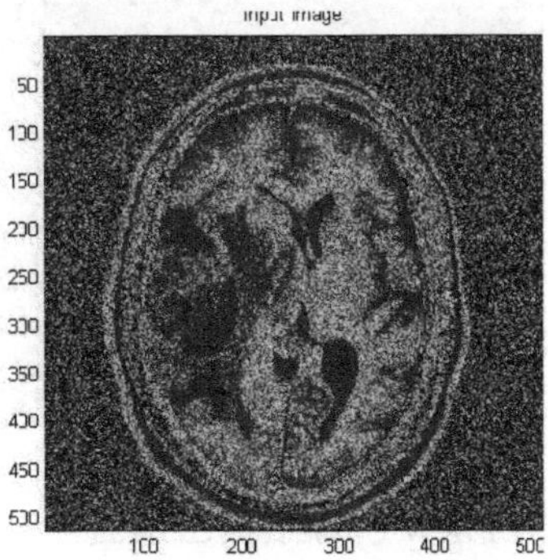

Fig. 3. Gaussian noise of variance 0.001 added to original Image

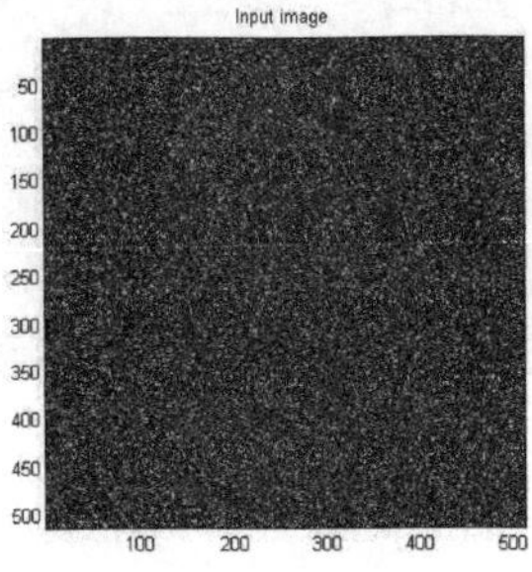

Fig. 4. Gaussian noise of 0.1 added to Original Image

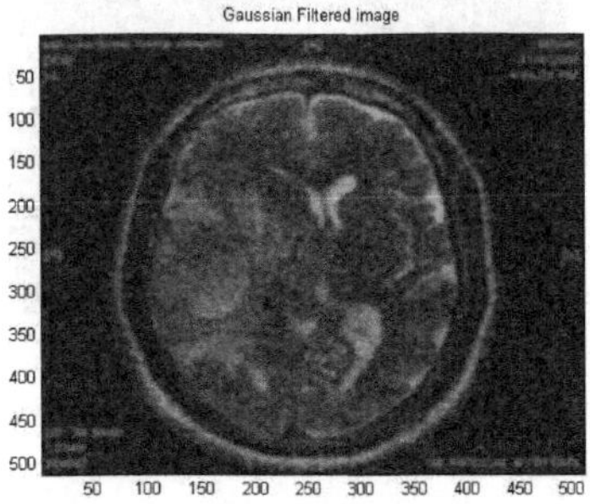

Fig. 5. Gaussian Filtered Image

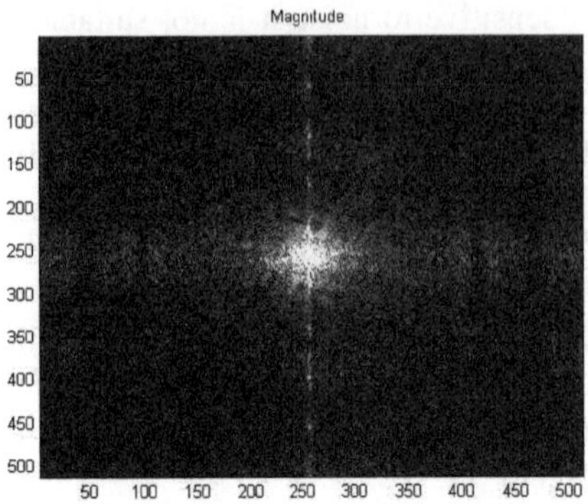

Fig. 6. Magnitude of Fourier Transformed Image

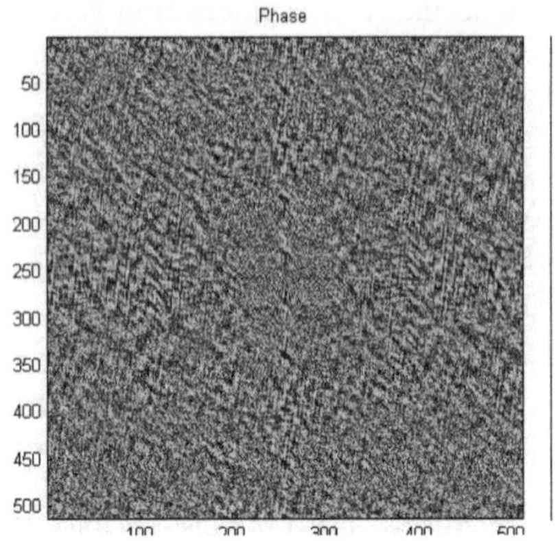

Fig. 7. Phase of Fourier Transformed Image

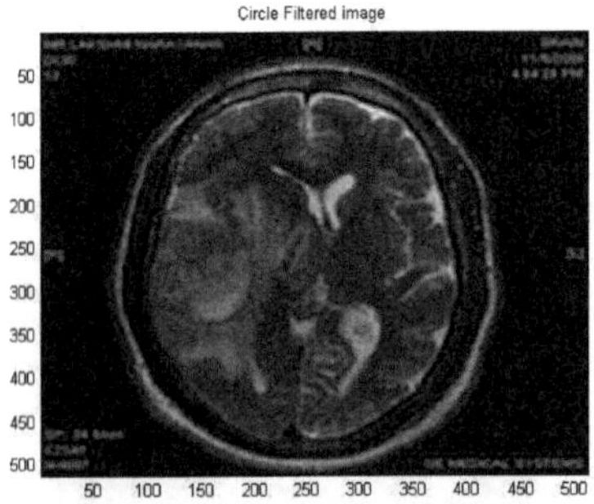

Fig. 8. Circle filtered Image

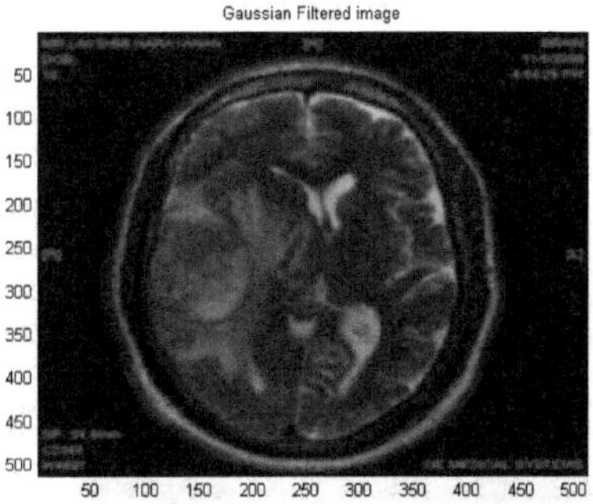

Fig. 9. Gaussian filtered Image

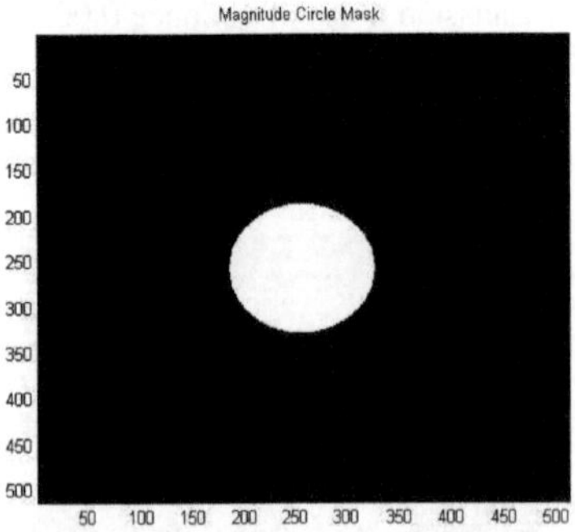

Fig. 10. Magnitude of Circle Mask

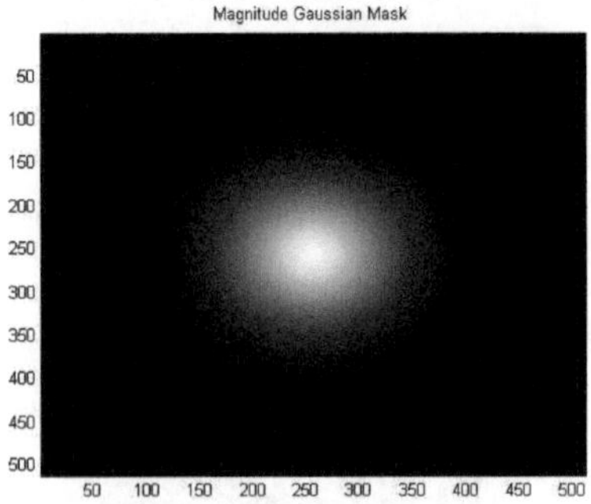

Fig. 11. Magnitude of Gaussian Mask

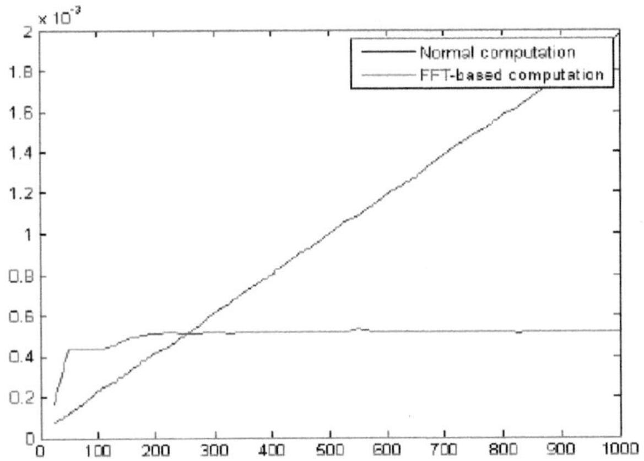

Fig. 12. Execution Times of convolution in DFT versus FFT

Table 1. Accuracies of EM,EM-GMM and FFT based EM-GMM when applied to MRI brain image

Noise level	**0.01**	**0.1**
EM	96%	87%
EM-GMM	97%	90
FFT based EM-GMM	98%	93

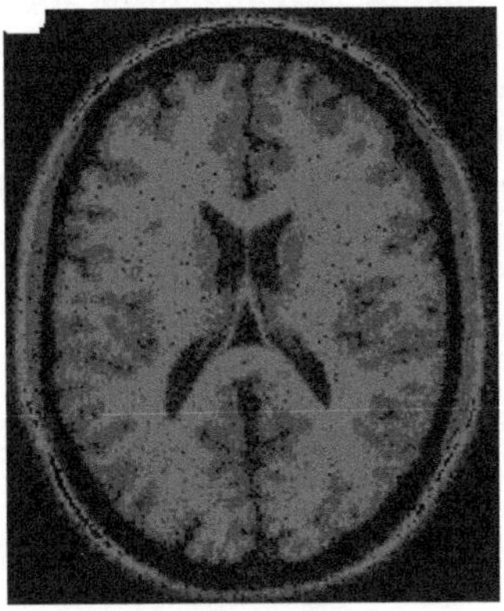

Fig. 13. Original Image with variance 0.1

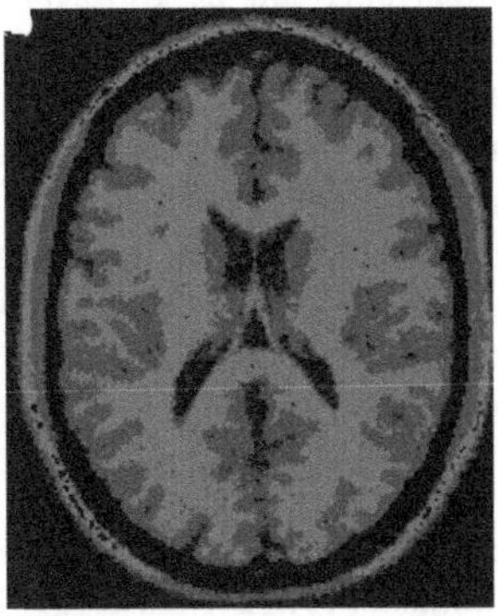

Fig. 14. Results obtained with FFT based EM-GMM

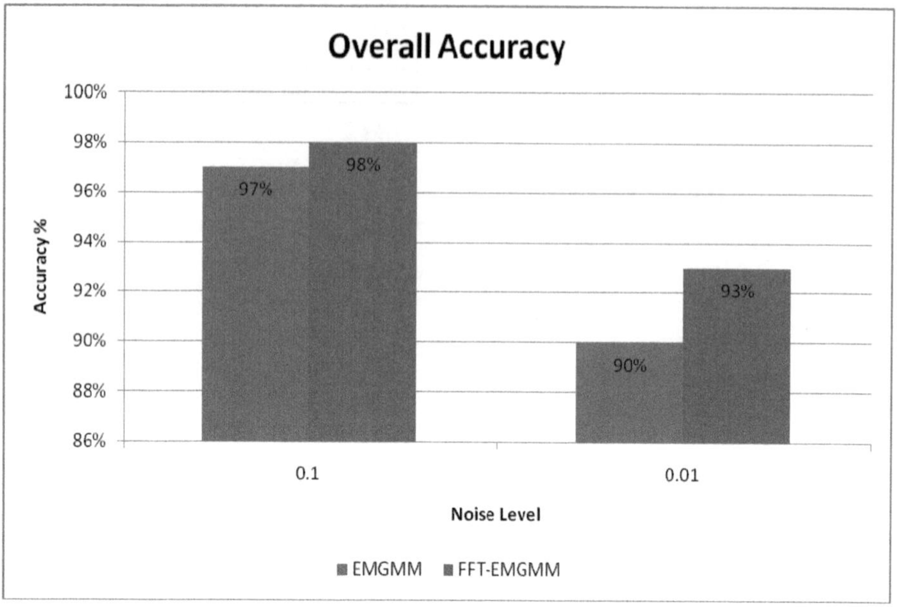

Fig. 15. Bar chart represents the comparision between EMGMM and FFT-EMGMM for different noise variance levels

5 Conclusion

A new FFT-based EM-GMM algorithm is proposed for the segmentation of white matter ,gray matter and CSF is proposed in this paper.The proposed algorithm is based on working with Fast Fourier Transform before applying EM-GMM algorithm for segmentation. Since convolution is done in frequency domain and image smoothing is faster in frequency domain as compared to spatial domain. It increases correlations between neighboring pixels so the disadvantage of conventional EM-GMM algorithm got eliminated. In the conventional EM-GMM algorithm no spatial correlation exists and because of this segmentation accuracy got reduced. This disadvantage overcome by FFT based EM-GMM algorithm which eliminates the misclassified pixels which are laying on the boundary between classes or tissues. Also the solution via FFT is significantly faster compared to the classical solution in spatial domain — it is just O(N log $_2$N) instead of O(N^2) .

References

1. Grossman, R.J., McGowan, M.C.: Perspectives on Multiple Sclerosis. Am. J. Neuroradiol. 19, 1251–1265 (1998)
2. Khayati, R., Vafadust, M., Towhidkhah, F., Massood Nabavi, S.: Fully Automatic Segmentation of Multiple Sclerosis Lesions In Brain MR FLAIR images using Adaptive Mixtures. Computers in Biology and Medicine 38, 379–390 (2008)

3. Soni, A.: Brain Tissue Classification of Magnetic Resonance Images Using Conditional Random Fields Department of Computer Sciences University of Wisconsin-Madison (2007)
4. Jagannathan: Classification of Magnetic Resonance Brain Images using Wavelets as Input To Support Vector Machine And Neural Network. Biomedical Signal Processing and Control 1, 86–92 (2006)
5. Maitra, M., Chatterjee, A.: Hybrid multiresolution Slantlet transform and fuzzy c-means clustering approach for normal-pathological brain MR image segregation. Med. Eng. Phys. (2007), doi:10.1016/j.medengphy.2007.06.009
6. Fletcher-Heath, L.M., Hall, L.O., Goldgof, D.B., Murtagh, F.R.: Automatic segmentation of non-enhancing brain tumors in magnetic resonance images. Artificial Intelligence in Medicine, 43–63 (2001)
7. Abdolmaleki, P., Mihara, F., Masuda, K., Buadu, L.D.: Neural Networks Analysis of Astrocytic Gliomas from MRI appearances. Cancer Letters 118, 69–78 (1997)
8. Rosenbaum, T., Engelbrecht, V., Kroll, W., van Dorstenc, F.A., Hoehn-Berlagec, M., Lenard, H.-G.: MRI abnormalities in neurofibromatosis type 1 (NF1): a study of men and mice. Brain & Development 21, 268–273 (1999)
9. Cocosco, C., Zijdenbos, A.P., Evans, A.C.: A Fully Automatic and Robust Brain MRI Tissue Classification Method. Medical Image Analysis 7, 513–527 (2003)
10. El-dahshan, E.-S.A., Salem, A.-B.M., Youni, T.H.: A Hybrid Technique For Automatic MRI Brain Images Classification, STUDIA UNIV. Babes_Bolyai. Informatica LIV(1) (2009)
11. Gelenbe, E., Feng, Y., Krishnan, K.R.R.: Neural network methods for volumetric magnetic resonance imaging of the human brain. Proc. IEEE 84, 1488–1496 (1996)
12. Hall, L.O., Bensaid, A.M., Clarke, L.P., Velthuizen, R.P., Silbiger, M.S., Bezdek, J.C.: A Comparison Of Neural Network And Fuzzy Clustering Techniques In Segmenting Magnetic Resonance Images of The Brain. IEEE Transactions on Neural Networks 3, 672–682 (1992)
13. Cocosco, C.A., Zijdenbox, A.P., Evans, A.C.: A Fully Automatic and Robust Brain MRI Tissue Classification Method. Medical Image Analysis 7(4), 513–527 (2003)
14. Ashburner, J., Friston, K.J.: Image Segmentation.: Human Brain Function, 2nd edn. Academic Press, London (2003)
15. Zhang, Y., Brady, M., Smith, S.: Segmentation of Brain MR Images Through a Hidden Markov Random Field Model and the Expectation-Maximization Algorithm. IEEE Transactions on Medical Imaging 20(1), 45–57 (2001)
16. Tolba, M.F., Mostafa, M.G., Gharib, T.F., Salem, M.A.: MR-Brain Image Segmentation Using Gaussian Multiresolution Analysis and the EM Algorithm. In: ICEIS, vol. 2, pp. 165–170 (2003)
17. Lustig, M., Tsaig, J., Lee, J.H., Donoho, D.: Fast Spiral Fourier Transform For Iterative MRImage Reconstruction. Stanford University, Stanford (2004)
18. Rowe, D.B., Logan, B.R.: A complex way to compute fMRI activation. NeuroImage 23, 1078–1092 (2004)
19. Rowe, D.B.: Modeling both the magnitude and phase of complex-valued fMRI data. NeuroImage 25, 1310–1324 (2005)
20. Rowe, D.B., Nencka, A.S., Hoffmann, R.G.: Signal and noise of Fourier reconstructed fMRI data. Journal of Neuroscience Methods 159, 361–369 (2007)
21. Zwicker, E., Fastl, H.: Psychoacoustics: Facts and Models, 2nd edn. Springer, Berlin (1999)
22. Kailath, T., Sayed, A.H., Hassibi, B.: Linear Estimation. Prentice-Hall, Inc., Englewood Cliffs (2000)

23. Gray, R.M., Davisson, L.D.: An Introduction to Statistical Signal Processing. Cambridge University Press, Cambridge (2003)
24. Paquet, E., Rioux, M., Arsenaul, H.: Range image segmentation using the Fourier transform. Optical Engineering 32(09), 2173–2180 (1993)
25. Li, C.T., Wilson, R.: Image Segmentation Using Multiresolution Fourier Transform.Technical report, Department of Computer Science, University of Warwick (1995)
26. Wu, H.S., Barba, J., Gil, J.: An iterative algorithm for cell segmentation usingshort-time Fourier transform. J. Microsc. 184(Pt 2), 127–132 (1996)
27. Escofet, J., Millan, M.S., Rallo, M.: Applied Optics 40(34), 6170–6176 (2001)
28. Zou, W., Wang, D.: Texture identification and image segmentation via Fourier transform. In: Zhang, T., Bhanu, B., Shu, N. (eds.) Image Extraction, Segmentation, and Recognition. Proc. SPIE, vol. 4550, pp. 34–39 (2001)
29. Harte, T.P., Hanka, R.: Number Theoretic Transforms in Neural Network Image Classification (1997)
30. Kunttu, I., Lepisto, L., Rauhamaa, J., Visa, A.: Multiscale Fourier Descriptor for Shape Classification. In: Proceedings of the 12th International Conference on Image Analysis and Processing (ICIAP 2003). IEEE, Los Alamitos (2003)
31. Rowe, D.B., Logan, B.R.: A complex way to compute fMRI activation. NeuroImage 24, 1078–1092 (2004)
32. Rowe, D.B.: Modeling both magnitude and phase of complex-valued fMRI data. NeuroImage 25, 1310–1324 (2005)
33. Rowe, D.B., Nencka, A.S., Hoffman, R.G.: Signal and noise of Fourier reconstructed fMRI data. Journal of Neuroscience Methods 159, 361–369 (2007)
34. Mezrich, R.: A perspective on K-space. Radiology 195, 297–315

Network Intrusion Detection Using Genetic Algorithm and Neural Network

A. Gomathy[1] and B. Lakshmipathi[2]

[1] PG Student, Dept of CSE, Anna University of Technology Coimbatore
gomathy.aucbegmail.com
[2] Assistant Professor, Dept of CSE, Anna University of Technology Coimbatore
lkpathi_2004@yahoo.co.in

Abstract. Intrusion detection is a classification problem where the classification accuracy is very important. In network intrusion detection, the large number of features increases the time and space cost. As the irrelevant features make noisy data, feature selection plays essential role in intrusion detection. The process of selecting best feature is the vital role to ensure the performance, speed, accuracy and reliability of the detector. In this paper we propose a new feature selection method based on Genetic Algorithm in order to improve detection accuracy and efficiency. Here the Genetic Algorithm is used for the best feature selection and optimization. The Back Propagation Neural Network is used to evaluate the performance of the detector in terms of detection accuracy. To verify this approach, we used KDD Cup99 dataset.

Keywords: Intrusion Detection, Feature Selection, Genetic Algorithm, Back Propagation Network.

1 Introduction

With the development of network and information technology, network is becoming increasingly important in daily life. In order to protect the network and information, intrusion detection is applied to network security issues. Intrusion detection is a kind of security technology to protect the network against the intrusion attacks. It includes two main categories. One is misuse detection and the other is anomaly detection. Misuse detection can exactly detect the known attacks, but it can do nothing against the unknown attacks. However, anomaly detection can detect the unknown and new attacks.

There are many methods that have been applied to intrusion detection such as wavelet analysis [1], fuzzy data mining [2] and intelligent Bayesian classifier [3]. But many experiments [4], [5], [6] show that there is a high detection accuracy when Support Vector Machine (SVM) is used in intrusion detection. But it is very critical to select features in intrusion detection. Because some features in data may be irrelevant or redundant. Furthermore, they may have a negative effect on the accuracy of the classifier. In order to improve intrusion detection performance, we must select appropriate features and optimize them. In this paper, we mainly study intrusion detection based on BPN, and use Genetic Algorithm (GA) to select and optimize features.

D.C. Wyld et al. (Eds.): ACITY 2011, CCIS 198, pp. 399–408, 2011.

An intrusion is an unauthorized access or use of computer system resources. Intrusion detection systems are software that detect, identify and respond to unauthorized or abnormal activities on a target system Intrusion detection techniques can be categorized into misuse detection and anomaly detection. Misuse detection uses patterns of well-known attacks or vulnerable spots in the system to identify intrusions. However, only known attacks that leave characteristic traces can be detected this way. Anomaly detection, on the other hand, attempts to determine whether deviations from the established normal usage patterns can be flagged as intrusions [7].

Although misuse detection can achieve a low false positive rate, minor variations of a known attack occasionally cannot be detected [7]. Anomaly detection can detect novel attacks, yet it sufferers a higher false positive rate. Earlier studies on intrusion detection have utilized rule-based approaches to intrusion detection, but had a difficulty in detection new attacks or attacks that had not previously define patterns[8][9][10].

In the last decade, the emphasis has shifted to learning by example and data mining paradigm. Neural Networks have been extensively used to detect both misuse and anomies pattern [9] [10] [11] [12] [13] [14] [15]. Recently, kernel-based methods such as support vector machine (SVM) and their variants are being used to detect intrusion [14] [16] [17]. One way in which fuzzy ARTMAP differs from many previously fuzzy pattern recognition algorithm is that it learns each input as it is received online, rather than performing an off-line optimization of a criterion function.

2 Related Works

The approach of information gain ratio and k-means classifier can be used in the feature selection. We used IGR measure as a means to compute the relevance of each feature and the k-means classifier to select the optimal set of MAC layer features.

In the experimental section, we study the impact of the optimization of the feature set for wireless intrusion detection systems on the performance and learning time of the classifier based on neural network [20]. In [21], explored the benefits of using a genetic algorithm that restricts the space search. This algorithm performs better than sequential algorithms, and is even superior to other unconstrained genetic algorithms.

In [23] we dealt with the problem of feature selection for SVMs by means of GAs. In contrast to the traditional way of performing cross-validation to estimate the generalization error induced by a given feature subset we proposed to use the theoretical bounds on the generalization error for SVMs, which is computationally attractive.

A balanced accuracy model is proposed to mitigate class bias during feature set evolution [24]. Experiments compare the selection performance of genetic algorithms using various fitness functions varying in terms of accuracy, balance, and feature parsimony.

A generic algorithm is proposed for feature selection with a Feature Quality Index (FQI) metric [25]. We generate feature vectors by defining fuzzy sets on Hough transform of character pattern pixels. Each feature element is multiplied by a mask vector bit before reaching the input of a multilayer perceptron (MLP). The genetic algorithm operates on the bit string represented by the mask vector to select the best set of features.

A method for automated classification of ultrasonic heart (echocardiography) images is proposed in [25]. The feature of the method is to employ an artificial neural network (ANN) trained by genetic algorithms (GA's) instead of the back propagation.

A two-step feature selection algorithm is proposed, [26] which utilizes data' statistical characteristic and depends on no intrusion detection algorithm. It firstly eliminates the irrelevant features and then eliminates the redundant features. And secondly Feature Selection for Sound Classification in Hearing Aids through Restricted Search Driven by Genetic Algorithms.

A hybrid method is proposed in [27], for the speech processing area, to select and extract the best features that represent a speech sample. The proposed method makes use of a Genetic Algorithm along with Feed Forward Neural Networks in order to either deny or accept personal access in real time

3 Methodology

3.1 Intrusion Detection

The Mass data comes from the Internet, which is partly extracted as behavioural data, and then the behavioural data is waiting for feature selection. Firstly, the extracted data is served with pre-treatment, including data discretion and data formatting. After this, the data usually is of very high dimension. It is requisite to transform the data into a lower dimension feature space through feature selection in order to eliminate any irrelevant or redundant features for improving the detection accuracy and efficiency of IDS.

The Feature Reduction module of Figure 1 plays that role. Then, classification rules are elicited according to the results of feature reduction. Finally, the Mass Data is classified complying with the classification rules. When the system detects any intrusion data which meets the alarm conditions, it will trigger the alarm system.

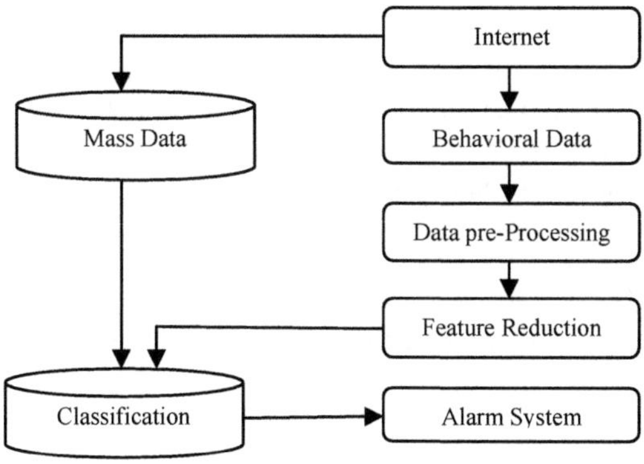

Fig. 1. Process of Intrusion Detection

3.2 Feature Selection

Feature selection is the most critical step in building intrusion detection models. During this step, the set of attributes or features deemed to be the most effective attributes is extracted in order to construct suitable detection algorithms. A key problem is how to choose the optimal set of features. As not all features are relevant to the learning algorithm, and in some cases, irrelevant and redundant features can introduces noisy data that distract the learning algorithm, severely degrading the accuracy of the detector and causing sloe training and testing processes. Feature selection was proven to have a significant impact on the performance of the classifier [20],[21],[22],[23],[26].

3.3 Feature Optimization with GA

GA is an adaptive method of global-optimization searching and simulates the behaviour of the evolution process in nature. It maps the searching space into a genetic space. That is, every possible key is encoded into a vector called a chromosome. One element of the vector represents a gene. All of the chromosomes make up of a population and are estimated according to the fitness function [22],[23],[24]. A fitness value will be used to measure the "fitness" of a chromosome. Initial populations in the genetic process are randomly created.

GA uses three operators to produce a next generation from the current generation: reproduction, crossover, and mutation. GA eliminates the chromosomes of low fitness and keeps the ones of high fitness [26],[27]. This whole process is repeated, and more chromosomes of high fitness move to the next generation, until a good chromosome (individual) is found.

(i) Chromosome Encoding

Encoding is the first step in GA. For a data record, we convert each value of its feature into a bit binary gene value, 0 or 1. In our experiments, we choose the subsets of KDD Cup99, 1999 kddcup.data_10_percent and corrected [8], as the training dataset and test dataset. Because the values of feature No.2, No.3, and No.4 are all symbols, it is not necessary to optimize these three features. It is just all right to eliminate them before encoding and add them to the record after optimization.

For feature that has a numeric value, if its value isn't 0, we convert it to 1; otherwise we convert it to 0. For example, a record (0,tcp,http, SF,181,5450,0,0,0,0,0,1,0,0,0,0,0,0,0,0,0,0,8,8,0.00,0.00,0.00,0.00,1.00,0.00, 0.00 ,9 ,9,1. 00, 0. 00, 0.11,0. 00, 0. 00,0. 00,0.00,0.00.can be converted (01100000100 00000000110 0001001110100000) after encoding.

(ii)Fitness Function

We adopt the value of fitness function to decide whether a chromosome is good or not in a population. The following equations are used to calculate the fitness value of every chromosome.

$$F(x)=Ax+\beta N0 \tag{1}$$

$$A= (\alpha 1, \alpha 2, .\alpha\ n)$$
$$X=(x1, x2\ldots xn)^T$$

Where N0 is the number of 0 in a chromosome, β is the coefficient, x_n means the nth gene (0 or 1), and α_n means the weight of the nth gene. We calculate the weight by

$$\alpha_n = \frac{N_n}{N_{all}} \tag{2}$$

Where N_n means the number of the nth feature in dataset when its value isn't 0, and N_{all} means the total number of the nth feature in dataset.

3.4 Back Propagation Network

Back propagation is a systematic method for training multi-layer artificial neural network. It has a mathematical foundation that is strong if not highly practical. It is multi-layer forward network using extend gradient-descent based delta-learning rule, commonly known as back propagation rule. Back propagation provides a computationally efficient method for changing the weights in a feed forward network, with differential activation function units, to learn a training set of input-output examples.

The network is trained by supervised learning method. The aim of this network is to train the net to achieve a balance between the ability to respond correctly to the input patterns that are used for training and the ability to provide good responses to the input that are similar

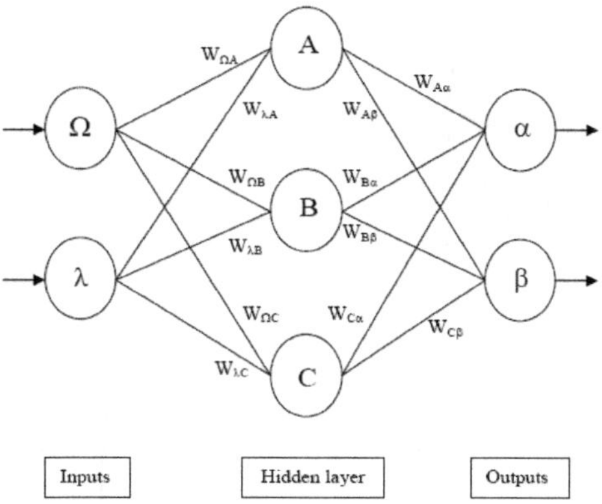

Fig. 2. Back Propagation Neural Network

Back propagation learning will be given by as follows:

1. Calculate errors of output neurons
$\delta\alpha = \text{out}\alpha\,(1 - \text{out}\alpha)\,(\text{Target}\alpha - \text{out}\alpha)$
$\delta\beta = \text{out}\beta\,(1 - \text{out}\beta)\,(\text{Target}\beta - \text{out}\beta)$

2. Change output layer weights
$W+A\alpha = WA\alpha + \eta\delta\alpha \text{ outA}$
$W+A\beta = WA\beta + \eta\delta\beta \text{ outA}$
$W+B\alpha = WB\alpha + \eta\delta\alpha \text{ outB}$
$W+B\beta = WB\beta + \eta\delta\beta \text{ outB}$
$W+C\alpha = WC\alpha + \eta\delta\alpha \text{ outC}$
$W+C\beta = WC\beta + \eta\delta\beta \text{ outC}$

3. Calculate (back-propagate) hidden layer errors
$\delta A = \text{outA} (1 - \text{outA}) (\delta\alpha WA\alpha + \delta\beta WA\beta)$
$\delta B = \text{outB} (1 - \text{outB}) (\delta\alpha WB\alpha + \delta\beta WB\beta)$
$\delta C = \text{outC} (1 - \text{outC}) (\delta\alpha WC\alpha + \delta\beta WC\beta)$

4. Change hidden layer weights
$W+\lambda A = W\lambda A + \eta\delta A \text{ in}\lambda$
$W+\Omega A = W+\Omega A + \eta\delta A \text{ in}\Omega$

$W+\Omega B = W+\Omega B + \eta\delta B \text{ in}\Omega$
$W+\lambda B = W\lambda B + \eta\delta B \text{ in}\lambda$

5 Overall System Architecture

The proposed intrusion detection system has four main phases which are data Pre-processing and feature selection, selection of an optimal parameters using Genetic algorithm, classification of attacks and testing of the IDS (fig 3).

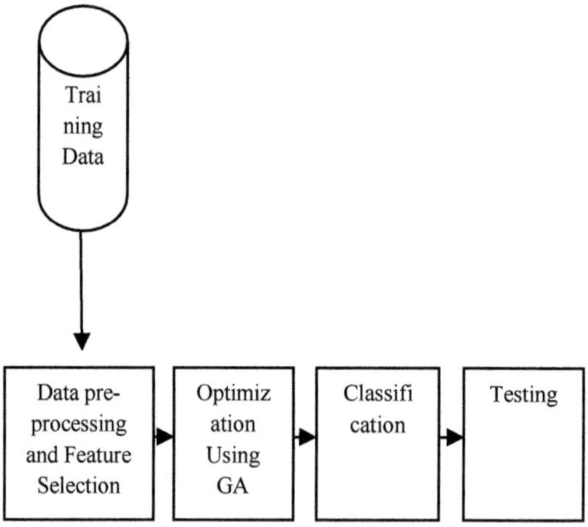

Fig. 3. Proposed IDS

4 Data Set

The data we used to train and test the classifier is DARPA KDD CUP99 and it is collected from [8]. The data set contains forty one features and it is reduced to six optimal set of features by applying Genetic Algorithm. The classifier is trained using the complete set of features (41 features), which are the full set of data attributes collected from [8], and the reduced set of features (six features).The complete and reduced set of features is given by the table1 and 2.

Table 1. Complete Feature Set

Duration	protocol type	service	Flag	src_bytes	dst_bytes	land
Wrong_fragment	Urgent	hot	num_failed_logins	logged_in	num_compromised	root_shell
su_attempted	num_root	num_file_creations	num_shells	num_access_files	num_outbound_cmds	is_host_login
is_guest_login	Count	srv_count	serror_rate	srv_serror_rate	rerror_rate	srv_rerror_rate
same_srv_rate	diff_srv_rate	srv_diff_host_rate	dst_host_count	dst_host_srv_count	dst_host_same_srv_rate	dst_host_diff_srv_rate
dst_host_same_src_port_rate	dst_host_srv_diff_host_rate	dst_host_serror_rate	dst_host_srv_serror_rate	dst_host_rerror_rate	dst_host_srv_rerror_rate	

Table 2. Optimal Feature Set

num_failed_logins	same_srv_rate
dst_bytes	Hot
Service	dst_host_rerror_rate

5 Experimental Result and Analysis

The optimal set of features is generated by using the fitness value of each feature [Table 3a to 3d].

The neural network based classifier (BPN) is trained using the complete set of features, which are the full set of data attributes, and the optimal set of features, from the experimental result we evaluate the performance of the classifier.

The performance evaluation of the classifier trained with the reduced set of features and the full set of features is given in Fig: 4

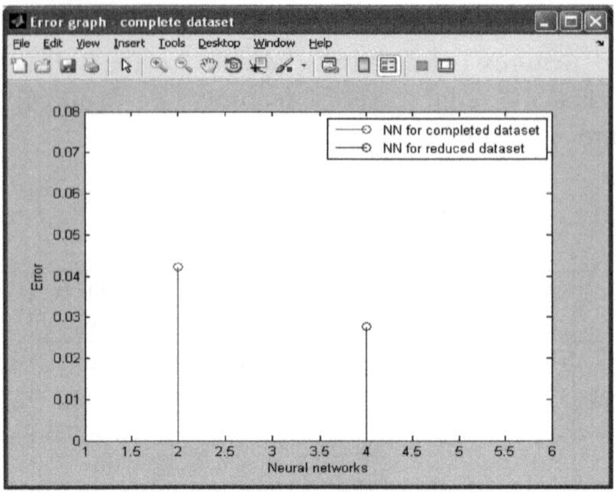

Fig. 4. Detection Accuracy

Table 3. Fitness Value for Feature 1 To 41

Table 3a. Fitness Value for Features 1 To 10

	F1	F2	F3	F4	F5	F6	F7	F8	F9	F10
Fitness1	0.0820	0.0656	0.0745	0.0745	0.0781	0.0656	0.0911	0.0713	0.0781	0.0820
Fitness2	0.0656	0.0781	0.0863	0.0656	0.0683	0.0713	0.0863	0.0713	0.0683	0.0820
Fitness3	0.0820	0.0863	0.0911	0.0656	0.1025	0.0781	0.0964	0.0607	0.0781	0.0863
Fitness4	0.0911	0.0911	0.0781	0.0964	0.0863	0.0713	0.0713	0.0781	0.1025	0.0745

Table 3b. Fitness Value for Features 11 To 20

	F11	F12	F13	F14	F15	F16	F17	F18	F19	F20
Fitness1	0.0781	0.0863	0.0820	0.0863	0.0683	0.0863	0.0863	0.0911	0.0820	0.0713
Fitness2	0.1093	0.0820	0.0713	0.0713	0.0713	0.0781	0.0565	0.0745	0.0745	0.0529
Fitness3	0.0964	0.0745	0.0745	0.1025	0.0863	0.0964	0.0781	0.0911	0.0911	0.0745
Fitness4	0.0656	0.0863	0.0863	0.1025	0.1025	0.0656	0.0911	0.0745	0.1025	0.0745

Table 3c. Fitness Value for Features 21 To 30

	F21	F22	F23	F24	F25	F26	F27	F28	F29	F30
Fitness1	0.0607	0.0781	0.0911	0.0781	0.0911	0.0713	0.0820	0.0656	0.0863	0.0781
Fitness2	0.0863	0.0781	0.0745	0.0820	0.0745	0.0683	0.0713	0.0745	0.0683	0.0863
Fitness3	0.0820	0.0964	0.0820	0.0745	0.0745	0.0586	0.0820	0.0820	0.0863	0.0683
Fitness4	0.0745	0.0911	0.0911	0.0863	0.0781	0.0863	0.0781	0.1171	0.0683	0.0863

Table 3d. Fitness Value for Features 31 To 41

	F31	F32	F33	F34	F35	F36	F37	F38	F39	F40	F41
Fitness1	0.0820	0.0820	0.1025	0.0683	0.0781	0.0683	0.0911	0.0863	0.0964	0.0863	0.0911
Fitness2	0.0820	0.0781	0.0713	0.0683	0.0745	0.0863	0.0631	0.0781	0.0631	0.0863	0.0781
Fitness3	0.0745	0.0863	0.0656	0.0820	0.0745	0.0781	0.0820	0.1025	0.0631	0.0820	0.0863
Fitness4	0.1025	0.0745	0.0781	0.0713	0.0781	0.0656	0.0781	0.0781	0.0781	0.0820	0.0781

6 Conclusion and Future Work

In this paper, we proposed an intrusion detection method based on GA and BPN. Because some features in data may be irrelevant or redundant, we first apply GA to select and optimize features, and then apply BPN to classify. The experimental results show that BPN can achieve good classification accuracy, and the accuracy can be improved obviously after feature selection and optimization.

In future a comparative study can be done on the impact of the reduced feature set on the performance of classifiers-based ANNs, in comparison with other computational models such as SVMs, MARSs, and LGPs.

References

[1] Rawat, S., Sastry, C.S.: Network Intrusion Detection Using Wavelet Analysis. In: Das, G., Gulati, V.P. (eds.) CIT 2004. LNCS, vol. 3356, pp. 224–232. Springer, Heidelberg (2004)

[2] Guan, J., Liu, D.-x., Wang, T.: Applications of Fuzzy Data Mining Methods for Intrusion Detection Systems. In: Laganá, A., Gavrilova, M.L., Kumar, V., Mun, Y., Tan, C.J.K., Gervasi, O. (eds.) ICCSA 2004. LNCS, vol. 3045, pp. 706–714. Springer, Heidelberg (2004)

[3] Bosin, A., Dessì, N., Pes, B.: Intelligent Bayesian Classifiers in Network Intrusion Detection. In: Ali, M., Esposito, F. (eds.) IEA/AIE 2005. LNCS (LNAI), vol. 3533, pp. 445–447. Springer, Heidelberg (2005)

[4] Kim, D.S., Park, J.S.: Network-based intrusion detection with support vector machines. In: Kahng, H.-K. (ed.) ICOIN 2003. LNCS, vol. 2662, pp. 747–756. Springer, Heidelberg (2003)

[5] Rao, X., Dong, C.-x., Yang, S.-q.: An intrusion detection system based on support vector machine. Journal of Software 4, 798–803 (2003)

[6] Zhang, K., Cao, H.-x., Yan, H.: Application of support vector machines on network abnormal intrusion detection. Application Research of Computers 5, 98–100 (2006)

[7] llgun, K.: USTAT: a real-time intrusion detection system for UNIX. In: Proceedings of the 1993 Computer Society Symposium on Research in Security and Privacy, pp. 16–29 (1993)

[8] KDD Cup99 Data, `http://kdd.ics.uci.edu/databases/kddcup99/kddcup99.html`

[9] Debar, H., Dorizzi, B.: An application of a recurrent network to an Intrusion Detection System. In: Proceedings of IJCNN, pp. 78–83 (1992)

[10] Ryan, J., Lin, M.J., Mikkulalan, R.: Intrusion Detection on NN. In: Advances in Neural Information Processing System. MIT Press, Cambridge (1997)

[11] Mitra, S., Pal, S.K.: SOM neural network as a fuzzy classifier. IEEE Transaction of Systems, Man and Cybernetics 24(3), 385–399 (1994)

[12] Mukkamala, S., Jonaski, A., Sung, A.T.: Intrusion Detection using neural network and SVM. In: Proceedings of the IEEE IJCNN, pp. 202–207 (2002)

[13] Mukkamala, S., Sung, A.H., Ajith, A.: Intrusion Detection using intelligent paradigm. Journal of Network and Computer Application 28, 167–182 (2005)

[14] Zhong, C., Jiong, J., Kanel, M.: Intrusion Detection using hierachical NN. Pattern Recognition Letters 26, 779–791 (2005)

[15] Marais, E., Marwala, T.: Predicting global Internet instability caused by worms using Neural Networks. In: Proc of the Annual Symposium of the Pattern Recognition Association of South Africa, South Africa, pp. 81–85 (2004)

[16] Hu, W., Liao, Y., Rao, V., Venurri, R.R.: Robust SVM for anomaly detection in Computer Security. In: Proceedings of the 2003 International Conf. on MC and Application, LA California (2003)

[17] Zhang, Z., Shen, H.: Application of Online training SVM for real time intrusion detection. Computer Communications 28, 14281442 (2005)

[18] Deepa, S.N.: Introduction to Neural Networks Using MATLAB 6.0

[19] Zhang, Z., Manikopoulos, C.: Investigation of Neural Network Classification of Computer Network Attacks. In: Proc. Int'l Conf. Information Technology: Research and Education, pp. 590–594 (August 2003)

[20] El-Khatib, K.: Impact of Feature Reduction on the Efficiency of Wireless Intrusion Detection Systems. IEEE Transactions on Parallel And Distributed Systems 21(8) (August 2010)

[21] IEEE Transactions on Audio, Speech, and Language Processing 15(8) (November 2007)

[22] Feature Selection for Support Vector Machines by Means of Genetic Algorithms

[23] Balanced Accuracy for Feature Subset Selection with Genetic Algorithms

[24] A Genetic Algorithm for Feature Selection in a Neuro-Fuzzy OCR System

[25] Classification Of Heart Diseases In Ultrasonic Images Using Neural Networks, E D By Genetic Algorithms Proceedings of Xsp 1998 (1998)

[26] A Two-step Feature Selection Algorithm Adapting to Intrusion Detection. In: 2009 International Joint Conference on Artificial Intelligence (2009)

[27] Feature Selection for a Fast Speaker Detection System with Neural Networks and Genetic Algorithms

Performance Evaluation of IEEE 802.15.4 Using Association Process and Channel Measurement

Jayalakhsmi Vaithiyanathan[1], Ramesh Kumar Raju[2], and Geetha Sadayan[3]

[1] Research Scholar, Dravidian University, Andhra Pradesh, India
jayasekar1996@yahoo.co.in
[2] Principal, Lalgudi Co-Operative Polytechnique College,Lalgudi, Tamil Nadu
rramesh1968@gmail.com
[3] Asst. Professor, Computer Applications Dept., Anna University of Technoloy, Thiruchirapalli, India
kasagee1971@yahoo.co.in

Abstract. IEEE 802.15.4 is a new standard addressing the needs of low-rate wireless personal area networks or LR-WPAN with a focus on enabling wireless sensor networks. The standard is characterized by maintaining a high level of simplicity, allowing for low cost and low power implementations. It operates primarily in the 2.4GHz ISM band, which makes the technology easily applicable and worldwide available. However, IEEE 802.15.4 is potentially vulnerable to interference by other wireless technologies working in this band such as IEEE 802.11 and Bluetooth. This paper gives a short overview of the IEEE 802.15.4 and carefully analyzes the properties and performance of IEEE 802.15.4 through simulation study and channel measurement. Furthermore, this paper analyzes one of the association scheme named Simple Association Process (SAP) and compares SAP with the original IEEE 802.15.4 protocol. The analytic results are validated via ns-2 simulations.

Keywords: IEEE 802.15.4, IEEE 802.11, ISM band, LR-WPAN, SAP.

1 Introduction

IEEE 802.15.4 is a new standard to address the need for low-rate low power wireless communication. In December 2000, IEEE standard committee set up a new group to develop the low-rate wireless personal area network (LR-WPAN) standard, called 802.15.4[1]. IEEE 802.15.4 is used to provide low complexity, low-cost and low-power wireless connectivity among inexpensive devices. This characteristic determines its huge potential in industry, agriculture, home networks, portable electronic system, medical sensor and so on. The task of this group is to establish the criterion of physical layer and MAC layer. The application of higher layer, connectivity test and marketing extension are handled by ZigBee alliance which was founded in August 2002. It can operate both as a PAN coordinator or a common device. RFD can only be used as a common device. Depending on the application requirements, the LR-WPAN may operate in either of two topologies: the star topology or the peer-to-peer topology.

The IEEE 802.15.4 standard was specifically developed to address a demand for low-power, low-bit rate connectivity towards small and embedded devices.

D.C. Wyld et al. (Eds.): ACITY 2011, CCIS 198, pp. 409–417, 2011.

Furthermore the standard is trying to solve some problems that were inadequately taken into account by Bluetooth technology. Since the release of the standard in 2003 and the emergence of the first products on the market there have been several analytical and simulation studies in the literature, trying to characterize the performance of the IEEE 802.15.4 [1], [2].Furthermore, a lot of effort has been put on the energy efficiency characterization and optimization of the protocol stack for wireless sensor networks [3]–[6]. Unfortunately there is not enough reported results on the practical insights gained from measurement campaigns. The IEEE 802.15.4 and IEEE 802.11b/g are envisioned to support complimentary applications and therefore it is very likely that they will be collocated. Since both types of devices operate in the 2.4GHz ISM frequency band, it is of great importance to understand and evaluate the coexistence issues and limitations of the two technologies. According to [7] the IEEE 802.15.4 network has little or no impact on IEEE 802.11's performance. However IEEE 802.11 can have a serious impact on the IEEE 802.15.4 performance if the channel allocation is not carefully taken into account [8]. Both of these studies are theoretical and simulation based.

Most nowadays researches are focused on analysis mathematically or simulation the performance of IEEE 802.15.4. Literature [9] evaluated the throughput and energy consumption of network in contention access period (CAP) in IEEE802.15.4. J. Misic et al. in [10] studied the uplink, downlink traffic and stability of IEEE 802.15.4 beacon network under different communication parameters. In [11], the throughput and energy efficiency performances of 802.15.4 were assessed by simulations.

This paper analyzes the initialization procedure of IEEE 802.15.4 network and the improved association scheme named *Simple Association Process* (SAP). SAP reduces redundant primitives, avoid collisions and decrease association delay. It is compared with original protocol and validated by simulations.

The reminder of the paper is organized as follows: section II gives an overview of the IEEE 802.15.4 standard. Section III gives the association scheme called Simple Association Scheme .Section IV gives the Simulation Study. In section V, we present results from measurements made to characterize the basic behavior of IEEE 802.15.4 Finally, we conclude the paper in section VI.

2 Overview of the IEEE 802.15.4

We shall now give a brief overview of the IEEE 802.15.4 standard [12], focusing on the details relevant to our performance study. For a more comprehensive introduction to the IEEE 802.15.4 technology, as well as some foreseen application scenarios, we refer the reader to [13]. The 802.15.4 is a part of the IEEE family of standards for physical and link-layers for wireless personal area networks (WPANs). The WPAN working group focuses on short range wireless links, in contrast to local area and metropolitan area coverage explored in WLAN and WMAN working groups, respectively. The focal area of the IEEE 802.15.4 is that of low data rate WPANs, with low complexity and stringent power consumption requirements. Device classification is used for complexity reduction. The standard differentiates between full function device (FFD), and reduced function device (RFD), intended for use in the simplest of devices. An RFD can only communicate with an FFD, whereas an FFD can communicate with both other FFDs, and RFDs. The IEEE 802.15.4 supports two PHY options. The 868/915MHz PHY known as low-band uses binary phase shift keying (BPSK) modulation whereas the 2.4GHz PHY (high-band) uses offset quadrature phase shift keying (OQPSK) modulation. Both modulation modes offer extremely good bit error rate (BER) performance at low Signal-to-Noise Ratios (SNR). Figure 1 compares the performance of the 802.15.4 modulation technique to Wi-Fi and Bluetooth. The graph clearly illustrates that IEEE 802.15.4 modulation is anywhere from 7 to 18 dB better than the IEEE 802.11 and IEEE 802.15.1 modulations , which directly translates to a range increase from 2 to 8 times the distance for the same energy per bit, or an exponential increase in reliability at any given range. The IEEE 802.15.4 physical layer offers a total of 27 channels, one in the 868MHz band, ten in the 915MHz band, and, finally, 16 in the 2.4GHz band. The raw bit rates on these three frequency bands are 20 kbps, 40 kbps, and 250 kbps, respectively. Unlike, for example, Bluetooth, the IEEE 802.15.4 does not use frequency hopping but is based on direct sequence spread spectrum (DSSS). In this paper we are focusing solely on measurement in the 2.4GHz frequency band as that is the area where inter-technology problems can be prominent and due to the fact that it is a tempting for larger scale sensor deployments.

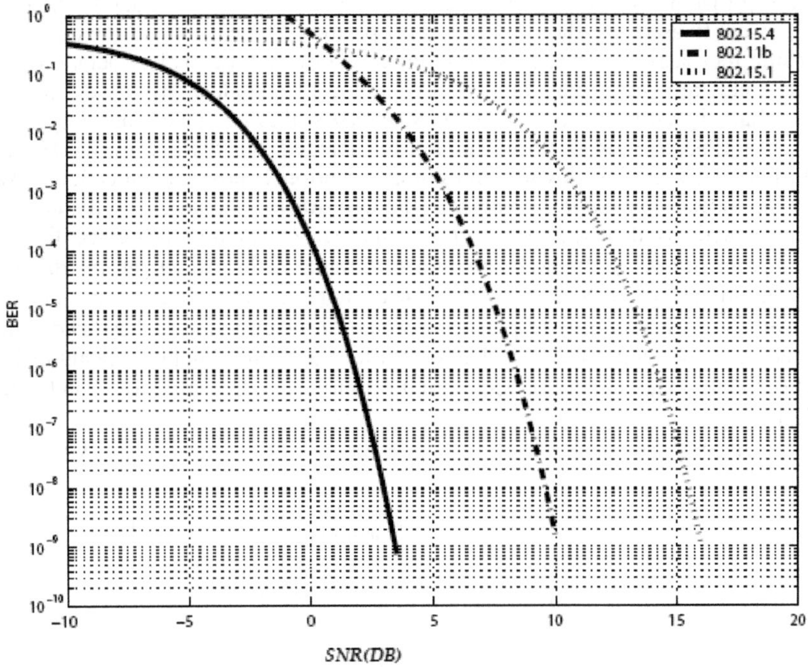

Fig. 1. Theoretical bit error rate in an AWGN channel for IEEE 802.15.4, IEEE 802.11b and IEEE 802.15.1

The IEEE 802.15.4 MAC layer is fundamentally that of CSMA/CA system together with optional time slot structure and security functionality. The network can assume either a star topology, or operate in peer-to-peer mode. In each case an FFD device acting as a coordinator manages the local network operations. The standard defines four frame types, namely beacon frames, data frames; acknowledgment frames and MAC control frames. Beacon frames are used by the coordinator to describe the channel access mechanism to other nodes. Two fields found in beacon frames are relevant for further discussion. The beacon order (*BO*) subfield specifies the transmission interval of the beacon, called the beacon interval (*BI*) by the identity $BI = B \times 2^{BO}$, where $B$is a base super frame duration, and 0 _*BO* _14. If $BO = 15$ the coordinator transmits beacon frames only when requested to do so, such as on receipt of a beacon request command. The super frame order (*SO*) subfield specifies the length of time during which the superframe is active, superframe duration (*SD*), as $SD = B \times 2^{SO}$ symbols. If $SO = 0$, the superframe following the transmission of the frame is not active. Data frames are used to send varying amount of payload (2–127 bytes), while acknowledgment frames are used to increase reliability for data frame and control frame transmissions. Finally, the control frames are used to carry out network management functions, such as association to and disassociation from the network.

3 Simple Association Process

According to the simulation, it can be seen that the time of device association is wasted by many redundant primitives in the original IEEE 802.15.4 protocol. Thus overfull collisions will occur and the coordinator will be overloaded when many devices want to associate the PAN in a short period of time. Some of the devices will retransmit their association request when meet failure and the total association time of all the nodes are increasing rapidly. SAP reduces redundant primitives. It can be found that *T_scan_duration* and *T_ResponseWaitTime* take the majority of association time. *T_scan_duration* can not be changed, but *T_ResponseWaitTime* can be decreased by cutting down some communication handshake procedures. When receiving *Association request command*, the coordinator should check resources and allocate an address, then send *Association response command* to the device directly.

This processing time should be an integer multiple of *T_beacon_period* and we use 2288s in simulation. In SAP, the device need not send *Data request command* and only wait for the a*ssociation response command* of the coordinator. SAP is developed to reduce association primitives and association delay.. The simulation result of T_{avg} is about 0.20438s. The number of association primitives is decreased to 57 and listed in Table 1.

Table 1. The number of association primitives in IEEE802.15.4 and SAP

Steps	nodes	number of primitives (original protocol)	number of primitives (SAP)
1	Device	7	7
2	Device	16	16
	Coordinator	7	7
3	Device	3	0
4	Device	16	0
	Coordinator	23	16
5	Device	8	8
	Coordinator	3	3
Total number		83	57

4 Simulation Study

In order to evaluate the performance of IEEE 802.15.4 association process, and to consider the application to the home network, the paper analyses the situation of various devices to associate PAN in star topology by using ns2 simulator. The experiment has totally *N* nodes, all of which use the identical interval (T_{inter}) to start associating for each independent simulation. Figures 2 (a) and 2 (b) show the impact of different intervals on the total time until all the nodes are associated within a variety of networks with different scales. We use T_{total} to denote the total time until all the nodes are associated. Let T_{di} be the time of the *i*th device associated the network.

4.1 Comparing the Original Protocol with the SAP

We can see that SAP can bring a significant improvement on decreasing the total time to join the PAN, as compared to the original protocol under the different parameter values. The two methods all increase with *N*. Each device of the original protocol costs about 0.5752s to associate PAN SAP used 0.20438s instead. As *N* is increasing, T_{inter} decreases, SAP performs better than the original protocol. On the contrary, the differences between two methods reduce as T_{inter} is increasing. Especially, when T_{inter} is bigger than 0.5s, the devices usually associate the network orderly without collisions and the T_{total} increases linearly. The difference between above two schemes is nearly fixed.

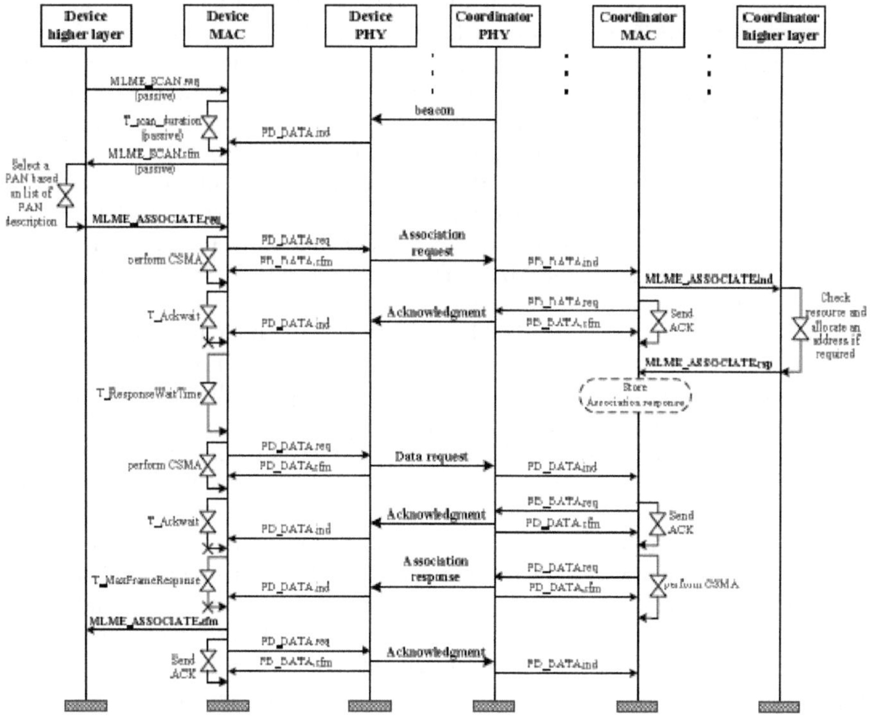

Fig 2. Association message sequence chart of the original 802.15.4 protocol

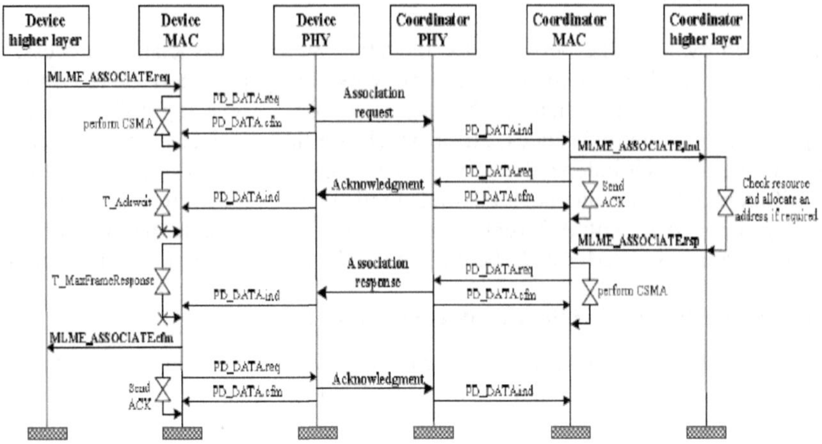

Fig. 3. Association message sequence chart of the SAP

5 Channel Measurements

Depending on the RF environment and the power output consumption required for a given application, IEEE 802.15.4 compliant wireless devices are expected to transmit in a range of 10–75 meters. In his section we evaluate through measurements, using off-the-shelf IEEE 802.15.4 radio, the PER (Packet Error Rate) and the RSSI (Received Signal Strength Indicator) both in indoor and outdoor environments in order to examine the basic characteristics of the IEEE 802.15.4 communication channel. Additionally we measured the run lengths distribution both in indoor and outdoor environments. We used the results to calibrate the error model in ns-2 in order to more realistically map the measurement and the simulation environment used for performance analysis of the MAC. The measurements for PER and RSSI in the indoor scenario were made up to 32 meter distance between the transmitter and the receiver with PSDU sizes of 20, 40, 80 and 127 bytes. For both the transmitter and the receiver we used the evaluation CC2420EB board from Chipcon [10]. The system operates at 2.4GHz band and offers a bit rate of 250 kbps. In the outdoor scenario the measurements were done up to maximum of 70 meters between the sender and the receiver and fixed packet size of 20 bytes. As a transmitter in this case, we used a Telos MoteIV running TinyOS [11]. In every measurement event 5000 packets were sent at a rate of 20 packets/s.

The results were averaged over several trials. The respective results are shown in Figure 4 for the indoor environment and Figure 5 for the outdoor environment. Packet error rate measurements indicate that the 802.15.4 radio has a rather good performance indoor since the PER is less than 3.5% at 32 m distance. It should be further mentioned that the indoor measurements were done in a softly partitioned office environment without any serious obstacles for the propagating signal. The outdoor measurements were performed only with the smallest possible packet length, because we wanted to test the behavior of the 802.15.4 for real outdoor applications where the aim is to send as little data as possible to be more energy efficient.

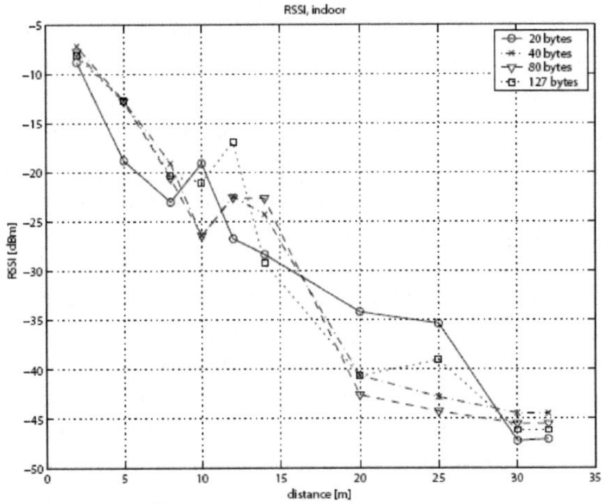

Fig. 4. RSSI in indoor environment

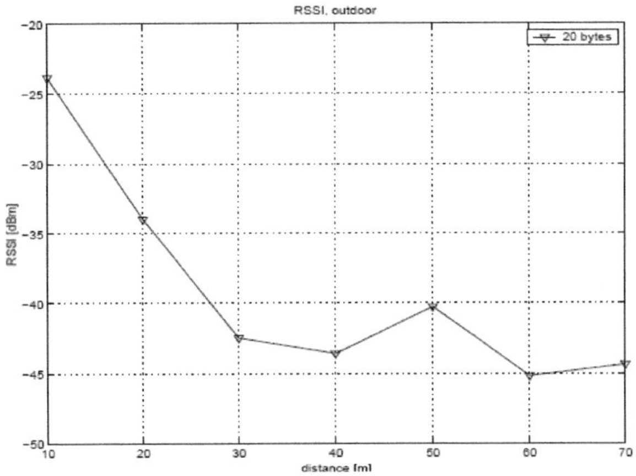

Fig. 5. RSSI in outdoor environment

Recent studies have revealed the existence of three different reception regions in a wireless link: connected, transitional and disconnected. The transitional region is often quite significantly characterized by high variances in the reception rates and the asymmetric connectivity [12]. It is particularly important concept, since we are ultimately interested in how to dimension reliably home and sensor networks. Being in the transitional region can have a significant impact on the performance of the upper-layer protocols and particularly on the routing protocols. The unpredictability in the transitional region (due to high variance of the link quality) itself makes many adaptive algorithms suboptimal or unfair. Figure 6 shows the packet reception rate ($PRR = 1{-}PER$) vs. distance for an off-the-shelf receiver in a real indoor and outdoor environment. Our results show that the outdoor channel is not very stable since the transitional region is rather large. We assume that this is due to multi-path fading the wireless link experienced during the measurements. As mentioned earlier in this section, in order to appropriately chose and error model for the simulation studies, we measured the run lengths distribution in a single IEEE 802.15.4 link in indoor and outdoor environment. We want to remind the reader that a run is defined as a sequence of error free packets. We compared the results with the Complementary Cumulative Distribution Function (CCDF) of the run lengths of the independent (Bernoulli)1 and two-state Markov (Gilbert-Elliot) error model2. It can be noticed that both error models reproduce the measured run lengths distribution very well for communication distance of 20m and packet size of 35 bytes (MAC load of 20 bytes). The reason for the good fit of the both error models, which are suitable for modelling of a wired channel, is the good reliability and stability of the 802.15.4 channel up to 30m (see Figure 4). In the outdoor environment (we do not show the results due to space limitations) both error models fit very well up to 20m, where the PER is less than 1%. For longer distances both the independent and the two-state Markov model do not closely follow the measured results. The model that fits better is the two-state Markov model with a transition probability from bad to bad state given by a parameter _= 0▷5. In the previously mentioned Markov model _was set to 0.001.

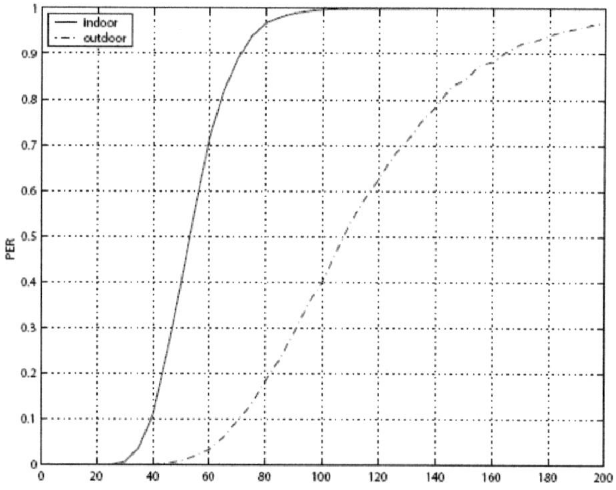

Fig. 6. Analytical prediction of the transitional region

6 Conclusion

The overall goal of this paper was to contribute and help through measurements and simulations towards dimensioning of the sensor networks for future applications using IEEE 802.15.4 technology. Using these measurements, we calibrated the ns-2 simulator in order to be able to produce more real simulation environment and evaluate the IEEE 802.15.4 in a reliable way. Our results clearly showed that the simulated throughput is far away from the maximum transmission capacity of the channel and higher throughput can be achieved by relatively small increase in the back off order. Comparing SAP with the original IEEE 802.15.4 protocol, the number of association service primitives in SAP is 31.3% less than in the original protocol, and the simulation results show that the association time decreases 64.5%. SAP will get better performance as the number of devices increases and the interval time of association request decreases. It can be widely used in home networks and sensor network applications.

References

[1] Callaway, E., Gorday, P., Hester, L., Gutierrez, J.A., Naeve, M., Heile, B., Bahl, V.: Home Networking with IEEE 802.15.4: A Developing Standard for Low-Rate Wireless Personal Area Networks. IEEE Communications Magazine 40(8), 70–77 (2002)

[2] Zheng, J., Lee, M.J.: Will IEEE 802.15.4 make ubiquitous networking a reality?: A discussion on a potential low power, low bit rate standard. IEEE Communications Magazine 27(6), 23–29 (2004)

[3] Bougard, B., Catthoor, F., Daly, D.C., Chandrakasan, A., Dehaene, W.: Energy Efficiency of the IEEE 802.15.4 Standard in Dense Wireless Microsensor Networks: Modeling and Improvement Perspectives. In: Proceedings of Design, Automation and Test in Europe (DATE 2005), vol. 1(1), pp. 196–201 (2005)

[4] Al-Karaki, J.N., Kamal, A.E.: Routing techniques in wireless sensor networks: A survey. IEEE Wireless Communications 11(6) (December 2004)

[5] Sadagopan, N., Krishnamachari, B., Helmy, A.: Active query forwarding in sensor networks (ACQUIRE). In: Proc. 1st IEEE Intl. Workshop on Sensor Network Protocols and Applications (SNPA) (May 2003)

[6] Heinzelman, W., Chandrakasan, A., Balakrishnan, H.: Energyefficient communication protocol for wireless microsensor networks. In: Proceedings of the Hawaii Conference on System Sciences (January 2000)

[7] Howitt, I., Gutierrez, J.A.: IEEE 802.15.4 Low Rate – Wireless Personal Area Network Coexistence Issues. In: Proceedings of WCNC, vol. 3, pp. 1481–1486 (March 2003)

[8] Shin, S., Choi, S., Park, H.S., Kwon, W.H.: Packet error rate analysis of IEEE 802.15.4 under IEEE 802.11b interference. In: Braun, T., Carle, G., Koucheryavy, Y., Tsaoussidis, V. (eds.) WWIC 2005. LNCS, vol. 3510, pp. 279–288. Springer, Heidelberg (2005)

[9] Das, I.R.A.K., Roy, S.: Analysis of the Contention Access Period of IEEE 802.15.4 MAC. UWEETR-2006- 0003, Department of Electrical Engineering, University of Washington (February 2006)

[10] Misic, J., Shafi, S., Misic, V.B.: Performance of a Beacon Enabled IEEE 802.15.4 Cluster with Downlink and Uplink Traffic. IEEE Transactions on Parallel and Distributed Systems 17(4), 361–376 (2006)

[11] Lu, G., Krishnamachari, B., Raghavendra, C.S.: Performance evaluation of the IEEE 802.15.4 MAC for lowrate low-power wireless networks. In: Proc. of the 23rd IEEE International Performance Computing and Communications Conference (IPCCC 2004), Phoenix, AZ, USA, April 15-17, pp. 701–706. IEEE, Los Alamitos (2004)

[12] IEEE Standard for Information Technology Part 15.4: Wireless Medium Access Control (MAC) and Physical Layer (PHY) Specifications for Low-Rate Wireless Personal Area Networks (LR-WPANs), IEEE Std 802 (April 15, 2003)

[13] TinyOS embedded operating system, `http://www.tinyos.net` (referenced September 13, 2005)

Efficient Personalized Web Mining: Utilizing the Most Utilized Data

L.K. Joshila Grace[1], V. Maheswari[2], and Dhinaharan Nagamalai[3]

[1] Research Scholar,Department of Computer Science and Engineering
[2] Professor and Head,Department of Computer Applications
[1,2] Sathyabama University, Chennai, India
[3] Wireilla Net Solutions PTY Ltd, Australia

Abstract. Looking into the growth of information in the web it is a very tedious process of getting the exact information the user is looking for. Many search engines generate user profile related data listing. This paper involves one such process where the rating is given to the link that the user is clicking on. Rather than avoiding the uninterested links both interested links and the uninterested links are listed. But sorted according to the weightings given to each link by the number of visit made by the particular user and the amount of time spent on the particular link.

Key words: Search Key word, User Profiling, Interesting links.

1 Introduction

While a search is being made for a particular word. Each user may have different views for a single word. For example if the search word is given as card. A child may be in need of some games in cards, an adult may want information regarding the ATM cards, an lay man would be in need of some ID card. So each person is in need of different information for a single word.

[4] Traditional approaches of mining user profiles are to use term vector spaces to represent user profiles and machine learning. [7] There are two kinds of method to learn users' interests. One method is the static method. The e-learning system sets questions or asks users to register, from which we can find out each user's information, such as age, major, courses to learn, courses learned, education background and so on. The other method is the dynamic method. The system observes each user's action through his session with the system. Then an analysis of his logs and queries are done to learn his interestingness.

Therefore the user profiling method was evolved. For performing search in a database or the web the user information like the name, address, occupation, Qualification, Area of interest etc are provided by the user. A separate data base table is maintained for the user. Whenever the user logs inside with his/her user name and password he would be able to do a personalized search. The search key given by the

D.C. Wyld et al. (Eds.): ACITY 2011, CCIS 198, pp. 418–426, 2011.

user would provide the list of links that are related. For the data file a separate database is present giving the keywords in the links. These key words will not include is, as, for, not etc. Only ten key words are considered. The search key matching the key words present in the database will get listed. The first time the user does the search he will get the normal list of links. The link that is clicked and used by the user is recorded in the database. So the next time the same user logs into the search engine and searches for the same search key the order of listing will change. The link that was clicked and used by the user would get the higher weightings, this gets into the first position in the list. Each time the search made by the user gets updated in the database. In this system not only the interested links but also the uninterested links gets displayed. But this may occupy the last few places in the list.

TextStat 3.0 software is used to find the key words in the document that has to be searched. This will give the frequently occurring words, omitting the is, was, the etc . this is the text where the match has to be found. These frequently occurring texts is called as the key word which are used to identify the particular link.

Incase of web usage mining the mining process is done based on the number of time the web site is visited and How much time spent on the web site[8][10][11].

- Preprocessing: Data preprocessing describes any type of processing performed on raw data to prepare it for another processing procedure. The different types of preprocessing in Web Usage Mining are:
  1. Usage Pre-Processing: Pre-Processing relating to Usage patterns of users.
  2. Content Pre-Processing: Pre- Processing of content accessed.
  3. Structure Pre-Processing: Pre-Processing related to structure of the website.
- Pattern Discovery: Data mining techniques have been applied to Extract usage patterns from Web log data. The following are the pattern discovery methods.

  1. Statistical Analysis
  2. Association Rules
  3. Clustering
  4. Classification
  5. Sequential Patterns
  6. Dependency

2 User Profiling

User profiling strategies can be broadly classified into two main approaches[2]:

1. Document-based
2. Concept-based approaches.

Document-based user profiling methods aim at capturing users' clicking and browsing behaviors. Users' document preferences are first extracted from the click through data, and then, used to learn the user behavior model which is usually represented as a set of weighted features.

On the other hand, concept-based user profiling methods aim at capturing users' conceptual needs. Users' browsed documents and search histories are automatically mapped into a set of topical categories. User profiles are created based on the users' preferences on the extracted topical categories.

3 Related Works

There are many algorithms present which would list only the interested links of that particular user. Therefore if the user is in need of some more options he has to either log out and perform a normal search or has to go for any other process of searching.

3.1 Weighted Association Rule (WAR)

Each item in a transaction is assigned a weight to reflect the interest degree, which extends the traditional association rule method. [3]Weighted association rule (WAR) through associating a weight with each item in resulting association rules.

Each Web page is assigned to a weight according to interest degree and three key factors, i.e. visit frequency, stay duration and operation time.

3.2 PIGEON

Personalized Web page recommendation model called PIGEON abbr. for PersonalIzed web paGe rEcommendatiON) via collaborative filtering and a topic-aware Markov model. [5]A graph-based iteration algorithm to discover users' interested topics, based on which user similarities are measured.

3.3 Single Level Algorithm

This is a New pattern mining algorithm, for efficiently extracting approximate behavior patterns so that slight navigation variations can be ignored when extracting frequently occurring patterns.[6] This algorithm is particularly useful with websites that have a large number of web – pages.

3.4 FCA (Formal Concept Analysis)

An approach that automatically mines web user profile based on FCA (formal concept analysis) methods from positive documents. [4]The formal concepts with their weights as patterns are represented to denote topics of interest. Based on the patterns discovered, the process of assessing documents relevance to the topics is found.

3.5 Other Method

- **Joachims'** method assumes that a user would scan the search result list from top to bottom.[2] If a user has skipped a document di at rank i before clicking on document dj at rank j, it is assumed that he/she must have scan the document di and decided to skip it. Thus, we can conclude that the user prefers document dj more than document di

- **Click through method** - Click through data are important implicit feedback mechanism from users.[2] This gives the clicks made by the user on the same link or the different link.
- **Open Directory Project (ODP) -** [2]If a profile shows that a user is interested in certain categories, the search can be narrowed down by providing suggested results according to the user's preferred categories
- **Personalized query clustering method**
  This method involves these activities [2]
  1. Filtering the result by user profile
  2. Re-rank the retrievals from search engine

4 Tables Generated

For maintaining all the information regarding the search various tables are created.

4.1 User Profile

This table consists of the details that are provided by the user when they create a new account to use the search engine. The details may be user name, password, address, occupation, area of interest etc., These information's are stored in this table.

4.2 Users Search Keys

This table consists of the search key words used by the particular user, The option selected from the list. The number of times the search made by the user for the same search key, The number of times the selection of the same link made, the time spent on that particular link etc., are updated to the table. According to this information the weights for the links is put up. These weights would help in giving higher preference while listing the most interested links of the user in the next time of search.

4.3 Keywords Matching the Document

This table consists of the key words of the document and the link of the document which has to be listed while searching for the particular search key is made by the user.

5 Search Process

Every time the user logs inside the search engine. The login is verified with the username and password in the user profile database. Once the verification is successful it would link to the personalized search screen and the user can perform a search for a particular search key.

First step the search key is compared with the Key words matching the document table to analyze what are the links that has to be listed for the user. After the list of options (links) being listed the user activity is being listened by updating the details of the link he / she is clicking on and time duration they use the link data. This update is made in the user search keys table. The search key along with the link clicked by the user is noted in the table. The time duration the user is using the particular link is also found. This information would also contribute in providing the weights for each link. Not only the frequently visited link but also the highly utilized link is used. According to this information the weights for the links is put up. These weights would help in giving higher preference while listing the most interested links of the user in the next time of search.

The interested links include the frequently used and the amount of time spent on the particular link. This link occupies the first position in the list during the next time of search for the next time of search for the same search key. The fig.1 shows the procedure done while the user logs inside the search engine for the first time. Starts from the creation of login to the list of search link matching the search key

The next time when the same user logs in and performs a search for the same search key. The same process is carried out. The search key is compared with the key words of the document in the "Key words matching the document" table and listing option is generated. But since the user has already searched for the same key word the order of listing is differed according to the weightings generated from the previous search.

The higher weighted link takes up the first position in the listing. The listing now will not only gives the interested link but also the uninterested link are listed.

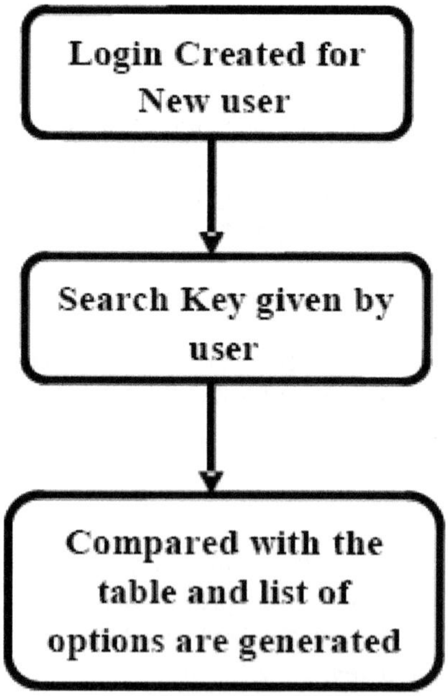

Fig. 1. Process for the first time of search

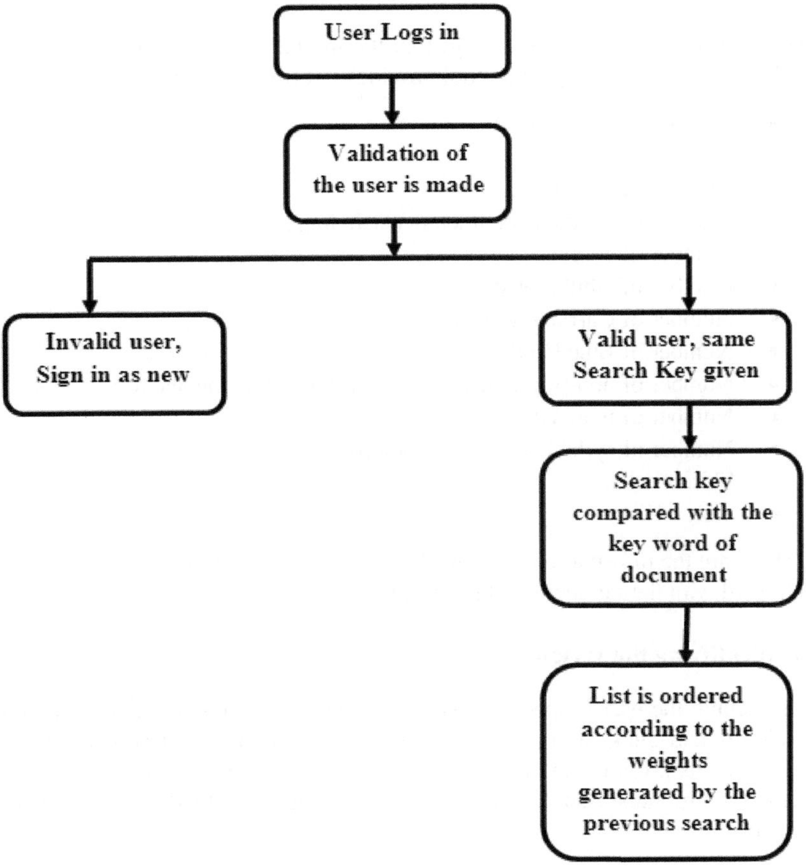

Fig. 2. Second time of search done by Same user for the same search key

6 Tools and Algorithm Used

For developing these type of system various tools and algorithms are Used. They are discussed below:

6.1 Validation of User

The user name and password is validated by comparing with the user Profile table. Only a valid user can perform this personalized search. Therefore the user who does not have a valid username and password has to sign in as a new user providing all the details. Then the user can continue with the personalized searching.

6.2 Extracting Key words from the Documents

TextStat 3.0 software tool is used to find the frequently used text omitting the words like is, was, are, the etc., [9] this tool provides information like

- Number of paragraphs:
- Number of words:
- Number of sentences:
- Number of printable characters (including spaces):
- Number of spaces:
- Number of tabulations:
- Number of Carriage Return:
- Number of Line Feed:
- Number of non-printable characters (others than the above):
- Number of words per sentence:
- Number of syllables per word (approximate):
- Flesch index:
- Start of list:

These are the information provided by the software. The last option gives the list of each word with the number of times repeated.

6.3 Identifying the Weights

By default the user is specified with a weight of zero. Each time the user puts on a search key and clicks an option the weight of that particular link gets incremented. These weights provide the interest of the user. Thus the next time of search made by the user for the same search key would have the high weighted link in the first option of the list.

7.4 Extracting Options from the Weights

The lists of options are generated not only by just considering the link that match the key word but also the weights of the link. These weights are considered only for the second time of search by the user for the same key word.

The original GSP algorithm [1]

```
F1={frequent 1-sequences};
        For (k=2;Fk-1?Ø;k=k+1) do
                Ck=Set of candicate k-sequences;
        For all input-sequences ε in the databse do
                Increment count of all α Ck contained in ε
                Fk={α Ck | α.sup?min_sup};
        Set of frequent sequences = kFk
```

The evolved WTGSP algorithm [1]

```
WTGSP {
F1={frequent 1-sequences};
```

```
        For (k = 2; fk-1 ? Ø; k = k+1) do
                Ck = Set of candicate k-sequences;
        For all input-sequences ε in the databse do
                Increment count of all α Ck contained
                in ε With GETWeight(α)
                Fk = {α Ck | α.sup ? min_sup};
        Set of frequent sequences = kFk
        }
    Real function GetWeight(Date ItemDate) {
        int AllRecordsDistance = MaxDate - MinDate;
        int ItemDistance = ItemDate - MinDate;
        Real Weight = ItemDistance / AllRecordsDistance + 0.3;
        Return Weight;
        }
```

The Proposed WMGSP Algorithm

```
        WMGSP {
    F1={frequent 1-sequences};
        For (k = 2; fk-1 ? Ø; k = k+1) do
                Ck = Set of candicate k-sequences;
        For all input-sequences ε in the databse do
                Increment count of all α Ck contained
                 in ε With GETWeight(α)
                Fk = {α Ck | α.sup ? min_sup};
        Set of frequent sequences = kFk
        }

    Real function GetWeight(Date ItemDate) {
        int AllRecordsDistance = MaxDate - MinDate;
        int Minutes = starttime – endtime;
        Real Weight = Minutes / AllRecordsDistance + 0.3;
        Return Weight;
        }
```

By utilizing the weight generated by the Weight Minute GSP algorithm. The efficiency of determining the weights are even more refined by analyzing the utilization time period of the particular link.

7 Conclusion

In this system the utilization concept is provided for a definite set of data set. If the web server is connected and utilize a wide range of data it would be even more efficient. The time duration is calculated in terms of minutes if they are done in seconds it would give an even more fine output. A very effective mining of highly utilized data are listed to the user. This decreases the time of search and provides the exact information the user is in need of. The user can get a very effective personalized searching mechanism done. It uses the information of the utilization of the link by the user which helps to sort information for the same user during the next time of search.

References

1. Djahantighi, F.S., Feizi-Derakhshi, M.-R., Pedram, M.M., Alavi, Z.: An Effective Algorithm for Mining Users Behaviour in Time- Periods. European Journal of Scientific Research 40(1), 81–90 (2010)
2. Leung, K.W.-T., Lee, D.L.: Deriving Concept-Based User Profiles from Search Engine Logs. IEEE Transactions on Knowledge and Data Engineering 22(7), 969–982 (2010)
3. Junyan, Z., Peiji, S.: Personalized Recommendation based on WAR. In: International Conference on Computer Application and System Modeling (ICCASM 2010) (2010)
4. He, H., Hai, H., Rujing, W.: FCA –Based Web User Profile Mining for Topics of Interest. In: International Conference on Integration Technology (2007)
5. Yang, Q., Fan, J., Wang, J., Zhou, L.: Personalizing Web Page Recommendation via Collaborative Filtering and Topic-Aware Markov Model. In: International Conference on Data Mining (2010)
6. Verma, B., Gupta, K., Panchal, S., Nigam, R.: Single Level Algorithm: An Improved Approach for Extracting User Navigational Patterns To Improve Website Effectiveness. In: Int'l Conf. on Computer & Communication Technology (2010)
7. Kuang, W., Luo, N.: User Interests Mining based on Topic Map. In: Seventh International Conference on Fuzzy Systems and Knowledge Discovery (2010)
8. Dhiyanesh, B., Gunasekaran, R.: Extracting User Profile. In: Dynamic Web Sites Using Web Usage Mining. In: National Intelluctual Conference On Research Perspective-NICORP (2010)
9. Joshilagrace, L.K., Maheswari, V., Nagamalai, D.: Web Log Data Analysis and Mining. In: Meghanathan, N., Kaushik, B.K., Nagamalai, D. (eds.) CCSIT 2011, Part III. Communications in Computer and Information Science, vol. 133, pp. 459–469. Springer, Heidelberg (2011)
10. Joshilagrace, L.K., Maheswari, V., Nagamalai, D.: Analysis of Web Logs and Web User in Web Mining. International Journal of Network Security & Its Application 3(1) (2011)
11. Software tools used TextStat 3.0

Performance Comparison of Different Routing Protocols in Vehicular Network Environments

Akhtar Husain[1], Ram Shringar Raw[2], Brajesh Kumar[1], and Amit Doegar[3]

[1] Department of Computer Science & Information Technology,
MJP Rohilkhand University, Bareilly, India
husainakhtar@yahoo.com, bkumar@mjpru.ac.in
[2] School of Computer and Systems Sciences,
Jawaharlal Nehru University, New Delhi, India
rsrao08@yahoo.in
[3] Department of Computer Science, NITTTR, Chandigarh, India
amit@nitttrchd.ac.in

Abstract. Due to mobility constraints and high dynamics, routing is a more challenging task in Vehicular Ad hoc NETworks (VANETs). In this work, we evaluate the performance of the routing protocols in vehicular network environments. The objective of this work is to assess the applicability of these protocols in different vehicular traffic scenarios. Both the position-based and topology-based routing protocols have been considered for the study. The topology-based protocols AODV and DSR and position-based protocol LAR are evaluated in city and highway scenarios. Mobility model has significant effects on the simulation results. We use Intelligent Driver Model (IDM) based tool VanetMobiSim to generate realistic mobility traces. Performance metrics such as packet delivery ratio and end-to-end delay are evaluated using NS-2. Simulation results shows position based routing protocols gives better performance than topology based routing protocols.

Keywords: VANET, Routing Protocols, AODV, DSR, LAR, City Scenario, Highway Scenario, Intelligent Driver Model.

1 Introduction

Vehicular ad hoc network is important technology for future developments of vehicular communication systems. Such networks composed of moving vehicles, are capable of providing communication among nearby vehicles and the roadside infrastructure. Modern vehicles are equipped with computing devices, event data recorders, digital map, antennas, and GPS receivers making VANETs realizable. VANETs can be used to support various functionalities such as vehicular safety [1], reduction of traffic congestion, office-on-wheels, and on-road advertisement. Most of the nodes in a VANET are mobile, but because vehicles are generally constrained to roadways, they have a distinct controlled mobility pattern [2]. Vehicles exchange information with their neighbors and routing protocols are used to propagate

D.C. Wyld et al. (Eds.): ACITY 2011, CCIS 198, pp. 427–436, 2011.

information to other vehicles. Some important characteristics that distinguish VANETs from other types of ad hoc networks include:

- High mobility that leads to extremely dynamic topology.
- Regular movement, restricted by both road topologies and traffic rules.
- Vehicles have sufficient power, computing and storage capacity.
- Vehicles are usually aware of their position and spatial environment.

Unlike conventional ad hoc wireless networks a VANET not only experiences rapid changes in wireless link connections, but may also have to deal with different types of network topologies. For example, VANETs on freeways are more likely to form highly dense networks during rush hours, while VANETs are expected to experience frequent network fragmentation in sparsely populated rural freeways or during late night. High and restricted node mobility, sort radio range, varying node density makes routing a challenging job in VANETs.

A number of routing protocols have been proposed and evaluated for ad hoc networks. Some of these are also evaluated for VANET environment, but most of them are topology based protocols. Position based protocols (like Location Aided Routing (LAR) [3] [4]), which require information about the physical position of the participating nodes, have not been studied that much and require more attention. The results of performance studies heavily depend on chosen mobility model. The literature shows that the results of many of performance studies are based on mobility models where nodes change their speed and direction randomly. Such models cannot describe vehicular mobility in a realistic way, since they ignore the peculiar aspects of vehicular traffic such as vehicles acceleration and deceleration in the presence of nearby vehicles, queuing at roads intersections, impact of traffic lights, and traffic jams. These models are inaccurate for VANETs and can lead to erroneous results.

In this paper performance evaluation of Ad Hoc OnDemand Distance Vector (AODV) [5], Dynamic Source Routing (DSR) [6], and LAR in city and highway traffic environments under different circumstances is presented. To model realistic vehicular motion patterns, we use the Advanced Intelligent Driver Model which is the extension of Intelligent Driver Model (IDM) [7]. We evaluate the performance of AODV, DSR, and LAR in terms of Packet Delivery Ratio (PDR) and End-to-End Delay (EED).

The rest of the paper is organized as follows: Section 2 presents related work, while section 3 briefly depicts the mobility model for VANETs. Section 4 presents simulation methodology and describes reported results. Finally, in section 5, we draw some conclusion remarks and outline future works.

2 Related Work

Routing protocols can be classified in two broad categories: topology based and position based routing protocols [8] [9]. Topology based approaches, which are further divided into two subcategories: reactive and proactive, use information about links to forward the packets between nodes of the network. Prominent protocols of this category are AODV, and DSR. Position-based routing (e.g. LAR) requires some information about the physical or geographic positions of the participating nodes. In this protocol the routing decision is not based on a routing table but at each node the routing decision is based on the positions of its neighboring nodes and the position of the destination node.

Several studies have been published comparing the performance of routing protocols using different mobility models, and different traffic scenarios with different performance metrics. A paper by Lochert et al. [10] compared AODV, DSR, and Geographic Source Routing (GSR) in city environment. They show that GSR which combines position-based routing with topological knowledge outperforms both AODV and DSR with respect to delivery rates and latency. A study by Jaap et al. [11] examined the performance of AODV and DSR in city traffic scenarios. Another study presented by Juan Angel Ferreiro-Lage et al. [15] compared AODV and DSR protocols for vehicular networks and concluded that AODV is best among the three protocols. LAR is described in [3] is to reduce the routing overhead by the use of position information. Position information will be used by LAR for restricting the flooding to a certain area called request zone. Authors found that LAR is more suitable for VANET.

3 Mobility Model

Simulation is a popular approach for evaluating routing protocols; however the accuracy of the results depends on the mobility model used. Mobility model has significant effects on the simulation results. Random waypoint (RWP) model, which is widely used for MANET simulations, is unsuitable for VANET simulations as the mobility patterns underlying an inter-vehicle communication are quite different. The mobility model used for studying VANETs must reflect as close as possible, the behavior of vehicular traffic. In this work, we discuss the Intelligent Driver Model (IDM).

3.1 The Intelligent Driver Model

The Intelligent Driver Model (IDM) [12] is a car-following model that characterizes drivers' behavior depending on their front vehicles. Vehicles acceleration/deceleration and its expected speed are determined by the distance to the front vehicle and its current speed. Moreover, it is also possible to model the approach of vehicles to crossings. Another advantage of the IDM is that it uses a small set of parameters that which can be evaluated with the help of real traffic measurements. The instantaneous acceleration of a vehicle is computed according to the following equation:

$$\frac{dv}{dt} = a\left[1 - \left(\frac{v}{v_0}\right) - \left(\frac{S^*}{S}\right)^2\right] \tag{1}$$

Where v is the current speed of the vehicle, v_0 is the desired velocity, S is the distance from the preceding vehicle and S^* is the desired dynamical distance to the vehicle/obstacle, which computed with the help of equation (2).

$$S^{*} = S_0 + \left[v\,T + \left(\frac{v.\Delta v}{2\sqrt{ab}}\right)\right] \quad (2)$$

Where desired dynamical distance S^* is a function of jam distance S_0 between two successive vehicles. T is the minimum safe time headway. The speed difference with respect to front vehicle velocity is Δv. a and b are maximum acceleration and maximum deceleration.

4 Experiments and Evaluations

Extensive simulations have been carried out to evaluate and compare the performances of LAR, AODV, and DSR in VANETs by using the network simulator NS-2 [13] in its version 2.32. It is freely available and widely used for research in mobile ad hoc networks. The movements of nodes are generated using VanetMobiSim tool. The awk programming is used to analyze the simulation results. It is assumed that every vehicle is equipped with GPS receiver and can obtain its current location.

4.1 System Model

Vehicles are deployed in a 1000m*1000m area. A Manhattan grid like road network is assumed to have eight vertically and horizontally oriented roads and 16 crossings. The vehicle moves and accelerates to reach a desired velocity. When a vehicle moves near other vehicles, it tries to overtake them if road includes multiple lanes. If it cannot overtake it decelerate to avoid the impact.

Table 1. Mobility model parameters

Parameter	Value
Maximum Acceleration	0.9 m/ s^2
Maximum Deceleration	0.5 m/ s^2
Maximum safe deceleration	4 m/ s^2
Vehicle Length	5 m
Traffic light transition	10s
Lane change threshold	0.2 m/ s^2
Politeness	0.5
Safe headway time	1.5 s
Maximum congestion distance	2 m

When a vehicle is approaching an intersection, it first acquires the state of the traffic sign. If it is a stop sign or if the light is red, it decelerates and stops. If it is a green traffic light, it slightly reduces its speed and proceeds to the intersection. The other mobility parameters are given in table 1.

Table 2. Simulation parameters

Parameter	Value
Simulation time	1500 seconds
Simulation area	1000m x 1000m
Transmission range	250m
Node speed	30 km/hr (city) and 100 km/hr (highway)
Traffic type	CBR
Data payload	512 bytes/packet
Packet rate	4 packets/sec
Node pause time	20 s
Bandwidth	2 Mbps
Mobility model	IDM based
Interface queue length	50 packets
No. of vehicles	10 to 80
MAC and Channel Type	IEEE 802.11, Wireless Channel

Vehicles are able to communicate with each other using the IEEE 802.11 DCF MAC layer. The transmission range is taken to be 250 meters. The traffic light period is kept constant at 60 seconds. Simulations are repeated varying the speed, that is, 30 km/h (city) and 100 km/h (highway) and varying the node density. The other simulation parameters are given in Table 2. Only one lane case is taken for city scenario. However, in highway scenario, first one lane case is considered and later it is generalized to multiple lanes.

4.2 Results and Discussion

The protocols are evaluated for packet delivery ratio and average end-to-end delay at varying node densities (10 to 80 vehicles). Hereafter the terms node and vehicle are used interchangeably.

4.2.1 Packet Delivery Ratio (PDR)

Packet delivery ratio is defined as the ratio of data packets received by the destinations to those generated by the sources. Mathematically, it can be defined as:

$$PDR = \frac{S_a}{S_b} \quad (3)$$

Where, S_a is the sum of data packets received by the each destination and S_b is the sum of data packets generated by the each source.

Fig. 1 depicts the fraction of data packets that are successfully delivered during simulations time versus the number of nodes. In city scenario, all the three protocols exhibit good performance for low node densities as shown in Fig. 1(a) and none of the protocols clearly outperforms the others. But with the increase in density, performance of the protocols decreases. It can be observed that the performance of the DSR reduces drastically while LAR is slightly better among the three.

In highway scenario all the protocols show relatively better performance as depicted by Fig. 1(b) and position based routing protocol clearly outperform the topology-based routing protocols with LAR exhibiting best results. Though, PDR again decreases with increasing density, but it is not that much low as observed in city scenario. Fig. 1(c) and Fig. 1(d) show that performance of the protocols degrades in highway scenario with lane changing (LC). It further slightly degrades with increase in the number of lanes. Again DSR is the worst and LAR has a slight edge over the other protocols.

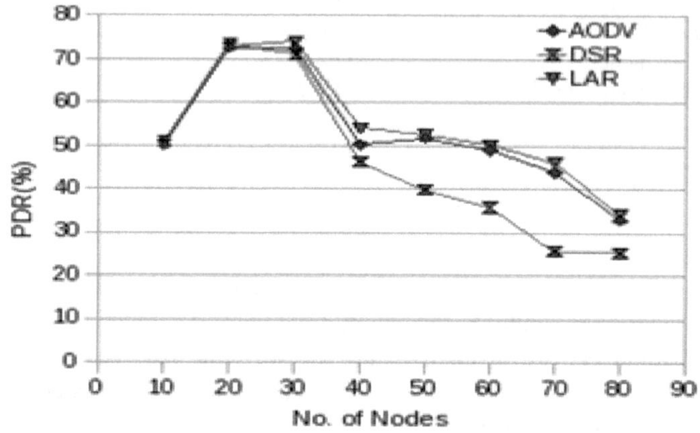

(a) City Scenario using IDM-IM

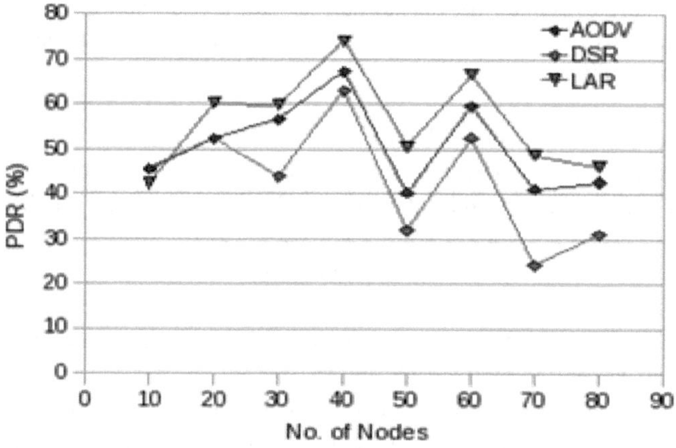

(b) Highway Scenario using IDM-IM

Fig. 1. PDR as a function of node density

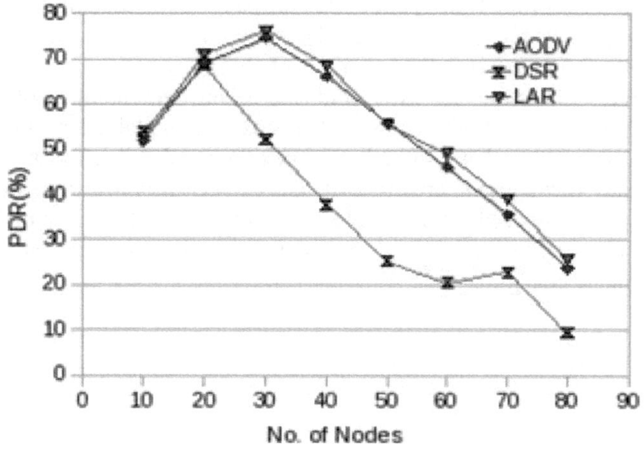

(c) Highway Scenario using IDM-LC (lane=2)

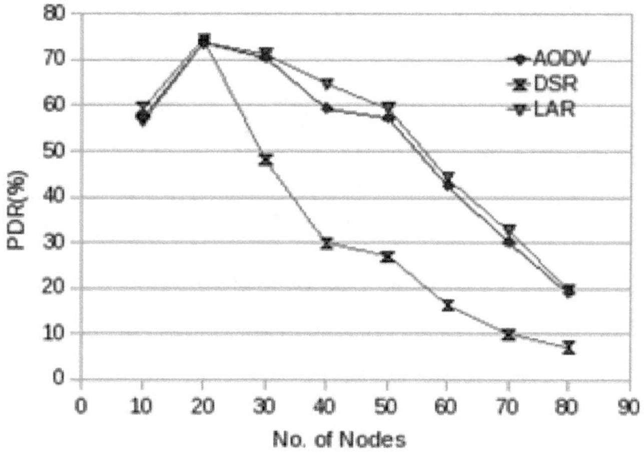

(d) Highway Scenario using IDM-LC (lane=4)

Fig. 1. *(continued)*

4.2.2 Average End-to-End Delay (EED)

The average time it takes a data packet to reach the destination. This includes all possible delays caused by buffering during route discovery latency, queuing at the interface queue, retransmission delay at MAC, and propagation delay. This metric is calculated by subtracting time at which first packet was transmitted by source from time at which first data packet arrived to destination. Mathematically, it can be defined as:

$$\text{Average EED} = \frac{S}{N} \quad (5)$$

Where S is the sum of the time spent to deliver packets for each destination, and N is the number of packets received by the all destination nodes.

Finally, Fig. 2 summarizes the variation of the average latency by varying node density. Average latency increases with increasing the number of nodes. DSR consistently presents the highest delay. This may be explained by the fact that its route discovery process takes a quite long time compared to other protocols. LAR has the lowest delay though compared to DSR and AODV it is low only slightly. In city scenario the position-based routing protocol exhibit lower delay compared to AODV especially at higher densities. Delay of all the protocols clearly increases in highway scenario with lane changing.

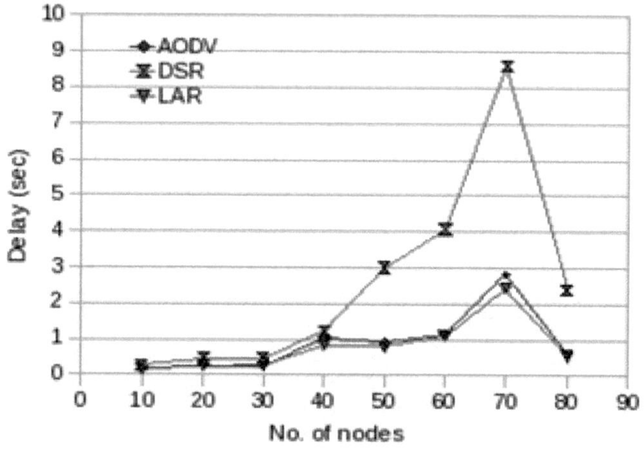

(a) City Scenario using IDM-IM

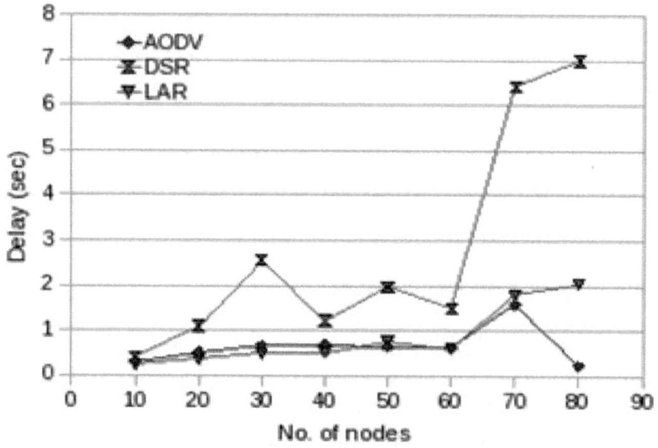

(b) Highway Scenario using IDM-IM

Fig. 2. Delay as a Function of Node Density

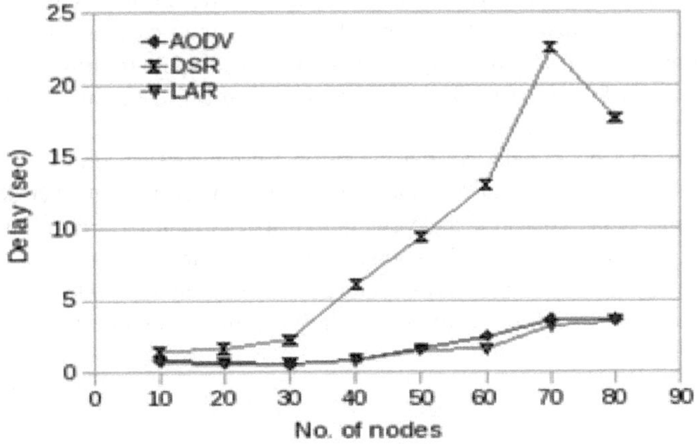

c) Highway Scenario using IDM-LC (lane=2)

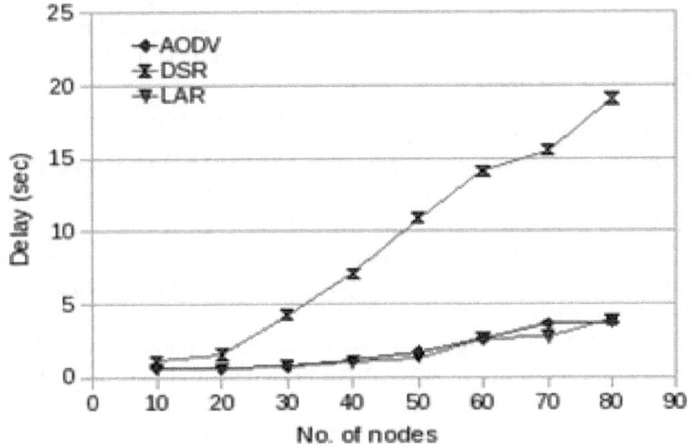

(d) Highway Scenario using IDM-LC (lane=4)

Fig. 2. Delay as a Function of Node Density

Overall, it can be concluded that LAR showed the best performance in the simulated scenarios with highest PDR. Moreover, it has the highest throughput and shown the lower delays also. We can say that DSR is not a suitable protocol for VANET whether it is city scenario or highway scenario. AODV also showed the good performance with better PDR and lower delays.

5 Conclusion and Future Work

In this paper, performance of three routing protocols AODV, DSR, and LAR were evaluated for vehicular ad hoc networks in city and highway scenarios. We used

Advanced Intelligent Driver Model to generate realistic mobility patterns. The three protocols were tested against node density for various metrics. It is found that position based routing protocol (LAR) outperforms topology based routing protocols (DSR and AODV) in different VANET environment. For most of the metrics LAR has the better performance.

Overall, it can be concluded that position based routing protocol gives better performance than topology based routing protocols in terms of packet delivery ratio and end-to-end delay for both the vehicular traffic scenarios. For future work, we want to study the impact of traffic signs, traffic lights and transmission range on the performance of the routing protocols. Future work will also include the evaluation of other position based routing protocols as they are more suitable in vehicular traffic environment.

References

1. Yang X., Liu J., Zhao F., Vaidya N.: A Vehicle-to Vehicle Communication Protocol for Cooperative Collision Warning. In: Int'l Conf. On Mobile and Ubiquitous Systems: Networking and Services (MobiQuitous 2004), pp. 44–45 (August 2004)
2. Bernsen, J., Manivannan, D.: Unicast routing protocols for vehicular ad hoc networks: A critical comparison and classification. Elsevier Journal of Pervasive and Mobile Computing 5(1), 1–18 (2009)
3. Ko, Y., Vaidya, N.: Location Aided Routing in Mobile Ad Hoc Networks. ACM Journal of Wireless Networks 6(4), 307–321 (2000)
4. Camp, T., Boleng, J., Williams, B., Wilcox, L., Navidi, W.: Performance Comparison of Two Locations Based Routing Protocols for Ad Hoc Networks. In: Proceedings of the IEEE INFOCOM, June 23-27, vol. 3, pp. 1678–1687 (2002)
5. Perkins, C.E., Royer, E.M.: Ad hoc on-demand distance vector routing. In: Proceedings of the 2nd IEEE Workshop on Mobile Computing Systems and Applications, New Orleans, I.A., pp. 90–100 (February 1999)
6. Johnson, D.B., Maltz, D.A., Broch, J.: Dynamic source routing protocol for wireless ad hoc network. IEEE Journal on Selected Areas in Communication 3(3), 431–439 (1985)
7. Haerri, J., Filali, F., Bonnet, C.: Performance comparison of AODV and OLSR in VANETs urban environments under realistic mobility patterns. In: 5th Annual IFIP Mediterranean Ad Hoc Networking Workshop (Med-Hoc-Net 2006), Lipari, Italy (June 2006)
8. Mauve, M., Widmer, J., Hartenstein, H.: A survey on position-based routing in mobile ad hoc networks. IEEE Network Magazine 15(6), 30–39 (2001)
9. Hong, X., Xu, K., Gerla, M.: Scalable Routing Protocols for Mobile Ad Hoc Networks. IEEE Network Magzine 16(4), 11–21 (2002)
10. Lochert C., Hartenstein H., Tian J.: A Routing strategy for vehicular ad hoc networks in city environments. In: Proceedings of IEEE Intelligent Vehicles Symposium, Columbus, USA, pp. 156–161 (June 2003)
11. Jaap, S., Bechler, M., Wolf, L.: Evaluation of routing protocols for vehicular ad hoc networks in city traffic scenarios. In: Proceedings of the 5th International Conference on Intelligent Transportation Systems Telecommunications (ITST), Brest, France (June 2005)
12. Trieber, M., Hennecke, A., Helbing, D.: Congested traffic states in empirical observations and microscopic simulations. Phys. Rev. E 62(2) (August 2000)
13. The Network Simulator NS-2 (2006), `http://www.isi.edu/nsnam/ns/`

A BMS Client and Gateway Using BACnet Protocol

Chaitra V. Bharadwaj[1], M. Velammal[2], and Madhusudan Raju[3]

[1] M.Tech, Dept of Computer Science and Engineering, The Oxford College of Engineering, Bangalore-560 062
chaitravb@gmail.com

[2] Asst. Professor, Dept of Computer Science and Engineering, The Oxford College of Engineering, Bangalore-560 062
velammaljegan@yahoo.co.in

[3] Technical Specialist, Robert Bosch Engineering and Business Solutions Limited, Bangalore-560 062
madhusudan.raju@in.bosch.com

Abstract. A Building Management System (BMS) is a computer-based control system installed in buildings that controls and monitors the building's mechanical and electrical equipments such as ventilation, lighting, power systems, fire systems, and security systems. The aim is at integrating elements of BMS using an open standard known as BACnet. BACnet stands for Building Automation Control and Network. It is the most widely used protocol in industry for automation control, which is used to control/monitor the status of different units. Any security system installed in a company can also be controlled using the same philosophy.

The main objective is to use BACnet protocol, an open standard protocol to develop BMS client application, capable of displaying, controlling and monitoring all BACnet entities, irrespective of the manufacturer and also to develop a gateway to interface Fire panels to communicate over network using BACnet protocol.

Keywords: Building Management System, BACnet Protocol, BACnet Client, BACnet Gateway.

1 Introduction

The word "BACnet" [1] has become recognizable in the building controls industry as the "Automation and Controls Network". However, do you really understand its capabilities? Do you know what benefits it brings to your buildings? BACnet is a very capable open protocol, but it does have its limits. This paper explores the role of BACnet as one of the leading protocol standards today, points out its current limitations, and shows where the standard is heading. You will also learn how to create a comfortable multi-protocol building today while planning for the secure BACnet system of tomorrow.

A Building Management System (BMS) [7] is a computer-based control system installed in buildings that controls and monitors the building's mechanical and electrical equipment such as ventilation, lighting, power systems, fire systems, and

D.C. Wyld et al. (Eds.): ACITY 2011, CCIS 198, pp. 437–449, 2011.

security systems. A BMS consists of software and hardware. A BMS is most common in a large building.

Organizations use multiple systems to monitor and control their buildings, ranging from Fire and Intrusion alarm to access control, video surveillance and building automation systems. But some of the 3rd party Building Management System (BMS) Clients available in market support different protocols for each of these systems. BACnet protocol is an industry standard protocol that is widely used in the heating and ventilation industry. It can also be applied to the security systems domain like a Fire Alarm System. Hence BACnet protocol is used to integrate Intrusion, Access control, CCTV, Fire alarm systems into a single operating system.

BACnet is a communications protocol for **B**uilding **A**utomation and **C**ontrol **net**works. It is an ASHRAE, ANSI, and ISO standard protocol. The BACnet protocol provides mechanisms for computerized building automation devices to exchange information, regardless of the particular building service they perform. The BACnet protocol defines a number of services that are used to communicate between building devices.

2 Motivation

The development of the proposed work is divided into two parts. First part is to develop a BACnet client capable of displaying all the BACnet entities present in the network. The scope of the client is to monitor as well as control (if required) the different BACnet entities present in the network. This development will be employing a third party BACnet stack (library) for making all the calls to BACnet entities. The BACnet client developed will be used to monitor fire alarm systems. Further it can be extended to any type of system. The second part is to develop a generic Gateway using BACnet protocol. The gateway is a software solution which communicates with the actual fire system in its proprietary protocol, and performs the complex job of creating and mapping BACnet objects into equivalent objects in the actual fire system. Gateway will be developed in generic nature, for Fire panels developed at BOSCH which can also be extended further for intrusion and video systems.

3 Literature Survey

3.1 The Safety Components

As climate control has several components, so does safety. Perhaps more! The main systems used to make a facility safe are physical and electronic security, fire and life safety, and emergency power and lighting. Physical security is the use of doors, locks, fences, gates, walls, etc., to keep intruders out or to provide containment. Physical security is made efficient by the use of electronic security, which in some implementations may eliminate the physical security requirements. Electronic security is the use of intrusion sensors, access control, and digital CCTV devices, including digital video recorders.

Fire and life safety systems are ready to go into action when excessive heat, smoke, or chemical levels are detected or when manually called upon. Response may come in the form of a call to the fire department, sprinkler, and chemical dousing methods, smoke evacuation, and room pressurization to contain chemical and biological hazards. Emergency power keeps critical building systems running. What is critical depends on the facility. Simple facilities may not require any emergency power. However, emergency backup power is becoming critical to more and more facilities such as hospitals, laboratories, and production facilities where a loss of power could endanger the building's occupants. Lighting systems are a simple but effective form of security. A well-lit parking lot or entrance deters incidences and provides instant comfort to those using the facility. Emergency lights assure a clear egress path during a fire or power loss event.

3.2 Building Management System

Building Management Systems (BMS) [2,3] had their genesis in simple monitoring and switch panels that allowed building managers to observe and control large building loads — such as heating, air conditioning, and lighting. Monitoring and control of these loads was performed through simple current loop systems, with very little qualitative information about these assets gathered. Building Management Systems have increased in sophistication over the years and now include operations such as building security, and feature characteristics such as modern communications networks based on TCP/IP and server based management platforms — including Web- based solutions. Building Management Systems are offered by a wide variety of vendors.

A BMS consists of software and hardware; the software program, usually configured in a hierarchical manner, can be proprietary, using such protocols as C-bus, Profibus, and so on. Vendors are also producing BMS's that integrate using Internet protocols and open standards such as DeviceNet, SOAP, XML, BACnet and Modbus. Its core function is to manage the environment within the building and may control temperature, carbon dioxide levels and humidity within a building. As well as controlling the building's internal environment, BMS systems are sometimes linked to access control or other security systems such as closed-circuit television (CCTV) and motion detectors. Fire alarm systems and elevators are also sometimes linked to a BMS, for example, if a fire is detected then the system could shut off dampers in the ventilation system to stop smoke spreading and send all the elevators to the ground floor and park them to prevent people from using them in the event of a fire.

Before the modern computer-controlled BMSs came into being, various electromechanical systems were in use to control buildings. Many facilities management offices had panels consisting of manual switches or more commonly, lights showing the status of various items of plant, allowing building maintenance staff to react if something failed. Some of these systems also include an audible alarm. Advancements in signal communications technology have allowed the migration of early pneumatic and "home run" hard wired systems, to modems communicating on a single twisted pair cable, to ultra fast IP based communication on "broad band" or "fiber optic" cable.

Functions of Building Management System

To create a central computer controlled method which has three basic functions:

- Controlling
- Monitoring
- Optimizing

the building's facilities, mechanical and electrical equipments for comfort, safety and efficiency.

Benefits of BMS

- Ease of information availability problem diagnostics
- Effective use of maintenance staff
- Computerized maintenance scheduling
- Good control of internal comfort conditions
- Save time and money during the maintenance
- Central or remote control and monitoring of building
- Increased level of comfort and time saving

Efficient and Simple - Monitoring, control, administration and maintenance of all these systems can be a huge challenge because individual systems only serve individual purposes. To completely secure and manage a building, you need a number of functions – and if you want them all, they have to run alongside each other. This approach is not only inefficient, unreliable and expensive, but also difficult to upgrade when your requirements change.

A single system-but still flexible - This is where the Building Integration System comes in. The idea is one solution that offers everything – combining different building management functions on one platform, and providing simple responses to difficult questions. But because every organization has unique building management requirements, the Building Integration System is modular. This means that, like with building blocks, you can add or remove single elements or create new combinations, which gives you maximum flexibility. This guarantees that you get the solution you need.

Complete solution for integrated building management - No matter how comprehensive and complex your building management requirements are, the BIS responds flexibly and is also extremely easy to use. The Building Integration System combines a number of technical systems: fire and intrusion alarm, video monitoring, access control and evacuation systems. All on one modular platform.

4 BACnet Protocol

Supported by the American Society of Heating, Refrigerating and Air Conditioning Engineers (ASHRAE) [4], BACnet was adopted as an ANSI standard in 1995. It has also been adopted as ISO 16484-5 and as European standard EN/ISO 16484-5. It is a software based protocol so it can run on current and future hardware platforms. Developed specifically for Building Services, BACnet defines how all the elements of the Building Management System interoperate. In BACnet terms, interoperate means that two or more BACnet devices may share the same communications networks, and ask each other to perform various functions on a peer-to-peer basis. Although BACnet does not require every system to have equal capabilities, it is possible for designers of system components at every level of complexity to have access to functions of other automation system peers. There are two key concepts in BACnet that are critical to understand. First, is the idea that BACnet is applicable to all types of building systems: HVAC, Security, Access Control, Fire, Maintenance, Lighting etc. The same mechanism that gives BACnet this flexibility has other important benefits: vendor-independence and forward-compatibility with future generations of systems. This is accomplished using an object-oriented approach for representing all information within each controller. The second key idea is that BACnet/IP can communicate with different Local Area Network (LAN) technology for transporting BACnet application messages via BACnet gateways.

Thus the key part of BACnet is its application layer and it defines the following:

- a method of abstracting the functionality of control and monitoring devices (objects)
- application layer messages (services)
- the encoding of BACnet application layer messages

The combination of these components delivers important benefits to owners and specifiers of BACnet systems.

4.1 BACnet's Method of Exchanging Messages

In defining the format for BACnet communications, the Standards Committee chose a flexible, object-oriented approach. All data in a BACnet system is represented in terms of "objects," "properties" and "services." This standard method of representing data and actions is what enables BACnet devices from different manufacturers to interoperate. Understanding this object-oriented approach and its terms is essential to understanding BACnet.

4.2 Objects

BACnet's object-oriented approach to accessing and organizing information provides a consistent method for controlling, examining, modifying and interoperating with different types of information in different types of devices, which is both vendor-independent and forward-compatible with future BACnet systems. All information in a BACnet system is represented in terms of objects. An object might represent information about a physical input or output, or it may represent a logical grouping of points that perform some function. Every object has an identifier (such as AI-1) that allows the BACnet system to identify it. In this regard, an object is much like what is now commonly known as a "data point" in the HVAC community. Where an object differs from a data point is that a data point would typically have a single value associated with it, whereas an object consists of a number of prescribed properties, only one of which is the present value. It is only through its properties that an object is monitored and controlled. All objects have some required properties and some that are optional.

4.3 Properties

As indicated in the discussion of objects above, objects are monitored and controlled only through their properties. BACnet specifies 123 properties of objects. Three properties-Object-identifier, Object-name, and Object-type-must be present in every object. BACnet also may require that certain objects support specific additional properties. The type of object and the type of device in which that object resides determine which properties are present. BACnet defines not only what the properties of standard objects are, but also what types of behavior are to be expected from each property.

Standard objects also have optional properties, which need not be implemented by every vendor, but if they are implemented then they must behave as the standard describes. These standard objects may also have proprietary properties that are added by vendors at their discretion to provide additional features. A BACnet device may also implement proprietary object types that can provide any type of feature or set of properties that the vendor chooses. The key to the object mechanism is that every object and every property, whether standardized or proprietary, is accessible in the same manner. Some properties can accept writes, and others can only be read.

4.4 Services

When a property is read or written to, that act is known as a service. Services are how one BACnet device gets information from another device, commands a device to perform certain actions (through its objects and properties, of course), or lets other devices know that something has happened. The only service that is required to be supported by all devices is the Read-property service. There are a total of 32 standard services on the application layer which is subdivided into 5 categories. Namely, Alarm and Event Service, Object Access Service, File Access Service, Remote Device Management Service, Virtual Terminal Service.

As a system developer or user, you don't need to be concerned with the execution or processing of service requests, which will be transparent and automatic. As a specifier or engineer, however, you will need to know what objects and services are supported by which devices. This information is found in the device's protocol implementation conformance statement (PICS).

4.5 Conformance Classes and the Device PICS

Because not all devices need to have the same level of functionality, BACnet defines conformance classes that categorize the capabilities and functionality of devices. All devices of a certain conformance class will have a minimum set of required features (in the form of objects and services). Some other features can be optional. BACnet insists that this information is made public in a **P**rotocol **I**mplementation **C**onformance **S**tatement (PICS)-basically a list of features that the software/device supports. The PICS lists what objects are present in the device and whether the device initiates a service request (asks or commands) or executes the request (responds or acts). The PICS also provides you with the conformance class of the device. By comparing a device's PICS with project requirements or with another vendor's PICS, you can determine how well a BACnet product "fits" a given application.

PICS Uses

PICS is a written document, created by the manufacturer of a device, that identifies the particular options specified by BACnet that are implemented in the device. A BACnet PICS is considered a public document that is available for use by any interested party.

The following are the important uses of PICS:

- the protocol implementer, as a check list to reduce the risk of failure to conform to the standard.
- the supplier and producer of the implementation, as a basis for what is desired and what is supplied.
- the user of the implementation, as a basis for initially checking the possibility of inter working with another implementation.
- a protocol tester, as the basis for selecting appropriate tests against which to assess the claim for conformance of the implementation.

"For the operator, the main advantages are that it offers a 'single seat' (one computer and one software interface) of control for all of their systems and allows multiple systems to use the same devices and interfaces in the occupied space," said Richard Westrick, Jr., Manager, Applications Engineering for Lithonia Lighting's Control Systems Division. In an effort to bridge the gap between existing control networks and the BACnet networks, and to appease engineers who are specifying BACnet because of its promise, some manufacturers have turned to BACnet Gateways [6]. The function of a BACnet Gateway is to convert data from the format used by one control network into the BACnet format. This allows the manufacturer to state that a product supports BACnet because BACnet packets can be received by the gateway and forward it to the non-BACnet system, and vice versa.

5 Existing Scenario

There are two types of Building Management Systems that are being used. One of them is shown below: In figure 1, the BMS Client will interface many of the building's mechanical and electrical equipments like Fire detection system, Access control etc. This client will interface all these systems to a single PC. This BMS uses OPC (**OLE** for **P**rocess **C**ontrol) as the protocol for the communication between equipments and the client. BMS uses OPC sever, which will be interconnected to the equipments. These equipments or the devices will send the information to the gateway and the gateway in turn will send the information to the BIS client for displaying. The client will display the information which can be easily understood by the client.

OPC protocol is a De-facto-Industry Standard, based on Microsoft COM (**C**omponent **O**bject **M**odel)/DCOM (**D**istributed **C**omponent **O**bject **M**odel) technology. No optional object properties are present. Configuration of DCOM in complex network environment can be tricky. Many times firewalls do not allow for port 15 (OPC/DCOM) to be open as several virus attacks (like W32Lovsan) will come through this port. The number of services offered is very less.

All these disadvantages forced the developers to use of different protocol. This became the reason for the use of BACnet Protocol in the industry.

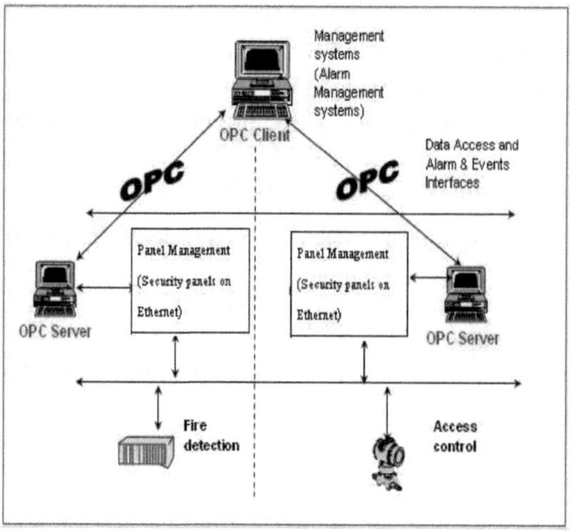

Fig. 1. Building Management System using OPC Protocol and Single Client

The other type of Building Management System that is used is shown below. In figure 2, each equipment like Fire/Smoke detectors system, Intrusion detection systems, access control etc will be separately connected to different clients. Each client will interface with the equipments through separate gateways. Every client will receive information only about the particular device to which it is connected. It will display information about that particular device. More clients are needed to interface with different types of equipments.

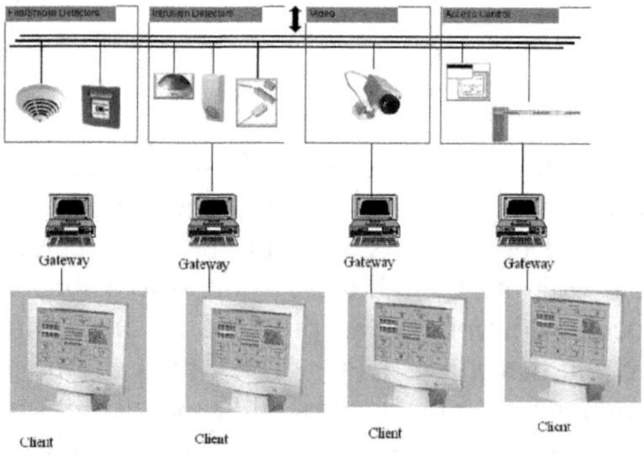

Fig. 2. Building Management System using Different Clients and Protocols

Having all the climate and safety systems installed and working within their realm of expertise will elevate the level of comfort within the facility. However, having each system work independently of the others will not provide the highest level of comfort. When all the systems are working in concert with one another, the safety of the facility is improved with the added intelligence. So, there is a need to unite all the systems in a building using a single open protocol. To accomplish this, BACnet protocol is used. Client should be generic in nature and should display information about all the systems in the building.

6 Uniting Buildings Under a Single Open Protocol

The goal is to have all these systems interoperate despite the existence of multiple protocols within a site. Here is where things get technical. The power meters may speak Modbus, the lighting panel may speak LonTalk, the fire panel and lights may speak BACnet or any other protocol, and the security system is a proprietary system. How can these all be linked up with your BACnet or proprietary HVAC system?

The oldest method of integration is to use hardwired points. Dependable, hardwired integration, however, is not always cost-effective or informative. With hardwired points, you are only getting an "off" or an "on" value and you need an input/output set for each point to be exchanged. Hardwiring is required for some life/ safety sequences, but you will want to limit its use to applications that require it.

The next method of integration is through software "drivers". Drivers integrate by translation. Drivers actually take a message from system A and translate using the language of system B to a mapped point. With drivers, it is possible to get more detailed information exchanged between systems. You may read and write analog, digital, and even text values. Some drivers even pass alarm information between systems. However, all drivers have their drawbacks. To configure a driver, often representatives from both vendor systems need to coordinate; and if one vendor upgrades their system after the initial setup, communication may be lost.

As a response to the difficulties of hardwired points and drivers, several open systems have been developed and utilized by manufacturers. With an open system, the protocol language is shared between two or more vendors. Since both systems speak the same language, interoperability is made a lot easier. Some open protocols like BACnet are designed to link systems of the same type whereas others attempt to link systems of many types. Furthermore, the levels of services offered by open protocols differ. Some open systems only permit data sharing whereas others are capable of offering rich services such as alarming, scheduling, trending, and device management between systems.

Interoperability is achieved most easily through the use of open protocol systems with rich services. Having rich services exchanged between systems enables one user interface to be the primary monitoring and response center for all events. A single user interface that can have graphics, schedules, alarms, and logs for trending, activity, and events is preferred over separate workstations for each system.

With one user interface for all building systems, there is a clearer assessment of each event. The user can monitor smoke evacuation and view video camera feeds while receiving fire alarm messages- all from the same screen.

The BMS Client can be any component (hardware/software) that understands BACnet protocol. The BMS client will be responsible for displaying BACnet objects created by the Gateway. Any change in the state of any BACnet object must be visible in the BMS Client. The BMS client should also be capable of sending commands to the Gateway (E.g.: Reset Command for a Life Safety Object). The Gateway and the BMS client communicate over Ethernet and must be uniquely addressed in a BACnet internetwork.

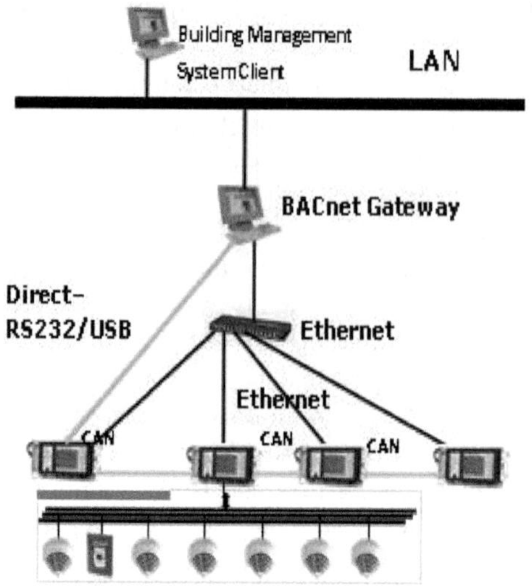

Fig. 3. BMS Client using BACnet Protocol

The Gateway will be a software component, installed on a PC. Gateways, also called protocol converters, can operate at network layer and above. Typically, a gateway must convert one protocol stack into another. It will be responsible for communicating with the fire panel on one side and the BMS BACnet Client on other side. It will act as an intermediary between fire panel and BMS BACnet Client. The Gateway must be capable of creating BACnet objects, updating their states and handle commands from the BMS BACnet client. BACnet Objects will be created based upon the SI (Security Item) Type of the Security Item. Each fire panel has an Ethernet port over which it reports the Security Items (SI) as well as their states. In a networked panel system with more than one fire panel connected, all panel ports must be connected to the Gateway via the Ethernet switch. Hence, the Gateway PC must have 2 Network Interface Cards, one for communicating with the Panel(s) and the other to communicate with the BMS client.

The commands would be converted and forwarded to the panel. Alarms/Events on the other hand would be interpreted on receipt by the gateway. These would then be converted into BACnet objects and passed onto the BMS application via the BACnet stack. The Gateway and the BMS client communicate over Ethernet and must be uniquely addressed in a BACnet internetwork.

Each Fire Panel has an Ethernet port over which it reports the SI Items as well as their states. In a networked panel system with more than one Fire Panels connected, all panel ports must be connected to the Gateway via the Ethernet switch. Hence, the Gateway PC must have 2 Network Interface Cards, one for communicating with the Panel(s) and the other to communicate with the BMS client.

Only one instance of the BACnet Client can be opened on one PC. Hence the Client application and BACnet Gateway server must not run on the same PC. BACnet stack should be installed in both client and the server PCs.

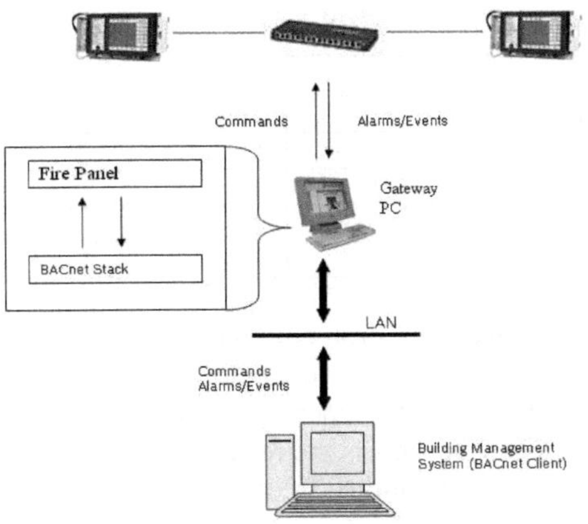

Fig. 4. Gateway using BACnet Protocol

7 BACnet – Open Protocol with Rich Services

Open protocols are capable of proving the best means of achieving interoperability between building systems. However there are different levels of openness. When evaluating an open protocol certain questions should be asked. The table below provides the results of applying these questions towards the BACnet protocol.

Table 1. What makes BACnet Protocol Open

	BACnet
Is the Protocol used by multiple vendors?	Yes
Is the protocol "freely" distributed?	Yes
Is the protocol hardware chip independent?	Yes
Is the protocol software dependent?	Yes
Is the standard developed in an open manner?	Yes

An important item that was incorporated into the BACnet standard by the committee was the concept of rich services, services that go beyond the standard data sharing functions. Without rich services, the total system looses functionality. When using a single user interface to manage an entire facility, you want to be able to receive alarms and trend data, edit schedules and manage devices. The table below shows the services that are offered by BACnet.

Table 2. BACnet Rich Services

	BACnet
Data Sharing (Read/Write points)	Yes
Scheduling	Yes
Trending	Yes
Alarm and Event Management	Yes
Device Management	Yes

The next point is how well the protocol “natively” interoperates. Although other protocol may offer the same range of building systems control; however, the integration level between these other open systems are not as high as the integration level between BACnet systems. This is the result of richness of BACnet services. The table below shows the interoperability of the systems in a building with BACnet protocol.

Table 3. BACnet’s Building System Support

	BACnet
HVAC	Yes
Smoke Control	Yes
Fire Annunciation Panels	Yes
Intrusion	Some
Access Control	Rare
CCTV	Yes
Power Monitoring	Yes
Lighting	Yes

8 Conclusion

This paper focuses on the use of BACnet Protocol to efficiently manage a building. BACnet makes a great core for building control. BACnet is a robust open protocol that is poised to be the total building protocol of the future with all the necessary security refinements. It also emphasizes on building a generic client, capable of communicating with any kind of BACnet device has to be developed which also will monitor and control different BACnet entities present in the network and this application will run irrespective of the manufacturer of BACnet server/BACnet supported devices. It also focuses on building a Gateway must be capable of creating BACnet objects, updating their states and handle commands from the BMS BACnet client. Safety and comfort go hand and hand. But only when climate, lighting, CCTV, access control, intrusion, and fire systems communicate with each other in a rich manner can the highest level of safety and comfort be achieved.

References

1. Schneider Electric: White Paper on BACnet Without Limits (2005)
2. Tennefoss, M.R.: White Paper on Implementing Open Interoperable Building Control Systems (2000)

3. Echlin, G.: White Paper on Building Management Systems and Advanced Metering
4. Cylon: White Paper on BACnet
5. BOSCH security systems, http://www.boschsecurity.co.in
6. BACnet protocol overview, http://www.en.wikipedia.org/wiki/BACnet
7. Building Management System, http://en.wikipedia.org/wiki/BuildingManagementSystem
8. Working of BACnet, http://www.aboutlightingcontrols.org/education/papers/bacnet.shtml

About the Authors

#1 Chaitra V Bharadwaj is currently persuing M.Tech in Computer Science and Engineering from the Oxford College of Engineering, Bangalore.

#2 Mrs. Vellamal M is currently working as Asst. Prof, Dept of Computer Science and Engineering in The Oxford College of Engineering. She has completed her M.Tech from The Anna University, Tamil Nadu, India.

#3 Mr. Madhusudan Raju is currently working as Technical Specialist in Robert Bosch Engineering and Business Solutions Limited.

Implementation of Scheduling and Allocation Algorithm

Sangeetha Marikkannan[1], Leelavathi[2], Udhayasuriyan Kalaiselvi[3], and Kavitha[4]

Karpaga Vinayaga College of Engineering and Technology, Chennai
{sang_gok}@yahoo.com

Abstract. This paper presents a new evolutionary algorithm developed for scheduling and allocation for an elliptic filter. It involves the scheduling of the operations and resource allocation for elliptic filter. The Scheduling and Allocation Algorithm is compared with different scheduling algorithms like As Soon As Possible algorithm, As Late As Possible algorithm, Mobility Based Shift algorithm, FDLS, FDS and MOGS using Elliptic Filter. In this paper execution time and resource utilization is calculated for different Elliptic Filter and reported that proposed Scheduling and Allocation increases the speed of operation by reducing the control step. The proposed work to analyse the magnitude, phase and noise responses for different scheduling algorithm in an elliptic filter.

Keywords: Data Flow Graph, Scheduling Algorithm, Elliptic Filter, Control Step.

1 Introduction

In this process, the scheduling and allocation algorithm is designed with an objective to minimize the control steps which in turn reduce the cost function. Elliptic filter is a signal processing filter with equalized ripple behavior in both the pass band and stop band. The process tasks are scheduling and allocation[1]. The first step in the scheduling and allocation algorithm design, which is the case of transforming elliptic filter program into structure, includes operation scheduling and resource allocation. The scheduling and allocation algorithm are closely interrelated. In order to have an optimal design, both task should be performed simultaneously. However, due to time complexity, many systems perform them separately or introduce iteration loops between the two subtasks. Scheduling involves assigning the operation to so- called control steps. A control step is the fundamental sequencing unit in the synchronous system; it corresponds to a clock cycle.

Allocation involves assigning the operation and values to resources i.e., providing storage, functional units and communication paths are specifying their usage. Therefore, allocation is usually further divided into three subtasks: variable binding, operation assignment and data transfer binding. Variable binding refers to the allocation of register to data, i.e., values that are generation one control step and used in another must be assigned to registers. Few systems have a one-to one correspondence between variables and registers, while other allow register sharing for those variables, which have disjoint life times. Operation assignment binds operation to functional units (e.g., an adder or an ALU). Data transfer bindings represent the

D.C. Wyld et al. (Eds.): ACITY 2011, CCIS 198, pp. 450–459, 2011.

allocation of connections (e.g., buses, multiplexer) between hardware components i.e., registers and functional units to create the necessary information paths as required by the specification and the schedule.

There is a variety of scheduling algorithms that differ in the way of searching for the best solution. Mostly they optimize only the number of functional units. In our evaluation process, it turned out that scheduling algorithm obtained the best results in terms of utilization of functional units and computation time [2]. Therefore it is reasonable to use the principles of the evolutionary algorithm to find some of the optimum solutions.

However, there are different approaches to sewing the same problem, but it is not important how close the algorithm comes to the optimum solutions: what matters is how those schedules are allocated in the final design. Therefore, since the subtasks of scheduling and allocation are heavily interrelated, the algorithm cannot be judged in terms of optimization until the final result of the allocation subtask is known. So, when a new scheduling algorithm is created the allocation criteria has to be taken in to account [3].

The main steps involved in scheduling and allocation algorithm for an elliptic filter.

Description of the behaviour of the system.

Translation of the description in to a graph (e.g., CDFG)[5].

Operation scheduling (each operation in the graph is assigned to a control step).

Allocation of the resources for the digital system (here the resources can be functional units assigned to execute operation derived from the graph CDFG).

Portioning the system behaviour in to the hardware and software module for the scheduled CDFG to estimate buffer size and delay.

Usually, allocation, scheduling and assignment are widely recognized as mandatory backbone tasks in high-level synthesis.

2 Previous Approach

Techniques for combined scheduling and check point insertion in high-level synthesis of digital systems. More generalized CDFGs are needed to be designed. Ravi kumar (1998) present an adaptive version of the well-known simulated annealing algorithm and described application to a combinatorial optimization problem arising in the high level synthesis of digital systems. It takes 29 registers for the 5 functional registers[4]. Scheduling method for reducing the number of scan register for a cyclic structure. In order to estimate the number of scan register during scheduling, and they proposed a provisional binding of operational units and showed a force-directed scheduling algorithm with the provisional binding [2] cluster based register binding is performed that binds each carrier of DFG to a register. A set of resources consisting of functional units and registers is assigned to each cluster, and instead of binding the resources to and sharing them among individual operations or carriers, the set of resources is bound to and shared among the clusters. Such as approach, help to reduce the average active cycles of those clocked elements [3]. Multi objective genetic scheduling(MCGS) algorithm which shows less cost function than other scheduling algorithm for an elliptic wave filter. The proposed scheduling and allocation algorithm shows less execution time and cost function [1].

3 Nodes Assignment

In general the nodes in a CDFG can be classified as one of the following types.

Operational nodes: These are responsible for arithmetic logical or relational operations.

Call nodes: This node denotes calls to sub program modules.

Control nodes: This node is responsible for applications like conditional and loop constructs.

Storage nodes: These nodes represent assignment applications associated with variables and signals.

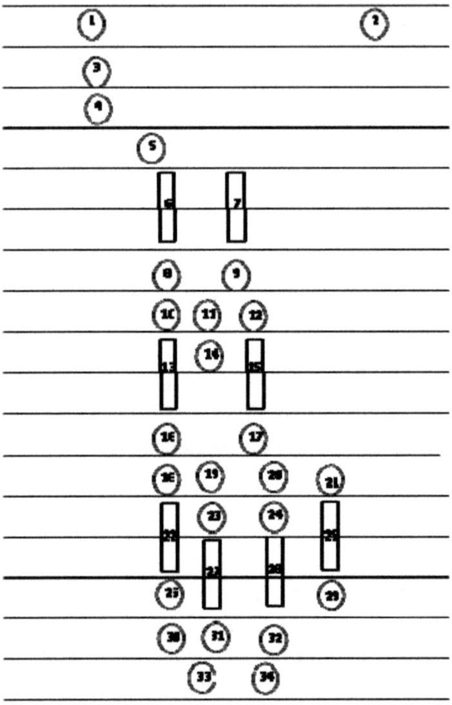

Fig. 1. Operational nodes for Elliptic wave filter benchmark

4 CDFG Generation

The control data flow graph is a directed a cyclic graph in which a node can be either an operation node or a control node (representing a branch, loop, etc.,).the directed edges in a CDFG represent the transfer of a value or control from one node to another. An edge can be condition, while implementing a if/care statements or loop constructs[4].The Table 1 shows the estimated functional units and registers for Hardware Oriented Approach.

Table 1. Hardware oriented approach

			Functional unit	Register
Binary partitioning	Proposed work	merging	1	4
Source level partitioning	Papa&silc(2000)	ASAP	8	11
	Papa&silc(2000)	ALAP	9	13
	Papa&silc(2000)	FDS	6	11
	Papa&silc(2000)	LS	6	11
	Papa&silc(2000)	FDLS	6	11
	Papa&silc(2000)	MOGS	6	11
	Proposed work	SAA	5	11
	Deniz Dal &NazaninMansouril (2008)	-	5	12

5 Hardware Components

A very essential hardware component is the functional unit (FU). This is a combinatorial or sequential logic circuit that realizes Boolean functions, such as an adder, a multiplexer or an arithmetic unit(ALU). Another essential component inherent to synchronous logic is the register, which makes it possible to store data in the circuit. Both FUs and registers operate on words, which means that each input or output is actually realized by a number of signals carrying a bit. A register is a simplest form of a memory element, separate registers are not very efficient, as individual wires have to be connected to each register. Registers are then combined to form register files. The simplest way to make connections between hardware components is by using wires. The hardware can be used much efficiently; it is possible to change the connection between the components during a computation. One way to realize this is to use multiplexing. Even more efficient hardware design is possible if buses and tri-state drivers are used.

6 Scheduling

Scheduling algorithm can be constructive or transformational (based on their approach). Transformational algorithms start with some schedule (typically parallel or maximally serial) and separately apply transformations in an attempt to bring the schedule closer to the design requirements[3]. The transformations allow operations to be parallelized or serialized whilst ensuring that dependency constraints between operations are not violated. In contrast, constructive algorithm builds up a schedule from scratch by incrementally adding operations. A simplest e.g., of the constructive approach scheduling is As Soon As Possible (ASAP) scheduling.

7 Scheduling and Allocation Algorithm

The data flow graph obtained from the input description to scheduled using As Soon As Possible scheduling and As Late As Possible scheduling. ASAP scheduling computes the earliest time at which an operation can be scheduled and ALAP can also be computed by adapting the longest path algorithm to work from the output backwards. Combining the information obtained in both ways of scheduling algorithm give rise to more powerful heuristics called mobility based scheduling. (according to the available functional units).

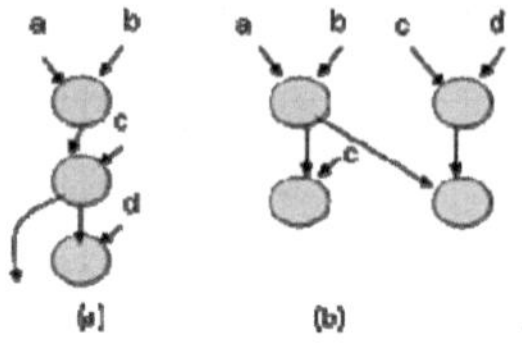

Fig. 2. (a) Most serial form (b) Most parallel form

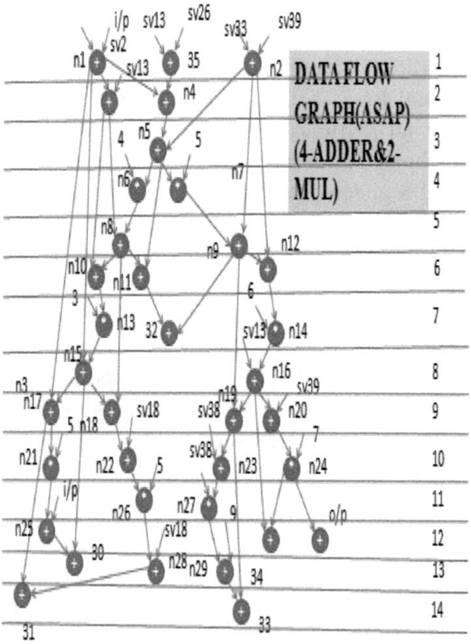

Fig. 3. Scheduling and Allocation Algorithm for Elliptic Wave Filter

The scheduling algorithm proposed take care of resource constrained synthesis and find a scheduling and assignment, such that, the total computation is completed in minimal time(resource constrained synthesis). The proposed scheduling reduces the critical path of the data flow graph.

The root nodes are calculated from the graphical description and the critical path is determined. The algorithm merges the node that has data dependency, which is of same type and has minimum two extend an input that is decomposed in to parallel form.

The condition is that, last node should have single output edge, if predecessors have one output edge than the both nodes are merged and formed in to single node. If the node has more than one output edge the node should not be disturbed and a cut in the path is set and the current node is moved to previous cycle where it meets the hardware constraint problem are shown in Fig.2. If the problem satisfies the condition, a node is inserted in the previous cycle else it chooses the critical path. If the critical path is cut, the control step of the CDFG is reduced, which leads to a reduction in clock cycle of the entire system without any change in the hardware constraint.

A cut in the critical path, i.e., between node 3and node 4 converts, the most serial is converted in to most parallel form, and leads to a reduction in a single control step without affecting the hardware constraints of 3 adder and 2 multiplier. Hardware is allocated according to data dependency of the nodes are shown in Fig.3.

8 Experimental Results

The proposed scheduling algorithm cost less and also has reduced control steps when compared to other scheduling algorithms and utilizes minimum number of hardware resources. A cut established between hardware and software partitioned nodes determines the edge cut and buffer size is determined from the life time of the edge. The proposed scheduling and allocation algorithm proves to achieve better solution for two way portioning. Table 2 shows the control step and Execution time. Table 3 represents the software Oriented Approach using ARM processor.

Table 2. Software oriented approach using LABVIEW

Algorithm	Number of Functional Unit		Number of Control Step	Number of Execution Time (ms)
	+	*		
ASAP	3	2	16	34.24
ALAP	3	2	16	38.88
MBS	3	2	16	39.52
SAA	4	2	13	22.56

Table 3. Software oriented approach using ARM processor

Algorithm	No. of Ripple	No. of cluster	Ripple execution time (0-1000) ms	Cluster Execution time (0-1000) ms
ASAP	6	4	32	98
ALAP	8	5	13	45
MBS	2	8	10	19
SAA	2	1	209	568

9 ASAP Scheduling Algorithm

In this Front panel of ASAP scheduling algorithm using ARM processor the analog inputs are connected and more ripple and cluster are analysed in between (0-1000) execution time. The number of ripple in ASAP is 6 and ripple execution time is 32ms. The number of cluster in between (0-1000) is 4 and cluster execution time is 98ms are shown in fig.4.

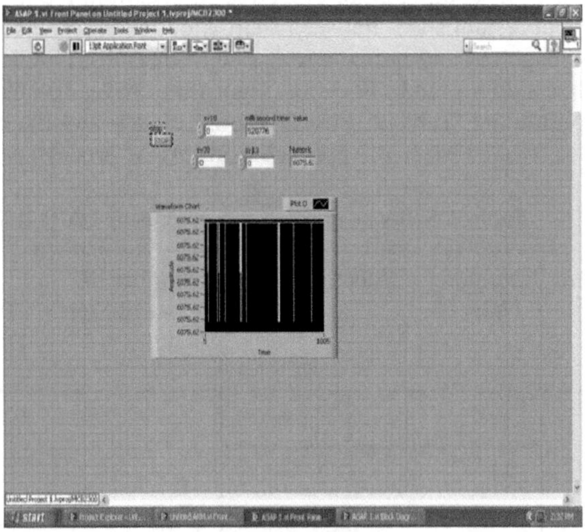

Fig. 4. Front panel of ASAP using ARM Processor

In this Front panel of ASAP scheduling algorithm the first figure shows the magnitude response are analysed using LABVIEW in which the ripple frequency is 10MHZ. The second figure shows the phase response of ASAP in which the ripple frequency is 11MHZ and third figure represents the noise response of ASAP are shown in fig.5.

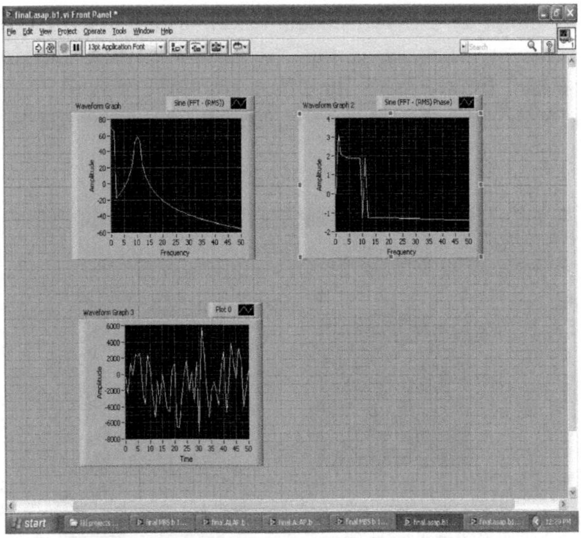

Fig. 5. Front panel for responses of ASAP using LABVIEW

10 ALAP Scheduling Algorithm

In this Front panel of ALAP scheduling algorithm using ARM processor the analog inputs are connected and more ripple and cluster are analysed in between (0-1000) execution time. The number of ripple in ALAP is 8 and ripple execution time is 24ms. The number of cluster in between (0-1000) is 5 and cluster execution time is 45ms are shown in fig.6.

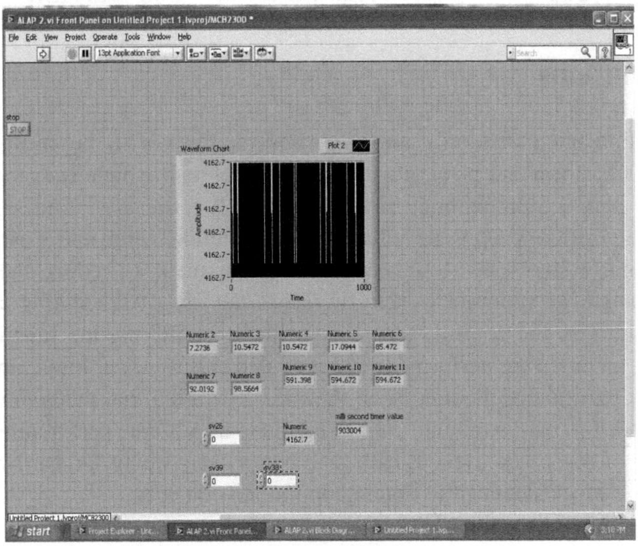

Fig. 6. Front panel of ALAP using ARM processor

In this Front panel of ASAP scheduling algorithm the first figure shows the magnitude response are analysed using LABVIEW in which the ripple frequency is 10MHZ. The second figure shows the phase response of ASAP in which the ripple frequency is 11MHZ and third figure represents the noise response of ASAP are shown in fig.7.

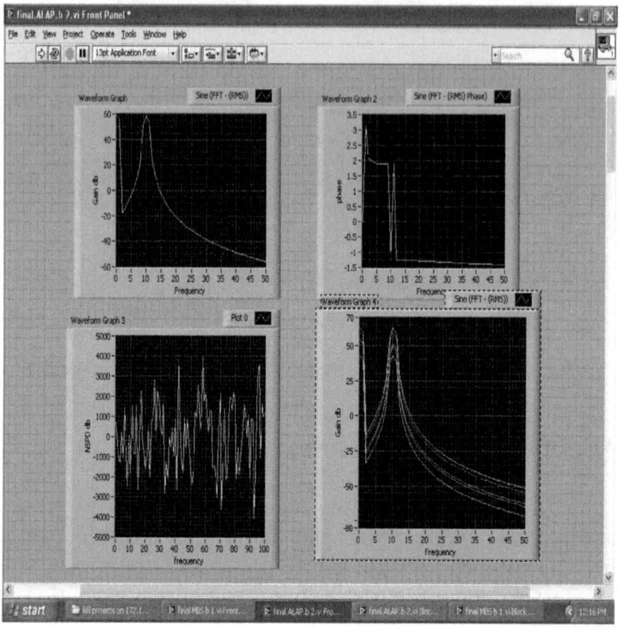

Fig. 7. Front panel for responses of ASAP using LABVIEW

11 Conclusions

The scheduling and allocation algorithm is designed by converting most serial form in to most parallel form and placing a cut in the serial path which leads to a decrease in the critical path length without any change in functionality. The scheduling and allocation algorithm proposed reduces the execution time and cost function by reducing control step (one step). An effort is not made to reduce the critical path length in the earlier reported works. However, the use of scheduling and allocation algorithm shortens the control step to 16 without modifying the functionality. Four partitioning methods are performed for scheduled control data flow graph. In the first method, the partitioning is done such that, the operation that takes more number of cycles is placed in hardware units. Other methods uses clique partitioning to minimize the number of resources used. Buffer size and system delay for hardware/ software partitioning is also calculated to obtain communication cost.

References

1. Papa, G., Silc, J.: Multi-objective genetic scheduling algorithm with respect to allocation in high-level synthesis. In: Proceedings of the 26th Euromicro Conference, vol. 1, September 5-7, pp. 339–346 (2002)
2. Papa, G., Silc, J.: Automated large-scale integrated synthesis using allocation-based scheduling algorithm, February 2. IEEE, Los Alamitos (2002)
3. You, M.-K., Song, G.-Y.: Implementation of a C-to-SystemC Synthesizer Prototype, School of Electrical and Computer Engineering Chungbuk National University, Cheongju Chungbuk, Korea, pp. 361–763 (2007)
4. Hughes, J.B., Moulding, K.W., Richardson, J., Bennett, J., Redman-White, W., Bracey, M., Soin, R.S.: Automated Design of Switched-Current Filter. IEEE Journal of Solid State Circuits 31(7) (July 1996)
5. Hansen, J., Singh, M.: A Fast Branch-and-Bound Approach to High-Level Synthesis of Asynchronous Systems. In: IEEE Symposium on Asynchronous Circuits and Systems (2010)

Sangeetha Marikkannan born in 1975 in Tamilnadu, India, received his B.E. degree from the Bharathidasan University, Trichy, in1996 and M.E. degree from the University of Madras in 1999. She is currently with Karpaga Vinayaga College of Engineering and Technlogy in the Department of Electronics and Communication Engineering and Ph.D. degree with the Anna University, Chennai, India. She is a member of the IEEE and ISTE. Her research interests are Hardware/Software Codesign and High Level Synthesis.

Interfacing Social Networking Sites with Set Top Box

Kulkarni Vijay[1] and Anupama Nandeppanavar[2]

[1] M.Tech (CSE) , Dept. of Computer Science and Engineering,
The Oxford College of Engineering
Vijaykulkarni.u@gmail.com
[2] Senior Lecturer, Dept. of Computer Science and Engineering,
The Oxford College of Engineering
anupama.nandeppanavar@gmail.com

Abstract. Today's viewers can be overwhelmed by the amount of content that is made available to them. In a world of hundreds of thousands, sometimes hundreds of millions of choices, we need powerful and effective interfaces to help viewers manage their viewing choices and find the content that's right for them.

The project explores how the merging of ubiquitous consumer electronics and the sociable web improve the user experience of these devices, increase the functionality of both, and help distribute content in a more sociable way. The source of motivation for this project is the very idea of providing 'lean back' mode to communicate via social networking sites that can be achieved using a remote control for T.V like device. All one needs to communicate in this mode is a T.V (with a remote), a STB that is provided with IP.

This project saves the time and money of customers as they need not have a computer or a dedicated internet connection to utilize services of social networking sites. This project also acts as a add-on feature from the service provider to the customers. This project can also be extended to include still more useful services of World Wide Web. The future fields would be to allow the customer to do TV shopping, Net surfing

Keywords: Set Top Box, Twitter, OAuth.

1 Introduction

Interactive television (generally known as ITV or sometimes as iTV when used as branding) describes a number of techniques that allow viewers to interact with television content as they view it.

Interactive television represents a continuum from low interactivity (TV on/off, volume, changing channels) to moderate interactivity (simple movies on demand without player controls) and high interactivity in which, for example, an audience member affects the program being watched. The most obvious example of this would be any kind of real-time voting on the screen, in which audience votes create decisions that are reflected in how the show continues. A return path to the program provider is not necessary to have an interactive program experience. Once a movie is downloaded for example, controls may all be local. The link was needed to download the program, but texts and software which can be executed locally at the set-top box

D.C. Wyld et al. (Eds.): ACITY 2011, CCIS 198, pp. 460–471, 2011.

or IRD (Integrated Receiver Decoder) may occur automatically, once the viewer enters the channel.

The term "interactive television" is used to refer to a variety of rather different kinds of interactivity (both as to usage and as to technology), and this can lead to considerable misunderstanding. At least three very different levels are important (see also the instructional video literature which has described levels of interactivity in computer-based instruction which will look very much like tomorrow's interactive television).

The simplest, Interactivity with a TV set is already very common, starting with the use of the remote control to enable channel surfing behaviors, and evolving to include video-on-demand, VCR-like pause, rewind, and fast forward, and DVRs, commercial skipping and the like. It does not change any content or its inherent linearity, only how users control the viewing of that content. DVRs allow users to time shift content in a way that is impractical with VHS. Though this form of interactive TV is not insignificant, critics claim that saying that using a remote control to turn TV sets on and off makes television interactive is like saying turning the pages of a book makes the book interactive. In the not too distant future, the questioning of what is real interaction with the TV will be difficult. Panasonic already has face recognition technology implemented its prototype Panasonic Life Wall. The Life Wall is literally a wall in your house that doubles as a screen. Panasonic uses their face recognition technology to follow the viewer around the room, adjusting its screen size according to the viewers distance from the wall. Its goal is to give the viewer the best seat in the house, regardless of location.

Interactive TV is often described by clever marketing gurus as "lean back" interaction, as users are typically relaxing in the living room environment with a remote control in one hand. This is a very simplistic definition of interactive television that is less and less descriptive of interactive television services that are in various stages of market introduction. This is in contrast to the similarly slick marketing devised descriptor of personal computer-oriented "lean forward" experience of a keyboard, mouse and monitor. This description is becoming more distracting than useful as video game users; for example, don't lean forward while they are playing video games on their television sets, a precursor to interactive TV. A more useful mechanism for categorizing the differences between PC and TV based user interaction is by measuring the distance the user is from the Device. Typically a TV viewer is "leaning back" in their sofa, using only a Remote Control as a means of interaction. While a PC user is 2 ft or 3 ft from his high resolution screen using a mouse and keyboard. The demand of distance, and user input devices, requires the application's look and feel to be designed differently. Thus Interactive TV applications are often designed for the "10ft user experience" while PC applications and web pages are designed for the "3ft user experience". This style of interface design rather than the "lean back or lean forward" model is what truly distinguishes Interactive TV from the web or PC. However even this mechanism is changing because there is at least one web-based service which allows you to watch internet television on a PC with a wireless remote control.

In the case of Two-Screen Solutions Interactive TV, the distinctions of "lean-back" and "lean-forward" interaction become more and more indistinguishable. There has been a growing proclivity to media multitasking, in which multiple media devices are used simultaneously (especially among younger viewers). This has increased interest in two-screen services, and is creating a new level of multitasking in interactive TV. In addition, video is now ubiquitous on the web, so research can now be done to see if there is anything left to the notion of "lean back" "versus" "lean forward" uses of interactive television.

For one-screen services, interactivity is supplied by the manipulation of the API of the particular software installed on a set-top box, referred to as 'middleware' due to its intermediary position in the operating environment. Software programs are broadcast to the set-top box in a 'carousel'. On UK DTT (Freeview uses ETSI based MHEG-5), and Sky's DTH platform uses ETSI based WTVML in DVB-MHP systems and for OCAP, this is a DSM-CC Object Carousel. The set-top boxes can then load and execute the application. In the UK this is typically done by a viewer pressing a "trigger" button on their remote control (e.g. the red button, as in "press red").

Interactive TV Sites have the requirement to deliver interactivity directly from internet servers, and therefore need the set-top box's middleware to support some sort of TV Browser, content translation system or content rendering system. Middleware examples like Liberate are based on a version of HTML/JavaScript and have rendering capabilities built in, while others such as OpenTV and DVB-MHP can load microbrowsers and applications to deliver content from TV Sites. In October 2008, the ITU's J.201 paper on interoperability of TV Sites recommended authoring using ETSI WTVML to achieve interoperability by allowing dynamic TV Site to be automatically translated into various TV dialects of HTML/JavaScript, while maintaining compatibility with middlewares such as MHP and OpenTV via native WTVML microbrowsers.

Typically the distribution system for Standard Definition digital TV is based on the MPEG-2 specification, while High Definition distribution is likely to be based on the MPEG-4 meaning that the delivery of HD often requires a new device or set-top box, which typically is then also able to decode Internet Video via broadband return paths.

2 Literature Survey

2.1 History

Before the mid-1950s all British television sets tuned only VHF Band I channels. Since all 5 Band I channels were occupied by BBC transmissions, ITV would have to use Band III. This meant all the TV sets in the country would require Band III converters which converted the Band III signal to a Band I signal. By 1955, when the first ITV stations started transmitting, virtually all new British Televisions had 13-channel tuners, quickly making Band III converters obsolete.

Before the All-Channel Receiver Act of 1962 required US television receivers to be able to tune the entire VHF and UHF range (which in North America was NTSC-M channels 2 through 83 on 54 to 890 MHz), a set-top box known as a UHF converter would be installed at the receiver to shift a portion of the UHF-TV spectrum onto low-VHF channels for viewing. As some 1960s-era twelve-channel TV sets remained in use for many years, and Canada and Mexico were slower than the US to require UHF tuners to be factory-installed in new TV's, a market for these converters continued to exist for much of the 1970s.

Cable television represented a possible alternative to deployment of UHF converters as broadcasts could be frequency-shifted to VHF channels at the cable head-end instead of the final viewing location. Unfortunately, cable brought a new problem; most cable systems could not accommodate the full 54-890 MHz VHF/UHF frequency range and the twelve channels of VHF space were quickly exhausted on most systems. Adding any additional channels therefore needed to be done by inserting the extra signals into cable systems on non-standard frequencies, typically either below VHF channel 7 (midband) or directly above VHF channel 13 (superband).

These frequencies corresponded to non-television services (such as two-way radio) over-the-air and were therefore not on standard TV receivers. Before cable-ready TV sets became common in the late 1980s, a set-top box known as a cable converter box was needed to receive the additional analog cable TV channels and convert them to frequencies that could be seen on a regular TV. These boxes often provided a wired or wireless remote control which could be used to shift one selected channel to a low-VHF frequency (most often channels 3 or 4) for viewing. Block conversion of the entire affected frequency band onto UHF, while less common, was used by some models to provide full VCR compatibility and the ability to drive multiple TV sets, albeit with a somewhat non-standard channel numbering scheme.

Newer television receivers greatly reduced the need for external set-top boxes, although cable converter boxes continue to be used to descramble premium cable channels and to receive digital cable channels, along with using interactive services like video on demand, pay per view, and home shopping through television. Satellite and microwave-based services also require specific external receiver hardware, so the use of set-top boxes of various formats never completely disappeared.

2.2 Technology Gap

Earlier the STBs were perceived as the equipments that used to convert the signal received from the service provider and then convert it into the format needed by the T.V.

However, these days with the advent of technology the STBs are supporting the IP protocol and they run JVM1.3 and support a hard disk it has become more of a platform for launching the end user application that can provide interaction when connected to IP.

3 Motivation

With the advent of the ubiquitous computing there has been a sharp increase in the need to decrease the communication gap between people.

Earlier, people used to write letters to communicate with people, with the advent of telegraph the whole communication scenario has changed very rapidly. However, with the advent of the telephone, there has been a huge increase in the need of communication in real-time. From the fixed land line the communication scenario has now arrived to 3G technology. In spite of all these the newer way of communicating with people i.e. through the social networking websites has attracted more attention.

However to communicate with people via the social networking sites, one needs a PC and an Internet connection. Since the user is required to be present in front of the PC to communicate , this approach is called 'lean forward' approach since the user has to lean forward to use the keyboard and mouse which are the input devices.

The source of motivation for this project is the very idea of providing '*lean back*' mode to communicate via social networking sites. The 'lean back' mode of communication / interaction is generally achieved through a remote i.e. like in case of T.V., thus providing the end users the access to social networking sites like twitter.com. All one needs to communicate in this mode is a T.V (with a remote), a STB that is provided with IP.

4 Existing System

The new STBs are designed around a set of protocols collectively known as Multimedia Home Platform (MHP) [4]. The multimedia home-software platform progressively integrates DVB digital-video processing protocols with Internet protocols in what is known as DVB-MHP (Digital Video Broadcasting with Multimedia Home Platform). The end user might have the features that we have come to expect, including:

- EPG (Electronic Programming Guide)
- Gaming
- Telebanking
- Home shopping
- PVR (Personal Video Record)
- Router functions (NAT, DHCP, routing, private addressing)
- Security features
- Distance Learning
- Video on Demand (VOD)
- Wireless Interface 802.11e
- Wireless Interface for phones at 900MHz

In addition to boasting a rich feature set, the STB needs to be able to make effective use of the bandwidth that it receives from the service provider. This box should be designed to fetch and store your programs when you are either away from home or not watching TV. These functions are currently available from TiVo services. Incorporating fetch-and-store functions on a set-top box will help to mitigate the limited bandwidth that ADSL or VDSL might provide.

5 System Architecture of a Developed STB

Fig.1 [1] shows the block diagram of the digital set-top box. It receives RF signals from the optical/coax hybrid cable, selects a particular frequency and demodulates 64QAh4 modulated MPEG-TS (transport stream) packets and passes them on to the MPEG-TS decoder. The decoder separates the stream into its component units; MPEG-2 video, MPEG-audio and private data and sends them to the appropriate units. For example private data send to the CPU, can contain graphic menus for movie selection. This is processed by the CPU, sent to the graphics generator and used to realize processor generated graphics. This is sent through the broad MPEG-TS channel ensuring fast response time. This can also be used to send data to the flash memory which contains basic software so software maintenance is easy. Upstream data from the CPU is sent to the Ethernet circuit, and then transferred to the telephony set-top-box.

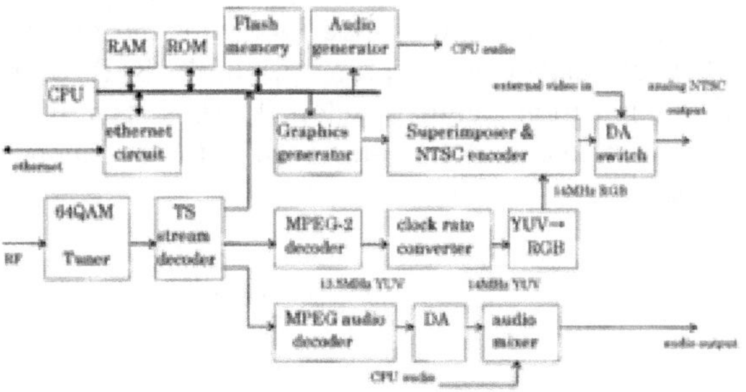

Fig. 1. Block Diagram of a developed Set Top Box

5.1 Software Architecture of Existing System

The new software [2] stack is shown in Fig. 2. It provides a uniformed API to the applications (Native API & JavaScript API), thus application developers can focus on their implementations, regarding the platform they are using. Besides, a porting interface is provided to shield the differences underlying.

The porting interface collects all the requirements from the upper modules, and a full implementation of which can makes all the modules platform-independent.

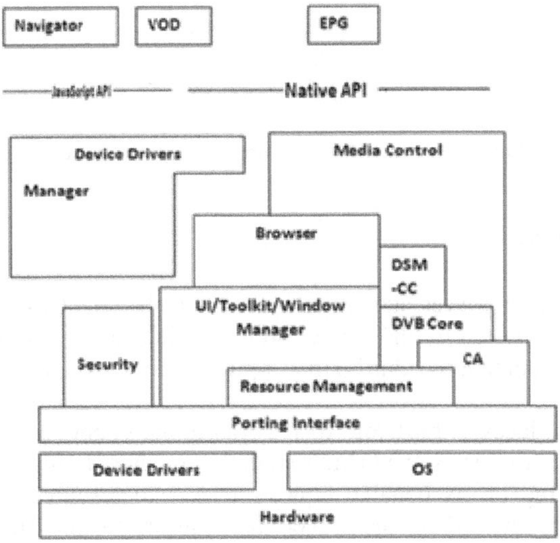

Fig. 2. Software Architecture of Developed Set Top Box

6 Proposed System

The proposed system as shown in fig 3 inherits all the features of the existing system; however, it provides the facility to connect to the social networking sites when the IP is provided to the STB.

It can be noticed that the change in the architecture of the proposed system is the incorporation of the Application being developed at the top most level.

The major advantage of this is that, the properties of the STB like the CA will also be applicable to the application being developed. Thus it provides value added services for the customer and controls the access to the application from the developer's point of view.

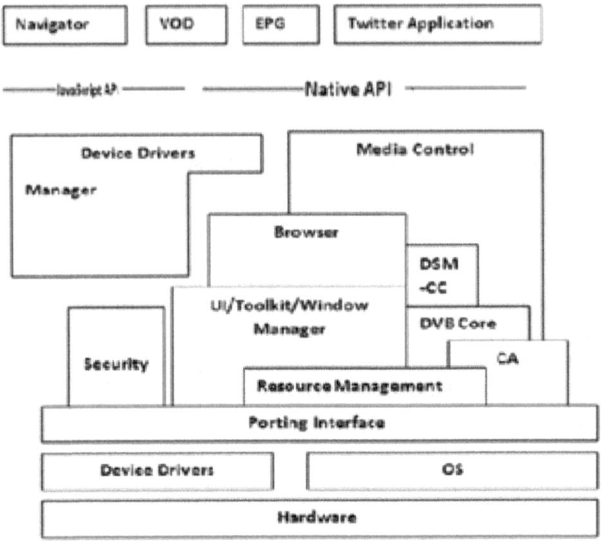

Fig. 3. Software Architecture of Proposed System

7 Protocol Used

In the traditional client-server authentication model, the client uses its credentials to access its resources hosted by the server. With the increasing use of distributed web services and cloud computing, third-party applications require access to these server-hosted resources.

OAuth [3] introduces a third role to the traditional client-server authentication model: the resource owner. In the OAuth model, the client (which is not the resource owner, but is acting on its behalf) requests access to resources controlled by the resource owner, but hosted by the server. In addition, OAuth allows the server to verify not only the resource owner authorization, but also the identity of the client making the request.

OAuth provides a method for clients to access server resources on behalf of a resource owner (such as a different client or an end- user). It also provides a process for end-users to authorize third- party access to their server resources without sharing their credentials (typically, a username and password pair), using user- agent redirections. For example, a web user (resource owner) can grant a printing service (client) access to her private photos stored at a photo sharing service (server), without

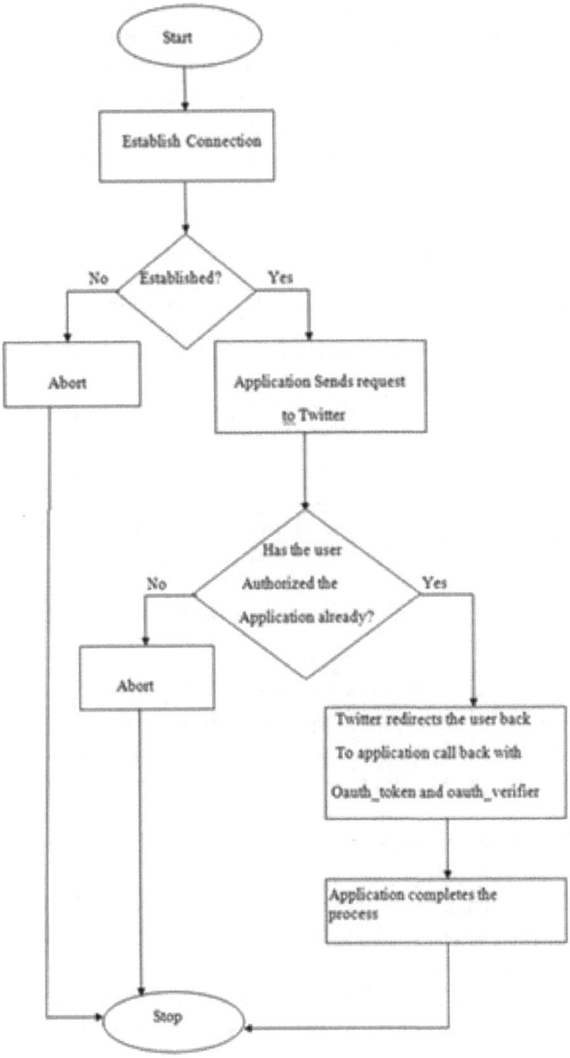

Fig. 4. The flowchart for the authentication process using OAuth1.0

sharing her username and password with the printing service. Instead, she authenticates directly with the photo sharing service which issues the printing service delegation-specific credentials.

In order for the client to access resources, it first has to obtain permission from the resource owner. This permission is expressed in the form of a token and matching shared-secret. The purpose of the token is to make it unnecessary for the resource owner to share its credentials with the client. Unlike the resource owner credentials,tokens can be issued with a restricted scope and limited lifetime, and revoked independently.

This specification consists of two parts. The first part defines a redirection-based user-agent process for end-users to authorize client access to their resources, by authenticating directly with the server and provisioning tokens to the client for use with the authentication method. The second part defines a method for making authenticated HTTP [RFC2616] requests using two sets of credentials, one identifying the client making the request, and a second identifying the resource owner on whose behalf the request is being made.

7.1 Advantages of Using OAuth

The advantages of using OAuth from the end user point of view:

- Don't have to create another profile on the net.
- Fewer passwords to remember.
- Do not have to submit a password to your application if he / she does not completely trust us.
- User can prevent access to the application from the OAuth Provider.
- Allows for exciting extra functionality and synergies when taking advantage of the social graph and other data and features made available by the OAuth provider.

From the developers / Service Providers Point of View the advantages of using OAuth are:

- Save time on developing authentication, display of user profile and social interaction as friends lists, status updates, profile, photos, etc.
- Do not need support for password renewal, forgotten password, authentication of users, and support to let users remove themselves from the service, etc.
- Lower risk and fewer bugs in connection to authentication when using a ready-made proven API.
- Low-risk for ID theft, etc. The service already has good support to prevent this. Authentication takes place at provider, the OAuth tokens is encrypted and not in our application.
- If the OAuth standard is extended with support for info cards or other functionality in the future, it would be supported in your application automatically.
- Easier to manage / maintain / configure
- Less data to store on your servers.

8 Design

Design is one of the most important phases of software development. The design is a creative process in which a system organization is established that will satisfy the functional and non-functional system requirements. Large Systems are always are decomposed into sub-systems that provide some related set of services. The output of the design process is a description of the Software architecture.

The application has a Graphical User Interface (GUI) that allows the User to navigate through the tweets and update the status. The application then process the commands from the Remote Control Unit (RCU) and communicates with the server.

8.1 Design Considerations

8.1.1 General Constraints

- It will be a set top box based application. In the present scenario, it will not be used as a web-based or a distributed application.
- The system needs to get an IP address from the home network.
- It will not be like a fully fledged browser system, since set top box does not support all features required by networking sites.
- In the present scenario, all the credentials and interaction with the user interface needs to happen over the set top box remote control.
- The box must use a middleware that conforms to the Open Middleware Standards.

8.2 Detailed Design

8.2.1 Level -0 Data Flow Diagram

The level 0 DFD is also known as the context level diagram. For this project the context level diagram shows the system as a whole which interacts with the social site. The user interacts with the system using the GUI displayed on the TV. The inputs to the system are the credentials and the input data given by the user through the remote control actions. The system sends the requests to the site server and received the response. All the interactions between user and site server passes through the system.

The level 0 DFD is also known as the context level diagram. For this project the context level diagram shows the system as a whole which interacts with the social site. The user interacts with the system using the GUI displayed on the TV. The inputs to the system are the credentials and the input data given by the user through the remote control actions. The system sends the requests to the site server and received the response. All the interactions between user and site server passes through the system.

The Level – 0 DFD is as shown in fig. 5.

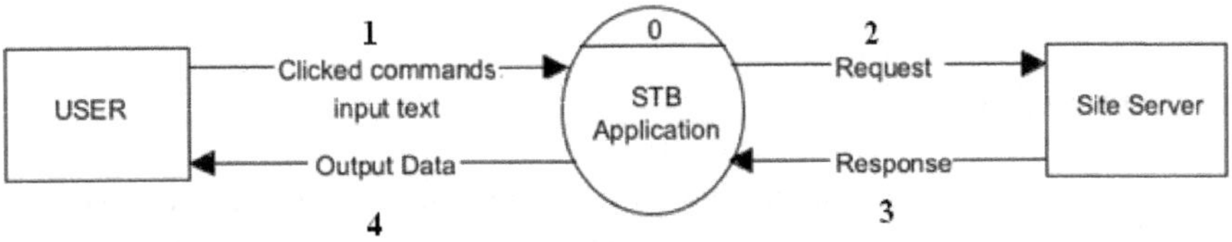

Fig. 5. Level – 0 DFD

8.2.2 Level –1 Data Flow Diagram

The level 1 DFD as shown in fig. 6 shows the sub modules of the system. The system is divided into four main components. The four components are Twitter API, REST API and Http/ OAuth and JSON.

The Twitter API mainly comprises of the Factory methods and the Twitter Exception Handling Mechanism and the functions like Updating / retrieving the statuses etc. The REST API consists of the RESTful services, which perform tasks analogous to session handling. The Http /OAuth module comprises of the Http Client implementation and the OAuth implementation. The Java Script Object Notation (JSON) provides static methods to convert comma delimited text into a JSONArray, and to covert a JSONArray into comma delimited text. Comma delimited text is a very popular format for data interchange. It is understood by most database, spreadsheet, and organizer programs. Each row of text represents a row in a table or a data record. Each row ends with a NEWLINE character. Each row contains one or more values. Values are separated by commas. A value can contain any character except for comma, unless is wrapped in single quotes or double quotes. The first row usually contains the names of the columns. A comma delimited list can be converted into a JSONArray of JSONObjects. The names for the elements in the JSONObjects can be taken from the names in the first row.

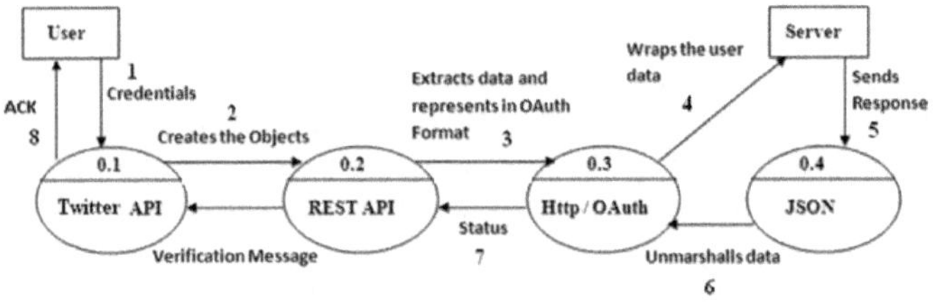

Fig. 6. Level – 1 DFD

The user passes the credentials to the TwitterAPI that creates the Twitter Objects and then sends them to the REST API for performing the tasks analogous to session handling. This extracts the data i.e. the credentials and then passes it to the Http / OAuth in the corresponding format. This module then wraps the user data and passes it to the server which sends the appropriate response. This response is then handled by the JSON and is converted into comma delimited text format.

9 Conclusion

This paper focuses on the integration of ubiquitous electronics with the web. It provides the user a seamless way of transition between TV Watching and usage of Social Networking Sites. In addition it also provides Value added service for the customer thereby, defining a new dimension to the level of interactivity of the interactive TV.

References

1. Kohiyama, S.K., Shirai, H., Ogawa, K., Manakata, A., Koga, Y., Ishizaki, M.: Fujitsu Laboratories Limited Fujitsu Limited.: Architecture Of Mpeg-2 Digital Set-Top-Box For Catv Vod, pp. 667–672 (1996)
2. Gao, C., Wang, L., Ni, H.: Software Design Methodology for Set-Top Box, pp. 302–305 (2009)
3. Hammer – Lahav, E.: Request for Comments: 5849 The OAuth 1.0 Protocol
4. `http://www.mhp.org` (dated February 10, 2011)

About the Authors

#1 Vijay Kulkarni – Vijay Kulkarni is currently pursing M.Tech in Computer Science and Engineering from The Oxford College of Engineering, Bangalore.

#2 Anupama. S. Nandeppanavar – is currently working as Senior Lecturer, Dept. of Computer Science and Engineering, in The Oxford College of Engineering. She has completed her M.Tech from Basaveshwar Engineering College, Bagalkot.

Comparison between K-Means and K-Medoids Clustering Algorithms

Tagaram Soni Madhulatha

Alluri Institute of Management Sciences
Warangal, Andhra Pradesh

Abstract. Clustering is a common technique for statistical data analysis, Clustering is the process of grouping similar objects into different groups, or more precisely, the partitioning of a data set into subsets according to some defined distance measure. Clustering is an unsupervised learning technique, where interesting patterns and structures can be found directly from very large data sets with little or none of the background knowledge. It is used in many fields, including machine learning, data mining, pattern recognition, image analysis and bioinformatics. In this research, the most representative algorithms K-Means and K-Medoids were examined and analyzed based on their basic approach.

Keywords: Clustering, partitional algorithm, K-mean, K-medoid, distance measure.

1 Introduction

Clustering can be considered the most important unsupervised learning problem; so, as every other problem of this kind, it deals with finding a structure in a collection of unlabeled data. A cluster is therefore a collection of objects which are similar between them and are dissimilar to the objects belonging to other clusters. Besides the term data clustering as synonyms like cluster analysis, automatic classification, numerical taxonomy, botrology and typological analysis.

There exist a large number of clustering algorithms in the literature. The choice of clustering algorithm depends both on the type of data available and on the particular purpose and application. If cluster analysis is used as a descriptive or exploratory tool, it is possible to try several algorithms on the same data to see what the data may disclose. In general, major clustering methods can be classified into the following categories.

1. Partitioning methods
2. Hierarchical methods
3. Density-based methods
4. Grid-based methods
5. Model based methods

D.C. Wyld et al. (Eds.): ACITY 2011, CCIS 198, pp. 472–481, 2011.

Some clustering algorithms integrate the ideas of several clustering methods, so that it is sometimes difficult to classify a given algorithm as uniquely belonging to only one clustering method category.

2 Partitional Clustering

Partitioning algorithms are based on specifying an initial number of groups, and iteratively reallocating objects among groups to convergence. This algorithm typically determines all clusters at once. most applications adopt one of two popular heuristic methods like

k-mean algorithm

k-medoids algorithm

2.1 K-Means Algorithm

K means clustering algorithm was developed by J. McQueen and then by J. A. Hartigan and M. A. Wong around 1975. Simply speaking k-means clustering is an algorithm to classify the objects based on attributes/features into K number of group. K is positive integer number. The grouping is done by minimizing the sum of squares of distances between data and the corresponding cluster centroid. Thus the purpose of K-mean clustering is to classify the data.

K-means demonstration

Suppose we have 4 objects as your training data points and each object have 2 attributes. Each attribute represents coordinate of the object.

Table 1. Sample data points

SNO	Mid-I	Mid-II
A	1	1
B	2	1
C	4	3
D	5	4

We also know before hand that these objects belong to two groups of Sno (cluster 1 and cluster 2). The problem now is to determine which Sno's belong to cluster 1 and which Sno's belong to the other cluster.

The basic step of k-means clustering is simple. In the beginning we determine number of cluster K and we assume the centroid or center of these clusters. We can take any random objects as the initial centroid or the first K objects in sequence can also serve as the initial centroid.

Then the K means algorithm will do the three steps below until convergence Iterate until stable (= no object move group):

1. Determine the centroid coordinate

2. Determine the distance of each object to the centroid
3. Group the object based on minimum distance

Suppose we have several objects (4 types of Sno) and each object have two attributes or features as shown in table below. Our goal is to group these objects into K=2 group of Student-number (Sno) based on the two features (Mid-I, Mid-II).

Each Sno one point with two attributes (X, Y) that we can represent it as coordinate in an attribute space as shown in the figure below.

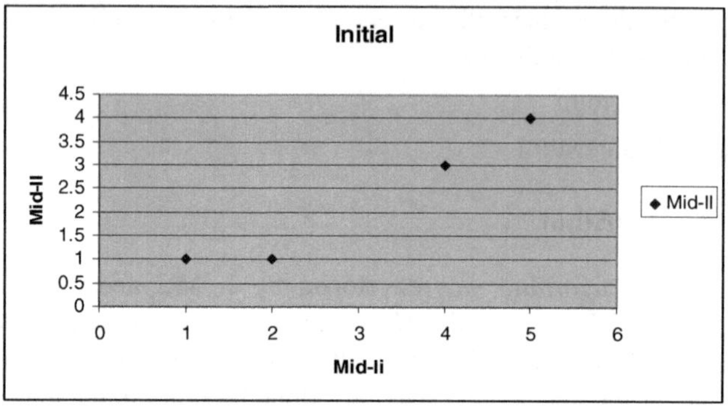

Fig. 1. Initial data points distribution on XY Scatter graph

1. Initial value of centroids : Suppose we use Sno A and Sno B as the first centroids. Let c_1 and c_2 denote the coordinate of the centroids, then $c_1 = (1,1)$ and $c_2 = (2,1)$

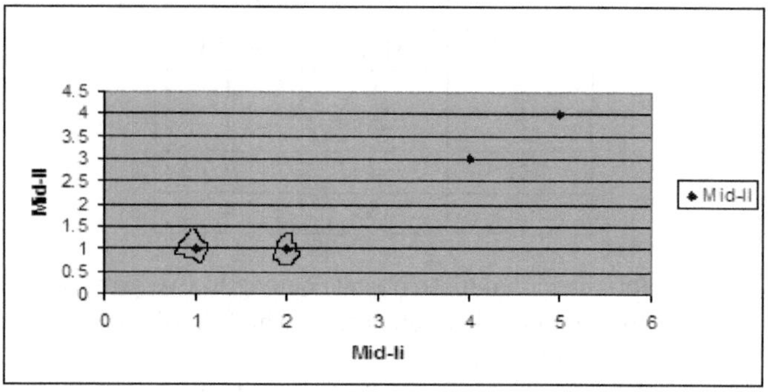

Fig. 2. Iteration0 data points distribution on XY Scatter graph

2. Objects-Centroid distance: we calculate the distance between cluster centroid to each object. Let us use Euclidean distance, then we have distance matrix at iteration 0 is

$$\mathbf{D}^0 = \begin{bmatrix} 0 & 1 & 3.61 & 5 \\ 1 & 0 & 2.83 & 4.24 \end{bmatrix} \quad \begin{matrix} \mathbf{c}_1 = (1,1) & group-1 \\ \mathbf{c}_2 = (2,1) & group-2 \end{matrix}$$

$$\begin{matrix} A & B & C & D \end{matrix}$$

$$\begin{bmatrix} 1 & 2 & 4 & 5 \\ 1 & 1 & 3 & 4 \end{bmatrix} \quad \begin{matrix} X \\ Y \end{matrix}$$

Each column in the distance matrix symbolizes the object. The first row of the distance matrix corresponds to the distance of each object to the first centroid and the second row is the distance of each object to the second centroid. For example, distance from medicine C = (4, 3) to the first centroid $\mathbf{c}_1 = (1,1)$ is $\sqrt{(4-1)^2+(3-1)^2} = 3.61$, and its distance to the second centroid $\mathbf{c}_2 = (2,1)$ is $\sqrt{(4-2)^2+(3-1)^2} = 2.83$, etc.

3. **Objects clustering** : We assign each object based on the minimum distance. Thus, medicine A is assigned to group 1, medicine B to group 2, medicine C to group 2 and medicine D to group 2. The element of Group matrix below is 1 if and only if the object is assigned to that group.

$$\mathbf{G}^0 = \begin{bmatrix} 1 & 0 & 0 & 0 \\ 0 & 1 & 1 & 1 \end{bmatrix} \quad \begin{matrix} group-1 \\ group-2 \end{matrix}$$

$$\begin{matrix} A & B & C & D \end{matrix}$$

4. **Iteration-1, determine centroids :** Knowing the members of each group, now we compute the new centroid of each group based on these new memberships. Group 1 only has one member thus the centroid remains in $\mathbf{c}_1 = (1,1)$. Group 2 now has three members, thus the centroid is the average coordinate among the three members: $\mathbf{c}_2 = (\frac{2+4+5}{3}, \frac{1+3+4}{3}) = (\frac{11}{3}, \frac{8}{3})$.

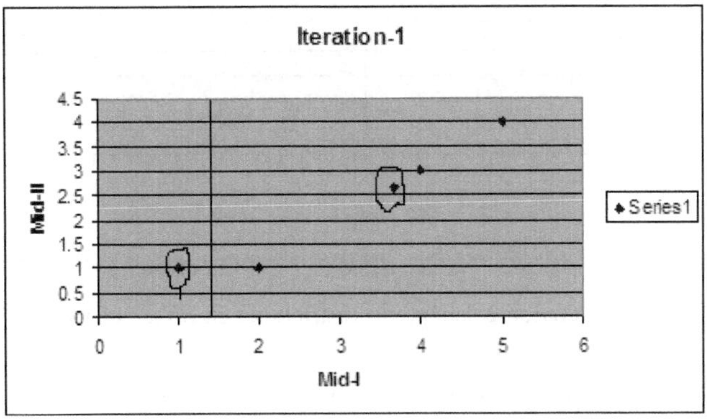

Fig. 3. Iteration 1 data points distribution on XY Scatter graph

5. Iteration-1, Objects-Centroids distances : The next step is to compute the distance of all objects to the new centroids. Similar to step 2, we have distance matrix at iteration 1 is

$$D^1 = \begin{bmatrix} 0 & 1 & 3.61 & 5 \\ 3.14 & 2.36 & 0.47 & 1.89 \end{bmatrix} \quad \begin{matrix} c_1 = (1,1) & group-1 \\ c_2 = (\frac{11}{3}, \frac{8}{3}) & group-2 \end{matrix}$$

$$\begin{matrix} A & B & C & D \end{matrix}$$

$$\begin{bmatrix} 1 & 2 & 4 & 5 \\ 1 & 1 & 3 & 4 \end{bmatrix} \begin{matrix} X \\ Y \end{matrix}$$

6. Iteration-1, Objects clustering: Similar to step 3, we assign each object based on the minimum distance. Based on the new distance matrix, we move the medicine B to Group 1 while all the other objects remain. The Group matrix is shown below

$$G^1 = \begin{bmatrix} 1 & 1 & 0 & 0 \\ 0 & 0 & 1 & 1 \end{bmatrix} \quad \begin{matrix} group-1 \\ group-2 \end{matrix}$$

$$\begin{matrix} A & B & C & D \end{matrix}$$

7. Iteration 2, determine centroids: Now we repeat step 4 to calculate the new centroids coordinate based on the clustering of previous iteration. Group1 and group 2 both has two members, thus the new centroids are $c_1 = (\frac{1+2}{2}, \frac{1+1}{2}) = (1\frac{1}{2}, 1)$ and $c_2 = (\frac{4+5}{2}, \frac{3+4}{2}) = (4\frac{1}{2}, 3\frac{1}{2})$

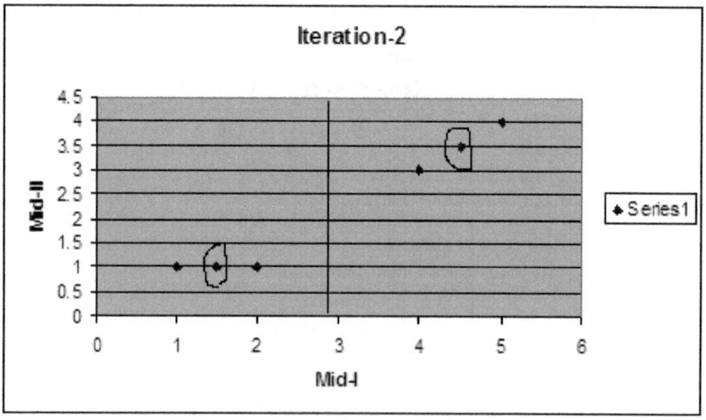

Fig. 4. Iteration 2 data points distribution on XY Scatter graph

8. Iteration-2, Objects-Centroids distances: Repeat step 2 again, we have new distance matrix at iteration 2 as

$$\mathbf{D}^2 = \begin{bmatrix} 0.5 & 0.5 & 3.20 & 4.61 \\ 4.30 & 3.54 & 0.71 & 0.71 \end{bmatrix} \begin{matrix} c_1 = (1\frac{1}{2}, 1) & group-1 \\ c_2 - (4\frac{1}{2}, 3\frac{1}{2}) & group-2 \end{matrix}$$

$$\begin{matrix} A & B & C & D \end{matrix}$$

$$\begin{bmatrix} 1 & 2 & 4 & 5 \\ 1 & 1 & 3 & 4 \end{bmatrix} \begin{matrix} X \\ Y \end{matrix}$$

9. Iteration-2, Objects clustering: Again, we assign each object based on the minimum distance.

$$\mathbf{G}^2 - \begin{bmatrix} 1 & 1 & 0 & 0 \\ 0 & 0 & 1 & 1 \end{bmatrix} \begin{matrix} group-1 \\ group-2 \end{matrix}$$

$$\begin{matrix} A & B & C & D \end{matrix}$$

We obtain result that $\mathbf{G}^2 = \mathbf{G}^1$. Comparing the grouping of last iteration and this iteration reveals that the objects does not move group anymore. Thus, the computation of the k-mean clustering has reached its stability and no more iteration is needed. We get the final grouping as the results

Table 2. Clustering Group formed after K-Means have applied

SNO	Mid-I	Mid-II	Group
A	1	1	1
B	2	1	1
C	4	3	2
D	5	4	2

2.2 K-Medoid

The **K-medoids algorithm** is a clustering algorithm related to the K-means algorithm. Both algorithms are partitional and both attempt to minimize squared error, the distance between points labeled to be in a cluster and a point designated as the center of that cluster. In contrast to the K-means algorithm K-medoids chooses data points as centers.

K-medoid is a classical partitioning technique of clustering that clusters the data set of n objects into k clusters. It is more robust to noise and outliers as compared to k-means. A medoid can be defined as that object of a cluster, whose average dissimilarity to all the objects in the cluster is minimal i.e. it is a most centrally located point in the given data set.

K-medoid clustering algorithm is as follows:

1) The algorithm begins with arbitrary selection of the k objects as medoid points out of n data points (n>k)

2) After selection of the k medoid points, associate each data object in the given data set to most similar medoid. The similarity here is defined using distance measure that can be Euclidean distance, Manhattan distance or Minkowski distance
3) Randomly select non-medoid object O'
4) Compute total cost, S of swapping initial medoid object to O'
5) If S<0, then swap initial medoid with the new one (if S<0 then there will be new set of medoids)
6) Repeat steps 2 to 5 until there is no change in the medoid.

Consider a data set of ten objects as follows, and Cluster the data set of ten objects into two clusters i.e k = 2.

Table 3. Sample data

SNO	Mid-I	Mid-II
X_1	2	6
X_2	3	4
X_3	3	8
X_4	4	7
X_5	6	2
X_6	6	4
X_7	7	3
X_8	7	4
X_9	8	5
X_{10}	7	6

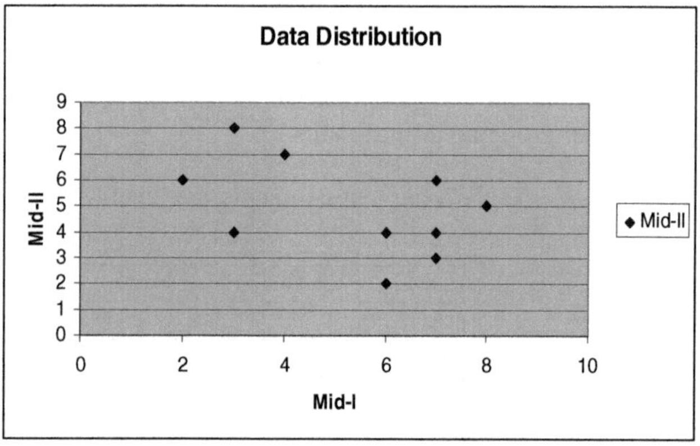

Fig. 5. Initial Data Distribution

Initialise *k* centre
Let us assume $c_1 = (3,4)$ and $c_2 = (7,4)$
So here c_1 and c_2 are selected as medoid.
Calculating distance so as to associate each data object to its nearest medoid. Cost is calculated using Minkowski distance metric with $r = 1$.
The Minkowski distance of order p=1 between two points $P=(x_1,x_2,x_3,\ldots\ldots\ldots x_n)$ and $Q=(y_1,y_2,y_3,\ldots\ldots\ldots y_n) € R^n$ is defined as:

$$\left(\sum_{i=1}^{n} \left| x_i - y_i \right|^P\right)^{1/p} \qquad (1)$$

Then so the clusters become:
$Group_1 = \{(3,4)(2,6)(3,8)(4,7)\}$
$Group_2 = \{(7,4)(6,2)(6,4)(7,3)(8,5)(7,6)\}$
Since the points (2,6) (3,8) and (4,7) are close to c_1 hence they form one cluster whilst remaining points form another cluster.

Table 4. Cluster 1 data

c_1		Data objects (X_i)		Cost (distance)
3	4	2	6	3
3	4	3	8	4
3	4	4	7	4
3	4	6	2	5
3	4	6	4	3
3	4	7	3	5
3	4	8	5	6
3	4	7	6	6

Table 5. Cluster 2 data

c_2		Data objects (X_i)		Cost (distance)
7	4	2	6	7
7	4	3	8	8
7	4	4	7	6
7	4	6	2	3
7	4	6	4	1
7	4	7	3	1
7	4	8	5	2
7	4	7	6	2

So the total cost involved is 20.
Where cost between any two points is found using formula where x is any data object, c is the medoid, and d is the dimension of the object which in this case is 2

$$\text{Cost}(x,c) = \sum_{i=1}^{d} \left| x - c \right| \qquad (2)$$

Total cost is the summation of the cost of data object from its medoid in its cluster so here:

Total Cost={ cost((3,4),(2,6))+ cost((3,4),(3,8))+ cost((3,4),(4,7))}
+ {cost((7,4),(6,2))+ cost((7,4),(6,4))+ cost((7,4),(7,3))
+ cost((7,4),(8,5)) + cost((7,4),(7,6))}
=20

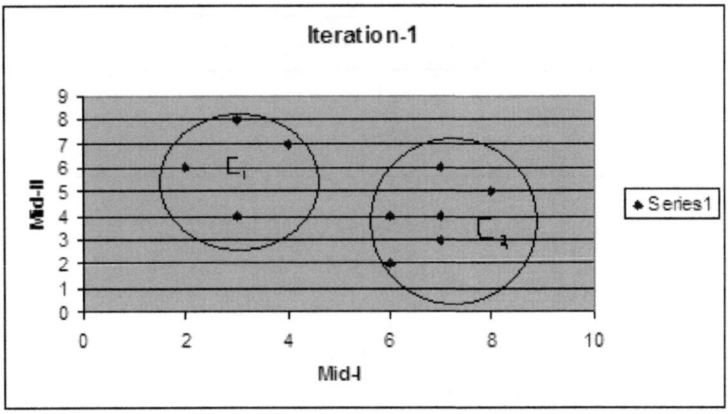

Fig. 6. K-Medoid result after iteration-1

Selection of nonmedoid O′ randomly
Let us assume O′ = (7,3)
So now the medoids are c_1(3,4) and O′(7,3)
If c1 and O′ are new medoids, calculate the total cost involved. By using the formula in the step 1.

Table 6. Cluster 1 after Iteration

c_1		Data objects (X_i)		Cost (distance)
3	4	2	6	3
3	4	3	8	4
3	4	4	7	4
3	4	6	2	5
3	4	6	4	3
3	4	7	4	4
3	4	8	5	6
3	4	7	6	6

Table 7. New Medoid data

O′		Data objects (X_i)		Cost (distance)
7	3	2	6	8
7	3	3	8	9
7	3	4	7	7
7	3	6	2	2
7	3	6	4	2
7	3	7	4	1
7	3	8	5	3
7	3	7	6	3

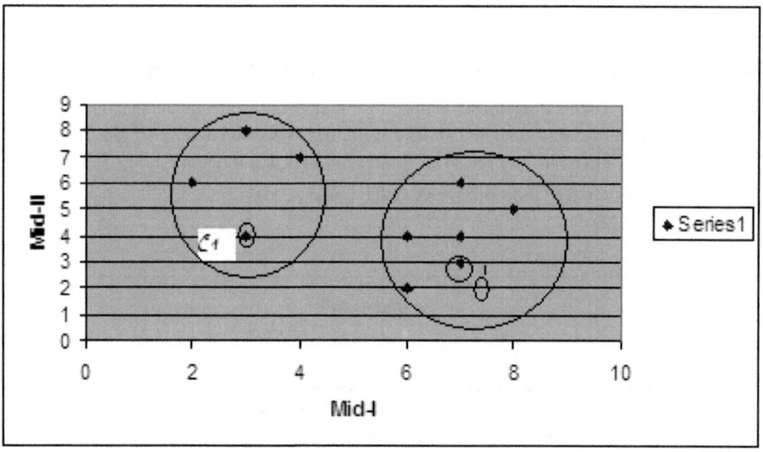

Fig. 7. New Medoid O^1 in cluster 2

Total Cost =3+4+4+2+2+1+3+3
= 22.

So cost of swapping medoid from c_2 to O′ is
S = current total cost – past total cost
= 22 – 20
= 2 >0.

So moving to O′ would be bad idea, so the previous choice was good and algorithm terminates here.It may happen some data points may shift from one cluster to another cluster depending upon their closeness to medoid.

3 Conclusion

The partition based algorithms work well for finding spherical-shaped clusters in small to medium-sized data points. The advantage of the K-Means algorithm is its favorable execution time. Its drawback is that the user has to know in advance how many clusters are searched for. It is observed that K-Means algorithm is efficient for smaller data sets and K-Medoids algorithm seems to perform better for large data sets. If the number of data points is less, then the K-Means algorithm takes lesser execution time. But when the data points are increased to maximum the K-Means algorithm takes maximum time and the K-Medoids algorithm performs reasonably better than the K-Means algorithm. The characteristic feature of this algorithm is that it requires the distance between every pair of objects only once and uses this distance at every stage of iteration.

References

1. Han, J., Kamber, M.: Data Mining: Concepts and Techniques. Academic Press, San Diego (2001)
2. Abbas, O.A.: Comparision between clustering algorithms
3. Pham, D.T., Afify, A.A.: Clustering techniques and their applications in engineering. Submitted to Proceedings of the Institution of Mechanical Engineers, Part C: Journal of Mechanical Engineering Science (2006)
4. Jain, A.K., Dubes, R.C.: Algorithms for Clustering Data. Prentice Hall, Englewood Cliffs (1988)
5. Bottou, L., Bengio, Y.: Convergence properties of the k-means algorithm
6. Grabmeier, J., Rudolph, A.: Techniques of cluster algorithms in data mining. DataMining and Knowledge Discovery 6, 303–360 (2002)
7. Jain, A.K., Murty, M.N., Flynn, P.J.: Data Clustering. A Review
8. Lee, R.C.T.: Cluster Analysis and Its Applications. In: Tou, J.T. (ed.) Advances in Information Systems Science. Plenum Press, New York
9. Velmurugan, T., Santhanam, T.: Computational Complexity between K-Means and K-Medoids Clustering Algorithms for Normal and Uniform Distributions of Data Points

Performance of Routing Lookups

S.V. Nagaraj

RMK Engineering College
RSM Nagar, Kavaraipettai 601 206, Tamil Nadu, India
http://www.rmkec.ac.in

Abstract. We look at the performance of routing lookups when techniques for restructuring binary search trees are applied. We try to obtain near-optimal routing lookups with bounded worst-case performance. For this, we look at the problem of constructing search trees so that the average lookup time is minimized while keeping the worst-case lookup time within a fixed bound.

Keywords: Routing lookups, restructuring binary search trees, performance.

1 Introduction

Internet routing is a complex process. For every incoming packet, a router must lookup a routing table so as to determine the packet's next hop destination. This process has become more difficult due to the constantly increasing size of routing tables. Routers perform a longest prefix match in order to find out the next hop of a packet. This is done as follows. A set of destination address prefixes is maintained in a routing table. For a given packet, the lookup operation consists of determining the longest prefix in the routing table that matches the first few bits of the destination address of the packet. A variety of data structures and algorithms have been employed for routing lookup (see [3], [4], [10], [11],[17], [21], [23]). The objectives have included minimization of lookup time as well minimization of space usage. It is reasonable to assume that the frequencies with which prefixes are likely to be accessed is known. This is reasonable provided there are no sudden bursts in the traffic. Given these, the aim is to design a routing lookup scheme for minimizing the average lookup time.

2 The Algorithm of Gupta et al.

Binary search trees may be used for designing routing lookup schemes that minimize the average lookup time. A binary search tree is a data structure that is extensively used for information storage as well as retrieval. The reader may refer [20] for a survey of binary search trees. A binary search tree T for a set of keys from a total order may be defined (as in [20]) as a binary tree in which each node has a key value and all the keys of the left subtree are less than the key at the root and all the keys of the right subtree are greater than the key at the root. This property must hold recursively for the left and right subtrees of the tree T.

D.C. Wyld et al. (Eds.): ACITY 2011, CCIS 198, pp. 482–487, 2011.

Assume that we are given n keys and also the probabilities of accessing each key and those occurring in the gap between two successive keys. The optimal binary search tree problem is to construct a binary search tree on these n keys that minimizes the expected access time. One important variant of this problem is when only the gaps have non-zero access probabilities. This problem is known as the optimal alphabetic search tree problem. Knuth studied the problem of building optimal binary search trees [16] and gave a quadratic time algorithm by using dynamic programming. There are numerous algorithms for building optimal binary search trees [20] as well as heuristics for building nearly-optimal binary search trees (see for example [1], [19], [20]). Algorithms are known for constructing optimal alphabetic binary search trees (see [9], [13], [14]). There are also many heuristics for building nearly-optimal alphabetic search trees [20].

Gupta et al. [11] make use of a binary search tree built on the intervals created by the routing table prefixes. They study the problem of constructing binary search trees to minimize the average lookup time while keeping the worst case lookup time within a fixed bound. It is easy to note that when binary search trees are used the worst-case depth of a binary search tree could be very prohibitive depending on the distribution of the access probabilities. This essentially means that we may encounter very long lookup times for some prefixes. Consequently, we must try to control the depth of the binary search trees to some reasonable value so that there is no significant degradation in performance in some bad cases. So we need to build depth-constrained binary search trees. The problem of building optimal binary search trees with restricted maximal depth was studied by [8].

The approach used by Gupta et al. [11] necessitates the construction of depth-constrained alphabetic binary search trees. Algorithms for constructing optimal depth-constrained alphabetic binary search trees were presented by [8], [15], [18] and [24]. Among these algorithms, the fastest algorithm in terms of computational complexity is due to Larmore and Przytycka [18]. This algorithm has a complexity of $O(nD \log n)$ where D is the worst-case number of memory accesses permissible and n is the number of prefixes. This algorithm is unfortunately rather complicated and difficult for implementation purposes. Gupta et al. [11] obtained an easy to implement algorithm that is nearly optimal and has a pre-processing time complexity of $O(n \log n)$. They considered the problem of finding the minimum average length alphabetic tree for an m-letter alphabet. Each letter corresponds to an interval (Note: Each prefix matching the incoming packet's destination address may be viewed as an interval on the number line. The leaves of the tree store the intervals created by the routing table prefixes). We need to obtain a small upper bound on the maximum depth of an alphabetic tree that may be used for performing routing lookups. The Larmore and Przytycka algorithm [18] is quite complicated but finds an optimal solution. However, it is not really necessary to find the optimal solution since an approximate solution that is close to the optimal solution is also acceptable in practice. Gupta et al. [11] argue that since the probabilities associated with the intervals induced by the routing prefixes change frequently and are not known exactly there is really no need to find an optimal solution. Since neither routing tables nor access patterns are static so the time taken to build the data structures is important. A good approximate solution is useful if it is easy to obtain and is close to the optimal solution. Gupta et al. [11] make use of a lemma stated by Yeung [25] (see Lemma 2 of their paper) that produces a near-optimal alphabetic tree which may or may not satisfy the depth constraint. They then suggest some steps so that this near-optimal alphabetic binary tree may be processed so that the depth constraint is satisfied. For this they solve an optimization problem.

3 Restructuring Ordered Binary Trees

Instead of taking the approach of Gupta et al. [11], it is possible to restructure the near-optimal tree (produced by the lemma 2 in their paper or for that matter by any algorithm for constructing optimal or nearly optimal alphabetic search trees) by applying the ideas in Evans and Kirkpatrick (see [5] and [6]). Evans and Kirkpatrick consider the problem of restructuring an ordered binary tree T so that the in-order sequence of its nodes is preserved with the objective of reducing its height to some target value h. Such a restructuring will no doubt cause the downward displacement of some of the nodes of T. Their article [5] describes efficient algorithms to achieve height-restricted restructuring while minimizing the maximum node displacement. Evans and Kirkpatrick [5] show that any L-leaf tree T with fixed but unknown leaf access frequencies can be restructured into a tree R of height at most $1 + \lg L$ such that the expected depth of R exceeds the expected depth of T by at most 2. Here lg denotes logarithm to the base 2. In their paper Gupta et al. [11] describe a heuristic for constructing near-optimal depth-constrained alphabetic trees. Unfortunately, it is not easy to prove any optimal properties of this heuristic, although, it seems to perform well in practice. As mentioned earlier, we may apply tree restructuring in this case too by first constructing near-optimal alphabetic trees using heuristics and then employing restructuring.

Theorem 2.1 of Evans and Kirkpatrick [5] shows that an optimal binary search tree with keys stored at leaves can be restructured to have worst-case search cost within one of optimal without increasing the average search cost by more than two. In fact, their result also applies to the average search cost of any key. Theorem 2.2 of their paper [5] is especially useful for routing lookups since it implies that even without any information regarding the key access frequencies, an optimal or near-optimal binary search tree can be restructured to have worst-case search cost within one of optimal at the expense of an additional increase of at most $\lg \lg L$ in the expected search cost for any L-leaf tree. In order to illustrate the usefulness of Theorems 2.1 and 2.2 of Evans and Kirkpatrick [5], we must explain the circumstances under which it is necessary to compute new trees when using the algorithm of Gupta et al [11]. The computation of a new tree when using the algorithm of Gupta et al. may be necessitated due to changes in the routing table or due to changes in the access patterns of the routing table entries. Gupta et al. [11] assume that the average frequency of routing updates may be of the order of a few updates per second. However, as mentioned by them in some cases the frequency of those updates could even be of the order of over hundred updates per second. Gupta et al. [11] suggest that several updates to the routing table be batched and the tree be computed accordingly. They believe that changes in the routing table structure are more easily managed than changes in the access frequencies which are harder to predict. Here we may employ Theorem 2.2 of Evans and Kirkpatrick [5] as mentioned earlier. This theorem does not require the knowledge of key access frequencies. So it is possible for us to employ tree restructuring periodically to control the depth of binary search trees and consequently the worst-case lookup time.

Gupta et al. [11] claim that well-known algorithms for constructing optimal alphabetic trees such as [9], [13] [14] cannot be used in their setting since they do not incorporate a maximum depth constraint. However, we can use these algorithms by first constructing optimal alphabetic trees and then employing tree restructuring to satisfy depth constraints. We must note that tree restructuring can be done in linear time (see [5], [6], [7]).

Gagie [7] obtained some improvements to the tree restructuring techniques of Evans and Kirkpatrick ([5] and [6]). Improvements to the results of Evans and Kirkpatrick ([5] and [6]) and Gagie [7] were obtained by Bose and Douieb [2]. In their paper, they argue that there is really no need to keep static search trees unbalanced. They demonstrate that a balanced tree is always a better option than an unbalanced one since the balanced tree has similar average access time and much better worst case access time. Bose and Douieb present several methods to restructure an unbalanced binary search tree T into a new tree R that preserves many of the properties of T while having a height of $\lg n + 1$ (which is one unit off of the optimal height). They show that it is possible to ensure that the depth of the elements in R is no more than their depth in T plus at most $\lg\lg n + 2$. They also guarantee that the average access time $P(R)$ in tree R is no more than the average access time $P(T)$ in tree T plus $O(\lg P(T))$. Bose and Douieb [1] developed a method to build a binary search tree in $O(n)$ time that gives the best known upper bound on the path length of a binary search tree and produces a near-optimal binary search tree. So their method is useful for constructing nearly optimal binary search trees quickly. Their method also improves on results in [22]. Bose and Douieb [2] present tree restructuring methods that focus on reducing the worst-case drop of any given key. They also develop a method that focuses on the relative drop. By this, they mean that in the worst case, the amount that a node will drop is proportional to its depth in the original tree instead of being proportional to the number of nodes in the tree. Finally, they develop a hybrid drop approach that combines the worst-case and relative drop approaches.

4 Conclusion

The application of restructuring ordered binary trees for routing lookups has been considered. We have considered tree restructuring as an alternative as well as supplementary approach to the algorithm of Gupta et al. [11] for constructing search trees so that the average lookup time is minimized while keeping the worst-case lookup time within a fixed bound. Tree restructuring helps to control the maximum depth of binary search trees without significant changes in the expected search cost.

Acknowledgement. The author is thankful to Pankaj Gupta and William Evans for having answered some of his queries.

References

1. Bose, P., Douïeb, K.: Efficient construction of near-optimal binary and multiway search trees. In: Dehne, F., Gavrilova, M., Sack, J.-R., Tóth, C.D. (eds.) WADS 2009. LNCS, vol. 5664, pp. 230–241. Springer, Heidelberg (2009)
2. Bose, P., Douïeb, K.: Should Static Search Trees Ever Be Unbalanced? In: Cheong, O., Chwa, K.-Y., Park, K. (eds.) ISAAC 2010. LNCS, vol. 6506, pp. 109–120. Springer, Heidelberg (2010)
3. Cheung, G., McCanne, S.: Optimal Routing Table Design for IP Address Lookups under Memory Constraints. In: Proceedings of IEEE Eighteenth Annual Joint Conference of the IEEE Computer and Communications Societies, INFOCOM 1999, vol. 3, pp. 1437–1444. IEEE Press, New York (1999)
4. Degermark, M., Brodnik, A., Carlsson, S., Pink, S.: Small forwarding tables for fast routing lookups. ACM SIGCOMM Computer Communication Review 27(4), 3–14 (1997)
5. Evans, W., Kirkpatrick, D.: Restructuring ordered binary trees. In: Proceedings of the Eleventh Annual ACM-SIAM Symposium on Discrete Algorithms, pp. 477–486. SIAM, Philadelphia (2000)
6. Evans, W., Kirkpatrick, D.: Restructuring ordered binary trees. Journal of Algorithms 50(2), 168–193 (2004)
7. Gagie, T.: Restructuring binary search trees revisited. Information Processing Letters 95(3), 418–421 (2005)
8. Garey, M.R.: Optimal binary search trees with restricted maximal depth. SIAM Journal on Computing 3(2), 101–110 (1974)
9. Garsia, A.M., Wachs, M.L.: A new algorithm for minimum cost binary trees. SIAM Journal on Computing 6, 622–642 (1977)
10. Gupta, P., Lin, S., McKeown, N.: Routing lookups in hardware at memory access speeds. In: Proceedings of IEEE Seventeenth Annual Joint Conference of the IEEE Computer and Communications Societies, INFOCOM 1998, vol. 3, pp. 1240–1247. IEEE Press, New York (1998)
11. Gupta, P., Prabhakar, B., Boyd, S.: Near-optimal routing lookups with bounded worst case performance. In: Proceedings of IEEE Nineteenth Annual Joint Conference of the IEEE Computer and Communications Societies, INFOCOM 2000, vol. 3, pp. 1184–1192. IEEE Press, New York (2000)
12. Gupta, P., Prabhakar, B., Boyd, S.: Near-optimal depth-constrained codes. IEEE Transactions on Information Theory 50(12), 3294–3298 (2004)
13. Hu, T.C.: Combinatorial Algorithms. Addison-Wesley, Reading (1982)
14. Hu, T.C., Tucker, A.C.: Optimal computer search trees and variable-length alphabetical codes. SIAM Journal on Applied Mathematics 21(4), 514–532 (1971)
15. Itai, A.: Optimal alphabetic trees. SIAM Journal on Computing 9(1), 9–18 (1976)
16. Knuth, D.E.: Optimum binary search trees. Acta Informatica 1(1), 14–25 (1971)

17. Lampson, B., Srinivasan, V., Varghese, G.: IP Lookups using Multiway and Multicolumn Search. In: Proceedings of IEEE Seventeenth Annual Joint Conference of the IEEE Computer and Communications Societies, INFOCOM 1998, vol. 3, pp. 1248–1256. IEEE Press, New York (1998)
18. Larmore, L.L., Przytycka, T.M.: A fast algorithm for optimum height-limited alphabetic binary trees. SIAM Journal on Computing 23(6), 1283–1312 (1994)
19. Mehlhorn, K.: A best possible bound for the weighted path length of binary search trees. SIAM Journal on Computing 6(2), 235–239 (1977)
20. Nagaraj, S.V.: Optimal binary search trees. Theoretical Computer Science 188(1–2), 1–44 (1997)
21. Nilsson, S., Karlsson, G.: IP-Address Lookup Using LC-Tries. IEEE Journal on Selected Areas in Communications 17(6), 1083–1092 (1999)
22. Prisco, R.D., Santis, A.D.: New lower bounds on the cost of binary search trees. Theoretical Computer Science 156(1-2), 315–325 (1996)
23. Srinivasan, V., Varghese, G.: Faster IP Lookups using Controlled Prefix Expansion. ACM Transcations on Computer Systems 17(1), 1–40 (1999)
24. Wessner, R.L.: Optimal alphabetic search trees with restricted maximal height. Information Processing Letters 4(4), 90–94 (1976)
25. Yeung, R.W.: Alphabetic codes revisited. IEEE Transactions on Information Theory 37(3), 564–572 (1991)

Multi Agent Implementation for Optimal Speed Control of Three Phase Induction Motor

Rathod Nirali[1] and S.K. Shah[2]

[1] Electrical Engg. Dept., S.V.I.T, Vasad, India
nirali_ee@yahoo.co.in
[2] Electrical Engg. Dept., Faculty of Technology & Engineering, M.S.U. Baroda, India
satishkshah_2005@yahoo.com

Abstract. Agent and Multi agent systems are becoming a new way to design and control of complex systems. Induction motor is widely used in industrial applications. But due to its highly non linear behavior its control is very complex. Recently by adapting non linear speed control techniques the dynamic performance of electric drives can be improved.

In this paper agent based approach is developed to control speed of Induction motor. Design and simulation of Multi Agent System is developed for Indirect vector controlled 3-phase Induction motor. To implement Multi Agent system classical controller (PI) & various intelligent controllers such as Fuzzy Logic & Neural Network are developed. The system is developed on simulink toolbox in MATLAB. The speed responses of controllers in terms of rise time, steady state error and overshoot are compared. And also results are compared with that of Multi Agent system.

Keywords: Induction motor, Vector control, Artificial Neural Network (ANN), PI controller, Fuzzy Logic (FLC), Multi Agent System (MAS).

1 Introduction

An agent represents an abstract entity that is able to solve a defined problem. Agents are combined into a multi-agent system, such that the overall multi-agent system can solve a more complex problem.

Induction motors are widely used in industries due to its robust construction, low maintenance and ease of availability in wide power range. But Induction Motors also suffer from disadvantage of controllability due to complex mathematical model and its nonlinear behavior.

In this paper the Multi Agent System is developed for indirect vector control of Three Phase Induction Motor in which motor is operated like separately excited D.C.Motor. This method enables the control of field and torque of Induction Motor independently.

2 Multi Agent System

Agent is a system, which has the ability to accomplish the tasks that the user has defined. A multi-agent system is a system comprising two or more agents or

D.C. Wyld et al. (Eds.): ACITY 2011, CCIS 198, pp. 488–496, 2011.

intelligent agents. Multi-Agent Systems (MAS) are systems where there is no central control: the agents receive their inputs from the other system or other agents and use these inputs to apply the appropriate actions.

Such systems are assembled from autonomously interacting agents. Agents are small software programs, which have some type of intelligence. Their individual behavior is able to control complex system. Coordination between agents is the one of the important element in the construction of MAS. [3]

The basic characteristics of MAS are lack of global control, decentralized data and asynchronous computation. Distributed problem, Robustness, Scalability, Simpler implementation, Parallism are some of the advantages of MAS. [3]

3 Indirect Vector Control

The Figure.1 shows Vector controlled Induction motor drive system. The Induction motor is fed by current controlled voltage source inverter. The motor current is decomposed into two components direct axis current i_{ds} and quadrature axis current i_{qs} with respect to synchronously rotating reference frame. These currents produce flux and torque respectively. To improve performance of Drive Indirect Vector control method is preferred. This method uses indirect procedure to ensure presence of rotor flux in the direct axis.

Indirect vector control is complex, but it is inherently four quadrant speed control. It can easily cover zero speed.

The inverter generates currents i_a,i_b,i_c as dictated by the corresponding command currents i_a^*, i_b^*,i_c^* from the controller. The machine terminal phase currents i_a, i_b, i_c are converted to i_{ds}^* and i_{qs}^* components by Park's transformation.

These current components are then converted to synchronously rotating reference frame by the unit vector components $\cos\theta_e$ and $\sin\theta_e$ before applying them to the d^e-q^e machine model. The controller makes two stages of inverse transformation, so that control currents i_{ds}^* and i_{qs}^* correspond to the machine currents i_{ds} and i_{qs} respectively.

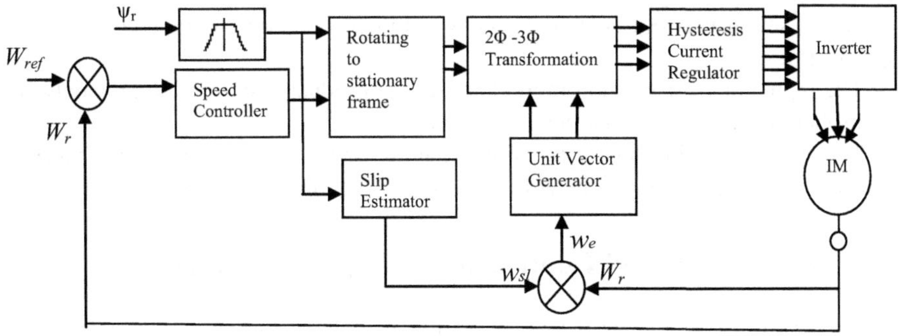

Fig. 1. Vector Control Scheme of Induction Motor

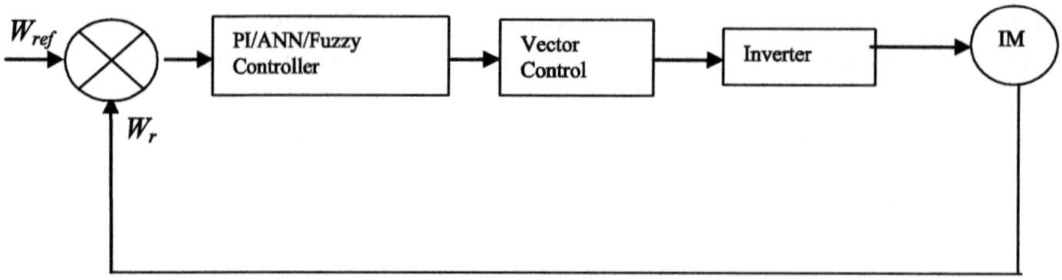

Fig. 2. Speed Control of Induction Motor using Intelligent Controller

When i_{qs}^* is controlled it affects the actual i_{qs} current only, but does not affect the flux Ψ_r. Similarly, when i_{ds}^* is controlled, it controls the flux only and does not affect the i_{qs} component of current. [1]

With the help of a classical controller PI and various Intelligent controller (FLC & Neural Network controller), the speed error is converted into a torque controlling current component i_{qs}, of the stator current. This current component is used to regulate the torque along with the slip speed. [1]

Figure.2 shows the block diagram of speed control system using different Controllers.

4 Artificial Neural Network

The ANN is an Artificial Intelligent technique which is machine like human brain with properties such as learning capability and generalization. It is a system of interconnecting neurons in a network which work together to form the output function. Neuron is a fundamental processing component of a neural network. [2] The performance of ANN relies on member neurons of network collectively. So that it can still perform its overall function even if some of the neurons are not functioning. Thus, they are very robust to error failure. It required a lot of training to understand the model of the system. To approximate complicated nonlinear functions is the basic property of ANN. [2]

Here, Neural network is used to produce torque producing component of current i_{qs}. [4], [5]

The input data (error) and output data (torque producing current component) of PI controller are used to train the neural network.

Tansig and Purelin transfer function are used for two input layers. Proper learning rate and proper training parameters are chosen to minimize error. [8]

5 Fuzzy Logic Speed Controller: Principle and Design

Basic structure of the fuzzy logic controller to control the speed of the induction motor consists of three important stages: Fuzzification, Decision Making Unit and Defuzzification Unit.

The inputs of the Fuzzification Unit are selected as error and rate of change of error. The output of the controller is torque controlling current component. The two input variables error and rate of change of error are calculated at every sampling instant say n.

$$e(\mathrm{n})=w_{\mathrm{ref}}(\mathrm{n})-w_{\mathrm{e}}(\mathrm{n})$$

$$\Delta e\ (\mathrm{n})=w(\mathrm{n})-w(\mathrm{n}-1)$$

Where, $w_{ref}(n)$ is the reference speed at instant n and $w_e(n)$ is measured speed at instant n.[7]

In Fuzzification stage the crisp variables e(n) and Δe(n) are converted into fuzzy variables which can be identified by membership function. The fuzzification maps the error and change in error to linguistic labels of fuzzy sets.

The proposed controller uses following linguistic labels: NB (Negative Big), NM (Negative Medium), NS (Negative Small), NVS (Negative Very Small), Z(Zero), PVS (Positive Very Small), PM(Positive Medium), PB(Positive Big).

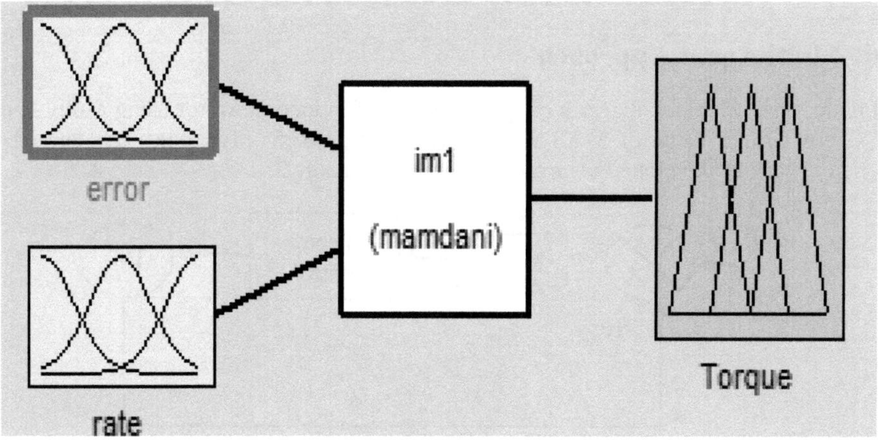

Fig. 3. Fuzzy Inference System

Here, the triangular membership functions are used to define both inputs (error and rate of change of error) and output (torque controlling current component).

In the second stage of FLC the input variables are processed by an inference engine that executes 49 rules as shown in Table 1.

Each rule can be interpreted as: if error is Negative Big and rate of change of error is Negative Big then output is Negative Big.

The output of the decision-making unit is given as input to the de-fuzzification unit and the linguistic format of the signal is converted back into the numeric form of data. In this paper, the center of gravity or centroids method is used to calculate the final output, which finally commands the induction motor via 2Φ-3Φ block.

Table 1. Rules of Fuzzy Logic Controller

e \ Δe	NB	NM	NS	Z	PS	PM	PB
NB	NB	NB	NB	NM	NS	NVS	Z
NM	NB	NB	NM	NS	NVS	Z	PVS
NS	NB	NM	NS	NVS	Z	PVS	PS
Z	NM	NS	NVS	Z	PVS	PS	PM
PS	NS	NVS	Z	PVS	PS	PM	PB
PM	NVS	Z	PVS	PS	PM	PB	PB
PB	Z	PVS	PS	PM	PB	PB	PB

6 Multi Agent Approach

Figure. 4 shows block diagram of speed control of Induction Motor using Multi Agent System. Frame work of MAS is as shown in figure. 5. Five rules are defined to operate various developed controllers as shown in Table 2.

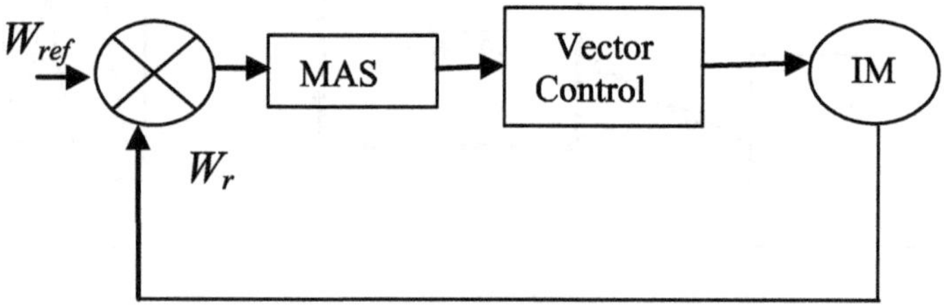

Fig. 4. Multi Agent System

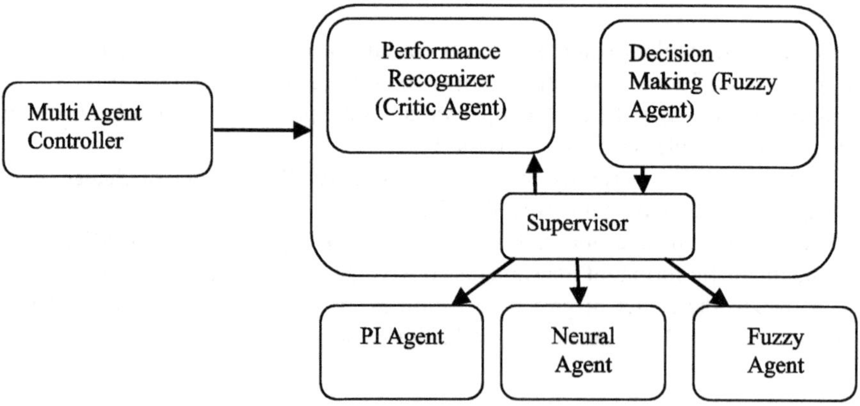

Fig. 5. Multi Agent Frame work

Table 2. Rules For MAS

Sr no.	Steady State eroor	Rise Time	Reference change	Controller
1	High	Low	Low	Neural
2	Low	High	Low	Fuzzy
3	Low	Low	High	Neural
4	High	High	High	Fuzzy
5	High	High	Low	PID

7 Results and Discussion

To implement Multi Agent system the conventional controller (PI), Neural Network Controller & Fuzzy Logic Controller are developed. All are constructed into MATLAB/SIMULINK environment. Simulation tests were carried out on the PI, Fuzzy and Neural Network Controller. Results are compared in terms of Time response.

Figure.6, figure.7 and figure.8 show speed response comparison of PI controller, ANN Controller and Fuzzy Logic Controller at set reference speed, 100 rad/sec. Here we can see that rise time and settling time of the drive using ANN Controller is very less compare to that of PI controller & Fuzzy Logic controller.

No overshoot is found with the use of ANN Controller and Fuzzy Logic Controller as compared to PI controller. The steady state error is also acceptable using ANN and Fuzzy Logic Controller. Simulink model is also tested using Multi Agent System.

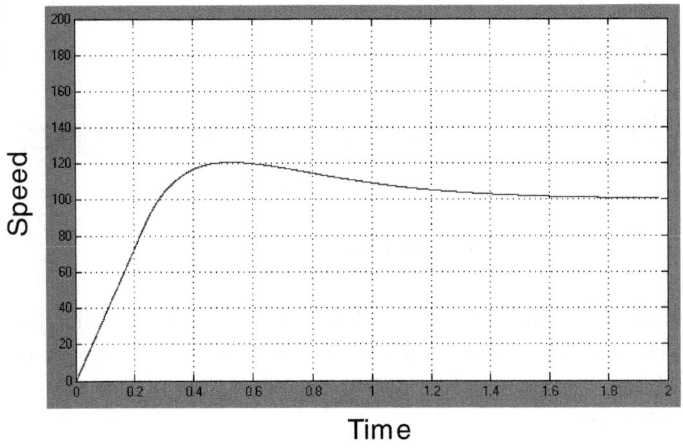

Fig. 6. Speed Response using PI Controller

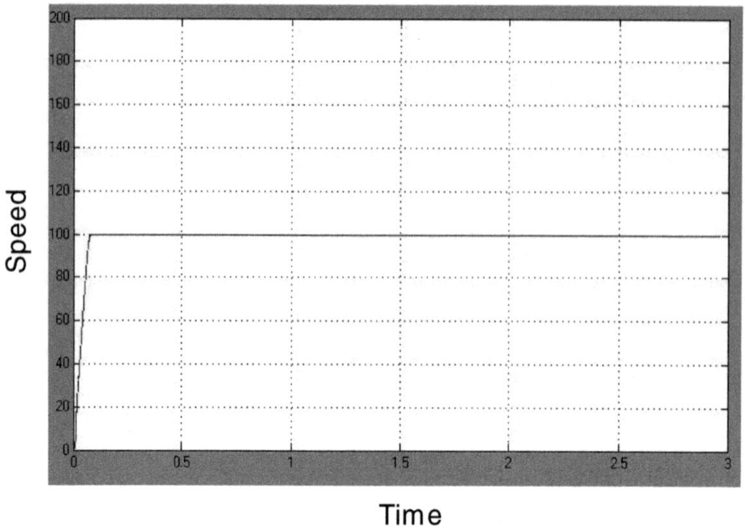

Fig. 7. Speed Response using ANN

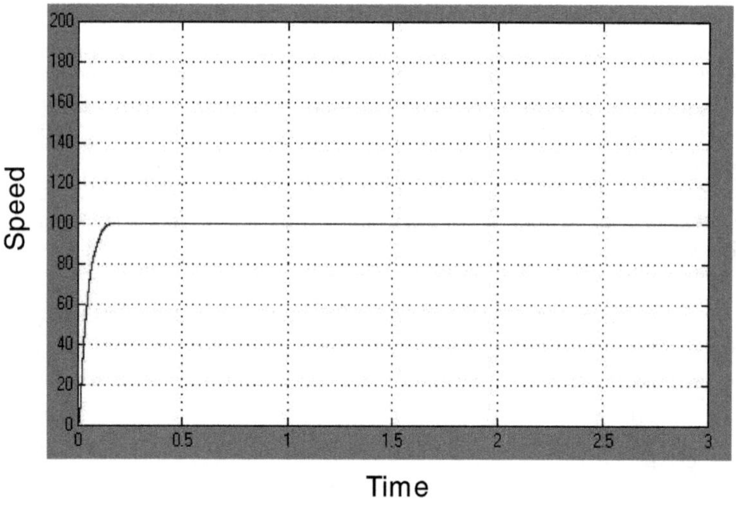

Fig. 8. Speed Response using FLC

Figure.9 shows speed response of MAS based on selection of Neural Network controller. The speed response is slower than that of Neural Network controller for the same reference speed which is due to operation time of Decision maker, Fuzzy agent and critic agent.

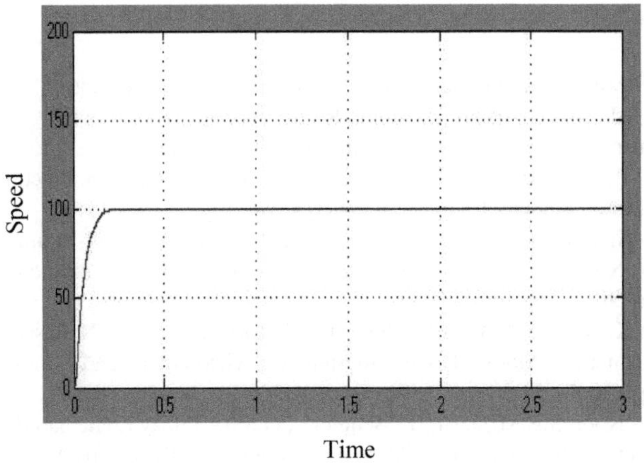

Fig. 9. Speed Response using MAS on the Selection of Neural Network Controller

Table 3. Comparison Table

Controller	PI Controller	NN Controller	FLC
Rise Time	High	Less compare to PI & FLC	Less compare to PI
Steady State Error	Large	Less compare to PI & FLC	Less compare to PI
Overshoot	20%	No overshoot	No overshoot

8 Conclusion

Vector control scheme to control speed of Induction motor is developed. To control speed of Induction motor classical controller (PI) and various Intelligent Controller such as Fuzzy Logic and Neural Network controller are developed and their responses are compared in terms of Rise time, Steady state error and overshoot. By using Fuzzy controller and Neural network controller the transient response of Induction machine has been improved greatly and dynamic response of the same is made faster.

Multi Agent framework is prepared. The Multi Agent System is implemented using three controllers (PI, FLC, Neural Network controller). The system is robust to the error failure.

By using Multi Agent System time required to reach steady state value is somewhat high compare to that of separate control because system will consider operational time of Decision maker, Fuzzy agent and critic agent is considerable.

References

[1] Bose, B.: Power Electronics and motor drives: Advances and Trends
[2] Chapman, S.J.: MATLAB programming for Engineers
[3] Van Breemen, A.J.N.: Agent based Multi-controller system
[4] Baruch, I., de la Cruz, I.P., Garrido, A.R.: An Indirect Adaptive Vector Control of the Induction Motor Velocity Using Neural Networks
[5] Wlas, M., Krzeminski, Z., Guzinski, J., Abu-Rub, H.: Artificial-Neural-Network-Based Sensorless Nonlinear Control of Induction Motors. IEEE Transactions On Energy Conversion 20(3) (September 2005)
[6] Sharma, A.K., Gupta, R.A., Srivastava, L.: Performance of ANN Based Indirect Vector Control Induction Motor Drive. Journal of Theoretical and Applied Information Technology (2007)
[7] Mariun, N., Noor, S.B.M., Jasni, J., Bennanes, O.S.: A Fuzzy Logic based controller for an Indirect Vector controlled Three- Phase Induction motor. IEEE, Los Alamitos (2004)
[8] http://www.mathwork.com

Indexing and Querying the Compressed XML Data (IQCX)

Radha Senthilkumar, N. Suganya, I. Kiruthika, and A. Kannan

Department of Information Technology, MIT Campus,
Anna University Chennai, India
{radhasenthil,kannan}@annauniv.edu

Abstract. Extensible Markup Language was designed to carry data which provides a platform to define own tags. XML documents are immense in nature. As a result there has been an ever growing need for developing an efficient storage structure and high-performance techniques to query efficiently. Though several storage structures are available, QUICX (Query and Update Support for Indexed and Compressed XML) compact storage structure proved to be efficient in terms of data storage. The major reason for performance loss in query processing is identified to be the storage structure used as well as the lack of efficient query processing techniques. The approach (IQCX) focuses on indexing and querying the compressed data stored in QUICX, thereby increasing the compression ratio. Proposed indexing technique exploits the high degree of redundancy exhibited by the XML documents. Thus indexing enhances the query performance, compared to querying without indexing.

Keywords: XML, XPath, Indexing, Query Processing.

1 Introduction

XML is flexible in managing data. Its design goals mainly focus on simplicity, and increasing the usability over the Internet. XML documents are huge in size thus an efficient storage structure is required. In the QUICX [9] structure, the XML document which is given as input is parsed and the details are stored in three different structures namely metatable, metadata and containers. Meta table stores the tag id, name of the node, level id, parent id and the file id. Meta data stores the tag id of the nodes in the same order as it is in the XML document. The actual data within the nodes is stored in containers and 50 records in each. This is how the entire XML document is divided and stored.

The proposed indexing technique is based on the redundant records found in the containers. If more redundant records are present in a container then it is chosen for indexing. The information available in the Meta data file is sometimes used for indexing. Once the file is indexed, the original container is removed and only the index is maintained. This is because the index file contains the data as well as the location where it is present in the original container. Hence, there will be no loss of

D.C. Wyld et al. (Eds.): ACITY 2011, CCIS 198, pp. 497–506, 2011.

data and the indexing technique leads to the deletion of some of the huge containers thereby reducing the memory wasted in storing them and increasing the compression ratio. Querying the XML data using index is carried. This proves that there is a decrease in the overall execution time though considerable amount of time is spent in creating the index file.

2 Related Work

Xlight [11] is used to store all types of XML documents and is composed of five tables. Document, Path, Data, Ancestor, Attribute. Querying becomes complex due to merging of tables for data retrieval. IQCX approach overcomes this problem by storing data in containers; the index file generated is used to retrieve only particular records required. DRXQP [7] technique stores the encoded value of element paths, attributes, contents of the element paths and attributes, and XML processing instructions in a dynamic relational structure termed as Multi-XML Data-Structure (MXDS). The encoded values are calculated based on the parent-child relationship. Encoding and query processing becomes complex when the size of the original XML document increases. RFX (Redundancy Free Compact Storage Structure) [8] Compact Storage is where the XML documents are stored, with no redundancy of elements. An entirely new technique is developed to process XPath queries in the RFX, exploiting the self optimized nature of Compact Storage, using Strategy List. QUICX[9] is an efficient compact storage structure that supports both query and update efficiently. Navigation-Free Data Instance [6] is the combination of the runtime generated path tables and token buffers of a given XQuery Q over data stream D. Token Buffers store the offset of nodes related to the query. Considerable amount of memory is wasted in storing the offsets and time is also wasted in calculating them. Indexing structure, extended inverted index technique [1], used in information retrieval is proposed for processing queries efficiently. Four types of indexes are defined and are stored in relational RDBMS. More memory space is required to store the details. A new methodology is proposed with multi dimensional approach for retrieving attributes [4]. Frequently occurring strings are given minimal length code and infrequent strings are given greater length code. Assigning such codes increases the memory requirement to store it. The XML compressor in XQzip, is proposed by imposing an indexing structure, which is called as Structure Index Tree (SIT) [2], on XML data. XQzip supports a wide scope of XPath queries such as multiple, deeply nested predicates and aggregation. But IQCX technique proves that executing aggregate queries using the index takes lesser time when compared to executing such queries in XQzip. IQCX also supports other queries.

3 Indexing XML Data

Redundancy found in data can be used to index files which enhance querying efficiency by reducing the time required to locate the record of interest. Once the index is generated, the original file can be removed. The indexing architecture shown in Fig. 1 involves getting the query as input from the user. Based on the query, the index file is searched for. If it is available, then it is loaded and the corresponding record is located using the index.

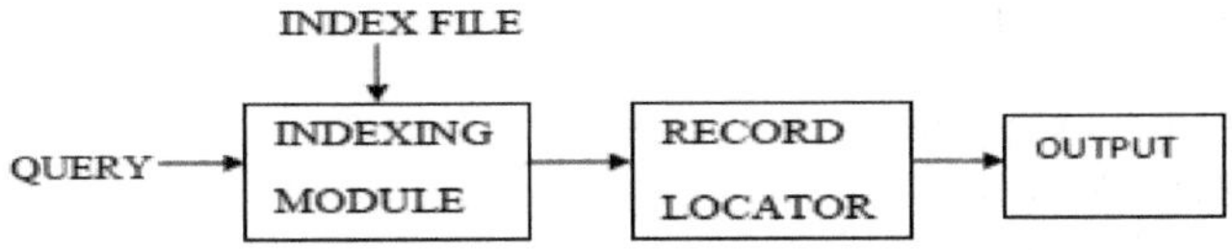

Fig. 1. Architecture for indexing XML data

```
Procedure index_without_Metadata()
/* generating index file */
Begin
1. Input the file to be indexed
2. Find out the records which are different
3. Find out the position numbers where each and every record is present.
4. For each and every record present
5. Write to the index file the record followed by '>'
 6. Append the position numbers (separated by '>') where the particular record is present.
End For
End
Procedure index_speaker_with_Metadata()
/* generating index file */
Begin
1. Input the file to be indexed
2. Input the Metadata file.
3. Traverse the Metadata file and count the number of lines spoken by each speaker.
   (i.e count the number of 21s after each 20)
4. For each and every speaker in the speaker container
5.  Write to the index file the name of the speaker followed by '>'
6.  For each and every set of line numbers
7.   Append the starting line number followed by '+' followed by total number of lines spoken at that instance – 1.
8.   Append '>'
    End For
  End For
End
```

The index file is created either using the Meta data file as shown in Fig. 2 or without using the Meta data file as shown in Fig. 3. Algorithm for creating the index files with or without using Meta data table is given below.

There are 58 containers (58 different tags) storing the data in the dataset Shakespeare. Let us take some sample records from the container 20.cont which has the names of the speakers, 21.cont which has the lines spoken by each speaker and the corresponding Meta data file.

Contents of 20.cont
PHILO>CLEOPATRA>MARK ANTONY>CLEOPATRA>DUKE VINCENTIO>
PHILO>
Contents of Meta data file
1>2>3>4>20>21>21>19>2>3>20>21>21>21>21>21>21>19>20>21>21>2>3>20>
21>20>21>21>21>19>20>21>21>21>21>
Contents of the Index file
PHILO>1+1>15+3>
CLEOPATRA>3+5>11+0>
MARK ANTONY>9+1>
DUKE VINCENTIO>12+2>

Fig. 2. Indexing Speaker Container using Meta data file

Contents of 15.cont
ACT I>ACT II>ACT III>ACT IV>ACT V>ACT I>ACT II>
Contents of the Index file
ACT I>1>6>
ACT II>2>7>12>
ACT III>3>
ACT IV>4>
ACT V>5>

Fig. 3. Indexing Title Container without using Meta data file

Meta data file is traversed once and the number of lines each and every speaker has spoken is found out. The speaker's name is written to the file. Then the starting line number and the line number to which he has spoken is written to the index file with a '-'(hyphen) in between. But it is found that, this technique increases the size of the index file which is greater than the original file if the original file is of huge size. Hence to optimize this technique, we find the total number of lines spoken by a speaker at a particular instance, we write the starting line number and the total number minus one to the file. These two numbers are separated by '+'. Now let us index the title container taking some sample records without using Meta data.

Likewise, the containers which can be indexed are found and once the index files are generated, the original files are removed. Querying can be done using the index file.

4 Querying XML Data

Querying involves loading the Meta table which stores the tag id, parent id, level id and name of the node in separate buffers. It is followed by query validation wherein the path, level and name of the node are checked. Then the container which has the desired record is found out, index file if available is opened and the records are located, the data is decompressed and retrieved. The querying architecture is shown in Fig. 4.

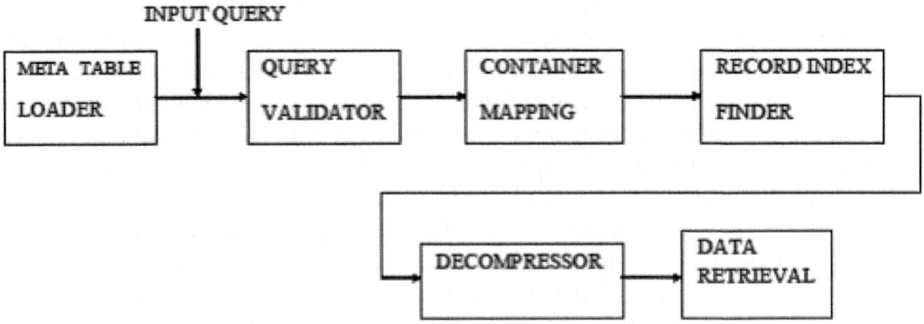

Fig. 4. Architecture for querying XML data

```
Procedure simple_query()
/* Simple query evaluation */
Begin
1. Con = tag id of the last node given in the query.
2. Open con.cont.cc file and the dictionary file.
/*Data retrieval*/
5. Load the dictionary
6. While not EOF
7.   Read the code from the container
8.   If (code = = '>')
       Print the text array
9.   Else if (code = ='<')
       Decode and print the number which says the count of empty records
10.  Else if (code < 256)
       Store the ASCII value in text array
11.  Else
   Find the prefix and append character of the code and store it in the text array
   End while
End
```

The procedure for executing a simple query is given above. In the case of other queries, condition (s) is extracted and desired records are displayed based on the given conditions. Let us see how different types of queries are executed.

For an aggregate query like
//PLAY/ACT/SCENE/SPEECH[count(LINE)>5]/SPEAKER
the query is obtained as input and validated. Since LINE tag is given as the argument for count function, index file for the entire speaker container is opened. For the index file given in Fig.2 the output will be
PHILO
CLEOPATRA
This is because, when the total number of lines spoken by PHILO is counted we get 6 (1+1 = 2 , 15 +3 gives 4 lines i.e starting from 15th line he has spoken 3 more lines). Likewise for CLEOPATRA it is 7.

For a conditional query like
//PLAY/ACT/SCENE/SPEECH[SPEAKER='PHILO']

The query is obtained as input and validated. Since SPEAKER tag is given in the condition, index file for the entire speaker container is opened. If we refer to the index file given in Fig. 2, initially the numbers 1,1,15,3 as mentioned for PHILO are stored in an array. Container to be opened is found from every even element and the number of lines to be printed in that container is identified from the successive odd element. Since 1%50 != 0, container to be opened is 1/50 +1 i.e. 1st container. Starting record number is 1/50=1. Number of records to be printed from there is arr[1] = 1. Thus records 1 and 2 are decompressed and displayed. Similarly starting from 15th line, 3 more lines are printed. Then, the tags (e.g.STAGEDIR) under SPEECH node are identified from the Meta data file and the corresponding records are printed.

Nested query has more than one query nested inside. There will be dependent and independent parts of the query. At first, the independent queries are extracted and executed and based on the value retrieved, dependent parts of the query are run. The records that satisfy the given conditions are located using the index and they are decompressed and displayed to the user.

```
Procedure nested_query()
Begin
1. Extract the independent part of the query
2. Execute the independent query and find the result
3. Have this result as the condition value for the dependent query
4. Find the index of the records required
5. Open the container with the desired records.
6. Traverse the records
7. for(i=0; i<index.length, i++)
8  if (index[i]%50 !=0)
    cont_no=index[i]/50+1
   record_no=index[i]%50
9  else
    cont_no=index[i]/50+1
    record_no=index[i]%50
    Decompress the record record_no in the container cont_no.cont.cc and print
    End for
End
```

For a nested query like

//PLAY/ACT/SCENE/SPEECH/SPEAKER=[//PLAY/ACT/SCENE/SPEECH[LINE= 'The office and devotion of their view']/SPEAKER]/LINE

The query is obtained as input and validated. The independent part of the query '//PLAY/ACT/SCENE/SPEECH[LINE='The office and devotion of their view']/SPEAKER' is separated and evaluated. LINE container is opened and the line number of the line 'The office and devotion of their view' is found out. Now, the index file is opened and the name of the speaker who has spoken that line and the index of the rest of the lines spoken by him are retrieved. Finally, LINE container is opened and the lines are decompressed and displayed to the user. This query can also be thought of as a correlation predicate query, because it compares a local context and an enclosing context. Correlation predicate queries in [5] are referred. Oracle takes time to execute nested queries because for each and every row in the outer table, it fetches each and every row in the inner table. Thus in order to reduce the execution time, a new approach [5] is proposed in which the inner query is executed first and then the outer query is executed with the result of the inner query.

5 Performance Analysis

The open source datasets, Shakespeare, SwissProt, dblp, lineitem are used to test and evaluate our system. Test machine was an Intel Pentium core 2 duo @ 2.53 GHz speed, running Windows XP. RAM capacity is 2GB.

5.1 Storage Size Comparison

Data sets are compressed and stored using various storage techniques and the compression ratio for IQCX and other compressors are shown in Table 1 and they are compared as shown in Fig. 5. It is proved that QUICX after indexing is efficient with highest compression ratio.

Table 1. Storage size comparison of IQCX with other queriable compressors

STORAGE TECHNIQUE	SHAKESPEARE	SWISSPROT	DBLP	LINEITEM
XBZIP INDEX	21.83	7.87	14.13	-
XBZIP	17.46	4.66	9.69	-
RFX	15.79	8.77	7.638	-
QUICX(Before Indexing)	36.96	57.8	61.8	74.5
IQCX(After Indexing)	37.82	67.9	68.3	80

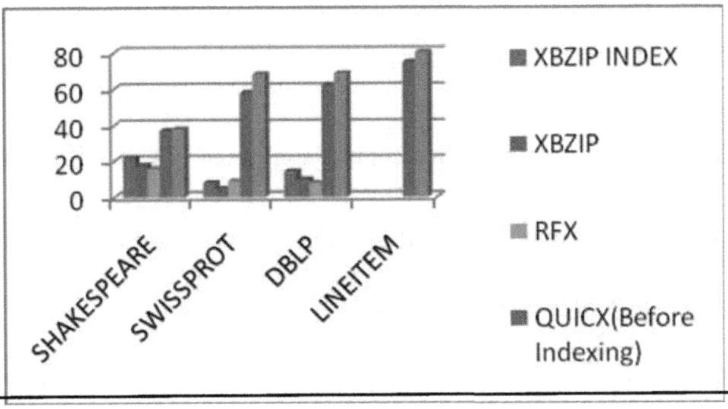

Fig. 5. Storage size comparison of IQCX with other queriable compressors

5.2 Querying Using the Index

Simple queries which do not use the index are executed and the querying time for IQCX and other compressors are shown in Table 2 and they are compared as shown in Fig. 6. Simple queries are taken from [3], [10].

Shakespeare.XML
Q1. /PLAYS/PLAY/TITLE
Q2. /PLAYS/PLAY/ACT/SCENE/STAGEDIR
Swissprot.XML
Q3. /root/Entry/@id
Q4. /root/Entry/Ref/Comment
Lineitem.XML
Q5. /table/T/L_ORDERKEY
Q6. /table/T/L_COMMENT
Dblp.XML
Q7. /dblp/article/cdrom

Table 2. Simple query execution time comparison of IQCX with other compressors

	Q1	Q2	Q3	Q4	Q5	Q6	Q7
XSAQCT	0.65	1.06	7.93	9.08	1.96	5.49	10.92
TREECHOP	1.56	1.44	17	16.63	5.06	6.22	15.49
IQCX	0.015	0.469	3.031	5.14	0.250	3.844	0.453

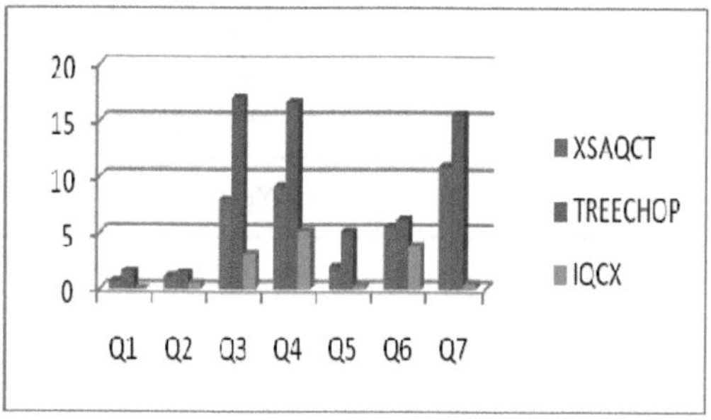

Fig. 6. Simple query execution time comparison of IQCX with other compressors

Aggregate query is executed using the index file generated and the querying times are shown in Table 3 and it is compared as shown in Fig. 7.

Q8. //SPEECH[![STAGEDIR]]/SPEAKER/$C
Q9. //L_DISCOUNT/$U
Q10. //PLAY/ACT/SCENE/SPEECH[count(LINE)>15]/SPEAKER

Table 3. Querying time comparison of Aggregate Queries

	Q8	Q9	Q10
Xqzip+	0.005	0.032	
IQCX	0.001	0.0063	0.187

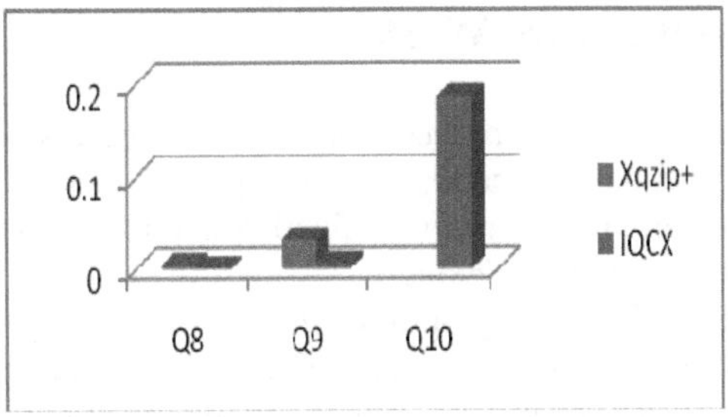

Fig. 7. Querying time comparison of aggregate queries

Conditional, compound queries from [2] are taken and the execution times are compared with other compressors as shown in Table 4 and Fig. 8.

Q11. //PLAY/ACT/SCENE/SPEECH[SPEAKER='PHILO']
Q12. /table/T[L_TAX='0.02']
Q13. /dblp/inproceedings[booktitle='SIGMOD Conference']
Q14.//PLAY/ACT/SCENE/SPEECH[SPEAKER>='MARK ANTONY'&&SPEAKER<'PHILO']
Q15. /table/T[L_TAX>='0.02'&&L_TAX<='0.04']
Q16. /dblp/inproceedings[year>='1998'&&year<='2000']
Q17. //PLAY/ACT/SCENE/SPEECH/SPEAKER=[//PLAY/ACT/SCENE/SPEECH[LINE='The office and devotion of their view']/SPEAKER]/LINE

Table 4. Querying time comparison of Conditional, Compound and Nested Queries

	Q11	Q12	Q13	Q14	Q15	Q16	Q17
XQZip-	0.038	0.044	0.345	0.039	0.075	9.541	-
XGRIND	1.620	2.890	26.108	2.312	3.210	50.344	-
IQCX	0.015	0.036	0.047	0.031	0.063	1.000	0.015

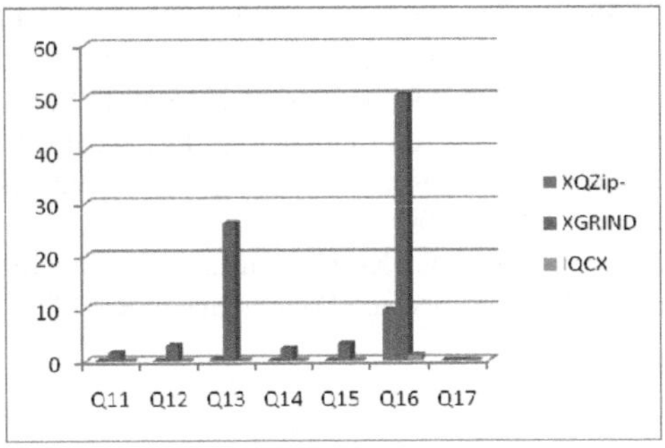

Fig. 8. Querying time comparison of Conditional, Compound and Nested Queries

6 Conclusion and Future Work

This indexing technique greatly reduces the overall storage size required. The index file is later used for evaluating queries. It is also proved that the overall time required to index the file once and use them for evaluating queries is lesser when compared to using the original files without indexing.

The future work involves query optimization and executing other types of queries using the index if required and prove that the overall execution time gets reduced if index file is used in locating records. It also involves runtime updation of the XML file and evaluating queries using Intra and Inter- documents.

References

[1] Ozgür, A., Gündem, T.İ.: Efficient indexing technique for XML-based electronic product catalogs. Electronic Commerce Research and Applications 5, 66–77 (2006)
[2] Cheng, J., Ng, W.: XQzip: Querying compressed XML using structural indexing. In: Proceedings of the International Conference on Extending Database Technologies, Heraklion, Greece, pp. 219–236 (2004)
[3] Leighton, G., Müldner, T., Diamond, J.: TREECHOP: A Tree-based Query-able Compressor For XML. In: Proceedings of the Ninth Canadian Workshop on Information Theory (CWIT 2005), pp. 115–118 (2005)
[4] Jin, L., Koudas, N., Li, C., Tung, A.K.H.: Indexing Mixed types for appropriate retrieval. In: Proceedings of the 31st VLDB Conference, Norway (2007)
[5] Brantner, M., Helmer, S., Kanne, C.-C., Moerkotte, G.: Kappa-join: Efficient Execution of Existential Quantification in XML Query Languages
[6] Li, M., Mani, M., Rundensteiner, E.A.: Efficiently loading and processing XML streams. In: Proceedings of the 2008 International Symposium on Database Engineering & Applications (2008)
[7] Monjurul Alom, B.M., Henskens, F., Hannaford, M.: DRXQP: A Dynamic Relational XML Query Processor. In: Seventh International Conference on Information Technology (2010)
[8] Senthikumar, R., Priyaa Varshinee, S., Manipriya, S., Gowrishankar, M., Kannan, A.: Query Optimization of RFX Compact Storage using Strategy List. In: ADCOM 2008 (2008)
[9] Senthilkumar, R., Kannan, A.: Query and Update support for Indexed and Compressed XML (QUICX), under publication in Springer lecturer notes
[10] Müldner, T., Fry, C., Miziołek, J.K., Durno, S.: XSAQCT: XML Queryable Compressor. Presented at Balisage: ThE Markup Conference 2009, Montréal, Canada (August 11-14, 2009); In: Proceedings of Balisage: The Markup Conference 2009. Balisage Series on Markup Technologies, vol. 3 (2009)
[11] Zafari, H., Hasani, K., Shiri, M.E.: XLight, An Efficient Relational Schema to Store and Query XML Data. In: Data Storage and Data Engineering, DSDE (2010)

Discovering Spatiotemporal Topological Relationships

K. Venkateswara Rao[1], A. Govardhan[2], and K.V. Chalapati Rao[1]

[1] Department of Computer Science and Engineering, CVR College of Engineering, Ibrahimpatnam RR District, Andhra Pradesh, India
{kvenkat.cse,chalapatiraokv}@gmail.com
[2] JNTUH College of Engineering, Jagityala, Karimnagar Dist, Andhra Pradesh, India
govardhan_cse@yahoo.co.in

Abstract. Discovering spatiotemporal topological relationships deals with the discovery of geometric relationships like disjoint, cover, intersection and overlap between every pair of spatiotemporal objects and change of such relationships with time from spatiotemporal databases. Spatiotemporal databases deal with changes to spatial objects with time. The applications in this domain process spatial, temporal and attribute data elements to find the evolution of spatial objects and changes in their topological relationships with time. These advanced database applications require storing, management and processing of complex spatiotemporal data. In this paper we discuss the design of spatiotemporal database and methodology for discovering various kinds of spatiotemporal topological relationships. Prototype implementation of the system is carried out on top of open source object relational spatial database management system called postgresql and postgis. The algorithms are experimented on historical cadastral datasets that are created using OpenJump. The results that are visualized using OpenJump software are presented.

Keywords: Spatiotemporal database, spatiotemporal relationships, spatiotemporal data analysis.

1 Introduction

Spatio-Temporal applications like temporal geographic information systems [1] and environmental systems [2] process spatial, temporal and attribute data elements of spatiotemporal objects for knowledge discovery. The spatial objects are characterized by their position, shape and spatial attributes. Spatial attributes are properties of space and spatial objects located in specific positions that inherit these attributes. Spatial attributes refer to the whole space and can be represented as layers and each layer represents one theme. The temporal objects are characterized by two models of time that are used to record facts and information about spatial objects. The two models of time are time points and time intervals. A time point is considered as one chronon, while a time interval has duration and is defined as set of chronons. Time points and time intervals can represent valid or transaction time. Valid time shows when a fact is true. There are two basic facts, events and states, for which time is recorded. An event occurs at an exact time point, i.e., an event has no duration. Example events are "car crash," "sunrise," etc. A state is defined for each chronon in a time interval, hence it has duration. For example, a "meeting" takes place from 9am until 11am.

D.C. Wyld et al. (Eds.): ACITY 2011, CCIS 198, pp. 507–516, 2011.

Spatiotemporal object captures simultaneously spatial and temporal aspects of data and deal with geometry changing over time. It can be represented by a four tuple - object id, geometry, time and attributes [3]. Recording a spatial object at a time point results in a snapshot of it. For example, capturing snapshots of a "landparcel" that changes its shape (e.g., split, expanded etc) during certain period of time. Recording a spatial object in a time interval is translated into capturing its evolution over time, i.e., capturing the possible changes of its shape over time. Consider the example of recording a "landparcel" in [2006, 2009], which changes shape.

Topology describes spatial relationships like intersects, meets, overlaps, equals etc, between spatial objects. The spatial objects may be point, line or polygon. Different types of spatial topological relationships between two objects are shown in fig., 1.

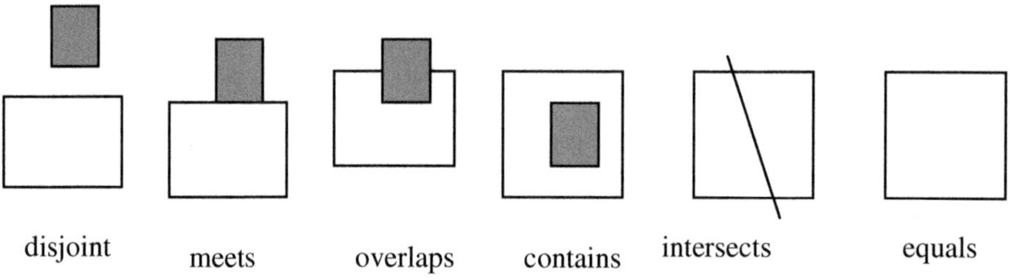

Fig. 1. Spatial topological relationships

But spatiotemporal topological relationships are far beyond this. Based on the semantics of spatiotemporal changes in the real world, they are classified into two categories [4] as given in fig., 2.

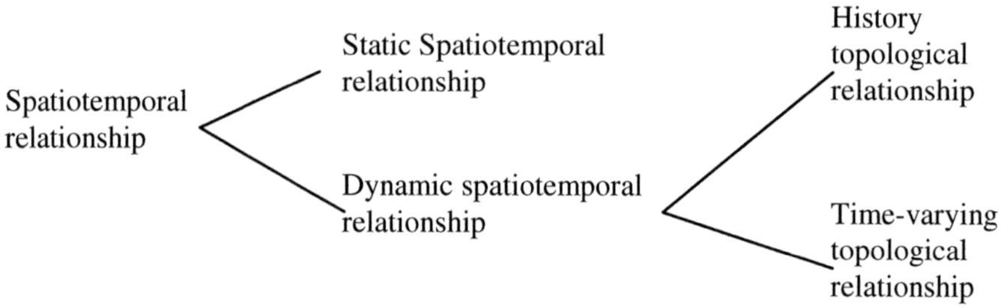

Fig. 2. Classification of spatiotemporal relationships

The static spatiotemporal relationship between two spatiotemporal objects, which is at a certain time instant, refers to the spatial topological relationship between these two objects at that time instant. It can be any one of the topological relationships shown in fig., 1. Dynamic spatiotemporal relationships refer to the topological relationship of spatiotemporal objects along the time line. This is mainly because a spatiotemporal object has life and topological changes. History topology is the spatiotemporal relationship between a spatiotemporal object and its "parents and children". It means where and how a spatiotemporal object comes from, and its life history. The history topology of land parcel objects from time t1 to t4 is shown in fig., 3. Time-varying topology is the changing history of spatial topological relationship between two spatiotemporal objects in a given time interval. It is shown in fig., 4 for two objects in a time interval [t1, t4].

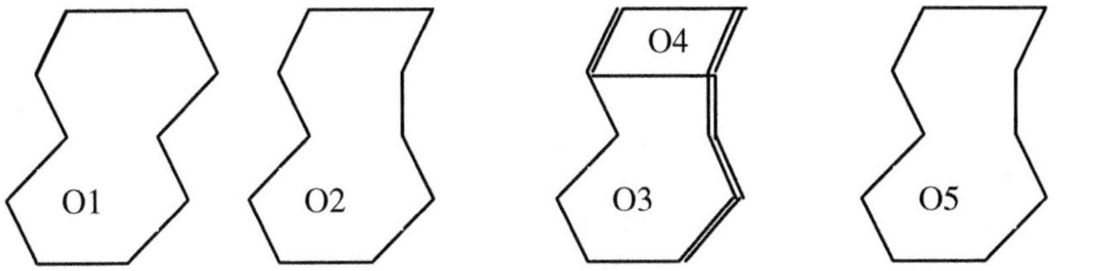

Object O1 at time t1 | O1 changes at time t2 | O2 splits at time t3 | O3 and O4 merges at t4

Fig. 3. History topology among land parcels in an interval [t1, t4]

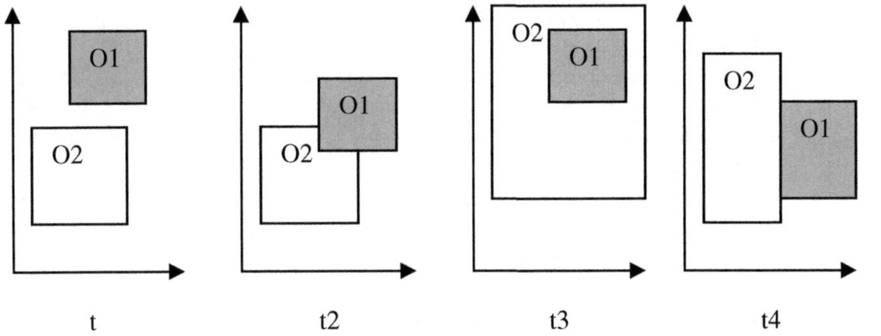

Fig. 4. Time-varying Topology in an interval [t1, t4]

The purpose of this research is to design an extendable spatiotemporal database and developing a methodology to discover spatiotemporal relationships from spatiotemporal data bases. Section 2 discusses the database design that can capture the changing geometry of spatiotemporal objects, section 3 describes methodology and algorithms for discovering spatiotemporal topological relationships, section 4 briefs about the implementation and section 5 provides the results a conclusion and some directions for future work are given in section 6.

2 Spatiotemporal Database Design

An object relational spatiotemporal database which consists of a set of tables and relationships among them is designed to facilitate the spatiotemporal data analysis and mining. Different sorts of spatiotemporal data to be handled are states, events and episodes. A state represents a version of an entity in a given moment. States can consist of different versions of an individual entity. An event is the moment in time when an occurrence takes place. Event causes one state to change to another. An episode is the length of time during which change occurs, a state exists or an event lasts. Two main strategies to represent multiple versions of an object are tracking the versions either at the level of objects or attributes. First one involves a different identifier (oid) to each new version and chaining the older versions to new oid. Second one involves a single object identity (oid) with versions actually associated with attributes. The attributes of spatiotemporal objects can be categorized as version significant, non-version significant and invariant. The version significant attribute values are to be updated in non-destructive manner, the non-version significant attribute values are to be updated in a destructive manner and invariant attributes values are not allowed to be changed. Following entities are designed to address these requirements.

1. Temporal_tab : This table stores timestamps which correspond to time at which change to any spatial object has taken place.
2. Spatial_obj_tab : This table contains spatiotemporal objects with unique identifier, geometry and existence time which has from time(st) and to time(et) as attributes. It also has other attributes to indicate category and type of spatial object, type of change. The events and episodes or processes are also considered as spatiotemporal objects and stored in this table.
3. split_tab: This composite entity is used to record splitting of any spatial object into multiple objects. It has object identifier that got split and new object identifiers for objects derived due to split and timestamp attribute that records time of split.
4. Merge_tab: This composite entity keeps the data related to merging of two or more objects into single object. It maintains object identifiers which are merged, new object identifier for object derived due to merge and timestamp attribute that records time of merge. The new objects created due to split or merge are stored in spatial_obj_tab with their new object identifiers.
5. Geom_version : This table records geometry changes by creating new object identifier for each change to the geometry of the object. It has oid of the object changed, new object identifier and timestamp attribute that records time of the change.The new object is stored in spatial_obj_tab table.
6. VsAttr_tab: This table manages version significant attributes of all objects in spatial_obj_tab. It has oid, attribute name, timestamp and attribute value as its fields.
7. VinAttr_tab: This table manages version insignificant and invariant attributes of all objects in spatial_obj_tab. It has oid, attribute name and attribute value as its fields.
8. Result_tab : This entity is used by analysis algorithms to store results back into database. This table can be accessed using OpenJump (An Open source GIS software) to visualize the results.

3 Knowledge Discovery Methodology

3.1 Methodology

The knowledge discovery considered in this paper includes discovering evolution of spatial objects with time and changes in topological relationships between pairs of spatial objects with time. This requires preprocessing the database objects in the given spatial region and mapping them to spatiotemporal data structures. The algorithms designed for this purpose are described below.

3.2 Algorithms

```
    Algorithm 1: Tracking Spatial object or History Topology
    Input: Spatiotemporal dataset (D),Spatial Object Identifier (oid), from time(f_t)
and to time(t_t)
    Output: The Object (oid) details changing with time.
    Method: Process(oid)
    Begin
       Obj = getobjdetails(oid) /* connect to dataset D and get spatial object details and
load them into variable  obj */
       Display(Obj)
       If ( Obj.et  <  t_t) Track(Obj)
    End

    Display(Obj)
    Begin
     If ( Obj.st > f_t and Obj.et < t_t )
        Print or save oid, geom, st, et, area, centroid and perimeter of Obj. The attribute
ChangeType of Obj indicates type of change the Obj has undergone at time et.
     Elseif ( Obj.st > f_t and Obj.et >= t_t )
        Print or save id, geom, st, t_t, area, centroid and perimeter of Obj.
     Elseif ( Obj.st <= f_t and Obj.et >= t_t )
        Print or save id, geom, f_t, t_t, area, centroid and perimeter of Obj.
     Elseif ( Obj.st <= f_t and Obj.et < t_t )
        Print or save id, geom, f_t, et, area, centroid and perimeter of Obj. The attribute
ChangeType of Obj indicates type of change the Obj has undergone at time et.
     Else Print " Obj is not valid between f_t and t_t"
    End

    Track(Obj)
    Begin
    Next = Obj.changeType
    Switch(Next)
    Begin
    Case C:
          Look into Geom_version table and find new object identifier (n_oid).
          Process(n_oid)
```

```
            Break;
    Case S:
            Look into split_tab and find list L of identifiers of objects which are result of
split of the Obj.
            For each object identifier e_oid in L, Process(e_oid)
            Break
    Case M:
            Look into Merge_tab and find the new object identifier (n_oid) which is the
result of merge of Obj with some other spatial object.
            Process(n_oid)
            Break
    Case default: break
    End
    End
```

Algorithm 2: Finding static spatiotemporal topological relationships between two objects.

Input: : Spatiotemporal dataset (D), Object Identifier (oid1, oid2) and time (t).

Output: Topological relationships between the oid1 and oid2.

Method :

Begin

1. Access the data set and get geometry details of the given objects oid1 and oid2 at given time t. Create an object of type GeometryRelation class for oid1 and oid2.
2. Using the methods of the class, compute topological relationships between the pair of objects.
3. Display or store the results.

End

```
Public class GeometryRelation
{
        PGgeometry obj1, obj2;
        Methods:
        PGgeometry Union();
        PGgeometry Intersection();
        Float Distance();
        Boolean isintersects()
        Boolean istouches()
        Boolean isequals()
        Boolean isdisjoint()
        Boolean iscrosses()
        Boolean isoverlaps()
        Boolean iscovers()
        Boolean iscoveredby()
}
```

All the methods of GeometryRelation class can be implemented using Postgis application programming interface.

Algorithm 3: Finding time-varying spatiotemporal topological relationships between two objects.

Input: : Spatiotemporal dataset (D), Object Identifier (oid1, oid2), from time(f_t) and to time(t_t)

Output: Topological relationship changes between the oid1 and oid2 from f_t to t_t

Method :

Begin

1. Using Algorithm1, track the objects oid1, oid2 and record all time points at which either oid1 or oid2 or their siblings have changed between f_t and t_t. Also use special data structure that manages valid identifiers of the objects for each of the time points.
2. For each of the time points, create an object of type GeometryRelation class and use its methods to compute topological relationships between the relevant pair of objects which are valid for the time point.
3. Display or store the spatiotemporal topological relationships for the given duration for the given objects.

End

4 Implementation

The system is implemented using postgresql [5], postgis [6], Java, JDBC and OpenJump [7] technologies. The object relational database is created and used in prototype implementation of the system for historical cadastral data analysis, static and time-varying spatiotemporal topological relationships discovery. The versions created due to split and merge processes or events are managed by considering each version as a new object. The linkage between parent and children objects is maintained using primary key foreign key relationship among the appropriate tables. Following is an example of table creation.

```
create table spatial_obj_tab(spobjid integer, category integer, st timestamp, et timestamp, objtype varchar(10),Changetype interger);
select AddGeometryColumn('spatial_obj_tab','objgeom',-1,'POLYGON',2);
```

The sample database objects are generated using OpenJump and loaded into the database. The modules for accessing the database and the designed algorithms are implemented in JAVA. The application programming interface provided by the postgis is used for all geometric related computations. The modules for loading the results back into the database for effective visualization using OpenJump software are developed.

5 Results

Case 1: Results for History Topology: Single Object Varying With Time:

Given object Id : 91
Starting time : 2000-01-01 12:12:12
Ending time:2000-12-31 12:12:12

Output:

The object 91 is changed to 151 at "2000-01-15 12:12:12". Then the object 151 is changed to 173 at "2000-04-15 12:12:12" and the object 173 is changed to 224 at "2000-08-26 12:12:12".

Object Id=91:
Ending time=2000-01-15 12:12:12.0
POLYGON((526 411,540 420,560 420,560 400,526 411))
Area: 430.0
centroid: POINT(547.2713178294573 411.72868217054264)
Perimeter: 92.378456

Object id=151:
Ending time=2000-04-15 12:12:12.0
POLYGON((526 411,540 420,555.6048020833342 411.7092239583335,560 400,526 411))
Area: 303.14026
centroid: POINT(544.3809692703338 410.3903727435555)
Perimeter: 82.55591

Object id=173:
Ending time=2000-08-26 12:12:12.0
POLYGON((526 411,540 420,555.9061650065141 417.272132796836,560 400,526 411))
Area: 361.783
centroid: POINT(545.6312040877306 411.0948951800529)
Perimeter: 86.2675

Object id = 224:
Ending time=2000-12-31 12:12:12.0
POLYGON((526 411,540 420,554.1993333333334 429.72733333333343,560 400,526 411))
Area: 469.26666
centroid: POINT(546.7926981736673 413.5161907152215)
Perimeter: 99.87812

Case 2: Results of static spatiotemporal topological relationships:
Given Two objects 4 and 5 and timestamp as input to algorithm. It generates following output.

Obj1	Obj2	intersects	contains	equals	touches	disjoint	overlaps	time
4	5	0	0	0	1	0	0	2000-01-08 12:12:12

Case 3: Results of time-varying spatiotemporal topological relationships:

Given Two objects 45 and 83 and two timestamps as input to algorithm. It generates following output. The object changes are tracked by creating new object in database for each change to its geometry.

Obj1	Obj2	intersects	contains	equals	touches	disjoint	overlaps	From time	To time
45	83	0	0	0	0	1	0	2000-01-08 01:10:15	2000-01-08 09:10:15
45	85	0	0	0	1	0	0	2000-01-08 09:15:15	2000-01-09 01:10:15
45	95	0	0	0	0	0	1	2000-01-09 01:15:15	2000-01-10 01:10:15
54	95	0	0	0	0	1	0	2000-01-10 01:15:15	2000-03-10 01:10:15

The algorithms can be used in applications like detection of land parcels that have undergone forestation, deforestation or flooding by using forest geometry or flood geometry objects respectively to discover their spatiotemporal topological relationships with the land parcel objects managed in the spatiotemporal database.

6 Conclusion and Furure Work

In this paper, the concepts of spatiotemporal topological relationships are reviewed and the design of spatiotemporal database design is discussed. The methodology and algorithms to discover various spatiotemporal topological relationships are described. The system is implemented using open source software postgresql, postgis. Spatiotemporal data sets are created using OpenJump. The algorithms are tested for their accuracy and the results of different analyses like history topology and time-varying topological relationships for cadastral database are provided. The system can be extended to provide multidimensional analysis at multiple granularities and spatiotemporal data mining tasks [8,9] such as characterization, association analysis [10], classification[11], trend prediction, clustering, outlier analysis and frequent pattern analysis.

References

1. Ping, Y., Xinming, T., Shengxiao, W.: Dynamic cartographic representation of Spatio-Temporal data. In: The International Archives of the Photogrammetry, Remote Sensing and Spatial Information Sciences, vol. XXXVII, part B2, Beijing (2008)

2. Obradovic, Z., Das, D., Radosavljevic, V., Ristovski, K., Vucetic, S.: Spatio-Temporal characterization of aerosols through active use of data from multiple sensors. In: ISPRS TC VII Symposium – 100 Years ISPRS, Vienna, Austria (July 5-7, 2010)
3. Pelekis, N., et al.: Literature Review of Spatio-Temporal Database Models. The Knowledge Engineering Review, 235–274 (2004)
4. Jin, P., Yue, L.: A Framework for the Description of Spatiotemporal Relationships. In: Proceedings of the Joint Conference on Information Sciences (October 2006)
5. `http://www.postgresql.org/docs/manuals/`
6. `http://postgis.refractions.net/documentation/`
7. `http://www.openjump.org/`
8. Chueh, H.-E.: Mining Target-Oriented Sequential Patterns with time-intervals. International Journal of Computer Science & Information Technology (IJCSIT) 2(4) (August 2010)
9. Ullah, I.: Data Mining Algorithms And Medical Sciences. International Journal of Computer Science & Information Technology (IJCSIT) 2(6) (December 2010)
10. Venkateswara Rao, K., Govardhan, A., Chalapati Rao, K.V.: An Object-Oriented Modeling And Implementation Of Spatio-Temporal Knowledge Discovery System. International Journal of Computer Science & Information Technology (IJCSIT) 3(2) (April 2011)
11. Bhargavi, P., Jyothi, S.: Soil Classification Using GAtree. International Journal of Computer Science & Information Technology (IJCSIT) 2(5) (October 2010)

A Novel Way of Connection to Data Base Using Aspect Oriented Programming

Bangaru Babu Kuravadi[1], Vishnuvardhan Mannava[1], and T. Ramesh[2]

[1] Department of Computer Science and Engineering, KL University, Vaddeswaram 522502, A.P, INDIA
bngrbbk@gmail.com, vishnu@klce.ac.in
[2] Department of Computer Science and Engineering, National Institute of Technology, Warangal, 506004, A.P, INDIA
rmesht@nitw.ac.in

Abstract. Over the recent years aspect-oriented programming (AOP) has found increasing interest among researchers in software engineering. Aspects are abstractions which capture and localise cross-cutting concerns. Although persistence has been considered as an aspect of a system aspects in the persistence domain in general and in databases in particular have been largely ignored. This paper brings the notion of aspects to object-oriented databases. Some cross-cutting concerns are identified and addressed using aspects. An aspect-oriented extension of an OODB is discussed and various open issues pointed out. In this paper we are using Aspect Oriented Programming (AOP) to enable dynamic adaptation in existing programs, to enable reusability during Data Base connections. We propose an approach to implement dynamic adaptability, reusability especially for connecting Data Base using AOP. We have used AspectJ; Java based language to create aspects in Eclipse supported framework.

Keywords: Dynamic Adaptability, Distribution, Aspect Oriented Programming, Object Oriented Data Base, AspectJ.

1 Introduction

Aspects are abstractions which serve to localise any cross-cutting concerns e.g. code which cannot be encapsulated within one class but is tangled over many classes. A few examples of aspects are memory management, failure handling, communication, real-time constraints, resource sharing, performance optimisation, debugging and synchronisation. In AOP classes are designed and coded separately from aspects encapsulating the cross-cutting code. An aspect weaver is used to merge the classes and the aspects. Aspect-orientation appears to be following the same development phases as objectorientation. Introduced through object-oriented programming in the late 1960s (SIMULA-67) object-orientation is now employed in a wide range of software development activities such as analysis, design, modeling, etc. It has also been successfully applied in the areas of databases and knowledge-bases. Likewise, research in aspect-orientation is now progressing from programming into other areas such as specification [3] and design [7]. Its applicability in the area of databases has,

D.C. Wyld et al. (Eds.): ACITY 2011, CCIS 198, pp. 517–525, 2011.

however, not yet been explored. Although persistence has been considered as an aspect of a system aspects in the persistence domain in general and in databases in particular have been largely ignored. This paper brings the notion of aspects to object-oriented databases in order to achieve a better separation of concerns. Reflecting on the fact that AOP is not limited to object-oriented programming languages, we are of the view that aspects can be employed in database technology other than OODBs [17] e.g. relational, object-relational, active databases, etc. This will, however, form the subject of a future paper. The discussion in this paper focuses on extending object-oriented databases with aspects.

Our experience with this system have been proved that use of AspectJ [22] language helps to modularize the crosscutting concerns and improved the productivity, reusability, dynamic adaptability, maintainability and code independence in our Data Base Connection using AOP.

Our paper is organized as follows. We review related work in section 2. Section 3 we describe the AOP paradigm and the need for a distributed framework to address the problem. Section 4 describes Aspects in database Systems. In Section 5, we propose the solution framework with a case study. Try to show the Efficiency of AOP by CPU Profiling in section 6. Section 7, Try to show the affect of 'Aspects' on application through Eclipse's Aspect Visualizer. We conclude the paper and future work in section 8.

2 Related Work

Although separation of concerns in object-oriented databases has not been explicitly considered, some of the existing work falls in this category. The concept of object version derivation graphs [12] separates version management from the objects. A similar approach is proposed by [13] where version derivation graphs manage both object and class versioning. Additional semantics for object and class versioning are provided separately from the general version management technique. [19] Employs propagation patterns [20] to exploit polymorphic reuse mechanisms in order to minimise the effort required to manually reprogram methods and queries due to schema modifications. Propagation patterns are behavioral abstractions of application programs and define patterns of operation propagation by reasoning about the behavioral dependencies among co-operating objects. [21] Implements inheritance links between classes using semantic relationships which are first class objects. The inheritance hierarchy can be changed by modifying the relationships instead of having to alter actual class definitions. In the hologram approach proposed by [13] an object is implemented by multiple instances representing its much faceted nature. These instances are linked together through aggregation links in a specialization hierarchy. This makes objects dynamic since they can migrate between the classes of a hierarchy hence making schema changes more pertinent.

3 Aspect Oriented Programming

Aspect-oriented programming (AOP) [1] has been proposed as a technique for improving separation of concerns in software AOP builds on previous technologies, including procedural programming and object-oriented programming that have already made significant improvements in software modularity.

The central idea of AOP is that while the hierarchical modularity mechanisms of object-oriented languages are extremely useful, they are inherently unable to modularize all concerns of interest in complex systems. Instead, we believe that in the implementation of any complex system, there will be concerns that inherently crosscut the natural modularity of the rest of the implementation. AOP does for crosscutting concerns what OOP has done for object encapsulation and inheritance. It provides language mechanisms that explicitly capture crosscutting structure as shown in Fig. 1.

This makes it possible to program crosscutting concerns in a modular way, and achieve the usual benefits of improved modularity: simpler code that is easier to develop and maintain, and that has greater potential for reuse. We call a well modularized crosscutting concern an aspect. AspectJ is a simple and practical aspect-oriented extension to Java.

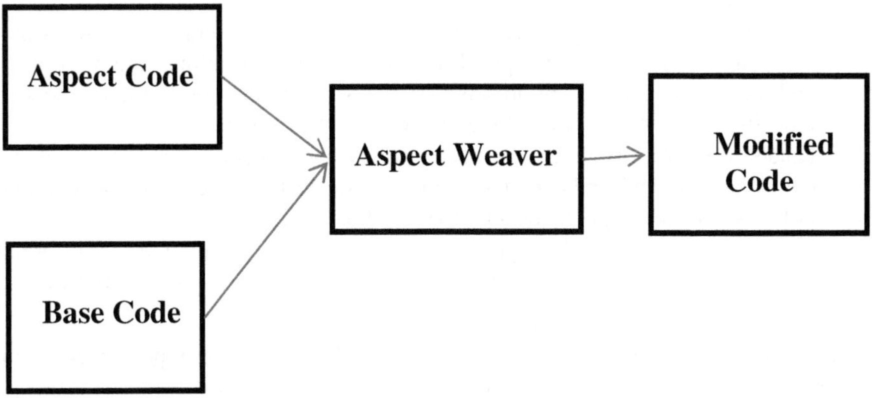

Fig. 1. Weaving of Aspect on source code

4 Aspects in Data Base System

Aspects in a database system can be classified in two levels:

- Database Management System (DBMS) level aspects, which provide features affecting the software architecture of the database system and allowing the tailoring of a database system architecture and features towards a specific system with which the database is going to work, and
- Database level aspects, which relate to the data maintained by the database and their relationship, i.e., the database schema.

We have identified a number of aspects in database systems on DBMS level by considering a feature as a crosscutting concern if it is spread over multiple subsystems, functions, and/or code modules of the database system, but performs the same function, or a part of the function, in the system. Based on these criteria, we have identified the following aspects that provide tailoring on the DBMS level:

- Synchronization, e.g., in a DBMS there exist many data areas spread over the entire DBMS that should be protected by semaphores, which can be encapsulated into aspects and automatically woven into the DBMS;
- failure detection, e.g., keeping data consistent in the database requires employing failure detection, which is typically spread over the entire DBMS in order to capture failures that can occur, and therefore can be considered as an aspect;
- Logging and recovery, e.g., in order to recover from a failure, logging is performed whenever database changes occur, and this often require logging routines to be spread out the entire software, and, thus, easily classified as an aspect;
- Error handling, e.g., different errors that can occur in the execution of the database software could be detected by monitoring the execution of a program by an error handling aspect;
- Transaction model, e.g., in real-time and embedded systems transactions are associated with different temporal properties such as deadlines and/or periods and these can be woven by means of aspects into a transaction model (hence, tailoring it to suit the needs of the underlying application);
- Database policies such as scheduling policy and concurrency control policy, e.g., real-time and embedded systems require different real-time scheduling policies that can be plugged-in by means of aspects; and
- Security, e.g., different encryption algorithms could be suitable for different database applications and these could be encapsulated into aspects and woven into the database to tailor it for a specific application.

Additionally, databases can make use of so-called development-type aspects such as debugging, which can also be classified as a DBMS level aspect.

5 Case Study

After completing some preliminary work, we are connecting to data base from AOP by cross cutting the OOP methods at compile time and send the results at run time through AOP. Following code represents above all specified things.

5.1 Reusable and Dynamic Aspect to Connect Data Base

- **DB.java**

```
public class db {
    public void display(String uid,String pwd){
    //This method cross cut by AspectDBConnect}
    public static void main( String args[])   {
          Scanner sc=new Scanner(System.in);
          db d=new db();
```

```
System.out.println("please enter database user id");
String uid=sc.next();
System.out.println("please enter database password");
String pwd=sc.next();d.display(uid,pwd);}}
```

- **AspectDBConnect.aj**

```
public aspect AspectDBConnect{
  // Cross cut display method of db class
  pointcut  display(db  d,String  uid,String  pwd):call(*
  db.display(..)) && target(d)&& args(uid,pwd);
  //Connection to Database and send request for display
  of desired table
  before(db d,String uid,String pwd): display(d,uid,pwd){
            Scanner sc=new Scanner(System.in);
            String tbname=null; int i=0,n=0;
  DriverManager.registerDriver(new
  oracle.jdbc.driver.OracleDriver());
  Connection
  con=DriverManager.getConnection("jdbc:oracle:thin:@loca
  lhost:1521:XE",uid,pwd);
  Statement st=con.createStatement();
  ResultSet rs=null;
  ResultSetMetaData rsmd=null;
  //request to display total tables of user
      String tables="Select * from tab";
      rs=st.executeQuery(tables);
      rsmd=rs.getMetaData();
      for(i=1;i<=1;i++) {
            System.out.print(rsmd.getColumnName(i));}
                  while(rs.next()){
                        for(int j=1;j<=1;j++){
                  System.out.print(rs.getString(j));}}
  //Request for display specified Table details
  System.out.println("please select table name from above
  displayed");
      tbname=sc.next();
      String q="select * from "+tbname;
      System.out.println("Searching for Table"+tbname);
      rs=st.executeQuery(q);
      rsmd=rs.getMetaData();
      n=rsmd.getColumnCount();
      for(i=1;i<=n;i++)
      System.out.print(rsmd.getColumnName(i)+"\t\t\t");
       for(i=1;i<=10;i++){
  while(rs.next()){
      for(int j=1;j<=n;j++){
            System.out.print(rs.getString(j)+"\t\t\t");
  }}}}}
```

In the above code, AspectDBConnect.aj is aspect oriented program, it will crosscut display method of db class which is specified in pointcut. Here we crosscut the display method of db class and add some additional code using before advice to implement database connection. Here we are using type 4 drivers to connect to oracle database.

In the above traditional java code, we are passing data base user id and password to the display method. Here Aspect code will cross cut the display method and then passes user id and password to database by using DriverManager, Connection classes of sql package.

In the Aspect code, we are selecting desire table name and then it will print total data of specified table. Everyone can use this aspect code by cross cutting their java class and then pass data base user id, password and desired table names to it. Here we strongly saying and practically proved that aspect support reusability as we explained above.

In the below Fig. 2, Aspect code has a data base connection. Here base code means traditional java code. Base code reuse that data base connection which is implemented in aspect code by cross cutting their methods in aspect code. Aspect weaver will generate class file by compile both base code and Aspect code together, later that class file is referred as modified code. Client can use modified code without knowing about aspect code details. We can run base code directly. Here output of base code is combination of aspect code and base code. Aspect Weaver will tangle aspect code to base code at compile time.

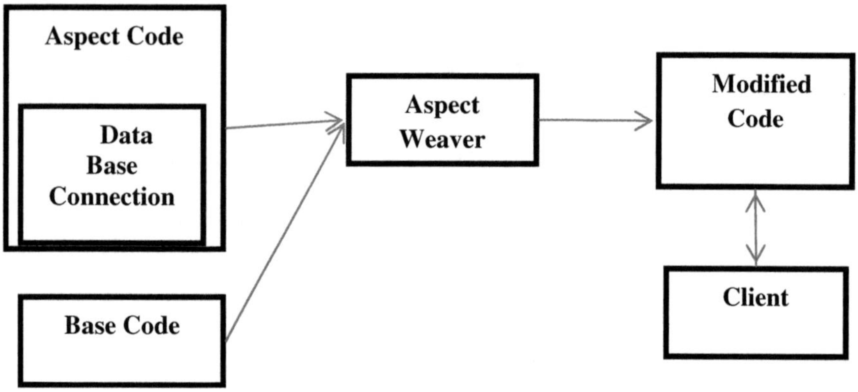

Fig. 2. Aspect with Data Base

6 Efficiency of AOP by CPU Profiling

In some cases, flexibility and reusability of the design comes with the price of decreased efficiency. At the same time, performance is often a key quality attribute of distributed applications. It is therefore beneficial to investigate whether AOP may influence performance of applications. The comparison of the differences between

AOP and OOP shows results that indicates influence of application quality, especially performance. To demonstrate this Data Base (DB) connection is applied and the CPU profiling data is collected. It took 13.86 ms to execute the program without AOP and 10.25 ms to execute when AOP is applied.

6.1 Profiling Statistics before Applying AOP

The main method execution took 13.86 ms with one time DB connection. The below figure 3 shows that the complete details of the DB connection and time spent by the processor in each time.

6.2 Profiling Statistics after Applying AOP

The main method execution took 10.25 ms with one time DB connection of each method defined. The below figure 3 shows that the complete details of the DB connection and the time spent by the processor in each method. By comparing these two call tree graphs we can say that the code having the AOP cross cutting is more efficient in terms of computation power usage.

Here, we have observed practically that execution time analysis comparison of Data Base Connection without AOP and With AOP by run the above code seven times shows in Fig 3. These both resulted has the same for memory usage.

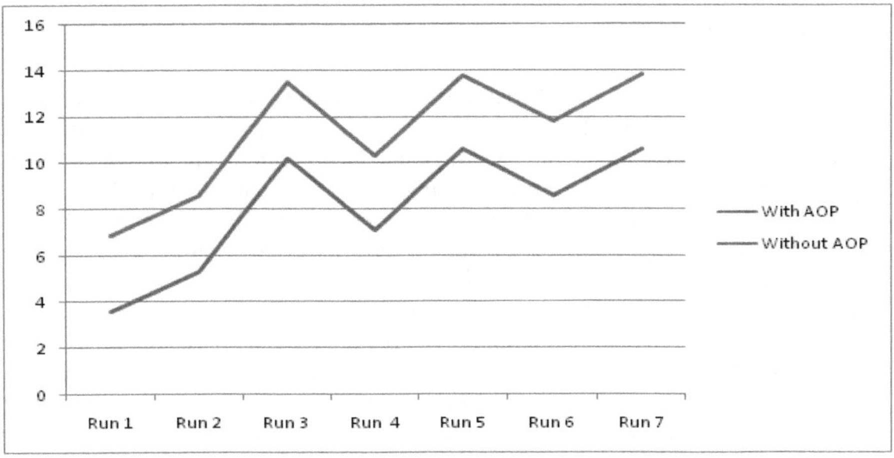

Fig. 3. Execution time analysis of Data Base Connection without AOP and With AOP

7 Eclipse's Aspect Visualiser

Aspect Visualiser is an extensible plugin that can be used to visualize anything that can be represented by bars and stripes. It began as the Aspect Visualiser, which was a part of the popular AspectJ Development Tools (AJDT) plug-in. It was originally created to visualize how aspects were affecting classes in a project. As in Figure 4 we have shown the member view of distribution, tracing, and profiling aspects with class

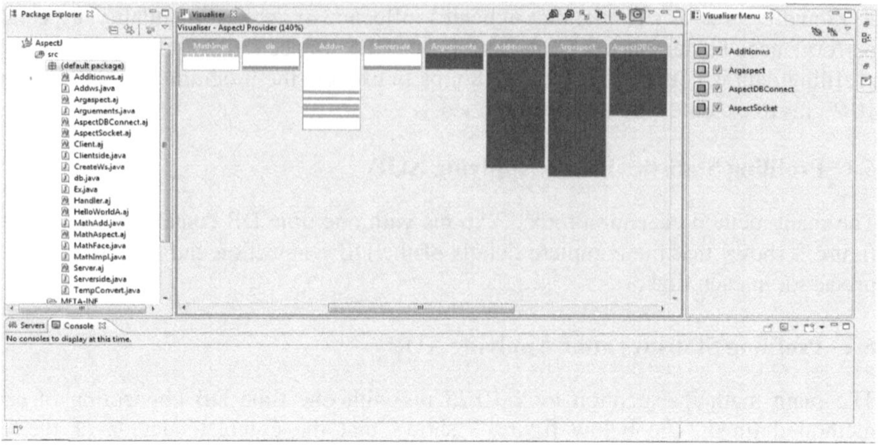

Fig. 4. Aspect Visualizer member view

AspectDBConnect in db class. Here bars represent classes and aspects in AOP code and black colored stripes represent advised join points in the execution flow of AOP code, which were matched with defined pointcuts in various aspects.

8 Conclusion

The use of AOP to achieve a better separation of concerns has shown promising results. Although some of the existing work in object-oriented databases implicitly addresses cross-cutting concerns, no attempts have been made to capture these explicitly. The novelty of our work is in extending the notion of aspects to object-oriented databases in order to capture these concerns explicitly. We have identified a number of cross-cutting features and discussed how these can be effectively addressed using aspects. Some examples have been discussed in order to demonstrate the effectiveness of aspects in localising the impact of changes, hence making maintenance easier. We have presented an aspect-oriented extension of an object database which is used to prototype the various examples. The extension is natural, seamless and does not affect existing data or applications. Our work in the immediate future will focus on persistent representations of aspects and development of efficient weaving mechanisms. In future, we will implement autonomic web services using aspect oriented programming and we will also address how Agent based java program communicates with aspect oriented java program with web services.

References

1. Kiczales, G., Lamping, J., Mendhekar, A.: Aspect-oriented programming. In: Aksit, M., Auletta, V. (eds.) ECOOP 1997. LNCS, vol. 1241, pp. 220–242. Springer, Heidelberg (1997)
2. Blair, L., Blair, G.S.: The Impact of Aspect-Oriented Programming on Formal Methods. In: Proceedings of the AOP Workshop at ECOOP 1998 (1998)

3. Blair, L., Blair, G.S.: A Tool Suite to Support Aspect-Oriented Specification. In: Proceedings of the AOP Workshop at ECOOP 1999 (1999)
4. Boellert, K.: On Weaving Aspects. In: Proc. of the AOP Workshop at ECOOP 1999 (1999)
5. Clarke, S., et al.: Separating Concerns throughout the Development Lifecycle. In: Proceedings of the AOP Workshop at ECOOP 1999 (1999)
6. Pazzi, L.: Explicit Aspect Composition by Part-Whole Statecharts. In: Proceedings of the AOP Workshop at ECOOP 1999 (1999)
7. Kendall, E.A.: Role Model Designs and Implementations with Aspect Oriented Programming. Proceedings of OOPSLA, ACM SIGPLAN Notices 34(10), 353–369 (1999)
8. Kenens, P., et al.: An AOP Case with Static and Dynamic Aspects. In: Proceedings of the AOP Workshop at ECOOP 1998 (1998)
9. Kersten, M.A., Murphy, G.C.: Atlas: A Case Study in Building a Web-based Learning Environment using Aspect-oriented Programming. Proc. of OOPSLA, ACM SIGPLAN Notices 34(10), 340–352 (1999)
10. Suzuki, J., Yamamoto, Y.: Extending UML for Modelling Reflective Software Components. In: France, R.B. (ed.) UML 1999. LNCS, vol. 1723, pp. 220–235. Springer, Heidelberg (1999)
11. Mens, K., Lopes, C., Tekinerdogan, B., Kiczales, G.: Aspect-Oriented Programming Workshop Report. In: Dannenberg, R.B., Mitchell, S. (eds.) ECOOP 1997 Workshops. LNCS, vol. 1357, pp. 483–496. Springer, Heidelberg (1998)
12. Loomis, M.E.S.: Object Versioning. JOOP, 40–43 (January 1992)
13. Rashid, A., Sawyer, P.: Facilitating Virtual Representation of CAD Data through a Learning Based Approach to Conceptual Database Evolution Employing Direct Instance Sharing. In: Quirchmayr, G., Bench-Capon, T.J.M., Schweighofer, E. (eds.) DEXA 1998. LNCS, vol. 1460, pp. 384–393. Springer, Heidelberg (1998)
14. Rashid, A.: SADES - a Semi-Autonomous Database Evolution System. In: Demeyer, S., Dannenberg, R.B. (eds.) ECOOP 1998 Workshops. LNCS, vol. 1543. Springer, Heidelberg (1998)
15. Rashid, A., Sawyer, P.: Toward 'Database Evolution': a Taxonomy for Object Oriented Databases. IEEE Transactions on Knowledge and Data Engineering Review
16. Rashid, A., Sawyer, P.: Evaluation for Evolution: How Well Commercial Systems Do. In: Proceedings of the First OODB Workshop, ECOOP 1999, pp. 13-24 (1999)
17. Rashid, A., Sawyer, P.: Dynamic Relationships in Object Oriented Databases: A Uniform Approach. In: Bench-Capon, T.J.M., Soda, G., Tjoa, A.M. (eds.) DEXA 1999. LNCS, vol. 1677, pp. 26–35. Springer, Heidelberg (1999)
18. Rashid, A., Sawyer, P.: Transparent Dynamic Database Evolution from Java. In: Proceedings of OOPSLA Workshop on Java and Databases: Persistence Options (1999)
19. Liu, L., Zicari, R., Huersch, W., Lieberherr, K.J.: The Role of Polymorphic Reuse Mechanisms in Schema Evolution in an Object-Oriented Database. IEEE Transactions of Knowledge and Data Engineering 9(1), 50–67 (1997)
20. Lieberherr, K.J., Huersch, W., Silva-Lepe, I., Xiao, C.: Experience with a Graph-Based Propagation Pattern Programming Tool. In: Proc. of the International CASE Workshop, pp. 114–119. IEEE Computer Society, Los Alamitos (1992)
21. Al-Jadir, L., Léonard, M.: If We Refuse the Inheritance .... In: Bench-Capon, T.J.M., Soda, G., Tjoa, A.M. (eds.) DEXA 1999. LNCS, vol. 1677, pp. 560–572. Springer, Heidelberg (1999)
22. Clement, A., Harley, G., Webster, M., Colyer, A.: Eclipse AspectJ: aspect oriented programming with AspectJ and the Eclipse AspectJ development tools. Addison Wesley Prof., Reading (2005)

Enhanced Anaphora Resolution Algorithm Facilitating Ontology Construction

L. Jegatha Deborah[1], V. Karthika[1], R. Baskaran[1], and A. Kannan[2]

[1] Department of Computer Science & Engineering, Anna University Chennai–25
{blessedjeny,Karthika2k6}@gmail.com,baaski@annauniv.edu
[2] Department of Information Science & Technology, Chennai-25
kannan@annauniv.edu

Abstract. Enormous explosion in the number of the World Wide Web pages occur every day and since the efficiency of most of the information processing systems is found to be less, the potential of the Internet applications is often underutilized. Efficient utilization of the web can be exploited when similar web pages are rigorously, exhaustively organized and clustered based on some domain knowledge (semantic-based) [1]. Ontology which is a formal representation of domain knowledge aids in such efficient utilization. The performance of almost all the semantic-based clustering techniques depends on the constructed ontology, describing the domain knowledge [6]. The proposed methodology provides an enhanced pronominal anaphora resolution, one of the key aspects of semantic analysis in Natural Language Processing for obtaining cross references [19] within a web page providing better ontology construction. The experimental data sets exhibits better efficiency of the proposed method compared to earlier traditional algorithms.

Keywords: Ontology, Anaphora resolution, semantic analysis, Natural Language Processing.

1 Introduction

Semantic Analysis is a technique of relating syntactic structure inclusive of phrases, clauses, sentences or paragraphs. Bridging the semantic gap between heterogeneous systems is a prerequisite to information retrieval. The basis of the above bridge is found in Ontology [1][2][5]. Ontology, in simple terms is a knowledge structure specifying the different terms and their relationships pertained to a particular domain. Earlier systems performed semantic analysis with the help of ontology that consists of terms and relationships related to synonyms, antonyms, hyponyms, hypernyms and Thesaurus [3-6]. In the midst of such inventions, identifying and resolving the presence of anaphors and cataphora among the sentences pertained to a particular domain was a milestone to be achieved until 1998. Limiting our methodology to anaphora resolution, where the process of "Anaphora Resolution" (AR) or Pronouns resolution is the problem of resolving earlier reference of a phrase or a word in the same real-world entity and is found to be one of the complicated problems in Natural Language Processing [11-13]. There is a possibility that one sentence in a single

D.C. Wyld et al. (Eds.): ACITY 2011, CCIS 198, pp. 526–535, 2011.

domain can be referred from another sentence and such kind of relationships between sentences is called as co-referencing relationship. Coreferencing involves the detection of anaphor, where it refers to word or phrase in a sentence used to refer to an entity introduced earlier in the discourse [13] [19] . Resolving anaphora finds the best place in many of the applications including information extraction, information retrieval, NLP applications, semantic and web ontology. The three predominantly occurring types of anaphora are pronominal anaphora, definite noun phrase anaphora and one anaphora used in different application domains. The anaphora resolution process relies on some of the factors like gender, number agreement, semantic consistency, syntactic parallelism, proximity, etc [13]. Most of the traditional systems attempted to resolve anaphora in a single sentence. To be very specific, the anaphora resolution done by those systems was predominantly intra-sentential (the antecedent is present in the same sentence as that of anaphor) [14]. Compound words in the input corpus attempt to give meaningful information in anaphora resolution. The key strength of the enhanced pronominal anaphora resolution algorithm proposed in this paper provides inter-sentential anaphora resolutions by uncovering compound nouns and resolving the POS for each and every word. The proposed algorithm is found to work better on many web input text corpus as well as standard corpus provided by many universities as well. The experimental result of the proposed algorithm is compared with some of the traditional existing anaphora resolution methodologies which proved to have a better performance [15].

The remainder of this paper is organized as follows. Section 2 conducts a brief summary of the existing systems. Section 3 exhibits the system architecture and the working of the proposed algorithm. Section 4 illustrates the experimental results of the proposed algorithm with the comparison results shown. Section 5 presents the concluding remarks of the work.

2 Related Works

Hobbs' algorithm [16] relies on a simple tree search procedure formulated in terms of depth of embedding and left-right order. The tree procedure selects and replaces the pronouns by selecting the first candidate encountered by a left right depth first search for the tree. The algorithm chooses as the antecedent of a pronoun P the first NP_i (Noun Phrase) in the tree obtained by left-to-right breadth-first traversal of the branches to the left of the path T. If an antecedent satisfying this condition is not found in the sentence containing P, the algorithm selects the first NP obtained by a left-to-right breadth first search of the surface structures of preceding sentences in the text. The algorithm is found to produce a success rate close to 80% for intrasentential anaphora resolution.

Shalom Lappin and Herbert Leass [17] report an algorithm for identifying the noun phrase antecedents of third person pronouns and lexical anaphors. The algorithm (hereafter referred to as RAP (Resolution of Anaphora Procedure) applies to the syntactic representations generated by McCord's Slot Grammar parser (McCord 1990, 1993) and relies on salience measures derived from syntactic structure and a simple dynamic model of attentional state to select the 12 antecedent noun phrase of a pronoun from a list of candidates . RAP algorithm concentrates more on resolving an intrasentential syntactic filter for ruling out anaphoric dependence of a pronoun on an NP on syntactic grounds. It employs an anaphor binding algorithm for identifying the possible antecedent binder of a lexical anaphor within the same sentence. The algorithm does not employ semantic conditions or real-world knowledge in choosing among the candidates. This algorithm is suited for intrasentential anaphora resolution, which will not be the case in most of the text corpus available in the WWW. RAP is also not suited in identifying the exact antecedents and replaces of such antecedents when the noun phrase is not a single but a compound noun phrase. The major limitation of the algorithm is that the performance in terms of resolving the entire set of anaphor is found to be very limited when the input corpus consists of a number of compound noun phrases, even though the algorithm employs a decision procedure for selecting the preferred element of a list of antecedent candidates for a pronoun.

C. Aone and S. Bennet [18] describe an approach to building an automatically trainable anaphora resolution system. The authors made use of a machine learning algorithm and used many training examples for anaphora resolution. This machine learning algorithm made use of a decision tree consisting of feature vectors for pairs of an anaphora and its possible antecedent. The feature vectors for the training samples include lexical, semantic, syntactic and positional features. The authors built 6 machine learning based anaphora resolvers and achieved about a precision close to 80%. However, the algorithm failed in cases when the machine learning algorithm has to resolve the anaphors between different sentences. The algorithm drastically showed lower performance when the intersentential anaphora resolution was performed.

3 Enhanced Pronominal Anaphora Resolution Algorithm (KADE) – Proposed Algorithm

The motivation of our enhanced Pronominal Anaphora Resolution algorithm KADE was from the theoretical background provided in the previous work done by Shalom Lappin and Herbert Leass [17], which was an attempt at providing the domain independent anaphora resolver. KADE follows the algorithmic steps similar to the algorithm given by the authors mentioned above with the exception that KADE resolves intersentential anaphors. The key power of KADE algorithm is that the existence of related anaphors found anywhere in the web input text corpus or standard corpus could be identified and replaced. Our proposed KADE algorithm, which is an enhancement of the previous one, is resolving the anaphors among the different sentences (intersentential anaphora detections). Increased efficiency in resolving the anaphors is obtained in this algorithm because the lexical knowledge with respect to a particular domain of the text corpus through Natural Language Processing is considered [5-6]. On performing many empirical tests on various input text corpus, the performance in retrieving the correct anaphors between different sentences (intersentential anaphors) was found to be better than many of the traditional works handled. Our proposed algorithm KADE however uses the output of Stanford Parser [21], but also found to work well on FDG parsers [22] and Charniak parsers too [23]. The overall architecture of the system is shown below:

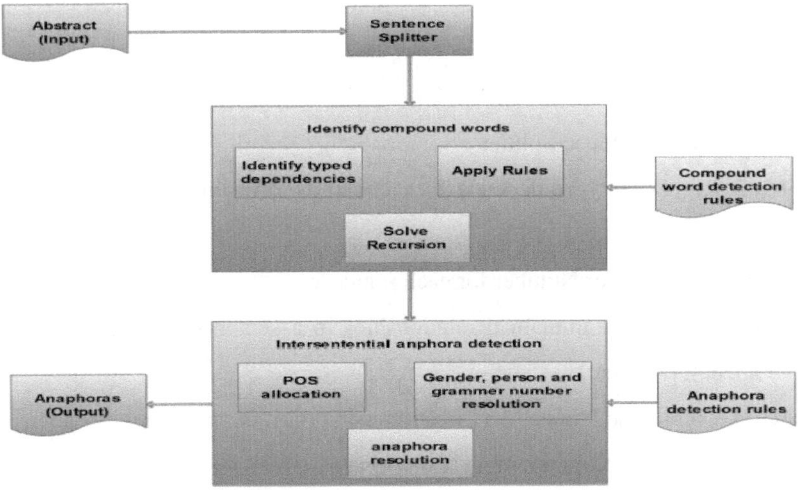

Fig. 1. KADE System Architecture

The input to the algorithm is any type of web input text corpus (web search engines) of any length. Initially, all the sentences of the text corpus are provided with an identification number for the purpose of easy referencing. The typed dependencies among the different words in the raw sentences of text corpus are resolved using the traditional Stanford Parser [21]. Many unwanted dependencies may exist when using the parser and such dependencies must be removed. The cleaning process from the typed dependencies obtained earlier, is done by writing specific rules for identifying the compound words, lemmatizing the words and removing the unwanted tags. The compound words in our algorithm is identified by writing the rules like, a noun followed by another noun and a noun prefixed by adverbial modifiers is considered to be a compound noun. Once, the compound nouns are identified for the entire corpus, the document is cleaned by just deleting the unwanted tags. The anaphors existing in different sentences are identified by allocating an identifier like, CC for coordinating conjunction, DET for determiner, JJ for adjectives, NN for noun singular, NNS for noun plural, RB for adverb, etc and resolving the POS for each word in the sentence. Such identifier allocation and POS tagging is done using the Penn Tree bank [24]. On completion of the execution of identifying POS tagging for every word in the sentence, the list of anaphors are displayed. The algorithmic steps of the enhanced anaphora resolution algorithm KADE follow the procedure given below:

Algorithmic Procedure:

Premise: Natural Language Processing

Domain: Text Corpus

Input: Any web input text corpus

Output: List of Anaphors found

Procedure:

Begin

do

{ // **Step 1**: Sentence Splitter

// **Step 2**: Resolving typed dependencies among the raw sentences

While (end of statement)

{ Assign Identifier Number for each sentence

Describe the grammatical relationships in a sentence among words (nsubj, nn, det, prep, etc) }

// **Step 3**: Compound Nouns Identification using rules description

For (every sentence from the input text corpus)

{ If a noun followed by another noun then it is a compound noun

If a noun prefixed by an adverbial modifier then it is a compound noun

For (every sentence after identifying compound nouns)

{ Replace the compound nouns in input text corpus}}

// **Step 4**: Resolving Anaphors among the sentences (intersentential anaphora detections)

While (end of statement)

{Identify the ID allocator and resolve POS using Penn Treebank (Stanford Parser)

}

End; While (end of document)}

4 Results and Discussions

The basic integrated development environment was developed to test the results for the experimental data sets done by KADE algorithm. The experimental tests were done on several raw input text corpuses. The performance efficiency in terms of correct retrieval of anaphors from the input corpus was found to be an average of 85%. Some of the sample data sets that were taken for the empirical tests for the exact retrieval of anaphors from the text corpus were Doctor Information System, Patient Information System, University Information System, Ontology Information Retrieval, etc [6]. The simplified screen shots for the algorithm evaluation are given below. Screen shots for a very small text corpus is shown.

Sample Input Text Corpus

Every patient has a patient number. This number is used to identify the record of the patient. For every record there is a separate slot to hold the details of doctors who checked the patient and the medicines that they should take.

Fig. 2. Anaphors Resolution

Fig. 3. List of Anaphors Resolved

The results of the KADE algorithm is compared with the other approaches and the graphical results below:

4.1 Result Set 1

KADE algorithm is compared with two approaches of Java RAP and Hobb algorithms. The algorithms are compared for the total number of anaphors present against the total number of anaphors retrieved.

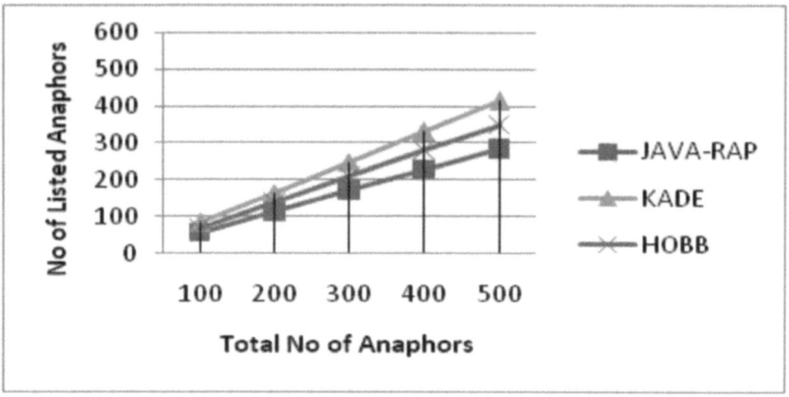

Fig.4. Comparison Results

4.2 Result Set 2

KADE algorithm is evaluated against the traditional performance parameters precision and recall. Precision evaluates the correct number of pronominal anaphors retrieved to the actual pronominal anaphors present in the corpus. Performance parameter recall evaluates the correct number of pronominal anaphors to the guessed pronominal anaphors in the corpus given by the domain expert. Precision and recall values are formulated as given below:

Assumption:

Let k be the number of actual anaphors present in the text corpus.
Let c be the number of correct anaphors obtained from the text corpus using any anaphora resolution algorithm.
Let g be the number of correct anaphors given by the user, preferably a domain expert.

$$\text{Precision} = c / k \quad (1)$$

$$\text{Recall} = c / g \quad (2)$$

The experimental results for different data sets, randomly collected abstract documents from the web engines viz. Doctor Information System (DIS), Patient Information System (PIS), Ontology Information Retrieval (ORS), and their corresponding graphical results are shown below:

Table 1. Evaluation Results – Precision and Recall

Text Corpus Files	Number of Actual Anaphors	Precision Value			Recall Value		
		Hobb	Java RAP	KADE	Hobb	Java RAP	KADE
Doctor Information System	77	0.7	0.77	0.88	0.77	0.85	0.9
Patient Information System	57	0.5	0.7	0.84	0.68	0.8	0.88
Ontology Information Retrieval	130	0.82	0.8	0.9	0.85	0.90	0.96

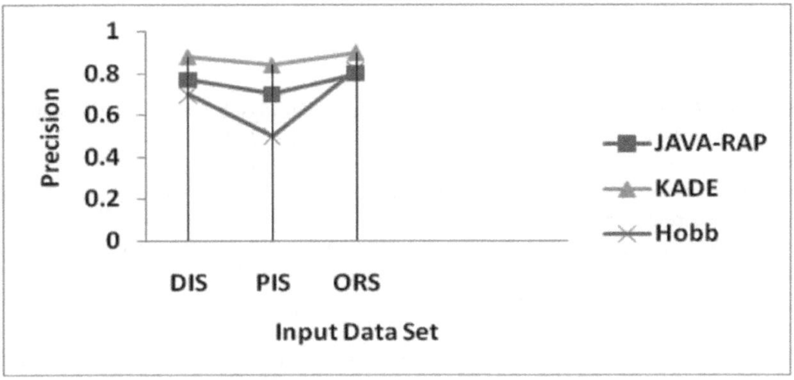

Fig. 5. Precision Comparison

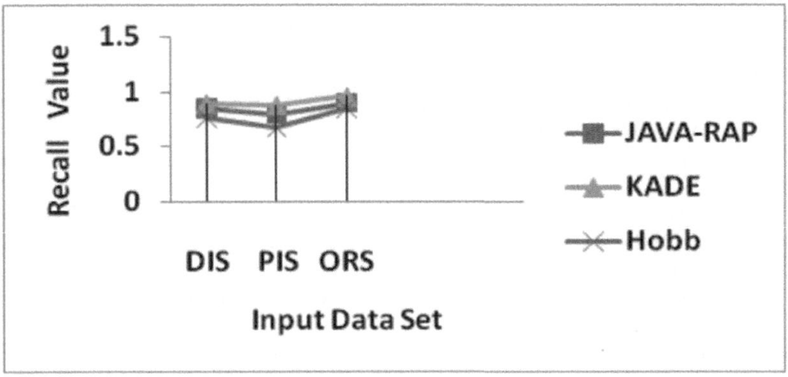

Fig. 6. Recall Comparison

5 Concluding Remarks

Ontology plays a vital role in clustering the web documents semantically to enhance the performance of many information extraction and information retrieval systems. Most of the systems given in the literature survey had the potential of constructing ontology based on synonyms, antonyms, hyponyms, anaphors and many more. This paper provides an enhanced pronominal anaphora resolution algorithm based on the results of Stanford Parser and Penn Treebank which works well on resolving anaphors existing among multiple sentences. The algorithm is tested against different data corpuses and is found to give better precision and recall values. The performance efficiency of the proposed algorithm in resolving intersentential anaphors is closer to 83%, compared to the traditional algorithms. This work provided a positive motivation and presents a wide research gap in the area of resolving cataphora in the raw text corpus which will be discussed in the future work.

References

1. Shu, G., Rana, O.F., Avis, N.J., Dingfang, C.: Ontology-based semantic matchmaking approach. Advances in Engineering Software 38, 59–67 (2007)
2. Assawamekin, N., Sunetnanta, T., Pluempitiwiriyawej, C.: Ontology based multiperspective requirements traceability framework. Knowledge and Information Systems Journal (2009)
3. Zhang, Y., Witte, R., Rilling, J., et al.: An ontology-based approach for traceability recovery. In: Proceedings of the 3rd International Workshop on Metamodels, Schemas, Grammars, and Ontologies for Reverse Engineering (ATEM 2006), Genoa, pp. 36–43 (2006)
4. Antoniol, G., Canfora, G., Casazza, G., et al.: Recovering traceability links between code and documentation. IEEE Trans. Softw. Eng. 28(10), 970–983 (2002)
5. Jurisica, I., Mylopoulos, J., Yu, E.: Ontologies for knowledge management: an information systems perspective. Knowl. Inf. Syst. 6(4), 380–401 (2004)
6. Pisanelli, D.M., Gangemi, A., Steve, G.: The role of ontologies for an effective and unambiguous dissemination of clinical guidelines. In: Dieng, R., Corby, O. (eds.) Knowledge Engineering and Knowledge Management Methods, Models, and Tools, pp. 129–139 (2000)
7. Ehrig, M., Staab, S.: Efficiency of ontology mapping approaches. In: International Workshop on Semantic Intelligent Middleware for the Web and the Grid at ECAI 2004, Valencia, Spain (2004)
8. Guarino, N., Welty, C.: Evaluating ontological decisions with OntoClean. Commun. ACM 45(2), 61–65 (2002)
9. Calvanese, D., De Giacomo, G., Lenzerini, M.: A framework for ontology integration. In: Proceedings of the 2001 International Semantic Web Working Symposium (SWWS 2001) CA, USA (2001)
10. Gangemi, A.: Some tools and methodologies for domain ontology building. Comp. Funct. Genom. 4, 104–110 (2003)
11. Winograd, T.: Understanding natural language. Academic Press, New York (1972)
12. Delmonte, R., Chiran, L., Bacalu, C.: Towards An Annotated Database For Anaphora Resolution. In: LREC, Atene, pp. 63–67 (2000)
13. Denis, P., Baldridge, J.: A ranking approach to pronoun resolution. In: The Proc. of IJCAI 2007 (2007)

14. Stuckardt, R.: Resolving anaphoric references on deficient syntactic descriptions. In: Proceedings of the ACL 1997/EACL1997 Workshop on Operational Factors in Practical, Robust Anaphora Resolution, Madrid, Spain, pp. 30–37 (1997)
15. Delmonte, R.: Getaruns: a Hybrid System for Summarization and Question Answering. In: Proc. Natural Language Processing (NLP) for Question-Answering, pp. 21–28. EACL, Budapest (2003)
16. Markert, K., Nissim, M.: Comparing Knowledge Sources for Nominal Anaphora Resolution. Association for Computational Linguistics 31(3) (2005)
17. Lappin, S., Leass, H.J.: An algorithm for Pronominal Anaphora Resolution. Association of Computational Linguistics (1994)
18. Aone, C., Bennet, S.: Evaluating auotamted and manual acquisition of anaphora resolution strategies: In: Proceedings of the 33rd Annual Metting of the Association of Computational Linguistics (ACL 1995), pp. 122–129 (1995)
19. Morton, T.S.: Coreference for NLP applications. In: Proc. of ACL 2000 (2000)
20. de Marneffe, M.C., Manning, C.D.: Stanford typed dependencies manual. Stanford Parser Library (2010)
21. The Stanford parser: a statistical parser (version 1.6). Stanford University, `http://www.nlp.stanford.edu/software/lex-parser.shtml`
22. The FDG parser: a statistical parser (version 3.7), `http://www.3d2f.com/download/11-349-parser-generator-free-download.shtml`
23. The Charniak parser: a statistical parser (version 1.0), `http://www-tsujii.is.s.u-tokyo.ac.jp/~tsuruoka/chunkparser`
24. Penn Tree bank Project, `http://www.ling.upenn.edu/courses/Fall_2003/ling001/penn_treebank_pos.html`

A New Data Mining Approach to Find Co-location Pattern from Spatial Data

M. Venkatesan[1], Arunkumar Thangavelu[2], and P. Prabhavathy[3]

[1]Assistant Professor (SG), School of Computing Science & Engineering,
VIT University, Vellore
mvenkatesan@vit.ac.in
[2]Professor (Assistant Director, AMIR), School of Computing Science & Engineering,
VIT University, Vellore
arunkumar.thangavelu@gmail.com
[3]Assistant Professor, School of Information Technology & Engineering,
VIT University, Vellore
pprabhavathy@vit.ac.in

Abstract. Spatial co-location patterns represent the subsets of Boolean spatial features whose instances are often located in close geographic proximity. These patterns derive the meaningful relation between spatial data. Co-location rules can be identified by spatial statistics or data mining approaches. In data mining method, Association rule-based approaches can be used which are further divided into transaction-based approaches and distance-based approaches. Transaction-based approaches focus on defining transactions over space so that an Apriori algorithm can be used. The natural notion of transactions is absent in spatial data sets which are embedded in continuous geographic space. A new distance –based approach is developed to mine co-location patterns from spatial data by using the concept of proximity neighborhood. A new interest measure, a participation index, is used for spatial co-location patterns as it possesses an anti-monotone property. An algorithm to discover co-location patterns are designed which generates candidate locations and their table instances. Finally the co-location rules are generated to identify the patterns.

Keywords: Co-location pattern, association rule, spatial data, participation index.

1 Introduction

Huge amount of Geo-spatial data leads to definition of complex relationship, which creates challenges in today data mining research. Geo-spatial data can be represented in raster format and vector format. Raster data are represented in n-dimensional bit maps or pixel maps and vector data information can be represented as unions or overlays of basic geometric constructs, such as points, lines and polygons. Spatial data mining refers to the extraction of knowledge, spatial relationships, or other interesting patterns not explicitly stored in spatial data sets. As family of spatial data mining, spatial Co-location pattern detection aim to discover the objects whose spatial features/events that are frequently co-located in the same region. It may reveal important

D.C. Wyld et al. (Eds.): ACITY 2011, CCIS 198, pp. 536–545, 2011.

phenomena in a number of applications including location based services, geographic information systems, geo-marketing, remote sensing, image database exploration, medical imaging, navigation, traffic control and environmental studies. Some types of services may be requested in proximate geographic area, such as finding the agricultural land which is nearest to river bed. Location based service providers are very interested in finding what services are requested frequently together and located in spatial proximity. The co-location pattern and the rule discovery are part of spatial data mining process. The differences between spatial data mining and classical data mining are mainly related to data input, statistical foundation, output patterns, and computational process. Co-location rules[12] are models to infer the presence of boolean spatial features in the neighborhood of instances of other boolean spatial features. Co-location rule discovery is a process to identify co-location patterns from large spatial datasets with a large number of boolean features. This paper discusses the detection of co-location pattern from the complex Geo-Spatial data by using event centric model approach. This paper is structured as follows: Section 2 discuses existing methods available to discover co-location pattern. Section 3 describes the model and the concepts of co-location pattern mining. Section 4 includes the proposed system design and co-location algorithm. Section 5 deals experimental execution of the co-location algorithm with the result implementation of each methodology. Section 6 summarizes the performance analysis and comparison our approach with the existing methods and Section 7 discusses the conclusions and future enhancements of the proposed system.

2 Literature Survey

Approaches to discovering co-location rules in the literature can be categorized into three classes, namely spatial statistics, data mining, and the event centric approach. Spatial statistics-based approaches use measures of spatial correlation to characterize the relationship between different types of spatial features using the cross-K function with Monte Carlo simulation and quadrant count analysis. Computing spatial correlation measures for all possible co-location patterns can be computationally expensive due to the exponential number of candidate subsets given a large collection of spatial boolean features. Data mining approaches can be further divided into a clustering-based map overlay approach and association rule-based approaches. Association rule-based approaches can be divided into transaction-based approaches and distance-based approaches Association rule-based approaches focus on the creation of transactions over space so that an apriori like algorithm [2] can be used. Transactions over space can use a reference-feature centric [3] approach or a data-partition approach [4]. The reference feature centric model is based on the choice of a reference spatial feature and is relevant to application domains focusing on a specific boolean spatial feature, e.g., incidence of cancer. Domain scientists are interested in finding the co-locations of other task relevant features to the reference feature [3]. Transactions are created around instances of one user specified reference spatial feature. The association rules are derived using the apriori[2] algorithm. The rules found are all related to the reference feature.

Defining transactions by a data-partition approach [4] defines transactions by dividing spatial datasets into disjoint partitions. A clustering-based map overlay approach [7], [6] treats every spatial attribute as a map layer and considers spatial clusters (regions) of point-data in each layer as candidates for mining associations. A distance-based approach [4],[5] was proposed called k-neighbouring class sets. In this the number of instances for each pattern is used as the prevalence measure [14], which does not possess an anti-monotone property by nature. The reference feature centric and data partitioning models materialize transactions and thus can use traditional support and confidence measures. Co-location pattern mining general approach [8] formalized the co-location problem and showed the similarities and differences between the co-location rules problem and the classic association rules problem as well as the difficulties in using traditional measures (e.g., support, confidence) created by implicit, overlapping and potentially infinite transactions in spatial data sets. It also proposed the notion of user-specified proximity neighborhoods[13][15] in place of transactions to specify groups of items and defined interest measures that are robust in the face of potentially infinite overlapping proximity neighborhoods .A novel Joinless approach[9] for efficient collocation pattern mining uses an instance-lookup scheme instead of an expensive spatial or instance join operation for identifying collocation instances. A Partial join approach [9] for spatial data which are clustered in neighbourhood area.

Mining co-location patterns with rare spatial features [10] proposes a new measure called the maximal participation ratio (maxPR) and shown that a co-location pattern with a relatively high maxPR value corresponds to a collocation pattern containing rare spatial events. A novel order-clique-based approach [11] is used to mine maximal co-locations. In this paper distance based approach is used to find the co-location patterns from the spatial data. The participation index is used to prune the data to accept only the interesting patterns.

3 Co-location Pattern Mining

Mining spatial co-location patterns is an important spatial data mining task. A spatial co-location pattern is a set of spatial features that are frequently located together in spatial proximity. Spatial co-location patterns represent relationships among events happening in different and possibly nearby grid cells. Co-location patterns are discovered by using any one of the model such as reference feature centric model, window centric model and event centric model. The prevalence measure and the conditional probability measure are called interesting measures used to determine useful co-location patterns from the spatial data. The interesting measures are defined differently in different models. Our approach is to find the co-location pattern from the spatial by using event centric model where the interesting measure is participation index.

3.1 Event Centric Model Approach

The event centric model is relevant to applications like ecology where there are many types of Boolean spatial features. Ecologists are interested in finding subsets of spatial features likely to occur in a neighborhood around instance of given subsets of event types.

Consider the figure 1, where the objective is to determine the probability of finding at least one instance of feature type B in the neighborhood of an instance of feature type A in figure 1. There are four instances of feature type A and two of them have some instances of type B in their 9 –neighbor adjacent neighborhoods. The conditional

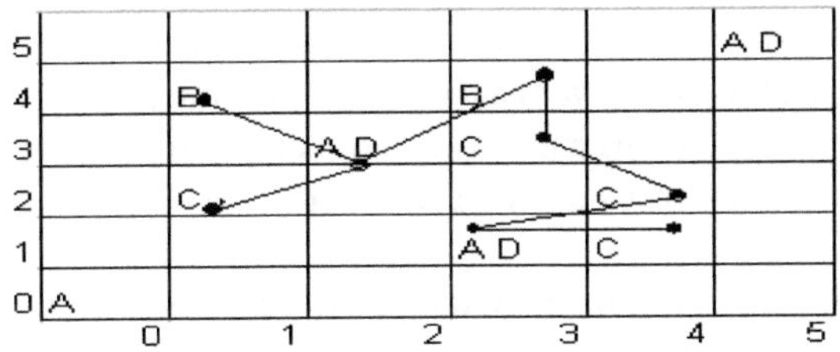

Fig. 1. Event Centric Model

probability for the co-location rule is: Spatial feature A at location 1 → spatial feature type B in 9 neighbor neighborhood is 50%.Neighbourhood is an important concept in the event centric model.

3.2 Basic Concepts and Mathematical Definition

For a spatial data set S, let F = { $f_1, \ldots, f_k$} be a set of boolean spatial features. Let i = {$i_1, \ldots, i_n$} be a set of n instances in S, where each instance is a vector <instance-id, location, spatial features>. The spatial feature f of instance i is denoted by i. f .We assume that the spatial features of an instance are from F and the location is within the spatial framework of the spatial database. Furthermore, we assume that there exists a neighborhood relation R over pair wise instances in S.

Case 1: (A Spatial Data Set) Figure 2 shows a spatial data set with a spatial feature set F = {A, B, C, D}, which will be used as the running example in this paper. Objects with various shapes represent different spatial features, as shown in the legend. Each instance is uniquely identified by its instance-id. We have 18 instances in the database

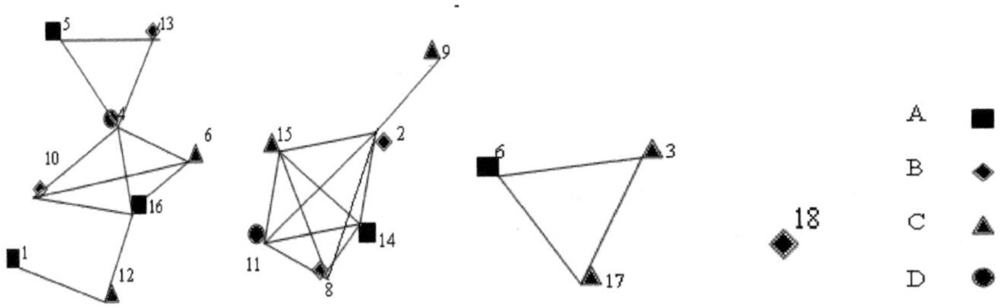

Fig. 2. Spatial data set

The objective of co-location pattern mining is to find frequently co-located subsets of spatial features. For example, a co-location {traffic jam, police, car accident} means that a traffic jam, police, and a car accident frequently occur in a nearby region. To capture the concept of "nearby," the concept of user-specified neighbor-sets was introduced. A neighbor-set L is a set of instances such that all pair wise locations in L are neighbors. A co-location pattern C is a set of spatial features, i.e., C ⊆ F. A neighbor-set L is said to be a row instance of co-location pattern C if every feature in C appears as a feature of an instance in L, and there exists no proper subset of L does so. We denote all row instances of a co-location pattern C by row set(C).

Case 2: (Neighbor-set, row instance and rowset) In Fig. 2, the neighborhood relation R is defined based on Euclidean distance. Two instances are neighbors if their Euclidean distance is less than a user specified threshold. Neighboring instances are connected by edges. For instance, {3, 6, 17}, {4, 5, 13}, and {4, 7, 10, 16} are all neighbor-sets because each set forms a clique. Here, we use the instance-id to refer to an object in Fig. 2. Additional neighbor-sets include {6, 17}, {3, 6}, {2, 15, 11, 14}, and {2, 15, 8, 11, 14}. {A, B,C, D} is a co-location pattern. The neighborhood-set {14, 2, 15, 11} is a row instance of the pattern {A, B,C, D} but the neighborhood-set {14, 2, 8, 15, 11} is not a row instance of co-location {A, B,C, D} because it has a proper subset {14, 2, 15, 11} which contains all the features in {A, B,C, D}.Finally, the rowset({A, B,C, D})= {{7, 10, 16, 4}, {14, 2, 15, 11},{14, 8, 15, 11}}.For a co-location rule R : A → B, the conditional probability cp(R) of R is defined as

$$\frac{|\{L \in \text{rowset}(A) \mid \exists L' \text{s.t.} (L \subseteq L') \wedge (L' \in \text{rowset}(A \cup B))\}|}{|\text{rowset}(A)|} \quad (1)$$

In words, the conditional probability is the probability that a neighbor-set in rowset(A) is part of a neighbor-set in rowset(A ∪ B). Intuitively, the conditional probability p indicates that, whenever we observe the occurrences of spatial features in A, the probability to find occurrence of B in a nearby region is p.

Given a spatial database S, to measure how a spatial feature f is co-located with other features in co-location pattern C, a participation ratio pr(C, f) can be defined as

$$\text{pr}(C, f) = \frac{|\{r \mid (r \text{¸} S) \wedge (r.f = f) \wedge (r \text{ is in a row instance of } C)\}|}{\{r \mid (r \text{¸} S) \wedge (r.f = f)\}} \quad (2)$$

In words, a feature f has a partition ratio pr(C, f) in pattern C means wherever the feature f is observed, with probability pr(C, f), all other features in C are also observed in a neighbor-set. A participation index was used to measure how all the spatial features in a co-location pattern are co-located. For a co-location pattern C, the participation index PI(C) = min f∈C{pr(C, f)}.In words, wherever any feature in C is observed, with a probability of at least PI(C), all other features in C can be observed in a neighbor-set. A high participation index value indicates that the spatial features in a co-location pattern likely occur together. The participation index was used because in spatial application domain there are no natural “transactions” and thus “support” is not well-defined. Given a user-specified participation index threshold min_prev, a co-location pattern is called prevalent if PI(C) ≥ min_ prev.

4 The Proposed System

The proposed system input mainly consists of a satellite image which is processed to derive the co-ordinates item instances. The image is processed in Matlab where the instance is identified by colour identification. The co-ordinates are stored in a text file. The text file is processed to convert the co-ordinates into program readable format. The co-location algorithm is used to generate item sets from those co-ordinates. When the algorithm is applied the co-ordinates are mapped in a grid map. The distance between the instances is calculated. The 2-item sets are calculated by comparing the neighbouring grid spaces. The 2-item sets are pruned if patterns don't have minimum participation index. The non-pruned item sets are used to calculate the 3-item sets. The interesting patterns are identified after pruning depending on the participation index.

4.1 Proposed Architecture

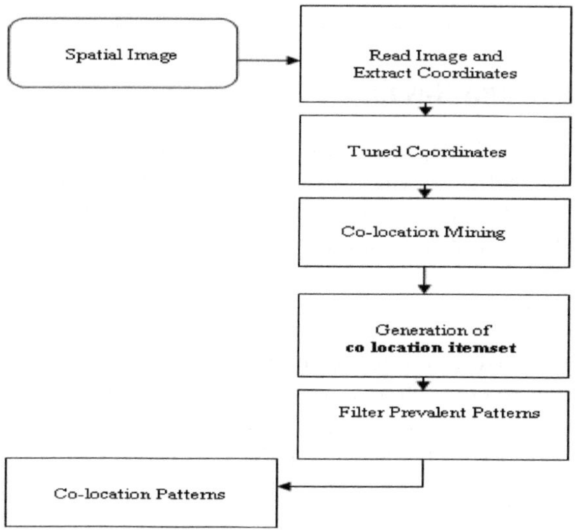

Fig. 3. General Architecture of Proposed System

4.2 Co-location Algorithm

One instance of an item is compared with all the instances of other item and checked for neighbourhood and participation index is found out and according to participation index the collocation pattern is predicted.

The collocation pattern is found out using participation index and using some pruning index value and some combinations are ruled out and final list of n-item set is proposed and only these combinations are taken to n+1-item set co-location analysis.

1. Write the coordinate vector values into temporary double array
   2. Initialize flag array with size of temporary array
   3. for each element in first row of array
   Compare each and every element in next row
   Find different in grid coordinates
   Check if difference leads to neighbor
   Mark true in flag array if collocated
     End loops
   4. Calculate participation index by diving number of true s by
     total number of instances
   5. Initialize pruning index
   6. Compare participation index value and pruning index and
     consider only the item set that are abovethe pruning index.
   7. The items that are pruned out in n-item set calculation are
     ruled out in n+1-item set calculation
8. End

5 Implementation and Result

The tools used for the implementation of co-location pattern mining are MATLAB 7.0, NET BEANS 6.1 and IE 7. The primary language of this experiment revolves around the largest open-source software JAVA. Hyper Text Markup Language (HTML) is used for displaying the result in a web browser.

5.1 Image Processing

In image processing we take an image which represent different objects and give it to MatLab for processing where each and every row is processed and different objects are identified and output is given to text file in raw format where x and y coordinates are separated by comma and each object is separated by type number.

Fig. 4. Type detection

5.2 Co-location Pattern Detection

Graphical User Interface allows user to browse the raw data file which is got through image processing. It has a method to take raw data as input and parse the whole text file and get x and y coordinates along with type value and write into another text file in a format that can be read by main program. This snapshot reflects the results of the co-location algorithm by grouping into item sets.

This is the final predictions of the algorithm after processing the coordinates to various item sets. This represents the various entities which are collocated together.

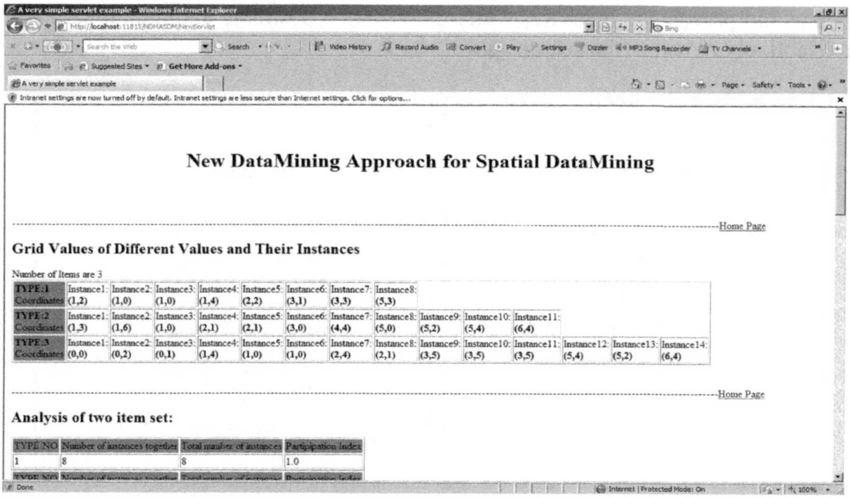

Fig. 5. Grid Coordinates

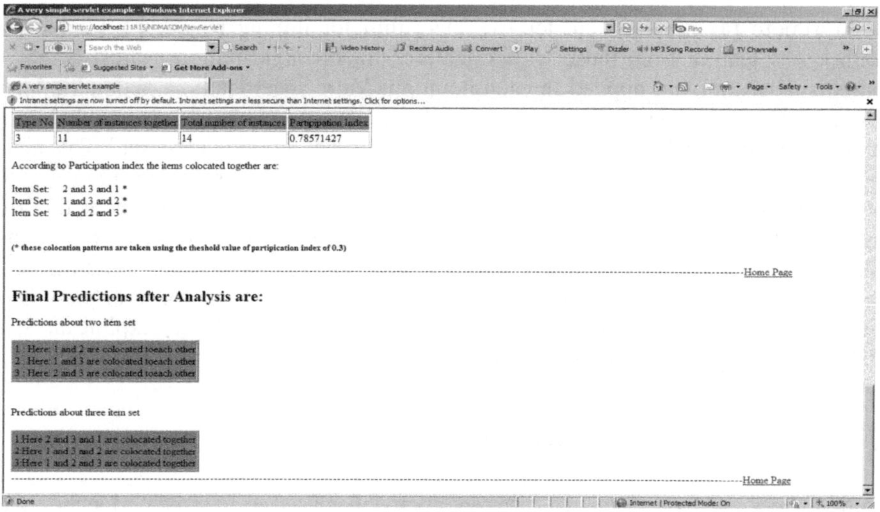

Fig. 6. Co-located Pattern

6 Performance Analysis

Apriori algorithm generates huge number of candidate itemset to find frequent patterns and also scans the transaction database number of time to calculate the support count of the item. Also it takes more time to generate more number of instances. Our Co-location algorithm takes minimum time to generate more number of instances in co-location pattern analysis. Figure 8.(a) and 8.(b) shows the comparison between apriori and collocation mining algorithm. Our approach does not need the constraint of "any point object must belong to only one instance" since we do not use the number of instances for a pattern as its prevalence measure. We propose the participation index as the prevalence measure, which possesses a desirable antimonotone property for effectively reducing the search space.

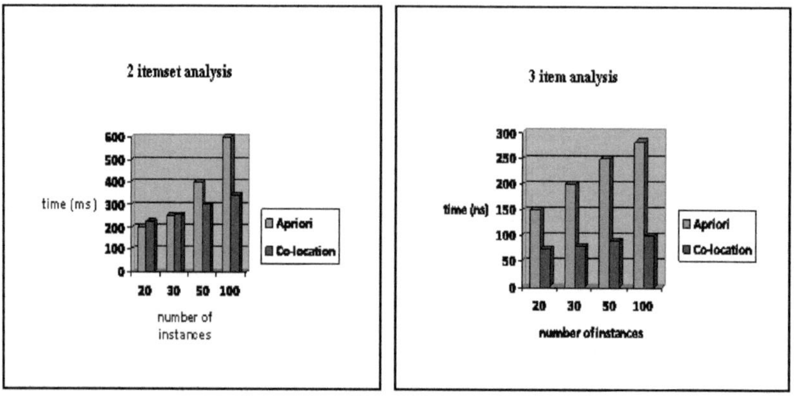

Fig. 7. (a) 2 itemset and (b) 3 itemset shows the comparison between Apriori and Co-location mining algorithm

Morimoto [4] provided an iterative algorithm for mining neighboring class sets with k + 1 feature from those with k features. In his algorithm, a nearest neighbor based spatial join was applied in each iteration. More specifically, a geometric technique, a Voronoi diagram, was used to take advantage of the restriction that "any point object must belong to only one instance of a k-neighboring class set." This algorithm considers a pure geometric join approach. In contrast, our co-location mining algorithm considers a combinatorial join approach in addition to a pure geometric join approach to generate size k+1 co-location patterns from size-k co-location patterns. Our experimental results show that a hybrid of geometric and combinatorial methods results in lower computation cost than either a pure geometric approach or pure combinatorial approach. In addition, we apply a multi resolution filter to exploit the spatial autocorrelation property of spatial data

7 Conclusions and Future Enhancements

In this paper, we have discussed different approaches used to find the co-location pattern from the spatial data. We also have shown the similarities and differences between the co-location rules problem and the classic association rules problem. A new interest measure, a participation index, is used for spatial co-location patterns as it possesses an anti-monotone property. The new Co-location algorithm to mine collocation patterns from the spatial data was presented and analyzed. In future, the collocation mining problem should be investigated to account categorical and continuous data and also extended for spatial data types, such as line segments and polygons.

References

1. Huang, Y., Shekhar, S., Xiong, H.: Discovering Colocation Patterns from Spatial Data Sets: A General Approach. IEEE Transactions on Knowledge and Data Engineering 16(12), 1472–1485 (2004)
2. Agarwal, R., Srikant, R.: Fast Algorithms for Mining Association Rules. In: Proc. 20th Int'l Conf. Very Large Data Bases (1994)
3. Koperski, K., Han, J.: Discovery of Spatial Association Rules in Geographic Information Databases. In: Proceedings of Fourth Int'l Symp. Spatial Databases (1995)
4. Morimoto, Y.: Mining Frequent Neighboring Class Sets in Spatial Databases. In: Proc. ACM SIGKDD International Conference on Knowledge Discovery and Data Mining (2001)
5. Shekhar, S., Huang, Y.: Co-location Rules Mining: A Summary of Results. In: Jensen, C.S., Schneider, M., Seeger, B., Tsotras, V.J. (eds.) SSTD 2001. LNCS, vol. 2121, p. 236. Springer, Heidelberg (2001)
6. Estivill-Castro, V., Lee, I.: Data Mining Techniques for Autonomous Exploration of Large Volumes of Geo-Referenced Crime Data. In: Proc. Sixth Int'l. Conf. Geo Computation (2001)
7. Estivill-Castro, V., Murray, A.: Discovering Associations in Spatial Data—An Efficient Medoid Based Approach. In: Wu, X., Kotagiri, R., Korb, K.B. (eds.) PAKDD 1998. LNCS, vol. 1394. Springer, Heidelberg (1998)
8. Huang, Y., Shekhar, S., Xiong, H.: Discovering Co-location Patterns from Spatial Data Sets: A General Approach. IEEE Transactions on Knowledge and Data Engineering 16(12) (December 2004)
9. Yoo, J.S., Shekhar, S.: A Joinless Approach for Mining Spatial Co-location patterns. IEEE Transactions on Knowledge and Data Engineering 18(10) (October 2006)
10. Huang, Y., Pei, J., Xiong, H.: Mining Co-Location Patterns with Rare Events from Spatial Data Sets. Geoinformatica 10, 239–260 (2006)
11. Wang, L., Zhou, L., Lu, J., Yip, J.: An order-clique-based approach for mining maximal co- locations. Information Sciences 179, 3370–3382 (2009)
12. Wang, Z.-Q., Chen, H.-B., Yu, H.-Q.: Spatial Co-Location Rule Mining Researc. In: Continuous Data. In: Proceedings of the Fifth International Conference on Machine Learning and Cybernetics, Dalian (August 13-16, 2006)
13. Qian, F., He, Q., He, J.: Mining Spatial Co-location Patterns with Dynamic Neighborhood Constraint. In: Buntine, W., Grobelnik, M., Mladenić, D., Shawe-Taylor, J. (eds.) ECML PKDD 2009. LNCS, vol. 5782, pp. 238–253. Springer, Heidelberg (2009)
14. Salmenkivi, M.: Efficient Mining of Correlation Patterns in Spatial Point Data. In: Fürnkranz, J., Scheffer, T., Spiliopoulou, M. (eds.) PKDD 2006. LNCS (LNAI), vol. 4213, pp. 359–370. Springer, Heidelberg (2006)
15. Celik, M., Shekhar, S., Rogers, J.P., Shine, J.A.: Mixed-Drove Spatiotemporal Co-Occurrence Pattern Mining. IEEE Transactions on Knowledge and Data Engineering 20(10) (October 2008)

Author Index

GPSR Compliance

The European Union's (EU) General Product Safety Regulation (GPSR) is a set of rules that requires consumer products to be safe and our obligations to ensure this.

If you have any concerns about our products, you can contact us on ProductSafety@springernature.com

In case Publisher is established outside the EU, the EU authorized representative is:

Springer Nature Customer Service Center GmbH
Europaplatz 3
69115 Heidelberg, Germany

Batch number: 10704693

Printed by Printforce, the Netherlands